Wrightsman's Psychology and the Legal System

SEVENTH EDITION

EDIE GREENE
University of Colorado at Colorado Springs

KIRK HEILBRUN
Drexel University

WADSWORTH
CENGAGE Learning

Australia • Brazil • Japan • Korea • Mexico • Singapore • Spain • United Kingdom • United States

WADSWORTH
CENGAGE Learning™

Wrightsman's Psychology and the Legal System, Seventh edition
Edie Greene and Kirk Heilbrun

Editor: Jon-David Hague

Development Editor: Kelly Miller

Assistant Editor: Trina Tom

Editorial Assistant: Kelly Miller

Media Editor: Lauren Keyes

Marketing Manager: Liz Rhoden

Marketing Communications Manager: Talia Wise

Project Manager, Editorial Production: Matt Ballantyne

Art Director: Vernon Boes

Print Buyer: Paula Vang

Permissions Editor (text): Bob Kauser

Permissions Editor (image): Robyn Young

Production Service: Pre-Press PMG

Photo Researcher: Sarah Evertson

Cover Designer: Larry Didona

Cover Image: Gary S Chapman/Getty Images

Compositor: Pre-Press PMG

For product information and technology assistance, contact us at
Cengage Learning Customer & Sales Support, 1-800-354-9706

For permission to use material from this text or product, submit all requests online at **cengage.com/permissions**
Further permissions questions can be emailed to
permissionrequest@cengage.com

Library of Congress Control Number: 2010920552

ISBN-13: 978-0-495-81301-9

ISBN-10: 0-495-81301-X

Wadsworth
20 Davis Drive
Belmont, CA 94002
USA

Cengage Learning is a leading provider of customized learning solutions with office locations around the globe, including Singapore, the United Kingdom, Australia, Mexico, Brazil, and Japan. Locate your local office at: **international.cengage.com/region**

Cengage Learning products are represented in Canada by Nelson Education, Ltd.

For your course and learning solutions, visit **academic.cengage.com**

Purchase any of our products at your local college store or at our preferred online store **www.CengageBrain.com**

Printed in the United States of America
1 2 3 4 5 6 7 14 13 12 11 10

*Dedicated to all the students in psychology and law
who will soon be our next generation of
researchers, practitioners, and informed citizens.*

Brief Contents

Contents

Preface

This is the 7th edition of *Psychology and the Legal System*. We hope that its longevity is some reflection of the commitment to rigorously presenting the various aspects of psychology and law described by Lawrence Wrightsman and his colleagues over the first five editions. Although Professor Wrightsman is no longer listed as an active author, the 6th (and now the 7th) editions incorporate his name into the title to honor his many contributions. The authorship has changed from the 6th to the 7th edition as well; Edie Greene and Kirk Heilbrun are now the sole authors.

We continue to believe that the law is inherently psychological. It is made by people with varying desires and ambitions, interpreted by individuals with different (sometimes contradictory) perspectives, and experienced—either directly or indirectly—by all of us. Both psychology and the law are about motivation and behavior. Indeed, for centuries the legal system has been a powerful influence on people's everyday activities. From the Supreme Court's school desegregation decision of 1954 to its recent decisions concerning the constitutionality of the death penalty for adolescents (all described in this book), the courts have had considerable impact on individual lives.

But as the second decade of the 21st century has dawned, we find it useful to describe the law from the perspective of psychology, a behavioral science that also has a significant applied component. Indeed, matters of law and psychology are often cited in the media. Whether they involve allegations of police brutality, criminal trials of the rich and famous, multi-billion-dollar civil litigation, charges of racism in the criminal justice system, or debates about the utility and morality of capital punishment, headlines and lead stories are often about some aspect of psychology and law. Although this attention appears to cater to an almost insatiable curiosity about crime and other types of legal disputes, it also promotes ambivalence about the law. Many citizens are suspicious of the police, but police are still the first responders in a crisis. Juries are frequently criticized for their decisions, but most litigants would prefer to have their cases decided by juries rather than judges. Citizens value their constitutionally-protected rights, but also demand security in a post-911 era.

The primary audiences for *Psychology and the Legal System* are those students taking a course in psychology and the law, forensic psychology, or the criminal justice system, and others who seek to learn more about the legally relevant science and practice of psychology. This book (and its individual chapters) may also be used as a supplement in psychology courses that emphasize applied psychology, social issues, or policy analysis. In addition, it covers a number of topics relevant to law school courses that introduce law students to social science research findings and applications.

We have attempted to find the right mix of psychology and legal analysis in the text. The book's emphasis remains on psychological science and practice, but we also summarize the legal history of many key topics and present the current status of relevant legal theories and court decisions. Specific topics that are covered for the first time in this edition include new forensic assessment measures, verbal and behavioral cues associated with deception, the diversion of mentally ill individuals using the Sequential Intercept model, cognitive aspects of trial judges' decisions, sentencing of juvenile offenders, and the community-based correctional rehabilitation of adult and juvenile offenders.

We continue to focus on the psychological dimensions of several topics that remain important in contemporary society, just as they were important when previous editions of this text were written. These topics include social influence effects of interrogations (involving children in investigative interviews and adults in interrogation rooms), clinicians' assessments of competence in various domains, reforms to eyewitness identification procedures based on research in perception and memory, recovery from victimization in light of our understanding of posttraumatic stress disorder, and racial influences on jury decision making. As in previous editions, we have updated each of these topics using the best available scientific evidence that has been published after our most recent edition went to press.

NEW FEATURES AND REVISIONS

We have made the following major changes from the last edition:

- We have made *Psychology and the Legal System* more "user friendly" by improving its readability and using more examples to illustrate the material.

- In each chapter, case summaries in boxes ("*The case of…*") have been updated. These summaries describe cases or trials that illustrate or explain an important legal concept or psychological principle covered in the chapter. Readers will be familiar with many of the recent cases, including those of Michael Vick, Terri Schiavo, and Michael Jackson, as well as cases involving the interrogation of terrorist suspects. We also feature the historic cases of Ernest Miranda, Clarence Gideon, John Hinckley, Ted Bundy, and others.

We have added a few cases that are either fictional (such as Dexter Morgan from the popular television series *Dexter*) or composites, but still applied them to illustrate the chapter material.

- We further sharpened our focus on the role of psychologists in the legal system and the ethical issues they face. Chapter 1 introduces the conflicts that pervade a psychological analysis of the law: the rights of individuals versus the common good, equality versus discretion as ideals that can guide the legal system, discovering the truth or resolving conflicts as the goals that the legal system strives to accomplish, and science versus the law as a source of legal decisions. We return to these conflicts several times throughout the book as we apply them to specific issues.

- We added a new chapter (chapter 15) devoted exclusively to the psychology of corrections. This chapter covers both adults and juveniles, and is heavily influenced by the importance of evidence-based practice. Accordingly, it describes both theoretical approaches and empirical evidence on assessing risk, identifying needs, and intervening accordingly.

- We distributed our coverage of children and adolescents among chapters that focus on the specific issues that sometimes involve young people (e.g., victimization, eyewitness reliability, forensic interviewing, adjudication and sentencing, corrections).

This edition includes a thorough, authoritative revision of every chapter in light of research and professional literature published since the last edition. Highlights include the following:

- Chapter 2, on players in the legal system, expands our discussion of the selection and retention of judges, and includes coverage of problem-solving courts like drug courts, mental health courts, and domestic violence courts.

- Chapter 4, on the psychology of police, includes updates on crisis intervention (police Crisis Intervention Teams) and police interactions with the mentally ill. There are also updates on the process involved in officer selection, and in the changes in policing in a post-911 era of enhanced concern about terrorism.

- Chapter 5 describes reforms to lineup procedures in cases involving eyewitness identification. These modifications, based on the scientific study of eyewitness memory, have now been implemented in several jurisdictions.

- Chapter 6 covers the evaluation of criminal suspects. It includes new studies on neuroimaging and brain wave analysis in deception detection, and highlights recent research on social influence factors in interrogations.

- Chapter 7, on issues that arise between arrest and trial, now covers psychological aspects of plea-bargaining in criminal cases and settlement negotiations in civil cases.

- Chapter 8, on forensic assessment in criminal cases, includes an expanded description of the topic of juvenile transfer, as well as updated material on the topics of competence to stand trial, insanity, and capital sentencing.

- Chapter 9 details forensic assessment in civil cases. It includes updated material illustrating problems with expertise and perceived bias (in a case against a pharmaceutical company stemming from the Columbine shootings). It also describes the difficulties experienced by an Arab-American police officer in an era in which terrorism is a major societal concern—and bias against certain groups may have increased accordingly.

- Chapter 11 describes psychological aspects of jury selection and representation and uses the Enron trial to illustrate important concepts regarding jury selection. It also describes recent research on how heterogeneity in the makeup of juries influences their deliberation experiences and the public's perceptions of fairness.

- Chapter 12 provides relevant updates regarding jury competence and concerns about juror bias. It also discusses jurors' use of technological advances such as Wikipedia, Twitter, Blackberries, and iPhones to seek and exchange information relevant to a trial and judges' attempts to curtail these activities.

- Chapter 13, on the psychology of victims, features new sections on the consequences of early victimization and offenders' experiences as victims of crime and violence.

- Chapter 14 addresses punishment and sentencing, including expanded coverage of restorative approaches to resolving conflicts. It also discusses the dual goals of juvenile court sentencing: ensuring public safety and meeting children's needs. As well, this chapter describes recent Supreme Court decisions regarding capital punishment of juvenile and mentally ill offenders—and the psychological research relevant to these decisions.

- Chapter 15 on correctional treatment is entirely new. It includes a description of a theoretically important approach to rehabilitation (the Risk-Need-Responsivity theory, or RNR) and how that approach has been applied with both juveniles and adults. Particular rehabilitation approaches are selected both for theoretical relevance and because they have been scientifically tested—and hence can be described as "empirically supported."

- The appendices for this book are now available online at www.cengage.com/psychology/greene. They include the Ethical Principles of Psychologists and Code of Conduct as well as the Specialty Guidelines for Forensic Psychologists, both of which provide ethical guidance for practice and research in forensic psychology. They also include the Bill of Rights, which describes the amendments to the United States Constitution.

For assistance in preparing this edition, Edie Greene thanks Jenny Robbins and Tracy Fuchs, and Kirk Heilbrun thanks Kento Yasuhara. The authors jointly thank Sarah Evertson for photo research, Melena Fenn who coordinated the production, and Wendy Heath who wrote the Instructors' Manual. Each was extremely helpful in crafting the 7th edition of *Psychology and the Legal System.*

About the Authors

Rebecca Siegel

Edie Greene is currently Professor of Psychology and Director of the Graduate Concentration in Psychology and Law at the University of Colorado (Colorado Springs). She earned her Ph.D. in cognitive psychology and law at the University of Washington in 1983 and served there as postdoctoral research associate between 1983 and 1986. From 1994-1995, Greene was a fellow in Law and Psychology at Harvard Law School. She has received several federally funded grants to support her research on legal decision making, eyewitness memory, and psycholegal aspects of aging. Greene received a college-wide award for Outstanding Research and Creative Works in 1999, university-wide award for Excellence in Research in 2001, and the Chancellor's Award for Distinguished Faculty in 2009. She has been invited to lecture at the National Judicial College and at continuing legal education programs nation-wide. She consults with lawyers on various trial-related issues including jury selection, trial strategies, and jury decisions and has, on numerous occasions, testified as an expert witness on jury behavior and eyewitness memory. In addition to serving as co-author for the 5th and 6th editions of *Psychology and the Legal System,* Greene is the author of a number of articles, columns, and book chapters and co-author of *The adversary system* (with Frank Strier, 1990), and *Determining damages: The psychology of jury awards* (with Brian Bornstein, 2003). She has served as President of the American Psychology-Law Society/APA Division 41 and, in 2008, received the Award for Outstanding Teaching and Mentoring from that Society.

Anna Heilbrun

Kirk Heilbrun is currently Professor and Head, Department of Psychology, Drexel University. He received his doctorate in clinical psychology in 1980 from the University of Texas at Austin, and completed postdoctoral fellowship training from 1981-82 in psychology and criminal justice at Florida State University. His current research focuses on juvenile and adult offenders, legal decision-making, and forensic evaluation associated with such decision-making, as well as primary prevention through academic-sport mentoring in youth. He is the author of a number of articles on forensic assessment, violence risk assessment and risk communication, and the treatment of mentally disordered offenders. In addition to serving as co-author for the 6th edition of *Psychology and the Legal System,* he has published five books (*Principles of Forensic Mental Health Assessment,* 2001; *Forensic Mental Health Assessment: A Casebook,* with Geff Marczyk and Dave DeMatteo, 2002; *Juvenile Delinquency: Prevention, Assessment, and Intervention,* with Naomi Goldstein and Rich Redding, 2005; *Foundations of Forensic Mental Health Assessment,* with Tom Grisso and Alan Goldstein, 2008; and *Evaluations for Risk of Violence in Adults,* in 2009). His practice interests also center around forensic assessment, and he directs a clinic within the department in this area. He is board certified in Clinical Psychology and in Forensic Psychology, American Board of Professional Psychology, and has previously served as president of both the American Psychology-Law Psychology/APA Division 41, and the American Board of Forensic Psychology. He received the 2004 Distinguished Contributions to Forensic Psychology award and the 2008 Beth Clark Distinguished Service award from the American Academy of Forensic Psychology.

1

Psychology and the Law
Choices and Roles

ORIENTING QUESTIONS

1. Why do we have laws and what is the psychological approach to studying law?
2. What choices are reflected in the psychological approach to the law?
3. How do recent laws reflect the contrast between due process and crime control in the criminal justice system?
4. What are five roles that psychologists may play in the legal system and what does each entail?

Consider the following stories, all of which were prominently featured in the news:

- In a string of brazen shootings in early 2009, 23 Americans died within a 48-hour period. Among them were 13 people shot by a troubled Vietnamese immigrant at an immigration center in New York State, 3 Pittsburgh police officers killed by a gun enthusiast recently discharged from the Marine Corps, and 5 children in Graham, Washington, whose father was distraught over the breakup of his marriage. Crime analysts advanced various explanations for the carnage, including the dismal state of the economy and the country's lax gun laws. But perhaps more telling is that each of the shooters had recently experienced a traumatic event—unemployment, a layoff, a separation—that may have unleashed an internal rage and desire for revenge.

- A drunken driver who killed a 10-year-old boy in suburban Dallas was sentenced to spend 180 days in jail over the next 10 years, including every Christmas Day, New Year's Day, and June 8, the child's birthday. The judge said he wanted to remind the defendant of the family's loss on these important family holidays.

- As part of its War on Terror, the U.S. government authorized psychologists employed by the CIA to design and monitor interrogation programs used on suspected terrorists in overseas prisons between 2002 and 2006. Their methods included confining detainees in small boxes, stripping them, slamming them against walls, blasting music into cold cells, using insects to induce fear, and waterboarding.

These techniques were justified by the desire to break detainees so they would provide sensitive information about Al Qaeda. But even some interrogators who imposed them were distressed by the torment they caused.

These stories illustrate a few of the psycholegal issues that we consider in this book: the motivations of offenders, discretion in sentencing decisions, and the nature and consequences of harsh interrogation techniques. They show the real flesh and blood of some of the issues we focus on throughout the book.

THE IMPORTANCE OF LAWS

These examples also illustrate the pervasiveness of the law in our society. But how does the law work? This book will help you understand how the legal system operates by applying psychological concepts, theories, findings, and methods to its study.

Laws as Human Creations

Laws are everywhere. They affect everything from birth to death. Laws regulate our private lives and our public actions. Laws dictate how long we must stay in school, how fast we can drive, when (and, to some extent, whom) we can marry, and whether we are allowed to play our car stereos at full blast or let our boisterous dog romp through the neighbors' yards and gardens. Given that the body of laws has such a widespread impact, we might expect that the law is a part of nature, that it was originally discovered by a set of archaeologists or explorers. Perhaps we think of Moses carrying the Ten Commandments down from the mountain.

But our laws are not chiseled in stone. Rather, laws are human creations that evolve out of the needs for order and conflict resolution. In addition, groups differ in what is considered acceptable behavior, so there are disagreements among people. When these disagreements occur, society must have mechanisms to resolve them. Thus societies develop laws and other regulations as conflict resolution mechanisms.

Laws Help Resolve Conflict and Protect the Public

Conflict—disagreement, argument, and dispute—is not necessarily bad; nor is it always good. Mainly, conflict is inevitable. It cannot be avoided, any more than you can avoid sneezing when the urge to sneeze begins. But society can establish procedures to control your behavior when your sneezing intrudes on another's rights. We recognize the need for mechanisms—laws, rules, and habits—to discourage a person from sneezing in people's faces or on their food. Customs and rules of etiquette evolve partly to deal with the conflict between one person's impulses and other people's rights. Similarly, laws are developed to manage and resolve those conflicts that cannot be prevented.

Public safety is always an important consideration in a civilized society. In earlier times, before laws were established to deter and punish unacceptable behavior, people "took the law" into their own hands, acting as vigilantes to secure the peace and impose punishment on offenders. Now, at least in the United States and most other nations, every governmental entity—states, counties, boroughs, municipalities, and even some neighborhoods—have enacted laws to protect the public.

The Changing of Laws

Because our society is so technologically developed, it is also constantly changing. As society changes, so does our day-to-day existence. The basic raw material for the construction and the revision of laws is human experience. Laws must be developed,

interpreted, reinterpreted, and modified to keep up with the rapid changes in our lives. As George Will (1984) put it, "Fitting the law to a technologically dynamic society often is like fitting trousers to a 10-year-old: Adjustments are constantly needed" (p. 6).

Certainly the framers of the U.S. Constitution, and even legislators of 30 years ago, never anticipated the possibility that frozen embryos and in vitro fertilization procedures would lead a man to sue a fertility clinic for wrongfully impregnating his ex-wife with a frozen embryo created years before. Although Richard Gladu consented to in vitro fertilization while still married, he claimed that he should have had a choice about what would happen to the embryos when his marriage was dissolved—and accused his ex-wife of using the frozen embryos without his consent. Similarly, no one could have anticipated the ways that DNA testing would change the scope of criminal investigations. Law enforcement officials have collected DNA samples from millions of Americans, including those who have simply been arrested and are awaiting trial. Officials claim that widespread testing will help them solve more crimes and exonerate people who were wrongly convicted. (We describe the role of DNA analysis in the exoneration of convicted criminals in Chapter 5.)

Recent widespread use of the Internet has caused legislators to consider what, if any, restrictions should be placed on its use. (Cyber-law, virtually unheard of 20 years ago, has become an important subfield in the law.) For example, the Children's Internet Protection Act, passed by Congress in 2000, required libraries that receive federal funding to use antipornography filtering software. Prosecutors have recently considered filing charges against teenagers for sexually abusing minors after nude and seminude pictures of the teens were distributed by cell phones (so-called "sexting"). Should laws regulate these activities? Some people claim that they interfere with constitutionally protected speech and privacy rights.

Car accidents (even minor ones) also cause conflicts over basic rights. The technological development of the automobile produced several new adversaries—including pedestrians versus drivers—and hence new laws. Consider a driver whose car strikes and injures a pedestrian. Does this driver have a legal responsibility to report the incident to the police? Yes. But doesn't this requirement violate the Fifth Amendment to the U.S. Constitution, which safeguards each of us against self-incrimination, against bearing witness in conflict with our own best interests?

Shortly after automobiles became popular in the first two decades of the 20th century, a man named Edward Rosenheimer was charged with violating the newly necessary reporting laws. He did not contest the charge that he had caused an accident that injured another person, but he claimed that the law requiring him to report it to the police was unconstitutional because it forced him to incriminate himself. Therefore, he argued, this particular law should be removed from the books, and he should be freed of the charge of leaving the scene of an accident. Surprisingly, the Court of General Sessions in New York State agreed with him and released him from custody.

Authorities in New York were, of course, unhappy with a court decision that permitted a person who had caused an injury to avoid being apprehended, so they appealed the decision to a higher court, the New York Court of Appeals. This court, recognizing that the Constitution and the recent law clashed with each other, ruled in favor of the state and overturned the previous decision. This appeals court concluded that rights to "constitutional privilege"— that is, to avoid self-incrimination—must give way to the competing principle of the right of injured persons to seek redress for their sufferings (Post, 1963). This example illustrates once more that the law is an evolving human creation, designed to arbitrate between values in opposition to each other. Before the advent of automobiles, hit-and-run accidents seldom occurred. However, once cars became a part of society, many new laws had to be enacted, and the courts obliged by holding the new laws to be constitutional.

THE PSYCHOLOGICAL STUDY

OF LAW

Laws and legal systems are studied by several traditional disciplines. For example, anthropologists compare laws (and mechanisms for instituting and altering laws) in different societies and relate them to other characteristics of these societies. They may be interested in how frequently women are raped in different types of societies and in the relationship between rape and other factors, such as the extent of separation of the sexes during childhood or the degree to which males dominate females (Sanday, 1997).

Sociologists, in contrast, usually study a specific society and examine its institutions (e.g., the family, the church, or the subculture) to determine their role in developing adherence to the law. The sociologist might study the role that social class plays in criminal behavior. This approach tries to predict and explain social behavior by focusing on groups of people rather than on individuals.

A psychological approach to the law emphasizes its human determinants. The focus in the psychological approach is on the individual as the unit of analysis. Individuals are seen as responsible for their own conduct and as contributing to its causation. Psychology examines the thoughts, actions, and impacts of the police officer, victim, juror, expert witness, corporate lawyer, judge, defendant, prison guard, and parole officer on the legal system. Psychology assumes that characteristics of participants in the legal system affect how the system operates, and it also recognizes that the law, in turn, can affect individuals' characteristics and behavior (Ogloff & Finkelman, 1999). By *characteristics*, we mean these persons' abilities, perspectives, values, and experiences—all the factors that influence their behavior. Will a defendant and his attorney accept a plea bargain, or will they go to trial? Will a Hispanic juror be more sympathetic toward a Hispanic defendant than toward a non-Hispanic defendant? Answers to these legally-relevant questions are determined by a person's multifaceted characteristics.

But the behavior of participants in the legal system is not just a result of their personal qualities. The setting in which they operate matters as well. Kurt Lewin, a founder of social psychology, proposed the equation $B = f(p, e)$: behavior is a function of the person and the environment. Qualities of the external environment and pressures from the situation affect an individual's behavior.

A prosecuting attorney may recommend a harsher sentence for a convicted felon if the case has been highly publicized, the community is outraged over the crime, and the prosecutor happens to be waging a reelection campaign. A juror holding out for a guilty verdict may yield if all the other jurors passionately proclaim the defendant's innocence. The social environment affects legally relevant choices.

This book concentrates on the behavior of participants in the legal system. As the examples at the beginning of this chapter indicate, we are all active participants in the system, even if we do not work in occupations directly tied to the administration of justice. We all face daily choices that are affected by the law—whether to speed through a school zone because we are late to class or whether to report the person who removes someone else's laptop from a table at the library. Hence, this book will also devote some attention to the determinants of our conceptions of justice and the moral dilemmas we all face.

But we will pay particular attention to the central participants in the legal system: defendants and witnesses, civil and criminal lawyers, judges and juries, convicts and parole boards. We will also focus on the activities of **forensic psychologists** who generate and communicate information to answer specific legal questions or to help resolve legal disputes (Heilbrun, Grisso, & Goldstein, 2008; Melton, Petrila, Poythress, & Slobogin, 2007). Most forensic psychologists are trained as clinical psychologists, whose specialty involves the psychological evaluation and treatment of others. Forensic psychologists are often asked to evaluate a person and then prepare a report for a court, and sometimes provide expert testimony in a hearing or trial. For example, they may evaluate adult criminal defendants or children involved with the juvenile justice system and offer the court information relevant to determining whether the defendant has a mental disorder that prevents him from going to trial, what the defendant's mental state was at the time of the offense, or what treatment might be appropriate for a particular defendant. But psychologists can play many other roles in the legal system, as well. We describe these roles later in the chapter.

BASIC CHOICES IN THE PSYCHOLOGICAL STUDY OF THE LAW

Just as each of us has to make decisions about personal values, society must decide which values it wants its laws to reflect. Choices lead to conflict, and often the resulting dilemmas cannot be resolved easily. Should the laws uphold the rights of specific individuals or protect society in general? For example, which should take precedence—your right to run a loud floor waxer at 3:00 a.m. or the right of everyone else in your apartment building to get a decent night's sleep? Is it better for ten murderers to go free than for one innocent person to be sentenced to death? The law struggles with the fact that rights desirable for some individuals may be problematic for others.

What kind of a society do we want? What laws will best achieve our society's goals? What functions should the legal system serve in our society? These questions highlight four basic choices that pervade the law as it applies to each of us in the United States, Canada, and many other countries. Each choice creates a dilemma and has psychological implications. No decision about these choices will be completely satisfactory because no decision can simultaneously attain two incompatible goals, both of which our society values. These four choices (and the tension inherent in their competing values) are so basic that they surface repeatedly throughout this book.

For example, our society champions freedom and equality, but it is hard to achieve both at the same time. A small-town civic organization that has always had a "males-only" policy at its Friday night dinners is also a vehicle by which prominent citizens transact their business. The men enjoy the "freedom" to act like "good ole boys" in the company of their own gender. But what if a woman starts a new insurance agency in town? Doesn't she have the right to "equality"—to full and equal participation in the civic organization that is influential in the success of any business in this community? It is hard to see how a resolution of this conflict could fully meet both of these goals (freedom of existing members and equality among all comers). The balance in such cases often shifts from one value to another, emphasizing the attainment of first one and then the other goal.

The First Choice: Rights of Individuals versus the Common Good

Consider the following:

- Smokers have long been restricted to smoky airport lounges and back sections of restaurants, and they often huddle together outside of workplace doors. But now some smokers are banned from lighting up in the confines of their own homes. Edith Frederickson, a two-pack-a-day smoker for 50 years, is one. She lives in an apartment complex for low-income seniors in Belmont, California, home to the nation's strictest antismoking law. "I'm absolutely outraged," said Ms. Frederickson. "They're telling you how to live and what to do, and they're doing it right here in America." But her neighbor, 84-year-old Ray Goodrich, who has a pulmonary disease and allergy problems, thinks otherwise. Mr. Goodrich and other neighbors complained to the city council about the effects of secondhand smoke, including persistent headaches, and a fire that broke out in one smoker's apartment fed by the smoker's oxygen tank (McKinley, 2009). Should cities be able to limit smoking in buildings where residents share walls, ceilings, and even the air? Whose rights prevail?

- In 2009, six states—Massachusetts, Connecticut, Vermont, Maine, New Hampshire, and Iowa—allowed same-sex marriage, and legislators in New York and New Jersey were debating the issue. Same-sex couples had been marrying in California prior to a constitutional amendment banning the practice in 2008. Yet laws and initiatives passed in several other states bar same-sex couples from marrying. Americans are clearly divided on this issue: According to a 2008 Gallup Poll, 54% favor civil unions (which grant gay and lesbian couples virtually the same rights and privileges as heterosexual couples), yet another poll conducted that same year showed that only about 40% of Americans favor same-sex marriage. This issue raises complex questions about individual rights versus traditional societal definitions of the family.

- In a less serious sort of dispute, a growing number of cities have made it a crime to wear "sagging pants" and some cases have actually gone to trial. Three defendants were charged with violating the "decency ordinance" in Riviera Beach, Florida. Their public defenders argued that the law violated principles of freedom of expression. But the town's mayor, Thomas Masters, said that voters "just got tired of having to look at people's behinds or their undergarments … I think society has the right to draw the line" (Newton, 2009).

A lesbian couple celebrating their marraige.

Values in Conflict. The preceding vignettes share a common theme. On the one hand, individuals possess rights, and one function of the law is to ensure that these rights are protected. The United States is perhaps the most individualistic society in the world. People can deviate from the norm, or "do their own thing," to a greater degree in the United States than virtually anywhere else. Freedom and personal autonomy are two of our most deeply desired values; "the right to liberty" is a key phrase in the U.S. Constitution.

On the other hand, our society also has expectations. People need to feel secure. They need to believe that potential lawbreakers are discouraged from breaking laws because they know they will be punished. All of us have rights to a peaceful, safe existence. Likewise, society claims a vested interest in restricting those who take risks that may injure themselves or others, because these actions can create burdens on society.

It is clear that two sets of rights and two goals for the law are often in conflict. The tension between the rights of the individual and the constraints that may be placed on the individual for the collective good is always present. We have seen it in various U.S. Supreme Court decisions since the 1960s with respect to the rights of criminal suspects and defendants versus the rights of crime victims and the power of the police.

The Supreme Court in the 1960s, headed by Chief Justice Earl Warren, established a number of principles that provided or expanded explicit rights for those suspected of breaking the law. The *Miranda* rule guaranteeing the right to remain silent (detailed in Chapter 6) was established in 1966. About the same time, the courts required that criminal defendants, in all cases in which incarceration is possible, have the right to an attorney, even if they can't afford to pay for one. These and other rights were established in an effort to redress a perceived imbalance in responding to important values.

The Supreme Court under Chief Justice Warren Burger, from 1969 to 1986, and Chief Justice William Rehnquist, from 1986 to 2005, trimmed the rights established by the Warren

Court by frequently ruling in favor of the police. (For example, in the 1996 case of *Whren v. United States*, the Supreme Court ruled that the police can properly stop a motorist whom they believe has violated traffic laws even if their ulterior motive is to investigate the possibility of illegal drug dealing. Because many motorists break the speed limit, most are subject to being pulled over and questioned about drug trafficking.) Chief Justice John Roberts has followed in the footsteps of his immediate predecessor and mentor, William Rehnquist, in his decisions (e.g., *United States v. Grubbs*, 2006).

Two Models of the Criminal Justice System. The conflict between the rights of individuals and the rights of society is related to a distinction between two models of the criminal justice system. This distinction is between the due process model and the crime control model (Packer, 1964).

The **due process model** places primary value on the protection of citizens, including criminal suspects, from possible abuses by the police and the law enforcement system generally. It assumes the innocence of suspects and requires that they be treated fairly (receive "due process") by the criminal justice system. It subscribes to the maxim that "it is better that ten guilty persons shall go free than that one innocent person should suffer." Thus the due process model emphasizes the rights of individuals, especially those suspected of crimes, over the temptation by society to assume suspects are guilty even before a trial.

In contrast, the **crime control model** seeks the apprehension and punishment of lawbreakers. It emphasizes the efficient detection of suspects and the effective prosecution of defendants, to help ensure that criminal activity is being contained or reduced. The crime control model is exemplified by a statement by former attorney general of the United States William P. Barr with respect to career criminals. He noted that the goal is "incapacitation through incarceration" (Barr, 1992)—that is, removing them permanently from circulation.

When the crime control model is dominant in society, laws may be passed that in other times would be seen as unacceptable violations of individual rights. The Racketeer Influenced and Corrupt Organizations (RICO) laws, passed by Congress in 1970, are an example. Although the original purpose of the RICO laws was to combat the growing influence of organized crime on legitimate business (Vise, 1989), they have been used to prosecute Wall Street executives for stock fraud and tax evasion charges, going beyond the usual definition of "racketeer."

Despite the drop in crime rates in recent years, the crime control model is clearly ascendant in the United States, more so than in Canada, Europe, or Australia. As we point out in Chapter 14, the United States incarcerates a higher percentage of its citizens than any other country (currently 751 of every 100,000 Americans are imprisoned, and the decade of the 1990s saw far more prisoners incarcerated than any decade in recorded history). According to the Center on Juvenile and Criminal Justice, the United States has only 5% of the world's population but nearly 25% of its prisoners.

Since 1993, several states and the federal government have passed laws that reflect the crime control model's goal of keeping lawbreakers off the streets. California's 1994 **three-strikes law** ("three strikes and you're out") is the most stringent. Under this law, criminals convicted of a third felony, no matter how minor, must be sentenced to either 25 years to life in prison or

triple the regular sentence, whichever is greater, if their first and second offenses were serious or violent. Persons convicted a second time of a serious or violent felony have their sentences doubled.

Although such laws are intended to increase the punishments for habitual criminals, they sometimes lead to results that make it doubtful whether the punishment fits the crime. For example, a California man with multiple convictions was sentenced to 25 years to life in prison for stealing a slice of pizza; another received the same sentence for impersonating his dead brother in a routine traffic stop. In fact, one study found that the vast majority of those receiving the stiff sentences had committed a nonviolent offense as their "third-and-out" crime. Almost 200 were sentenced for marijuana possession, compared to 40 who were convicted of murder, 25 of rape, and 24 of kidnapping. "We're worried about Willie Horton [a convicted sex offender], and we lock up the Three Stooges," said Professor Franklin Zimring of the University of California at Berkeley (quoted by Butterfield, 1996, p. A8).

Another study found that seven years after it was enacted, the three-strikes law had contributed to the aging of the prison population but had no apparent effect on the state's crime rate. This study estimates that by 2026, California will have 30,000 inmates serving sentences of 25 years to life, at a cost to taxpayers of at least $750 million, and that more than 80% of them will be 40 or older (King & Mauer, 2001).

Psychology, as an approach to the law, provides methods for assessing public support for these laws and the models of criminal justice. In one survey, 72% approved of a three-strikes law. In another survey, 50% responded "true" to the following: "In a criminal trial, it is up to the person who is accused of the crime to prove his innocence." This is a false statement—the accused doesn't even have to offer a defense, other than to plead "not guilty"—but half the respondents answered incorrectly, implicitly advocating the crime control view.

Their error does not mean that the crime control model is wrong. The values underlying each of the contrasting models are legitimate, and the goal of our society is to achieve a balance between them. As you will see throughout this book, governments and courts constantly struggle to offer a mix of laws that reasonably reflects each set of values.

The Second Choice: Equality versus Discretion

Kenneth Peacock was a long-distance trucker who was caught in an ice storm and came home at the wrong time. He walked in the door to find his wife Sandra in bed with another man. Peacock chased the man away and some four hours later, in the heat of an argument, shot his wife in the head with a hunting rifle. Peacock pled guilty to voluntary manslaughter and was sentenced to 18 months in prison. At the sentencing, Baltimore County Circuit Court Judge Robert E. Cahill said he wished he did not have to send Peacock to prison at all but knew that he must to "keep the system honest" (Lewin, 1994). He continued, "I seriously wonder how many men … would have the strength to walk away without inflicting some corporal punishment."

Move the clock ahead one day. A female defendant pleads guilty to voluntary manslaughter in a different Baltimore courtroom. She killed her husband after 11 years of abuse and was given a three-year sentence, three times longer than that sought by prosecutors (Lewin, 1994). Some people find no inconsistency in the severity of these punishments, believing that each case should be judged on its own merits. However, psychology analyzes these decisions as examples of a choice between the goals of equality and discretion.

What should be the underlying principle guiding the response to persons accused of violating the law? Again, we discover that two equally desirable values are often incompatible and hence create conflict—and psychology provides concepts through which this conflict can be studied and better understood.

The principle of **equality** means that all people who commit the same crime or misdeed should receive the same consequences. Fundamental to our legal system is the assumption advanced by the founders of the American republic that "all men are created equal." In fact, the "equal protection clause" of the Fourteenth Amendment states that no state shall "deny to any person within its jurisdiction the equal protection of the laws." This statement is frequently interpreted to mean that all people should be treated equally and that no one should receive special treatment by the courts simply because he or she is rich, influential, or otherwise advantaged. We cherish the belief that in the United States, politically powerful or affluent people are brought before the courts and, if guilty, convicted and punished just like anyone else who commits similar offenses. Consider the example of disgraced financier Bernard Madoff. A former chairman of the NASDAQ Stock Exchange, Madoff pled guilty in 2009 to perpetrating the largest investor fraud in history, and exchanged his three homes and a yacht on the French Riviera for a cell in the federal prison system.

But this value of equality before the law is not always implemented. In the last two decades, Americans have witnessed a series of incidents that—at least on the surface—seemed to indicate unequal treatment of citizens by the legal system. A common practice among police and state patrols in the United States is *profiling*—viewing certain

Bernard Madoff

characteristics as indicators of criminal behavior. African American and Latino motorists have filed numerous lawsuits over the practice of profiling, alleging that the police, in an effort to seize illegal drugs and weapons or to find undocumented immigrants, apply a "race-based profile" to stop and search them more frequently than White drivers. The plaintiffs in one Maryland case assembled an impressive set of statistics: Although 75% of drivers on Interstate 95 are White, only 23% of the people stopped and searched between 1995 and 1997 were White. Conversely, although only 17% of drivers on the interstate are Black, 70% of those pulled over were Black. Said Michigan Congressman John Conyers, Jr., "There are virtually no African-American males—including Congressmen, actors, athletes and office workers—who have not been stopped at one time or another for … driving while black" (Barovick, 1998). (Indeed, State Senator Kevin Murray of California was pulled over and questioned by police as he drove through Beverly Hills on the very night he won his Senate primary in 1998.) Nor is the issue limited to driving. It affects people when they shop, eat in restaurants, travel in trains and airplanes, hail a cab, and walk through their neighborhoods.

Many police agencies now gather statistics on the racial makeup of people targeted for traffic stops, border inspections, and other routine searches, and some courts have ruled that a person's appearance may not be the basis for such stops. Psychologists also have a role to play on this issue, gathering data on the psychological consequences to victims of racial profiling, improving police training so that cultural and racial awareness is enhanced, and examining how decision makers form implicit judgments of others on the basis of race.

In keeping with the laudable goal of equality under the law, the U.S. Supreme Court has occasionally applied a **principle of proportionality**; that is, the punishment should be consistently related to the magnitude of the offense. More serious wrongdoing should earn more severe penalties. If a relatively minor crime leads to a harsh punishment, then the fundamental value of equality has been violated.

The Supreme Court has also applied this concept in the realm of civil law, specifically in the amount of punitive damages that can be assessed against a defendant (*BMW of North America v. Gore*, 1996). The objective of punitive damages is to punish the defendant and deter future wrongdoing. After plaintiff Ira Gore bought a new BMW, he discovered that the car had been repainted to counteract the effects of acid rain. Gore sued, and an Alabama jury awarded him $4,000 in compensatory damages (to offset the lost value of the car) and $4 million in punitive damages. Although the Alabama Supreme Court reduced the punitive award to $2 million, the U.S. Supreme Court deemed even that amount "excessive." Noting that the punitive damages award was 500 times larger than the compensatory award and that Gore's financial injury was relatively insignificant, the Supreme Court ruled that such a large award violated the Fourteenth Amendment due process clause. In essence, the punitive damage award was disproportionate to the extent of the damage.

Yet the Supreme Court has also upheld the constitutionality of California's three-strikes law, setting aside arguments that at least in some cases, the punishment is grossly disproportionate to the severity of the offense (*Ewing v. California*, 2003). Even the highest court in the land struggles with the meaning of equality and its application to diverse sets of facts.

Although equality often remains an overriding principle, society also believes that **discretion** is appropriate. Rigid application of the law can lead to injustices. By discretion, we mean the use of judgments about the circumstances of certain offenses that lead to appropriate *variations* in how the system responds to these offenses. Many players in the legal system have the opportunity to exercise discretion, and most do so regularly. Police officers show discretion when they decide not to arrest someone who has technically broken the law. Prosecutors exercise discretion when they decide which of many arrestees to charge and for what particular crime. Juries exercise discretion in not convicting defendants who have killed under circumstances that may have justified their actions (e.g., self-defense, heat of passion).

B o x 1.1   THE CASE OF STANLEY TOOKIE WILLIAMS AND A GOVERNOR'S DISCRETION

In 1979, Stanley Tookie Williams was convicted of four murders committed in the course of botched robberies in Los Angeles and sentenced to death. Several years earlier, Williams had cofounded the Crips street gang. While imprisoned, he was involved in various fights and escape attempts. These facts do not portend a life of peace or decency. But through a series of personal transformations in the early 1990s, Williams became a powerful voice from prison of the perils of gang violence. In a series of children's books, lectures, and a memoir, Williams denounced violence, apologized for his role in the Crips, and urged young people to resist the allure of gangs. His story was told in the 2004 television movie, "Redemption," starring Jamie Foxx.

This apparent transformation captured the public's attention and led to numerous calls for clemency in the months leading up to Williams's scheduled

AP Images/Louis Lanzano, file

Supporter of Stanley "Tookie" Williams

execution in 2005. National and international rallies and vigils were held on his behalf, and activist campaigns took up his cause. But California Governor Arnold Schwarzenegger was not swayed; he rejected arguments that Williams deserved mercy because of claims of redemption. Williams was executed at San Quentin State Prison on December 13, 2005.

Although not usually considered formal participants in the justice system, state governors also have the opportunity to exercise discretion when they decide whether to commute a death sentence to life imprisonment (a process called granting clemency) or to allow an execution to proceed as planned. California Governor Arnold Schwarzenegger faced that stark choice in 2005 (see Box 1.1). He had to decide whether death row inmate Stanley Tookie Williams, who had become a symbol of peace and redemption in prison, should be executed by lethal injection or allowed to live. This case raises interesting questions about both discretion and the role of rehabilitation in the criminal justice system.

Discretion may be most obvious in the sentences administered by judges to convicted criminals. In many cases, judges are able to consider the particular circumstances of the defendant and of the crime itself when they determine the sentence. It would seem that this use of discretion is good, yet as we describe in Chapter 14, it can also lead to **sentencing disparity**, the tendency for different judges to administer a variety of penalties for the same crime. The contrasting sentences handed out by judges in the Baltimore cases we

described earlier provide one example of sentencing disparity.

Sentencing disparity is also apparent in the penalties given to African Americans and members of other minority groups. A thorough survey of the sentences given to convicted murderers in Philadelphia (Baldus, Woodworth, Zuckerman, Weiner, & Broffitt, 1998) found that African Americans were significantly more likely than people of other races to receive the death penalty, even when controlling for the severity of the crime (see Chapter 14). But inequality in punishment is not limited to the most serious crimes. A study of prison and jail incarceration rates (across *all* crime categories) for 2007 revealed that African Americans were more than six times more likely than Whites to be imprisoned. This disparity can also be seen for Hispanics—one in six Hispanic males and one in 45 Hispanic females can expect to be imprisoned in his or her lifetime, more than double the rates of those who are not Hispanic (Mauer & King, 2007).

A simple explanation for this disparity is **racial bias**, whereby police officers, prosecutors, jurors, and judges use an individual's race as a basis for judgments of his or her behavior. But the situation may actually be more complex. Some studies have shown that once decision makers are made aware of the potential for racial bias, they can largely avoid it, and racial injustices in the criminal justice system have declined in recent years (Spohn, 2000). A subtler, more insidious form of race-based judgments may still be prevalent in the justice system, however. Social psychological research has shown that individuals of the same race may be stereotyped and discriminated against to different degrees, depending how "typical" of their group they appear (Maddox & Gray, 2002). Thus, African Americans who possess more Afrocentric facial features may be subjected to more prejudicial treatment. Indeed, an analysis of criminal sentencing in Florida showed that among Black defendants, those with more Afrocentric features were given longer sentences than those with less distinctive Afrocentric features (Blair, Judd, & Chapleau, 2004).

To counteract sentencing disparity, many states implemented what is known as **determinate sentencing**; the offense determines the sentence, and judges and parole commissions have little discretion. But judges have been frustrated by the severe limitation on their discretion. One federal judge who resigned his appointment in protest over mandatory sentencing rules said, "It's an unfair system that has been dehumanized. There are rarely two cases that are identical. Judges should always have discretion. That's why we're judges. But now we're being made to be robots."

The pendulum has now begun to swing away from determinate sentencing and toward allowing judges more discretion. The Supreme Court ruled that both state (*Blakely v. Washington*, 2004) and federal sentencing guidelines (*United States v. Booker*, 2005) violate a defendant's right to a jury trial because the guidelines require judges to decide questions that are normally reserved for juries, such as the quantity of drugs involved in a narcotics case. Sentencing guidelines are now merely advisory. Permitting judges more leeway to consider factors such as the defendant's background, motivations for committing the crime, and any psychological disorders may strike a balance between the sentencing uniformity that the guidelines intended and the judicial discretion that some judges prefer.

The Third Choice: To Discover the Truth or to Resolve Conflicts

What is the purpose of a trial or a hearing before a judge? Your first reaction may be "To find out the truth, of course!" Determining the truth means learning the facts of the case, including events, intentions, actions, and outcomes. All this assumes that "what really happened" between two parties can be determined.

Finding out the truth is a desirable goal, but it may also be lofty and sometimes impossible. The truth often lies somewhere between competing versions of an event. Given that it is difficult for even well-meaning people to ascertain the true facts in certain cases, some observers have proposed that the real purpose of a hearing or trial is to provide social stability by resolving conflict. Supreme Court Justice Louis Brandeis once wrote that "it is more important that the applicable rule of law be settled than [that] it be settled right" (*Burnet v. Coronado Oil and Gas Co.*, 1932). This is a shift away from viewing the legal system's purpose as doing justice toward viewing its goal as "creating a sense that justice is being done" (Miller & Boster, 1977, p. 34).

Because truth is elusive, the most important priority of a hearing or a trial—whether it is to determine child custody or an alleged drug dealer's guilt—may be to provide a setting in which all interested parties have their "day in court." Justice for all parties replaces truth as the predominant goal. In fact, attorneys representing the opposing parties in a case do not necessarily seek "the truth." Nor do they represent themselves as "objective." They reflect a different value—the importance of giving their side the best representation possible, within the limits of the law. (The Code of Ethics of the American Bar Association even instructs attorneys to defend their clients "zealously.") Because lawyers believe the purpose of a hearing or trial is to win disputes, they present arguments supporting their client's perspective and back up their arguments with the best available evidence.

One argument in favor of the adversary system, in which a different attorney represents each party, is that it encourages the attorneys to discover and introduce all evidence that might induce the judge or jury to react favorably to their client's case. When both sides believe that they have had the chance to voice their case fully and their witnesses have revealed all the relevant facts, participants are more likely to feel they have been treated fairly by the system, and the system is more likely to be considered an effective one. This is an important part of a theory known as **procedural justice**, a concept we consider in Chapter 2.

"Conflict resolution" and "truth," as goals, are not always incompatible. When each participant ensures that his or her concerns and supporting documentation are presented in court, the goal of learning the truth often becomes more attainable. But frequently a tension between these goals exists. In some instances, the satisfactory resolution of a conflict may be socially and morally preferable to discovering an objectively established truth. But when conflict resolution compromises truth, the outcome can often be unsatisfactory.

This was the case for Richard Jewell, a security guard at the 1996 Summer Olympics in Atlanta. Shortly after a bombing that disrupted the Games, the Federal Bureau of Investigation (FBI) began to question Jewell, who discovered the bomb. Although at first the FBI denied that he was a suspect, they treated him like one, and his name and photograph were widely publicized. The pressure to find the person responsible for this terrifying act—and the desire to give people a sense that no more bombings would occur because the perpetrator had been caught—doubtless influenced the premature focus on Richard Jewell. Despite relentless FBI investigation, no charges were brought against Jewell, and in 2005, Eric Rudolph, a fugitive who lived in the hills of North Carolina for years after the bombing, pleaded guilty to that charge.

Truth versus Conflict Resolution in Plea Bargaining and Settlement Negotiations. The legal system is a massive bureaucracy, and in every bureaucracy, there is a temptation to value pragmatic efficiency rather than correct or just outcomes. The heavy reliance on plea bargaining is often criticized because it appears to give priority to conflict resolution over truth seeking. As we describe in Chapter 7, between 90% and 95% of defendants never go to trial; they accept the offer of the prosecutor and plead guilty to a lesser charge. Even some innocent persons plea-bargain after being convinced that the evidence against them is overwhelming. Indeed, plea bargaining remains an integral part of the criminal justice system. The state benefits by avoiding the expense and trouble of trial and the possibility of an acquittal, and often by obtaining the testimony of the accused against others involved in the crime. The defendant benefits by receiving some kind of reduction in the penalty

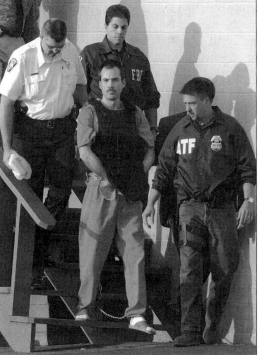

Eric Rudolph, a North Carolina fugitive, who pled guilty in 2005 to a bombing at the 1996 Olympics in Atlanta.

imposed. Many would argue that, in addition to these pragmatic benefits, justice is furthered by a system that rewards a show of remorse (which usually accompanies a guilty plea) and enables the prosecutor and defense counsel, together with the judge, to negotiate a resolution appropriate to the degree of wrongdoing (Kamisar, LaFave, & Israel, 1999). Nonetheless, the process shows how the goal of maintaining stability and efficiency in the system is achieved at some cost—the public's opportunity to determine the complete truth.

The civil justice system uses a procedure similar to plea bargaining to resolve about 90% of the conflicts between a plaintiff and a defendant. **Settlement negotiation** involves a sometimes lengthy pretrial process of give-and-take, offer-and-demand that ultimately ends with a plaintiff agreeing to accept what a defendant is willing to offer to end their legal disagreement.

Settlement negotiations also offer an opportunity for defendants to apologize for unforeseen outcomes experienced by the plaintiff. Although some defendants are loath to apologize because they fear that their apologies could be interpreted by judges and juries as admissions of responsibility, recent research shows that apologies may actually advance settlement negotiations and have other positive effects. In one study, people who were asked to take on the role of an injured person and evaluate a settlement offer were more likely to accept the offer when it was accompanied by an apology (Robbennolt, 2003). Apologies may also reduce plaintiffs' inclinations to sue (Greene, 2008), dissipate tension and antagonism in the settlement process (Shuman, 2000), and enhance jurors' perceptions of defendants (Bornstein, Rung, & Miller, 2002).

The Fourth Choice: Science versus the Law as a Source of Decisions

When one discipline (in our case, psychology) seeks to understand another (the law), a dilemma is likely to arise because each approaches knowledge in a different way. When asked, "How do you know whether that decision is the right one?" each relies on different methods, even though both share the goal of understanding human experience.

As you read this book you will learn that the U.S. Supreme Court and other courts have considered data and conclusions presented by psychologists and other social scientists in many recent decisions. In several cases, the American Psychological Association (APA) prepared a supporting brief or written document, called an *amicus curiae* ("friend of the court") **brief**, for consideration by an appellate court. Such *amicus curiae* briefs provide the courts with information from psychological science and practice relevant to the issues in a particular case. In many of its decisions, the Supreme Court has incorporated input from the *amicus curiae* brief, although in other cases it disregarded the social science data altogether. This inconsistency reflects the fact that the justices sometimes use different procedures and concepts from those of social science in forming their judicial opinions (Grisso & Saks, 1991).

In addition to employing different procedures, each profession may use idiosyncratic, or unique, concepts to describe the same phenomenon. An attorney and a social scientist will see the same event from different perspectives. Neither is necessarily more accurate than the other; the differences are the results of exposure to and training in different points of view. The following subsections illustrate such differences in more detail (see also Ogloff & Finkelman, 1999).

Law Relies on Precedents; Psychology Relies on Scientific Methods. Psychology, in contrast to the law, is generally committed to the idea that there is an objective world of experience that can be understood by adherence to the rules of science—systematic testing of hypotheses by observation and experimental methodology. As a scientist, the psychologist should be committed to a public, impersonal, objective pursuit of truth, using methods that can be repeated by others and interpreting results by predetermined standards. Although this traditional view of psychology's approach to truth is sometimes challenged as naive and simplistic because it ignores the importance of the personal, political, and historical biases that affect scientists as much as nonscientists (Gergen, 1994), it still represents the values and methods in which most psychologists are trained. (It also represents the authors' beliefs that the scientific method and the research skills of psychologists are the most essential and reliable tools available for examining the many important legal questions we address throughout the book.)

By contrast, when they establish new laws, legal experts rely heavily on **precedents**—rulings in previous cases (as well as the Constitution and the statutes) for guidance. **Case law**—the law made by judges ruling in individual cases—is very influential; statutes and constitutional safeguards do not apply to every new situation, so past cases often serve as precedents for deciding current ones. The principle of *stare decisis* ("let the decision stand," reflecting the importance of abiding by previous decisions) is also important in this process. Judges typically are reluctant to make decisions that contradict earlier ones, as the history of the Supreme Court's school desegregation cases indicates.

When the U.S. Supreme Court voted unanimously in 1954, in *Brown v. Board of Education*, that public school segregation was contrary to the law, many reports claimed that it "supplanted" or even "overturned" a ruling in the 1896 case of *Plessy v. Ferguson*. But intermediate decisions by the Court permitted this seemingly abrupt change to evolve gradually. A brief history of rulings that led up to the *Brown v. Board of Education* decision illustrates this phenomenon.

During a train trip in Louisiana in the 1890s, Homer Plessy sat down in a railroad car labeled "Whites Only." Plessy's ancestry was mostly Caucasian, but he had one Negro great-grandparent. Therefore, according to the laws of Louisiana at that time, Plessy was considered Black (or *colored*, the term used at that time). Plessy refused to move to a car designated for "colored" passengers, as a recently passed state law required. He took his claim to court, but a New Orleans judge ruled that, contrary to Plessy's argument, the statute that segregated railroad cars by race did not violate the Fourteenth Amendment to the Constitution. In other words, it did not fail to give Plessy "equal protection under

the law." Plessy persisted in his appeal, and eventually, in 1896, the U.S. Supreme Court upheld the decision of the judge and the lower courts. Judge Henry Billings Brown, speaking for the majority, declared that laws that had established separate facilities for the races did not necessarily imply that one race was inferior to the other.

Although this opinion was a far cry from the 1954 *Brown* decision, which highlighted the detrimental effects of segregation on the personality development of Black children, cases decided after *Plessy* and before *Brown* would foreshadow the Court's eventual leanings. One case was brought by George McLaurin, the first Black student admitted to the University of Oklahoma's Graduate School of Education. Although McLaurin was allowed to enroll, he was segregated from all his classmates. His desk was separated from all the others by a rail, to which the sign "Reserved for Colored" was attached; he was given a separate desk at the library; and he was required to eat by himself in the cafeteria. In the 1950 case of *McLaurin v. Oklahoma State Regents*, the U.S. Supreme Court ruled unanimously that these procedures denied McLaurin the right to equal protection of the law. The Court concluded that such restrictions would "impair and inhibit his ability to study, to engage in discussion and exchange of views with other students." But the Court did not strike down *Plessy v. Ferguson* in this decision.

With the appointment of Earl Warren as chief justice in 1953, however, there was enough momentum to reverse *Plessy v. Ferguson*. Justice Warren was less concerned with the fine points of the law than with whether the law was just. He liked to ask, "What is fair?" It was Warren who spearheaded the unanimous decision that finally overturned the idea that separate facilities can be "equal." He wrote that separating Black children "from others of similar age and qualifications solely because of their race generates a feeling of inferiority as to their status in the community that may affect their hearts and minds in a way unlikely to ever be undone" (*Brown v. Board of Education*, 1954).

The school desegregation cases show that lawyers reason from case to case. They locate

---

B o x 1.2   THE CASE OF FORMER ASTRONAUT LISA NOWAK: INSANE OR NOT?

Former astronaut Lisa Nowak

Lisa Nowak might prefer to be known as the flight engineer and robotics specialist who took several space-
walks during Space Shuttle *Discovery*'s trip to the
International Space Station in 2006. But most people
know her as the (former) astronaut who, on February
4–5, 2007, drove 900 miles from her home in Houston
to confront Colleen Shipman, the girlfriend of a fellow
astronaut with whom Nowak had been romantically
linked. On confronting the woman in a parking
garage at the Orlando airport, Nowak tried to enter
her car and squirted her with pepper spray. Nowak
was detained and arrested on charges of battery,
attempted kidnapping, and attempted murder. Based

on the evidence found in her car—black gloves, a BB
gun and ammunition, rubber tubing, a wig, a hooded
trench coat, and large garbage bags—the prosecutor
argued that Nowak had a detailed plan to kidnap and
perhaps injure Shipman. She was terminated by National
Aeronautics and Space Administration (NASA) in 2007.

In a pretrial motion, Nowak's attorneys indicated
that they would pursue an insanity defense. As we describe in Chapter 8, the insanity defense is used in cases
in which the defendant may not have known, at the
time of the crime, that her conduct was wrong—or (in
some states) may have been unable to conform her
conduct to the requirements of the law. We also explain the elusive nature of one's mental state at the
time of a crime and that the goals of clinical psychologists—diagnosis and treatment—do not correspond
well to the legal system's need for clarity on the issue
(i.e., was she, or was she not "insane" when she committed these acts?). Nowak's lawyer claim that she suffered from major depression, obsessive-compulsive
disorder, insomnia, and a "brief psychotic disorder
with marked stressors" at the time of the incident. She
eventually pled guilty to less serious crimes.

---

cases that are similar to the one at hand and then
base their arguments on the rulings from these
legal precedents. Psychologists, on the other hand,
value the scientific method, rely on experimental
and evaluation studies, and prefer to gather data
that describe large numbers of people. Just as
psychologists are cautious of findings based on very
small samples, lawyers are hesitant to decide a
person's fate on the basis of aggregate data drawn
from other people (Ellsworth & Mauro, 1998).

**Law Deals with Absolutes; Psychology Deals
with Probabilities.** Lawyers think in terms of
"either–or": A person was either fit or unfit to be a
parent; a person was either insane or not insane
when he or she committed a particular act
(Ellsworth & Mauro, 1998). Psychologists are not
comfortable reasoning in absolutes. They prefer to
think in terms of probabilities (e.g., that
a defendant's delusional thinking could indicate a

psychiatric disorder, that a White eyewitness to a
crime is more likely to misidentify a Black
perpetrator than a White perpetrator). Although
the law looks to psychologists for "either–or"
answers (e.g., "Is the defendant competent to stand
trial?" and "Was the defendant insane at the time
of the crime?"), psychologists usually prefer to
answer in terms of likelihoods or quantified
"maybes." Lawyers may have difficulty with such
inconclusive responses because they need a final
resolution to a dispute. We describe an "either–or"
choice in Box 1.2.

**Law Supports Contrasting Views of Reality;
Psychology Seeks One Refined View of Reality.**
As indicated earlier, judges and jurors must decide
which of two conceptions of the truth is more
acceptable in light of conflicting facts. Attorneys
assemble all the facts that support their side and
argue forcefully that their version of the facts is the

correct one. Although this procedure is similar to some scientific activities (a psychologist may do a study that compares predictions from two theories), the psychologist is trained to be objective and open to all perspectives and types of data. The psychologist's ultimate goal is to integrate or assimilate conflicting findings into one refined view of the truth, rather than choosing between alternative views.

Some observers have likened this difference between psychology and law to the difference between scaling a mountain and fighting in a boxing match. As psychologists gain a clearer understanding of a topic (e.g., the causes of domestic violence), they scale a figurative mountain, at the top of which lies true and complete understanding. Although they may never actually reach this pinnacle of knowledge, psychologists highly value the accumulation of data, the development of psychological theory, and the quest for "truth." By contrast, lawyers are less interested in ascertaining the objective truth about a topic and are more concerned with winning against their adversary. Lawyers strive to resolve the dispute in favor of their clients. Of course, for most lawyers, scoring a knockout would be even better.

Such distinctions only scratch the surface of the differences between law and psychology. In Chapter 2 we consider differing notions of justice in the two fields, and in subsequent chapters we will discuss the implications of these differences. As with the previous choices, selecting one domain over the other does not always yield a satisfactory resolution. The use of both perspectives moves us closer to an adequate understanding than does relying only on one. We should remain aware of the limits of our own perspective and realize that other viewpoints are essential for a fuller understanding of complex behavioral issues in the law.

But the contrast in knowledge-generating procedures does raise difficult procedural questions. For example, given the differences in approach, how should a psychologist respond to the challenge of studying the law? What roles should the psychologist play in the legal system? What ethical concerns are associated with psychologists' involvement in the legal system?

PSYCHOLOGISTS' ROLES IN THE LAW

Most courses in psychology portray only two roles for psychologists: that of the scientist who conducts basic research about the causes and development of behavior, and that of the applied psychologist (usually the clinical psychologist) who tries to understand and assist individuals or groups in addressing their problems. The possibilities are more elaborate, however, when the psychologist is involved in the legal system. We describe five distinct roles for psychologists in the legal system: basic scientist, applied scientist, policy evaluator, forensic evaluator, and consultant. The work inherent in these roles ranges from isolated academic research in psychology that may be relevant to law, on one end, to active collaboration with people who work in the legal system, on the other end.

As you will see, the five roles vary in several respects. But whatever role a psychologist chooses, it carries standards about what is acceptable and unacceptable behavior. Professionals often develop explicit statements of ethical standards of behavior; for psychologists, those principles have been published by the APA (2002). Recent modifications to the guidelines now specify, for example, what psychologists should tell their patients about treatments for which generally recognized procedures have not yet been established, when psychologists should terminate treatment and how to do it, and how to safeguard the privacy rights of graduate students enrolled in programs that require psychotherapy as part of their training.

But making the right choice is complicated. Sometimes, the principles specified by these ethics codes conflict with the psychologist's legal responsibilities. The most explicit illustration of this dilemma is the ethical obligation to protect clients' confidentiality when they have threatened to harm others. Should psychologists be required to report these threats? This conflict was most apparent in the controversial *Tarasoff* decision by the Supreme Court of California, described in Box 1.3.

B o x 1.3   THE CASE OF TATIANA TARASOFF: THE DUTY TO PROTECT

Few legal decisions have had as much impact on the practice of psychotherapy as the now-famous case of *Tarasoff v. Regents of the University of California.* The decision focuses on the duties required of psychotherapists whose clients threaten violence.

Prosenjit Poddar was a graduate student at the University of California who became infatuated with Tatiana Tarasoff. Poddar was inexperienced in romantic relationships and was confused about Tatiana's on-again–off-again behavior; she was friendly toward him one day but avoided him completely the next night. After Poddar went to the university counseling center and became a client of a staff psychologist, he confided that he intended to kill a girl who had rebuffed him. The psychologist told his supervisor of this threat and then called the campus police, requesting that they detain Poddar. They did so but soon released him, believing his promise that he would stay away from Tatiana, who was out of the country at the time. Poddar didn't keep his promise. Two months later, he went to Tatiana's home and stabbed her to death. He was eventually convicted of murder.

Tatiana Tarasoff's parents sued the university, the psychologists, and the campus police for failing to warn them or their daughter about Poddar's threats. After a lower court decided in favor of the university, the parents appealed to the California Supreme Court, which ruled in the parents' favor by deciding that the university had been negligent. The first *Tarasoff* decision (1974) established a duty on psychotherapists to warn the victims of therapy patients' violence when the therapist "knows or should have known" that the patient presented a threat to that victim. The court established a standard that therapists have a duty to use "reasonable care" to protect identifiable potential victims from clients in psychotherapy who threaten violence. After the second *Tarasoff* decision in 1976 broadened this duty to include the protection of third parties from patient violence, courts in several other states extended this duty to the protection of property and the protection of all foreseeable victims, not just identifiable ones.

The *Tarasoff* case still governs psychologists' conduct in multiple states. Many psychologists feel caught in a no-win situation: They can be held responsible for their clients' violence if they do not warn potential victims, but they can also be held responsible for breaching their clients' confidentiality if they do.

In the following sections, we describe the various roles that psychologists assume in relation to the legal system and the ethical issues that arise in each context. A footnote on psychologists' relationship to the law: Students often wonder how they can become involved in this field as basic scientists, applied scientists, policy evaluators, forensic evaluators, or consultants. What career paths should one pursue, and what professional opportunities exist at the ends of those trails? How might a developmental psychologist, a cognitive neuropsychologist, or a clinician (for example) interact with the legal system? To answer these questions, the American Psychology-Law Society (a division of the APA) has published a guide entitled *Careers in Psychology and Law.* It can be accessed from the Society's web page (**www.apls.org**). Those undertaking careers in psychology and law will also need to familiarize themselves with the ethical requirements pertaining to their professions.

The Psychologist as a Basic Scientist of the Law

A **basic scientist** pursues knowledge for its own sake. Basic scientists study a phenomenon for the satisfaction of understanding it and contributing to scientific advances in the area. They do not necessarily seek to apply their research findings; many have no concern with whether the knowledge they generate will be used to resolve real-world problems. Yet often their results can address important practical issues, including some that arise in the law. For example, though not specifically conducted for use in the courtroom, laboratory research on visual perception can help us understand the accuracy of eyewitness testimony about a crime or accident. Psychologists who test different theories of memory promote a better understanding of whether repression can cause long-term forgetting of traumatic events. Basic research on the relationship

between social attitudes and behavior can clarify why people obey or disobey the law. Research in personality psychology can help to show what kind of person will become a follower in a terrorist group and what kind of person will be a leader. Studies of adolescents' brain development may be relevant to their decisions about whether to commit petty crimes. Finally, research can assess whether psychologists' attitudes about the causes of crime affect their professional evaluations of criminal defendants.

The Ethics of the Basic Scientist. Like all scientists, psychologists who do basic research must adhere to standards of conduct in how they undertake and report their studies. In practical terms, this means that they cannot fabricate or forge data, plagiarize, or present a skewed selection of the data to hide observations that do not fit their conclusions. They must treat human subjects in an ethical manner. (All institutions that receive federal research funding have review boards that evaluate the way scientists treat human and animal subjects.) Basic researchers sometimes have a conflict of interest when faced with competing concerns such as honestly reporting their research findings versus making a profit or "getting

published." In these situations, they should learn to recognize and be honest about potential conflicts of interest and communicate them to interested parties before undertaking the research.

The Psychologist as an Applied Scientist in the Law

Applied scientists are dedicated to applying knowledge to solve real-life problems. Most of the public's awareness of a psychologist's work reflects this role, whether this awareness comes from viewing TV's Dr. Phil or watching a psychologist testify as an expert witness in a trial televised on truTV. Indeed, an important role for psychologists who are interested in applying the findings of their profession involves serving as an expert witness in a legislative hearing or in a courtroom.

Juries, judges, and legislators cannot be expected to be well versed in every topic from abscesses to zinfandel wine. An **expert witness** is someone who possesses special knowledge about a subject, knowledge that the average juror does not have. Psychologists may testify as expert witnesses during a trial based on their knowledge of scientific evidence (this information is called **social framework testimony**). Either side, as part of its presentation of the evidence, may ask the judge to allow expert witnesses to testify. The judge must be convinced that the testimony any expert will present is of a kind that requires special knowledge, skill, or experience and that the testimony will help promote better legal decision making. (When psychologists testify concerning a particular individual based on the results of a forensic evaluation, they take on a different role, one we describe later in this chapter.)

The psychological topics that call for scientific expertise are almost limitless. As expert witnesses, psychologists have been called on to testify in many types of cases. For example, expert testimony may be useful in understanding:

- Employee discrimination through selection and promotion procedures

- The accuracy of identifications by eyewitnesses

- The effects of posting warning signs or safety instructions on potentially dangerous equipment

- The factors that may cause a suspect to make a false confession

- The effects of suggestive questions on children's memory of alleged abuse

The Ethics of the Applied Scientist/Expert Witness.   The psychologist as expert witness represents a profession that stands for objectivity and accuracy in its procedures. Even though expert witnesses are usually hired (and paid) by one side, they are responsible for reporting all their conclusions, regardless of whether these favor the side paying them. Furthermore, it violates the ethical standards of both psychologists and lawyers for expert witnesses to accept payment that is contingent on the outcome of the case.

But achieving objectivity is not easy. Jurors may perceive the psychologist as an advocate rather than as an unbiased scientist (Horgan, 1988). Regardless of this perception, a psychologist, when asked to testify, has an ethical responsibility to be candid and explicit with the court about his or her opinions. Still, psychologists may be tempted to sympathize with the side that has employed them. This sympathy may not even be conscious; instead, the psychologist may simply filter the facts of the case through perceptions motivated by a spirit of helpfulness to his or her client.

Another ethical dilemma arises whenever the adversary system forces an expert to make absolute "either–or" judgments. Has the pretrial publicity caused potential jurors to be biased against the defendant? In a custody case stemming from a divorce, which parent would be better for the child to live with? Does the evaluation of a defendant indicate that she is mentally ill? In all of these situations, the law requires the psychologist to reach a firm conclusion on the witness stand, regardless of ambiguity in the evidence (Sales & Shuman, 1993).

Admissibility of Expert Testimony.   In some cases, judges fear that an expert witness's testimony will be so powerful that it will usurp (or take over) the jury as the fact finder in the case. Thus, judges sometimes refuse to let experts testify—particularly if they are convinced that the topic is one that most laypeople are familiar with.

On other occasions, judges have disallowed expert testimony as irrelevant or immaterial. Consider the case of unlucky Pedro Gil. On a night of wild abandon in the fall of 1993, Gil hoisted a bucket of plaster over the wall of a Manhattan rooftop. It dropped seven stories to the ground and hit and killed a police officer standing on the street below. Gil claimed that he expected the bucket to drop unceremoniously onto an unoccupied street directly below him, rather than to continue forward as it fell and land on the street where the police officer was positioned. To support his naive belief that objects drop straight down, Gil's attorneys attempted to introduce the testimony of cognitive psychologist Michael McCloskey, an expert in intuitive physics, who was prepared to testify that people commonly misunderstand physical laws. The trial judge did not let McCloskey testify, claiming that intuitive physics was irrelevant to the issues under contention. The jury convicted Gil of second-degree manslaughter.

Judges have discretion about many kinds of decisions in their courtrooms. Whether to allow expert testimony is one of the most important, and often most controversial, examples of this discretion. The U.S. Supreme Court has indicated (*Daubert v. Merrell Dow Pharmaceuticals, Inc.*, 1993) that judges' decisions about the admissibility of expert testimony based on "scientific" knowledge must turn on the validity of the science in question. In essence, judges are supposed to function as "gatekeepers" who must evaluate potential expert testimony by the standards of science. The *Daubert* decision listed four factors that judges should consider in assessing the validity—and subsequent admissibility—of the expert's testimony: (1) whether the expert's theory or technique can be and has been tested, a concept known as falsifiability; (2) whether it has been evaluated by peer review; (3) the reliability and error rate of the claims; and (4) the extent to which the expert's techniques and claims have been generally accepted by the relevant scientific community. The Court also decided, in a separate case, that these criteria apply to testimony based on technical or nonscientific knowledge (*Kumho Tire C. v. Carmichael*, 1999).

One clear implication of the *Daubert* decision is that judges must become savvy consumers of science if they are to decide which opinions qualify as "scientific." Since the *Daubert* case, the admissibility of expert evidence has become an important pretrial issue and judges are more likely to scrutinize the reasoning and methodology underlying experts' opinions (Cecil, 2005). This is probably a good thing because jurors assume that judges carefully evaluate the evidence before admitting it at a trial, and put more weight on expert scientific evidence presented in the context of a trial than the same evidence presented outside of a courtroom context (Schweitzer & Saks, 2009).

The Psychologist as a Policy Evaluator in the Law

In addition to their knowledge of substantive problems, psychologists have methodological skills that they use in assessing or evaluating how well an intervention has worked. Psychologists and other social scientists have been asked so frequently in the last several decades to conduct evaluation studies that a separate subfield called policy evaluation, or evaluation research, has emerged. The **policy evaluator** provides data to answer questions such as "I have instituted a change; how do I know whether it was effective?" Or, more laudably, "I want to make a change in our organization's procedures, but before

I do, how do I design it so I will be able to determine later whether it worked?" Psychologists working as policy evaluators might be asked whether changing the laws for teen drivers by restricting the number of passengers they can carry will reduce traffic accidents, or whether the chemical castration of released rapists will reduce the rate of sexual violence.

The law enforcement and criminal justice systems frequently alter their operating procedures. For example, police departments may change from automobile patrols to foot patrols to increase surveillance and to improve relations between police and community. Often these innovations are introduced without adequate planning about how they can be evaluated; hence their outcomes, whether good or bad, cannot be determined (Reppucci & Haugaard, 1989). The methodological skills of the psychologist as policy evaluator are essential in designing an innovation so that its effects can be tested.

Psychologists have been involved in evaluating changes in the federal law that governs special education. The Individuals with Disabilities Education Act (IDEA) guarantees children with disabilities the opportunity to receive a free and appropriate public education. Recent revisions in the law change the way that schools determine whether a child has a learning disability. The traditional method, in use since the 1970s, identified students as having a learning disability when their scores on achievement tests were significantly lower than their IQ would suggest they should be. But with the dramatic increase in the number of students identified as learning disabled in recent years, many people have begun to suspect that learning disabilities are overidentified. (Some conjecture that parents have pushed for this label so that schools will be forced to provide services for their academically struggling students.) When children struggle for reasons unrelated to a learning disability—poor instruction or speaking English as a second language, for example—shunting them into special education courses is of little value. Therefore, the new version of IDEA provides for alternative methods of identification, something that psychologists have been evaluating for some time (Bailey, 2003).

The Ethics of the Policy Evaluator. The psychologist who evaluates the impact of new or proposed legislation, court reforms, and other changes in the legal system faces ethical responsibilities similar to those of the expert witness. The standard rules of scientific procedure apply, but because of the source of payment, there are pressures to interpret results of evaluation studies in a certain way.

Consider, for example, a large state correctional system that wants to improve its parole process. Correctional officials have identified a problem with releasing those eligible for parole who are heavy drug users. If released into society, they are likely to commit further crimes to maintain their drug habit, and are therefore likely to return to prison. Accordingly, the system seeks to introduce and evaluate an innovative halfway house program for parolees with a history of narcotics addiction. It hires a policy evaluator to design a study and evaluate the effects of this innovation. The correctional system provides funding to carry out the study, and officials are sincerely committed to its goals. Assume the psychologist concludes that the halfway house does not significantly reduce drug use by parolees. The authorities are disappointed and may even attack the integrity of the policy evaluator. Yet, as scientists, program evaluators must "call 'em like they see 'em," regardless of the desirability of the outcome.

Even if the program is successful, the policy evaluator faces other ethical dilemmas. To assess such an innovative program, the researcher might have to deny some parolees access to the program and place them in a "status quo" control group. The ethical dilemma becomes more critical when some potentially lifesaving innovation is being evaluated. But often it is only through such research methods that a potentially helpful new program can be convincingly demonstrated to be effective.

The Psychologist as a Forensic Evaluator in Litigation

In addition to evaluating policies and programs, psychologists may be asked to evaluate individuals involved in civil and criminal cases, to report their findings to a judge, and on occasion, to testify about

the results in court. Forensic evaluators assess matters such as:

- The competence of a defendant to proceed with adjudication of charges (often called "competence to stand trial," although most criminal charges are adjudicated through plea bargaining rather than trial)

- The mental state of a defendant at the time of an alleged offense (often called "sanity at the time of the offense")

- The degree of emotional or brain damage suffered by a victim in an accident

- The effects on a child of alternative custody arrangements after divorce

- The risk of future violent or otherwise criminal behavior

- The prospects for a convicted defendant's rehabilitation in prison or on probation

There are two different ways that mental health professionals become involved in litigation as a **forensic evaluator**: they are either court-appointed, or hired by one of the parties involved in the litigation (defense, prosecution, or plaintiff). Serving in the court-appointed role involves receiving an order from the judge authorizing the mental health professional to evaluate a given individual for a specific purpose. The judge may also specify additional considerations such as how the results are to be communicated. In this role, there is typically the expectation that the resulting forensic evaluation will be considered by the judge without being introduced by either side.

Forensic evaluators for one of the parties involved in the litigation have a different expectation: That particular party may control when (and whether) the forensic assessment findings are actually introduced as evidence in the case. Some referrals for forensic assessment come from attorneys who authorize the evaluations without resorting to any kind of court authority. (This kind of right is usually associated with the defense in a criminal prosecution; the prosecutor cannot request a **forensic mental health assessment** unless it is approved by the court—and therefore known to the defense.) These tasks will be discussed in much more detail in Chapters 8 and 9 of this book. They are also described in detail elsewhere (Heilbrun et al., 2008; Melton et al., 2007).

The Ethics of the Forensic Evaluator. The ethical considerations associated with the role of forensic evaluator are fairly formal and specifically described in several documents. The Ethical Principles of Psychologists and Code of Conduct (EPPCC) (APA, 2002) is the ethics code applicable to all psychologists, including those involved in litigation. It describes a series of broad principles followed by a more specific set of standards; adherence to the standards is mandatory for psychologists. Violations can result in sanctions up to and including expulsion from the APA. The APA expulsions for ethical reasons are provided to state licensure boards. A state board that limits the conditions under which a licensed psychologist may practice can directly affect that individual's livelihood.

Two other sets of ethical guidelines affect the practice of forensic assessment in this role. Neither is "enforceable" in the sense that the EPPCC is. Nonetheless, both serve as important sources of authority, and may affect the judgments of courts regarding the admissibility and weight of forensic assessment evidence. These two documents are the Specialty Guidelines for Forensic Psychologists (Committee on Ethical Guidelines for Forensic Psychologists, 1991) and the Guidelines for Child Custody Evaluations in Divorce Proceedings (APA, 1994).

Between the three documents, there is substantial emphasis on providing evaluations that are (1) clear in their purpose; (2) conducted by individuals who are competent by virtue of their education, training, and experience; (3) respectful of appropriate relationships (and avoid multiple relationships, such as both forensic evaluator and therapist, in the same case); (4) provide the appropriate level of confidentiality consistent with circumstances and the applicable legal privilege; (5) use methods and procedures that are accurate, current, and consistent with science and standard of practice; and (6) communicated appropriately.

The Psychologist as a Consultant in Litigation

The final role for psychologists in the law is that of consultant. The field of trial consulting provides one example of this role for a psychologist working in the legal arena. Social scientists who began this work in the 1970s used so-called scientific jury selection procedures (further described in Chapter 11) to assist defense lawyers in highly politicized trials resulting from antiwar activities in the United States. Since then, these techniques have been refined and expanded. Today the field of trial consulting is a booming business and involves far more than jury selection; **trial consultants** also conduct community attitude surveys, prepare witnesses to testify, advise lawyers on their presentation strategies, and conduct mock trials.

The national media devoted extensive coverage to the use of trial consultants in the celebrity-status trials of Martha Stewart and O. J. Simpson, and research on community attitudes was also influential in the 2001 conviction of a former Ku Klux Klansman for the 1963 bombing of a Birmingham, Alabama church. (We describe this case in more detail in Chapter 11.) The jury consultant hired by the prosecution suggested that the case should not be cast as an attack on the Ku Klux Klan (KKK) because research showed that the Klan had little relevance to jurors today. Rather, he urged prosecutors to emphasize that the bombing singled out children (four girls were killed in the attack) and a place of worship. The jury took only two hours to convict the defendant (Sack, 2001).

Critics have argued that these techniques essentially rig the jury (Kressel & Kressel, 2002), but at least in the realm of jury selection, there are few, if any, convincing demonstrations that scientific jury selection is more effective than routine jury selection (e.g., Wallendael & Cutler, 2004). Consultants suggest that they are simply borrowing techniques commonly used in politics and bringing them into the courtroom. Politicians hire people to help them project a better image, so why shouldn't a lawyer do the same? They also argue that in an adversarial system, attorneys should be able to use every tool available to them.

Another role for psychologists as consultants involves working with attorneys to prepare clients for direct and cross-examination, present expert witnesses, cross-examine opposing experts, and better understand the empirical and professional literature (Posey & Wrightsman, 2005). Like the trial consultant, this role is undertaken with the assumption that the psychologist is assisting the attorney in winning the case. There is no expectation of impartiality as there would be for psychologists acting in the role of basic scientist, applied scientist, policy evaluator, or forensic evaluator. However, the psychologist must still provide the attorney with good information in order to promote more effective performance in litigation. A good example of the kind of information that might be provided to an attorney in this kind of consultation is contained in the series of books written by Jay Ziskin and David Faust (1988; 1995).

The Ethics of the Consultant in Litigation. As we noted earlier, when the psychologist becomes a consultant for one side in the selection of jurors, there may be ethical questions. Just how far should the selection procedures go? Should jurors have to answer consultants' intrusive questions about their private lives? Should their private lives be investigated? Should consultants be able to sculpt the jury to their clients' advantage? Do these techniques simply constitute the latest tools in the attorney's arsenal of trial tactics? Or do they bias the proceedings and jeopardize the willingness of citizens to participate in the process? These questions deal with fairness, and scientific jury selection may conflict with the way most people interpret the intent of the law.

But are psychologists who work for an advertising agency unethical when they use professional knowledge to encourage consumers to buy one brand of dog food rather than another? Many of us would say no; the free-enterprise system permits any such procedures that do not falsify claims. Is this example analogous to jury selection? Probably, given that rival attorneys—whether they employ jury consultants or not—always try to select jurors who will sympathize with their version of the facts. The adversarial system rests on the expectation that each side will eliminate those jurors most favorable to the other side and that an unbiased jury will result. As long as the adversarial system permits attorneys from each side to eliminate some prospective jurors without giving reasons, it does not seem unethical for psychologists to assist these attorneys, as long as their advocacy is consistent with the law and the administration of justice.

The same might be said about consultants retained by attorneys to provide information to support the effective presentation of the case. It might be appropriate to provide this information in a balanced way, but there is no expectation that the consultant needs to do so. In our adversarial system of justice, how the attorney decides to use such information is within that attorney's discretion.

When psychologists become trial consultants, they also subscribe to the ethical code of the attorneys, who, after all, are in charge of the trial preparation. The Ethics Code of the American Bar Association admonishes its members to defend their clients to the best of their abilities, short of lying or encouraging lying. Every litigant—whether a defendant or a plaintiff—regardless of the heinousness of the crime or the nature of the evidence presented, is entitled to the best legal representation possible, including the use of psychological techniques to assess the relative favorability of prospective jurors and to enhance case presentation.

SUMMARY

1. **Why do we have laws and what is the psychological approach to studying law?**

   Laws are human creations that have as their major purpose the resolution of human conflict.

   As society changes, new conflicts surface, leading to expansion and revision of the legal system. A psychological approach focuses on individuals as agents within a legal system, asking how their internal qualities (personality, values, abilities, and experiences) and their environments, including the law itself, affect their behavior.

2. **What choices are reflected in the psychological approach to the law?**

Several basic choices must be made between pairs of options in the psychological study of the law. These options are often irreconcilable because each is attractive, but both usually cannot be attained at the same time. The choices are (1) whether the goal of law is achieving personal freedom or ensuring the common good, (2) whether equality or discretion should be the standard for our legal policies, (3) whether the purpose of a legal inquiry is to discover the truth or to provide a means of conflict resolution, and (4) whether it is better to apply the methods of law or those of science for making decisions.

3. **How do recent laws reflect the contrast between the due process model and the crime control model of the criminal justice system?**

Recent laws in several states, including "three-strikes" laws, reflect the increased salience of a crime control model, which seeks to contain or reduce criminal activity. Large increases in prison populations over the past few decades stem from this objective.

4. **What are five roles that psychologists may play in the legal system and what does each entail?**

Five possible roles are identified in this chapter: the psychologist as (1) a basic scientist, interested in knowledge related to psychology and law for its own sake; (2) an applied scientist who seeks to apply basic research knowledge to a particular problem in the legal system; (3) a policy evaluator who capitalizes on methodological skills to design and conduct research that assesses the effects of innovations and program changes in the legal system; (4) a forensic evaluator who is either appointed by the court or retained at the request of one of the parties in the litigation to perform a psychological evaluation related to a legal question; and (5) a consultant who works on behalf of a party or position in litigation. Each role entails its own set of ethical dilemmas.

KEY TERMS

amicus curiae brief	due process model	policy evaluator	settlement negotiation
applied scientists	equality	precedents	social framework testimony
basic scientist	expert witness	principle of proportionality	*stare decisis*
case law	forensic evaluator	procedural justice	three-strikes law
crime control model	forensic mental health assessment	racial bias	trial consultants
determinate sentencing	forensic psychologists	sentencing disparity	
discretion			

2

The Legal System
Issues, Structure, and Players

ORIENTING QUESTIONS

1. What is the difference between the adversarial and inquisitorial models of trials?

2. How do notions of morality and legality differ?

3. How do different models of justice explain people's level of satisfaction with the legal system?

4. What is commonsense justice?

5. What are some examples of problem-solving courts? How do they differ from traditional courts?

6. What is alternative dispute resolution (ADR)? What are some types of ADR?

7. How are judges selected and how do their personal characteristics influence their decisions?

8. How does the experience of law school affect its students?

9. What have been the experiences of women and minorities in the legal profession?

10. What are some of the common criticisms of lawyers?

In Chapter 1, we described the different roles that psychologists can assume when they interact with the legal system. In this chapter, we focus on the legal system itself. We describe the nature of the adversary system and address psychological aspects of legality, morality, and justice. We discuss courts, including traditional trial courts and newer, problem-solving courts, as well as **alternative dispute resolution** (ADR) involving arbitration and mediation. We also examine the roles played by the major players in the legal system—judges and lawyers. An understanding of the workings of the legal system will help make it clear how psychologists study and assist judges, lawyers, and ordinary citizens involved in the law.

THE ADVERSARIAL SYSTEM

American legal procedures—whether in criminal or civil cases—involve an **adversarial system** of justice. Exhibits, evidence, and witnesses are assembled by representatives of one side or the other to convince the fact finder that their side's viewpoint is the truthful one. During a trial, the choice of what evidence to present is within the discretion of those involved in the litigation and their attorneys (Lind, 1982). Judges rarely call witnesses or introduce evidence on their own. In bench trials (trials without a jury), judges often question witnesses, but in jury trials, judges hesitate to question witnesses because they do not want to appear to favor one side over the other. Traditionally jurors have not been permitted to question witnesses (Heuer & Penrod, 1988), but a majority of states now allow jurors to submit written questions to the judge, who then decides whether the questions should be asked—either by the judge or by one of the attorneys (Munsterman & Hannaford-Agor, 2004). When the American College of Trial Lawyers, a prestigious organization of experienced trial lawyers, polled its members on this topic, 49% of those responding said juror questioning (by submitting questions to the judge) improved the quality of justice, whereas 33% viewed juror questioning negatively. We consider this issue in greater depth in Chapter 12.

The adversarial system is derived from English common law. This approach contrasts with the

inquisitorial approach used in Europe (but not in Great Britain), in which the judge has more control over the proceedings. Lind (1982) described the procedure in France as follows: "The questioning of witnesses is conducted almost exclusively by the presiding judge. The judge interrogates the disputing parties and witnesses, referring frequently to a dossier that has been prepared by a court official who investigated the case. Although the parties probably have partisan attorneys present at the trial, it is evident that control over the presentation of evidence and arguments is—firmly in the hands of the judge" (p. 14). In the inquisitorial system, the two sides do not have separate witnesses; the witnesses testify for the court, and the opposing parties are not allowed to prepare the witnesses before the trial (Sheppard & Vidmar, 1980).

The adversarial model has been criticized for promoting a competitive atmosphere that can distort the truth surrounding a dispute (Lind, 1982). Jurors may have to choose between two versions of the truth, neither of which is completely accurate, because witnesses often shade their testimony to favor the side of the lawyer who interviews them first (Sheppard & Vidmar, 1980).

However, research on these contrasting approaches reveals several benefits of the adversarial model. A research team led by a social psychologist, John Thibaut, and a law professor, Laurens Walker (Thibaut & Walker, 1975; Walker, La Tour, Lind, & Thibaut, 1974), conducted programmatic research and concluded that the adversarial system led to less biased decisions that were more likely to be seen as fair by the parties in dispute. One possible explanation for this more favorable evaluation of the adversarial system is that it is the system with which Americans are most familiar. But people who lived in countries with nonadversarial systems (France and West Germany) also rated the adversary procedure as fairer (Lind, Erickson, Friedland, & Dickenberger, 1978). Why? Perhaps because the adversarial system motivates attorneys to identify all the evidence favorable to their side. When law students, serving as experimental subjects, believed that the weight of the information and evidence favored the opposing side, they conducted more

thorough investigations of the case. Thus, when the case was presented to the judge, the arguments appeared more balanced than the original distribution of facts would have warranted (Lind, 1975; Lind, Thibaut, & Walker, 1973).

The primary advantage of the adversarial system is that it gives participants plenty of opportunity to present their version of the facts so that they feel they have been treated fairly (Lind & Tyler, 1988). Sheppard and Vidmar (1983) noted that any method of dispute resolution that fosters this belief is more likely to be viewed favorably than alternatives that do not. This finding comports with the procedural justice perspective described later in this chapter.

LEGALITY VERSUS MORALITY

Laws are designed to regulate the behavior of individuals—to specify precisely what conduct is illegal. But do these laws always correspond to people's sense of right and wrong?

Consider the case of Lester Zygmanik. Lester was charged with murdering his own brother, George, but only because George had demanded that Lester kill him. A motorcycle accident a few days earlier had left George, age 26, paralyzed from the neck down. He saw a future with nothing but pain, suffering, and invalidism; as he lay in agony, he insisted that his younger brother Lester, age 23, swear he would not let him continue in such a desperate state. (Other family members later verified that this had, in truth, been George's wish.) So, on the night of June 20, 1973, Lester slipped into his brother's hospital room and shot him in the head with a 20-gauge shotgun. Dropping the gun by the bed, he turned himself in moments later. There was no question about the cause of death; later, on the witness stand during his murder trial, Lester told the jury that he had done it as an act of love for his brother. Because New Jersey had no laws regarding mercy killing, the prosecution thought a case could be made for charging Lester with first-degree murder.

The state believed it had a good case against Lester. His actions met every one of the elements that the law required for his guilt to be proved. First, there was premeditation, or a plan to kill. Second, there was deliberation (as defined in the New Jersey criminal code—"the weighing of the 'pros' and 'cons' of that plan"). Third, there was willfulness ("the intentional carrying out of that plan"). Lester had even sawed off the shotgun before hiding it under his coat, and he had packed the bullets with candle wax, which compacted the explosion and made it more deadly. Lester forthrightly admitted to his lawyer: "I gave it a lot of thought. You don't know how much thinking I did on it. I had to do something I knew that would definitely put him away" (Mitchell, 1976, p. vii). At his trial, Lester took the stand and described his motivations, explaining that he did what his brother wanted.

If you had been a juror in this trial, how would you have voted? College students usually split just about evenly between verdicts of "guilty of first-degree murder" and "not guilty." Those who vote guilty often hope that the sentence will be seen as a humanitarian one, but they believe it is their duty to consider the evidence and apply the law. Certainly, this was an act of murder, they say, regardless of Lester's good intentions. But those who vote not guilty often feel that it is appropriate, on occasion, to disregard the law when mitigating circumstances are present or when community standards argue for forgiveness.

Both reactions are reasonable, and they illustrate the dilemma between treating similar defendants equally and showing discretion if circumstances warrant. They also demonstrate important differences between judgments based on **black letter law** and those based on one's conscience or personal sentiments about a given situation. By "black letter law" (sometimes referred to as the *law on the books*), we mean the law as set down by our founding fathers in the Constitution, as written by legislators, and as interpreted by judges (Finkel, 1995). According to the black letter law, Lester Zygmanik was guilty. But there is another way to judge his actions—by focusing on his altruistic motives and the desire to help his brother, rather than to harm him.

As Lester Zygmanik's trial began, the prosecutor was confident that he would be found guilty. The jury, composed of seven men and five women, was tough, conservative, and blue-collar. The judge had even ruled that the term *mercy killing* could not be used in the trial. But after deliberating for fewer than three hours, the jury found Lester Zygmanik not guilty. The jurors focused, apparently, on the relationship between Lester and his brother, and they concluded that Lester had been overcome by grief, love, and selflessness. Their decision implicitly acknowledged that moral considerations such as the commitment to care for others were more important to their decision than following the strict guidelines of the law.

Obviously, the Lester Zygmanik trial is not the only one in which a defendant claimed his act was a mercy killing. Helping terminally ill patients to commit suicide (so-called assisted suicide) is usually justified by the "offender" as an act of compassion or mercy, ending the "victim's" pain and suffering. Yet in all but two states—Oregon and Washington—helping someone to commit suicide is a crime. (Even in those states, assisted suicide is legal only if performed by a physician under narrowly defined circumstances.) Still, many people are loath to call the perpetrators of these acts criminals, and proponents of assisted suicide often hail them as heroes.

Mercy killings and assisted suicides are examples of **euthanasia**, the act of killing an individual for reasons that are considered merciful. They illustrate the often-tragic differences between what an individual feels is the morally right or just thing to do and what the law describes as the illegal act to avoid. Should someone who voluntarily, willfully, and with premeditation assists in killing another human *always* be punished? Or should that person, in some circumstances, be treated with compassion and forgiveness? Many people can imagine exceptional circumstances in which individuals who have technically broken the law should be exonerated. Often, these circumstances involve a lack of intention to harm another person and the desire to help a person who is suffering. The topic of euthanasia highlights the inconsistency between legality and people's perceptions of what is moral, ethical, and just.

Citizens' Sense of Legality and Morality

We might assume at first that what is defined as "legal" and what is judged to be "morally right" would be synonymous. But in the Zygmanik case, what the jury considered to be a moral action and what the system required as the proper legal resolution were inconsistent. Legislators and scholars have argued for centuries whether the law should be consistent with citizens' sense of morality. In fact, inconsistencies abound. For example, prostitution is universally condemned as immoral, yet it is legal in parts of Nevada and in some European countries. Acts of civil disobedience, whether performed in racially segregated buses in Montgomery, Alabama five decades ago or more recently to protest the war in Iraq, are applauded by those who consider some laws and policies to be morally indefensible.

Psychologists have now conducted a number of studies that illustrate the differences between citizens' sense of morality and justice, on the one hand, and the legal system's set of formal rules and laws, on the other. At first glance, it may seem nearly impossible to study people's views about the legitimacy of formal laws because there are so many variations in laws and so many different penalties for violating those laws. (Because criminal penalties are decided on a state-by-state basis in the United States, there could be 50 different penalties for the same crime.) Fortunately, though, a large majority of states base their criminal laws on the Model Penal Code drafted by the influential American Law Institute in the 1960s. Thus we can ask whether the principles embodied in the Model Penal Code are compatible with citizens' intuitions about justice and legality. Do people tend to agree with the Model Penal Code or does their sense of right and wrong diverge from this black letter law? One set of studies has examined the category of attempted crimes and the important role that intention plays in these cases.

Attempted Crimes and the Concept of Intention in Law and Psychology.   Consider the following fundamental question of criminal law: How should attempted (but not completed) crimes be punished?

An attempt may be unsuccessful because the perpetrator tries to commit a crime but fails (e.g., he shoots but misses) or because the attempt is interrupted or abandoned (e.g., robbers are about to enter a bank with guns drawn when they see a police officer inside).

The Model Penal Code says that attempts should be punished in the same way as completed crimes. If the offender's conduct strongly corroborates his criminal **intention**—showing that he not merely thought about the crime but actually tried to accomplish it—the Model Penal Code holds that he should be punished to the same degree as the successful offender. In keeping with the central role of intent, the Model Penal Code assigns the same penalty to attempted crimes as to completed crimes. Thus, the inveterate pickpocket who thrusts his hand into another person's pocket, only to find it empty, is just as guilty (and just as deserving of punishment) as the pickpocket who makes off with a fat wallet. Regardless of the outcome of this act, he tried to steal—and so, by definition, a crime was committed. A similar situation arose in the case of *State v. Damms* (1960), described in Box 2.1.

According to the Model Penal Code, an offender who tries but fails is just as culpable as an offender who tries and succeeds. But do ordinary people think about intent and attempted crimes this way? Do they think that *trying* to break into a store is as serious as *actually* breaking into the store?

Psychologist John Darley and his colleagues asked respondents to read short scenarios that described people who had taken one or more steps toward committing either robbery or murder and to assign punishment for those people (Darley, Sanderson, & LaMantha, 1996). They found that people's intuitions differed in predictable ways from the position of the Model Penal Code. In situations where the person depicted in the scenario had taken only preliminary action (e.g., examining the store he planned to burgle or telling a friend about his plan), few respondents thought he was guilty of any offense, and punishments were generally mild. (Yet, according to the Model Penal Code, this person is just as guilty as one who actually completed the burglary.) When the scenario described a person who had reached the point of "dangerous proximity" to the

Box 2.1 THE CASE OF RALPH DAMMS AND THE UNLOADED PISTOL

Prior to the events in question, Marjory Damms had initiated divorce proceedings against her husband Ralph, and the two were living apart. On April 6, 1959, Ralph Damms drove to a location in Milwaukee where his estranged wife usually boarded a bus to go to work. He lured her into his car by falsely claiming that her mother was ill and dying. He then took his wife for a car ride, stopped the car, and brandished a gun. Marjory Damms ran away, but Ralph caught her and raised the pistol to her head. Slowly, deliberately, he pulled the trigger. The gun did not fire. He had forgotten to load it! Two police officers witnessed the event and heard Damms exclaim, after he pulled the trigger of the unloaded gun, "It won't fire. It won't fire." (It was not clear whether the exclamation was made in a tone of assurance, disappointment, surprise, or desperation.) Damms was found guilty of attempted murder, but he appealed his conviction on the ground that it was impossible to kill his wife with an unloaded gun. The court upheld his conviction, concluding that the mere fact that the gun was unloaded when Damms pulled the trigger did not absolve him of attempted murder if he actually believed the gun was loaded at the time. Intention is the central issue here; at least for the charge of attempted murder, it is more important than the consequences of the act. The judge concluded that Damms assumed he had put bullets in the gun. If he had, his wife would have been dead.

crime, punishments increased, but they still were only half as severe as those assigned to the person who actually completed the crime. Apparently people do not accept the view that intent to commit an act is the moral equivalent of actually doing it. Their notions about criminality and the need for punishment were more nuanced, less "black and white" than what the Model Penal Code prescribed.

Psychology's focus on mental states also reflects more differentiations and less clear-cut distinctions than those of the legal system. Psychology considers a spectrum of behavior, motivated by a variety of influences and ranging from accidents to behavior influenced by stress, peer pressure, immature judgment, to actions that are deliberate and carefully planned.

Even this continuum may oversimplify variations in intention because it minimizes the importance of the environmental and cultural influences that affect people differently. The social context in which behavior occurs can strongly influence a person's intention to behave in certain ways. Different contexts can make it very hard for an individual to conceive of certain behavioral options. Therefore, one person's ability to intend a given behavior might be much more limited than that of another person who has more behavioral alternatives.

Psychologists have also studied how people assign causes, including intentions, to the behavior of others and themselves. A well-established theory in social psychology, **attribution theory**, has led to a number of discoveries, including the following:

- Attributions tend to vary along three dimensions: *internality*—whether we explain the cause of an event as due to something within ourselves or to something that exists in the environment; *stability*—whether we see the cause of a behavior as enduring or merely temporary; and *globalness*—whether we see the cause as specific to a limited situation or applicable to all situations. An individual who makes internal, stable, global attributions about an act of misconduct ("He is so evil that he doesn't care what anyone thinks or feels about him") will see an offender as more culpable and more deserving of punishment than a person who offers external, unstable, specific explanations for the same act ("As a result of hanging out with a rough crowd, she was in the wrong place at the wrong time").

- When making inferences about what caused another person's behavior—especially behavior that has negative consequences—we tend to attribute the cause to stable factors that are internal to the person. That is, we are inclined to believe that others are disposed to act the way they do. But when our own actions lead to negative outcomes, we are more likely to blame the external environment for the outcome, suggesting an unstable cause for our behavior that will probably change in the future.

Consequences of Citizen–Code Disagreements.
What difference does it make if laws do not comport with people's sense of right and wrong? Can people simply ignore the laws they believe to be immoral? Indeed, we can find many examples of situations in which people opt not to obey laws and legal authority. When parents fail to make child support payments or when people violate restraining orders, it is often because they do not accept the legitimacy of a judge's decision. When people use illegal drugs or cheat on their income tax returns, it is often because they do not believe that the laws regulating these behaviors are just or morally right. During the era of prohibition in the United States, when alcohol consumption was outlawed, honest citizens became "criminals," entire illicit industries were created, and gang membership and gang-related violence increased significantly.

But there may be more significant and more general consequences of discrepancies between citizens' sense of morality and the legal system's sense of legality. For the law to have any authority, it must be consistent with people's shared sense of morality. When that consistency is lacking, citizens may feel alienation from authority and become less likely to comply with laws they perceive as illegitimate (Darley, Fulero, Haney, & Tyler, 2002). Initial disagreement with one law can lead to contempt for the legal system as a whole, including the police who enforce laws and the judges who punish wrongdoers. If the law criminalizes behaviors that people do not think are immoral, it begins to lose its legitimacy (Darley et al., 2002). In the words of Oliver Wendell Holmes, "[The] first requirement of a sound body of law is that it should correspond with the actual feelings and demands of the community" (1881, pp. 41–42).

WHAT IS JUSTICE?

More than 2,000 years ago, at the beginning of the *Republic*, Socrates posed this question and we continue to ponder it today. Definitions of justice have changed throughout history; in the Old Testament and in Homer's *The Iliad*, justice meant something like revenge. By the time of the Golden Age of Athens in the fifth century B.C.E., the concept of justice came to be less about vengeance and more about achievement of the well-being of individuals (Solomon, 1990). The development of Christianity and Islam accentuated a conception of justice within religious traditions of morality. As a result, people began to see matters of social injustice (e.g., the suffering of the poor and the oppressed) as issues of concern, along with offenses against one's person or one's family (Solomon, 1990).

Distributive and Procedural Justice

Our discussion so far has assessed perceptions of legitimacy in the *outcomes* of legal disputes, such as whether the would-be pickpocket who came up empty-handed should be punished as severely as the one who got the loot. This focus on the fairness of the outcome in a legal dispute is the main concern of **distributive justice** models. According to the principles of distributive justice, a person will be more accepting of decisions and more likely to believe that disputes have been resolved appropriately if the outcomes seem just (or if the outcomes—in the same sense as salaries or promotions—seem distributed equitably, hence the term *distributive justice*).

A series of classic studies in psychology and law showed that although distributive justice theories were correct, there was clearly more to the story. This work, conducted by a psychologist and a law professor, suggests that disputants' perceptions of the fairness of the *procedures* are vitally important to the sense that "justice" was done (Thibaut & Walker, 1975). Such an orientation leads us to think of justice not only as punishment for wrongdoing, but also as a process by which people receive what they deserve or are due. **Procedural justice** models suggest that if individuals view the procedures of dispute resolution or decision-making as fair, then they will view the outcome as just, regardless of whether it favors them or not. According to this perspective, an important question in a contested divorce is the means by which each person was wronged. In a dispute with an insurance company over an accident claim, one might ask whether the injured party was treated unfairly.

Generally, individuals perceive a decision-making process as fair to the extent that they believe they have a voice in how the process unfolds, are treated with dignity and respect during the process, and trust the authorities in charge of the process to be motivated by concerns about fairness (Sydeman, Cascardi, Poythress, & Ritterband, 1997). A full opportunity to state one's viewpoint and to participate actively and personally in the decision makes a strong contribution to an assessment of fairness, probably because it allows people to feel that they retain some control over their affairs (Ebreo, Linn, & Vining, 1996).

Can we apply these findings to the real-world interactions that occur in police stations and courtrooms? Police officers and judges are not likely to generate warm feelings in the community when they give people less than what those people feel is deserved, or when they limit people's abilities to act as they wish. Do citizens have a better view of police officers and judges (and, by extension, of the entire legal system) if they perceive that they are being treated fairly? Will this make it more likely that they will comply with the law?

To answer these questions, Tom Tyler and Yuen Huo (2002) interviewed 1,656 individuals in Oakland and Los Angeles. Those interviewed were chosen because they indicated that they had had at least one recent experience with a police officer or a judge. The authors attempted to over-sample members of minority groups and ended with approximately equal numbers of whites, African Americans, and Hispanics as participants in their study. The researchers asked about the fairness of the outcomes of those encounters with authorities, as well as about the fairness of the procedures that were used to achieve the outcomes. They also measured people's trust in the motives of a particular authority figure by asking participants whether they felt that their views had been considered, whether they could trust the authority, whether the authority tried to do the right thing, and whether the authority cared about their concerns.

As one might expect, the favorability of the outcomes that participants received shaped their responses to this encounter. (We feel better about situations and people when we get what we want from those situations and from those individuals.) But importantly, the willingness to accept the decision of a police officer or judge was strongly influenced by perceptions of procedural fairness and trustworthiness: When people perceived that police officers and judges were treating them fairly and when they trusted the motives of these officials, they were more likely to accept their decisions and directives.

Commonsense Justice: Everyday Intuitions about Fairness

Another approach to the study of justice—one closely aligned with the analysis of citizens' agreement with the criminal code—is to learn about the intuitions that average people hold about culpability, fairness, and justice. Psychologist Norman Finkel has examined the relationship between the "law on the books" and what he calls **commonsense justice**—ordinary citizens' basic notions of what are just and fair. This work has much to say about inconsistencies between the law and public sentiment in the types of cases we have examined in this chapter—assisted suicide and euthanasia—as well as in cases involving self-defense, the insanity defense, the death penalty, and felony murder (Finkel, 1995). Commonsense justice is also reflected in cases in which a jury refuses to convict a defendant who is legally guilty of the crime charged—the phenomenon known as jury nullification (discussed in Chapter 12).

According to Finkel and others who have studied commonsense justice (e.g., Haney, 1997a; Olsen-Fulero & Fulero, 1997), there is evidence that the "black letter law" on the books may be at odds with community sentiment. This work is an important contribution to the field of law because it explains *how* jurors' sentiments depart from legal concepts and procedures. There are three identifiable discrepancies.

1. *The commonsense context is typically wider than the law's.* Ordinary people tend to consider the big picture: Their assessment of the event in question extends backward and forward in time (including, for example, the defendant's conduct prior to the incident and behavior after the crime), whereas the law allows consideration of a more limited set of circumstances. For example, in a date rape case or other case in which the victim and defendant knew each other, jurors would be likely to consider the history of the individuals, both together and apart. Is the incident one in a series of troublesome encounters in a tumultuous relationship? Have these events been alleged by other partners?

Although jurors contemplate the wider context of the story, the law freezes the frame at the time of the act and then zooms in on that relatively finite moment. Reasoning that this narrower perspective will result in a cleaner and more precise judgment, the law then asks jurors to determine culpability on the basis of the defendant's actions and intentions within this narrow window. But jurors would often rather learn about the big picture; for many, viewing only the last act does little to reveal the entire drama (Finkel & Groscup, 1997).

2. *Jurors' perspectives on the actions of the defendant and the victim are more subjective than the law allows.* In cases that involve two people with a prior history, jurors construct a story about what happened, and why, by stepping into the shoes of the defendant and viewing the events through that person's eyes. The stories they construct typically describe the hidden motives of the defendant. But, as Finkel notes, "such a subjective, discretionary enterprise grounds the law not on terra firma but on the unstable and invisible, where all we have are constructions, interpretations and stories constructed by jurors and judges" (Finkel, 1995, p. 327).

The concern, of course, is that too much subjectivity will result in lawlessness, that jurors' judgments will be rooted in illusion rather than in the more objective premises of the law. But jurors do not yield indiscriminately to their imaginations. In fact, when the individuals in a case are strangers to each other (as is often the situation), jurors tend to judge the circumstances and the actors' intentions objectively rather than subjectively.

3. *Jurors take a proportional approach to punishment, whereas the law asks them to consider the defendant in isolation.* Imagine a situation in which an armed robber enters a convenience store while his female accomplice watches guard outside the store. Further imagine that things go awry— the robber ends up shooting the cashier, and the cashier dies. The robber has certainly committed a crime, but what about the accomplice?

According to the felony-murder doctrine (which applies in about half the states), the accomplice is as culpable as the triggerman. Yet, as Finkel points out, this egalitarian approach seems to contradict the notion of proportional justice, in which a defendant's actions and intentions are assessed in comparison to others and the more culpable defendants are dealt with more severely. Jurors make distinctions among types of crimes and criminals, and they usually want more severe punishment for those they find most blameworthy.

COURTS

We now turn our attention to the reality of resolving legal disputes and the structures our society has enacted to do so. Disputes that reach the legal system are often resolved in court and different kinds of courts have been created to handle specific issues.

Federal Courts

Federal courts have jurisdiction over cases arising under the Constitution or laws of the United States but typically do not have jurisdiction over cases arising under state law, unless the plaintiff and defendant are from different states. Federal courts include trial courts, appellate courts, and the U.S.

Supreme Court. When Congress passes a law regarding federal crime (for example, the statute making carjacking a federal crime), the effect is to increase the case load of the federal courts.

Federal trial courts are called United States district courts. There is at least one district in every state; some states (California, for example) have several districts. The number of judges per district varies according to the district's case load.

The federal appellate courts are called the United States courts of appeals. There are 13 federal courts of appeals, divided into geographical "circuits"; there is a circuit for the District of Columbia, 11 circuits for the rest of the country, and a circuit for appeals from federal agencies (the Federal Circuit). In population, the largest circuit is the Ninth Circuit which includes California, and the smallest is the First Circuit which includes only a few New England states. The number of judges on each of the appellate courts depends on the case load of the particular court. There are 21 active judges on the Ninth Circuit and only 11 on the First Circuit, for instance.

Appeals are assigned to three-judge panels. The three judges assigned to a particular case examine the record (documents that the lawyers believe the judges need in order to decide the case), read the briefs (the lawyers' written arguments), and listen to the oral argument (the lawyers' debate about the case) before voting. The panel decides the case by majority vote (either 3–0 or 2–1), and one of the judges writes an opinion explaining why the court decided as it did. The opinion is sent to the parties and published in bound volumes (called Reporters). Opinions can be accessed through the Internet (for some courts) and through Westlaw and Lexis, which are computer-assisted legal research services. Very important cases are sometimes heard *en banc*— meaning that all the judges on the particular court of appeals decide the case.

Nine justices make up the United States Supreme Court, which has the authority to review all cases decided by the federal appellate courts. The Supreme Court also has the authority to review state court decisions based on the Constitution or on laws of the United States. When a state court decision involves a Constitutional or federal law issue, lawyers and judges refer to the decision as *raising a federal question*. The Supreme Court reviews only those cases that the justices view as most significant. When the Court decides to review a case, the order granting review is called a **writ of *certiorari***. The Court reviews only a small percentage of the cases it is asked to consider.

Justices of the Supreme Court, like other federal judges, are appointed by the president and confirmed by the Senate. Federal judges are granted a lifelong tenure to allow them to be impartial, not influenced by the whims of political or legislative interests. But an important Supreme Court decision in 2004 tested the independence of the judiciary. We describe the case of Terri Schiavo in Box 2.2.

State Courts

State court systems are typically divided into "lower" courts and trial courts. Lower courts have jurisdiction only over specific matters such as probate of wills (proving that a will was properly signed), administration of estates (supervising the payment of the deceased's debts and the distribution of his or her assets), family matters, and cases involving juvenile offenders. Family courts handle cases involving divorce, child custody, and child dependency, issues that we cover in Chapter 8. Juvenile courts deal with legal questions concerning delinquency; we discuss these in Chapter 14. Both family courts and juvenile courts tend to focus on helping people rather than punishing them. In fact, juvenile courts have functioned for many years to protect children from the rough-and-tumble world of adult criminal courts and to resolve cases in a supportive, nonadversarial way. (Over the past two decades, though, public opinion has become more punitive and many people now clamor for "adult time for adult crimes.")

Trial courts typically decide any case that concerns state laws. Most criminal cases (e.g., those involving drunken driving, armed robbery, and sexual assault) are tried in state trial courts.

In addition to lower courts and trial courts, state court systems typically include one or more

---

B o x 2.2   THE CASE OF TERRI SCHIAVO: A THREAT TO JUDICIAL INDEPENDENCE?

For a few weeks in March 2005, headlines about the Iraq war were replaced by front-page stories chronicling the battle over the life and death of Terri Schiavo. In 1990, Schiavo suffered a heart attack that caused permanent brain damage, described by her doctors as a "persistent vegetative state." She could breathe on her own and her eyes were open at times, but she could not eat or drink and her responses were random. Michael Schiavo, Terri's husband, claimed she had said she would not want to live "like that," and asked that her feeding tube be withdrawn. But Terri's parents, Bob and Mary Schindler, objected to removal of the feeding tube.

REUTERS/Carlos Barria/Landov

Protesters in the Terri Schiavo case

---

courts of appeal, similar to the federal appellate courts, and a state supreme court. Like the United States Supreme Court, state supreme courts review only those cases deemed to be important. Published opinions are found in state Reporters, and all opinions are accessible online.

"Problem-Solving Courts"

Fed up with "revolving door" justice (certain offenders are summoned back to court time and again), states and communities increasingly are creating "problem-solving" courts, combining the justice system with treatment-oriented principles to address underlying causes of antisocial behavior (Casey & Rottman, 2005). The premise of problem-solving courts is that the legal system should help troubled individuals cope with the problems that brought them to court. This approach, in which the law is used as a vehicle to improve people's lives, is called **therapeutic jurisprudence**. Examples of problem-solving courts include drug courts, mental health courts, homeless courts, and domestic violence courts.

In these courts, judges become social workers and cheerleaders as much as jurists. Rather than imposing punishment, they offer opportunities for people to deal with their addictions, violent tendencies,

The Schindlers and Michael Schiavo fought over Terri for seven years—in state and federal court, the halls of the U.S. Congress, and the court of public opinion. Ultimately, the courts ruled that Michael Shiavo could decide for Terri because she could not decide for herself. The tube was withdrawn on March 14, 2005, and she died two weeks later.

In addition to its public spectacle, the Shiavo case was extraordinary because of the important concerns it raised about the independence of the judiciary from legislative "oversight." In 1998, Michael Schiavo filed suit to have the tube removed. The Schindlers opposed the request, but a Florida judge ordered the tube removed, and the Florida appellate courts affirmed his decision. The Schindlers didn't give up. They fought this decision in the Florida courts for five years, and when the last appeal was lost and the tube removed in October 2003, they took their cause to then-Governor Jeb Bush and the Florida legislature. A few days later, the legislature responded with an extraordinary statute ("Terri's law"), giving the governor the authority to reinsert the feeding tube. Governor Bush signed the law that same day, and the feeding tube was reinserted.

Michael Shiavo then sued the governor in state court, claiming that the legislature and governor had violated the principle of separation of powers as embodied in the Florida Constitution and had encroached on the power and authority of the judiciary. The courts agreed. It is basic to the American system of government that, in the words of the Florida Supreme Court, legislatures pass laws and courts decide cases. By attempting to reverse the decision in the Schiavo case, the legislature had exceeded its authority in violation of the state constitution (*Bush v. Schiavo*, 2004).

After further litigation in both state and federal courts, the tube was removed again in March 2005. But then the U.S. Congress did an extraordinary thing: The Congress passed a law, which President George W. Bush signed, entitled "An Act for the relief of the parents of Theresa Marie Schiavo." The act directed the federal court in Florida to consider the Schindlers' request to have the feeding tube reinserted, notwithstanding the many opinions upholding the decision that the tube be removed. When a judge refused to consider reinserting the feeding tube, the Schindlers pressed on, buoyed at this point by throngs of supporters holding vigil outside the hospice where Terri lay. They filed several more appeals and suffered more defeats, including one the day before Terri died. In one of the last opinions in this case, a federal judge scolded Congress for telling a court how to exercise its duties:

[W]hen the fervor of political passions moves the Executive and the Legislative branches to act in ways inimical to basic constitutional principles, it is the duty of the judiciary to intervene. If sacrifices to the independence of the judiciary are permitted today, precedent is established for the constitutional transgressions of tomorrow. ... Accordingly, we must conscientiously guard the independence of our judiciary and safeguard the Constitution, even in the face of the unfathomable human tragedy that has befallen Mrs. Schiavo and her family. ...." (*Schiavo ex rel. Schindler v. Schiavo*, 2005, p. 14).

and squabbles with their landlords (Hartley, 2008). Judges are trained in their courts' specialty and may have a psychologist on their staff. Although some aspects of these courts are traditional—for instance, judges wear robes—many characteristics of problem-solving courts are unconventional. For example, the people who appear in court are often called clients rather than defendants. These "clients" are able to speak directly to the judge, rather than communicating through their attorneys. Judges often have a great deal of information about the clients and may interact with them over a number of years. On occasion, a friendly relationship develops, as described in Box 2.3.

Drug Courts. The most common form of problem-solving court is drug court, created to deal with offenders whose crimes are related to addiction. Drug courts developed in response to an increase in anti-drug law enforcement efforts and stiffer sanctions for drug offenders during the 1980s and 1990s. By 2008 there were more than 2,100 drug courts in the 50 states and many more in the planning phase (Eckholm, 2008).

Drug courts were developed to address the abuse of alcohol and other drugs and criminal activity related to addictions. Drug courts offer treatment programs and extensive supervision to drug-addicted offenders. In exchange for successful completion of

---

B o x 2.3   THE CASE OF A "CLIENT" OF JUSTICE MATTHEW D'EMIC

An immigrant from Barbados in his early 20s arrived in the New York courtroom of Justice Matthew D'Emic in 2003, facing a serious charge of arson after starting a fire that damaged a small public housing complex (Eaton & Kaufman, 2005). The man was delusional, believing that he was the son of God; he had been hospitalized nine times in five years. In a traditional courtroom, the case would have been disposed of by a guilty plea or verdict, and the defendant would have been sent to prison. But in the mental health court over which Justice D'Emic presided, something very different happened. The judge decided that the young man could safely return to live with his mother, provided that he continues to take his medications. Later, when the man complained of stomach cramps and began to miss appointments, the judge suggested that he change his medicine. The judge insisted that the man sign up for job training, allowing him to "graduate" from court with only a misdemeanor on his record. Most remarkably, Justice D'Emic gave the client his cell phone number and urged him to call if he got into a jam. The man said he used it just once, to ask the judge for advice about a woman he was considering marrying.

---

the program, the court may dismiss the original charge, reduce or set aside a sentence, assign some lesser penalty, or make a combination of these adjustments. The ultimate goal, in addition to improving the lives of drug-addicted individuals, is to reduce the number of drug offenders in prisons.

Writing in 2001, a team of authors headed by Arthur Lurigio described drug courts' team approach, in which the prosecutor, defender, judge, treatment providers, and probation officers work together to monitor offenders and hold them accountable for rule infractions through a series of graduated sanctions. The five common elements of drug courts are "immediate intervention, a non-adversarial process, a hands-on judicial role, drug treatment with clearly defined rules and goals, and a team approach" (Lurigio, Watson, Luchins, & Hanrahan, 2001, p. 186).

How successful are drug courts in reducing drug-related criminal activity? We describe studies that address this question in Chapter 15 but suffice to say that the findings are encouraging. A 2003 study of drug courts in New York found that "graduates" were about a third less likely to be rearrested on subsequent drug charges than similar defendants in traditional court (Eaton & Kaufman, 2005). Recently, drug courts have begun to target high-risk and violent offenders (in addition to first-time low-level offenders), and evidence suggests that even some serious violent offenders can be

helped by drug courts (Saum & Hiller, 2008). In fact, drug courts may be more effective than virtually any other intervention with drug offenders (Marlowe, DeMatteo, & Festinger, 2003).

According to Seattle Judge J. Wesley Saint Clair, "Drug courts work, and not because they're fuzzy—let me tell you, I can be a hard man to deal with." One offender to appear in Judge Saint Clair's courtroom was 36-year-old Jenifer Paris who, after 22 years or heroin and cocaine use and stretches of prostitution and homelessness, was now clean. "You guys are the first people to believe in me … I'm full of gratitude for the opportunity and for you not kicking me out," she said, tearfully. Replied Judge Saint Clair with a hint of a smile, "We're not done yet" (Eckholm, 2008).

Mental Health Courts.   The number of individuals hospitalized for mental illness dropped from 559,000 in 1960 to 60,000 in 1999 (Trupin, Richards, Wertheimer, & Bruschi, 2001). But **deinstitutionalization**, the long-term trend of closing mental hospitals and transferring care to community-based mental health treatment facilities, has left many mentally ill individuals without services or medication. As a result, the mentally ill have experienced higher rates of homelessness, unemployment, alcohol and drug use, and physical and sexual abuse. A sizeable number of people with severe mental illness are incarcerated in jails and prisons. Mental health courts were developed for offenders dealing with serious mental illness. By 2005, there were 125 mental health courts in the United States with more in the planning stage (The Criminal Justice/Mental Health Consensus Project, 2005).

Following the drug court model, the first decision is whether to divert the offender from the regular criminal courts to a mental health court. This decision, which usually requires the consent of both the offender and the victim, is made after an evaluation of the offender and by considering the nature of the offense. If the offender is diverted, the mental health team prepares a treatment plan to lead to long-term psychiatric care and reintegration into society. Close monitoring is essential. Defendants are often assigned to a probation officer who is trained in mental health and who carries a greatly reduced caseload in order to provide a more intensive level of supervision and expertise. The charges are dismissed if the offender follows the treatment plan (Lurigio et al., 2001). Preliminary evaluations of mental health courts suggest that they have been somewhat effective in linking participants to treatment services and in reducing recidivism rates (Redlich, Steadman, Monahan, Robbins, & Petrila, 2006).

Homeless Courts. Homeless courts were started in southern California with much the same design as mental health courts, and New York has created a variant on this approach termed *community courts* in Times Square and the Red Hook area of Brooklyn (Post, 2004a). Meeting in a refurbished Catholic school, the judges, prosecutors, and defenders in the Red Hook community court see their goal as bettering the quality of life for citizens. They know the people of the community and make it a point to know the offenders and to make sure the offenders know them. "The clerk of court has been known to stop her car at street corners and tell defendants the judge has issued a warrant for them and they'd best get over to court" (Carter, 2004, p. 39). The result is a reduction in low-level crime and decreased recidivism by offenders. Some courts aim to reduce homelessness by dealing with landlord and tenant issues and addressing the underlying

causes of homelessness—mental illness, poor job skills, and language barriers.

Domestic Violence Courts. Historically, legal response to domestic violence cases has been fragmented with different court divisions issuing restraining orders, prosecuting perpetrators, and protecting children. Victims have been considered merely "witnesses" and the needs of children have been largely ignored (Casey & Rottman, 2005). In recent years though, domestic violence courts have coordinated efforts to hold perpetrators accountable, enhance victim and child safety, and promote informed judicial decision-making. Domestic violence court personnel work with community-based agencies to strengthen the entire community's response to domestic violence (Sack, 2002). There are now more than 300 domestic violence courts in the United States (Casey & Rottman, 2005).

Like other problem-solving courts, domestic violence courts involve judges and staff specially trained in the relevant domain, coordination among community resources, and close monitoring of the perpetrator both before and after case disposition. But domestic violence courts differ from other problem-solving courts in important respects. They start from the premise that offenders' behavior is learned rather than rooted in a treatable addiction or illness. Therefore, court proceedings are primarily adversarial rather than therapeutic. They often involve both victim and offender attempting to reach agreement on protection orders. The needs of children are considered, and co-occurring child abuse and neglect is addressed.

Victims, perpetrators, advocates, and judges have generally reacted positively. Both victims and perpetrators express satisfaction with the court processes and outcomes. Compared with traditional courts, domestic violence courts process cases faster and have higher rates of guilty pleas. In addition, perpetrators are more likely to comply with judge-ordered conditions (Casey & Rottman, 2005).

Criticisms of Problem-Solving Courts. Despite the apparent successes of problem-solving courts, they have also been criticized. One concern is that middle-class judges inevitably reflect their middle-class values and may become inappropriately paternalistic in what they require of people (Eaton & Kaufman, 2005). Some have argued that problem-solving courts lack legitimacy because threatening punishment to coerce rehabilitation is unfair and because guilt or innocence is not determined by a trial (Casey, 2004). Prosecutors and public defenders have expressed concern over the "social worker" roles inherent in drug court philosophy; prosecutors feel pressured to favor rehabilitation of the offender over protection of society, and defenders feel pressured to plead their clients guilty and to inform the court of clients' failure to comply with the terms of probation (Feinblatt & Berman, 2001).

In spite of these criticisms, problem-solving courts have shown remarkable growth and the ability to effectively address some of the contributors to criminal offending that respond to interventions. As a result, they have the potential to reduce recidivism rates. Problem-solving courts will very likely continue to develop and evolve, focusing on the reasons why people are in court in the first place.

ALTERNATIVE DISPUTE RESOLUTION

From watching cable and online news and entertainment, one might get the impression that most lawsuits are resolved in trial by jury. In fact, most cases are resolved through negotiation or by ADR and fewer cases are being settled in trials. In a 2001 study of courts in 46 randomly selected counties in 22 states, the National Center for State Courts found that the number of cases tried had decreased by 50% in 10 years, a decrease of about 5% per year in a period when the number of cases filed increased by 1% a year (Post, 2004c).

The decrease in trials in the federal courts is even more dramatic. In 1962, 50,320 civil cases were disposed of in federal courts, and 11.5% of them were decided by trial. By 2002 the number of dispositions had climbed to 258,876, and the number of dispositions by trial had *decreased* to just 1.8% of the total (Galanter, 2004). On the criminal side, trials also decreased, though not as sharply. In 1962, when the cases of 33,110 defendants were disposed of, 15.39% were decided by trials; in 2002 the cases of 76,827 defendants were resolved, yet only 4.65% involved a trial (Galanter, 2004).

This decline is attributable to several factors, principally the perceived cost of litigation—the "transaction costs," in economists' language. Lawyers' fees to prepare for and try a case often make a trial economically unfeasible (Galanter, 2004). In addition, federal courts pressure litigants to settle or, in the case of criminal defendants, plead guilty. The federal sentencing guidelines give criminal defendants an incentive to plead guilty rather than stand trial because judges can decrease the length of a sentence on the basis of "acceptance of responsibility" (which normally requires a guilty plea) (Galanter, 2004).

In civil cases, federal judges are required to attempt to resolve disputes through ADR, and in both state and federal courts, judges are empowered to require litigants to try to settle their cases without going to trial. Increasingly, American courts assume that cases will be settled, not tried, to the point where a trial is viewed "as a failure of the system" (Sanborn, 2002, p. 25). Edmund Ludwig, a judge with over 30 years of experience, describes it this way:

> Litigation represents a breakdown in communication, which consists in the civil area of the inability of the parties to work out a problem for themselves and in the criminal area, of ineffectively inculcating society's rules and the consequences for violating them. Trials are the method we have ultimately used to deal with those breakdowns. However, the goal of our system is not to try cases. Rather, it is to achieve a fair, just, economical, and expeditious result by trial or otherwise, where communication has previously failed (Ludwig, 2002, p. 217).

Many cases are settled by **negotiation**, without the assistance of a third party. (Technically, ADR involves the use of a third person, or persons, to help resolve the controversy, so negotiation is actually not a method of ADR.) Negotiation might be formal, as happens when management and union representatives negotiate a labor contract, or informal, as when attorneys go back and forth in a series of phone calls to settle a personal injury claim.

As with trials, procedural justice considerations are important in successful negotiations. People care about both the outcome of negotiations and the fairness of the process. In a study in which law students role-played attorneys in a simulated negotiation about a contract dispute, participants thought negotiations were fair when they believed that they had been listened to and treated with courtesy, and when they perceived the other party as trustworthy (Hollander-Blumoff & Tyler, 2008).

Arbitration

One form of ADR, binding **arbitration**, bears the closest resemblance to a trial. When the parties agree to binding arbitration, they agree to accept the decision of an arbitrator. Salary arbitration in major league baseball is a good example of binding arbitration. The contract between the owners and the players' union provides that players' salary disputes are settled by binding arbitration, and it further provides that the arbitrator must accept either the owner's offer or the player's offer but cannot split the difference. The parties have an incentive to make an offer as close as possible to the player's "value" (their estimate of the arbitrator's valuation of the player's worth). Although many cases require binding arbitration, other cases are resolved by nonbinding arbitration. If one of the parties is dissatisfied with the arbitrator's decision, that person may ask that the case be tried before a judge or jury.

Arbitration, whether binding or nonbinding, uses trial-like procedures. The parties present evidence and argue the case, and the arbitrator makes a decision. Arbitration provides a speedy, flexible, and informal alternative to litigation, and arbitration clauses are often made part of contracts (Cox, 1999).

Litigants are usually satisfied with the outcome of arbitration. In a Georgia survey, 90% of attorneys said that arbitrators in their cases were fair. Though many attorneys did not agree with the outcome (45% believed that the damages awarded by arbitrators were at least somewhat unfair), attorneys were inclined to

accept (not appeal) the arbitrators' decisions because the hearings were perceived as fair—another example of the importance of procedural justice. Litigants usually want to resolve their disputes, not protract them, and the arbitrator's decision serves that function.

Summary Jury Trial

The **summary jury trial** is an interesting variation on arbitration. Developed in 1980, the summary jury trial is much like a conventional jury trial, though shorter. A jury is empanelled, and the lawyers tell the jurors what the witnesses would say if they were present. The lawyers argue the case and try to answer the jurors' questions about the facts. The judge tells the jury what the law is and tries to answer jurors' questions about the law. The jurors then deliberate and decide the case. Although the "verdict" does not bind the parties, the process educates the lawyers and clients on how a conventional jury might view the facts and the law. Once educated, the lawyers and their clients are more amenable to settling the case (Lambros, 1993).

The *American Bar Journal* has reported favorable comments from lawyers and judges who had availed themselves of this form of ADR (McDonough, 2004). Commenting on the summary jury trial, federal judge William Bertelsman said:

> I believe that substantial amounts of time can be saved by using summary jury trial in a few select cases. Also … the summary jury trial gives the parties a taste of the courtroom and satisfies their psychological need for a confrontation with each other. Any judge or attorney can tell you that emotional issues play a large part in some cases. When emotions are high, whether between attorneys or parties, cases may not settle even when a cost-benefit analysis says they should. A summary jury trial can provide a therapeutic release of this emotion at the expenditure of three days of the court's time instead of three weeks. After the emotions have been released the parties are more likely rationally to do the cost-benefit

analysis, and the case may then settle. (*McKay v. Ashland Oil Inc.*, 1988, p. 49)

Mediation

Mediation is the use of a neutral person (the mediator) to work with the litigants and their lawyers to achieve a settlement of the controversy. The mediator does not have authority to decide the controversy but, rather, acts as a facilitator. Mediation often involves *shuttle diplomacy*, a term associated with former Secretary of State Henry Kissinger. Much as Kissinger would "shuttle" between the two sides in international diplomacy, the mediator goes back and forth between the parties, meeting first with one side, then with the other, in an attempt to broker an agreement between the two.

One thinks of lawyers as eager to do battle—to slay their opponents with rhetorical swords. The facts, however, indicate otherwise: Lawyers prefer mediation over arbitration and trial by jury (Reuben, 1996). Why? Like most people, lawyers are **risk averse**; they work to avoid taking risks. They prefer that controversies be *settled by them* rather than *decided for them*. A mediator can assist to facilitate settlement and attorneys prefer the certainty of a settlement over the uncertainty of arbitration or trial.

Mediation in divorce and child custody disputes is now common practice and psychologists have assessed whether it leads to more desirable outcomes than litigation. One remarkable study assessed parent–child contact and coparenting in families whose custody disputes had been resolved 12 years earlier by either mediation or litigation (Emery, Laumann-Billings, Waldron, Sbarra, & Dillon, 2001). Families who mediated custody showed more cooperation and flexibility than families who litigated. In particular, nonresidential parents who mediated had more contact with their children and were more intimately involved in parenting, and fathers who mediated were much more satisfied with their custody arrangements. Mediation apparently encourages parents to comply with divorce agreements, remained involved in their children's lives, and renegotiate relationships in a more adaptive way.

Beliefs about Alternative Dispute Resolution

What form of ADR do people tend to favor? The answer to this question is important because ADR procedures will be accepted and used only if they are respected and considered legitimate. A recent study investigated the preferences of role-playing participants for different dispute resolution features. People evaluated civil disputes and indicated their preferences for a particular process, set of rules, and decision (Shestowsky, 2004). The most consistent finding was that participants favored options that offered them control (e.g., a neutral third party helping disputants to arrive at *their own* resolutions, processes that allow disputants to control *their own* presentation of evidence, and their agreement in advance on the rules that govern the decision).

Should courts force litigants to try ADR before setting a case for trial? The reports from courts that mandate ADR are generally positive. Attorneys like the process, believing that it is fair and saves clients' time and money (Boersema, Hanson, & Keilitz, 1991). The counter argument is that litigants have a right to trial by judge or jury. Judges are paid to enforce that right; mandating ADR undermines it. According to Federal Judge G. Thomas Eisele (1991), mandatory ADR leads to an unintended effect: Some lawyers (he calls them "piranhas") file meritless claims, knowing that their claims will have "settlement value" in mediation.

PLAYERS IN THE LEGAL SYSTEM: JUDGES

How Are Judges Selected?

We discussed judicial independence—the insulation of judges from the court of public opinion—in the context of the Schiavo case. Though the Schiavo case might suggest otherwise, U.S. federal judges, who are appointed by the president and serve for life, are shielded from the sometimes fickle inclinations of politicians and the public. They can be removed from office only if impeached for "high crimes and misdemeanors."

The vast majority of state court judges face elections. Typically, the governor makes an initial appointment and the judge is then retained (or not) in a popular election. If retained, the judge serves a number of years, after which he or she again runs for retention. Supporters maintain that this system makes judges accountable to the public and that a judge who makes unpopular decisions can be removed from the bench. Of judges surveyed in 10 states, 86% favored retention elections. The judges reported their behavior was improved by knowing that they would have to face the electorate; they were less likely to be arrogant to jurors and litigants and more likely to explain their decisions (Aspin & Hall, 1994).

But like other elections, judicial retention elections may invite pressure from special interest groups. In fact, some judicial races have been hotly contested in recent years, with special interest groups pouring money into advertising, often negative advertising, to elect judges thought to favor their positions. In 2004, Illinois voters experienced what critics called "the race to the bottom": $10 million was spent on a race for the state supreme court, with attack ads featuring the opponents' alleged leniency toward violent offenders in such graphic terms as to almost "make you believe the candidate committed the crime" (Carter, 2005).

There is also concern that judicial elections pose a threat to fairness and impartiality of the courts. The Fourteenth Amendment (Due Process Clause) requires judges to avoid even the appearance of bias. For that reason, former Supreme Court Justice Sandra Day O'Connor has condemned the practice of electing judges, stating that "you're not going to get fair and impartial judges that way" (Liptak, 2008). One judge whose impartiality has been questioned is West Virginia Supreme Court Justice Brent Benjamin, who decided a case in favor of a company that contributed $3 million to his election campaign. Many observers thought he should recuse himself (disqualify himself because of his personal involvement with a

party in the case). The U.S. Supreme Court tackled the issue in 2009, ruling by a 5–4 majority that Benjamin should have recused himself due to the apparent conflict of interest (*Caperton v. A. T. Massey Coal*, 2009).

According to one study, judges become more punitive as elections near (Huber & Gordon, 2004). Using sentencing data from more than 22,000 criminal cases in the 1990s, researchers found that judges added more than 2,700 years of additional prison time in aggravated assault, rape, and robbery cases when they are standing for election.

The politicization of judicial races is unfortunate. Judges are not accountable to the electorate in the same way as other elected officials. What is a virtue in a legislative office—keeping a campaign promise—is a vice in a judicial office. Judges who promise in a campaign not to probate offenders either break their promise to the voters by probating an offender who deserves probation, or violate their obligation as judge by denying probation. No judicial candidate should state or imply that he or she would favor one side over the other or decide an issue on anything other than the facts and the law.

There is no easy answer to the issue of judicial selection. Perhaps the balance between public accountability and judicial independence can best be struck by a system that combines merit appointments with retention elections in which voters are provided with an evaluation of the judge's entire tenure in office by a nonpartisan judicial qualifications commission. Such a system is in place in a handful of states.

Influences on Judicial Judgments

Although women make up more than half of the U.S. populace, until recently federal judges were almost exclusively male. Racial minorities were also vastly underrepresented on the bench. This imbalance began to change during the presidencies of Jimmy Carter and Bill Clinton whose appointments were 21% and 49% women or minorities, respectively. Although former President George W. Bush did not match those numbers, his appointments were more inclusive than other Republican presidents of the last half century. State courts are also increasingly diverse.

Do male and female judges view cases differently? One commentator has compared judges to baseball umpires by proposing that although judges' decisions are constrained by procedural rules and precedents, there is still opportunity for personal discretion (Quinn, 1996). This would suggest that the life experiences of women and members of racial minorities predispose them to make decisions that differ from those of their White male counterparts, particularly in cases related to gender and race (e.g., sexual offenses, harassment, and discrimination).

But the powerful forces associated with years of legal education and practice may trump the influence of personal characteristics. Legal socialization broadens attorneys' knowledge base and increases their respect for precedent and legal compliance. Because judges have typically practiced law for many years before assuming the bench, their personal characteristics may not exert a strong influence on their decisions (Kulik, Perry, & Pepper, 2003; Quinn, 1996). In fact, despite claims that women and racial minorities will be more sensitive to the concerns of plaintiffs in sexual harassment cases, a study of 292 federal cases decided between 1981 and 1996 showed no effects of judges' gender or race on their decisions (Kulik et al., 2003). Men and women, Whites and non-Whites were equally likely to rule in favor of the plaintiff in cases of sexual harassment.

There is some evidence that female judges do not handle stress as well as male judges. In a 2001 study using the Occupational Stress Inventory—Revised (OSI-R), female judges' scores on nine out of ten stressors were higher than those of their male counterparts (the only stressor on which men scored higher was responsibility) and female judges' scores were lower than men's on coping mechanisms (recreation, self-care, and social support) (Bremer & Todd, 2004).

But for both male and female judges, the stresses of judgeship are considerable. Not only do most judges have sizable caseloads, but because they make unpopular decisions—at least in the eyes of some who appear in their courtrooms—they become objects of public scorn and even, on occasion,

fear for their safety. Within a one-month period in 2005, the husband and mother of a Chicago judge were gunned down in their home (apparently in retaliation for the judge's handling of a case), and an Atlanta judge was shot to death in his courtroom. Both of the assailants were disgruntled defendants.

Trial judges, as human beings, reflect their own experiences, assumptions, and biases when reaching decisions from the bench, especially when the decision involves some leeway (e.g., a sentencing range). They may have biases for or against certain groups—homosexual persons, racial minorities, and older adults—that affect the way they process evidence and make decisions. Judges who have been prosecutors may maintain their sympathy with the state's evidence in criminal trials; conversely, judges who were once defenders may be biased in favor of defendants.

Appellate judges face a different task. Rather than assessing the credibility of certain witnesses and rendering a verdict, their job is to determine if the law has been correctly applied in previous decisions by trial judges and juries. There are two "schools of thought" about appellate decision-making. The **legal model of decision-making** is exemplified by Supreme Court Justice Clarence Thomas's assertion that "There are right and wrong answers to legal questions" (Thomas, 1996). It suggests that judges dispassionately consider the relevant laws, precedents, and constitutional principles, and that judicial bias has no part in decision-making. Yet Supreme Court justices tend to vote in predictable ways on cases that reflect basic values such as free speech and civil liberties: Decisions by federal judges appointed by Democratic presidents differ from those of judges appointed by Republican presidents. This suggests that judges' attitudes and predispositions *do* influence their decisions. Indeed, most social scientists now reject the legal model and instead favor an **attitudinal model of decision-making** in which judges view the facts of the case "in light of the ideological attitudes and values of the justices" (Segal & Spaeth, 1993, p. 32).

How Do Judges Decide?

Cognitive psychologists have proposed various two-process models of human judgment. Though the details vary, all distinguish between **intuitive processes** that occur spontaneously, often without careful thought or effort (as described by Malcolm Gladwell in his best-selling book *Blink)*, and **deliberative processes** that involve mental effort, concentration, motivation, and the application of learned rules.

A team of law professors has used a two-process model to explain trial judges' decision-making (Guthrie, Rachlinski, & Wistrich, 2007). They claim that although judges try to make decisions by relying on facts, evidence, and legal rules rather than personal biases or emotions, because they are ordinary people (who happen to wear robes), judges tend, like all of us, to have intuitive reactions. And though quick judgments can be overridden by complex, deliberative thoughts, judges must expend the effort to do so.

The researchers asked approximately 300 trial judges to take the Cognitive Reflection Test (Frederick, 2005), a brief test designed to measure intuitive and deliberative processing. Each question has a correct answer that one can recognize on reflection, yet an intuitive—and incorrect—response comes easily to mind. Here is an example:

A bat and a ball cost $1.10 in total. The bat costs $1.00 more than the ball.

How much does the ball cost?

Many people will immediately say "10 cents." But this intuitive answer is incorrect because if the ball costs 10 cents and the bat costs $1.00 more, the bat will cost $1.10 and together, they would cost $1.20, not $1.10. Upon reflection, the correct answer (the ball costs 5 cents and the bat costs $1.05) becomes apparent. Many judges tended to favor the intuitive, rather than the deliberative, response on all questions on the test, though some judges used more deliberate processes. Although judges undoubtedly exercise more care in thinking about issues that arise in their courtrooms than in responding to this short test, they commonly rely on intuitive reactions on the job, as well. The same team of law professors has shown that judges use intuitive decision processes to respond to suggested damage awards, descriptions of litigants' conduct, and inadmissible evidence (Guthrie, Rachlinski, & Wistrich, 2001; Wistrich, Guthrie, & Rachlinski, 2005). The authors suggest that judges should verify their intuitive decisions through careful analysis and that the justice system should take steps to make it likely they will do so.

PLAYERS IN THE LEGAL SYSTEM: LAWYERS

Lawyers are plentiful in the United States. Over 70% of the world's lawyers live in the United States, three times as many per capita as in Great Britain and more than 25 times as many per capita as in Japan. The American Bar Association (ABA) reported that there were 1,162,124 active lawyers in the United States as of 2008—enough to populate a fair-sized city (www.abanet.org). With law school enrollments stabilized at about 125,000, approximately 40,000 new lawyers are sworn in annually, more than are needed to replace those who leave the practice.

The National Association of Law Placement (www.nalp.org) provides statistical information on the employment of recent law graduates. A 2007 survey of information about 40,416 graduates showed that six months after graduation, 92% were employed. About 56% of those employed were in private practice, with the balance spread out in government, business, and academic endeavors. The median reported starting salaries were $62,500 for women and $70,000 for men.

Lawyers' Work Settings

Lawyers in law firms work for the firm's clients. Some lawyers specialize (e.g., labor law or intellectual property), and others are generalists, trying to handle most of their clients' legal matters. Some lawyers work for corporations and have only one client—their corporate employers.

Many lawyers work for the government—on the federal, state, or local level. Like attorneys for

---

Box 2.4   THE CASE OF CLARENCE GIDEON, HIS FAMOUS PAUPER'S PLEA, AND THE RIGHT TO AN ATTORNEY

Clarence Earl Gideon, Petitioner

vs.

H.G. Cochran, Jr., Director, Division of Corrections. State of Florida, Respondent

"Answer to respondent's response to petition for Writ of Certiorari."

Petitioner, Clarence Earl Gideon recieved a copy of the response of the respondent in the mail dated sixth day of April, 1962. Petitioner can not make any pretense of being able to answer the learned Attorney General of the State of Florida because the petitioner is not a attorney or versed in law nor does not have the law books to copy down the decisions of this Court. But the petitioner knows there is many of them. Nor would the petitioner be allowed to do so. According to the book of Revised Rules of the Supreme Court of the United States sent to me by Clerk of the same Court. The response of the respondent is out of time (Rule #24). Under this rule the respondent has thirty days in which to make a response. The respondent claims that a citizen can get a equal and fair trial without legal counsel. That the constitution of the United States does not apply to the State of Florida. Petitioner thinks that the fourteenth amend. makes this so. Petitioner will attempt to show this Court that a citizen of the State of Florida cannot get a just and fair trial without the aid of Counsel. Petitioner when he wrote his petition for Writ of Habeas Corpus to the Florida Supreme Court and his petition to this Court for a Writ of Certiorari and this brief was and is not allowed to send out a prepared petition. Petitioner is required to write his petition under duress or as the attorney General states, under physical restrain. If the petitioner had a attorney he could send out any kind of a petition he was so minded too, which shows he can not have equal rights to the law unless he does have a attorney. The same thing applies to the lower court. If the petitioner would of had a attorney there would not of been allowed such things as hear say perjury or Bill of attainer against him. Petitioner claims that there was never the crime of Breaking and Entering ever comitted. At that time he call to the The Federal Bureau of Investigation for help at Panama City, Fla., But was told they could not do nothing about it. Respondent claims that I have no right to file petition for a Writ of Habeas Corpus. Take away this right to a citizen and there is nothing left. It makes no difference how old I am or what color I am or what church I belong too if any. The question is I did not get a fair trial. The question is very simple. I requested the court to appoint me attorney and the court refused. All countrys try to give there Citizens a fair trial and see to it that they have counsel. Petitioner asks of this court to disregard the response of the respondent because it was out of Time and because the Attorney General did not have one of his many assistant attorney Generals to help me a citizen of the State of Florida to write my petition or this brief. But instead force me to write these petitions under duress. On this basis it is respectfully urged that the petition for a Writ of Certiorari shall be issue.

Clarence Earl Gideon
Petitioner

---

corporations, government lawyers have only one client: the governmental unit for which they work. Prosecutors are government lawyers responsible for prosecuting individuals charged with crime. Federal prosecutors (called U.S. Attorneys) are appointed by the president. (The widely publicized scandal over the dismissal of nine U.S. Attorneys in 2006 led to the resignation of then-Attorney General Alberto Gonzales because he was believed to have ordered the firings.) The head prosecutors for cities and counties, called States' Attorneys, are elected, often in partisan elections.

Because many people accused of crime cannot afford to hire a lawyer, most defendants are represented by public defenders who are also government employees. The history of public defenders dates from the 1963 case of *Gideon v. Wainwright*, in which the Supreme Court held that the State of Florida was obligated to pay for a lawyer for Clarence Earl Gideon, a small-town thief who lived on the fringes of society. His story is detailed in Box 2.4.

States responded to the Gideon case by appointing and paying lawyers to represent indigent

At age 51, Clarence Earl Gideon was tried for breaking into a pool hall and stealing money from a cigarette machine and a jukebox. At his trial, Gideon asked the judge to appoint an attorney to defend him because he had no money to pay for one. The judge, following the laws in Florida, refused.

Gideon did not have a lawyer during his trial. Though no stranger to a courtroom, having been convicted on four previous occasions, he lost this case as well. Eventually, from his prison cell, Gideon filed a pauper's appeal to the U.S. Supreme Court. His contention, laboriously printed in pencil, was that the U.S. Constitution guaranteed the right of every defendant in a criminal trial to have the services of a lawyer. Gideon's effort was a long shot; well over 1,500 paupers' appeals are filed each term, and the Supreme Court agrees to consider only about 3% of them. Furthermore, 20 years earlier, in the case of *Betts v. Brady* (1942), the Supreme Court had rejected the very proposition that Gideon was making by holding that poor defendants had a right to free counsel only under "special circumstances" (e.g., if the defendant was very young, illiterate, or mentally ill).

Yet, ever since its adoption, the doctrine of *Betts v. Brady* has been criticized as inconsistent and unjust. The folly of requiring a poor person to represent himself is exemplified by Gideon's cross-examination of the most important witness for the prosecution:

Q. Do you know positively I was carrying a pint of wine?

A. Yes.

Q. How do you know that?

A. Because I seen it in your hand. (Lewis, 1964)

When Gideon's case was argued before the Supreme Court in January 1963, he was represented by Abe Fortas, a Washington attorney later appointed to the Supreme Court. Fortas argued that it was impossible for defendants to have a fair trial unless they were represented by a lawyer. He also observed that the "special circumstances" rule was very hard to apply fairly.

In 1963, the Supreme Court ruled unanimously that Gideon had the right to be represented by an attorney, even if he could not afford one. As Justice Hugo Black put it, "[that] the government hires lawyers to prosecute and [that] defendants who have the money hire lawyers to defend are the strongest indications of the widespread belief that lawyers in criminal cases are necessities, not luxuries" (*Gideon v. Wainwright*, 1963, p. 344). Nearly two years after he was sentenced, Clarence Gideon was given a new trial. With the help of a free court-appointed attorney, he was acquitted. The simple handwritten petition of a modest man had forever changed the procedures of criminal trials.

defendants on a case-by-case basis and by establishing public defender programs, with lawyers hired by the state to represent those who cannot afford to hire them. Public defenders know the law, the system, and the other players in the system (the judge, the prosecutor, the probation officer), and though they have large caseloads, they often obtain excellent results for their clients.

Occasionally one reads of a public defender or appointed attorney who goes far beyond what can reasonably be expected of someone who is overworked and underpaid. Abbe Smith, now a law professor at Georgetown University, recently wrote a book about her experience in representing Patsy Kelly Jarrett over a span of 25 years (Smith, 2008). Smith first met Jarrett in 1980, three years after Jarrett received a life sentence for driving the getaway car as a result of a 1973 felony-murder conviction in New York. Convinced that Jarrett (whose conviction was based on eyewitness testimony) was innocent, Smith agreed to represent her and became a tireless advocate over the next 25 years in trying to secure her freedom. Her conviction was eventually overturned.

Clarence Earl Gideon

Patsy Kelly Jarrett

Law Schools and Legal Education

American lawyers of the 18th and 19th centuries typically learned to practice law through the apprentice method: An enterprising young man (the first female lawyer graduated in 1869) would attach himself to an attorney for a period of time, until both he and the lawyer were satisfied that he was ready to be "admitted to the bar." He would then be questioned, often superficially, by a judge or lawyer and pronounced fit to practice (Stevens, 1983).

Powerful forces shaped legal education as we know it today. States began to require those aspiring to be lawyers to pass meaningful examinations. Influenced by the ABA, the states also gradually increased the educational requirements for admission to these exams, first requiring some college, then some law school, and finally graduation from an accredited law school.

But while legal education may foster analytic skills and deepen knowledge of the law, it may take a toll on students' well-being. Studies show that attending law school tends to undermine students' values, motivation, and mental health (Sheldon & Krieger, 2004; 2007). Prior to law school, students are comparable to students in other professional fields in terms of psychological functioning. But soon after law school commences they report large increases in anxiety, depression, hostility, and paranoia. Some attribute these symptoms to law schools' excessive workload, intimidating teaching practices, competitive grading systems, status-seeking job placement services, and the lack of concern about personal feelings, values, or subjective well-being.

Researchers Kennon Sheldon and Lawrence Krieger (2004, 2007) suggest that psychological dysfunction is related to changes in motivation that occur over the course of one's law school career. They focus on the **self-determination theory of optimal motivation** (Deci & Ryan, 2000) which describes situational and personality factors that cause positive and negative motivation and, eventually, changes in subjective well-being. Sheldon and Krieger (2004) found that the increase in psychiatric symptoms in the first year of law school was correlated with a decrease in **intrinsic motivation** (engaging in an activity because it is interesting and enjoyable). Over the course of that year, students moved from pursuing their professional goals for reasons of interest and enjoyment (i.e., because of their intrinsic motivation) to pursuing goals that would please and impress others (i.e., for reasons of **extrinsic motivation**).

In other words, they felt less self-determined at the end of the year than they had at the beginning. Importantly, students who perceived that faculty supported their autonomy showed fewer declines in psychological well-being in the first year of law school and had higher grades in the third year (Sheldon & Krieger, 2007).

Professional Satisfaction among Lawyers

The practice of law may also be less satisfying than one might hope. Though some data show that lawyers report general satisfaction with the substance of their work (e.g., Kay & Hagan, 2004), other findings are rather grim. Seventy percent of lawyers who responded to a 1992 *California Lawyer* magazine poll stated that they would change careers if the opportunity arose. A survey on lawyer satisfaction conducted by the ABA's Young Lawyers Division in 2000 also revealed apparent discontent: More than 65% of respondents indicated that they would consider switching jobs within two years, 20% were dissatisfied with their current positions, and 25% were dissatisfied with the practice of law generally. Lawyers are generally less satisfied with their jobs than judges or law professors, suggesting that situational forces inherent in the practice of law (e.g., the hierarchical structure of many law firms, the obligation to bill a certain number of hours each week), rather than the discipline itself, may be to blame.

Lawyers who do not possess typical "lawyer traits" may be most discontented by the practice of law. A particular constellation of characteristics distinguishes lawyers from the general adult population: a preference for dominance, competitiveness, the need for achievement, and interpersonal insensitivity (Daicoff, 1999). According to law professor Susan Daicoff, these traits fit well with traditional forms of legal practice that value winning, analytical reasoning, and the elevation of concerns about clients' legal rights (Daicoff, 1999). Certainly not all lawyers possess these traits and not all legal issues require an adversarial, "I win–you lose" mentality. But attorneys who are not highly competitive, achievement-oriented, or motivated by dominance may experience the legal profession as a harsh and inhospitable place to work.

Fortunately, some legal institutions (including problem-solving courts and juvenile diversion programs) have begun to integrate principles of therapeutic jurisprudence, mentioned earlier in this chapter, with traditional legal structures and procedures. Therapeutic jurisprudence identifies emotional consequences of legal matters and asks whether the law can be interpreted, applied, or enforced in ways that maximize its therapeutic, or healing, effects. Therapeutic use of the law to enhance people's well-being may promise a less adversarial future for lawyers and the practice of law.

Women and Minorities in Law School and the Legal Profession

Women were denied admission to elite law schools well into the 20th century. As late as 1975, only 5% of American lawyers were women (Lentz & Laband, 1995). By 1980, however, women made up almost 40% of law students, a percentage that gradually increased to 49% in 2000 and then leveled off. Because women came into the profession in large numbers only recently, the percentage of women lawyers is still lower than the percentage of female law students. The 2000 census reports that 29% of attorneys are female.

Women lag behind men in pay, partnership numbers, and retention in law firms. For example, although surveys reveal gains in the percentage of partners who are female (rising from 6% in 1985 to 17% in 2004), still only 5% of managing partners are women (Rhode, 2001). According to this author, Stanford Law Professor Deborah Rhode, "women's opportunities are limited by traditional gender stereotypes, by inadequate access to mentors and informal networks of support, by inflexible workplace structures, and by other forms of gender bias in the justice system" (p. 14). Some firms may present social barriers to the advancement of women. As described in a 1996 article:

> "Often … women lawyers don't get a chance to build relationship in the firm or

with the client … Attaining new business, key to the coveted equity partnership, requires a fair amount of socializing. But social events tend to be male-centered: golf, ball games, and 'nights on the town when everyone ends up in a room smoking cigars' as one woman lawyer who asked not to be identified put it" (Klein, 1996, p. 1).

The fact that the percentage of female partners continues to increase suggests that demographic factors (e.g., age; older lawyers are predominately male), rather than overt discrimination, might be the cause of underrepresentation of women in positions of power within law firms. Yet women continue to perceive differential treatment. In a 2000 survey of Mississippi lawyers and judges, 80% of female respondents believed they were treated differently because of their gender by other lawyers, and 53% perceived gender differences in how judges responded. The women described patronizing references (e.g., "honey"), sexual innuendos, and the belief that engaging in appropriately aggressive behavior labeled them as "bitches" (Winkle & Wedeking, 2003).

With regard to minorities, in 1930, there were only six Black lawyers in Mississippi, a state with a Black population of more than 1 million (Houston, 1935). By 1966, the number had grown only to nine (Gellhorn, 1968). This rate reflected national trends; in 1988, only about 1% of the nation's lawyers were Black (McGee, 1971). Jim Crow laws and practices barred Blacks from southern law schools; Thurgood Marshall, who later became a justice on the U.S. Supreme Court, was denied admission to the University of Maryland Law School and attended Howard University, a predominantly Black school in the District of Columbia (Rowan, 1993).

Not until 1951 did the Association of American Law Schools (AALS) take a position against racial discrimination in admissions (Cardozo, 1993), and not until 1964 could the AALS state that none of its member schools reported denying admission on the basis of race. Nonetheless, in that year only 433 out of more than 50,000 students in predominantly White law schools were Black (ABA, 1992).

The number of minority lawyers in the United States has grown steadily since the mid-1960s, although the numbers still lag far behind the percentage of minorities in the general population. In 1960, less than 1% of lawyers in the United States were African Americans. In 1990, 3.3% of American attorneys were Black, and in the next decade, the percentage of African American attorneys increased only to 3.9% (ABA Commission on Racial and Ethnic Diversity, 2006). As of 2007, 5.4% of partners and 18% of associates at law firms were minorities. Additionally, over one-third of law firms reported no minority partners (www.nalp.org).

Minority admissions into law schools and the role of affirmative action programs were at the core of a case considered by the U.S. Supreme Court in 2003. The plaintiff was a White female applicant to the University of Michigan Law School by the name of Barbara Grutter (see Box 2.5).

Corporate America has made a commitment to diversity and might be minority lawyers' best friend. In choosing their lawyers, large corporations increasingly look for firms with women and minorities. Roderick Palmore, general counsel for Sara Lee, asked his counterparts in other corporations to use their positions to persuade the legal community not only to hire minorities and women but also to give them positions of responsibility. As of 2005, 73 large corporations had pledged to give work to diverse law firms and to avoid using firms that weren't making progress in that area (McDonough, 2005).

Criticisms of Lawyers

The legal profession has been criticized for several reasons. Chief among these are criticisms that the legal profession is relatively indifferent to the middle class, has a tendency to make the law overly complicated so that no one but a lawyer can understand it, often indulges the filing of frivolous lawsuits, and disregards the truth. Lawyers, it is claimed, fail to adequately serve the "middle 70%" of the population. Wealthy criminal defendants can afford expensive law firms to represent them; corporations have the resources to pay for extensive legal research and preparation. At the other end of the

---

B o x 2.5   THE CASE OF BARBARA GRUTTER AND HER ADMISSION TO LAW SCHOOL

Barbara Grutter, a White resident of Michigan, applied in December 1996 for admission into the first-year class of the University of Michigan Law School for the fall of 1997. At the time of her application, Grutter was 43 years old and had graduated from college 18 years earlier. She applied with a 3.8 undergraduate grade point average and a Law School Admission Test (LSAT) score of 161, representing the 86th percentile nationally. In June 1997, her application was rejected. Grutter believed that she was the victim of reverse discrimination—that she would have been admitted if she had been African American. The Center for Individual Rights, an organization opposed to affirmative action, agreed with her and sponsored a lawsuit on her behalf against the University of Michigan in federal court.

The trial lasted 15 days, during which Grutter relied on statistical evidence that the University admitted African American applicants with credentials inferior to hers, and the University defended its policy as one of diversity, not quotas (*Grutter v. Bollinger*, 2001). The trial court ruled in favor of Grutter, the federal court of appeals ruled against her, and the case came to the Supreme Court in 2003. In a 5–4 opinion, the Court also ruled against her, holding that the Law School could, in the name of diversity, prefer minority students of inferior numerical credentials over White applicants. Justice

O'Connor wrote the majority opinion, reasoning that diversity is a legitimate educational goal—that the Law School's admission policy, "promotes cross-racial understanding, helps to break down racial stereotypes, and enables students to better understand persons of different races," which in turn "better prepares students for an increasingly diverse workforce and society."

Turned away by the Court, the Center for Individual Rights took the fight to the voters, sponsoring a ballot initiative that amended the Michigan constitution to prohibit the state from extending preferential treatment to any group or individual based on race, gender, ethnicity, or national origin. Barbara Grutter was a spokesperson for the initiative—not an easy task, for she was greeted with "boos, hisses, and picket signs" and "frequently interrupted by jeers and murmurs of disapproval" (www.adversity.net).

In California, passage of Proposition 209 in 1995 also required state law schools to admit on a color-blind basis. At highly rated Boalt Hall (the law school at the University of California at Berkeley), the number of African Americans admitted dropped sharply in the wake of Proposition 209's passage but rebounded when Boalt changed the way it considered students' records (grades from all undergraduate institutions are now weighted the same) (Ward, 1998).

---

economic scale, poor people are provided lawyers without cost if they are defendants in criminal trials, and they may rely on legal aid clinics, including volunteer private attorneys, if they are involved in civil suits. It is middle-class individuals who have the most difficulty obtaining legal assistance, because attorneys' fees of $150 to $600 an hour quickly become prohibitive.

Lawyers are also charged with complicating the law unnecessarily so that consumers must hire an attorney to interpret the law for them. In apparent response to this criticism, the Florida Bar Association developed a procedure that allows childless couples who agree to divide their assets and debts to receive a divorce at a cost of less than $100 in filing fees, without the assistance of an attorney. In this example, a public institution arguably protected consumers from overly complicated legal maneuverings.

Another frequent criticism of lawyers is that they abuse the system by filing frivolous suits. Horror stories abound: pro football fans suing a referee over a bad call, umpires suing baseball managers over name calling, an adult man suing his parents for lack of love and affection, a man suing his former girlfriend over injuries he received during consensual sex, one prisoner suing his guards for "allowing" him to escape, and another inmate suing prison officials for denying him the chance to contribute to a sperm bank.

The reality, however, is that the extent of litigation involving claims of personal injury has been nearly constant since 1975 and has actually decreased since 1990. Most of the 10 million cases litigated each year are divorce cases and contract and property claims. At the same time, there is considerable evidence that some litigants and their lawyers seek compensation for nonexistent injuries. From 1980 to 1989, rates of motor vehicle accidents fell, and the number of claims made for property damages per million miles traveled also decreased 12%. With safer cars, the rate of claims for bodily injuries should have dropped even faster. Instead, the rate of bodily injury claims rose 15%.

A final criticism of lawyers is the public's perception that lawyers, as a group, do not have the same regard for the truth as the public supposedly has. Sometimes the criticism focuses on some lawyers' willingness to hide behind legalisms to bend the truth. President Clinton (a skilled lawyer) amused us by contending that oral sex wasn't sex and by denying a sexual relationship with Monica Lewinsky because of the tense of the verb in a question posed to him. As noted by political scientist Austin Sarat, he "played into every stereotype of taking refuge in narrow legalisms.... He's a caricature of the overly prepared witness. As for the public view of lawyers, this does damage to the profession" (Carter, 1998, p. 42). President Clinton escaped being removed from office by the Senate following his impeachment in the House of Representatives.

Often, lawyers are said to encourage falsity by consciously shaping a witness's recollection. Consider this description of famed lawyer Edward Bennett Williams' interviewing technique:

> As a rule, Williams didn't bother to take notes of the initial interview because he knew the client was lying. Slowly he'd probe for the truth. ... The fact is, however, that Williams did not always want the truth—at least the whole truth. ... He would ... help the client come up with a plausible theory to explain away incriminating facts. This was done subtly, through leading questions and a certain amount of winking and nodding (Thomas, 1991, p. 405).

As another example, the Dallas law firm of Baron & Budd sent clients allegedly suffering from asbestosis (a constellation of symptoms related to exposure to asbestos), instructions for depositions (pretrial questioning of a witness by an attorney hired by the other party). The instructions went beyond the usual "make sure you understand the question" advice and clearly were designed to tell the workers how to testify:

- It is important to emphasize that you had NO IDEA ASBESTOS WAS DANGEROUS when you were working around it.

- It is important to maintain that you NEVER saw any labels on asbestos products that said WARNING or DANGER (Rogers, 1998).

These examples are exceptions, not the rule, however. Most lawyers understand that their job is not to create the facts but to present the facts in the most favorable light to the client.

SUMMARY

1. *What is the difference between the adversarial and inquisitorial models of trials?* The trial process in the United States and several other countries is called the adversarial model because all the witnesses, evidence, and exhibits are presented by one side or the other. In contrast, in the inquisitorial model used in much of Europe, the judge does nearly all questioning of witnesses. Although the adversarial model has been criticized for instigating undesirable competition between sides, in empirical studies it has been judged to be fairer and to lead to less biased decisions.

2. *How do notions of morality and legality differ?* What is considered moral is not always what is ruled legal, and vice versa. When determining right and wrong, some people rely on the law almost entirely, but many people have internalized principles of morality that may be inconsistent with the laws.

3. *How do different models of justice explain people's level of satisfaction with the legal system?* According to the distributive justice model, people's acceptance of a legal decision is related to whether they think the outcome, or

decision, is fair. According to the procedural justice model, fairness in the procedures is a more important determinant of satisfaction.

4. *What is commonsense justice?* Commonsense justice reflects the basic notions of everyday citizens about what is just and fair. In contrast to black letter law, commonsense justice emphasizes the overall context in which an act occurs, the subjective intent of the person committing the act, and a desire to make the legal consequences of the act proportionate to the perceived culpability of the actor.

5. *What are some examples of problem-solving courts? How do they differ from traditional courts?* Drug courts and mental health courts are two examples of problem-solving courts. They differ from traditional courts in their focus on the underlying causes of people's legal difficulties and in their attempt to assist people with these problems (e.g., drug addiction, mental illness), rather than to punish them.

6. *What is alternative dispute resolution (ADR)? What are some types of ADR?* Alternative dispute resolution (ADR) is an umbrella term for alternatives to the court and jury as a means of resolving legal disputes. The most common forms are arbitration, in which a third party decides the controversy after hearing from both sides, and mediation, in which a third party tries to facilitate agreement between the disputants. The summary jury trial is another ADR mechanism.

7. *How are judges selected and how do their personal characteristics influence their decisions?* Federal judges are appointed for life. Most state court judges are appointed and then run on their records in retention elections. Judges' demographic characteristics tend not to influence their decisions, probably because the experiences of law school and years of work as a lawyer are powerful socializing forces. On the other hand, judges' biases and predisposition do tend to influence their judgments.

8. *How does the experience of law school affect its students?* Attending law school tends to undermine students' values, motivation, and psychological health because it reduces their intrinsic motivation and sense of self-determination.

9. *What have been the experiences of women and minorities in the legal profession?* Women are accepted in every facet of the legal profession, although they are not yet on par with men in terms of pay or access to positions of power in law firms. Minorities are underrepresented, and law schools' affirmative action programs are under attack, although the University of Michigan program was deemed constitutional by the U.S. Supreme Court.

10. *What are some common criticisms of lawyers?* Criticisms include lawyers' efforts to complicate legal matters unnecessarily in order to secure business, their supposed disregard for the truth, and the filing of frivolous lawsuits.

KEY TERMS

adversarial system

alternative dispute resolution

arbitration

attitudinal model of decision-making

attribution theory

black letter law

commonsense justice

deinstitutionalization

deliberative processes

distributive justice

euthanasia

extrinsic motivation

inquisitorial approach

intention

intrinsic motivation

intuitive processes

legal model of decision-making

mediation

negotiation

procedural justice

risk averse

self-determination theory of optimal motivation

summary jury trial

therapeutic jurisprudence

writ of *certiorari*

3

Psychology of Crime

ORIENTING QUESTIONS

1. Theories of crime can be grouped into four categories. What are they?
2. Among sociological explanations of crime, how does the subcultural explanation differ from the structural explanation?
3. What is emphasized in biological theories of crime?
4. What psychological factors have been advanced to explain crime?
5. How do social-psychological theories view crime?

OFFENDING IN THE UNITED STATES

Crime is a serious problem in our society. How often are crimes committed? What are the important influences to consider in understanding such offending? Questions about the causes of crime are the concern of **criminology**, which is the study of crime and criminal behavior. In this chapter, we summarize the major theories of crime, beginning with a brief review of the historical predecessors of 20th-century criminology. We will give examples of particularly serious and troubling offenses, and discuss why they occur.

Serious Offending

Rates of serious crime have been steadily declining in the United States. This decrease is confirmed by both victimization studies and official police statistics. According to the National Crime Victimization Survey (Bureau of Justice Statistics, 2005b), the rate of violent crime has been steadily dropping since 1994, and in 2005, the total violent crime rate decreased to the lowest level recorded by the National Crime Victimization Survey since 1973. There is a similar pattern for property crimes; however, the statistics suggest that these rates have started to level off since 2003.

Despite this downturn in crime rates, many Americans continue to list crime and the fear of crime as one of their most serious concerns. If the rate of crime is declining, why do so many individuals continue to perceive crime as a major threat in their lives? For one reason, the rate of violent crime is still relatively high despite recent decreases: 22 out of every 1,000 residents age 12 or older and living in an urban area were victimized by violent crime in 2003. The average citizen's fear of crime is also heightened by the highly publicized crimes of a few individuals that conjure up images of an epidemic of random violence beyond the control of a civilized society. The media provide extensive coverage of heinous crimes, contributing to a heightened state of public fear.

Consider these examples:

- In early 2004, Charles Allen McCoy, Jr., dubbed the Ohio Highway sniper, committed an estimated 24 acts involving firing at cars from an overpass, killing a woman, and terrorizing many more.

- Beginning on October 2, 2002, John Allen Muhammed and Lee Boyd Malvo paralyzed the Washington, D.C., area during a three-week shooting spree that left 10 people dead and 3 more critically wounded.

Perhaps even more troubling than overall crime rate or highly publicized crime sprees is the frequency of serious criminal activity among young people. Although the number of serious violent offenses committed by persons ages 12 to 17 declined by 61% from 1993 to 2005, juveniles continue to be responsible for committing about 24% of violent crimes. Specifically, youths under 18 years old commit approximately 12% of sexual assaults, 18% of robberies, and 22% of aggravated assaults.

In 2002, juveniles were involved in approximately 8% of all homicides. Although the number of murders involving juveniles has steadily decreased since 1994, juveniles continued to be involved in high-profile fatal events.

- In February 2009, an eighth grader named Lawrence King was shot in the head in his Oxnard, California, classroom while classmates looked on, horrified. Police allege that the shooter, 14-year-old Brandon McInerney, and some other boys had previously taunted King because he was gay. At the time of this death, King was living in a shelter for abused and troubled children.

- In 2006, Daytona Beach teen Warren Messner and three other boys brutally beat a homeless man to death because they were bored. The boys, who jumped on the man's chest and crushed his ribcage, were sentenced to between 22 and 35 years in prison.

- In April 1999, two students at Columbine High School in Littleton, Colorado, shot 12 of their classmates and a teacher before killing themselves.

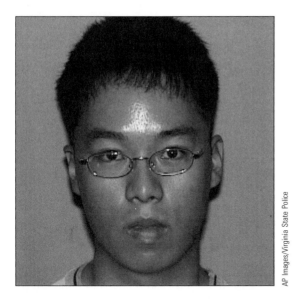

Seung-Hui Cho

AP Images/Virginia State Police

School Violence

The public becomes especially fearful about crime when they perceive it is occurring in traditionally safe environments. In the past two decades, crime in the workplace and violence in our schools have caused great national concern. DeKalb, Illinois; Blacksburg, Virginia; Red Lake, Minnesota; and Littleton, Colorado—these four communities share something that sets them apart from thousands of other American towns. In each, one or more students went to school one day, armed with guns, and proceeded to kill and wound their classmates. The grizzly totals from these four shootings: more than 60 dead and dozens wounded.

High-profile shootings occur both in high schools and on college campuses. Seung-Hui Cho was a child of South Korean immigrants who moved to the United States in 1992. Cho's mother thought that her son had autism, although he was eventually diagnosed as having "selective mutism" instead. In his earlier school days, he was often so uncommunicative that he would not even respond when his teacher took the roll. He enrolled at Virginia Tech but did not continue the treatment

he had received in middle and high school—and the university was not entitled to know about his diagnosis under federal privacy laws. Cho did not seek disability accommodation at Virginia Tech. On April 16, 2006, at 7:15 A.M., Cho shot and killed two students in a campus dormitory. Later that morning, he took the two handguns and ammunition he had obtained off-campus and went from room to room in Norris Hall, a building on campus with a number of classrooms. He killed 30 people before turning one of his guns on himself. Police responded quickly to an emergency call placed at 9:43 A.M., but by the time they were able to break into the building 8 minutes later (Cho had chained several doors shut), Cho and 30 students and faculty members were dead.

The school shooting fatalities had experts, parents, teachers, and youngsters themselves trying to understand what motivates school shootings and what can be done to prevent them. Are school environments to blame? Is the ready availability of guns one explanation? Were the killers mentally ill or emotionally disturbed misfits? Were they driven by violent music and gory video games? Did their parents fail to support and supervise them adequately?

Statistics about school violence, and the case histories of those boys who have murdered their classmates at school, provide some possible answers. First, according to a national survey of public schools in 1999–2000, 71% of students reported experiencing one or more violent incidents, and 20% reported *serious* violent incidents, which include rape, sexual battery other than rape, physical fight with a weapon, and robbery with or without a weapon. However, only about 36% of these schools reported one or more of these incidents to the police (National Center for Education Statistics, 2004). These events occurred more often in high schools than in elementary or middle schools, and high schools reported these events to police more often than did elementary or middle schools (National Center for Education Statistics, 2004). One survey conducted in 2001 (National Center for Education Statistics, 2003) revealed that 17% of high school students had carried a weapon (a gun, knife, or club) at least once in the previous month, and about 6% of these students carried the weapon to school. Additionally, in the 2005–2006 school year, 17% of public schools experienced at least one serious violent incident at school. A smaller percentage of primary schools (67%) than middle schools (94%) or high schools (95%) experienced a violent incident in 2005–2006.

School-ground homicides remain very rare, but when they do occur, they attract a great deal of speculation about the motives of the shooters (Cornell, 2006). Based on the small sample of cases, a few common characteristics have been identified in the backgrounds of the boys responsible for recent killings (Cloud, 1998; Verlinden, Hersen, & Thomas, 2000). Such boys tend to have

- had more than the usual experience with firearms, showing a persistent fascination with guns.
- felt isolated from, rejected by, or even tormented by classmates and had particular difficulty relating comfortably with girls.
- been preoccupied with various forms of graphically violent media, including music, Internet sites, and video games.
- suffered teasing because of their physical appearance—most of these assailants are either frail or somewhat obese.
- a history of angry brooding, often over their real or perceived status as social outcasts.
- developed a detailed plan for their aggression, which was often communicated to others in the days or weeks prior to the event.

Whether we will ever be able to explain this kind of crime is not clear. In retrospect, many of these individuals' classmates and teachers report that they now recognize that there were warning signs—although these signs do not necessarily reflect a forthcoming school shooting.

A number of reforms and programs have been attempted: requiring school uniforms, beefing up security measures, passing tougher gun laws, offering violence prevention programs, and restricting access to violent movies, among others. Another practice has involved "profiling" to predict which students are likely to commit violent crimes. However, this practice causes many students to be unjustly targeted, often on the basis of features not related to criminal behavior (e.g., clothing, music preferences). Furthermore, profiling in schools (even if it were very accurate in identifying those who are likely to commit homicides, which it is not) encounters the problem of "low base rates." That is, because school shootings are so rare, profiling would "overpredict," identifying many students who would actually not have committed a shooting. Instead, some researchers have proposed that increasing communication between students and school administrators may be a more productive approach to resolving the issues surrounding school violence and weapons (Mulvey & Cauffman, 2001). They note, "Students who are committed to school, feel that they belong, and trust the administration are less likely to commit violent acts than those who are uninvolved, alienated, and distrustful … Establishing school environments where students feel connected and trusted will build the critical link between those who often know when trouble is brewing and those who can act to prevent it."

Additional research on secondary school and campus shootings (Cornell, 2003, 2006; Flynn & Heitzmann, 2008; Heilbrun, Dvoskin, & Heilbrun, 2009; Reddy et al., 2001) would suggest several important points:

- The most prevalent problem with aggression in education settings is not shootings. In school contexts, it is bullying; on college campuses it is more likely to be date rape and hazing. Much of this aggression is unreported and hence underestimated by official records.
- Most of those who make implied or direct threats will not go on to commit serious violence. Threatening communications are made for a variety of reasons, including angry disputes, fear, jealousy, and ideology.
- "Zero tolerance" policies are both ineffective and have the potential to stigmatize and harm a variety of mistakenly identified individuals.
- A different approach, termed **threat assessment** involves carefully considering the nature of the threat, the risk posed by the individual, and the needed response to reduce the risk of

---

Box 3.1 THE CASE OF DEXTER MORGAN: A FICTIONAL PSYCHOPATH?

Dexter Morgan is playful, handsome, and has a wonderfully ironic sense of humor. He is the fictional star of novels (*Dearly Devoted Dexter* and *Darkly Dreaming Dexter*) and television series ("*Dexter*"). To his coworkers and fiancée, he is the blood-splatter analyst for the Miami Police Department. Privately, however, he is a selective serial killer who is guided by an internal companion whom he calls "the Dark Passenger." Dexter was trained by his adoptive father, a Miami cop, to present himself as "normal"—and to kill only those who deserve it, and according to a strict set of rules designed to avoid detection.

Can a fictional character such as Dexter tell us anything about reality? Are there real-life, nonfictional Dexter Morgans out there? Perhaps not, but reading about and watching Dexter can illustrate genuine phenomena. Engaging in a heinous act such as the killing of neighborhood pets, and needing to be taught to act "as if" one feels certain emotions, are associated with a kind of personality disorder known as **psychopathy**. This disorder provides the framework for the first-person narrative used in books and television series about Dexter Morgan. Would a real measure of this disorder (the Hare Psychopathy Checklist-Revised, or PCL-R; Hare, 2003) classify the fictional Dexter as a psychopath? Let's consider how some of the PCL-R items might apply.

PCL-R Item	Dexter
Glibness/superficial charm	<ul><li>Flirts with women to keep up appearances</li><li>Talks his way out of difficult situations easily</li></ul>
Pathological lying	<ul><li>Lies often, but presumably for self-preservation rather than without any understandable motivation</li></ul>
Conning/manipulative	<ul><li>Able to obtain files from clerks with flirting and donuts</li><li>Plans his killings carefully, using ruses and cons to capture and subdue his victims</li></ul>
Lack of remorse or guilt	<ul><li>Does not describe feeling these things for his victims</li><li>Also does not feel remorse or guilt for anything he does with coworkers or his fiancée or her children, although he feigns these emotions to fit in</li></ul>
Callous/lack of empathy	<ul><li>Shows no empathy for his victims</li></ul>

---

harmful action. Threat assessment has been refined by organizations such as the U.S. Secret Service in their work with threats of targeted violence toward those they protect (such as the U.S. president and vice-president, and their families). It can also be modified for use in other settings such as schools and colleges.

Highly publicized acts of violence at school or in the workplace threaten fundamental assumptions about personal security and the safety of our children and have a major effect on how individuals feel about their quality of life. For these reasons, policymakers and social scientists must pay particular attention to

workplace and school violence, although neighborhood violence continues to be a concern.

The fluctuations in the crime rate give rise to much speculation about what factors are most responsible for affecting crime. When crime is on the rise, the figures are used to justify requests for new policies and budget priorities. When the crime rate falls, the statistics are taken as an indication that one's favorite programs have been effective and need to be expanded.

Behavioral scientists argue that to ease the crime problem, we must first understand its causes. Why does crime happen? What motivates people to commit illegal acts? Bad genes? Inadequate parents? Failed

PCL-R Item	Dexter
Promiscuous sexual behavior	▪ No. Dexter describes himself as disinterested in all aspects of sexuality, including both physical and emotional intimacy
Need for stimulation/ proneness to boredom	▪ Describes this as a hunger for killing, which he must satisfy periodically ▪ Has a professional position involving the inspection of highly stimulating phenomena (homicide crime scenes) ▪ In other respects, however, he is not a great stimulation seeker, nor does he portray himself as easily bored
Parasitic lifestyle	▪ No. He has a steady job and does not rely on others for assistance
Poor behavioral controls	▪ No. He is careful and calculating, the antithesis of an impulsive offender
Irresponsibility	▪ No. He is gainfully employed and does his job well ▪ He is committed to his fiancée and her family, although not attracted to the intimacy ▪ He uses both his job and his relationships as a cover for his "avenging angel" role
Early behavior problems	▪ Showed behavior that could have resulted in arrest (e.g., killing neighborhood pets, taping up and threatening a classmate)
Criminal versatility	▪ No. Dexter is a "specialist" whose offending is limited to abducting and killing his victims

In some respects, the fictional Dexter Morgan (Phillips, 2006) is quite similar to those who have the personality disorder of psychopathy. These similarities are most apparent in his superficial emotions and absence of the capacity for deep emotional attachments. But Dexter does not possess some of the other characteristics and much of the history that are core elements of psychopathy. We might conclude that Dexter Morgan is a charming fictional character who can communicate what it's like to have difficulty feeling deep emotions—but it's not clear whether he would be classified as a psychopath.

Michael Hall plays Dexter Morgan

schooling? Twisted impulses? Harsh environments? Delinquent friends? Social disadvantage? Drug addiction? Some combination of these factors? Can crime be predicted from knowing about a person's early life? Or are many people capable of crime under the wrong circumstances—an unfortunate mix of intoxication, anger, and unprotected victims which come together, in the words of novelist Daniel Woodrell (1996), "like car wrecks that you knew would happen … almost nightly, at the same old crossroads of Hormones and Liquor" (p. 27)? Are some crimes, like those of Dexter Morgan (see Box 3.1), so extreme that they defy scientific explanation or can behavioral scientists make sense of them?

THEORIES OF CRIME AS EXPLANATIONS OF CRIMINAL BEHAVIOR

Theories of crime are as old as crime itself. Aristotle claimed that "poverty is the parent of revolution and crime." But most ancient explanations of crime took a religious tone; crime was either equivalent to or due to sin, a view that was popular throughout the Middle Ages and lives on today in many religious belief systems.

In the 17th century, Sir Francis Bacon argued that "opportunity makes a thief." During the 1700s, philosophers and social critics such as Voltaire and Rousseau emphasized concepts such as free will, hedonism, and flaws in the social contract to explain criminal conduct. These principles ultimately grew into the **classical school of criminology**.

The two leading proponents of classical criminology were the Italian intellectual Cesare Beccaria and the British philosopher Jeremy Bentham, who believed that lawbreaking occurred when people freely chose to behave wrongly when faced with a choice between right and wrong. People chose crime when they believed that the gains from crime outweighed the losses it entailed. Classical theorists were interested in reforming the harsh administration of justice in post-Renaissance Europe, and they believed that punishment of criminals should be proportionate to the crimes committed—that punishment should fit the crime.

Classical theory influenced several principles of justice in Western societies (e.g., the U.S. Constitution's Eighth Amendment ban against "cruel and unusual punishment"). It still exerts an important effect on modern correctional philosophy.

Modern theories of crime developed from the **positivist school of criminology**. Rather than focusing on individuals' free will, positivists emphasized factors that they believed determined criminal behavior. They sought to understand crime through the scientific method and the analysis of empirical data. Some stressed sociological factors, whereas others preferred biological, psychological, or environmental explanations. Additionally, some positivistic theories try to explain how people choose between criminal and noncriminal behaviors, thereby sharing some common ground with classical theories.

An early positivist was Adolphe Quetelet, a Belgian statistician who studied crime data and concluded that crime occurred more often in certain geographic areas and under specific social conditions. Lombroso (1876) and Garofalo (1914), other theorists who relied on scientific data, emphasized the physical characteristics of criminals and proposed a strong biological predisposition to crime. Although the early positivists thought of themselves as scientists, their science was crude by current standards and led to conclusions that are not taken seriously today. Positivists believed that punishment should fit the criminal rather than the crime. This position foreshadowed rehabilitation as a correctional priority and the indeterminate sentence as a means for achieving it.

Most modern theories of criminal behavior—including those of biology, genetics, psychology, sociology, economics, anthropology, and religion—are a legacy of the positivist tradition. The validity of these theories varies greatly. Most can account reasonably well for certain types of crime, but none explains all forms of criminality—and some explain very little. Empirical data, rational analyses, moral values, and political ideologies all play a role in shaping preferences for the leading theories in criminology.

For the most part, criminologists have concentrated on those crimes that frighten the average citizen—violent acts (e.g., robbery, rape, assault, and murder) or aggressive behavior against property (e.g., burglary, theft, and arson). But many other kinds of legally prohibited conduct—environmental plunder, price fixing, and business fraud, for example—can cause great damage to individuals and society. (Consider the securities fraud perpetrated by Bernard Madoff, the hedge fund trader and former chairman of the Nasdaq Stock Market, who may have plundered up to $50 billion of his clients' money.) However, these crimes are not the typical focus of criminologists, nor are they the kind of offenses considered by the general public when it debates the "crime problem."

Most theories of crime have focused on men. This may be reasonable, given that about three-quarters of all arrests are of men and that almost 85% of violent crimes are committed by men. However, the factors that influence female criminality deserve attention, at least in part because crime by females has increased relative to crime by males over the past decade. The rate of growth in the female inmate population has outpaced that of the male inmate population since 1995. Between 1995 and 2005, the annual growth rate of women in the prison populations increased by an average of 4.6%, compared to about 3.0% for men. The increase in females as a proportion of all incarcerated offenders in the United States during this period—from 6.1% to 7.0%—reflects an increase of nearly 15% (Harrison & Beck, 2006). In 2001, about 17% of women arrestees were charged with a violent offense, compared to 15% in 1996 (James, 2004). Despite these increases in violent criminal behavior, women are most often arrested for larceny and theft. Such arrests often involve collaborating with a male partner. One implication of this pattern is that explanations of female crime need to carefully consider the role of coercion, especially as it is exerted in close relationships.

In this chapter, we review criminological theories that attempt to explain aggressive crimes. We define these crimes as legally proscribed behavior in which one or more persons deliberately inflict or attempt to inflict physical injury on others or intentionally take or destroy the property of others. We group these theories into four categories: sociological, biological, psychological, and social-psychological. There are important distinctions among these four approaches.

Crime may appear to result from an individual's experience with his or her environment. This belief is explained through **sociological theories**, which maintain that crime results from social or cultural forces that are external to any specific individual; exist prior to any criminal act; and emerge from social class, political, ecological, or physical structures affecting large groups of people (Nettler, 1974).

Alternatively, criminal behavior may appear to result from an individual's biological characteristics. **Biological theories of crime** stress genetic influences, neuropsychological abnormalities, and biochemical irregularities. But as we shall see, there is little empirical evidence that either sociological or biological theories independently predict criminal behavior. Instead, current theories of crime incorporate a combination of environmental and biological factors to understand the causes of offending behaviors.

Some **psychological theories** emphasize that crime results from personality attributes that are uniquely possessed, or possessed to a special degree, by the potential criminal. For example, psychoanalysts have proposed several variations on the theme that crime is the result of an ego and superego that are too weak to control the sexual and aggressive instincts of the id. Other psychological approaches have focused more on patterns of thinking—particularly with respect to recognized risk factors such as pro-criminal attitudes or certain kinds of personality disorders.

Social-psychological theories (or social process theories; Nettler, 1974; Reid, 1976) bridge the gap between the environmentalism of sociology and the individualism of psychological or biological theories. Social-psychological theories propose that crime is learned, but they differ about *what* is learned and *how* it is learned.

Sociological Theories of Crime

Sociological theories may be divided into **structural** and **subcultural explanations**. Structural theories emphasize that dysfunctional social arrangements (e.g., inadequate schooling, economic adversity, or community disorganization) thwart people's efforts toward legitimate attainments and result in their breaking the law. Subcultural theories hold that crime originates when various groups of people endorse cultural values that clash with the dominant, conventional rules of society. In this view, crime is the product of a subculture's deviation from the accepted norms that underlie the criminal law.

Structural Explanations. A key concept of structural approaches is that certain groups of people suffer fundamental inequalities in opportunities to achieve the goals valued by society. Differential opportunity, proposed by Cloward and Ohlin (1960) in their book *Delinquency and Opportunity*, is one example of a structural explanation of crime. This theory can be traced to Émile Durkheim's ideas about the need to maintain moral bonds between individuals in society. Durkheim thought that life without moral or social obligations becomes intolerable and results in **anomie**, a feeling of normlessness that often precedes suicide and crime. One implication of anomie theory was that unlimited aspirations pressure individuals to deviate from social norms.

According to Cloward and Ohlin (1960), people in lower socioeconomic subcultures usually want to succeed through legal means, but society denies them legitimate opportunities to do so. For example, consider a person from Nicaragua who immigrates to the United States because of a sincere desire to make a better life for his family. He faces cultural and language differences, financial hardships, and limited access to the resources that are crucial for upward mobility. It remains more difficult for poor people to obtain an advanced education, despite advances in the practice of need-blind admissions and tuition adjustments based on need that are now offered by some U.S. universities. In addition, crowding in large cities makes class distinctions more apparent.

When legal means of goal achievement are blocked, intense frustration results, and crime is more likely to ensue. Youthful crime, especially in gangs, is one outgrowth of this sequence. The theory of differential opportunity assumes that people who grow up in crowded, impoverished, deteriorating neighborhoods endorse conventional, middle-class goals (e.g., owning a home). Thus, crime is an illicit means to gain an understandable end.

Consistent with this view, Gottfredson (1986) and Gordon (1986), a sociologist team, attempted to explain the higher crime rate of lower-class black youth in terms of their poorer academic performance. Denied legitimate job opportunities because of low aptitude scores or grades, these youth discover that they can make several hundred dollars a week dealing crack cocaine. In fact, with the advent of crack cocaine, arrests of juveniles in New York City, Detroit, Washington, and other cities tripled in the mid- to late 1980s.

The theory of differential opportunity has several limitations (Lilly, Cullen, & Ball, 1989). First, a great deal of research indicates that seriously delinquent youth display many differences from their law-abiding counterparts other than differing educational opportunities, and they tend to show these differences as early as the beginning of elementary school. Second, there is no evidence that lower-class youth find limited success in school to be more frustrating than do middle-class youngsters. On the contrary, the exact opposite is likely to be true. The assumption that lower-class juveniles typically aspire to membership in the middle class is also unproved. Furthermore, the major terms in the theory, such as *aspiration*, *frustration*, and *opportunity*, are defined too vaguely; the theory does not explicitly explain what determines adaptation to blocked opportunities (Sheley, 1985). Last and most apparent, crimes are often committed by people who have never been denied opportunities; in fact, they may have basked in an abundance of good fortune. Think of Winona Ryder's shoplifting incident at a high-end department store. Many other examples come readily to mind: the head of a local charity who pockets donations for personal enrichment, the pharmacist who deals drugs under the counter, the politician who accepts bribes for votes. Indeed, think of many white-collar offenses, motivated not by lack of opportunity but by the desire to expand what are already tremendous opportunities and resources even further.

Subcultural Explanations. The subcultural version of sociological theory maintains that a conflict of norms held by different groups causes criminal behavior. This conflict arises when various groups endorse subcultural norms, pressuring their members to deviate from the norms underlying the criminal law (Nietzel, 1979). Gangs, for example, enforce unique norms about how to behave. For many youths, a gang replaces the young person's parents as the main source of norms, even when parents attempt to instill their own values.

This theme of cultural conflict is illustrated by Walter Miller's theory of **focal concerns**. Miller explains the criminal activities of lower-class adolescent gangs as an attempt to achieve the ends valued in their culture through behaviors that appear best suited to obtain those ends. Thus, youth must adhere to the traditions of the lower class. What are these characteristics? Miller (1958) lists six basic values: trouble, toughness, smartness, excitement, fate, and autonomy. For example, lower-class boys pick fights to show their toughness, and they steal to demonstrate their shrewdness and daring (Sheley, 1985). Hundreds of juvenile homicides occur each year; many are committed to demonstrate macho toughness or relieve boredom (Heide, 1997). However, the theory of focal concerns does not explain crime by individuals who are not socially disadvantaged, such as the rich hotel owner, the television evangelist, or the Wall Street swindler. In addition, key concepts in the theory are vague.

Like structural theories of crime, subcultural explanations have not demonstrated a strong theoretical or empirical basis. Questions remain. How do cultural standards originate? How are they transmitted from one generation to the next? How do they control the behavior of any one individual? The most troublesome concept is the main one—subculture. Some critics reject the assumption that different socioeconomic groups embrace radically different values.

Biological Theories of Crime

Biological theories of crime search for genetic vulnerabilities, neuropsychological abnormalities, or biochemical irregularities that predispose people to criminal behavior. These dispositions, biological theorists believe, are then translated into specific criminal behavior through environments and social interactions. Research on biological theories commonly focuses on twin and adoption studies to distinguish genetic from environmental factors.

In twin studies, the researcher compares the **concordance rate** (the percentage of pairs of twins sharing the behavior of interest) for **monozygotic twins** (identical twins) and **dizygotic twins** (commonly called fraternal twins). If the monozygotic concordance rate is significantly higher, the investigator concludes that the behavior in question is genetically influenced, because monozygotic twins are genetically identical whereas dizygotic pairs share, on average, only 50% of their genetic material.

In one study of 274 adult twin pairs, participants were asked to complete several questionnaires about past criminal behaviors, such as destroying property, fighting, carrying and using a weapon, and struggling with the police. Results reflected a finding of 50% heritability for such violent behaviors (Rushton, 1996) suggesting that inherited tendencies may play a "preponderant part" in causing crime (Lange, 1929). However, studies that distinguish between crimes against property and violent crimes against persons have found that although heredity and environment play important roles in both types of crime, the influence of heredity is higher for aggressive types of antisocial behavior (e.g., assaults, robberies, and sexual offenses) than for nonaggressive crimes such as drug taking, shoplifting, and truancy (Eley, 1997).

Adoption studies also support the contention that genetic factors play some role in the development of criminality. Cloninger, Sigvardsson, Bohman, and von Knorring (1982) studied the arrest records of adult males who had been adopted as children. They found that men whose biological parents had a criminal record were four times more likely to be criminal themselves (a prevalence rate of 12.1%) than adoptees who had no criminal background (2.9%) and twice as likely to be criminal as adoptees whose adoptive parents had a criminal history. More recently, researchers conducted a review of several twin and adoption studies in this area and found similar results (Tehrani & Mednick, 2000).

An interesting possibility regarding a biological contributor to offending was first raised by a 1993 study (Brunner, Nelen, Breakefield, Ropers, & van Oost, 1993). Studying individuals who had committed offenses, the investigators noted five participants who showed both borderline mental retardation and impaired control of impulsive aggression. These individuals each showed a complete absence of activity of a certain enzyme (monoamine oxidase A, or MAOA) which in turn affects important neurotransmitters. This absence resulted from a mutation on the X chromosome in the gene coding for MAOA.

Without replication, this finding—involving a small number of affected individuals—would not have implications for the broader scientific and legal fields (Appelbaum, 2005). However, a second study with a large cohort (1,037 individuals followed since birth in Dunedin, New Zealand) has replicated and extended these findings (Caspi et al., 2002). The investigators considered both the levels of MAOA and the history of maltreatment between the ages of 3 and 11. Using multiple measures of antisocial behavior, they reported that the 12% of their participants who had both low MAOA and maltreatment accounted for 44% of the total convictions for violent offenses, with 85% of individuals with both low MAOA and maltreatment later showing some form of antisocial behavior.

These findings may begin to answer the question that has always been present in connection with the possibility that genetic factors influence crime: What influences what? There is a lengthy list of likely candidates (Brennan & Raine, 1997; DiLalla & Gottesman, 1991; Moffitt & Mednick, 1988), but five possibilities are emphasized:

1. *Low MAOA in combination with a history of maltreatment.* Further replication is needed, but this initial finding shows promise in helping to explain how a combination of an adverse experience (child maltreatment) and a biological risk factor (low MAOA) could affect impulsivity and propensity to antisocial behavior.

2. *Neuropsychological abnormalities.* High rates of abnormal electroencephalogram (EEG) patterns have been reported in prison populations and in violent juvenile delinquents. These EEG irregularities may indicate neurological deficits that result in poor impulse control and impaired judgment. Studies of violent offenders have shown slow-wave EEG (underarousal) (Mark & Ervin, 1970; Milstein, 1988; Williams, 1969). Although a high percentage of persons in the general population also have EEG abnormalities, recent research does describe a somewhat higher rate of EEG abnormalities in delinquent youth (Raine, Venables, & Williams, 1989; Satterfield & Schella, 1984).

More promising results have been reported concerning abnormalities in four subcortical regions of the brain—the amygdala, hippocampus, thalamus, and midbrain—specifically in the right hemisphere of the brain, which has been linked to the experience of negative emotions. In one study (Raine, Meloy, & Buchshaum, 1998), brain scans of a group of homicide offenders showed that, compared with normal controls, the offenders experienced excessive activity in the four subcortical structures. Excessive subcortical activity may underlie a more aggressive temperament that could, in turn, predispose an individual to violent behavior.

A review of the neuropsychological literature supports a relationship between deficits in the prefrontal cortex, a region of the brain responsible for planning, monitoring, and controlling behavior, and antisocial behavior (see Raine, 2002). Damage to the prefrontal cortex may predispose individuals to criminal behavior in one of several ways. Patients with impairment in this region of the brain have decreased reasoning abilities that may lead to impulsive decision making in risky situations (Bechara, Damasio, Tranel, & Damasio, 1997). In addition, prefrontal impairment is associated with decreased levels of arousal, and individuals may engage in stimulation seeking and antisocial behaviors to compensate for these arousal deficits (Raine, Lencz, Bihrle, Lacasse, & Colletti, 2000).

Other lines of research suggest that impaired functioning in the prefrontal cortex contributes to aggressive behavior. Offenders, on average, have about an 8- to 10-point lower IQ (intelligence quotient) than nonoffenders. This difference is mainly due to verbal (as opposed to performance) functioning, suggesting that offenders are less able to (1) postpone impulsive actions, (2) use effective problem-solving strategies (Lynam, Moffitt, & Stouthamer-Loeber, 1993), and (3) achieve academic success in schools as a route to socially approved attainments (Binder, 1988).

In one longitudinal study of 411 London boys, low IQ at ages 8 through 10 was linked to persistent criminality and more convictions for violent crimes up to age 32 (Farrington, 1995). This relationship persists even after controlling for the effects of social class, race, and motivation to do well on tests (Lynam et al., 1993).

3. *Autonomic nervous system differences.* The autonomic nervous system (ANS) carries information between the brain and all organs of the body. Because of these connections, emotions are associated with changes in the ANS. In fact, we can "see" the effects of emotional arousal on such ANS responses as heart rate, skin conductance, respiration, and blood pressure. Some offenders—particularly those whose offending is most chronic—are thought to differ from noncriminals in that they show chronically low levels of autonomic arousal and weaker physiological reactions to stimulation (Mednick & Christiansen, 1977). These differences, which might also involve hormonal irregularities (see the next section), could cause this group of offenders to have (1) difficulty learning how to inhibit behavior likely to lead to punishment and (2) a high need for extra stimulation that they gratify through aggressive thrill seeking. These difficulties are also considered an important predisposing factor by some social-psychological theorists that we discuss later.

4. *Physiological differences.* A number of physiological factors might lead to increased aggressiveness and delinquency (Berman, 1997). Among the variables receiving continuing attention are (1) abnormally high levels of testosterone, (2) increased secretion of insulin, and (3) lower levels of serotonin (DiLalla & Gottesman, 1991). Research on testosterone has yielded inconsistent results (Archer, 1991), but depleted or impaired action of serotonin has received considerable support as a factor underlying impulsive aggression (Coccaro, Kavoussi, & Lesser, 1992).

One study using animal models provides further support for the role of these physiological variables in aggressive behavior. Researchers found that rats with increased production of testosterone and lower levels of serotonin exhibited more aggressive behaviors; these rats displayed an increased number of attacks and inflicted a greater number of wounds on other rats compared to rats with lower testosterone and higher serotonin levels (Toot, Dunphy, Turner, & Ely, 2004). Such findings may be helpful in understanding the biological contributions to human aggression as well. Low levels of serotonin might be linked to aggressiveness and criminal conduct in any of several ways—for example, through greater impulsivity and irritability, impaired ability to regulate negative moods, excessive alcohol consumption, or hypersensitivity to provocative and threatening environmental cues (Berman, Tracy, & Coccaro, 1997).

5. *Personality and temperament differences.* Several dimensions of personality, known to be heritable to a considerable degree, are related to antisocial behavior. Individuals with personalities marked by undercontrol, unfriendliness, irritability, low empathy, and a tendency to become easily frustrated are at greater risk for antisocial conduct (Nietzel, Hasemann, & Lynam, 1999). We discuss some of these characteristics more fully in the next section on psychological theories of crime.

Psychological Theories of Crime

Psychological explanations of crime emphasize individual differences in the way people think or feel about their behavior. These differences, which can take the form of subtle variations or more extreme personality disturbances, might make some people more prone to criminal conduct by increasing their anger, weakening their attachments to others, or fueling their desire to take risks and seek thrills.

Psychoanalytic Theories. Psychoanalysts believe that crime results from a weak ego and superego that cannot restrain the antisocial instincts of the id. Each individual's unique history should reveal the specific factors that produced a defective ego or superego, but the factor most commonly blamed is inadequate identification by a child with his or her parents. Freud believed that the criminal suffers from a compulsive need for punishment to alleviate feelings of guilt stemming from the unconscious, incestuous feelings of the Oedipal period. He wrote, "In many criminals, especially youthful ones, it is possible to detect a very powerful sense of guilt which existed before the crime, and is therefore not its result but its motive. It is as if it was a relief to be able to fasten this unconscious sense of guilt onto something real and immediate" (1961, p. 52).

Other psychoanalysts have suggested that criminal behavior is a means of obtaining substitute gratification of basic needs such as love, nurturance, and attention that have not been normally satisfied within the family. John Bowlby (1949, 1953; Bowlby & Salter-Ainsworth, 1965) suggested that disruptions of the attachment between mother and infant or parental rejection of the developing child account for a majority of the more intractable cases of delinquency and repetitive crime (Bowlby, 1949, p. 37).

Psychoanalytic theories often trap their adherents in tautological circles, and they are no longer favored in modern criminology. What have been called "antisocial instincts" may simply be alternative names for the behaviors they are intended to explain. Another major problem with psychoanalytic interpretations of crime is that they are contradicted by patterns of real criminal conduct. Freud's idea that criminals commit crimes in order to be caught and punished, and thus to have their guilt reduced, ignores the obvious extremes to which most offenders go to avoid detection of their wrongdoing. Most offenders do not appear frustrated or guilt-ridden by the fact that their "crimes pay," at least some of the time. In fact, the success of their crimes seems to be a major source of gratification. Finally, psychoanalytic descriptions are at odds with the observation that many forms of crime are more calculated than compulsive, and more devised than driven.

Criminal Thinking Patterns. In a controversial theory spawned from their frustration with traditional criminological theories, Samuel Yochelson and Stanton E. Samenow (1976; Samenow, 1984) have proposed that criminals engage in a fundamentally different way of thinking than noncriminals. They wrote that the thinking of criminals, though internally logical and consistent, is erroneous and irresponsible. In short, consistent lawbreakers see themselves and the world differently from the rest of us.

Yochelson and Samenow rejected sociological, environmental, and psychoanalytic explanations of criminality, such as a broken home, unloving parents, or unemployment. Rather, they argued that criminals become criminals as a result of choices they start making at an early age. These patterns, coupled with a pervasive sense of irresponsibility, mold lives of crime that are extremely difficult to change. Yochelson and Samenow described the criminals they studied as very much in control of their own actions, rather than being victims of the environment or being "sick." These criminals were portrayed as master manipulators who assign the blame for their behavior to others. They are such inveterate liars that they can no longer separate fact from fiction. They use words to manipulate reality, not to represent it.

Yochelson and Samenow's conclusions are based on intensive interviews with a small number of offenders, most of whom were incarcerated offenders or men who were hospitalized after having been acquitted of major crimes by reason of insanity. But no control groups of any sort were studied. Furthermore, Yochelson and Samenow portray only one type of criminal; their analysis does not accurately represent the majority of lawbreakers. Finally, the "criminal thinking pattern" theory does not explain how these choices are made in the beginning (Pfohl, 1985), although in other publications Samenow hints at genetic predispositions to crime. In fact, in this way and others, this theory is similar to the notion of the psychopathic personality, to which we now turn.

Personality-Based Explanations. Three major personality dimensions have been described: **extroversion**, **neuroticism**, and **psychoticism** (Eysenck & Gudjonsson, 1989). Extroverted people are active, aggressive, and impulsive. Persons high in neuroticism are restless, emotionally volatile, and hypersensitive. Persons high in psychoticism are troublesome, lacking in empathy, and insensitive to the point of cruelty.

Extroversion, neuroticism, and psychoticism are inherited to a substantial degree and also are associated with important physiological differences, some of which we will describe in the discussion of psychopathy later in this section. High extroverts have relatively low levels of arousal that slow their conditioning. Such conditioning is also impaired because physiological arousal dissipates more slowly in extroverted people and psychopaths. As a result, avoiding a previously punished act may be less reinforcing for such people because they experience less reduction in fear following their avoidance of the taboo behavior (Mednick, Gabrielli, & Hutchings, 1984).

Persons high in neuroticism tend to overreact to stimuli. Therefore, high neuroticism interferes with efficient learning because of the irrelevant arousal that is evoked. In addition, high neuroticism leads to greater restlessness and drive to carry out behavior of all sorts, including crimes.

Eysenck (1964) believes that high extroversion and neuroticism result in poor conditioning and, consequently, inadequate socialization. Poor conditioning leads to a faulty conscience, which in turn produces a higher risk for criminality. Finally, if the person is high on psychoticism, he

or she will be more of a primary, "tough-minded" psychopath.

Research on the links between criminal offending and personality supports a positive association between high levels of extroversion and increased offending. However, the role of neuroticism and psychoticism is less clear; in fact, neuroticism may be lower in most psychopaths than in normal controls (Doren, 1987). Another problem is that Eysenck has not clearly separated the predisposition to be conditioned from the different conditioning opportunities that children experience. Genetic differences are accompanied by different conditioning histories. A family of extroverts can transmit a potential for crime not only through inherited personality traits but also through laissez-faire discipline that is too scarce or inconsistent to be effective.

Psychopathy. Many individuals attribute crime to personality defects, typically in the form of theories that posit the criminal's basic antisocial or psychopathic nature. The concept of *psychopathy* has a long history. As we mentioned previously, this term refers to individuals who engage in frequent, repetitive criminal activity for which they feel little or no remorse. Such persons appear chronically deceitful and manipulative; they seem to have a nearly total lack of conscience that propels them into repeated conflict with society, often from a very early age. They are superficial, arrogant, and do not seem to learn from experience; they lack empathy and loyalty to individuals, groups, or society (Hare, Hart, & Harpur, 1991). Psychopaths are selfish, callous, and irresponsible; they tend to blame others or to offer plausible rationalizations for their behavior.

The closest diagnostic label to psychopathy is **antisocial personality disorder**. The two disorders are similar in their emphasis on chronic antisocial behavior, but they differ in the role of personal characteristics, which are important in psychopathy but are not among the diagnostic criteria for antisocial personality disorder. About 80% of psychopaths are men, and their acts sometimes are well publicized (see Box 3.2).

B o x **3.2**   THE CASE OF TED BUNDY: A REAL-LIFE PSYCHOPATH

Born in 1946, Theodore Robert Bundy seemed destined for a charmed life; he was intelligent, attractive, and articulate (Holmes & DeBurger, 1988). A Boy Scout as a youth and then an honor student and psychology major at the University of Washington, he was at one time a work–study student at the Seattle Crisis Clinic. Later he became assistant to the chairman of the Washington State Republican Party. It is probably around this time that he claimed his first victim, a college-age woman who was viciously attacked while sleeping, left alive but brain-damaged.

From 1974 through 1978, Bundy stalked, attacked, killed, and then sexually assaulted as many as 36 victims in Washington, Oregon, Utah, Colorado, and Florida. Apparently, some of the women were taken off guard when the good-looking, casual Bundy approached, seeming helpless walking with crutches, or having an apparent broken arm. He usually choked them to death and then sexually abused and mutilated them before disposing of their bodies in remote areas (Nordheimer, 1989).

It is characteristic of many people with psychopathy to maintain a facade of charm; acquaintances often describe them (as they did Bundy) as "fascinating," "charismatic," and "compassionate." Beneath his superficial charm, though, Bundy was deceitful and dangerous. Embarrassed because he was an illegitimate child and that his mother was poor, he constantly sought, as a youth, to give the impression of being an upper-class kid. He wore fake mustaches and used makeup to change his appearance. He faked a British accent and stole cars in high school to help maintain his image. He constantly sought out the company of attractive women, not because he was genuinely interested in them but because he wanted people to notice and admire him.

At his trial for the murder of two Chi Omega sorority sisters in their bedrooms at Florida State University, he served as his own attorney. (Bundy had attended two law schools, although he did not graduate from either.) He was convicted; he was also found guilty of the kidnapping, murder, and mutilation of a Lake City, Florida, girl who was 12 years old. Bundy was sentenced to death.

© Bettman/CORBIS

Serial killer Ted Bundy

Shortly before he was executed on January 24, 1989, Bundy gave a television interview to evangelist James Dobson in which he blamed his problems on pornography. He said, "Those of us who are … so much influenced by violence in the media, in particular pornographic violence, are not some kind of inherent monsters. We are your husbands, and we grew up in regular families" (quoted by Lamar, 1989, p. 34).

Bundy claimed that he spent his formative ages with a grandfather who had an insatiable craving for pornography. He told Dr. Dobson, "People will accuse me of being self-serving but I am just telling you how I feel. Through God's help, I have been able to come to the point where I, much too late, but better late than never, feel the hurt and the pain that I am responsible for" (quoted by Kleinberg, 1989, p. 5A).

The tape of Bundy's last interview, produced by Dobson and titled "Fatal Addiction," has been widely disseminated, especially by those who seek to eliminate all pornography. But Bundy's claim that pornography was the "fuel for his fantasies" should be viewed skeptically. It may merely have been one last manipulative ploy to buy more time. In none of his previous interviews, including extensive conversations in 1986 with Dorothy Lewis, a psychiatrist he had come to trust, did he ever cite "a pornographic preamble to his grotesqueries" (Nobile, 1989, p. 41).

Psychopathy as measured by the Hare PCL and PCL-R (Hare, 1991, 2003) has been well established as a risk factor for offending and for violent offending. Perhaps the best demonstration of this relationship comes from a meta-analysis on this topic (Leistico, Salekin, DeCoster, & Rogers, 2008). The authors integrated 95 nonoverlapping studies (N = 15,826 participants) to summarize the relation between the

Hare Psychopathy Checklists and antisocial conduct. Their results indicated that higher PCL Total scores and the scores on Factor 1 (describing interpersonal characteristics) and Factor 2 (describing chronic antisocial behavior) were moderately associated with increased antisocial conduct. These results depended on the setting from which the participants were drawn. Checklist scores were more strongly associated with offending in the community than with serious misconduct in correctional facilities and secure hospitals.

There are a multitude of theories about what causes psychopathic behavior. One view is that psychopathic persons suffer a cortical immaturity that makes it difficult for them to inhibit behavior. Robert Hare (Hare & McPherson, 1984) has proposed that psychopaths may have a deficiency in the left hemisphere of their brains that impairs **executive function**, the ability to plan and regulate behavior carefully (Moffitt & Lynam, 1994). Considerable research supports a strong relationship between antisocial behavior and impaired executive functioning (Morgan & Lilienfeld, 2000).

Compared to normal controls, psychopaths experience less anxiety subsequent to aversive stimulation and are relatively underaroused in the resting state as well. This low autonomic arousal generates a high need for stimulation. Consequently, the psychopath prefers novel situations and tends to pay less attention to many stimuli, thereby being less influenced by them.

One study demonstrated this by examining EEG readings of brain waves in 35 hospital patients who met diagnostic criteria for antisocial personality disorder and compared those readings with a matched control group of 35 hospital patients who met criteria for diagnoses other than antisocial personality disorder (Dewolf, Duran, & Loas, 2002). The neurophysiologist interpreting the readings was blind to the patients' diagnoses. Findings revealed that the patients with psychopathy showed significantly slower waves and more abnormalities than the controls, even during a state of excitement. The authors question, however, whether these abnormalities are a result of brain development that leads to this type of personality disorder or of risky behaviors (i.e., head trauma) that are often associated with conduct disorder.

Another study with 89 right-handed males found a relationship between antisocial personality disorder and EEG activity. Findings showed that greater right hemisphere activity, lower left hemisphere activity, or both were associated with diagnosis of antisocial personality disorder (Deckel, Hesselbrock, and Bauer, 1996).

Herbert Quay (1965) advanced the **stimulation-seeking theory**, which claims that the thrill seeking and disruptive behavior of the psychopath serve to increase sensory input and arousal to a more tolerable level. As a result of such thrill seeking, the psychopathic person seems "immune" to many social cues that govern behavior. Eysenck (1964) proposed a theory that emphasizes the slower rate of classical conditioning for persons classified as psychopaths. He argued that the development of a conscience depends on acquisition of classically conditioned fear and avoidance responses, and that psychopathic individuals' conditioning deficiencies may account for their difficulties in normal socialization.

Another popular explanation for psychopathy involves being raised in a dysfunctional family (Loeber & Stouthamer-Loeber, 1986; Patterson, 1986). Arnold Buss (1966) identified two parental patterns that might foster psychopathy. The first is having parents who are cold and distant. The child who imitates these parents develops an unfeeling, detached interpersonal style that conveys a superficial appearance of social involvement but lacks the empathy required for stable, satisfying relationships. The second pattern involves having parents who are inconsistent in their use of rewards and punishments, making it difficult for the child to imitate a stable role model and develop a consistent self-identity. A child in this situation learns to avoid blame and punishment but fails to learn the finer differences between appropriate and less appropriate behavior.

The major drawback of psychopathy as an explanation for crime is that it describes only a small percentage of offenders. It might be tempting to classify most offenders as psychopaths and feel content that their crimes had been explained with that terminology. But in fact, most offenders are not psychopathic. One study found that only about 25% of a correctional sample could be classified as psychopathic, and this percentage was even smaller for women than for men (Salekin, Trobst, & Krioukova, 2001).

In addition, there is controversy about using the PCL and revised versions of the instrument as diagnostic tools on which legal decisions are based (Zinger & Forth, 1998). First, although the PCL-R has an excellent inter-rater reliability when carried out in accordance with instructions (indicating that two raters using the PCL-R would tend to reach the same conclusion), a lack of training and possible biases on the part of the clinician may contribute to disparities in scores. Slight differences in scores may account for differences in courts' dispositions of these cases.

Evidence suggests that expert testimony about an offender's psychopathy or *psychopathic traits* (the preferred term for adolescents showing features of psychopathy) is associated with an increase in severity of the court's disposition (Zinger & Forth, 1998), although other evidence with juveniles suggests that the "antisocial behavior" label has a stronger effect than "psychopathic traits" on the judgments of juvenile probation officers (Murrie, Cornell, & McCoy, 2005). Potential jurors were most influenced in their decisions regarding juveniles by descriptions of antisocial behavior, psychopathic traits, or the colloquial use of the term *psychopath* (Boccaccini, Murrie, Clark, & Cornell, 2008).

Furthermore, because the PCL is a self-report measure, the administrator is subject to relying on inaccurate information. As a safeguard against potentially erroneous information, the administrator must have access to collateral information to compare with information obtained from the examinee. Because the number of judicial decisions that rely on the PCL-R appears to be on the rise, the ongoing training efforts for this measure are particularly important.

Yet another criticism of the use of these psychopathy assessment instruments in criminal proceedings revolves around their use in cases involving adolescent and female offenders. Although some evidence suggests that these instruments can be successfully used with women

offenders (Loucks & Zamble 1994; Neary, 1990; Salekin, Rogers, & Sewell, 1997; Vitale & Newman, 2001) and male adolescent offenders (Chandler & Moran, 1990; Forth, 1995; Forth & Burke, 1998; Forth, Hart, & Hare, 1990; Trevethan & Walker, 1989), more research is needed. Nonetheless, it is fair to say that these psychopathy assessment tools offer a valuable way of assessing personal characteristics and history that are related to criminal offending by some offenders. But there are other contributors as well, including social influences, to which we now turn.

Social-Psychological Theories of Crime

Social-psychological explanations view crime as being learned through social interaction. Sometimes called social-process theories in order to draw attention to the processes by which an individual becomes a criminal, social-psychological theories fall into two subcategories: control theories and direct learning theories. **Control theory** assumes that people will behave antisocially unless they learn, through a combination of inner controls and external constraints on behavior, not to offend. **Learning theory** stresses how individuals directly acquire specific criminal behaviors through different forms of learning.

Control Theories.   Control theories assume that people will behave antisocially unless they are trained not to by others (Conger, 1980). Young people are bonded to society at several levels. They differ in (1) the degree to which they are affected by the opinions and expectations of others, (2) the payoffs they receive for conventional behavior, and (3) the extent to which they subscribe to the prevailing norms. Some people never form emotional bonds with significant others, so they never internalize necessary controls over antisocial behavior.

Walter Reckless's (1967) **containment theory** is an example of a control theory. Reckless proposes that it is largely external containment (i.e., social pressure and institutionalized rules) that controls crime.

If a society is well integrated, has well-defined limits on behavior, encourages family discipline and supervision, and provides reinforcers for positive accomplishments, crime will be contained. But if these external controls weaken, control of crime must depend on internal restraints, mainly an individual's conscience. Thus, a positive self-concept becomes a protective factor against delinquency. Strong inner containment involves the ability to tolerate frustration, be motivated by long-term goals, resist distractions, and find substitute satisfactions (Reckless, 1967).

Containment theory is a good "in-between" view, neither rigidly environmental nor entirely psychological. Containment accounts for the law-abiding individual in a high-crime environment. But this theory explains only a part of criminal behavior. It does not apply to crimes within groups that are organized around their commitment to deviant behavior.

The British psychologist Hans Eysenck (1964) proposes a related version of containment theory in which "heredity plays an important, and possibly a vital, part in predisposing a given individual to crime" (p. 55). Socialization practices then translate these innate tendencies into criminal acts. Socialization depends on two kinds of learning. First, **operant learning** explains how behavior is acquired and maintained by its consequences: Responses that are followed by rewards are strengthened, whereas responses followed by aversive events are weakened. Immediate consequences are more influential than delayed consequences. However, according to Eysenck (1964), in the real world the effects of punishment are usually "long delayed and uncertain [whereas] the acquisition of the desired object is immediate; therefore, although the acquisition and the pleasure derived from it may, on the whole, be less than the pain derived from the incarceration which ultimately follows, the time element very much favors the acquisition as compared with the deterrent effects of the incarceration" (p. 101).

Because of punishment's ineffectiveness, the restraint of antisocial behavior ultimately depends on a strong conscience, which develops through **classical conditioning**. Eysenck believes that conscience is conditioned through repeated, close pairings of a child's undesirable behaviors with the prompt punishment of these behaviors. The taboo act is the **conditioned stimulus**, which, when associated frequently enough with the **unconditioned stimulus** of punishment, produces unpleasant physiological and emotional responses. Conscience becomes an inner control that deters wrongdoing through the emotions of anxiety and guilt. Whether conditioning builds a strong conscience depends on the strength of the autonomic nervous system. According to Eysenck, conditioned responses have a genetically determined tendency in some people to develop slowly and extinguish quickly. In others, conditioning progresses rapidly and produces strong resistance to extinction.

Learning Theories. Learning theory focuses on how criminal behavior is learned. According to Edwin H. Sutherland's (1947) **differential association approach**, criminal behavior requires socialization into a system of values conducive to violating the law; thus, the potential criminal develops definitions of behavior that make deviant conduct seem acceptable. If definitions of criminal acts as being acceptable are stronger and more frequent than definitions unfavorable to deviant behavior, then the person is more likely to commit crimes. It is not necessary to associate with criminals directly to acquire these definitions. Children might learn pro-criminal definitions from watching their father pocket too much change or hearing their mother brag about exceeding the speed limit.

Using the differential association approach, Sutherland and Cressey (1974) propose various explanations of criminal behavior, including these:

1. Criminal behavior is learned in interaction with other persons in a process of communication.

2. When criminal behavior is learned, the learning includes (a) techniques of committing the crime, which are sometimes very complicated but at other times simple; and (b) the specific direction of motives, drives, rationalizations, and attitudes.

3. A person becomes delinquent because of an excess of definitions favorable to violation of law over definitions unfavorable to violation of law.

Sutherland's theory has been translated into the language of operant learning theory as developed by B. F. Skinner. According to **differential association reinforcement theory** (Akers, Krohn, Lanz-Kaduce, & Radosevich, 1996; Burgess & Akers, 1966), criminal behavior is acquired through operant conditioning and modeling. A person behaves criminally when such behavior is favored by reinforcement contingencies that outweigh punishment contingencies. The major contingencies occur in families, peer groups, and schools, which control most sources of reinforcement and punishment and expose people to many behavioral models (Akers et al., 1996).

Differential association attempts to explain crime in places where it would not, on first blush, be expected (e.g., among lawbreakers who grew up in affluent settings). But it has difficulty explaining impulsive violence, and it does not explain why certain individuals, even in the same family, have the different associations they do. Why are some people more likely than others to form criminal associations?

Social Learning. **Social learning theory** acknowledges the importance of differential reinforcement for developing new behaviors, but it assigns more importance to cognitive factors and to observational or **vicarious learning**. Its chief proponent, Albert Bandura (1986), claims that "most human behavior is learned by observation through modeling" (p. 47). Learning through modeling is more efficient than learning through differential reinforcement. Sophisticated behaviors such as speech and complex chains of behavior such as driving a car require models from which to learn. In all likelihood, so does crime. Observational learning depends on (1) *attention* to the important features of modeled behavior, (2) *retention* of these features in memory to guide later performance, (3) *reproduction* of the observed behaviors, and (4) *reinforcement* of performed behaviors, which determines whether they will be performed again.

The most prominent attempt to apply social learning theory to criminal behavior is Bandura's (1973) book *Aggression: A Social Learning Analysis* (see also Platt & Prout, 1987; Ribes-Inesta & Bandura, 1976). The theory emphasizes modeling of aggression in three social contexts.

1. *Familial influences.* Familial aggression assumes many forms, from child abuse at one extreme to aggressive parental attitudes and language at the other. It is in the arena of discipline, however, where children are exposed most often to vivid examples of coercion and aggression as a preferred style for resolving conflicts and asserting desires.

2. *Subcultural influences.* Some environments and subcultures provide context that supports aggression and an abundance of rewards for their most combative members. "The highest rates of aggressive behavior are found in environments where aggressive models abound and where aggressiveness is regarded as a highly valued attribute" (Bandura, 1976, p. 207).

3. *Symbolic models.* The influence of symbolic models on aggression has been attributed to the mass media, particularly television. A large number of studies have investigated the effects of televised violence on viewers, especially on children.

A longitudinal study, conducted over a 15-year period, suggests that there are significant long-term effects from watching violent television in childhood (Huesmann, Moise-Titus, Podolski, & Eron, 2003). Results from this study revealed a significant relationship between watching violence on television as children and aggressive behavior in adulthood. This pattern held for male and female participants, although the types of aggressive behavior differed. Males engaged in more overt aggression (e.g., domestic violence, physical fights), whereas women engaged in more indirect aggression (e.g., traffic violations). Women who watched violent television as children were also four times more likely than other women to be victims of domestic violence. Furthermore, the study found that early exposure to violence on television significantly predicted aggression in adulthood regardless of the level of aggression the individual displayed in childhood.

Researchers also hypothesized that viewing television violence in childhood can lead to other

---

B o x 3.3   THE CASE OF "TEENAGE AMUSEMENT," A MURDER, AND A VIDEOGAME

A 2006 report from the National Coalition for the Homeless noted a disturbing trend: 122 attacks and 20 murders of homeless people in 2005, several of them by teenage perpetrators. According to the Coalition's Executive Director Michael Stoops, "It's disturbing to know that young people would literally kick someone when they're already down on their luck. We recognize that this isn't every teenager, but for some this passes as amusement."

Three teenage perpetrators from Milwaukee, 16-year-old Luis Oyola, 17-year-old Andrew Ihrcke, and 15-year-old Nathan Moore claimed that killing Rex

Baum was never part of their plan. But yet, the trio, who had been drinking with Baum at his campsite, suddenly began punching and kicking the 49-year-old man and then hurled anything they could find—rocks, bricks, even a barbeque grill, at the hapless victim. After smearing him with feces, cutting him, and bragging about their actions, they were arrested. One of the teens told police that killing "the bum" reminded him of playing the violent videogame "Bumfights" that depicts homeless people pummeling each other to make a few bucks.

---

potentially harmful effects. For instance, children may become desensitized to the effects of violence (e.g., may care less about others' feelings) or experience a heightened fear of victimization. Children younger than 8 years old may be especially vulnerable to the effects of viewing violence because of their cognitive limitations in distinguishing fantasy and cartoon violence from reality. Of more recent interest is the question of whether movies and videogames, which often feature much more graphic depictions of violence than those allowed on TV, exert stronger modeling effects on aggression. We describe a relevant case in Box 3.3.

Social learning theory also points to several environmental cues that increase antisocial behavior. These "instigators" signal when it might be rewarding to behave antisocially (rather than risky to do so). Six instigators deserve special mention:

1. *Models.* Modeled aggression is effective in prompting others to behave aggressively, particularly when observers have been previously frustrated or when the modeled aggression is seen as justified.

2. *Prior aversive treatment.* Assaults, threats, blocking of goal-directed behaviors, and perceptions of inequitable treatment can lead to increased aggression and can enhance the perceived rewards of aggression.

3. *Incentive inducements.* Antisocial behavior can be prompted by the anticipated rewards of misbehavior. Habitual offenders often overestimate their

chances of succeeding in criminal acts and ignore the consequences of failing.

4. *Instructions.* Milgram's (1963) famous experiment demonstrating widespread willingness to follow orders to inflict "pain" on another person suggests that antisocial behavior can be instigated by commands from authorities. The strength of instructional control is limited to certain conditions, and it is not a common source of instigation in most crimes. However, it may play a role in some hate crimes, in which the perpetrator believes he or she is doing the will of a religious or patriotic fanatic.

5. *Delusions.* Individuals occasionally respond aggressively to hallucinated commands or paranoid jealousies and suspicions. People who suffer delusional symptoms also tend to be socially isolated, a factor that sometimes minimizes the corrective influences that a reality-based environment could have on them.

6. *Alcohol and drug use.* Alcohol and drugs can be potent instigators to antisocial conduct. There is a strong, positive association between crime and alcohol use, especially for violent crime (Parker, 2004; Richardson & Budd, 2003). By depressing a person's responsiveness to other cues that could inhibit impulsive or aggressive behavior, alcohol often leads to an increase in antisocial behavior even though it is not a stimulant (Chermack & Giancola, 1997). Narcotics use, by virtue of its cost and deviant status, also acts as a catalyst to or amplifier of criminality, especially property crime.

According to social learning theorists, people also regulate their behavior through self-reinforcement. Individuals who derive pleasure, pride, revenge, or self-worth from an ability to harm or "con" others enjoy an almost sensual pleasure in the way criminal behavior "feels" (Katz, 1988). Conversely, people will discontinue conduct that results in self-criticism and self-contempt.

People can also learn to exempt themselves from their own conscience after behaving antisocially. These tactics of "self-exoneration" assume many forms: minimizing the seriousness of one's acts by pointing to more serious offenses by others, justifying aggression by appealing to higher values, displacing the responsibility for misbehavior onto a higher authority, blaming victims for their misfortune, diffusing responsibility for wrongdoing, dehumanizing victims so that they are stripped of sympathetic qualities, and underestimating the damage inflicted by one's actions.

The major strength of social learning theory is that it explains how specific patterns of criminality are developed by individual offenders. A second strength is that the theory applies to a wide range of crimes. The major limitation of social learning theory is that little empirical evidence indicates that real-life crime is learned according to behavioral principles. Most of the data come from laboratory research where the experimental setting nullifies all the legal and social sanctions that actual offenders must risk incurring. A second problem is that the theory does not explain why some people fall prey to "bad" learning experiences and others resist them. Learning might be a necessary ingredient for criminality, but it is probably not a sufficient one. Individual differences in the way people respond to reinforcement need to be considered. The theory we review next does so.

Multiple-Component Learning Theory. Some theorists have integrated several learning processes into comprehensive, learning-based explanations of criminality (e.g., Feldman, 1977). The most influential and controversial multiple-component learning theory is James Q. Wilson and Richard Herrnstein's (1985) book *Crime and Human Nature*. Wilson and Herrnstein begin by observing that criminal and noncriminal behavior have both gains and losses.

Gains from committing crime include revenge, excitement, and peer approval. Gains associated with not committing crime include avoiding punishment and having a clear conscience. Whether a crime is committed depends, in part, on the net ratio of gains and losses for criminal and noncriminal behavior. If the ratio for committing a crime exceeds the ratio for not committing it, the likelihood of the crime being committed increases.

Wilson and Herrnstein argue that several individual differences influence these ratios and determine whether an individual is likely to commit a crime. Like Eysenck, they propose that individuals differ in the ease with which they learn to associate, through classical conditioning, negative emotions with misbehaviors and positive emotions with proper behaviors. These conditioned responses are the building blocks of a strong conscience that increases the gains associated with noncrime and increases the losses associated with crime.

Another important factor is what Wilson and Herrnstein call *time discounting*. All reinforcers lose strength the more remote they are from a behavior, but people differ in their ability to delay gratification and obtain reinforcement from potential long-term gains. More impulsive persons have greater difficulty deriving benefits from distant reinforcers. Time discounting is important for understanding crime because the gains associated with crime (e.g., revenge, money) accrue immediately, whereas the losses from such behavior (e.g., punishment) occur later, if at all. Thus, for impulsive persons, the ratio of gains to losses shifts in a direction that favors criminal behavior.

Equity is another important influence on criminality. *Equity theory* states that people compare what they feel they deserve with what they observe other people receiving. Inequitable transactions are perceived when one's own ratio of gains to losses is less than that of others. Judgments of inequity change the reinforcing value of crime. If one perceives oneself as being unfairly treated by society, this sense of inequity increases the perceived gains associated with stealing because such behavior helps restore one's sense of equity.

Another major component in Wilson and Herrnstein's theory is a set of constitutional factors, including gender, intelligence, variations in physiological arousal, and the aforementioned impulsivity, all of which conspire to make some persons more attracted to wrongdoing and less deterred by the potential aversive consequences of crime.

Of several social factors linked to criminal behavior, Wilson and Herrnstein believe that family influences and early school experiences are the most important. Families that foster (1) *attachment* of children to their parents, (2) *longer time horizons*, where children consider the distant consequences of their behavior, and (3) *strong consciences* about misbehavior will go far in counteracting criminal predispositions.

The work of Gerald Patterson and his colleagues is important here as well. On the basis of elaborate observations of families with and without aggressive and conduct-disordered children, Patterson (1982, 1986) identified four family interaction patterns associated with later delinquency: (1) disciplinary techniques involving either excessive nagging or indifferent laxness, (2) lack of positive parenting and affection toward children, (3) ineffective parental monitoring of a child's behavior, and (4) failure to employ adequate problem-solving strategies, thereby increasing stress and irritability within a family.

Research on parenting practices and the quality of the parent–child relationship underscores the relevance of familial interaction to childhood delinquency. Findings from a qualitative study with juvenile offenders and their parents revealed that their familial interactions were characterized by poor communication and high levels of conflict between children and parents. These interactions were associated with children's perceptions of lack of parental concern and warmth (Madden-Derdich, Leonard, & Gunnell, 2002). In addition, an intergenerational study examining the effect of parenting styles on antisocial behavioral patterns across generations suggests that familial interactions have far-reaching implications; parental conflict and highly demanding, unresponsive parents were related to childhood behavioral problems in two successive generations (Smith & Farrington, 2004).

The remedies to these harmful patterns involve warm supportiveness combined with consistent enforcement of clear rules for proper behavior. Unfortunately, these methods are least likely to be practiced by parents whose own traits reflect the predispositions they have passed to their children. Therefore, many at-risk children face the double whammy of problematic predispositions coupled with inadequate parental control and support.

Biological factors interact with family problems and early school experiences to increase the risks of poorly controlled behavior even more. Not only are impulsive, poorly socialized children of lower intelligence more directly at risk for criminality, but their interactions with cold, indifferent schools that do not facilitate educational success can further discourage them from embracing traditional social conformity. Consistent with this part of the theory is a long line of research studies showing that children officially diagnosed with early conduct problems and/or attention deficit/hyperactivity disorder face a heightened likelihood of becoming adult offenders (Nietzel et al., 1999).

Because they took hereditary and biological factors seriously, Wilson and Herrnstein have come under heavy fire from critics who portray their ideas as a purely genetic theory. It is not. Instead, it is a theory that restores psychological factors (some inheritable, some not) and family interaction variables to a place of importance in criminology, which for decades was dominated by sociological concepts.

Social Labeling. The most extreme version of a social-psychological theory of crime is the **social labeling** perspective. Its emergence as an explanation reflects (1) frustration about the inability of prior approaches to provide comprehensive explanations and (2) a shift in emphasis from why people commit crimes to why some people are labeled "criminals" (Sheley, 1985).

Some examples will illustrate this shift. In one study conducted during the turbulent 1970s, a group of college students in Los Angeles—all of whom had perfect driving records in the last year—had "Black Panther" bumper stickers put on their cars. Within hours, they began to get pulled over for traffic violations such as improper lane changes, implying that the Los Angeles police officers were labeling behavior differently on the basis of the presence of the bumper sticker (Heussanstamm, 1975).

A more contemporary illustration of this troubling phenomenon is the allegation that police use **racial profiling** as a basis for making a disproportionate number of traffic stops of minority motorists, particularly African Americans. As we noted in Chapter 1, this practice has often been justified by police as a tool for catching drug traffickers, but arresting motorists for "driving while black" as a pretext for additional criminal investigations clearly raises the risk of harmful and inappropriate labeling, to say nothing of its discriminatory impact. The outcry over racial profiling has resulted in a call for federal legislation that would prohibit the practice and has led to several lawsuits, including one in which the Maryland State Police agreed to pay damages to four African American drivers who had been targets of profile stops.

The basic assumption of labeling theory is that deviance is created by the labels that society assigns to certain acts. Deviance is not simply based on the quality of the act; rather, it stems also from an act's consequences in the form of society's official reactions to it. Social labeling theory makes a distinction between **primary deviance**, or the criminal's actual behavior, and **secondary deviance**, or society's reaction to the offensive conduct (Lemert, 1951, 1972). With regard to primary deviance, offenders often rationalize their behavior as a temporary mistake, or they see it as part of a socially acceptable role (Lilly et al., 1989). Whether or not that self-assessment is accurate, secondary deviance serves to brand them with a more permanent "criminal" stigma.

The main point of the **social labeling theory** is that the stigma of being branded a deviant can create a self-fulfilling prophecy (Merton, 1968). Even those ex-convicts who seek an honest life in a law-abiding society are spurned by prospective employers and by their families and are labeled "ex-cons." Frustrated in their efforts to make good, they may adopt this label and "live up to" its pejorative connotations by engaging in further lawbreaking (Irwin, 1970). According to this perspective, the criminal justice system produces much of the deviance it is intended to correct.

The social labeling approach raises our awareness about the difficulties offenders face in returning to society. Moreover, it reminds us that some lawbreakers (e.g., those who live in crime-ridden neighborhoods where the police patrol often) are more likely to be caught and "criminalized" than are others. But the social labeling approach does not explain most criminal behavior. Primary deviance (i.e., a law violation in the first place) usually has to occur before secondary deviance takes its toll, and many lawbreakers develop a life of crime before ever being apprehended (Mankoff, 1971). Behavioral differences between people exist and persist, despite the names we call them.

INTEGRATION OF THEORIES OF CRIME

Where do all these theories leave us? Do any of them offer a convincing explanation of crime? Do they suggest how we should intervene to prevent or reduce crime? Although many commentators decry the lack of a convincing theory of crime, knowledge about the causes of serious crime has accumulated and now provides certain well-supported explanations for how repeated, violent criminality develops. Serious criminality is extraordinarily versatile, involving careers that include violent behavior, property offenses, vandalism, and substance abuse.

One implication of this diversity is that individuals travel several causal pathways to different brands of criminality. No single variable causes all crime, just as no one agent causes all fever or upset stomachs. However, several causal factors are associated reliably with many types of criminality. Any one of these factors may sometimes be a sufficient explanation for criminal behavior, but more often they act in concert to produce criminality. Our attempt to integrate these various factors (see Figure 3.1) emphasizes four contributors to crime that occur in a developmental sequence.

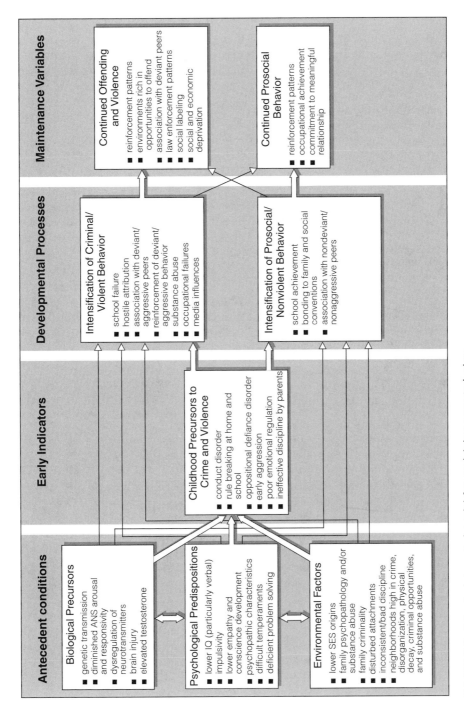

FIGURE 3.1 An integrated model for explaining repeated crime

NOTE: Thick arrows indicate probable paths; thin arrows indicate less likely paths.

Our model emphasizes what we believe are the variables best supported by criminological research as causal factors in crime.

1. *Antecedent conditions.* Chances of repeated offending are increased by biological, psychological, and environmental antecedents that make it easier for certain individuals to learn to behave criminally and easier for this learning to occur in specific settings. The leading candidates for biological risk are genetic inheritance, neurochemical abnormalities, brain dysfunction, and autonomic nervous system irregularities.

Among psychological variables, poor social skills; lower verbal intelligence; the personality traits of irritability, impulsiveness, and low empathy; and deficiencies in inner restraint (or conscience) leave some people well stocked in attitudes, thinking, and motivations that encourage antisocial behavior and that also render them relatively immune to negative consequences for misconduct. These psychological factors may accompany biological risks or may convey their own independent vulnerability to crime.

Finally, certain environments are rife with opportunities and temptations for crime and help translate biological or psychological predispositions toward criminal behavior into ever-stronger antisocial tendencies. Such environments function this way because of social impoverishment and disorganization, fundamental economic inequalities, a tradition of tolerating if not encouraging crime, social dissension and strife, and an abundance of inviting targets and easy victims of crime (Heide, 1997; Patterson, 1986). Crime-causing environments encourage offending because they are replete with antagonists who provoke violence, easy targets to be victimized by violence, and high rates of alcohol and substance abuse that lower inhibitions against violence (Chermack & Giancola, 1997).

Within family environments, high levels of mental disorders, criminality, parental absenteeism, and substance abuse also lead to more violence. These links may be forged through any one of several factors: genetic influence, modeling, increased hostility against a constant backdrop of harsh living conditions, disturbed attachments with parents, or lax or overly punitive discipline that does not teach youngsters how to control behavior. Research suggests that early exposure to harsh family living conditions can aggravate some of the biological factors that contribute to aggression, such as a child's physical and emotional reactions to threat (Gallagher, 1996).

2. *Early indicators.* Repetitive antisocial conduct is disconcertingly stable over time. Aggressive children often grow up to be aggressive adults, and the precedents for adult violence and substance abuse are often seen as early indicators of aggressiveness in preschool and elementary school children (Lynam, 1998; Slutske et al., 1998). Although there are tools that can identify youth who are at elevated risk for behavioral problems, it remains difficult to predict whether these individuals will commit serious, violent acts later in life (Sprague & Walker, 2000). Relatively few at-risk youth commit serious, violent offenses, but many display major long-term adjustment problems. For instance, youth identified as at risk in childhood may experience drug and alcohol abuse, domestic and child abuse, divorce or multiple relationships, employment problems, mental health problems, dependence on social services, and involvement in less serious crimes (Obiakor, Merhing, & Schwenn, 1997).

Although not all chronic offenders were violent children, many repetitively aggressive adults began to exhibit that pattern early; in fact, most psychologists who study aggression believe that severe antisocial behavior in adulthood is nearly always preceded by antisocial behavior in childhood. These early indicators include officially diagnosed conduct disorder, oppositional defiant disorder, and attention deficit/hyperactivity disorder (Lynam, 1996; McGee, Feehan, Williams, & Anderson, 1992).

Developmental models have enhanced our understanding of the onset and maintenance of antisocial behavior. For instance, one model suggests two subtypes of adolescent offenders: those who display behavioral problems later in adolescence and desist in early adulthood, and the relatively smaller group who display conduct-disordered behaviors earlier in adolescence that persist into adulthood. Adolescent offenders in the latter group are more likely to develop antisocial personality disorder than those in the former group.

Another model suggests that early emergence of conduct-disordered behavior that is displayed across multiple and diverse settings may predict the development of antisocial personality disorder in adulthood. One study found that early indicators of a diagnosis of antisocial personality disorder included a formal diagnosis of conduct disorder by age 10, participation in frequent and varied conduct-disordered behavior at an early age, and significant drug use in childhood or early adolescence (Myers, Stewart, & Brown, 1998).

Long-term longitudinal studies have demonstrated that aggression in childhood predicts violence in adulthood. Huesmann, Eron, and Yarmel (1987) measured aggression in childhood and tracked the boys and girls for 22 years. They found that aggression began to crystallize around the age of 8 and remained stable into adulthood (Eron, 1990; Huesmann, Eron, Lefkowitz, & Walder, 1984). Aggressive boys turned into men who were more likely to commit serious crimes, abuse their spouses, and drive while intoxicated. Aggressive girls turned into women who were more likely to punish their children harshly.

3. *Developmental processes.* Whether early indicators of criminal offending harden into patterns of repeated adult crime or soften into prosocial nonviolent conduct depends on several developmental processes. These processes occur in families, schools, peer groups, and the media—and in the thinking of the youth themselves.

Delinquency is often associated with poor school achievement. Grades in school begin to predict delinquency around age 15. As adolescent youth fall further and further behind in school, they have fewer and fewer opportunities or reasons to stay bonded to school and to strive for academic success (Cernkovich & Giordano, 1996). School failure seems to narrow the options for prosocial behavior because it decreases the chances of employability and job success.

Modeling and peer pressure also promote criminality. Crime increases when peers support it, as is sometimes the case in the criminal justice system itself when, by virtue of its official processing of offenders, "beginning" criminals are thrown together with more serious offenders. Furthermore, the more delinquent friends a youth has, the more likely he or she is to behave criminally (Elliott, Huizinga, & Ageton, 1985).

Other research suggests that the association between delinquency and negative peer influences may be even more complex than previously thought. One study found that poor parental monitoring and supervision, as well as increased social stress and poor social skills, affected the relationship between adolescents' delinquent behavior and negative peer affiliation (Kimonis, Frick, & Barry, 2004). On the basis of these findings, the authors concluded that intervening with training in parenting skills and social skills, specifically encouraging more parental involvement and monitoring of their child's behavior, may be especially important in reducing negative peer affiliation and decreasing delinquency.

Modeling influences can also be mediated through the media. One investigator (Murray, 2008) noted that 50 years of research strongly suggested a relationship between TV violence and the increase in aggressive attitudes, values, and behaviors among children. There was the further suggestion that these changes may be mediated by neurological changes in children who view frequent TV violence. It is, of course, difficult to know whether there is a causal relationship between such TV and other media violence and such behavior. What makes this even more difficult is that most of the studies in this area are not experimental. But another set of authors (Glymour, Glymour, & Glymour, 2008) considered these difficulties and concluded, in light of the existing evidence, that there is likely (but not certainly) a causal relationship between exposure to TV violence and subsequent adult aggression.

Another intensifier of aggression is alcohol and substance abuse (Murdoch, Pihl, & Ross, 1990). Numerous mechanisms could account for the tendency for substance abuse to lead to more crime. Alcohol is a depressant, so it might suppress the ability of certain areas of the brain to inhibit behavior effectively. The more time a youth spends abusing drugs and alcohol, the less time he or she has for prosocial, academic activities. Substance abuse typically results in more associations with deviant peers, thereby increasing the opportunities for antisocial behavior to be reinforced. Repeated substance abuse during adolescence serves as one more "trap" that shuts off many youngsters' options for prosocial behavior. These limits, in turn, increase the reinforcing potential of antisocial conduct.

Unfortunately, these developmental processes tend to compound one another. The impulsive, low-IQ child is more likely to fail at school. School dropouts increasingly associate with antisocial peers. Parents who fail to monitor and sanction their children when they misbehave tend not to show much concern about what movies their children watch or what videogames they play. Finally, early conduct and academic problems are strongly related to later substance abuse. When it comes to crime, at-risk youth stay at risk.

4. *Maintenance factors.* Violent offending can become an entrenched way of life when one or more of the following maintenance factors are in place: The short-run positive payoffs for offending are stronger and more probable than the long-term risks of apprehension and punishment. The person lives in environments that are rich in opportunities for offending and low in the chances of being detected. As a result of the inevitable arrests and incarcerations that repeat offenders experience, their associations with aggressive peers increase, just as contacts with law-abiding citizens decrease. As the long-run consequence of many earlier estrangements from conventional norms and values, delinquents begin to feel growing resentment and contempt for social rules. These maintenance factors do not cause crime so much as solidify it. Once they start to work their influence, the battle is often already lost, because criminal conduct has become a basic part of a person's identity.

An implication of our integrative model is that preventing crime might be a better way of fighting the "crime problem" than rehabilitating criminals. Certainly, with the help of treatment programs that strengthen their social skills, build better cognitive controls, model prosocial behavior, and reinforce law-abiding conduct, some people can "turn around" a life of violent offending (Andrews & Bonta, 2006). But however promising the rates of "success" in correctional rehabilitation might eventually become, it is still likely that some who are arrested and incarcerated will continue to offend throughout their lives.

This should not be surprising. After a protracted history of learning antisocial behavior, rejecting prosocial behavior, and facing closed doors to legitimate opportunity, repeat offenders will not yield easily to attempts to suppress criminal conduct. That is why prevention becomes so important. If most at-risk youth can be reliably identified, we can then intervene in multiple areas—with individuals, families, schools, peer groups, and neighborhoods—to interrupt those processes that eventually ensnare youth into antisocial lifestyles. Brought about by hostile environments and the decisions of youth themselves, these processes include experimenting with alcohol and drugs, dwelling on violent media and subcultures, dropping out of school, failing at legitimate employment, and associating with other lawbreakers. They are the pathways to deviance that must be blocked early before they become too well traveled for any change to occur.

SUMMARY

1. **Theories of crime can be grouped into four categories. What are they?** The most common theories can be classified into four groups: sociological, biological, psychological, and social-psychological.

2. **Among sociological explanations of crime, how does the subcultural explanation differ from the structural explanation?** The structural explanation for crime emphasizes chronic barriers to conventional success that certain people face;

these barriers include cultural and language differences, financial hardships, and limited access to those resources crucial to upward mobility. In contrast, the subcultural explanation proposes that certain groups, such as gangs, adhere to norms that conflict with the values of others in society and encourage criminal conduct.

3. *What is emphasized in biological theories of crime?* Both genetic and physiological factors are emphasized in biological explanations of criminal behavior. Hereditary factors influence criminal behavior, but the mechanisms through which this influence is exerted are unclear. The most likely candidates involve neurotransmitters, such as serotonin, and certain subcortical and cortical brain structures, particularly the prefrontal cortex, which

is responsible for monitoring behavioral inhibition, planning, and decision making. A more specific prospect involves a mutation on the X chromosome in the gene coding for MAOA, in combination with maltreatment as a child.

4. *What psychological factors have been advanced to explain crime?* Psychological theories of criminal behavior emphasize criminal thinking patterns or a personality defect, such as psychopathy.

5. *How do social-psychological theories view crime?* Social-psychological theories view criminal behavior as a learned response resulting from classical conditioning, reinforcement, observation or modeling, and social labeling.

KEY TERMS

anomie

antisocial personality disorder

biological theories of crime

classical conditioning

classical school of criminology

concordance rate

conditioned stimulus

containment theory

control theory

criminology

differential association approach

differential association reinforcement theory

dizygotic twins

executive function

extroversion

focal concerns

learning theory

monozygotic twins

neuroticism

operant learning

positivist school of criminology

primary deviance

psychological theories (of crime)

psychopathy

psychoticism

racial profiling

secondary deviance

social labeling theory

social learning theory

social-psychological theory (of crime)

sociological theories (of crime)

stimulation-seeking theory

structural explanations

subcultural explanations

threat assessment

unconditioned stimulus

vicarious learning

4

Psychology of Police

ORIENTING QUESTIONS

1. What is the role of the police in our society?
2. What procedures are used to select police?
3. How has the training of police officers expanded into new areas?
4. Describe the different activities of the police. Is law enforcement central?
5. What stressors do the police face?
6. Is there a police personality?
7. What is the relationship between the police and the communities they serve?

In any survey of public concerns, "crime" is usually near the top. This ranking stems from the pervasiveness of crime in our country, as well as from the fear that crime typically instills. Despite the decreasing crime rate over the last 15 years, about 2% of Americans were victims of personal crime and 15% of households were victimized by property crime in 2007 (Bureau of Justice Statistics, 2008). These figures also indicate that at least twice as many violent crimes and three times as many property crimes occur as are officially reported to the police. Only crimes that are detected and reported to the police find their way into the criminal justice system. However, the physical, financial, and psychological effects of being a victim of crime persist even when the victimization is never reported to the police. Whether measured in lost cash, damaged property, medical expenses, emotional trauma, or lost income due to injuries, the annual economic impact of crime runs to the billions of dollars.

The road from reporting a crime to convicting and punishing an offender can be long and tortuous, but in most cases the police are the officials in the criminal justice system with whom citizens have the most contact. The police must confront criminal activities face-to-face, and we expect them to keep our streets safe and our homes secure. They are the "thin blue line" that stands between the law-abiding citizen and public disorder. The visibility of the police is heightened by the uniforms they wear, the weapons they carry, and the special powers they are given. This visibility makes the police convenient targets for the public's frustrations with the criminal justice system. At the same time, many people place enormous trust in the police, and police are the first people who most citizens call in emergencies. Consequently, the public holds conflicting attitudes about the police. It demands protection from them at the same time that it resists interference from them.

The major purpose of this chapter is to describe the selection, training, and behavior of police officers. This chapter also serves as an introduction to the next two chapters, on crime investigation and detection.

Police perform a complex set of tasks in the criminal justice system. To succeed at their jobs, street officers must combine physical prowess, perceptual acuity, interpersonal sensitivity, and intelligent discretion. They need to make quick judgments about all sorts of human behavior, often under very stressful conditions. They should be well versed in the law and should have at least some familiarity with the social sciences. Despite the complexity of these demands, police are usually overworked and underappreciated. These factors, along with the job pressures they face, the criminal offenders they encounter, and the isolation in which they often work, can make officers susceptible to bribery, corruption, and abuses of power.

When we consider the police from a psychological perspective, we encounter each of the dilemmas introduced in Chapter 1. Law enforcement in a democratic society must strike a balance between protecting citizens through crime prevention and investigation while simultaneously respecting Constitutional rights. Police officers investigate crime—their job is to find out what happened—but they must also make arrests and maintain an image of stability in society. Operating within this balance can be very difficult, particularly when domestic terrorism, cyber crime, and other relatively recent challenges are added to the traditional kinds of criminal offending. But when this balance is not achieved, then either effective crime control or civil liberties/criminal rights can suffer.

Another conflict arises when social scientists question the validity of techniques that the police often use, such as lineup identifications and lie detector tests. Last, but of great importance to the police, is the dilemma of equality versus discretion. When should an arrest be made, and when should only a warning be issued? How much force can legitimately be used in an arrest? Should all suspects be treated the same way?

SELECTION OF POLICE OFFICERS

One purpose of this chapter is to examine the police officer from a psychological perspective. How are police officers selected? Do the selection criteria work? Is there a set of personality characteristics that police officers share? How are the police trained, and does training improve their performance on the job? Can the police officer's image in the community be improved?

These questions took on a special urgency in the 1990s as a result of several highly publicized cases in which police officers had brutally beaten suspects in their custody. Many of these cases involved white officers attacking black citizens, raising the possibility that racial bias was a motive.

Beginning with the prosecution of the Los Angeles police officers who were videotaped beating Rodney King (described in Box 4.2), which was followed by other, similar incidents, concerns have grown over police brutality. For instance, in June 2004, videotapes showed Stanley Miller, a suspect in an auto theft, apparently trying to surrender while Los Angeles officers tackled him and began kicking and repeatedly hitting him in the head (CNN, 2004).

This kind of incident has been reported in several cities throughout the country, including Detroit, New York, Louisville, Pittsburgh, and Miami. Perhaps no case sparked such heated national debate over the relationship between minorities and the police as the assault against Abner Louima, the Haitian immigrant who was beaten and sodomized with a bathroom plunger by New York City police officer Justin Volpe, as a second officer, Charles Schwarz, held him down. After Volpe pled guilty, a federal jury convicted Schwarz of conspiracy to sodomize and of violating Louima's civil rights, but it acquitted three other officers who had also been charged in the beating. Although it is tempting to view this case as an isolated incident, similar cases have occurred often enough to raise the possibility that they reflect a broader problem. Are certain police officers prone to these kinds of attacks? If so, can they be identified in advance and screened out of police work?

The brutal police assault of Abner Louima by several New York City police officers led to their conviction on federal criminal charges

Psychological evaluation of police personnel began in 1916 when Lewis Terman, the Stanford University psychologist who revised Alfred Binet's intelligence scales to produce the Stanford–Binet intelligence test, tested the intelligence of 30 applicants for police and firefighter jobs in San Jose, California. Terman (1917) found that the average IQ among these applicants was 84 and recommended that no one with an IQ below 80 be accepted for these jobs. A few years later, L. L. Thurstone tested the intelligence of 358 Detroit policemen, using the Army Alpha Intelligence Examination. Like Terman, he reported below-average IQ scores, and he also found that police of higher ranks scored lower than entry-level patrolmen.

Throughout the years, psychologists continued to assess police candidates, although in a way that was often unsystematic and poorly evaluated. As late as 1955, only 14 American cities with populations greater than 100,000 formally tested police candidates; by 1965, 27% of local police agencies reported some psychological evaluation of applicants (Ostrov, 1986). In the 1960s and 1970s, the period when police psychology became an established specialty, several national commissions, including the 1967 President's Commission on Law Enforcement and the Administration of Justice and the 1973 National Advisory Committee on Criminal Justice Standards, recommended formal psychological assessment of police personnel in all departments. By the mid-1980s, 11 states required psychological screening of police candidates, and more than 50% of the country's departments psychologically screened beginning police officers (Benner, 1986). By the 1990s, formal assessment of police candidates had become routine, due in part to attempts by municipal governments to prevent or defeat lawsuits claiming that they were liable for dangerous or improper conduct by their police employees.

Psychological evaluation of police applicants can focus on selecting those candidates who appear most psychologically fit or on eliminating individuals who appear least suited for police work. Most selection methods concentrate on screening out disturbed candidates, because it is very difficult to agree on the "ideal" police profile. Despite concerns about the validity of psychological evaluations in police selection, many experts (Arrigo & Claussen, 2003; Bartol & Bartol, 2006; Gowan & Gatewood, 1995; Ostrov, 1986; Reiser & Klyver, 1987; Scogin, Schumacher, Gardner, & Chaplin, 1995) believe that psychological screening is useful in the selection process and should be included. However, the current standards for screening may not be sufficient. Psychological tests are currently used to assess levels of psychopathology that may interfere with officers' abilities to perform their duties rather than focusing on risk assessment, situational testing, or job simulations that could detect potential problem behaviors or attitudes (such as racism) (Scrivner, 1994).

In general, the courts have upheld the legality of psychological screening of police candidates as long as the evaluation and testing involved do not violate the provisions of various civil rights acts or the Americans with Disabilities Act and are in compliance with federal guidelines.

If it were your task to select police officers from a pool of applicants, what psychological qualities would you look for? Your answers probably reflect your values, as well as your image of what police officers do. Among the psychological characteristics usually cited in such a list are the following:

- *Incorruptible:* A police officer should be of high moral character. Reports of officers taking bribes or framing innocent suspects are especially disturbing, because the police officer must treat all citizens fairly within the rules of law.

- *Well-adjusted:* A police officer should be able to carry out the stressful duties of the job without becoming seriously and continuously affected by the stress. Officers are always in the public view. They need to be thick-skinned enough to operate without defensiveness, yet they must be sensitive to the needs of others. They also need to cope with the dangers of their jobs, including the constant awareness that injury or death could occur at any time. In 2008, a total of 140 officers were killed in the line of duty, down from 181 killed in 2007.

- *People-oriented:* A police officer's major duty is service to others. An officer needs to have a genuine interest in people and compassion for them. At a commencement program of the New York City Police Academy, new officers were told, "There is one thing we cannot teach you and that is about people. The bottom line is to treat people as people and you'll get by" (quoted by Nix, 1987, p. 15).

- *Free of overly emotional reactions:* Although a degree of caution and suspiciousness may be desirable for the job, the police officer should be free of impulsive, overly aggressive reactions and other responses in which emotions overcome the discipline imposed by training. Restraint is essential because officers are trained to take an active stance in crime detection and are even encouraged by their superiors to be wary of

---

B o x 4.1   THE CASE OF THE UNIDENTIFIED SKELETON

Al Seedman, former chief detective of the New York City Police Department, once explained to an interviewer that he had been helping some detectives from a small Connecticut town investigate a case. "In the woods just outside town they found the skeleton of a man who'd been dead for three months or so. They figured they'd find out who he was as soon as his family reported him missing, but it's been three months since he was found—which makes six months since he died—and nobody has claimed him. They don't know what to do.... Once I got the answer to one question I was able to give them a method. I asked whether this skeleton showed signs of any dental work, which usually can be identified by a dentist. But according to the local cops, they said no, although the skeleton had crummy teeth. No dental work at all. Now, if he'd been wealthy, he could have afforded to have his teeth fixed. If he'd been poor, welfare would

have paid. If he was a union member, their medical plan would have covered it. So this fellow was probably working at a low-paying non-unionized job, but making enough to keep off public assistance. Also, since he didn't match up to any family's missing-person report, he was probably single, living alone in an apartment or hotel. His landlord had never reported him missing, either, so most likely he was also behind on his rent and the landlord probably figured he had just skipped. But even if he had escaped his landlord, he would never have escaped the tax man. The rest was simple. I told these cops to wait until the year is up. They can go to the IRS and get a printout of all single males making less than $10,000 a year but more than the welfare ceiling who paid withholding tax in the first three quarters but not the fourth. Chances are the name of their skeleton would be on that printout" (quoted in Seedman & Hellman, 1974, pp. 4–5).

---

what is happening around them (Greenberg & Ruback, 1982). A new police officer, reflecting on the effect of his training, said, "I've always been suspicious. [But now] I find myself looking up at the roofs of buildings to see if people are going to throw anything off" (quoted by Nix, 1987, p. 15). A study of police officers by Ruby and Brigham (1996) supports this police officer's reaction; they found that, compared to laypersons, police are more attentive toward indications that people's actions might be criminal.

- *Dedicated:* Officers should be committed to their jobs, and not inclined toward frequent lateness, absenteeism, or have personal problems that interfere with this commitment in an ongoing way.

- *Disciplined:* Police officers should be team players, able to function effectively within a chain of command. This includes the ability to give orders to supervisees and accept orders from superior officers.

- *Logical:* Police officers should be able to examine a crime scene and develop hypotheses about what happened and what characteristics might

be present in the lawbreaker. This deductive ability is apparent in the actions of Al Seedman, whose work is described in Box 4.1.

Keep these characteristics in mind as we now discuss particular approaches to evaluating police candidates. To what extent can each of these characteristics be accurately assessed? There are several reported purposes for evaluating police candidates, including screening out those who are (1) chronically late or absent; (2) disciplinary problems; (3) at risk for inflicting needless harm on citizens; and (4) otherwise reckless or irresponsible (Shusman, Inwald, & Landa, 1984). Psychological evaluation is not likely to identify "ideal" candidates—but it can be used to screen out those with specific problems that would interfere with their effective functioning as police officers.

Psychologists who evaluate police candidates rely on three tools: (1) personal interviews, (2) observations of candidates performing in special situations set up to reflect real-world characteristics of police work, and (3) psychological tests. How much emphasis different psychologists place on these tools depends on several factors, including their professional background and training, the resources available for the evaluation, and the focus of the assessment (e.g., different strategies will be used for assessing mental disorders than for predicting what type of person will do best in which kind of position).

A national survey of municipal police departments sought to identify selection and psychological assessment practices for police officers (Cochrane, Tett, & Vandecreek, 2003). Of the 355 police agencies surveyed, a total of 155 (43%) responded. The majority of police departments used selection measures that included a background investigation, medical exam, interview with applicant, drug test, physical fitness exam, and polygraph test. More than 90% required some kind of psychological evaluation of applicants.

The Interview

Personal interviews are the most widely employed tool, despite evidence that interviews are subject to distortion, low reliability, and questionable validity. The extent to which an interview yields the same information on different occasions or with different interviewers (*reliability*) and the degree to which that information is accurately related to important criteria (*validity*) have not been clearly established for most police selection interviews.

However, there is good evidence that reliability, at least, is increased by the use of **structured interviews**—those in which the wording, order, and content of the interview are standardized (Rogers, 2001). One semi-structured interview for the psychological screening of law enforcement candidates (the Law Enforcement Candidate Interview) uses content from other measures for screening law enforcement personnel and for assessing personality. Modest inter-rater reliability and prediction of performance in the police academy was achieved (Varela, Scogin, & Vipperman, 1999).

Interviews are a necessary part of an evaluation, according to guidelines recommended by police psychologists (Blau, 1994). They are also valuable as a rapport-building introduction to the evaluation process. They increase applicants' cooperation at the same time that they reduce apprehension. Interviews

are also popular because they are flexible and economical. However, because they are subject to distortions and impression management by candidates, interviews are still more useful for orienting candidates to the evaluation than for predicting subsequent performance.

Situational Tests

Situational tests incorporate tasks that are similar to those that will actually be undertaken by officers on the job. They are designed to predict performance in the training academy and on the job. For example, Mills, McDevitt, and Tonkin (1966) administered three tests that simulated various police abilities to a group of Cincinnati police candidates. The Foot Patrol Observation Test required candidates to walk a six-block downtown route and then answer questions about what they remembered having just observed. In the Clues Test, candidates were given 10 minutes to investigate a set of planted clues about the disappearance of a city worker from his office. They were observed as they performed this task and were graded on the information they assembled. The Bull Session was a two-hour group discussion of several topics important in police work. Performance on the Clues Test correlated significantly with class ranking in the police academy, but scores from the Foot Patrol Observation Test did not. Although "grades" for the Bull Session were not derived, it was viewed as an important measure of emotional and motivational qualities. A more recent example of a screening measure with a situational component is the National Police Officer Selection Test (POST) (http://www.kacp.cc/misc/post.pdf), which involves writing an incident report as part of the screening process.

Situational tests have an intuitive appeal as selection devices. There is some evidence that such ability tests, involving situational exercises, are somewhat better predictors of job performance than other measures (Hunter & Hunter, 1984; Schmidt, Hunter, McKenzie, & Muldrow, 1979). However, situational measures are also time-consuming and expensive. For that reason, they are used only by a small minority of police departments in screening candidates.

Psychological Tests

Many standardized psychological tests have good reliability and can be objectively scored and administered to large groups of subjects at the same time. Consequently, they are important in police screening. Two types of tests are included in most selection batteries: tests of cognitive or intellectual ability and tests of personality traits, integrity, or emotional stability.

Police officers tend to score in the average to above-average range on intelligence tests (Brewster & Stoloff, 2003; Poland, 1978), and intelligence tends to correlate fairly strongly with the performance of police recruits in their training programs. However, intelligence scores are only weakly related to actual police performance in the field (Bartol, 1983; Brewster & Stoloff, 2003). These results point to the problem of predictive validity, which is a pervasive difficulty that we discuss in the next section.

The Minnesota Multiphasic Personality Inventory (MMPI; the 1989 revision of this test is called the MMPI-2) is the test of personality most often used in police screening; it is followed by the California Psychological Inventory (CPI) and the Sixteen Personality Factor Questionnaire (16PF). Evidence for the validity of these tests in screening out candidates unsuitable for police work is mixed. There is research supporting the validity of the MMPI (Bartol, 1991), the MMPI-2 (Weiss, Davis, Rostow, & Kinsman, 2003), and the CPI (Ho, 2001), although others (e.g., Hogg & Wilson, 1995) have questioned the general value of psychological testing of police recruits.

One personality test designed specifically to identify psychologically unsuitable law enforcement candidates is the Inwald Personality Inventory (Detrick & Chibnall, 2002; Inwald, 1992; Inwald, Knatz, & Shusman, 1983). It consists of 26 scales that tap past and present behaviors presumed to have special relevance for law enforcement applicants; examples include Lack of Assertiveness, Trouble with Law and Society, Undue Suspiciousness, and Driving Violations. This instrument demonstrates good reliability, and some research suggests that its predictive validity is significantly better than that of the MMPI (Scogin et al., 1995).

Another written tool developed for the selection of entry-level police officers is the POST, noted earlier as having a situational component. In addition to incident report writing, the POST measures arithmetic and reading comprehension. It has demonstrated adequate reliability and criterion-related validity in some research (Henry & Rafilson, 1997; Rafilson & Sison, 1996). It has also been mandated as a statewide screening measure in several states, and adopted by the police chiefs associations in some jurisdictions.

An excellent study of psychological test validity for police selection purposes (Beutler, Storm, Kirkish, Scogin, & Gaines, 1985) examined the relationship between several tests (including the MMPI and five other standardized tests) and various measures of performance for 65 subjects who had been accepted for police work. Of these officers, 22 were employed in an urban police department, 27 worked in a department associated with a major state university, and 16 were from a community college police department. The researchers gathered an extensive list of criteria on how well each officer performed on the job. Ratings were obtained from supervisors, and seven indicators of performance (e.g., different kinds of reprimands, commendations, grievances, and suspensions) were collected from each officer's personnel record. The results suggest that performance on the different criteria was predictable by psychological tests, and these predictions even generalized across different types of police departments. The MMPI profile was particularly effective in predicting reprimands, grievances, and suspensions.

THE VALIDITY OF POLICE SCREENING

Although experts disagree on the usefulness of psychological screening of police, they all agree that good empirical research on this topic is difficult to conduct (Bartol, 1996; Gaines & Falkenberg, 1998; Inwald, 1986). Studies of **predictive validity** using actual police performance in the field as the criterion are so time-consuming and expensive that most departments cannot afford them. Instead, they settle for research that examines the relationship between screening results and performance by police recruits in police academies or training schools. This relationship is usually positive, but success or failure in training is not the criterion of real interest. One fairly inexpensive form of assessment is to gather peer ratings from trainees as they progress through their training classes together; these ratings have been shown to correlate with job retention of police officers, but not with most other measures of job performance or with supervisor ratings (Gardner, Scogin, Vipperman, & Varela, 1998).

Another problem with studies of validity is that the police candidates who do poorly on screening evaluations are eliminated from the pool of trainees and potential employees. Although this decision is reasonable, it makes it impossible to study whether predictions of poor performance by these individuals were valid.

In addition, applicants for police work, like applicants for most jobs, are likely to try to present an unrealistically positive image of themselves. They may deny or underreport symptoms of mental illness, answer questions to convey a socially desirable impression, and respond as they believe a psychologically healthy individual generally would. If evaluators fail to detect such "fake good" test-taking strategies, they may mistakenly identify some psychologically disturbed candidates as well-adjusted applicants. For these reasons, tests such as the MMPI-2 and the Inwald include various **validity scales** intended to detect test takers who are trying to "fake good" (Baer, Wetter, Nichols, Greene, & Berry, 1995). Research on these scales has shown that they are useful in detecting defensiveness and deception by some candidates for police positions (Borum & Stock, 1993; Weiss et al., 2003).

Finally, selecting adequate criteria to measure effective police performance is notoriously difficult. Supervisor ratings are often inflated or biased by factors that are irrelevant to actual achievements or problems. In some departments, especially smaller ones, the individual police officer will be expected to perform so many diverse functions that it becomes unreasonable to expect specific cognitive abilities or psychological traits to be related in the same way to various aspects of performance. In addition, if we are interested in predicting which officers will act in risky, dangerous, or inappropriate ways, our predictions will be complicated by the fact that such behaviors occur only rarely in any group of people. As a consequence, these assessments, if offering such predictions, will yield many "false positives"—erroneous predictions in which predicted events do not take place.

FITNESS-FOR-DUTY EVALUATIONS

Another type of psychological assessment of police officers is the **fitness-for-duty evaluation**. As a result of stress, a life-threatening incident, a series of problems, injuries, or other indicators that an officer is psychologically impaired, police administrators can order an officer to undergo an evaluation of fitness to continue performing his or her duties.

These evaluations pose difficulties for everyone involved. Administrators must balance the need to protect the public from a potentially dangerous officer against the legal right of the officer to privacy and fair employment. Clinicians have to navigate a narrow path between a department's need to know the results of such an evaluation and the officer's expectation that the results will be kept confidential. Finally, the officers themselves face a dilemma: They can be honest and reveal problems that could disqualify them from service, or they can distort their responses to protect their jobs and consequently miss the opportunity for potentially beneficial treatment.

Two different models of fitness-for-duty evaluations have been used. In the first, departments use the same psychologist to perform the evaluation and to provide whatever treatment is necessary for the officer. In other departments, the psychologist who evaluates the officer does not provide any treatment; this avoids an ethical conflict between keeping the therapy confidential (as part of duty to the patient) and disclosing an officer's psychological functioning to supervisors (as part of duty to the department). The second approach is endorsed in the "Guidelines for Fitness for Duty Evaluations" distributed by the Police Psychological Services Section of the International Association for Chiefs of Police (*Psychological Fitness-for-Duty Evaluation Guidelines*, 2004, which are still current in 2009).

TRAINING OF POLICE OFFICERS

Once candidates have been selected, they participate in a course of police training that usually lasts several months. Many major American cities require 24 weeks of training, with 40 hours of training per week. Smaller jurisdictions have training programs averaging 14 to 16 weeks. An increasing number of departments are now requiring that police officers complete at least some college education.

Two types of criticism of police training programs are common. One is that after rigorous selection procedures, few trainees fail the training. For example, of 1,091 recruits who began the training program in New York City in 1987, only about 6% dropped out or were dismissed for a variety of reasons, including physical or academic inadequacies (Nix, 1987). In a smaller sample of 93 cadets who began training in 2003, only about 10% either dropped out or failed mandatory academic or physical endurance exercises (Phillips, 2004). Advocates count this rate of success as an indication that the initial selection procedures were valid, but critics complain that graduation is too easy, especially given the burnout rate of on-the-job police officers.

A second criticism is that there is insufficient training in the field, as well as a lack of close supervision of trainees during the time they spend on patrol. The limited time that trainees spend with veteran training officers on patrol may give them a false sense of security (Beck, 1987) and deprive them of opportunities to learn different ways of responding to citizens from various cultural backgrounds or resolving disputes other than through arrests.

However, it is also possible that there are limits to the benefits of extensive supervision by senior officers. It is possible that such contacts teach new officers to be cynical about law enforcement, to "cut corners" in their duties, and, above all, to identify almost exclusively with the norms of police organizations rather than with the values of the larger and more diverse society (Tuohy, Wrennall, McQueen, & Stradling, 1993).

TRAINING IN CRISIS INTERVENTION

The police are often asked to maintain public order and defuse volatile situations involving persons who are mentally ill, intoxicated, angry, or motivated by politically extreme views. Because of the instability of the participants in such disputes, they pose great risks to the police as well as to bystanders. In this section, we examine three types of crisis situations to which police are often called: incidents involving mentally ill citizens, family disturbances, and the taking of hostages. Psychologists have made important contributions to each of these areas by conducting research, designing interventions, and training the police in crisis intervention skills.

Interactions with Mentally Ill Citizens

For the past two decades, several factors have forced mentally ill persons from residential mental health facilities, where they formerly lived, into a variety of noninstitutional settings, including halfway houses, community mental health centers, hospital emergency rooms, detoxification facilities, "flophouses," the streets, and local jails. As we mentioned in Chapter 2, deinstitutionalization itself is an admirable goal; spending much of one's life in an institution breeds dependency, despair, and hopelessness. People with mental illness should receive treatment in the least restrictive environment possible, allowing them to function in and contribute to their local communities. However, the evidence on how people with mental illness have fared suggests that deinstitutionalization in the United States has not achieved its lofty goals. The problems stem from two fundamental difficulties.

First, even under ideal conditions, severe mental illness is difficult to treat effectively. The impairments associated with disorders such as schizophrenia and serious mood disorders can be profound, and relapses are common. For example, less than a third of nonhospitalized persons with schizophrenia are employed at any given time. Second, sufficient funding for alternative, noninstitutional care has not been provided in the United States. As a result, community-based treatment of severely mentally ill persons seldom takes place under proper circumstances, despite the fact that the economic costs of severe mental disorders rival those of diseases such as cancer and heart disease and could be reduced considerably if proper care were provided.

The deinstitutionalization movement resulted from four historical forces: (1) advances in antipsychotic medications, which first became available in the 1950s, that enabled persons to function better outside of hospitals; (2) increased legal restrictions on the involuntary commitment of the mentally ill to hospitals; (3) reductions in the length of the average psychiatric hospitalization; and (4) decreased public funding for mental health programs throughout the 1980s and 1990s (Kiesler, 1982; Teplin, 1984). The rise of the homeless population, among whom problems of substance abuse and mental illness are frequent and severe (Fischer & Breakey, 1991; McNiel & Binder, 2005), is also linked to declining availability of publicly supported mental health treatment.

One consequence of deinstitutionalization is that supervising people with mental illness has become a primary responsibility for the police. In medium-size to large police departments, about 7% of all police contacts involve citizens with mental illness, and it is estimated that the police are responsible for up to one-third of all mental health referrals to hospital emergency rooms. In one survey, nine out of ten police officers had responded to a call involving a mentally ill individual in the past month, and eight out of ten had responded to two or more such calls in the same time period (Borum, Deane, Steadman, & Morrissey, 1998). Another survey found that 33% of all calls made to a police district in a one-year period were for mental health-related situations (Steadman,

Deane, Borum, & Morrissey, 2000). Research on how the police handle mentally ill persons has focused on the discretion that officers use in crisis incidents. Will they arrest the citizen, or will they have the person hospitalized? Will they offer on-the-spot counseling, refer the citizen to a mental health agency, or return the person to a safe place, to relatives, or to friends?

Some research on these questions suggests that the police are reluctant to arrest the mentally ill or to require their emergency hospitalization unless their behavior presents an obvious danger to themselves or others (Bittner, 1967; Lamb, Weinberger, & DeCuir, 2002). These findings are consistent with research on the use of discretion by police in general, which suggests that they tend to avoid an arrest in minor incidents unless the suspect is disrespectful to the officer, the complaining party prefers that an arrest be made, or the officer perceives the benefits of arresting the subject to outweigh the perceived costs.

However, a very large study (Teplin, 1984) clearly indicated that the presence of mental illness increases rather than decreases the probability of arrest. This study assembled a team of psychology graduate students and trained them to observe and code the interactions of police officers with citizens over a 14-month period in two precincts in a large U.S. city. Observers used a symptom checklist and a global rating of mental disorder to assess mental illness in the citizens observed. Teplin studied 884 nontraffic encounters involving a total of 1,798 citizens, of whom 506 were considered suspects for arrest by the police. Arrest was relatively infrequent, occurring in only 12.4% of the encounters; in terms of individuals (some incidents involved several suspects), 29.2% were arrested. The observers classified only 30 (5.9%) of the 506 suspects as mentally ill. The arrest rate for these 30 persons was 46.7%, compared to an arrest rate of 27.9% for suspects who were not rated as having mental disorders. Mentally ill suspects were more likely to be arrested regardless of the type or seriousness of the incident involved.

Teplin (1984, 2000) concluded that the mentally ill were being "criminalized" and that this outcome was the result not only of the provocative nature of their psychological symptoms but also of the inadequacies of the mental health system in treating them, and the lack of training in mental illness for some police officers. As a result, the criminal justice system has become a "default option" for patients whom hospitals refuse to accept for treatment because they are too dangerous to adjust to a hospital setting, are not dangerous enough to be involuntarily committed, or suffer a disorder that the hospital does not treat. Not surprisingly, the rate of severe mental disorders in jail populations, often combined with diagnoses of substance abuse and personality disorder in the same individuals, is alarmingly high (Teplin, 1994; Teplin, Abram, & McClelland, 1996).

Another study examined police responses to incidents involving individuals with mental illness in three jurisdictions differing in the level of mental health training that police received. Findings suggested that the jurisdictions with specialized mental health training were especially effective in crisis intervention and made fewer arrests. However, the officers' decisions about how to handle the situation depended on the overall resources available; jurisdictions with mobile crisis units were able to transport mentally ill individuals to treatment locations to ensure that they obtained treatment, while those without crisis units could only refer individuals for treatment (Steadman et al., 2000).

The Memphis Police Department started the Memphis **Crisis Intervention Team** (CIT) program, which has now become known as the "Memphis Model" for crisis intervention (CIT National Advisory Board, 2006). This program was designed to increase officer and consumer safety while attempting to redirect those with mental illness from the judicial system to the mental health system. Along with these broad goals, the program provides law enforcement officers the tools and skills necessary in dealing with mentally ill persons. Many police departments around the country have started their own CIT programs, some based on this "Memphis Model." A pilot program for crisis intervention was started in Philadelphia, which made the news because two officers, recently trained in CIT, were able to use their newly acquired skills in communicating with people with mental disorders. Encountering a man who was very depressed and had

climbed up on a bridge, these officers talked to him—and convinced him to come down, preventing a possible suicide.

One study (Skeem & Bibeau, 2008) addressed the question of whether CIT intervention decreases the risk of violence. The investigators reviewed police reports ($N = 655$) for CIT events that occurred between March 2003 and May 2005. They were able to classify 45% of these events as reflecting a danger to self, and another 26% in which the individual involved was dangerous to others. The research showed that officers were more likely to use force when the individual was perceived as threatening to others. However, consistent with CIT training, the officers were inclined to use low-lethality force—even when encountering individuals presenting a high risk for violence. Some 74% of these events resulted in hospitalization, while only 4% were concluded by arrest. These results are consistent with the potential for CIT to result in safe and treatment-oriented resolution of high-risk situations involving individuals with mental disorder.

A review of the existing studies on CIT (Compton, Bahara, Watson, & Oliva, 2008) yielded several conclusions. First, this research did provide support for the notion that CIT may be an effective way to link individuals with mental illnesses with indicated mental health treatment. Second, the training component of CIT may have a favorable impact on officers' attitudes, beliefs, and knowledge about these interactions; CIT-trained officers report feeling better prepared for their encounters with individuals with mental illnesses. Finally, CIT may have a lower arrest rate and lower associated criminal justice costs than other diversionary approaches.

The importance of evaluating how police interact with individuals with mental illness is underscored by the prevalence of mentally ill offenders in prisons and jails. Estimates suggested that in the 1990s, 16% of state prison inmates, 7% of federal prison inmates, and 16% of those in local jails suffered from mental illness (Ditton, 1999). However, by mid-year 2005, the Bureau of Justice Statistics (BJS) (2006) estimated that 56% of state prisoners, 45% of federal inmates, and 64% of those incarcerated in jails had a mental health problem. This definition of "mental health problem" was somewhat broader than that used in the earlier study (hospitalization or self-report used in Ditton, 1999; a clinical diagnosis or treatment or display of a psychiatric symptom in the BJS report). Even so, this appears to reflect an increase in the proportion of individuals incarcerated in the United States with mental health problems.

The jailing of mentally ill persons does not reflect improper behavior by the police as much as a failure of public policy regarding the treatment and protection of people with chronic mental illness. More and better training of police officers in the recognition and short-term management of mentally ill persons is necessary, but an adequate resolution of this problem requires better organization and funding of special services for those with serious mental illness (Abram & Teplin, 1991; Teplin, 2000).

One possibility is to increase the use of **jail diversion programs**, in which mentally ill individuals who have been arrested and jailed are considered for supervised release to the community, where they will presumably have better access to treatment and support services. One evaluation of a jail diversion program found that two months after arrest, approximately one in five diverted participants (20%) had been rearrested. In the same time period, about 50% of nondiverted subjects either had been rearrested or had never been released from jail (Steadman, Cocozza, & Veysey, 1999). More recently, an evaluation of a jail diversion program for offenders with mental illness found that diverting the individuals to crisis stabilization units rather than incarcerating them reduced recidivism from 70% to 11%. Although recidivism was slightly higher a year later (18%), the program appeared to be effective in maintaining reduced rates of reoffending (Buchan, 2005).

Domestic Disturbances

When violence erupts in a family or between a couple, the police are often the first people called to the scene. What will they encounter when they arrive? Are the participants armed? Are they intoxicated or psychologically disturbed? How much violence has already taken place? What is certain is that responding to family disturbances is one of the most dangerous activities that police perform. The level of danger involved when intervening in a domestic dispute is not surprising, considering that people "are more likely to be killed, physically assaulted, hit, beat up, slapped, or spanked in their own homes by other family members than anywhere else, or by anyone else, in our society" (Gelles & Cornell, 1985, p. 12).

Police spend a great deal of time investigating domestic disturbances, and these are high risk situations for officers. A large-scale study investigating the circumstances of 1,550 assaults on police in Baltimore County, Maryland between 1984 and 1986 (Uchida & Brooks, 1988) indicated that about 25% of these assaults occurred during the investigation of a domestic disturbance. Perpetrators were more likely to use blunt objects than guns or knives. However, such data are clearly inconsistent with the historical trend in police academies to play down the risk of investigating domestic disturbances. For this reason, and because participants may decline to cooperate and otherwise be antagonistic toward officers (even when they do not assault them), police are often reluctant to investigate such disturbances.

Empirical research is increasing our understanding of domestic violence. We are now better able to recognize the false assumptions underlying how many perceive family violence. These were first described by Gelles and Cornell (1985).

Myth 1: Family Violence Is Rare. It is difficult to obtain accurate statistics on child abuse and other forms of family violence because no agency systematically gathers such data. But family violence is not a rare phenomenon; it is estimated that 14% of children in the United States are abused within their families each year and that the lifetime prevalence of spouse abuse may be as high as 50% of married couples. Nor is family violence exclusively or even largely restricted to male perpetrators. Studies in both the United States and New Zealand suggest that women are as likely as men to be violent toward their partners (Magdol et al., 1997; Steadman et al., 1998).

The question of how gender affects partner violence reveals an important aspect of the approaches used in researching such problems. The answers will vary—sometimes to a great extent—depending on the types of individuals who participate in the research. The initial studies of family violence relied on *clinical samples* of women who sought physical or psychological help for the injuries they suffered, or male batterers who had been ordered into treatment or arrested because of their violence. Not surprisingly, these studies suggested that male perpetrators far outnumbered females.

More recent studies have used *community surveys* of large cohorts of people, selected at random rather than because they have been referred for assistance or charged with an offense. These studies suggest that the rates of partner violence are substantial among both male and female abusers. Each of these approaches addresses a slightly different question (Magdol et al., 1997). If one is interested in studying the consequences of especially severe partner violence, clinical samples are preferable. If one is trying to outline the epidemiological patterns and general risk factors for partner violence, then community surveys are likely to yield the more trustworthy answers.

Myth 2: Family Violence Is Confined to Mentally Disturbed or Sick People. When we hear or read that a woman has plunged her 2-year-old son into a tub of boiling water or that a man has had sexual intercourse with his 6-year-old daughter, our first reaction might be, "That person is terribly sick!" The portrayal of family violence in the mass media often suggests that "normal people" do not harm family members. In reality, however, family violence is too widespread to be adequately explained by mental illness, although perpetrators of serious domestic violence often experience depression or personality disorder (Andrews, Foster, Capaldi, & Hops, 2000).

Myth 3: Family Violence Is Confined to Poor People. Violence and abuse are more common among families of lower socioeconomic status, but they are by no means limited to such families. There are risk factors associated with poverty (e.g., unemployment, limited education, and sparse social support) that are associated with the risk for family violence (Barnett, Miller-Perrin, & Perrin, 2005; Magdol et al., 1997).

Myth 4: Battered Women Like Being Hit; Otherwise, They Would Leave. This belief combines two myths. First, as noted earlier, family violence is perpetrated by both males and females, although violence by men against women tends to produce more serious injuries. But faced with the fact that many female victims of partner violence do not leave even the most serious of abusers, people seek some type of rational explanation.

A common belief is that women who remain in violent relationships must somehow provoke or even enjoy the violence. This form of "blaming the victim" (see Chapter 13) is not a useful explanation. The concept of **learned helplessness** can explain why so many women endure such extreme violence for so long (Walker, 1979). Psychologist Lenore Walker observed that women who suffer continued physical violence at the hands of their partners have a more negative self-concept than women whose marriages are free from violence. She proposed that the repeated beatings leave these women feeling that they won't be able to protect themselves from further assaults and that they are incapable of controlling the events that go on around them (Gelles & Cornell, 1985). Under such circumstances, they give in to the belief that there is nothing they can do to change their circumstances and that any effort at starting a new life not only will be futile but also will lead to even more violence against them. We discuss battered spouses in more detail in Chapter 13.

Myth 5: Alcohol and Drug Abuse Are the Real Causes of Violence in the Home. "He beat up his children because he was drunk" is another popular explanation of domestic violence, and most studies do find a considerable relationship between drinking and violence (Gerber, Ganz, Lichter, Williams, & McCloskey, 2005; Magdol et al., 1997), especially among male perpetrators. Perhaps as many as half of the incidents of domestic violence in the past have involved alcohol or drugs (Gelles & Cornell, 1985); in the case of violence directed toward a spouse, both the offender and the victim may have been drinking heavily before the violence.

This observation appears to be as accurate today as it was nearly 25 years ago. In a longitudinal study considering the relationships among drinking, alcohol-related problems, and recurring incidents of partner violence over a five-year period (Caetano, McGrath, Ramisetty-Mikler, & Field, 2005), investigators found that the rate of domestic violence among men who drink more than four drinks at a time at least once per month was three times higher than that among men who abstain or drink less often and less frequently. This pattern also held for women. But does the substance cause the violence? Some assume that alcohol is a disinhibitor of behavior and that it therefore facilitates the expression of violence. Although there is certainly some truth to this, reactions in those who have been drinking are also a function of social expectations and "blaming the bottle" ("I was drunk and didn't know what I was doing"). Furthermore, those who have trouble controlling their aggressive behavior while drinking can certainly anticipate this and take steps to manage their risk (e.g., drinking in moderation or not at all).

Because of their danger and frequency, family disturbances pose a difficult challenge for the police. Can these encounters be handled in a manner that protects potential victims, reduces repeat offenses, and limits the risk of injury to responding officers?

The first project on crisis intervention with domestic disputes was developed by Morton Bard, a psychologist in New York City. Bard (1969; Bard & Berkowitz, 1967) trained a special group of New York City police officers (nine black and nine white volunteers) in family disturbance intervention skills for a project located in West Harlem. The month-long training program focused on teaching officers how to intervene in family disputes without making arrests. The training emphasized the psychology of family conflict and sensitivity to cross-racial differences. Role playing was used to acquaint officers with techniques for calming antagonists, lowering tensions, reducing hostilities, and preventing physical violence.

For two years after the training, all family crisis calls in the experimental precinct were answered by the specially trained officers. They performed 1,375 interventions with 962 families. Evaluation of the project concentrated on six desired outcomes: (1) a decrease in family disturbance calls, (2) a drop in repeat calls from the same families, (3) a reduction of homicides in the precinct, (4) a decline in homicides among family members, (5) a reduction of assaults in the precinct, and (6) a decrease in injuries to police officers. But results indicated that the intervention affected only two of these outcomes. Fewer assaults occurred in the precinct, and none of the trained officers was injured (compared with three police officers who were not part of the program but were injured while responding to family disturbances).

Evaluations of similar domestic crisis units in other cities have yielded mixed results (Pearce & Snortum, 1983). Specially trained officers typically rate their resolutions of disturbance calls more favorably than do officers without special training. However, the long-term effects of the special interventions are less positive; sometimes they lead to an increase in repeat callers, but in other cases this effect is not observed.

In recent years, as more is learned about domestic violence, crisis intervention and other nonarrest alternatives for resolving family disturbances have come in for increased criticism. Women's rights groups have filed lawsuits against law enforcement agencies that have not arrested seriously assaultive domestic batterers. These critics maintain that when actual assaults have taken place in a family, arrest is the most appropriate response to protect victims and reduce future violence (Dutton, 1987).

In response to these concerns and to their own evaluation of the problem of domestic assaults, many police departments have shifted policies and now advocate the arrest and prosecution of domestic batterers. Is this a better alternative than crisis intervention or counseling?

The first well-controlled evaluation of the effects of arresting domestic batterers was the Minneapolis Domestic Violence Experiment (Sherman & Berk, 1984). In this experiment, police officers' responses to domestic violence were randomly assigned to be (1) arresting the suspected batterer, (2) ordering one of the parties to leave the residence, or (3) giving the couple immediate advice on reducing their violence. Judging on the basis of official police records and interviews with victims, subsequent offending was reduced by almost 50% when the suspect was arrested, a significantly better outcome than that achieved by the two nonarrest alternatives. These findings quickly changed public and expert opinion about the value of arresting domestic batterers, and soon many cities had replaced informal counseling with immediate arrest as their response to domestic violence cases.

Since the initial Minneapolis Experiment, at least five other jurisdictions—Charlotte, Colorado Springs, Miami, Omaha, and Milwaukee—have conducted studies designed to test whether arresting batterers is the best deterrent to repeated domestic violence. The results of these projects, collectively known as the Spouse Assault Replication Program, have been mixed. In some cases, arrests reduced recidivism; in other cases, they increased recidivism; and in a few instances, the effect was different depending on whether official arrest records or victim interviews were considered (Brame, 2000; Garner, Fagan, & Maxwell, 1995). These inconsistencies may be attributed to differences in methodologies and analyses across the various sites. However, a more comprehensive analysis integrating the data from all five sites revealed that arresting the violent partner significantly reduced future victimization independent of other criminal justice sanctions or individual factors (Maxwell, Garner, & Fagan, 2002). Thus, even though one large-scale study supports the conclusion that arrests reduce recidivism, the search continues for factors that could resolve the inconsistent results. Another caveat to those interpreting these findings is that deterrent effects associated with arrest tend to diminish over time (Mills, 1998).

What conclusion should we reach about the value of arrest as a deterrent to future spouse abuse? At this point, the jury is still out. Deterrence is achieved in some cases but is too inconsistent an outcome to justify the enthusiastic claims that are often made for arrest programs.

Questions about how best to quell domestic violence illustrate an interesting phenomenon often encountered with social reforms. Social problems and well-intentioned efforts to modify them tend to revolve in cycles rather than moving in a straight line toward progress and increased sophistication. A reform in vogue today, aimed at correcting some social evil, often fosters its own difficulties or inequities and ultimately becomes itself a problem in need of reformation.

Crisis intervention was originally preferred over arrest as a more psychologically sophisticated response by police to family disturbances; however, this intervention fell out of favor and was criticized as an inadequate response to serious domestic violence. Official arrest was then championed as the most effective intervention, but as additional data are gathered about its effectiveness, new questions are raised about whether arrest and prosecution are the best answers for domestic violence.

Hostage Negotiation

Although hostage incidents are at least as old as the description in Genesis of the abduction and rescue of Abraham's nephew Lot, most experts agree that the massacre of 11 Israeli athletes taken hostage and murdered by Palestinian terrorists at the 1972 Munich Olympic Games spurred the creation of new law enforcement techniques for resolving hostage incidents. Developed through extensive collaboration among military, law enforcement, and behavioral science experts, these hostage negotiation techniques are still being refined as more is learned about the conditions that lead to effective negotiations.

One study of 120 hostage-related incidents found that the perpetrator used a barricade to separate himself and his hostage from police in over half of the incidents (55.8%) (Feldmann, 2001), creating a complicated situation for negotiation strategies because police could not be fully aware of the perpetrator's activities and intentions. Soskis and Van Zandt (1986) have identified four types of hostage incidents that differ in their psychological dynamics and techniques for resolution (see also Gist & Perry, 1985; Hatcher, Mohandie, Turner, & Gelles, 1998).

More than half of hostage incidents involve *persons suffering a mental disorder* or experiencing serious personal or family problems (Feldmann, 2001). In these situations, the hostage takers often have a history of depression, schizophrenia, or other serious mental illness, or they harbor feelings of chronic powerlessness, anger, or despondency that compel a desperate act. Disturbed hostage takers pose a high risk of suicide, which they sometimes accomplish by killing their hostage(s) and then themselves. In other situations, they try to force the police to kill them; such victim-precipitated deaths are termed **suicide by cop**. This underscores the importance of incorporating mental health consultants' expertise into the effort to peacefully negotiate and resolve these hostage situations.

A second common type of hostage situation involves the *trapped criminal*. Here, a person who is trapped by the police while committing a crime takes, as a hostage, anyone who is available and then uses the hostage to bargain for freedom. Because these incidents are unplanned and driven by panic, they tend to be, especially at their early stages, very dangerous to the victims and the police.

The third type of hostage situation, also involving criminals, is the *takeover of prisons* by inmates who capture prison guards or take other inmates as hostages. In these incidents, the passage of time tends to work against non-violent resolution because the hostage takers are violent people, working as an undisciplined group with volatile leadership.

The fourth type of hostage taking, and the one that is most widely publicized, is **terrorism**. Terrorists use violence or the threat of violence "to achieve a social, political, or religious aim in a way that does not obey the traditional rules of war" (Soskis & Van Zandt, 1986, p. 424; see also Lake, 2002).

Terrorists usually make careful plans for the kidnapping of hostages or the taking of property, and they are typically motivated by extremist political or religious goals. These goals may require their own deaths as a necessary but "honorable" sacrifice for a higher cause. For this reason, terrorists are less responsive to negotiation techniques that appeal to rational themes of self-preservation. Therefore, new ways of responding to this type of terrorism must be sought.

One terrorism specialist suggested that a country has three options in responding. At the lowest level of response, it may increase its internal security to prevent further attacks, as anyone who has flown in an airplane the last few years knows only too well. A more proactive response may be to attempt to capture or eliminate the terrorists in a limited operation targeting the leaders of the terrorist organizations. Lastly, a country may implement a military retaliation with the aims of eradicating the terrorists and their organizations and deterring future attacks from other groups (Lake, 2002).

The 1990s saw an outbreak of right-wing domestic terrorism and sieges in the United States. In the most visible of these incidents (e.g., the mass death of the Branch Davidian sect under the leadership of David Koresh; the three-month standoff between the FBI and the antigovernment Freemen group in Montana), conventional negotiation techniques did not prove effective. The reasons why negotiations were not successful are not clear; the American public seems divided between those who believe the government was too aggressive and those who think officials were too restrained in their handling of these incidents. This remains true for the U.S. government's response to the attacks on the World Trade Towers and the Pentagon on September 11, 2001; again, the nation is divided between support for the war on terror and opposition to it.

The new millennium has brought additional forms of terrorism that redefine what it means to be "taken hostage." For example, **bioterrorism**, in which biological "weapons" such as viruses and bacteria are released or threatened, could hold far larger populations hostage than conventional guns or bombs. One study examined public distress following the anthrax-related incidents that occurred shortly after the September 11, 2001, attacks.

Findings suggested that even for individuals not actually exposed to the anthrax, initial media exposure to the anthrax attacks was a significant predictor of distress. Levels of distress were especially high when the attacks were first detected (Dougall, Hayward, & Baum, 2005). Effective countermeasures to such threats require new collaborations among law enforcement officials, public health experts, and behavioral scientists.

Successful hostage negotiation requires an understanding of the dynamics of hostage incidents so that these dynamics can be manipulated by the negotiator to contain and ultimately end the incident with a minimum of violence (Vecchi, Van Hasselt, & Romano, 2005). For example, in many hostage situations, a strong sense of psychological togetherness and mutual dependency develops between the hostages and their kidnappers. These feelings emerge from (1) the close, constant contact between the participants, (2) their shared feelings of fear and danger, and (3) the strong feelings of powerlessness induced by prolonged captivity. This relationship, dubbed the **Stockholm syndrome**, involves positive feelings by the hostages toward their kidnappers as well as reciprocated positive feelings by the kidnappers toward their hostages. Hostage negotiators try to take advantage of this dynamic by becoming a part of it themselves. First attempting to become a psychological member of the hostage group who nevertheless maintains important ties to the outside world, negotiators will then try to use their outside contacts to persuade terrorists to bring the crisis to a peaceful end.

Successful negotiators make contact with hostage takers in as nonthreatening a manner as possible and then maintain communication with them for as long as necessary. Generally, the negotiator attempts to isolate the hostage takers from any "outside" communication in order to foster their dependency on the negotiator as the crucial link with other people. Once communication is established, the negotiator tries to reduce the hostage takers' fear and tension so that they will be more willing to agree to a reasonable solution. Negotiators structure the situation in ways that maximize predictability and calm. For example, they may offer help with any

medical needs the hostage group has, thereby fostering positive components of the Stockholm syndrome. Finally, through gradual prompting and reinforcement, the negotiator tries to encourage behaviors that promote negotiation progress. Examples of such behaviors include increased conversation between the negotiator and the hostage taker, the passage of deadlines without threatened violence taking place, and less violent content and fewer threats in the speech of hostage takers.

The term *Stockholm syndrome* derives from a 1973 event in which hostages held in a Swedish bank developed a close emotional attachment to their captors (Eckholm, 1985). Hostages may come to sympathize with the lawbreakers and even adopt, at least temporarily, their captors' ideological views. The behavior of Patricia Hearst, a newspaper heiress who was kidnapped in 1974 and later helped her captors rob a bank, has been explained through this syndrome. It was also seen in 1985, when 39 passengers from Trans World Airlines (TWA) Flight 847 were detained as hostages for 17 days by hijackers in Beirut. Allyn Conwell, the spokesperson for the hostages in the hijacking, was criticized for his statements expressing "profound sympathy" for his captors' Shiite position, but he explicitly denied that he was influenced by the Stockholm syndrome (Eckholm, 1985).

According to Martin Symonds, a New York psychiatrist and expert on terrorism, the Stockholm syndrome (which is one of several that is known to form among hostages, hostage takers, and negotiators) is more likely to emerge when the hostages are purely "instrumental" victims of no genuine concern to the terrorists except as means to obtain leverage over a third party. In such situations, the captors say, "We'll let you go if our demands are met," and the captives begin "to misperceive the terrorist as the person who is trying to keep you alive" (quoted in Eckholm, 1985, p. 6). For this reason, it is especially important for the police to determine the motivations of any hostage takers, as well as their specific goals.

Increasingly, police departments have developed special crisis/hostage negotiation teams that usually include a psychologist as a consultant or adviser (Bartol & Bartol, 2006). In this capacity, the psychologist helps select officers for the team, provides on-the-scene advice during hostage incidents, profiles the hostage taker's personality, and assesses the behavior of the hostages themselves.

Do psychologist-consultants make a difference? In the one study evaluating the effects of psychological consultation in hostage incidents, Butler, Leitenberg, and Fuselier (1993) found that using a psychologist resulted in fewer injuries and deaths to hostages and more peaceful surrenders by hostage takers. However, empirical evidence regarding the effectiveness of specific negotiation techniques has yet to be gathered (Vecchi et al., 2005).

THE POLICE OFFICER'S JOB

In the eyes of most citizens, the job of the police officer is to catch criminals and enforce the law, just as the officers on *The Wire* and *Law and Order* do weekly on TV. But the police are responsible for more functions than these. The major duties of the police are divided into three general areas:

- *Enforcing the law,* which includes investigating complaints, arresting suspects, and attempting to prevent crime. Although most citizens perceive law enforcement to be the most important function of the police, it accounts for only about 10% of police activity.

- *Maintaining order,* which includes intervening in family and neighborhood disputes and keeping traffic moving, noise levels down, rowdy persons off the streets, and disturbances of the peace to a minimum. It is estimated that three out of every ten requests for police officers involve this type of activity.

- *Providing services,* such as giving assistance in medical and psychological emergencies, finding missing persons, helping stranded motorists, escorting funerals, and rescuing cats from trees.

Most studies indicate that the largest percentage of police activities fall into the third category. According to one review (Klockars, 1985), the typical day's duty for a police officer in the high-crime areas of three of the nation's largest cities—Boston, Chicago, and Washington, D.C.—did not see the arrest of a single person!

Should the police spend so much time on community services? The major objections to community services are that they waste police resources and distract the police from the crucial roles of law enforcement and public protection for which they are specially trained. In the 1990s, special initiatives were taken to increase the time police commit to crime-fighting activities. Federal legislation providing funds for cities to hire thousands of new police officers was justified with the promise that additional police would lead to more arrests of criminals. Urban police forces have found that concentrating more police officers in high-crime areas and instructing them to arrest all lawbreakers (even for relatively minor offenses such as loitering and public drunkenness) have resulted in lowered crime rates. This **zero tolerance** policy demands that police officers concentrate more time on apprehension and arrest activities. Although it has been credited with bringing about reductions in crime, the zero tolerance policy has also been linked to increases in citizen complaints and lawsuits against the police (Greene, 1999). For instance, a 12-year-old boy in Florida was handcuffed after he stomped in a puddle and splashed his classmates, and a 13-year-old boy in Virginia was suspended and required to attend drug awareness classes after accepting a breath mint from a classmate (Koch, 2000).

There are two advantages to the police continuing to provide an array of social services. First, short of spending massive amounts of money to train and employ a new cadre of community service workers, there is no feasible alternative to using the police in this capacity. Second, by providing these services, the police create a positive identity in the community that carries goodwill, respect, and cooperation over to their crime-fighting tasks.

These "side effects" also serve as a buffer that gives the police opportunities to interact with people who are not behaving criminally, thereby reducing the tendency of police to develop cynical, suspicious attitudes toward others. They also may encourage citizens to perceive the police in a less threatening and less hostile manner.

STRESS AND THE POLICE

Not only is the police officer's job composed of multiple duties, but the requirements of these duties may lead to feelings of stress, to personal conflicts, and eventually to psychological problems. Scores of books, technical reports, and journal articles have been written on the causes and treatment of police stress (e.g., Ford, 1998; Harpold & Feemster, 2002), and entire Web sites (e.g., the Police Stressline: www.stressline.com) are now devoted to this topic.

All of this raises the question: Is police work more stressful than other occupations? Although the stereotype of police work is that it must be extremely stressful because it entails a constant threat of danger and exposure to criminals, surprisingly little is known about whether policing is inherently stressful. The National Institute on Workers' Compensation lists police work among the "ten toughest jobs" (Miller, 1988, p. 43), but one large-scale survey of Australian police officers indicated that police felt no more stress as a group than the average citizen or college student (Hart, Wearing, & Headey, 1995). Whether this same finding would characterize American police officers is not certain. Also, the reasons for the relatively high level of psychological well-being reported by these officers are not clear. It might be because most of them were males, and males report fewer stressful feelings than females. It might be due to a reluctance of police officers to admit to feeling stressed. Or it could reflect the fact that preemployment screening of police candidates eliminated easily stressed individuals.

Regardless of this survey's findings, no one would suggest that a police officer's job is easy. Certain factors make the occupation particularly difficult. One problem that comes with being a police officer is the "life in a fishbowl" phenomenon. Officers are constantly on public view, and they realize that their every act is being evaluated.

Often they perform their job differently than the public wants, and they are then likely to hear an outcry of protest and condemnation (Lefkowitz, 1975). Police are sensitive to public criticism, and this criticism also leads their spouses and children to feel isolated and segregated.

Several investigators have divided the stress of police work into different categories according to the sources of the stress or the type of problem involved (Harpold & Feemster, 2002; Ostrov, 1986; Spielberger, Westberry, Grier, & Greenfield, 1980). Project Shield, a large-scale study conducted by the National Institute of Justice, asked police officers to respond to a series of questions about the negative effects of stress in several different categories, including psychological, physical, behavioral, and organizational public health (Harpold & Feemster, 2002).

Results from the surveys showed that officers reported an increased vulnerability to alcohol abuse and heightened levels of anxiety within the first five years of employment. In addition, approximately 1% of officers in the study reported having contemplated suicide at some point. Compared to the general population, officers reported more experiences of physical and medical problems over their lifetime, including cancer, heart disease, hypertension, acute migraine headaches, reproductive problems, chronic back problems, foot problems, and insomnia. They also reported increased behavioral problems in their personal lives, such as physical abuse of their spouses and children, as a result of job-related stress. Officers reported the highest levels of organizational, or job-related, stress when faced with making split-second decisions with serious consequences, when hearing media reports of police wrongdoing, when working with administrators who did not support the officers, and when not having enough time for personal or family responsibilities.

Another study (Solomon and Horn, 1986) examined the effects of shooting incidents in the line of duty with 86 police officers. These officers, 53% of whom had been involved in a shooting in which a person was killed, were attending a three-day workshop on postshooting incident trauma at the time. Participants were asked to report whether they experienced 18 different postincident reactions. More than half reported a heightened sense of danger after the incident (58%), many reported feeling angry (49%), feeling isolated or withdrawn (45%), having difficulty sleeping (46%), experiencing flashbacks or intruding thoughts about the incident (44%), emotional numbing (43%), depression (42%), and alienation (40%). Other common postincident reactions included guilt or remorse (37%), nightmares (34%), family problems (27%), substance abuse (14%), and suicidal thoughts (11%). In addition, participants reported several perceptual distortions, including perceiving the event to occur in slow motion (67%), perceiving the event to occur in rapid motion (15%), and tunnel vision during the event (37%).

According to questionnaire studies of police stress, the following three categories of stress are most commonly encountered by the police:

1. *Physical and psychological threats.* Included here are events related to the unique demands of police work, such as using force, being physically attacked, confronting aggressive people or grisly crime scenes, and engaging in high-speed chases. Danger can emerge from even apparently innocuous circumstances. Three police officers in Inkster, Michigan, made a routine call at a motel to serve a warrant for writing a bad check. They were met with a fusillade of gunfire; all three were killed. Patrolman Gary Lorenzen was one of the first officers to discover the bodies. "I haven't had anyone here I could talk to—I'm hurting like a son of a bitch inside but I have to be strong for the other officers," he said (Clancy, 1987, p. 1A).

2. *Evaluation systems.* These stressors include the ineffectiveness of the judicial system, court leniency with criminals, negative press accounts of the police, the public's rejection of the police, and put-downs and mistreatment of police officers in the courts. This source of stress is a major problem in countries other than the United States. For example, in France, where the public is particularly contemptuous of the police, the rate of suicide is 35 for every 100,000 officers, a rate exceeding that in most major U.S. cities. However, even in the United States, many more police officers die as a result of suicide than of homicide.

3. *Organizational problems and lack of support.* Examples of these stressors include bureaucratic hassles, inadequate leadership by police administrators, weak support and confused feedback from supervisors, lack of clarity about job responsibilities, and poor job performance by fellow officers. In the survey of Australian police cited earlier (Hart et al., 1995), as well as in other studies (Stinchcomb, 2004; Violanti & Aron, 1994), organizational problems proved to be one of the most important sources of stress—more influential even than physical danger, bloody crime scenes, and public scrutiny.

A certain degree of stress is inevitable, given the demands placed on the police. Yet police officers often find it hard to acknowledge that the stressful nature of their job is affecting them. There is a stigma about admitting a need for professional help. Too often, police officers believe that if they acknowledge personal problems or ask for assistance, they will be judged to be unprofessional or inadequate.

These fears are not entirely unreasonable. Officers found to have psychological problems are sometimes belittled by other officers or are relieved of their weapons and badges and assigned to limited-duty tasks. Fear of these consequences induces some officers to hide the fact that they are suffering from job-related stress.

Stressful working conditions also lead to **burnout**, which has been defined as "a syndrome of emotional exhaustion, depersonalization, and reduced personal accomplishment that can occur among individuals who work with people in some capacity" (Maslach & Jackson, 1984, p. 134). Emotional exhaustion reflects feelings of being emotionally overextended and "drained" by one's contact with other people. Depersonalization frequently takes the form of a callous or insensitive response to other people, particularly crime victims and others requesting police assistance. Reduced personal accomplishment is manifested in a diminished sense

© CNN/Getty Images

Arresting a high-risk suspect after a car chase

of competence at the end of a day's work with other people (Maslach & Jackson, 1984).

Burnout also affects behavior off the job. In Jackson and Maslach's (1982) study of police officers and their families, emotional exhaustion was found more likely than any other factor to affect behavior at home. Police officers were described by their wives as coming home upset, angry, tense, and anxious. High rates of substance abuse, domestic battering, and divorce are regarded as occupational hazards of police work. A subsequent study (Hawkins, 2001) replicated Maslach's finding regarding emotional exhaustion, and its relationship to burnout in police. Depersonalization was another factor that was strongly related to burnout among the 452 officers (in four departments) who were surveyed.

Burnout may also result from working many years at the same job. Patrol officers sometimes speak of the "seven-year syndrome." Initially, officers are eager and anxious about their job performance. The tasks are initially interesting and challenging. But after several years, some officers lose interest; the job feels stale. Enthusiasm plummets.

What can be done to reduce stress and burnout in police officers? From their analysis of the research on organizational behavior, Jackson and Schuler (1983) have hypothesized four organizational qualities

that increase employee burnout: (1) lack of rewards (especially positive feedback), (2) lack of control over job demands, (3) lack of clear job expectations, and (4) lack of support from supervisors. Although each of these is especially problematic for police officers, certain interventions can reduce the likelihood of burnout. For example, the police officer seldom hears when things go well but often hears of the complaints of enraged citizens. Police officials could create opportunities for citizens to express their appreciation of what police officers are doing daily.

Officers often feel a lack of control in their jobs. They must react to calls; they cannot change the flow of demands. Furthermore, citizens expect them to respond immediately. Although the level of demands cannot be changed, officers can be given greater flexibility in how they respond to these demands. Their daily duties can be restructured so as to increase their sense of choice among activities. The importance of discretion can be emphasized to the officers, because they must exercise such discretion when dealing with suspected offenders. Officers do not always make an arrest, even when they catch a suspect breaking the law. LaFave (1965) provides one illustration:

> A traffic officer stopped a car that had been going 15 m.p.h. over the speed limit. The driver was a youth, but he had a valid driver's license. Although the 15 m.p.h. excess was beyond the ordinary toleration limit for speeding violations, the officer only gave the youth a severe warning. The officer knew that the law required suspension of the license of a juvenile driver for any moving violation (p. 138).

One strategy for decreasing burnout among police is the use of **team policing**. Team policing involves a partial shift of decision making from a centralized authority to front-line officers and their immediate supervisors, who share the responsibility of setting policing priorities and making management decisions. Teams are often organized around neighborhoods, where they focus their efforts for extended periods of time. Within a neighborhood team, members perform several different functions so that they come to realize how important each team member is to the overall success of the group. In addition, because the team stays in the neighborhood, citizens should come to know the officers more closely and develop a better understanding of them.

In addition to team policing, many police agencies have developed their own stress management programs or referred their officers to other agencies for counseling to reduce burnout. These programs emphasize the prevention of stress through various techniques, including relaxation training, stress inoculation, detection of the early signs of stress, and effective problem solving (Reiser & Geiger, 1984). As useful as these types of techniques may be, the stigma associated with obtaining mental health treatment may be strong enough to discourage officers from going to these agencies.

But despite attempts to prevent stress and to change organizations in positive ways, some officers will experience stress-related problems that require counseling. Psychological treatment of police officers is complicated because police officers are often reluctant to become involved in therapy or counseling, for several reasons. First, they tend to believe that capable officers should be able to withstand hardships—and failure to do so shows a lack of professionalism or emotional control. Second, police fear that counseling will brand them with the stigma of mental disorder and thus diminish their peer officers' respect for them. Finally, officers are justifiably concerned that the department's need to know their psychological status related to fitness for duty will override their rights of confidentiality and lead to embarrassing disclosures of personal information.

Police departments have developed several alternatives for providing psychological counseling to their officers. Each addresses some of the obstacles that arise in police counseling programs. Peer counseling, involving the delivery of services by police officers, has the potential to overcome the stigma of being involved in treatment with a psychiatrist or psychologist. Describing their experiences with peer counseling in the Los Angeles Police Department (LAPD), Reiser and Klyver (1987) reported that 200 trained peer counselors conducted about 5,000 hours of counseling with their fellow officers in one year alone. Most of this counseling

was aimed at relationship problems and job dissatisfaction in the LAPD, which pioneered the development of peer counseling with police officers.

A second method is to provide counseling targeted at problems specific to police officers. The most noteworthy example of these focused interventions is with officers who have been involved in the use of deadly force (Blau, 1986). The emotional aftermath of shooting incidents is among the most traumatic experiences the police encounter and can often lead to symptoms of posttraumatic stress disorder (Hatch, 2002; Solomon & Horn, 1986). Providing post-incident counseling is a common service of police psychologists; in many departments, counseling for officers involved in shooting incidents is mandatory (Hatch, 2002). The goals of this counseling, which often also relies on peer support, are to reassure officers that their emotional reactions to incidents are normal, to give them a safe place to express these emotions, to help them reduce stress, and to promote a timely return to duty. Many departments also try to make counseling services available to the family of officers who have been involved in traumatic incidents.

There are several ethical considerations involved in psychological counseling for police officers (D'Agostino, 1986), and some of the most difficult concern confidentiality. Police counseling services are usually offered in one of two ways: by an "in-house" psychologist who is a full-time employee of the police department, or by an "outside" psychologist who consults with the department on a part-time basis. In-house professionals are more readily available and more knowledgeable about police issues. Outside consultants, because of their independence from the department, may be better able to protect the confidentiality of their clients' disclosures.

IS THERE A POLICE PERSONALITY?

Given that the work of a police officer entails a number of challenging tasks and that the job is highly visible, the public has a tendency to label police officers as having a certain set of qualities. Is there a distinct "police personality?" Do police officers share a cluster of personality characteristics that distinguishes them from other people? If there is a police personality, how does it come about? Are police officers, by nature, a homogeneous group? Do they differ from other occupational groups and from the general population in terms of inherited personality traits? Or is the personality of police officers shaped gradually over their careers as a result of common occupational demands and experiences?

Different answers have been given to these questions, but the consensus is that career socialization is a stronger influence than preexisting differences in temperament. One of the earlier influential conceptions of a police personality is Lefkowitz's description of the psychology of the police. After studying a host of variables, Lefkowitz concluded that the police do not differ from other groups in terms of psychological disorders or intelligence, but he also suggests that there are other important differences. According to Lefkowitz (1975):

> There exists a constellation of traits and
> attitudes or a general perspective on the
> world which particularly characterizes
> the policeman. This constellation …
> presumably [comprises] such interrelated
> traits as authoritarianism, suspiciousness,
> physical courage, cynicism, conservatism,
> loyalty, secretiveness, and
> self-assertiveness (p. 6).

Lefkowitz and others (Charles, 1986; Muir, 1977) have identified two clusters of personality traits that have been viewed as characteristic of police officers, but not in any pathological way. Cluster 1 includes the traits of isolation and secrecy, defensiveness and suspiciousness, and cynicism. These traits suggest a close-knit group whose occupational isolation and accompanying secrecy lead to strong feelings of being misunderstood by outsiders, who are in turn viewed with suspiciousness and cynicism by the police. Feelings of insecurity develop in response to this isolation and sense of being different; such feelings underlie the officers' desire for a uniform and badge as symbols to bolster

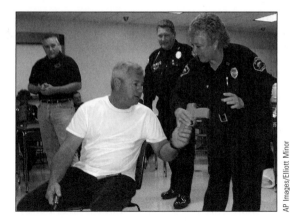

Crisis Intervention Team Training for Police

their self-esteem and to meet the extraordinary challenges of their jobs. In fact, being misunderstood by the public is one of the three most frequent problems reported by police officers. The segregation that results from wearing a uniform daily and from their role in the community leads to what Lefkowitz (1975) calls socio-occupational isolation, which only intensifies the individual's solidarity with other police officers.

Another manifestation of this cluster is what has been called the "blue wall of silence," the tendency for police officers to cover up the wrongdoing of fellow officers. The extent of this problem is unknown, but increased attention has been paid to it ever since Alan Dershowitz, one of O. J. Simpson's attorneys, charged that officers are routinely trained at the police academy to lie on the witness stand. This charge is easier to make than to verify, but it may be that some police officers shade the truth or ignore it altogether to protect themselves and obtain convictions. In fact, allegations of police misconduct, including the planting of evidence, have become a mainstay argument among criminal defense attorneys. Moreover, this argument works; convictions have been overturned because the police either faked or suppressed evidence. For instance, in 2004, Laurence Adams, who was convicted of killing a transit worker during an attempted robbery, was released after 30 years on death row. Mr. Adams's attorney presented evidence that Boston police withheld key documents in the case, including reports of other individuals' confessions of their involvement in the murder (Lindsay, 2004).

Lefkowitz's second cluster includes the qualities of **authoritarianism**, status concerns, and violence. This cluster is much more controversial than cluster 1 and includes a penchant for violence and several dimensions of authoritarianism. Authoritarianism, as conceived by Adorno, Frenkel-Brunswik, Levinson, and Sanford (1950), is a set of beliefs that reflect identification with and submissiveness to authorities, an endorsement of power and toughness, intolerance of out-groups and minorities, pressure for conformity to group norms, and rejection of anything unconventional as "deviant" or "sick." Although the police appear submissive to authority and tend to be politically conservative, they do not as a group score as particularly authoritarian on the California F Scale of Authoritarianism or as particularly rigid on Rokeach's Dogmatism Scale (Carlson, Thayer, & Germann, 1971; Fenster & Locke, 1973). In some studies, they score lower on these dimensions than college students and teachers. If police officers are authoritarian, it is primarily in the sense of exhibiting middle-class conventionality.

Police may also become more aggressive when they perceive their personal authority to be questioned and when they work at a job in which the use of force is justifiable. Police also appear to be more responsive to politically powerful figures than to powerless ones. In a provocative investigation, Wilson (1978) asked police officers how they would respond if they saw a car with a very low license number (such as NY-2) speeding. Such low-number plates are offered to politicians in many states. Police officers in two New York communities, Amsterdam and Newburgh, responded without hesitation that they would "mind our own business."

Two large meta-analyses have demonstrated the applicability of the "big five" personality dimensions (conscientiousness, agreeableness, extraversion, neuroticism, and openness to experience) in predicting police job performance. These studies (Barrick & Mount, 1991; Tett, Jackson, & Rothstein, 1991) suggest that the strongest of these five factors predicting police job performance is conscientiousness.

The labels *authoritarian* and *violent* may be justified for police officers, but in a narrower sense than is usually applied. Police officers do tend to be a politically conservative, conventional group, very loyal to one another, and concerned with assertively maintaining the status quo. They are authoritarian, primarily in the sense of respecting the higher authority of the law, the nation, and the government they serve.

A primary psychological motivation to become a police officer appears to be the preference for order and security, which probably reflects the working-class backgrounds from which many police officers come (Copes & Forsyth, 1994). A second important motive is a desire to provide social services to others. Police officers also report a desire for a job that allows them to exercise independent thought, to be creative, and to learn new things (Lurigio & Skogan, 1994).

Research indicates that police officers do not possess pathological extremes of personality. Most studies indicate that as a group, they are healthy in their adjustment but have a highly stressful occupation.

POLICE–COMMUNITY RELATIONS

Police officers are justified in feeling that they live in a "fishbowl." Their performance is constantly being reviewed by the courts and evaluated by the public. Several amendments to the U.S. Constitution impose limits on law enforcement officers; such limits are part of the first ten amendments, known as the Bill of Rights (see Chapter 1). The Fourth Amendment protects against unreasonable search and seizure of persons or property. The Fifth Amendment provides guarantees for persons accused of a crime; for example, no such person "shall be compelled in any criminal case to be a witness against himself, nor be deprived of life, liberty, or property, without due process of law." Limits on police activities are frequently reevaluated on the basis of current court interpretations of these amendments. The Sixth Amendment guarantees a defendant "the right to a speedy and public trial" and "the assistance of counsel for his defense." These amendments also have implications for police procedures. Protection against "cruel and unusual punishment" is provided under the Eighth Amendment, and the Fourteenth Amendment guarantees all citizens "due process." These amendments also govern and constrain several police activities.

During the last 25 years, citizens' groups have become increasingly critical of the police. Two types of concerns can be identified. The first deals with the manner in which the police perform certain duties (e.g., arrests and interrogations); the second concerns the prevalence of police brutality.

Historically, the interrogation practices used by the police to elicit confessions from suspects have been a major focus of concern. Police are often criticized for using manipulative tactics to induce confessions from suspects. As we describe in Chapter 6, the most common approach is "to overwhelm the suspect with damaging evidence, to assert a firm belief in his or her guilt, and then to suggest that it would be easier for all concerned if the suspect admitted to his or her role in the crime" (Kassin & Wrightsman, 1985, p. 75). Along with this tactic, police often express concern for the suspect's welfare. Undue physical force is used far less than in the past, but promises of lowered bail, reduced charges, and leniency by the judge, as well as vague threats about harsher treatment, are common. These techniques are sometimes supplemented with exaggerated or trumped-up evidence to scare suspects into confessing (Kassin & Kiechel, 1996).

A police technique that has caused widespread concern and condemnation more recently is racial profiling—the practice of making traffic arrests of a larger percentage of minority than nonminority motorists. Although some law enforcement officials have defended this procedure as a reasonable crime control tool, the public outcry over its potential for abuse has led several states to abandon it.

The second major concern of some community groups is excessive force or brutality by the police (Holmes & Smith, 2008). During the protests of the 1960s that took place in Watts (a section of Los Angeles), in Detroit, and throughout the South, massive demonstrations were held by American citizens, mostly African Americans, against what they believed was racially motivated harassment by the police.

The police officer has come to be viewed in predominantly African American neighborhoods as a representative of a member of an "out-group," subject to distortions in the same respect that many police officers may view lower socioeconomic status (SES) urban minority citizens in a unitary fashion (Holmes & Smith, 2008). Part of this perception involves the history of overwhelming authority and power exerted by white males in the United States. Although law enforcement officers are trained to act within legally prescribed boundaries and to do so equally toward all citizens, charges of "police brutality" have continued as concerns in the United States. In 2000, the U.S. Civil Rights Commission, an independent, bipartisan agency established by Congress, reviewed the findings of its 1981 report on police practices and concluded that many of its 1981 findings still applied in alleged police brutality, harassment, and misconduct toward people of color, women, and the poor.

In the past 15 years, the beating or killing of suspects by the police again commanded national attention. For example, the spotlight shone on three New Orleans police officers who, in the aftermath of Hurricane Katrina, were captured on film beating a black man in the French Quarter. Another particularly vivid case—also involving police brutality filmed by a bystander—is described in Box 4.2.

More recent events suggest that the King case was not an isolated incident; minority citizens can point to many cases justifying their concerns that they are often not treated fairly by the police (Weitzer & Tuch, 1999). In 2001, the shooting and killing of Timothy Thomas by Cincinnati police officers sparked riots followed by days of civil unrest (Larson, 2004). In a two-month period prior to the shooting, Thomas, a 19-year-old African American man, was pulled over a total of 21 times and ticketed for either not wearing a seatbelt or driving without a license. Then, in the early morning hours of April 7, 2001, a police officer who reportedly recognized Thomas from having ticketed him, spotted him

B o x   4.2   THE CASE OF RODNEY KING: VIDEOTAPED POLICE BRUTALITY?

In March 1991, police chased a black motorist who they alleged was speeding through a Los Angeles suburb in his 1988 Hyundai. As the unarmed man emerged from his car, a police officer felled him with a blast from a 50,000-volt stun gun, and three patrolmen proceeded to beat and kick him while a police helicopter hovered overhead. As a result of this attack, which was witnessed by at least 11 other police onlookers, Rodney King—a 25-year-old man who, it was later learned, was on parole—lay seriously injured with multiple skull fractures, a broken ankle, a cracked cheekbone, and several internal injuries.

One special feature of this attack was that a nearby citizen captured the entire episode on his video camera; within hours, the tape of this terrifying beating was played across the country on network news programs. Soon thereafter, local, state, and federal agencies launched investigations into the beating and into the entire LAPD. Three of the four officers who were charged with beating King were initially acquitted of all criminal charges, an outcome that

AP Images/George Holliday/
Courtesy of KTLA Los Angeles

The violent arrest of Rodney King

shocked millions of Americans. But in a second trial, brought in federal court, two of the officers were found guilty of depriving King of his civil rights and were sentenced to prison.

King was awarded $3.8 million in a civil case and used part of this money to start a record label. He has, since then, been involved with the police on several other occasions, involving several arrests and sentences to prison. King's latest television appearance was on the second season of Celebrity Rehab with Dr. Drew, which premiered in October 2008.

---

outside a local nightclub. When the officer approached Thomas, he ran. The officer called for backup, stating that he was chasing a suspect who had approximately 14 warrants. Thomas ran into a dark alley and the officer followed, firing a single shot that killed Thomas. The officer reported shooting because Thomas was reaching for a gun, but no gun was ever found.

Other cases publicized in the national media include the sodomy and torture of Abner Louima, which we described earlier; the shooting and killing of Amadou Diallo, a West African immigrant, by four plainclothes New York City police officers; and the shooting of Javier Franciso Ovando by two Los Angeles police officers, who then planted a gun on the paralyzed victim to frame him for a crime he did not commit.

Even the U.S. Supreme Court has found it necessary to restrict the use of deadly force by police (see Box 4.3).

How can we explain incidents in which officers have used excessive force? One popular explanation is that police excesses stem from the personality

problems of a "few bad apples." In this view, brutality reflects the extreme of the aggressive, tough pole of the authoritarian personality that we have already discussed. A contrasting explanation is that brutality is the unfortunate price occasionally paid for situations in which rising numbers of violent, even deadly, criminals demand forceful responses from the police. A third explanation is that police brutality reflects a fundamental sociological pathology—that the deep strains of racism are still apparent in society. Which view is correct?

Police brutality is another example of a problem for which psychology seeks explanations in the *interactions* between persons and the situations in which they function, rather than simply in the individual's characteristics or the situational influences. From this perspective, we begin with police officers who typically are strongly committed to maintaining the conventional order and to protecting society. We repeatedly put them into potentially dangerous situations, we arm them well, we urge them to be "tough on crime," and we train and authorize them to use appropriate force. The result

---

B o x 4.3   THE CASE OF EDWARD GARNER AND LIMITS ON THE USE OF DEADLY FORCE

In the 1985 case of *Tennessee v. Garner*, the United States Supreme Court struck down a Tennessee law that allowed police to shoot to kill, even when an unarmed suspect fleeing a crime scene posed no apparent threat (Duning & Hanchette, 1985; Fyfe, 1982). In October 1974, Edward Garner, then 15, fled when the police arrived just after he had broken the window of an unoccupied house. He was pursued by Officer Elton Hymon.

As Garner scaled a 6-foot fence at the back of the property, Officer Hymon yelled, "Police—halt!" Garner didn't halt, and Officer Hymon, knowing that he was in no shape to catch the fleeing youth, shot and killed him with a bullet to the back of the head.

Garner's father sued public officials and the city of Memphis, alleging that the police had violated his son's civil rights by the use of excessive force. The city defended itself on the basis of a state statute giving peace officers the right to use deadly force if necessary to stop a fleeing felon. The lower courts agreed with the city, but 11 years later the United States Supreme Court struck down the statute in a 6–3 decision (*Tennessee v. Garner*, 1985).

The majority held that shooting a person, even one suspected of a felony, violates that person's Fourth Amendment right to be free from unreasonable searches and seizures. The majority opinion added, however, that deadly force would be justified if the officer had reason to believe that the suspect posed an immediate threat to him or others.

---

of mixing this type of person with these types of situations is not surprising: In some encounters, the police will use excessive force against citizens who are suspected of wrongdoing that threatens public safety. In addition, police justifications for extreme force can be motivated by stereotypes, mistaken information, and the mutual mistrust that can develop between individuals from different cultural and ethnic backgrounds.

As it turns out, many episodes of police brutality occur following high-speed chases, when (as with Rodney King) police react with violence after pursuing a suspect they consider belligerent or threatening. In a 2000 incident that has been compared to the Rodney King beating, three Philadelphia police officers punched and kicked one man 59 times in 28 seconds while trying to arrest him (Associated Press, 2000). In such tension-charged situations, police are prone to let their emotions dictate their actions. Some police departments are now concentrating on the problem of high-speed pursuits as triggers for police overreaction. They try to teach police to remain focused during these incidents, maintaining the discipline instilled in their training and not responding primarily out of fear or anger.

Since the 1970s, but particularly since the Rodney King episode, a number of attempts have been made to improve police relations with people in the community, especially in neighborhoods with large numbers of ethnic minorities. We have already described team policing as one effort to make the police officer's job less stressful and to respond to some community concerns about the way police perform; however, one of the most important innovations in police work during the last 25 years is **community-based policing**.

In this approach, police officers develop a proactive, problem-solving approach with active collaboration from local citizens who support the police in the effort to combat crime, promote safety, and enhance the overall quality of neighborhoods. This type of policing was designed to enhance the working relationship between the police and the public (Zhao, Lovrich, & Thurman, 1999).

In most versions of community policing, there are more foot patrols by officers who stay in the same neighborhoods. As a result, community-based policing seeks to humanize police and citizens in one another's eyes and to broaden the roles that police play in a community. For example, Chicago's version of community policing contains six basic features (Lurigio & Skogan, 1994):

1. *A neighborhood orientation,* in which officers forge friendships with individual residents in a community, identify the "hot spots" for

crime, and develop partnerships with community organizations for fighting crime

2. *Increased geographic responsibility,* which means that officers regularly walk a given neighborhood "beat" and become highly visible, well-known experts about problems in that area

3. *A structured response to calls for police service,* in which emergency calls are handled by a special-response team, thereby permitting beat officers to stay available for routine calls and maintain a high-profile presence

4. *A proactive, problem-oriented approach,* whereby more effort is devoted to crime prevention (e.g., closing down drug houses, breaking up groups of loitering youth) than responding to discrete disturbances or criminal activities

5. *Brokering more community resources for crime prevention,* as police enlist the help of other city agencies to identify and respond to local community problems

6. *Analysis of crime problems,* which enables officers to focus their attention on the highest-risk areas by using computer technology to keep accurate track of crime patterns.

Some opponents of the practice have criticized community policing as expensive and as seeking to turn police officers into "social workers with guns" (Worsnop, 1993). Nonetheless, as of June 30, 2000, two-thirds of all local police departments and over half of the sheriffs' offices across the country had full-time officers engaging in community-based policing activities (Bureau of Justice Statistics, 2005a).

Does community policing work, or is it just a fad, long on rhetoric but short on success? As with most social reform projects, the results have been mixed. Some cities that have introduced community-policing initiatives report large improvements in the public's attitude toward their police departments (Adams, Rohe, & Arcury, 2005; Peak, Bradshaw, & Glensor, 1992) and sizable reductions in rates of serious crimes.

Residents of small to midsize cities were questioned about the effects of community-oriented policing. Findings revealed that awareness of this type of policing, compared to more conventional

Community policing is a philosophy designed to increase the amount and quality of specific police officer's contact with citizens and to involve police more in crime prevention and community maintenance activities

policing focused on arresting offenders, was associated with greater self-protection efforts (e.g., putting bars on windows), lower fear of crime, and stronger feelings of attachment to the community (Adams et al., 2005). This finding held regardless of the respondents' history of victimization; participants associated community-oriented policing with a lower fear of crime even when they had previously been a victim of crime.

In the early 1990s, the city of Chicago reorganized its police force to incorporate community policing. In a study of the impact of this program, Skogan (2006) considers its impact on crime, neighborhood residents, and the police. The 13-year study revealed distinctive problems for African American, white, and Latino citizens. Skogan described very substantial improvements in the city's predominately African American districts, where crime and fear dropped significantly. The city's largely white neighborhoods were already supportive of police, but they also made significant gains in these areas. However, for Latinos, there were differences according to whether the neighborhood contained long-term residents and had been integrated for some time (good outcomes) versus predominantly Spanish-speaking people (poorer outcomes on crime, disorder, and neighborhood decay). Although the overall results were promising, it will be important to find a way to assist the city's newest citizens.

Other evaluations indicate that police officers themselves remain skeptical about community policing. In Chicago's program, police officers initially doubted that community-based policing would reduce crime or improve relationships with racial minorities, and believed it would require more work on their part and possibly undercut their authority in the community (Lurigio & Skogan, 1994). In general, police administrators endorse the value of community policing and believe that its advantages (improved physical environment, more positive attitudes toward police, fewer citizen complaints) outweigh its disadvantages (displacement of crime to a non-community-policing area, more opportunities for officer corruption, resistance from rank-and-file officers).

SUMMARY

1. *What is the role of the police in our society?* Policing is necessary in any society concerned with maintaining public order, even though it is important in a democratic society to balance public safety with civil liberties and criminal rights. Police officers daily face the dilemma of equality versus discretion: whether to treat all suspects or lawbreakers equally or to temper justice with mercy.

2. *What procedures are used to select police?* Selection of police officers usually includes the completion of psychological tests and a clinical interview. Another assessment device is the use of situational tests, in which the candidate role-plays responses to real-life challenges that would face a police officer, such as intervening in a dispute between a wife and her husband or writing an incident report. Although responses to these situational tasks are valuable additions to psychological testing and interviewing, they are also costly and time-consuming.

3. *How has the training of police officers expanded into new areas?* Training of police officers usually involves a variety of activities, including criminal law, human relations training, self-defense, and the use of firearms. Most training programs last at least six months. Police officers are now frequently trained in crisis intervention, including handling situations involving individuals with mentally illness, resolving family disputes, and responding to hostage-taking situations.

4. *Describe the different activities of the police. Is law enforcement central?* The police officer's job is multifaceted. Law enforcement (including investigation of complaints, arrest and prosecution of suspects, and efforts at crime prevention) accounts for only about 10% of police activity. Maintaining order (intervening in family and neighborhood disputes, keeping traffic moving, responding to disturbances of the peace) accounts for about 30% of police activity. Providing social services to the community is even more time-consuming.

5. *What stressors do the police face?* Three problems are especially significant: the "life in a fishbowl" phenomenon, job-related stress, and burnout. Job duties and perceptions of police work can be modified to reduce burnout. Special psychological interventions are also available to counteract stress reactions experienced by the police.

6. *Is there a police personality?* There is no specific "police personality," but research suggests that there are two clusters of relevant traits: (1) isolation and secrecy, defensiveness and suspiciousness, and cynicism; and (2) authoritarianism, status concerns, and aggression. The evidence for the existence or strength of the second cluster is less convincing than for the first, and there is no indication that police officers as a group exhibit pathological personalities.

7. *What is the relationship between the police and the communities they serve?* Some community groups have been critical of police behavior, focusing on unequal and sometimes brutal treatment of the poor and racial minorities. Efforts to

improve police–community relations include team policing, crisis intervention training, reorganization of the police department that restructures the traditional chain of command, and community-based policing. These interventions have had some success.

KEY TERMS

authoritarianism

bioterrorism

burnout

community-based
 policing

Crisis Intervention
 Team

fitness-for-duty
 evaluation

jail diversion programs

learned helplessness

predictive validity

Stockholm syndrome

structured interviews

suicide by cop

team policing

terrorism

validity scales

zero tolerance

5

Crime Investigation

Witnesses

Repressed and Recovered Memories

ORIENTING QUESTIONS

1. What psychological factors contribute to the risk of mistaken identifications in the legal system?
2. How do jurors evaluate the testimony of eyewitnesses, and can psychologists help jurors understand the potential problems of eyewitness testimony?
3. Can children accurately report on their experiences of victimization? What factors affect the accuracy of their reports?
4. Can memories for trauma be repressed, and if so, can these memories be recovered accurately?

As we saw in Chapter 4, the police investigate crimes and accumulate evidence so that suspects can be identified and arrested. At the early stages of an investigation, eyewitnesses to those crimes provide important information to police. Sometimes they provide the only solid leads. Eyewitnesses also play a vital role in later stages of a prosecution. According to defense attorney David Feige, "It's hard to overstate the power of eyewitness testimony in criminal cases. In thousands of cases every year, testimony of a single eyewitness, uncorroborated by forensic or any other evidence, is used to sustain serious felony charges, including robbery and murder" (Feige, 2006). The National Institute of Justice (Department of Justice, 1999) estimates that approximately 75,000 defendants are implicated by eyewitnesses in the United States every year.

But in their attempts to solve crimes—and especially in their reliance on eyewitness observers—police and prosecutors face a number of challenges.

Although many eyewitnesses provide reliable reports, some make mistakes. Sometimes the desire to get a case "nailed down" overshadows the goal of discovering the truth. The recollections of eyewitnesses can lead the police down blind alleys or cause them to arrest the wrong suspect, sometimes resulting in wrongful convictions by judges and juries.

It is now apparent that eyewitness errors create problems for the justice system (and for the people mistakenly identified!). DNA procedures developed in the 1980s make it possible to take a new look at evidence left at a crime scene. Unfortunately, only a small fraction of crimes—most notably murders and sexual assaults—have DNA-rich evidence. Even when DNA is present, it is often not tested or is destroyed, though new state laws grant inmates some degree of access to DNA evidence.

According to the Innocence Project, the largest and most prominent organization devoted to proving wrongful convictions, 75% of the first 218 people exonerated on the basis of DNA analysis had been mistakenly identified (Innocence Project, 2008). A study by Professor Samuel Gross and his colleagues estimated that of 121 exonerated prisoners who were wrongly sentenced for rape between 1989 and 2003, fully 88% were victims of erroneous eyewitness testimony (Gross, Jacoby, Matheson, Montgomery, & Patil, 2005). Mistaken eyewitness identifications account for more wrongful convictions than do false confessions, problems with snitches, and defective or fraudulent science combined (Innocence Project, 2008).

Concern about eyewitnesses' accuracy is not restricted to criminal cases or to the identification of persons (Wells & Loftus, 1984). The results of civil lawsuits are also often affected by the reports of eyewitnesses, and law enforcement officials know that eyewitness descriptions of unusual events cannot always be trusted. Consider the reports from eyewitnesses to the assassination of President Abraham Lincoln as documented by historian Bruce Catton. All witnesses agreed that John Wilkes Booth pulled the trigger and then leaped from the presidential box where Lincoln was seated and onto the stage. But their descriptions of Booth's actions from that point vary widely:

> … he made a 15-foot leap, ran swiftly off-stage, and vanished … he slid down a flag-pole (which did not actually exist), and more or less crept away … [he limped] painfully across the stage moaning incoherently … [he stalked] off calmly, dropping his "*Sic simper tyrannis*" as a good actor might … [he ran] furiously, saying nothing at all … he went off-stage on his hands and knees, making noises … (Catton, 1965, p. 105)

EXAMPLES OF MISTAKEN EYEWITNESS IDENTIFICATION

Cases of wrongful convictions based on faulty eyewitness testimony abound. The ordeal of Calvin C. Johnson, Jr., is a good example. Johnson, a college graduate with a job at Delta Airlines, spent 16 years behind bars for a rape he did not commit. He is not

alone. In fact, Johnson was the 61st person in the United States to be exonerated through the use of DNA testing. Tests in Johnson's case proved definitively that he was not the man who raped and sodomized a College Park, Georgia, woman in 1983. Yet the victim picked Johnson out of a photographic lineup and identified him as the rapist at trial. The all-White jury convicted Johnson, who is Black, despite the fact that forensic tests excluded him as the source of a pubic hair recovered from the victim's bed. The jury also apparently chose to disregard the testimony of four alibi witnesses who claimed that Johnson was home asleep at the time. One of the jurors stated that the victim's eyewitness testimony had been the most compelling evidence in the case.

One reason why mistakes are so common is that when eyewitnesses make a tentative identification, police often stop investigating other leads and instead look for further evidence that implicates the chosen suspect. This is an example of **confirmation bias**, whereby people look for, interpret, and create information that verifies an existing belief. In terms of eyewitness identification, the goal of finding the truth is neglected, often unintentionally, in a rush to solve the crime. In Johnson's case, police pushed ahead with the case even after the victim picked someone else at a live lineup (conducted after the photographic lineup). She testified at trial that she had picked the wrong person at the lineup because looking at Johnson was

An example of a sketch drawn by a police artist

© Bettmann/CORBIS

B o x 5.1   THE CASE OF THOMAS LEE GOLDSTEIN: HOW TO VALUE 24 YEARS LOST TO PRISON

Thomas Goldstein (right), whose conviction was overturned after 24 years in prison

Thomas Lee Goldstein emerged from prison in California in April 2004 as a homeless, white-haired man of 55, clad only in a jail jumpsuit and cheap slippers, without a cent to his name. He had spent the previous 24 years in prison for a murder he did not commit, sent there through the testimony of a supposed eyewitness to a 1979 murder in Long Beach and by a jury convinced of his guilt. The eyewitness since recanted his story, saying that he was overeager to help the police and coached by investigators to identify Goldstein.

Over the years he was imprisoned, Goldstein slowly lost his sense of disbelief, bitterness, and even revenge fantasies until all he was left with was a sense of numbness (Broder, 2004). Sadly, even his exit from prison was numbing: His first stop was a Veterans Affairs office where he hoped to get a few clothes, some money, and a place to live. But the office computers were down, and officials could locate no record of his three

years of service as a Marine. He drove away with his attorney, still homeless and penniless. When asked the next day how he spent his first night of freedom after nearly a quarter-century, Goldstein replied that he "called up an old girlfriend hoping for a day of wild sex. Of course, she wasn't home so I went to the law library instead."

Goldstein had become quite a legal scholar in the years he spent behind bars, filing many petitions for his release and eventually earning a paralegal certificate. Those petitions caught the attention of a federal judge in 1996, and in 2002 a federal magistrate determined that Goldstein had been wrongly convicted and ordered him released. He now spends his days as a paralegal in a small Pasadena law firm, and has sued the city of Long Beach, the county of Los Angeles, four Long Beach police officers, and the district attorney's office for his incarceration. In pondering the size of the claim, his attorney, Ronald Kaye, asks, "How do you really evaluate in financial terms what 24 years of life are worth? He was locked up from age 30–55. He didn't get a chance to find a wife, have children, build a career. I ask you, is $25 million enough? Is $50 million enough?" As for Goldstein, his "sustaining fantasy" is of a farm in Kansas: "I dream of owning a large plot of land in the Midwest with a house and a dog and a huge field of flowers and a grassy area. I want to just sit back there and look at the fields and fields of nothing, the antiprison" (Broder, 2004).

---

too much for her: "I just pushed my eyes away and picked someone else," she reported (Boyer, 2000). Another example of mistaken identification that led to a wrongful conviction and imprisonment—the case of Thomas Lee Goldstein—is chronicled in Box 5.1.

You might think that people like Calvin Johnson and Thomas Goldstein would have some recourse— that they could get something back for the time they lost in prison. But Johnson received nothing for his years behind bars because Georgia did not have a law providing compensation for people who were wrongly convicted. Although Congress passed legislation in 2004 that included payments of $50,000 per year of imprisonment to people exonerated of federal crimes and encouraged states to follow its lead, only Vermont has done so (Roberts & Stanton, 2007).

Approximately 20 other states now provide some compensation for the exonerated. Many people who were wrongly incarcerated get either nothing or a token sum from these funds. One commentator has suggested that the new crime is how little these lost lives are worth (Higgins, 1999).

HOW MISTAKEN EYEWITNESS IDENTIFICATIONS OCCUR

Mistakes in the process of identification can occur the moment the crime is committed. It may be too dark, events may move too swiftly, or the encounter may

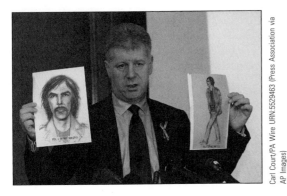

Sketches based on eyewitnesses' recollections

Carl Court/PA Wire URN:5529463 (Press Association via AP Images)

in perception and memory. We are all prone to making errors in perceiving and remembering events that we experience. But eyewitnesses must remember experiences that are typically brief, complicated, and sometimes very frightening. So they are especially prone to error. To illustrate these errors, we consider the steps involved in acquiring and recalling information from the outside world—steps an eyewitness must take to record a memory.

BASIC INFORMATION PROCESSING

We have all had the experience of greeting someone we recognize, only to realize that we were wrong—that the person is actually a stranger. Similar mistakes can be made when crimes are observed. To process information about a crime, we must first perceive a stimulus and then retain it in our minds at least momentarily. But failures and errors can emerge at any step along the way.

Perception

Although our perceptual abilities are impressive (Penrod, Loftus, & Winkler, 1982), we do make errors. We tend to overestimate the height of criminals. We overestimate the duration of brief events and underestimate the duration of prolonged incidents. When watching a short film, we notice more about the actions than about the persons doing the acting.

If a weapon is present when a crime is committed, we may devote more attention to it than to the facial features or other physical aspects of the person who has the weapon. This **weapon focus effect** appears to be caused not by emotional arousal but by the novelty of the weapon that draws witnesses' attention (Hope & Wright, 2007). This limits the amount of attention they can pay to other aspects of the situation, such as physical features of the perpetrator (Shaw & Skolnick, 1999).

The presence of a weapon can also affect the processing of auditory information. Professor Kerri Pickel

be too brief for the victim to perceive the incident accurately. Yet when they are questioned by police, victims are asked to give their impressions of the criminal's height, hair color, voice, and other identifying features.

Mistakes can also occur during the investigation of a crime. In cases that involve eyewitnesses, police often ask these witnesses to examine a series of photos (called a **photographic lineup** or **photospread**) or a physical lineup of suspects and decide whether the perpetrator is present. At this point, eyewitnesses want to help the police solve the crime; they may feel implicit pressure to identify someone, even if the police do not explicitly encourage them to do so. Although accurate identifications are more likely than inaccurate identifications, we know that innocent people are sometimes selected and guilty people are sometimes overlooked.

During trial, jurors may watch an eyewitness confidently identify the defendant as the perpetrator. Not only will they assume that this identification is accurate, they will also assume that the victim was confident about the initial description or identification of the perpetrator. These assumptions fail to recognize the many problems that can undermine the accuracy of a criminal identification (Wells & Olson, 2003). We describe several such problems in this chapter.

The study of eyewitness identification grew out of our understanding of the basic principles involved and her colleagues showed a film of a man holding either a weapon (e.g., a gun, a switchblade knife) or a neutral object (e.g., a soda pop bottle, a ballpoint pen) and speaking to a woman in such a way that his words were either easy or difficult to understand (Pickel, French, & Betts, 2003). Witnesses had difficulty understanding the man's speech in the latter condition, and the presence of a weapon further impaired their comprehension. A reasonable explanation is that their focus on the weapon and their attempt at language comprehension competed for limited processing time. They had a hard time doing both things at once. In general, when people must divide their attention between two or more stimuli, they are more suggestible (Lane, 2006).

Memory

Cognitive psychologists subdivide the building of a memory into three processes: encoding, storage, and retrieval. We describe the memory of eyewitnesses in each of these three stages.

Encoding. **Encoding** refers to the acquisition of information. Many aspects of a stimulus can affect how it is encoded; stimuli that are only briefly seen or heard cannot be encoded fully, of course. The complexity of a stimulus also affects its encoding. As the complexity of an event increases (consider an earthquake, explosion, or tsunami), some aspects of the event probably will be misremembered, while others will be accurately recalled.

Contrary to what many people believe, a stressful situation does not necessarily enhance the encoding of events. Although mild stress or arousal may indeed heighten alertness and interest in a task, extreme stress usually causes the person to encode the information incompletely or inaccurately (Deffenbacher, Bornstein, Penrod, & McGorty, 2004). Performance on many tasks is best when the level of arousal is sufficient to ensure adequate attention but not so high as to disrupt accuracy.

A study of the accuracy of eyewitness memory in highly stressful military survival school interrogations provides good evidence of the effects of stress on memory (Morgan et al., 2004). Survival school interrogations are one of the greatest training challenges that active duty military personnel experience. (These interrogations are intended to test one's ability to withstand exploitation by the enemy, and to train people to hold up under the physical and mental stresses of capture.) Participants in this study were 500 soldiers, sailors, and pilots who were placed in mock prisoner of war (POW) camps and deprived of food and sleep for approximately 48 hours prior to interrogation. During 40 minutes of intense questioning, half of them were physically threatened and all participants were tricked into giving away information. One day later, they were asked to identify their interrogators from an eight-picture photographic lineup (chance accuracy is therefore 1/8, or 12.5%). The results were startling. Among soldiers who experienced moderate stress (without the threat of physical injury), 76% were correct in identifying the target. But only 34% of participants who experienced the high stress of a physically threatening situation were correct.

Characteristics of the witness also affect encoding. We all differ in visual acuity and hearing ability. When we have experience perceiving a stimulus we usually notice its details better than when we perceive something new. This is why experienced judges notice flaws in a gymnast's performance that the rest of us can detect only in a slow-motion replay. Different expectancies about upcoming events also influence how they are encoded; in general, we have a tendency to see what we expect to see.

Storage. The second step in building a memory is the **storage** of stimulus information. How well do we retain what we encode? Many years ago, psychologist Hermann Ebbinghaus showed that memory loss is rapid. In a recent study, eyewitnesses attempted to recall details of a video one, three, or five weeks after viewing it. Eyewitnesses who recalled the video for the first time five weeks after seeing it were significantly less accurate than eyewitnesses who attempted recall after one or three weeks, supporting the notion that memory fades as the **retention interval**, the period of time between viewing an event and being questioned about it, increases (Odinot & Wolters, 2006). Meta-analyses

---

Box 5.2   THE CASE OF LARRY FULLER AND THE VICTIM WHO "NEVER WAVERED"

Six o'clock on a foggy April morning in 1981, 45 minutes before sunrise in Dallas. A woman awakens to find a Black man with a knife atop her. The only light in the room comes from a digital alarm clock. The intruder cuts her and rapes her. Shortly afterwards, hospital personnel collect sperm in a rape kit. Two days later the victim looks at photographs of possible suspects; Larry Fuller's picture is among them. Because she cannot make an identification, the investigating officer recommends that the investigation be suspended. But other detectives persist, showing the victim a second photospread several days later. Importantly, Fuller's picture is the only one in the second photospread that was also in the first. At this point, the victim positively identifies him and he is arrested. Subsequent to a trial during which the prosecution claimed that the victim "never wavered," Fuller is convicted and sentenced to 50 years in prison.

Larry Fuller was 32 years old at the time, raising two young children. He had served two tours of duty in Vietnam where he was shot down several times. After being honorably discharged, he pursued a degree in the arts while working several jobs. From prison he petitioned the Innocence Project to take his case but the Dallas District Attorney's Office opposed requests for DNA testing, as it had done many times before. After a judge ordered testing that excluded Fuller as the perpetrator, he became the 186th person exonerated through DNA analysis.

---

of 53 studies showed that the longer the retention interval, the more memory loss for previously seen faces (Deffenbacher, Bornstein, McGorty, & Penrod, 2008).

A second phenomenon—a surprising and potentially disturbing one—also occurs during the storage phase. Activities that eyewitnesses carry out or information they learn after they observe an event, which is termed **postevent information**, can alter their memory of the event. For example, simply talking to other witnesses can introduce new (not always accurate) details into one's memory. We know that most witnesses *do* share information about serious events such as crimes. A survey of Australian undergraduates who witnessed actual assaults or robberies revealed that 86% discussed the event with cowitnesses, sometimes encouraged to do so by the police (Paterson & Kemp, 2006).

The now-classic studies of Elizabeth Loftus (1975, 1979) showed how exposure to postevent information can affect memory. In one study, participants viewed a film of an automobile accident and were asked questions about it. The first question asked either how fast the car was going "when it ran the stop sign" or how fast it was going "when it turned right." Then all subjects were asked whether they had seen a stop sign in the film. In the first group, which had been asked about the speed of the car "when it ran the stop sign," 53% said they had

seen a stop sign, whereas only 35% of the second group said they had seen the sign. The effect of the initial question was to "prompt" a memory for the sign. In a second study, Loftus included a misleading follow-up question that mentioned a nonexistent barn. When questioned one week later, 17% of the subjects reported seeing the barn in the original film. In essence, the new information that was conveyed simply as part of a question was added to the memory of the original stimulus.

Viewing photographs of suspects after witnessing a crime can also impair an eyewitness's ability to recognize the perpetrator's face in a lineup. According to a recent meta-analysis, exposure to photographs reduces both correct identifications (identifying the actual perpetrator when he is present in the lineup) and correct rejections (rejecting the choices in a lineup when the perpetrator is absent), and increases false alarms (identifying someone who is not the perpetrator) (Deffenbacher, Bornstein, & Penrod, 2006). The case of Larry Fuller, described in Box 5.2, provides an example of the effects of postevent exposure to photographs.

Retrieval.   The third and final step in establishing memory is the **retrieval** of information. This process is not as straightforward as it might seem. We all have experienced the "tip of the tongue" phenomenon, when we know an answer or a person's name but can't dredge it out of our memory store. The wording of questions can also influence retrieval (Wells, Wright, & Bradfield, 1999). For example, consider the question "What was the man with the mustache doing with the young boy?" Assume that the man in question had no mustache. This form of the question may not affect the eyewitness's report of the man's actions, but it may influence memory of the man's appearance. Later, if asked to describe the man, eyewitnesses may incorporate the detail (in this case, the mustache) that was embedded in the original question (Leippe, Eisenstadt, Rauch, & Stambush, 2006; Loftus & Greene, 1980).

In recalling information from our memory, we often generate memories that are accurate but are not relevant to the task at hand. Victims sometimes pick from a lineup the person whom they have seen before but who is not the actual criminal. For example, a clerk at a convenience store who is the victim of a late-night robbery may mistakenly identify an innocent shopper who frequents the store. In an actual case, a Los Angeles judge who was kidnapped and attacked while jogging picked a suspect's picture from a photographic lineup. She later stated that she had not remembered the suspect appearing before her in court for similar offenses four years earlier, and that she had sentenced him to unsupervised probation (Associated Press, 1988).

This phenomenon, called **unconscious transference**, was demonstrated by Psychology Professor David Ross and his colleagues, who showed two versions of a filmed robbery to college student witnesses (Ross, Ceci, Dunning, & Toglia, 1994). Half of the witnesses saw the film with an innocent bystander in the background, and the other half saw the same film without the bystander. When witnesses were asked whether they could identify the robber from a lineup (in this particular lineup, the bystander was present but the assailant was missing), eyewitnesses in the first group were three times more likely to misidentify the bystander than eyewitnesses in the second group. The majority of people who selected the bystander thought that the assailant and the bystander were the same person. This is one reason that innocent persons are sometimes charged with a crime and eventually convicted.

Common Research Methods in Eyewitness Identification

We have already described studies of the various influences on eyewitness memory. We now expand on two techniques that psychologists use to study eyewitness issues, and describe their advantages and disadvantages. Knowing how the studies are conducted can help you to understand what we can justifiably conclude from them.

Experimental methodology, in which a researcher stages a crime or shows a filmed crime to unsuspecting participant witnesses, is the dominant research method. In an experiment, the researcher manipulates some variable (e.g., the presence or absence of an instruction to participant witnesses, prior to viewing a lineup, that the perpetrator "may or may not be in the lineup") and measures its effects (e.g., the likelihood of choosing someone from the lineup). The value of an experiment is that the researcher knows exactly what the witnesses experienced (termed **ground truth**) and can measure, fairly precisely, how the manipulated variable affected what the witnesses remember. In other words, an experiment can establish cause-and-effect relations. But any individual experiment may lack **ecological validity**, meaning that the study may not approximate the real-world conditions under which eyewitnesses observe crimes and police interact with eyewitnesses. Still, if a number of experiments conducted under varying conditions and with different populations tend to reach the same conclusion, we can be fairly certain that the result would apply to the "real world."

A second way to study eyewitness identification is via **archival analysis** that involves after-the-fact examination of actual cases involving eyewitnesses. Archival analysis has been particularly helpful in examining choices from lineups (Wells, Memon, & Penrod, 2006). One might wonder, for example, how often filler faces are chosen instead of a suspect's face. An archival study of 119 lineups conducted around London showed that 21.5% of the eyewitnesses selected fillers (Valentine, Pickering, & Darling, 2003). The value of archival analysis is that it uses real-life situations as the backdrop; the disadvantage is that it can only document what happened in those cases and it cannot explain why.

THE VARIABLES THAT AFFECT EYEWITNESS ACCURACY

Building on the research on basic information processing and using these methodologies, psychologists have identified several other variables that can influence the validity of identifications. Professor Gary Wells, a prolific researcher in the area of eyewitness identification, introduced a useful taxonomy to categorize these variables (Wells, 1978). He coined the term **system variable** to refer to those factors that are under the control of the criminal justice system (e.g., the instructions given to eyewitnesses when they consider a lineup and the composition of that lineup). The term **estimator variable** refers to factors that are beyond the control of the justice system and whose impact on the reliability of the eyewitness can only be estimated (e.g., the lighting conditions at the time of the crime and whether the culprit was wearing a disguise). A third variable—a **postdiction variable**—does not directly affect the reliability of an identification, but is a measurement of some process that correlates with reliability (Wells et al., 2006). The confidence that a witness feels for an identification or the speed with which a witness identifies someone from a lineup are examples of postdiction variables.

Because system variables hold more promise for preventing errors in eyewitness identification (they are, after all, controllable), many psychologists have focused their research efforts on those variables. But research on estimator variables is important because it can help us understand situations in which eyewitnesses experience problems in perception and memory, and studies of postdiction variables allow an after-the-fact assessment of eyewitness accuracy. The next sections review these kinds of variables, all relevant in different ways to our understanding of the psychology of eyewitness identification.

Assessing the Impact of Estimator Variables

We have already described two estimator variables—the witness's stress level at the time of the crime and the presence of a weapon. Other factors also come into play.

Race of the Eyewitness.   Eyewitnesses are usually better at recognizing and identifying members of their own race or ethnic group than members of another race or ethnic group. The chances of a mistaken identification have been estimated to be 1.56 times greater when the witness and suspect are of different races than when they are of the same race (Meissner & Brigham, 2001). This phenomenon, termed the **other-race effect**, has been examined extensively in experimental studies, and archival analysis of DNA exoneration cases shows that it is also a significant problem in actual cases. In their analysis of 77 known cases of mistaken identification, Scheck, Neufeld, and Dwyer (2000) reported that 35% of these cases involved White victims or witnesses who misidentified Black suspects, whereas only 28% of cases involved White victims or witnesses who misidentified White suspects.

Understanding the reasons for the other-race effect has vexed psychologists for some time. Racial attitudes are apparently not related to this phenomenon (people with prejudicial attitudes are not more likely to experience the other-race effect than are people with unbiased attitudes). Recent explanations of the other-race effect have tended to involve both cognitive and social processes.

Cognitive interpretations hold that there are differences between faces of one race and faces of another race in terms of the variability in features, something called **physiognomic variability**. Faces of one race differ from faces of another race in terms of the *type* of physiognomic variability. For example, White faces show more variability in hair color, and Black faces show more variability in skin tone. For eyewitnesses to correctly identify members of other races, they must focus on the characteristics that distinguish that person from other people of the same race. Thus, Black eyewitnesses would be better off noticing and encoding a White perpetrator's hair color than her or his skin tone, whereas White eyewitnesses could more profitably pay attention to a Black assailant's skin tone. But most of us have more experience with members of our own race, so our natural inclination is to focus on the features that distinguish members of *our own group*. We have less practice distinguishing one member of another race from other people of that race.

Social psychologists have also tried to explain the other-race effect. One reasonable hypothesis is based on social perception and **in-group/out-group differences** (Sporer, 2001). When we encounter the face of a person from another race or ethnic group (the out-group), our first job is to categorize the face as a member of that group (e.g., "That person is Asian"). Attentional resources that are directed toward categorization come at the expense of attention to facial features that would distinguish that person from other members of the out-group. But when we encounter the face of a person from our in-group, the categorization step is eliminated, so we can immediately devote attention to distinguishing that person from other members of the in-group. Because identifying people of other races involves both a cognitive and a social process, both explanations may be right.

Age and Gender of the Eyewitness. Do males make better eyewitnesses than females and do young people make better eyewitnesses than older people? The age and gender of an eyewitness are also estimator variables; we can't control their influence but we can estimate them.

The evidence for gender effects is not overwhelming: A meta-analysis showed that although women are slightly more likely to make accurate identifications, they also make slightly more errors than men because they are more likely to choose someone from a lineup (Shapiro & Penrod, 1986). So there is no clear evidence that one gender is superior to the other in ability to identify people from lineups.

There is stronger evidence that the age of the eyewitness matters: Older eyewitnesses and young children make more errors than younger and middle-aged adults (Wilcock, Bull, & Vrij, 2007).

In addition, the errors of older adults and young children are fairly predictable. They are more likely to choose someone from a lineup in which the culprit is absent and, hence, make more mistaken identifications than young and middle-aged adults (Memon, Bartlett, Rose, & Gray, 2003). But when the lineup contains the culprit, young children and elderly people perform as well as adults. We describe the issues associated with children as witnesses later in the chapter.

Controlling the Impact of System Variables

System variables are those factors in an identification over which the justice system has some control. In general, system variables tend to come into play after the crime, usually during the investigation. They are associated with how a witness is questioned and how a lineup is constructed and shown to the eyewitness. We have already described two system variables: the influence of postevent information and the effects of questions posed to eyewitnesses. Other system variables are also important. Research on these variables can suggest changes to procedures that investigators use with eyewitnesses.

To explain why system variables and procedures are so important, it may be helpful to draw an analogy to the steps used by researchers doing an experiment (Wells & Luus, 1990). Like scientists, crime investigators begin with a hypothesis (that the suspect actually committed the crime), test the hypothesis (by placing the suspect in a lineup), observe and record the eyewitness's decision, and draw conclusions from the results (e.g., that the suspect was the assailant).

There are certain principles that are essential to good experimental design (e.g., that observers should be unbiased), and violation of those principles affects the usefulness of the experiment's findings. In similar fashion, violating the principles of good criminal investigation affects the results of the investigation. For example, if the suspect appears to be different from the other people in the lineup in some obvious way, or if the person conducting the lineup conveys his or her suspicions to the eyewitness, then the results of that identification procedure can be erroneous. Applying the analogy of an experiment to criminal investigations enables us to evaluate critically the steps involved in these investigations.

REFORMING IDENTIFICATION PROCEDURES

One important aspect of a system variable is that because it is controllable, it can be modified. In 1999, the U.S. Department of Justice (DOJ) recommended new procedures for collecting eyewitness evidence that were based on psychological research. In her introduction to these procedures, then-Attorney General Janet Reno wrote, "Eyewitnesses frequently play a vital role in uncovering the truth about a crime. The evidence they provide can be critical in identifying, charging, and ultimately convicting suspected criminals. That is why it is absolutely essential that eyewitness evidence be accurate and reliable. One way of ensuring we, as investigators, obtain the most accurate and reliable evidence from eyewitnesses is to follow sound protocols in our investigations" (U.S. Department of Justice, 1999, p. iii). Reno cited the "growing body of research in the field of eyewitness identification" as support for the revised procedures.

The Justice Department recommended procedures for conducting lineups. These recommendations have two important goals: maximize accurate identifications and minimize eyewitness errors. Because the police want to catch the real culprits and avoid mistakes, we expect that many departments will eventually incorporate these recommendations. Already, police in a half-dozen states and several large cities have embraced these recommendations, and others are being trained in their use (Moore, 2007). In this section, we describe what psychologists have learned about five system variables: (1) interviewing strategies, (2) instructions to eyewitnesses, (3) selection of filler photos, (4) lineup presentation methods, and (5) influence of feedback during a lineup.

Interviewing Eyewitnesses

Because police typically want more information from eyewitnesses than those witnesses can provide (Kebbell & Milne, 1998), police have asked psychologists to devise ways to enhance information gathering. The **cognitive interview**, an interviewing protocol based on various concepts of memory retrieval and social communication, was the result (Fisher & Geiselman, 1992). Before describing the cognitive interview, we describe a standard police interview so you can understand why a new method was needed.

A "standard" police interview relies on a predetermined set of questions with little opportunity for follow-up, an expectation that the witness will be willing and able to answer all of the questions, repeated interruptions, and time constraints. By contrast, in a cognitive interview, the interviewer first engages the witness in order to develop rapport, asks the witness to provide a narrative account of the event, and finally, probes for details with specific questions. The interviewer allows the witness to direct the subject matter and flow of the questioning, interrupts infrequently, and listens actively to the witness's responses.

Perhaps the most distinctive element of a cognitive interview (and the reason for its name) is its reliance on a set of cues developed from research on memory retrieval. Cognitive psychologists have observed that reinstating the context in which a witness encoded an event increases accessibility of information stored in memory. With this objective in mind, the interviewer may cue a witness to mentally reconstruct the physical and emotional experiences that existed at the time of the crime. The interviewer may direct the witness to form an image of the situation, recollect sights, sounds, smells, and physical conditions (e.g., heat, cold, darkness), and recall any emotional reactions experienced at the time. When the witness has mentally reconstructed the event, the interviewer asks for a detailed narrative and then uses follow-up questions to probe for specific information. Witnesses are sometimes asked to recall events in different temporal orders (e.g., describing the event from the end to the beginning), from different perspectives, or from the point of view of different people.

Studies of the effectiveness of the cognitive interview show that it can generate approximately 34% more detail than the traditional interview method (Kohnken, Milne, Memon, & Bull, 1999), though it can also produce more incorrect details. Personnel from organizations including the Federal Bureau of Investigation (FBI), Department of Homeland Security, National Transportation Safety Board, and some state and local police departments have been trained on cognitive interviewing procedures. However, many other agencies have been slow to adopt them (Fisher & Schreiber, 2007). As a result, psychologists have asked for more resources to train police officers in cognitive interviewing (Milne & Bull, 2006).

Lineup Instructions

There is ample evidence that when conducting a lineup, an investigator should instruct the witness that the offender may or may not be present (Malpass & Devine, 1981). Without this instruction, eyewitnesses may assume that their task is to pick someone, so they choose the person who looks most like the perpetrator. This instruction may be especially important for older eyewitnesses who are less likely to remember the instruction and less apt to make a correct identification (Rose, Rull, & Vrij, 2005). The vast majority of police officers report that they give eyewitnesses the option of not making a selection from the lineup (Wogalter, Malpass & McQuiston, 2004).

Based on her analysis of studies that examined the presence of a "might or might not be present" instruction, Psychology Professor Nancy Steblay found that this instruction reduced the rate of mistaken identifications (i.e., saying that the offender was present in the lineup when he was not) by 42% (Steblay, 1997). The rate of accurate identifications may be slightly harmed by the instruction but that decline is much smaller than the decline in mistaken identifications (Clark, 2005).

Selection of Fillers

Police departments differ in the care they give to creating lineups. To their credit, most police officers constructing a lineup try to have all members of this lineup look fairly similar (Wogalter et al., 2004). But others may place the suspect in a lineup of people who differ from that suspect in height, weight, physique, hair style, and other significant features mentioned in the witness's description of the offender.

If an innocent suspect fits the witness's description of the perpetrator and the fillers do not, then he or she can be easily picked out. For example, if the victim of a robbery recalled that the robber had acne and the lineup showed only one person (namely, the suspect) with acne, the victim can easily eliminate the fillers and settle on the suspect. Suspects can stand out from other people in the lineup in a number of different ways: They might be the only person in the lineup with a prominent facial feature; their pictures might be a different size than the others or use a different background; or the suspect might be shown in jail clothes whereas the fillers might appear in street clothes. The general recommendation for selecting fillers is to find people who generally match the witness's description and to take whatever additional steps are needed to ensure that the suspect does not stand out (Wells et al., 1998). Defense attorneys who suspect that their clients stand out from the fillers can now perform a do-it-yourself test on the fairness of a lineup. Online instructions are provided by Professor Roy Malpass from the Eyewitness Identification Research Laboratory at the University of Texas at El Paso (http://eyewitness.utep.edu/diy.html).

Lineup Presentation Method

In the traditional police lineup, all eyewitnesses see the suspect and the fillers simultaneously. (In a photographic lineup, six photos are typically arrayed on a single page. In a live lineup, the suspect and fillers are shown together, standing in a line.) This procedure is termed **simultaneous presentation**. An alternative procedure, now used occasionally, is to show suspects and fillers sequentially—one at a time

(Lindsay & Wells, 1985)—in a procedure called **sequential presentation**. The witness makes a decision about each lineup member before seeing the next lineup member.

The manner in which a lineup is presented can affect the accuracy of identification. Cutler and Penrod (1988) showed a one-minute videotape of a staged liquor store robbery and varied the way in which the lineup was constructed. When the six members of the lineup were shown simultaneously, witnesses falsely selected an innocent person 39% of the time. However, when suspects were shown sequentially, witnesses picked the wrong individual only 19% of the time.

A compilation of 25 studies that compared simultaneous and sequential presentation showed that the chances of mistaken identifications were reduced by nearly half when presentations were sequential (Steblay, Dysart, Fulero, & Lindsay, 2001). However, that good news comes with a trade-off: The identification of actual perpetrators is *also* reduced when lineups are shown sequentially. In general, sequential lineups result in fewer identification attempts, so both mistaken and accurate identifications are reduced (Meissner, Tredoux, Parker, & MacLin, 2005).

Psychologists now suspect that the effects of sequential lineup presentation may depend on how the lineup is constructed and presented (McQuiston-Surrett, Malpass, & Tredoux, 2006). Sequential presentation may be advantageous in situations in which the composition of the lineup is unfair—for example, when an innocent suspect matches the description of the perpetrator better than do any of the fillers. In a simultaneous presentation of this lineup, the innocent suspect will stand out and may be misidentified. This is less likely to occur when the same lineup is shown sequentially (Carlson, Gronlund, & Clark, 2008).

Why are there more mistaken identifications in a simultaneous lineup? In the simultaneous presentation of individuals in a lineup, eyewitnesses tend to identify the person who, in their opinion, looks most like the culprit *relative to* other members of the group. In other words, they make a **relative judgment**. As long as the perpetrator is in the lineup, the relative-judgment process works well. But what

happens when the actual culprit is not shown? The relative-judgment process may still yield a positive identification because someone in the group will always look *most* like the culprit (Wells et al., 1998).

Contrast this situation with a lineup in which the members are presented sequentially, one at a time. Here, the eyewitness compares each member in turn to his or her memory of the perpetrator and, on that basis, decides whether any person in the lineup is the individual who committed the crime. In other words, they make an **absolute judgment**. The value of sequential presentation is that it decreases the likelihood that an eyewitness will make a relative judgment in choosing someone from the lineup.

Psychology Professor Gary Wells cleverly demonstrated the use of relative-judgment processes in his "removal without replacement" study (Wells, 1993). In this procedure, all eyewitnesses watched a staged crime. Some were shown a photographic lineup that included the actual culprit and five fillers. Another group saw the same photographic lineup with one exception: The culprit's photo was removed and was not replaced with another photo. If identifications of the culprit by the culprit-present group are based solely on their recognition of him, then the percentage of people in that group who identified him *plus* the percentage who said "not there" should be exactly the same as the percentage in the culprit-absent group who said "not there." Wells tested this idea by showing 200 eyewitnesses to a staged crime either a culprit-present lineup or a lineup in which the culprit was absent but was not replaced by anyone else (see Table 5.1). When the culprit was present in the lineup, 54% of eyewitnesses selected him, and 21% said "not there." Did 75% of eyewitnesses in the "target-absent" lineup say "not there"? Unfortunately, no. The "not there" response was given by only 32% of people in that group; the others all mistakenly identified someone else from the lineup. Why? Through a process of relative judgment, eyewitnesses apparently select whoever looks most like the perpetrator. The weaker one's memory, the more likely one is to use a relative judgment in this situation (Clark & Davey, 2005).

T A B L E   5.1   **Rates of choosing lineup members when a culprit is present versus removed without replacement**

	Lineup Member						
	1	2	3 (culprit)	4	5	6	No Choice
Culprit present	3%	13%	54%	3%	3%	3%	21%
Culprit removed (without replacement)	6%	38%	—	12%	7%	5%	32%

SOURCE: "What do we know from witness identification?" from G. Wells. (1993). *American Psychologist, 48*, 553–571.

The Influence of Feedback

Recall our analogy between a criminal investigation and a scientific experiment. One of the cardinal rules of a good experiment is that the person conducting the experiment should not influence the results, a problem referred to as **experimenter bias**. To avoid such bias, experimenters should know little about the study's hypotheses and less about the experimental condition in which any participant is placed. Nearly all clinical drug trials adhere to these rules—neither the patient taking the pills nor the doctor assessing the patient's health know whether the pills are actually a new drug or a placebo. These so-called **double-blind testing procedures**, commonplace in medicine and other scientific fields, have gone largely unheeded in criminal investigations, although some jurisdictions have recently begun to adopt them (Moore, 2007).

The lineup is typically conducted by the detective who selected the fillers and knows which person is the suspect (Wogalter et al., 2004). Does the detective's knowledge of the suspect affect the eyewitness in any way? The answer, based on several recent studies, is yes. A lineup administrator's knowledge of the suspect can affect both the likelihood that an eyewitness will choose someone from the lineup (Phillips, McAuliff, Kovera, & Cutler, 1999) and the confidence that the eyewitness attaches to that choice (Semmler, Brewer, & Wells, 2004). Furthermore, eyewitnesses who have frequent contact with the administrator—either because they are in close physical contact or because they have extensive interactions—are likely to make decisions consistent with the

administrator's expectations (Haw & Fisher, 2004). An obvious solution to this situation is to have the lineup administered by someone who does not know which person in the lineup is the suspect.

Eyewitnesses sometimes express increased certainty in their identifications as a result of events that happen after they choose someone from the lineup. For example, if eyewitnesses receive confirming feedback from the lineup administrator ("Good, you identified the suspect"), this increases their certainty in their initial identifications, compared to eyewitnesses who received no such feedback (Neuschatz et al., 2007). This inflation of confidence is actually greater for eyewitnesses who are mistaken in their identifications than for eyewitnesses who are correct (Bradfield, Wells, & Olson, 2002). It occurs both in experiments and in archival studies of actual eyewitnesses to real crimes (Wright & Skagerberg, 2007). Remarkably, confirming feedback also bolsters eyewitnesses' retrospective reports concerning their certainty at the time of the identification, ease of making an identification, willingness to testify, and clarity of the image of the perpetrator (Douglass & Steblay, 2006).

Even *without* confirming feedback, eyewitnesses infer from the facts of an ongoing investigation and eventual prosecution that they must have picked the suspect from the lineup. Hence, their confidence increases. This enhanced confidence is troubling because of the repeated finding that the confidence expressed by eyewitnesses during their trial testimony is one of the most compelling reasons why jurors believe such identifications are accurate (Brewer & Burke, 2002). We would expect that the rape victim described in Box 5.2 was more confident of her identification of Larry Fuller at his trial than she was when viewing his photograph.

Witness confidence is a postdiction variable that correlates at some level with witness accuracy. But studies have shown that witness confidence is not a very strong predictor of whether the witness's identification is accurate (Sporer, Penrod, Read, & Cutler, 1995). Another problem with eyewitness's confidence is its apparent malleability: After making a false identification from a photographic lineup, witnesses who were told that another witness identified the same person became highly confident in their false identifications (Luus & Wells, 1994). Furthermore, when witnesses were questioned about a simulated crime scene, their rated confidence depended on whether they might be contradicted by a cowitness. Confidence increased when there was no chance of contradiction and decreased when there was (Shaw, Appio, Zerr, & Pontoski, 2007).

One result of feedback from the lineup administrator—whether it conveys to the witness that he or she picked the suspect or tells the witness that another person picked the same suspect—is a sense of false confidence. Can the development of false confidence be prevented? Asking witnesses to provide a statement of their degree of certainty *before* giving them any feedback can be an effective way to eliminate the problem of false confidence (Jones, Williams, & Brewer, 2008). This recommendation, along with suggestions to use unbiased instructions and similar-looking fillers, is included in the Justice Department guidelines.

defendant, 18% convicted him. But when an eyewitness's identification of the defendant was presented as well, 72% of the mock jurors convicted him. It is hard to overstate the power of confident eyewitnesses to convince a jury of the correctness of their testimony.

Jurors overestimate the accuracy of eyewitnesses because they appear to be unaware of several of the factors that compromise eyewitness accuracy. For example:

- Jurors have little awareness of estimator variables that interfere with accurate retention, such as weapon focus, unconscious transference, retention interval, and other-race bias (Benton, Ross, Bradshaw, Thomas, & Bradshaw, 2006).

- Jurors show a lack of sophistication about the problems inherent in typical lineups used by the police to test witness recognition (Benton et al., 2006).

- Jurors are usually not told about those eyewitnesses who could not identify a suspect; even the defendant's attorney may not be aware of these misses (Wells & Lindsay, 1980).

- Jurors pay attention to factors, including the confidence with which an eyewitness testifies, that may not help them distinguish accurate from inaccurate testimony. This creates a dangerous situation for an innocent defendant because it means that a confident eyewitness can be persuasive to jurors, even when he or she is wrong (Wells, Olson, & Charman, 2002).

THE EYEWITNESS IN THE COURTROOM

Despite limitations on the reliability of eyewitness identifications, jurors put a great deal of weight on testimony from an eyewitness. In a study showing this influence, Loftus (1974) gave subjects a description of an armed robbery that resulted in two deaths. Of mock jurors who heard a version of the case that contained only circumstantial evidence against the

SAFEGUARDS AGAINST MISTAKEN IDENTIFICATION

Are there remedies to jurors' overreliance on eyewitness identification? One possibility is that jurors could be informed about whether investigators followed the DOJ guidelines for conducting lineups. This would allow jurors to gauge whether the procedures and outcome warrant their trust. A mock jury study tested this idea (Lampinen, Judges, Odegard, &

Hamilton, 2005). Some jurors were informed that detectives violated DOJ guidelines and others were not so informed. Those who learned about guideline violations thought the prosecution's case was weaker and were less likely to convict the defendant, suggesting that failure to adhere to DOJ guidelines could discredit the prosecution.

Until the guidelines are consistently applied, some other mechanism should be available to educate jurors and judges about the problems inherent in eyewitness reports. We discuss two ways this might be done. One solution would allow psychologists who are knowledgeable about the relevant research on perception and memory to testify to juries about their findings. As a second remedy, judges could instruct juries about the potential weaknesses of eyewitness identifications and suggest how to interpret this testimony.

Expert Testimony

Psychologists occasionally testify about experimental research on eyewitness identification, typically on behalf of the defendant. Their testimony focuses on factors that influence eyewitness accuracy. For example, such testimony might indicate that (1) extreme stress tends to inhibit encoding, (2) feedback from a lineup administrator can increase an eyewitness's confidence, and (3) differences in the way lineups are constructed and presented to witnesses affect eyewitness accuracy. Note that the expert witness does not tell the jury what to believe about a particular eyewitness or whether the eyewitness is accurate. Rather, the expert's task is to provide the jury with a scientifically based frame of reference within which to evaluate the eyewitness's evidence.

In most states, the decision about whether an expert psychologist can testify is left to the presiding judge—an example of the breadth of discretion that the legal system grants to judges. Some judges are reluctant to let psychological experts testify. Some believe that such testimony is a matter of common sense, and therefore not helpful to jurors. Others fear that admitting expert testimony would open the gates to conflicting expert

testimony, setting the scene for a confusing and uninformative "battle of the experts." (Such battles are actually rare in cases involving eyewitnesses.) Finally, judges worry that this type of testimony might make jurors skeptical of *all* eyewitnesses, even those who witnessed a crime or accident under good viewing conditions and who were not subjected to suggestive identification procedures. But studies show that expert testimony sensitizes jurors to problems in witnessing and identification procedures and does not make them generally skeptical of all witnesses (e.g., Devenport, Stinson, Cutler, & Kravitz, 2002).

A report of one actual crime lends anecdotal support to the conclusion that the testimony of an expert witness has impact. Loftus (1984) described the trial of two Arizona brothers charged with the torture of three Mexicans. Two juries were in the courtroom at the same time, one deciding the verdict for Patrick Hanigan, the other deciding the fate of his brother, Thomas. Most of the evidence was from eyewitnesses, and it was virtually identical for the two defendants. However, expert testimony about the inaccuracy of eyewitnesses was introduced in Thomas's trial only. (The jury hearing Patrick Hanigan's case waited in the jury room while this evidence was presented.) Patrick Hanigan was convicted by one jury; his brother was acquitted by the other. This is as close to a "natural experiment" as the legal system has offered for assessing the influence of a psychologist in the courtroom. But unfortunately, even when allowed, expert testimony is an expensive safeguard that is available in only a small fraction of the cases that come to trial each year (Wells et al., 1998). Are there other, more readily available remedies?

Jury Instructions

Another option for alerting jurors to the limitations of eyewitnesses is through a jury instruction delivered by the judge at the end of a trial. The defense typically requests that such an instruction be given and the judge decides whether to grant the request.

What effects do cautionary instructions have on jurors' beliefs about eyewitness accuracy? One study compared the effectiveness of the so-called *Telfaire* instruction, a frequently used instruction based on the case of *United States v. Telfaire* (1972), and an instruction modeled after typical expert testimony regarding eyewitness reliability (Ramirez, Zemba, & Geiselman, 1996). The researchers were interested in the "sensitivity versus skepticism" concerns that we mentioned with regard to expert psychological testimony. The *Telfaire* instruction reduced mock jurors' sensitivity to eyewitness evidence, probably because that instruction mentions only vague directives and gives little indication how jurors should evaluate the evidence. However, an instruction that incorporated information likely to be delivered by an expert preserved jurors' sensitivity to the factors that influence eyewitness reliability.

Although appellate courts encourage trial judges to instruct jurors on the possible mistakes of eyewitnesses (*Neil v. Biggers*, 1972) and research suggests that instructions can be effective, some judges are reluctant to do so. Only about one-quarter of judges said they would give instructions on issues about which jurors lack knowledge (e.g., confidence malleability, lineup presentation format) (Wise & Safer, 2004). As a result, many jurors are not informed about the possibility of suggestive lineup procedures, the effects of stress on eyewitness memory, and a host of other factors that reduce the accuracy of eyewitness reports.

CHILDREN AS WITNESSES

Sometimes a child is the only witness to a crime—or its only victim. A number of questions arise in cases where children are witnesses. Can they remember the precise details of these incidents? Can suggestive interviewing techniques distort their reports? Is it appropriate for children to testify in a courtroom? Society's desire for criminals to be prosecuted and punished may require that children testify about their victimization, but defendants should not be convicted on the basis of inaccurate testimony. In this section we focus on the accuracy of children as witnesses, and on concerns about children testifying in court.

Children as Eyewitnesses to Crimes

Like adults, children are sometimes asked to identify strangers or to describe what they witnessed regarding crimes. In kidnappings and assaults, the child may be the only witness to a crime committed by a stranger. To test children's eyewitness capabilities, researchers create situations that closely match real-life events. In these studies, children typically interact with an unknown adult (the "target") for some period of time in a school classroom or a doctor's office. They are later questioned about what they experienced and what the target person looked like, and they may attempt to make an identification from a lineup.

Two general findings emerge from these studies. First, children over the age of 6 can make reasonably reliable identifications from lineups, provided that the perpetrator is actually in the lineup and the child had extended contact with the perpetrator (Gross & Hayne, 1996). Second, children are generally less accurate than adults when making an identification from a lineup in which the suspect is absent. In these situations, children tend to select someone—usually a foil—from the lineup, thereby making a "false-positive" error (Lindsay, Pozzulo, Craig, Lee, & Corber, 1997). Such mistakes are troubling to the police because they thwart the ongoing investigation.

Psychologists have attempted to devise identification procedures for children that will maintain identification accuracy when the suspect is in the lineup but reduce false-positive choices when the suspect is absent. Allowing children to practice on target-absent lineups (e.g., lineups that include the child's parents) can be helpful, as can instructions telling the child that it is acceptable to *not* choose anyone from a lineup (Cordon, Saetermoe, & Goodman, 2005).

Children as Victims of Child Sexual Abuse

The most likely reason for a child to become involved with the legal system is child sexual abuse (CSA). Here the issue is not who committed the crime. Rather, it involves what happened to the child. Most CSA cases rest solely on the words of the victim because these cases typically lack any physical evidence. (The most frequent forms of sexual abuse perpetrated on children are fondling, exhibitionism, and oral copulation.) Yet anyone who has spent time with young children knows that their descriptions of situations can sometimes be fanciful mixes of fact and fantasy. There are concerns about whether preschoolers and even older children can be trusted to provide accurate details and to disclose experiences of abuse. Developmental psychologists have investigated these issues over the past few decades, typically relying on staged events and interviews of the children who watched those events, or interviews with actual abuse victims.

One feature of CSA cases is crucial to the accuracy of child witnesses: the investigative interview. Good interviewers first ask a child to describe the events in his or her own words ("You said there was a man. Tell me about him.") Analysis of responses to these so-called **open-ended questions** suggests that many preschool children recall little, even when they just witnessed the event (Fivush & Shukat, 1995), either because they are shy or because they fail to understand the questions. Older children can provide more detail, of course, provided they are not asked about something that was ambiguous or confusing to them.

Some interviewers now use a structured questioning protocol that encourages children to first provide details in their own words and discourages the use of **suggestive questions** (questions that assume information not disclosed by the child or that suggest the expected answer, such as "He touched you, didn't he?"). Police officers trained in this protocol interviewed 4- to 8-year-old children who claimed that they had been abused. Most children (83%) freely disclosed their experiences in response to open-ended questions (Lamb et al., 2003). These findings suggest that central details (the "gist") of experiences can be remembered well if they are elicited by open-ended questions.

After a child has recounted an experience in his or her own words and in response to open-ended questions, investigators may ask specific questions about the event. For example, if a child said that she was touched, a follow-up question might be "Where were you touched?" Although children tend to provide more detail in response to specific questions than to open-ended questions, the use of specific questions comes at a cost: Children are less accurate in answering specific questions. This difficulty is not restricted to very young children. After seeing a stranger in their classroom handing out candy the previous week, two groups of children (4- to 5-year-olds, and 7- to 8-year-olds) were asked specific, misleading questions (e.g., "He took your clothes off, didn't he?"). Older children were just as likely as younger children to assent to these suggestions (Finnila, Mahlberga, Santtilaa, Sandnabbaa, & Niemib, 2003).

Children are less accurate in answering specific questions than more general queries because specific questions demand precise memories of events that the child may never have encoded or may have forgotten (Dickinson, Poole, & Laimon, 2005). Additionally, the child may answer a question that she or he does not fully understand in order to appear to be cooperative (Waterman, Blades, & Spencer, 2001). Finally, the more specific the question, the more likely it is that the interviewer will accidentally include information that the child has not stated.

A sizeable number of children experience multiple incidents of sexual abuse, and although the central features of the experiences may be constant, peripheral details may change. But before prosecutors can file multiple charges, they must provide evidence that reflects the critical details of each separate incident. In other words, the child has to "particularize" his or her report by providing precise details about each specific allegation (Dickinson et al., 2005). Can a child do this? Studies that examine children's recall of repeated events typically expose them to a series of similar incidents with certain constant features and some details that vary across episodes. Although source-monitoring (identifying the source of a memory) improves with age (Quas & Schaaf, 2002), children often recall information from one event as having occurred in another (Roberts, 2002). In fact, exposure to

---

B o x 5.3   THE CASE OF MARGARET KELLY MICHAELS: REAL OR SURREAL MEMORIES?

In the spring of 1985, while having his temperature taken rectally at a doctor's office, a 4-year-old student at the Wee Care Nursery School in Maplewood, New Jersey told the nurse, "That's what my teacher does to me at school." That afternoon, the boy's mother notified child protective services. Two days later, during questioning by a prosecutor, the boy inserted his finger into the rectum of an anatomical doll (a tool used by professionals to help reluctant children enact sexual acts that were allegedly perpetrated on them) and stated that other boys also had their temperatures taken this way by their teacher, Margaret Kelly Michaels.

The Wee Care Nursery distributed a letter to all parents, alerting them to the investigation and encouraging them to examine their children for genital soreness. Various therapists and investigators interviewed the children and their families over the next two months. Many of the children were interviewed several times and, after persistent questioning, began to disclose some bizarre and horrifying details: that Michaels had licked peanut butter off their genitals, made

Margaret Kelly Michaels

children drink her urine and eat her feces, and raped children with knives, forks, spoons, and Lego blocks. Although the acts had not been reported by the children or noticed by other staff at the time they were alleged to have occurred, Michaels was convicted of 115 counts of sexual abuse against 20 children and was sentenced to 47 years in prison. She served 5 years of her sentence before her conviction was reversed on grounds that the interrogations of the children were coercive and highly suggestive (State v. Michaels, 1994).

---

recurring events is a double-edged sword: Repetition enhances memory for aspects of the incident that are held constant but impairs the ability to recall details that vary with each recurrence (Dickinson et al., 2005).

The Effects of Suggestive Questioning

In some cases, children may be reluctant to disclose abusive experiences and may even deny them when asked. Some people believe that suggestive questions are needed to elicit reports or details from sexually abused children who feel embarrassed, ashamed, or guilty about the abuse and hesitate to talk about it. But questioning in a suggestive manner sometimes elicits false reports. In fact, many people have speculated that suggestive questioning led to the notorious allegations of bizarre and ritualistic abuse in day care centers across the United States in the 1980s, including the McMartin Preschool in California, Little Rascals Day Care Center in North Carolina, and Wee Care Day Nursery in New Jersey (see Box 5.3).

Suggestive questions introduce new information that the child has not already provided. Consider the following exchange between an investigator in the *Michaels* case and R.F., a 3-year-old girl:

Detective: Do you think Kelly can hurt you?

  R.F.: No.

Detective: Did Kelly say she can hurt you? Did Kelly ever tell you she can turn into a monster?

  R.F.: Yes.

Detective: What did she tell you?

  R.F.: She was gonna turn into a monster.

Psychologists have known for many years that suggestive questions reduce children's accuracy. Children questioned in a suggestive manner have been led to remember events they did *not* experience—for example, getting their finger caught in a mousetrap (Ceci, Huffman, Smith, & Loftus, 1994) and seeing a thief steal food from a day care center (Bruck, Ceci, & Hembrooke, 2002).

One factor that characterizes suggestive interviewing is **interviewer bias**. When interviewers have some preconceived notions about a certain event, they can ask questions that elicit responses that are consistent with their beliefs. Biased interviewers would probably not ask children open-ended questions such as "What happened?" Rather, they would use suggestive questions that presuppose the answer. Consider this example from the Michaels case: "How do you think she hurt boys and girls, with a fork?" If the child does not immediately provide the desired answer, the question will be repeated until that answer is given (Bruck et al., 2002).

Social influence can also play a role in these interviews. Regardless of the nature of the questions, the manner in which they are asked can matter. Some interviewers may be warm and supportive; others may be hostile and intimidating. Children interviewed by a highly supportive interviewer may be more resistant to suggestive questions (Davis & Bottoms, 2002), perhaps because supportive interviewers reduce children's anxiety, improving their memory (Almerigogna, Ost, Jull, & Akehurst, 2007). But highly supportive interviewers can lose their impartiality if they selectively reinforce statements that are consistent with their beliefs and ignore statements that are inconsistent. This can happen when the interviewer gives praise, rewards, or approval to a child who says something desirable or expresses disappointment when a child says something that is undesirable.

Professor Maggie Bruck and her colleagues (Bruck, Ceci, & Hembrooke, 1998) discovered that interviewers really do reward children who provide the desired answer and punish those who don't. They analyzed interview transcripts provided by attorneys, judges, parents, and medical and mental health professionals who had concerns about the suggestive nature of a particular interview. Although Bruck and colleagues (Bruck et al., 1998) acknowledged that their sample may not be representative of the vast number of interviews conducted with children, their conclusion is still troubling. A **content analysis** (a careful, sometimes painstaking analysis of the content of a discussion or conversation) of 20 interviews from the *Michaels* case as well as other

cases involving alleged CSA showed that the interviews included several suggestive procedures (Wood et al., 1998).

Is Suggestive Questioning Necessary?

Are such heavy-handed tactics necessary? How likely are children to disclose sexual abuse without them? Professor Kamala London and her colleagues identified adults with documented histories of CSA and learned that only 33% had disclosed the abuse during their childhood (London, Bruck, Ceci, & Shuman, 2005). This means two things: (1) The majority of children fail to disclose their abuse when they are young, and (2) reported cases of CSA are the tip of a large iceberg (Ceci, Kulkofsky, Klemfuss, Sweeney, & Bruck, 2007).

But this study also showed that when asked directly about being abused, the vast majority of participants neither denied it nor recanted their stories. In fact, children can remember significant details of abuse experiences and, if asked directly, can describe them accurately. For example, developmental psychologists contacted approximately 200 adolescents and young adults who, during the 1980s, had been involved in a study of the effects of criminal prosecutions on victims of CSA. Participants had been 3 to 17 years old at the time of the original data collection (Alexander et al., 2005). All of them had been sexually abused. Upon renewing contact years later, psychologists provided a list of traumatic events (including CSA) and asked respondents to indicate which events happened to them and, among those events, which was the most traumatic. Respondents who designated CSA as their most traumatic experience were remarkably accurate in reporting details of their experiences. These data suggest that memory for emotional, even traumatic, victimization experiences can be retained quite well even decades after the events occurred.

Let's return to the question of whether suggestive questioning is necessary to elicit reports from children who may be too frightened or ashamed to disclose their victimization. We now know that most children will reveal abuse experiences if asked in an open-ended manner (e.g., "Tell me what happened." "You said it happened at the store. Tell me about the store.") (Lamb et al., 2003). Children probably do not need to be bombarded with suggestive questions to talk about their experiences of victimization because most of them will disclose when asked directly (Ceci et al., 2007).

The Child Witness in the Courtroom

Though only a small percentage of CSA cases result in a trial (many more end in admissions of guilt or plea bargains), tens of thousands of children, often preschoolers, must testify in sexual abuse trials each year. In one study, although only 18% of all CSA cases involved children 5 years old or younger, 41% of the cases that went to trial involved children of this age (Gray, 1993). Two questions arise: What is the effect on the child of having to discuss these issues in court, and how do jurors weigh the testimony of a child witness?

Talking about victimization in a public setting may increase the trauma for many children. Professor Gail Goodman and her colleagues examined the short- and long-term outcomes for children who testified in CSA cases, initially interviewing a group of 218 CSA victims when their cases were referred for prosecution (Goodman et al., 1992) and reinterviewing many of them 12 years later (Quas et al., 2005). The experience of testifying was quite traumatic for some children. They had nightmares, vomited on the day of their appearance in court, and were relieved that the defendant had not tried to kill them (Goodman et al., 1992). Twelve years later, when compared to a group of individuals with no CSA history, CSA victims who had been involved in criminal cases showed some long-term negative consequences. Most affected psychologically were those who were young when the case started, those who testified repeatedly, and those who opted not to testify when the perpetrator received a light sentence.

How do jurors perceive child witnesses? Do they tend to doubt the truthfulness of children's testimony, reasoning that children often make things up and leave things out? Or do they tend to "believe the children," as a popular bumper

sticker would like us to do? In mock jury studies, child eyewitnesses are generally viewed as less credible than adult eyewitnesses (Goodman, Golding, Helgeson, Haith, & Michelli, 1987). But something quite different happens in CSA cases. Here, younger victims are viewed as *more* credible than adolescents or adults, probably because jurors suspect that younger children lack the sexual knowledge to fabricate an allegation (Bottoms & Goodman, 1994). Jurors are also beginning to recognize the effects of suggestive questioning; mock jurors who read a transcript of a highly suggestive forensic interview tended to discount the child's testimony (Castelli, Goodman, & Ghetti, 2005).

Procedural Modifications When Children Are Witnesses

Judges allow various courtroom modifications to protect children from the potential stress of testifying. One innovation is the placement of a screen in front of the defendant so the child witness cannot see him or her while testifying. This arrangement was used in the trial of John Avery Coy, who was convicted of sexually assaulting two 13-year-old girls. Coy appealed his conviction on the grounds that the screen deprived him of the opportunity to confront the girls face-to-face, a reference to the **confrontation clause** of the Sixth Amendment that guarantees defendants the right to confront their accusers. The right to confrontation is based on the assumption that the witness will find it more difficult to lie in the presence of the defendant. In a 1988 decision, the Supreme Court agreed with Coy, saying that his right to confront his accusers face-to-face was not outweighed "by the necessity of protecting the victims of sexual abuse" (*Coy v. Iowa*, 1988).

But just two years later, in the case of *Maryland v. Craig* (1990), the Court upheld a law permitting a child to give testimony in a different part of the courthouse and have the testimony transmitted to the courtroom via close-circuit TV (CCTV). The law applied to cases where the child was likely to suffer significant emotional distress by being in the presence of the defendant. *Craig* thus modified the rule of the *Coy* case.

Proponents of CCTV claim that in addition to reducing the trauma experienced by a child, this technology will also provide more complete and accurate reports. Opponents claim that the use of CCTV violates the defendant's right to face-to-face confrontation of witnesses. Professor Gail Goodman and her colleagues conducted an elaborate study to test these ideas (Goodman et al., 1998). Each child in this study individually played with an unfamiliar male confederate. In the "defendant guilty" condition, the confederate helped the children place stickers on bare skin (e.g., the children's arm, toes, belly button). In the "defendant not guilty" condition, the confederate helped the children place stickers on their clothes. Each child then testified in a separate mock trial held in a courtroom. The child's testimony was presented either live in open court or via CCTV. Mock jurors viewed the trials, rated the child witness and the defendant, and deliberated to a verdict.

The use of CCTV generally promoted more accurate testimony by children. On the basis of these findings, one might argue for its use in every case in which a child feels anxious about testifying. But things aren't quite so simple. Children who testified via CCTV were viewed as less believable than children who testified in open court, despite the fact that they were more accurate. It appears that jurors want to see children in person in order to assess the truthfulness of their reports. Clearly, the impact of CCTV on jurors' decisions in CSA cases is complex. Perhaps it should be reserved for cases in which the prospect of testifying is so terrifying to children that they would otherwise become inept witnesses—or would not testify at all.

Judges make other accommodations in cases in which children must testify. Some provide an advocate who can familiarize the child with the courtroom setting, others permit a support person to sit with the child during testimony, and still others make structural changes to the courtroom (Myers, 1996).

Finally, we should note that although testifying has the potential to inflict further trauma on the child, it can be a therapeutic experience for some children. It can engender a sense of control over events, and if the defendant is convicted, provide some satisfaction to the child. One 15-year-old girl

said, "If I, as a young person, were a victim of a sexual abuse or rape case, I would *want* to testify before a full court. I might be scared at first or a little embarrassed, but I'd want to be present to make my assailant look like a complete fool. I'd want to see him convicted—with my own eyes. It would make me stronger" (quoted in Gunter, 1985, p. 12A).

REPRESSED AND RECOVERED MEMORIES

Retrieving memories over short time periods, as eyewitnesses must do, is a complex task. Yet it pales in comparison with retrieving memories that have been stored over lengthy intervals. Two basic processes need to be distinguished in understanding long-lost memories. The first is natural forgetting, which tends to occur when people simply do not think about events that happened years earlier. Just as you might have trouble remembering the name of your fourth-grade teacher, witnesses to crimes, accidents, and business transactions are likely to forget the details of these events, if not the entire event, after the passage of months or years. Such forgetting or misremembering is even more likely when the event is confused with prior or subsequent experiences that bear some resemblance to it. No one disputes the reality of natural forgetting.

Significantly more controversial is a second type of lost "memory"—the memories that are presumed to have been repressed over long time periods. This process involves events that are thought to be so traumatizing that individuals bury them deeply in their unconscious mind through a process of emotionally motivated forgetting called **repression**. For example, soldiers exposed to the brutal horrors of combat and individuals who experienced a natural disaster such as an earthquake are sometimes unable to remember the traumas they obviously suffered. In such cases, repression is thought to serve a protective function by sparing the individual from having to remember and relive horrifying scenes. These repressed memories sometimes stay unconscious, and hence forgotten, unless and until they are spontaneously

---

B o x 5.4   THE CASE OF FATHER PAUL SHANLEY AND HIS ACCUSER'S RECOVERED MEMORIES

On February 11, 2002, Paul Busa received a phone call from his girlfriend, telling him of a newspaper article that described accusations of CSA against Father Paul Shanley, a controversial and charismatic Roman Catholic priest. With this prompting, Busa began to recall his own abuse at the hands of Father Shanley two decades earlier, memories that had apparently been repressed for years. The accuser then began to speak openly about his abuse and agreed to testify in the criminal case against the former priest. Father Shanley, 74 at the time of the trial, was accused of pulling Busa out of Sunday school classes and orally and digitally raping him.

At the trial, the alleged victim, a barrel-chested Massachusetts firefighter, gave emotional—even teary—testimony about the multiple incidents of abuse in the church bathroom, pews, rectory, and even the confession booth. Busa testified that he was so traumatized by the memories that surfaced years later that he was unable to continue to function at his job. Despite some inconsistencies in his recollections and testimony from a defense expert witness who explained how false memories can be created in susceptible minds, the jury was apparently convinced by Busa's seemingly heartfelt testimony. They convicted

Father Paul Shanley being taken into custody shortly after his conviction on charges of raping an alter boy years before.

Father Shanley on two counts of rape and two counts of indecent assault on a child. He was sentenced to 12 to 15 years in prison though in 2009 the Massachusetts Supreme Judicial Court agreed to consider Shanley's argument that the recovered memory evidence should not have been admitted into evidence.

---

recalled or retriggered by exposure to some aspect of the original experience. (The smell of gasoline might remind a soldier of the battlefield, or the sight of an unusual cloud formation might remind an earthquake victim of the sky's appearance on the day of the disaster.) But the notion of repression is highly controversial; some suggest that repression has never been proven to exist and that the inability to remember traumatic effects can be explained by ordinary forgetting.

A related unconscious process is **dissociation**, in which victims of abuse or other traumas are thought to escape the full impact of an experience by psychologically detaching themselves from it. This process is thought to be particularly strong in children, who, because they are still forming integrated personalities, find it easier to escape from the pain of abuse by fantasizing about made-up individuals and imagining that the abuse is happening to those others. Many clinical psychologists believe that such early episodes of dissociation, involving unique ideas, feelings, and

behavior, form the beginning of the altered personalities that are found in dissociative identity disorder (formerly called multiple personality disorder).

Repressed Memories and Memory Recovery Therapy

Most of the reports of repressed and recovered memories involve claims of CSA. The theory is that individuals (1) suffered sexual/physical abuse as children, often at the hands of parents or other trusted adults, (2) repressed or dissociated any memory of these horrors for many years as a form of unconscious protection, and (3) eventually recovered their long-lost memories of the abuse. Some of the allegations of priest abuse that came to light and plagued the Roman Catholic Church in the 1990s and early 2000s, including the case of Father Paul Shanley, followed this pattern (Box 5.4).

One of the most widely cited studies on this topic suggests that it may be possible for people to forget horrible events that happened to them in childhood. Linda Williams (1994) interviewed 129 women who had experienced well-documented cases of CSA. She asked detailed questions about the abuse experiences that occurred an average of 17 years earlier. More than one-third of the women did not report the abuse they had experienced in childhood. Of course, this does not prove that the forgetting was due to repression. It is possible that when the abuse occurred, the women were too young to be fully aware of it; in addition, some of the women might have been unwilling to report sexual abuse to an interviewer, who was a relative stranger, even if they did remember it.

Sometimes, repressed memories are recovered only after a person participates in "memory-focused" psychotherapy that applies techniques such as hypnosis, age regression, sodium amytal ("truth serum"), guided visualization, diary writing, or therapist instructions to help clients remember past abuse (Lindsay & Read, 1995). Such "derepression" techniques have been advocated by popular books on incest (e.g., *The Courage to Heal* by Ellen Bass and Laura Davis, now in its 20th anniversary fourth edition) and by therapists who believe that unless severe childhood traumas are recalled, confronted, and defused, they will cause mental problems (Blume, 1990). Some therapists suspect clients of harboring repressed memories of abuse and ask the clients highly suggestive questions, such as, "You show many of the signs of childhood sexual abuse; can you tell me some of the things you think might have happened to you when you were a very young child?"

Many researchers and therapists question the validity of memories that resurface years after the alleged incidents and then only after the individual has been in therapy (Gerry, Garry, & Loftus, 2005). (These professionals are not denying the reality of CSA, of course. Not only does it occur, but it is a very serious problem both in the United States and throughout the world. It appears that children who were abused are at increased risk to suffer mental disorders in adulthood.) The real question is whether allegations of child abuse that first surface only after searching for them in therapy are trustworthy (Bottoms, Shaver, & Goodman, 1996). In a clever study designed to compare memories of abuse recovered in therapy to memories recovered outside of therapy and memories never forgotten, Professor Elke Geraerts and her colleagues sought independent corroboration of the abuse from other people who were abused by the same perpetrator, individuals who learned of the abuse soon after it occurred, or from perpetrators themselves. They were able to corroborate 45% of the abuse memories that had never been forgotten, 37% of the memories that were recalled out of therapy, but 0% of the memories that were recalled in therapy (Geraerts et al., 2007).

Those who question the validity of repressed memories also point out that most people who suffer severe trauma do not forget the event; in fact, many of them suffer intrusive recollections of it for years afterward. Skepticism is further fueled by the fact that some alleged victims claim to have recalled traumas that happened when they were less than 1 year old. Yet nearly all research on childhood memory and amnesia shows this is not possible, for reasons related to neurological development.

So what should we make of the sudden recall of events that a person claims to have repressed for years? Do recollections of past abuse stem from actual traumatic events, or are they false memories? If they are false, from where did they originate? Even psychologists are deeply divided on these questions. In fact, the Working Group on Investigation of Memories of Childhood Abuse, appointed by the American Psychological Association, was so deeply divided that the group was forced to issue two reports. One report, written by clinical psychologists (Alpert, Brown, & Courtois, 1998), suggests that intolerable emotional and physical arousal can lead a child victim to use dissociative coping strategies and that these strategies may interfere with or impair encoding, storage, and retrieval of memories. A second report, authored by experimental research psychologists (Ornstein, Ceci, & Loftus, 1998), points out that suggestive and misleading information can degrade memory, that memory for traumatic experiences can be highly malleable, and that it is relatively easy to create false memories for events that never occurred.

Can we be sure that alleged abuses took place? Is it possible that some memories, especially those that appear to have been repressed for years and then re-covered through aggressive "memory work" therapy, are imagined or made up? Although it is difficult to assess the authenticity of any individual's memories, evidence is accumulating that false memories can be implanted and that people can be led through sug-gestion and misinformation to believe such memories are real.

Creating False Memories

During the 2008 presidential campaign, Senator Hillary Clinton described the harrowing experience of landing in war-torn Bosnia under sniper fire in 1996, and running on an airport tarmac with her head down to get to a waiting vehicle. But photo-graphs and video of her arrival showed a very dif-ferent reality: Clinton greeting smiling Bosnian officials and being kissed by an 8-year-old girl. To what should we attribute Clinton's "memory"? Was this an intentional fabrication to bolster her image as someone who has undertaken dangerous missions? Or was it a genuinely false memory? In recent years, many psychologists have used labora-tory research and real-life cases to document how false memories can be created. There is now general agreement that given the right set of circumstances, people can create memories of incidents that never occurred.

One way that psychologists have been able to implant false memories is by enlisting the help of family members, who suggest to adult research par-ticipants that these relatives recall a fabricated event. In a now-classic study, Loftus and Pickrell (1995), with help from participants' relatives, constructed a false story that the participant had been lost during a shopping trip at the age of 5, was found crying by an elderly person, and was eventually reunited with

family members. After reading this story, partici-pants wrote what they remembered about the event. Nearly 30% of participants either partially or fully remembered the made-up event, and 25% claimed in subsequent interviews that they remem-bered the fictitious situation.

Psychologists have used other experimental procedures to examine the malleable nature of **au-tobiographical memory** (memory for one's past experiences). These include interpreting partici-pants' dreams to suggest that they had experienced a critical childhood event such as being harassed by a bully before the age of 3 (Mazzoni, Loftus, Seitz, & Lynn, 1999) and doctoring family photo-graphs by inserting childhood portraits to portray events such as hot-air balloon rides that never took place (Wade, Garry, Read, & Lindsay, 2002). Merely viewing a photo associated with a fabri-cated event can dramatically increase the rate of false memories. In one study, researchers provided false suggestions to adults about various school-related pranks (for example, putting Slime on a teacher's desk in Grade 1 or 2). Some participants viewed group class photos from that time and others did not. The rate of false memory reports was substantially higher among participants who viewed the photographs (Lindsay, Hagen, Read, Wade, & Garry, 2004). This is concerning because some memory-focused therapists recommend that adults who think they have been abused should view family photo albums to cue long-forgotten memories of abuse.

Simply imagining an event from one's past can also affect the belief that it actually occurred, even when the event is completely implausible—for example, proposing marriage to a Pepsi machine (Seamon, Philbin, & Harrison, 2006) or shaking hands with Bugs Bunny at a Disney theme park (Braun, Ellis, & Loftus, 2002). (The Bugs Bunny character was created by Warner Brothers, not Disney.)

How can we account for this "imagination in-flation" effect? One possibility is **source confusion**.

B o x 5.5   THE CASE OF GARY RAMONA, HIS DAUGHTER'S FALSE MEMORIES, AND THE THERA-PISTS WHO SUGGESTED THEM

The first parent who successfully sued a therapist for im-planting a false memory of abuse was Gary Ramona, a winery executive from Napa County, California. Ramona accused a family counselor and a psychiatrist of planting false memories in his 19-year-old daughter, Holly, when she was their patient. Ramona claimed that the thera-pists told Holly that her bulimia and depression were caused by having been repeatedly raped by her father when she was a child. According to Ramona, the psychi-atrist gave Holly sodium amytal to confirm the validity of her "recovered memory."

At their trial, the therapists claimed that Holly suffered flashbacks of what seemed to be real sexual abuse. She also became increasingly depressed and bulimic after reporting these frightening images. But the scientific experts who testified on Ramona's be-half criticized the therapists for using risky and dan-gerous techniques including suggestive questioning and sodium amytal. The jury decided that Holly's therapists had indeed acted improperly and awarded Gary Ramona damages in the amount of $500,000. In the words of his attorney, "If [therapists] use nonsensical theories about so-called repressed memo-ries to destroy people's lives, they will be held accountable."

The act of imagining may make the event seem more familiar, but that familiarity is mistakenly re-lated to childhood memories rather than to the act of imagination itself. The creation of false memo-ries is most likely to occur when people who are having trouble remembering are explicitly encour-aged to imagine events and discouraged from thinking about whether their constructions are real. But keep in mind that even though false childhood memories can be implanted in some people, the memories that result from suggestions are not always false. Unfortunately, without cor-roboration, it is very hard to know which distant memories are true and which were implanted via suggestion.

False Memories in Court

Evidence that false memories are a significant problem for the law comes in several forms. First, accusations that arise from recovered "memories" sometimes result in litigation. Because the ac-cused are often related to the victims, other fam-ily members may be forced to take sides, causing strain and animosity within a family. Second,

some accusers have retracted their claims of re-pressed memories for abuse. One of the most highly publicized retractions involved another case of al-leged priest abuse, this time against Cardinal Joseph Bernardin who was once the senior-ranking Roman Catholic official in the United States. Ironically, Bernardin was well known for his work helping children who had been sexually abused by priests. His accuser ultimately dropped the lawsuit after admitting that his charges were based on false memories.

More recently, parents have sued therapists who used aggressive memory recovery techniques to help the adult children of these parents recover supposedly repressed memories of CSA. The claims in these malpractice lawsuits usually take the following form: (1) The abuse never occurred, (2) therapists created and implanted false memo-ries of abuse through their uncritical use of mem-ory retrieval techniques, and (3) clients ultimately came to believe the false memories and accused their parents of the abuse. These cases have some-times resulted in large financial settlements to those who were falsely accused, including Gary Ramona (see Box 5.5).

SUMMARY

1. ***What psychological factors contribute to the risk of mistaken identifications in the legal system?*** Evidence produced by eyewitnesses often makes the difference between an unsolved crime and a conviction. In the early stages of a crime investigation, eyewitness accounts can provide important clues and permit suspects to be identified. But witnesses often make mistakes, and mistaken identifications have led to the conviction of numerous innocent people. Errors can occur at the moment the crime is committed or at any of the three phases of the memory process: encoding, storage, and retrieval. Furthermore, subsequent questioning and new experiences can alter what is remembered from the past. In describing the factors that affect the reliability of eyewitness memory, psychologists assess (1) estimator variables whose impact on an identification can only be estimated and not controlled, (2) system variables that are under the control of the justice system, and (3) postdiction variables that correlate with the accuracy of an identification. Much recent research has focused on a particular set of system variables related to the way lineups are conducted.

2. ***How do jurors evaluate the testimony of eyewitnesses, and can psychologists help jurors understand the potential problems of eyewitness testimony?*** Jurors are heavily influenced by the testimony of eyewitnesses, and they tend to overestimate the accuracy of such witnesses, relying to a great extent on the confidence of the eyewitness. To alert jurors to these problems, two types of special interventions have been tried. Some trial judges permit psychologists to testify as expert witnesses about the problems inherent in eyewitness memory. Laboratory evaluations of mock juries find that such testimony generally sensitizes jurors to factors that affect an eyewitness's reliability. The other intervention is for the judge to give the jurors a "cautionary instruction," sensitizing them to aspects of the testimony of eyewitnesses that they should consider.

3. ***Can children accurately report on their experiences of victimization? What factors affect the accuracy of their reports?*** Suggestive interviewing techniques can influence the accuracy of a child's report of abuse. When children are questioned in a nonsuggestive manner and are asked open-ended questions, the resulting report will be more accurate than when suggestive interrogation procedures are used.

4. ***Can memories for trauma be repressed, and if so, can these memories be recovered accurately?*** Memories of trauma are sometimes repressed and later recalled. But the accuracy of repressed and then recovered memories is suspect when the recollections occur in the context of therapies that use suggestive memory retrieval techniques. Recent research shows that people can "remember" events that never happened, sometimes simply by imagining them. Litigation involving the recovery of repressed memories involves lawsuits brought by victims claiming that therapists led them to believe that they were abused in the past and lawsuits brought by the accused claiming that therapists promoting such false recollections are guilty of malpractice.

KEY TERMS

absolute judgment	autobiographical memory	cognitive interview	confrontation clause
archival analysis		confirmation bias	content analysis

dissociation

double-blind testing procedures

ecological validity

encoding

estimator variable

experimental methodology

experimenter bias

ground truth

in-group/out-group differences

interviewer bias

open-ended questions

other-race effect

photographic lineup

photospread

physiognomic variability

postdiction variable

postevent information

relative judgment

repression

retention interval

retrieval

sequential presentation

simultaneous presentation

social influence

source confusion

storage

suggestive questions

system variable

unconscious transference

weapon focus effect

6

Evaluating Criminal Suspects

ORIENTING QUESTIONS

1. What are some psychological investigative techniques used by the police?
2. What is criminal profiling?

3. What cues do people use to detect deception and how accurate are these judgments?

4. Is the polygraph a valid instrument for lie detection? What are some problems associated with it?

5. What brain-based techniques are used to detect deception and how well do they work?

6. How valid is confession evidence? What kinds of interrogation procedures can lead to false confessions?

7. What are some of the reforms proposed to prevent false confessions?

In Chapter 5, we discussed psychological findings on the accuracy of eyewitness reports and claims of repressed memory. In this chapter, we discuss three other activities in which psychology can assist law enforcement: profiling criminal suspects, assessing the truthfulness of suspects, and evaluating the validity of their confessions. The common thread that ties these topics together is the assumption that psychological theory and techniques can be used to improve police officers' evaluations of criminal suspects.

These contributions occur in a logical sequence. Psychological profiling is usually performed at the beginning of a criminal investigation when the police need help focusing on certain types of people who might be the most likely suspects.

Once suspects have been identified, law enforcement officials use other procedures to determine whether any of them should be charged. While questioning suspects, police rely on various visual and verbal cues to determine whether they are giving truthful responses. But as you will learn, people are not especially adept at detecting deception by relying on these kinds of cues.

Suspects are sometimes given so-called lie detection (or polygraph) tests to provide more information about their guilt or innocence and, sometimes, to encourage them to confess. However, assumptions about the effectiveness of polygraph procedures conflict with some psychological findings about their accuracy. Though results of a lie detection test are sometimes admitted into evidence, many psychologists question the objectivity of the procedure as it is

usually administered and, hence, the validity of its results.

Increasingly, law enforcement agents and industry personnel are using brain-based technologies, including neuroimaging and brain-wave measurements, to detect deception. Although promising, these techniques have not yet been subjected to the kind of rigorous, real-world testing that is required before they become commonplace investigatory tools.

The police interrogate suspects and encourage them to confess because confessions make it more likely that suspects will be successfully prosecuted and eventually convicted. But in the quest for conviction, confessions can be coerced. Courts have tried to clarify when a confession is truly voluntary but psychological findings often conflict with the courts' evaluations of confessions—again reflecting the final dilemma described in Chapter 1.

Thus, a consistent theme throughout this chapter is the conflict between the legal system and psychological science regarding ways of gaining knowledge and evaluating truth. A related conflict is subordination of the goal of truth to the desire to resolve conflict.

PROFILING OF CRIMINAL SUSPECTS

Do criminals commit their crimes or choose their victims in distinctive ways that leave clues to their psychological makeup, much as fingerprints point to their physical identity or ballistics tests reveal the kind of gun they used? There is some evidence that psychological characteristics are linked to behavioral patterns and that these links can be detected by a psychological analysis of crime scenes. Behavioral scientists and police use **criminal profiling** to narrow criminal investigations to suspects who possess certain behavioral and personality features that were revealed by the way the crime was committed. (Another way to think about profiling is that it involves the attempt to "reverse engineer" a final product—the crime scene—in the attempt to gain leads about the individual(s) who created that final product.)

Profiling, which has also been called "criminal investigative analysis," does not identify a specific suspect. Instead, profilers offer a general psychological description of the most likely type of suspect, including personality and behavioral characteristics suggested by a thorough analysis of the crimes committed, so that the police can concentrate their investigation of difficult cases in the most profitable directions. (Profiles also help investigators search for persons who fit descriptions known to characterize hijackers, drug couriers, and undocumented aliens; Monahan & Walker, 2005.) The results of a careful profile may provide specific information about suspects, including psychopathology, characteristics of their family history, educational and legal history, and habits and social interests (Woodworth & Porter, 2000). Although profiling can be used in diverse contexts, it is considered most helpful in crimes in which the offender has demonstrated some form of repetitive behavior with unusual aspects, such as sadistic torture, ritualistic or bizarre behavior, evisceration, or staging or acting out a fantasy (Woodworth & Porter, 2000).

A successful profiler should possess several key attributes, including both an understanding of human psychology and investigative experience (Hazelwood, Ressler, Depue, & Douglas, 1995). There is some controversy regarding who should be considered a successful profiler. Because of the importance of investigative experience in criminal profiling, some have suggested that mental health professionals may not be fully qualified to engage in profiling (Hazelwood et al., 1995; see also Hazelwood & Michaund, 2001). Others maintain that clinical (forensic) psychologists possess a level

of expertise that contributes to the effectiveness of criminal profiling (Copson, Badcock, Boon, & Britton, 1997; Gudjonsson & Copson, 1997). Certainly any professional who attempts to conduct profiling should be knowledgeable and experienced with offenders and the process of criminal investigation, which typically means that individuals must have experience as a criminal investigator.

Many famous fictional detectives have been portrayed as excellent profilers because they could interpret the meaning of a small detail or find a common theme among seemingly unrelated features of a crime. Lew Archer, the hero in Ross MacDonald's popular series of detective novels, frequently began his search for a missing person (usually a wayward wife or a troubled daughter) by looking at the person's bedroom, examining her reading material, and rummaging through her closet to discover where her lifestyle might have misdirected her. Helen McCloy's Dr. Basil Willing, the psychiatrist/detective featured in novels such as *The One That Got Away*, boasts, "Every criminal leaves psychic fingerprints and he can't wear gloves to hide them." Profiling has even infiltrated popular culture through TV programs such as *Law and Order* and its offspring (*Criminal Intent* and *Special Victims Unit*), as well as *Criminal Minds*.

One of the earliest cases of criminal profiling involved the 1957 arrest of George Metesky, otherwise known as the Mad Bomber of New York City. Over an eight-year period, police had tried to solve a series of more than 30 bombings in the New York area. They finally consulted Dr. James Brussel, a Greenwich Village psychiatrist, who, after examining pictures of the bomb scenes and analyzing letters that the bomber had sent, advised the police to look for a heavyset, middle-aged, Eastern European, Catholic man who was single and lived with a sibling or aunt in Connecticut. Brussel also concluded that the man was very neat and that, when found, he would be wearing a buttoned double-breasted suit. When the police finally arrested Metesky, this composite turned out to be uncannily accurate—even down to the right type of suit.

Not all early profiles were so useful, however. For example, the committee of experts charged with the task of profiling the Boston Strangler predicted that the killer was not one man but two, each of whom lived alone and worked as a schoolteacher. They also suggested that one of the men would be homosexual. When Albert De Salvo ultimately confessed to these killings, police discovered that he was a married construction worker who lived with his wife and two sons and was not homosexual (Porter, 1983).

The major source of research and development on criminal profiling has been the FBI's Behavioral Science Unit (the BSU), which has been working on criminal profiles since the 1970s. The BSU is currently one of the instructional components of the FBI's Training and Development Division located at the FBI Academy in Quantico, Virginia. It provides training, conducts research, and offers consultation in the behavioral and social sciences. The BSU also coordinates with other FBI units, such as the National Center for the Analysis of Violent Crime (NCAVC), which provides operational assistance to FBI field offices and law enforcement agencies (http://www.fbi.gov/hq/td/academy/bsu/bsu.htm). The NCAVC now has separate units that focus on crimes against adults, crimes against children, apprehension of violent criminals, and counterterrorism and threat assessment. Its mission involves combining investigative and operational support, research, and training (without charge) to federal, state, local, and foreign law enforcement agencies—particularly involving investigation of unusual or repetitive violent crimes. The NCAVC also provides support through expertise and consultation in nonviolent matters such as national security, corruption, and white-collar crime investigations.

Following September 11, 2001, the FBI placed a higher priority on counterterrorism (FBI Academy, 2002). Profiling terrorist suspects in the United States has proved challenging, and no reliable profile has been developed. Initial profiles of suspected suicide bombers include Arab males between 18 and 40 years old, wearing baggy clothing or clothing inappropriate to the weather (cited in Nunn, 2004). However, focusing only on individuals who match this vague description not only violates Americans' civil liberties, but would produce an overwhelmingly large number of "false positives" (those who are predicted to present a threat but who actually do not).

FBI Academy in Quantico, Virginia

Much of the historical focus of the BSU was on violent offenders, especially those who commit bizarre or repeated crimes (Jeffers, 1991). Special attention has been given to rapists (Ressler, Burgess, & Douglas, 1988), arsonists (Rider, 1980), sexual homicides (Hazelwood & Douglas, 1980), and mass and serial murderers (Porter, 1983). A key to this research has involved interviewing those who have committed a specific type of offense in order to learn how they select and approach their victims, how they react to their crimes, what demographic or family characteristics they share, and what personality features might predominate among them. For example, as part of its study of mass and serial killers, the FBI conducted detailed interviews with some of the United States' most notorious homicide offenders—among them Charles Manson, Richard Speck, and David Berkowitz—to determine the similarities among them.

Classifying Homicide Offenders: Mass and Serial Murderers

On the basis of this research, behavioral scientists have been able to classify mass murderers and add to the portrait of contemporary American homicide offenders. Historically, most homicides were committed by killers who were well acquainted with their victims, had a personal but rational motive, killed once, and were then arrested. In the past two decades, however, increased attention is being paid to patterns of homicide involving killers who attack multiple victims, sometimes with irrational or bizarre motives, and who are much less likely to be apprehended than in former days. The criminal trail of these murderers may center on one locale and period of time or cross through different locations and stretch over a longer period of time. This does not mean, of course, that the patterns of homicide offending have necessarily changed. It is quite likely that changes in mass communication technology have changed the *awareness* of our citizens about a topic as notorious as homicide offending with multiple victims. (See the "Mass Murder Website" at www.fortunecity.com/roswell/hammer/73/index.html for a description of multiple homicide offenders dating back nearly 200 years.) Indeed, mass murderers have been a favorite subject of lurid "true crime" books such as *The Only Living Witness* (about Ted Bundy), *The Co-Ed Killer* (Edmund Kemper), *Killer Clown* (John Gacy), and *Bind, Torture, Kill* (Dennis Rader), as well as of more scholarly, comparative studies of multiple homicides (Fox & Levin, 1998; Levin & Fox, 1985; Meloy et al., 2004).

Although experts differ on what precise number of victims to use in defining multiple homicides, Fox and Levin's (1998) criterion of "the slaying of four or more victims, simultaneously or sequentially, by one or a few individuals" is probably the most widely accepted opinion. It is difficult to estimate how many double homicides are committed each year, but the consensus is that they are increasing, and this increase does not reflect merely greater media attention or police apprehension rates.

Mass murders remain relatively rare, however, which makes it virtually impossible to formulate predictive statistical models that are accurate. The particular problem with trying to predict such rare events is the "false-positive" error rate—even approaches that have a good overall accuracy rate in prediction will identify a relatively large number of false positives (those who are predicted to be violent, but actually will not be). As an alternative to prediction, current research aimed at understanding factors related to these behaviors has focused on identifying characteristics of these homicide offenders and examining patterns between individuals. One study comparing 30 adult with 34 adolescent mass murderers found striking similarities between the two groups (Meloy et al., 2004). Three-quarters of the entire sample were Caucasian (75%), the majority of both the adolescents (70%) and adults (94%) were described as "loners," almost half of the adolescent sample (48%) and almost two-thirds of the adult sample (63%) demonstrated a preoccupation with weapons and violence, and about 43% of both groups had a violent history. There were also several differences between the adolescent and adult offenders. Adolescents were significantly more likely to abuse substances than their adult counterparts (62% compared to 10%), and nearly twice as many adults (50%) as adolescents (23%) had a psychiatric history.

Two types of multiple homicides have been identified: mass murders and serial murders, which share some similarities but are marked by several differences (Meloy & Felthous, 2004). The **mass murderer** kills four or more victims in one location during a period of time that lasts anywhere from a few minutes to several hours. It is estimated that about two mass murders are committed every month in the United States, resulting in the deaths of 100 victims annually (Fox & Levin, 1998). Although most mass murderers are not severely mentally ill, they do tend to harbor strong feelings of resentment and are often motivated by revenge against their victims.

Contrary to popular myth, the majority of mass murderers do not attack strangers at random; in almost 80% of studied mass murders, the assailant was related to or well acquainted with the victims, and in many cases, the attack was a carefully planned assault rather than an impulsive rampage. For every Charles Whitman, who shot and killed 16 people and wounded more than 30 other strangers from a tower on the University of Texas campus, there are many more people like Bruce Pardo who, dressed as Santa Claus, opened fire at a Christmas party at the home of his ex-in laws and killed nine people before killing himself. Most mass murders are solved by law enforcement; the typical assailant is killed at the

Dennis Rader, the "BTK Killer"

location of the crime, commits suicide, or surrenders to police. **Spree killers** are a special form of mass murderers in which the attacker kills victims at two or more different locations with no "cooling-off" interval between the murders. The killing constitutes a single event, but it can either last only a short time or go on for a day or more.

Serial murderers kill four or more victims, each on separate occasions. Unlike mass murderers, **serial killers** usually select a certain type of victim who fulfills a role in the killer's fantasies. There are cooling-off periods between serial murders, which are usually better planned than mass or spree killings. Some serial killers (such as Angel Maturino Resendiz, called the Railway Killer because the murders he was charged with took place by railroad tracks) travel frequently and murder in several locations. Others (such as Gary Ridgway, the so-called Green River Killer who confessed to killing 48 women, mostly prostitutes, and dumping their bodies along the Green River in Washington State) are geographically stable and kill within the same area. The Unabomber, who apparently remained in one place but chose victims who lived in different parts of the country to receive his carefully constructed mail bombs, reflected an unusual combination of serial killer characteristics.

Because they are clever in the way they plan their murders, capable of presenting themselves as normal members of the community, kill for idiosyncratic reasons, and frequently wait months between killings, serial murderers are difficult to apprehend. It took 30 years for Wichita police to figure out that Dennis Rader, a Boy Scout leader and president of Christ Lutheran Church, was a brutal serial killer who used the moniker "BTK"—bind, torture, kill. He confessed to 10 counts of first-degree murder in 2005.

Social scientists have gained some knowledge about these criminals, who may number as many as 100 in the United States. One study compiled a list of characteristics from 157 serial offenders and found that most were white males in their early 30s (Kraemer, Lord, & Heilbrun, 2004). More than half of the offenders were employed at the time of the offense, and approximately one-third were married. The average offender had an 11th-grade education. Victims of these offenders were most often white females in their early to mid-30s who were strangers to their killers. More than half of the murders were sexually motivated. These characteristics differ from single-homicide offenders who more often know their victims and kill for emotional reasons such as anger or sexual jealousy (Kraemer et al., 2004).

Serial killers tend to select vulnerable victims of some specific type who gratify their need to control people. Consistent with the motive of wanting to dominate people, they prefer to kill with "hands-on" methods such as strangulation and stabbing, rather than with guns, which is the preferred weapon for mass murderers. They are often preoccupied with sadistic fantasies involving capture and control of their victims; these fantasies are frequently sexualized, as was the case with Jeffrey Dahmer. Many serial killers use pornography and violent sexual fantasies intensively as "rehearsals" for and "replays" of their crimes, and they often keep souvenirs (sometimes in the form of body parts from victims) to commemorate their savage attacks. Despite the apparent "craziness" of their behavior, serial killers are not typically psychotic individuals. Most of them, however, have personality disorders with deficits in their capacities to experience empathy and remorse. In fact, serial

T A B L E 6.1   **Generic examples of motivations for multiple murder**

Motivations for Multiple Murder	Type of Multiple Murder	
	Serial Murder	Mass Murder
Power	Inspired by sadistic fantasies, a man tortures and kills a series of strangers to satisfy his need for control and dominance.	A pseudo-commando, dressed in battle fatigues and armed with a semiautomatic weapon, turns a shopping mall into a "war zone."
Revenge	Grossly mistreated as a child, a man avenges his past by slaying women who remind him of his mother.	After being fired from his job, a gunman returns to the work site and opens fire on his former boss and coworker.
Loyalty	A team of killers turns murder into a ritual for proving their dedication and commitment to one another.	A depressed husband/father kills his family and himself to spare them from a miserable existence and bring them a better life in the hereafter.
Profit	A woman poisons to death a series of husbands to collect on their life insurance policies.	A band of armed robbers executes the employees of a store to eliminate all witnesses to their crime.
Terror	A profoundly paranoid man commits a series of bombings to warn the world of impending doom.	A group of antigovernment extremists blows up a train to send a political message.

SOURCE: From Fox & Levin, 2005, p. 20.

killers often revel in the publicity that their crimes receive. Over the course of their criminal careers, serial killers may become less organized in how they plan and commit their murders.

Fox and Levin (2005) have provided examples of different motivations for serial and mass murder (including power, revenge, loyalty, profit, and terror), along with brief vignettes illustrating these motivations (see Table 6.1).

Similar examples of possible motivations for homicide, as well as additional information (e.g., signature aspects of violent crime, staging and undoing at crime scenes, and recommendations for interrogation) are contained in the *Crime Classification Manual* (Douglas, Burgess, Burgess, & Ressler, 2006). As you might suspect, the classification with respect to offender motivation can be complex. For example, was Seung-Hui Cho, the Virginia Tech student who went on a shooting rampage on April 16, 2007, killing a total of 32 students and faculty before committing suicide, motivated by power? What about revenge? Some evidence suggests that both may have influenced him. This example vividly illustrates the point that many influences and motivations may

come together in the rare and tragic context of multiple homicide.

Steps Involved in Criminal Profiling

Douglas, Ressler, Burgess, and Hartman (1986) divided the FBI's profiling strategy into five stages, with a final, sixth stage being the arrest of the correct suspect. The six phases, as they evolve in a murder investigation, are as follows:

1. *Profiling inputs.* The first stage involves collecting all information available about the crime, including physical evidence, photographs of the crime scene, autopsy reports and pictures, complete background information on the victim, and police reports. The profiler does not want to be told about possible suspects at this stage, because such data might prejudice or prematurely direct the profile.

2. *Decision process models.* In this stage the profiler organizes the input into meaningful questions and patterns along several dimensions of criminal activity. What type of homicide has been

committed? What is the primary impetus for the crime—sexual, financial, personal, or emotional disturbance? What level of risk did the victim experience, and what level of risk did the murderer take in killing the victim? What was the sequence of acts before and after the killing, and how long did these acts take to commit? Where was the crime committed? Was the body moved, or was it found where the murder was committed?

3. *Crime assessment.* On the basis of the findings in the previous phase, the profiler attempts to reconstruct the behavior of the offender and the victim. Was the murder *organized* (suggesting an intelligent killer who carefully selects victims against whom to act out a well-rehearsed fantasy) or *disorganized* (indicating an impulsive, less socially competent, possibly even psychotic killer)? Was the crime staged to mislead the police? What motivation is revealed by such details as cause of death, location of wounds, and position of the body? Criminal profilers are often guided by the following hypotheses: (a) Brutal facial injuries point to killers who knew their victims, (b) Murders committed with whatever weapon happens to be available are more impulsive than murders committed with a gun and may reveal a killer who lives fairly near the victim, and (c) Murders committed early in the morning seldom involve alcohol or drugs.

4. *Criminal profile.* In this stage, profilers formulate an initial description of the most likely suspects. This profile includes the perpetrator's race, sex, age, marital status, living arrangements, and employment history; psychological characteristics, beliefs, and values; probable reactions to the police; and past criminal record, including the possibility of similar offenses in the past. This stage also contains a feedback loop whereby profilers check their predictions against stage 2 information to make sure that the profile fits the original data.

5. *Investigation.* A written report is given to investigators, who concentrate on suspects matching the profile. If new evidence is discovered in this investigation, a second feedback process is initiated, and the profile can be revised.

6. *Apprehension.* The intended result of these procedures, arrest of a suspect, allows profilers to evaluate the validity of their predictions. The key element in this validation is a thorough interview of the suspect to assess the influences of background and psychological variables.

The Validity of Criminal Profiles

Is there any evidence that psychological profiling is valid? Are profilers more accurate than other groups in their descriptions of suspects, or is this activity little more than a reading of forensic tea leaves? Do profilers use a different process in evaluating information than other investigators?

In a review of criminal profiling, Homant and Kennedy (1998) concluded that different kinds of crime scenes can be classified with reasonable reliability and that differences in these crimes do correlate with certain offender characteristics, such as murderers' prior relationships and interactions with victims (Salfati & Canter, 1999), organized versus disorganized approaches, and serial versus single offenders (e.g., Knight, Warren, Reboussin, & Soley, 1998). At the same time, this research suggests several reasons for caution: (1) Inaccurate profiles are quite common, (2) many of the studies have been conducted in-house by FBI profilers studying a fairly small number of offenders, and (3) the concepts and approaches actually used by profilers have often not been objectively and systematically defined.

One study (Pinizzotto & Finkel, 1990) investigated the effectiveness of criminal profiling as practiced by real-life experts. In this investigation, four different groups of participants evaluated two criminal cases—a homicide and a sex offense—that had already been solved but were completely unknown to the subjects. The first group consisted of four experienced criminal profilers who had a total of 42 years of profiling experience and six police detectives who had recently been trained by the FBI to be profilers. The second group consisted of six police detectives with 57 years of total experience in criminal investigations but with no profiling experience or training. The third group was composed of six clinical psychologists who had no profiling or criminal investigation experience. The final group consisted of six undergraduates drawn from psychology classes.

All participants were given, for each case, an array of materials that profilers typically use. These materials included crime scene photographs, crime scene descriptions by uniformed officers, autopsy and toxicology reports (in the murder case), and descriptions of the victims. After studying these materials, participants were asked to write all the details they could recall for each crime and to indicate the importance of these details to completing a profile. Three tests of profiling quality were used: All subjects prepared a profile of a suspect in each case, answered 15 questions about the identity (e.g., gender, age, employment) of the suspects, and were asked to rank-order a written "lineup" of five suspects, from most to least likely to have committed each of the crimes.

The results indicated that, compared with the other three groups, the profiler group wrote longer profiles that contained more specific predictions about suspects, included more accurate predictions, and were rated as more helpful by other police detectives. Although they did not differ substantially in the way they thought about the evidence, profilers were more accurate than the other groups in answering specific questions about the sex offense suspect. The groups did not differ in their accuracy about the homicide suspect. Similar results were found with the "lineup" identification: Profilers were the most accurate for the sex offense, whereas there were no differences for the homicide case.

This study suggests that profilers can produce more useful and valid criminal profiles, even when compared to experienced crime investigators. This advantage may be limited, however, to certain kinds of cases or to the types of information made available to investigators. One study found that individuals (senior police officers and forensic professionals) perceive ambiguous statements, when presented as an "offender profile," as being accurate descriptions of suspects (Alison, Smith, & Morgan, 2003).

Another study (Canter, Alison, Alison, & Wentink, 2004) tested the "organized/disorganized"

dichotomy by using specialized statistics to analyze 39 aspects of serial killing derived from murders committed by 100 U.S. serial killers. There was no distinct subset of offense characteristics associated with this dichotomy. Researchers did find a subset of organized features that were characteristic of most serial killings, but disorganized features were far more unusual and did not form a distinct type. The investigators suggested that these results cast doubt on the reliability and validity with which killings can be classified using this dichotomy.

Based on the absence of empirical scientific data supporting the process of profiling, some (e.g., Note, 2008; Risinger & Loop, 2002) have argued that profiling lacks the requisite scientific support to allow experts to testify to the findings of profiles in the course of litigation. Given the limited extent to which the profiling process has been studied, there does not appear to be an adequate scientific foundation for expert testimony. Whether courts admit profiling evidence will probably continue to depend on the leanings of the particular judge.

How do psychologists themselves view criminal profiling? In a survey of 152 police psychologists, 70% questioned the validity of crime scene profiling (Bartol, 1996). Nonetheless, despite such reservations, profiling is gaining popularity among law enforcement officials and is now practiced, in some form or other, in several countries (Woodworth & Porter, 2000; Homant & Kennedy, 1998).

DETECTING DECEPTION

The simplest way to determine whether someone is lying is with behavioral cues. Throughout history, many societies have assumed that criminals can be detected by the physical manifestations of their denials. Ever since King Solomon tried to discover which of two women who claimed to be the mother of an infant was lying by watching their emotions when he threatened to cut the baby in half and divide it between them, people have believed that the body will reveal when the mind is lying.

We all make frequent judgments of others' truthfulness by observing their behavior, often without conscious awareness of doing so. In late-night conversations, parents gauge the veracity of their teenagers' stories about where they had been and with whom. During job interviews, employers make quick judgments of the candor and honesty of prospective employees.

One context in which judgments of truthfulness and lying are ever present is law enforcement. Police officers and other officials know that deception is common in that setting, and that it is their responsibility to separate fact from fiction, truth from lies. Their ability to detect deception has profound implications for the people who pass through the criminal justice system. Being deemed "deceptive" can launch someone—perhaps an innocent person—into a criminal prosecution and toward eventual conviction and imprisonment. Being deemed "truthful" can absolve guilty people of suspicion, allowing them to remain on the streets to commit more crimes. How well law enforcement officials can assess deception is vitally important to the fair and effective operation of the justice system. Fortunately, psychologists have provided tools to help them. In this section, we describe what psychologists have learned about people's ability to detect deception unaided, using only their eyes and ears. In these studies, people must judge deceit based only on verbal and behavioral cues.

It is difficult to be certain when someone is fibbing and when he or she is telling the truth (at least as he or she believes it), and then to assess other people's judgments of his or her honesty. For this reason, psychologists have developed research protocols that mimic real-world lying and truth-telling. In these studies, researchers instruct some participants to lie and others to tell the truth about a particular experience, as observers (often with little or no training) watch or listen to videotapes or audiotapes and then judge the truthfulness of those statements (Vrij, 2000). Scientists measure the ability to detect deception—that is, realizing that a truthful person is telling the truth and that a liar is lying—as the percentage of correct judgments. In a simple two-alternative forced choice, the chance level of an accurate decision is 50%.

How accurately can people detect deception? In a meta-analysis that evaluated the decisions of nearly 25,000 observers in hundreds of studies,

Bond and DePaulo (2006) determined that people are correct only 54% of the time, hardly more than chance. The analysis revealed several other interesting clues to how people judge deception. For example, it uncovered a **truth bias,** meaning that people were biased toward judging statements as being truthful. We tend to take most assertions at face value, assuming that they are true unless their authenticity is called into question for some reason. (Think about asking someone for the time of day.) As a result, subjects in the meta-analysis correctly classified 61% of truthful statements as nondeceptive but only 47% of lies as deceptive. Not surprisingly, the truth bias is not apparent in judgments of the veracity of children. We don't assume that children always (or even usually) tell the truth (Edelstein, Luten, Ekman, & Goodman, 2006).

Many of the people making judgments in deception studies were college students who had no expertise or specialized training (and perhaps little desire) to do this task well. Might people who have more experience judging deception be better at it? When playwright Tennessee Williams wrote that "mendacity is the system we live in" he may have been referring to people whose occupations expose them to multiple lies on a daily basis: police officers, judges, customs officials, border patrol, and the like. Perhaps being exposed to frequent deceit would eventually make one a better lie catcher. Surprisingly, the data show otherwise. With few exceptions, people who have experience judging deceit are no better at it than those with no experience (Stromwall & Granhag, 2003). What expertise *does* provide is skepticism. Judges and other experts are less likely than laypeople to exhibit a truth bias and are less inclined to believe that others are truthful (Meissner & Kassin, 2002).

Distinguishing Liars and Truth-Tellers

How would you expect liars to act? What would you expect them to say? People can fairly easily conjure up an image of liars. Perhaps your image is of people who are shifty, avert their gaze, fidget, and look tense. Are these beliefs correct or are they based on stereotypes and misconceptions?

One reason that people are poor deception detectors is that they tend to focus on the wrong cues, both verbal and nonverbal, when judging another person's truthfulness. Instead of focusing on **diagnostic cues**—cues that can accurately distinguish a truth-teller from an imposter—people tend to fall back on stereotypes and biases about what deceptive behavior looks like. Studies of beliefs about deception have shown that people (laypeople and experts alike) tend to have mistaken beliefs about verbal and nonverbal cues to deception. For example, many people assume that avoiding eye contact is a sign of lying. Yet research on objective, diagnostic cues to deception shows that this trait is not a predictor of deceptive behavior (DePaulo et al., 2003) except in circumstances where liars have a lot to lose—like spouses, money, or reputations. People also mistakenly believe that fidgety movements mean a person is being deceitful. Although a prominent guide to interrogations, Zulawski and Wicklander's *Practical Aspects of Interview and Interrogation* (2001) asserts that a liar's movements tend to be "jerky and abrupt," the data show otherwise.

In fact, psychologists have found very few reliable nonverbal cues to deception, perhaps because people who are asked to tell the truth may also show signs of nervousness. Aldert Vrij, a psychologist at the University of Portsmouth, has said that there is nothing as obvious as Pinocchio's growing nose to alert us to a lie.

Psychologists have had more success determining which *verbal* cues can reliably predict deceptive behavior. For example, because it is difficult to quickly fabricate details that do not exist in memory, a large amount of reported detail should be indicative of truthful reports. Indeed, scientists have learned that truthful statements tend to be longer than lies. And though we are suspicious of memory lapses in the real world, truth-tellers are more likely than liars to say they can't recall certain details. Liars also tend to speak in a higher-pitched voice and make more speech errors (e.g., slips of the tongue, repeated words, and incomplete sentences) than truth-tellers (Sporer & Schwandt, 2006).

Though stereotypic beliefs may hinder our ability to distinguish fabricators from honest responders,

cognitive load interviews can enhance our ability to make those distinctions. Cognitive load interviews are designed to mentally tax a person so that it becomes difficult to simultaneously answer a question and maintain a lie. Lying is cognitively taxing. Liars must first formulate their fabrications and then remember what they said earlier and to whom. They need to avoid providing any new information to interviewers. Because they know they are being deceitful, they may have to pay more careful attention to their own demeanor and to reactions from the interviewer to see if they are getting away with their lies. Finally, they have to suppress the truth. All of these activities require mental effort which, when compounded by the need to answer interviewers' questions, can confound and confuse deceitful subjects.

Among the techniques that effectively increase cognitive load are asking subjects to recall a series of events in reverse chronological order and requiring them to perform a secondary task during the interview such as determining whether a figure that reappears on a computer screen is similar to a target figure shown earlier. By making a subject think harder in an interview, investigators have been able to more accurately discriminate liars from truthful interviewees (Vrig, Fisher, Mann, & Leal, 2006). Another technique that uses cognitive load may be seen in a standard measure of malingering, the Structured Interview of Reported Symptoms (Rogers, 1992). In this test, which is administered to individuals who are suspected of falsely reporting symptoms of mental illness that are not actually experienced, individuals are asked a number of detailed questions about their symptoms in rapid-fire fashion. It is very difficult to remember what has been reported if it was not actually experienced.

Using the Polygraph to Detect Deception

Over the years, people suspected of wrongdoing have faced various tests of their veracity. Suspects in India were once required to submit to "trial by sacred ass." After mud was put on the tail of an ass in a tent, the alleged suspects were required to enter the tent one by one and pull the ass's tail; they were told they would be deemed innocent if the ass didn't bray. The logic of this method was that the innocent man, having nothing to hide, would immediately yank the tail and get mud on his hands. A guilty suspect, however, would try to hide guilt by not pulling the tail. In the end, the suspect considered guilty was the one with the clean hands. The ancient Hindus forced suspects to chew rice and spit it out on a leaf from a sacred tree. If the rice was dry, the suspect was deemed guilty. The Bedouins of Arabia required conflicting witnesses to lick a hot iron; the one whose tongue was burned was thought to be lying (Kleinmuntz & Szucko, 1984). These procedures reflect activity of the sympathetic nervous system (under emotional states, salivation usually decreases) and thus are crude measures of emotion. But emotion and lying are not the same, and this distinction is at the root of concerns about using the polygraph, a relatively modern tool, to detect deception.

Emergence of the Polygraph. For many years, the standard way to detect deception was to measure signs of physiological arousal in combination with a specific questioning strategy. The **polygraph** (sometimes referred to as the *lie detector*) was developed around 1917 by William Marston, a complex and colorful figure who claimed that he could detect lying by noting increases in subjects' blood pressure when they told untruths. For much of the 20th century scientists granted little credibility to Marston's ideas, yet polygraphs were often used in law enforcement settings.

In the 1930s, a California police officer named John Larson built a forerunner of the modern polygraph that could measure pulse rate, blood pressure, and respiratory changes during questioning. Here we see the origins of the polygraph concept (*poly-* means "many"). Unfortunately for Marston, Larson, and others who sought a specific "lie response," the physiological manifestations of various negative emotions (e.g., fear, guilt, anger) are all very similar; suggesting that assessments of a person's credibility based on physiological responses alone may be problematic. Simply being suspected of committing a crime, even if you are innocent, may generate a great deal of surplus emotion that should not be taken as a sign of guilt.

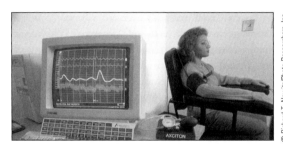

A polygraph examination

Although scientific research has contributed to the advancement of polygraph techniques over the past half-century, concerns about their validity still linger. Nonetheless, the polygraph enjoys fairly widespread application within the criminal justice system. Most of the polygraph machines used now are digital computer-based systems that record and evaluate physiological responses to various types of questions. The typical polygraph instrument measures respiration, blood pressure, and electrodermal activity on the surface of the skin.

Polygraph Techniques. In the 1940s, John Reid pioneered the **Control Question Test** (CQT, sometimes referred to as the *Comparison Question Test*), which has become the most popular approach to polygraphic examinations (Honts, 2004). This exam begins with an interview in which the examiner gathers biographical information from the subject and attempts to impress on the subject that he or she must be honest at all times during the test. The examiner tries to convince the subject that the polygraph is an infallible instrument; this strategy is meant to threaten guilty subjects at the same time that it reassures the innocent.

When the test begins, the polygrapher asks a series of questions and is especially interested in subjects' responses to two kinds of questions. *Relevant questions* inquire about the crime under investigation (e.g., "Did you steal the law school's TV set?"). *Comparison questions* are not directly concerned with the crime under investigation but are calculated to induce an emotional reaction because they cover common misdeeds that nearly all of us have committed (e.g., "Prior to the age of 21, did you ever try to hurt someone you disliked?"). Most polygraphers consider these "known lies." But subjects will deny them, thereby providing a characteristic physiological response to a lie.

The expectation is that guilty subjects should be more aroused by the relevant questions (to which they must respond with a lie in order to maintain their innocence), whereas innocent subjects should be more aroused by the comparison questions (because they will worry that admitting to a past misdeed might make them look more like a criminal at the present time). Therefore, this procedure works best when innocent subjects lie or at least show greater emotional turmoil in response to the comparison questions, and guilty subjects lie and become more emotionally aroused in response to the relevant questions.

An alternative to the CQT is the **Guilty Knowledge Test** (GKT), which was developed in 1991 by University of Minnesota psychologist, David Lykken. Both the procedure and the purposes of this method are fundamentally different from the control question approach. The goal is to detect the presence of guilty knowledge in the suspect's mind, not to detect lying. The procedure relies on the accumulation of facts that are known only by the police, the criminal, and any surviving victims. For example: In what room was the victim's body found? What was the weapon? What strange garment was the victim wearing? What was the victim clutching in his hand?

The polygrapher creates a series of multiple-choice questions and presents them to the suspect. Each alternative would appear equally plausible to an innocent person. But the true criminal will, in theory, be revealed by heightened physiological reactions that accompany recognition of guilty knowledge. Obviously, this technique can be used only when the details of the crime have been kept from the public. Even then, it is conceivable that the suspect is not the perpetrator but, rather, was told about the crime by the true criminal and therefore possesses "guilty" knowledge. It is possible that some guilty subjects are so distraught or pay so little attention to the details of their crimes that they actually lack the required knowledge on which this method relies. Some critics of the GKT suggest that

it can be conducted properly in only a small percentage of real-life cases.

Regardless of the test used, the final step in a polygraph exam is interpretation of the physiological measurements. Most polygraph examiners are trained to score responses by using a combination of rule-based subjective judgments and objective measures of physiological responses. They may also rely on observations of the subject's behavior throughout the test (Kleiner, 2002).

Validity of the Polygraph.   Examiners are accurate when they expose liars and believe truthful suspects. They err when they believe that a liar is truthful (a *false negative*) and that a truthful subject is lying (a *false positive*). The level of examiners' accuracy has been a central question in ongoing debates about the validity of the polygraph.

Advocates of polygraph procedures claim very high rates of accuracy. Reid and Inbau (1966) asserted that their success rate was 99%. F. Lee Bailey proposed that out of every 100 polygraph tests administered, 96 are accurate, 3 are inconclusive, and only 1 will be in error (quoted in Lykken, 1985, p. 96). Using mock crime methodology, some researchers have shown that accuracy rates far exceed chance (e.g., Raskin & Honts, 2002) and can be as high as 90% (Offe and Offe, 2007).

A claim of high accuracy—for example, 96% accuracy—can be misleading, however. Imagine that a major theft has occurred in a factory with 50 employees. One is the thief; 49 are honest. The examiner gives a polygraph test to each of the employees, and each denies being the thief. The polygrapher misclassifies one of the innocent people as the thief (false positive). He also fails to detect lying by the true thief (false negative). Thus he has erred in two cases, but he has been correct in classifying the 48 others as truthful. His accuracy rate is 48 of 50, or 96%. But he has still erred on the crucial determination; despite the 96% overall "accuracy rate," his answer to the referral question (Who stole?) is wrong.

The polygraph has several other shortcomings. First, as we've mentioned, the test cannot distinguish emotions such as fear, anger, nervousness, and excitement. This means that an innocent person, aware that the question "Did you kill your wife?" is relevant to the investigation, may respond with heightened arousal that stems from nervousness rather than deception. Nonetheless, that heightened response could lead to a false-positive error.

A second concern is that the questioning methods used by polygraphers are not standardized (Ben-Shakhar, 2002). More generally, few professional standards regulate professional polygraphers. Some states have no regulations or licensing requirements whatsoever. This means that the quality of polygraphy can vary widely from one jurisdiction to another.

Another concern about the accuracy of the polygraph is the fact that deceptive subjects can be trained to "beat" the test by taking **countermeasures** to avoid detection. Effective use of countermeasures should increase the rate at which examiners believe that a guilty subject is telling the truth (a false negative). Among the countermeasures suggested on the Internet (see www.wikihow.com/Cheat-a-Polygraph-Test) are these:

Develop a breathing strategy by altering the rate of breathing during relevant questions and comparison questions

Do complex calculations in your head

Think of something exciting or frightening

Bite the side of your tongue hard enough to cause pain but not so hard as to draw blood

Insert a small tack in your shoe and press down on it during the comparison questions

Contract your anal sphincter muscle when answering comparison questions

To determine whether using some of these countermeasures allows subjects to "beat" the test, researchers trained participants to bite their tongue or press their toes to the floor (physical countermeasures) or to count backwards by 7 (a mental countermeasure) during CQT administration (Honts, Raskin, & Kircher, 1994). The mental and physical countermeasures were both effective, enabling approximately 50% of subjects to defeat the test. Moreover, the polygraph examiners were not particularly suspicious; they detected only 12% of the physical countermeasures and none of the mental countermeasures.

The Cheat-a-Polygraph Web site now warns that astute examiners are wise to these tactics. For example, rather than settling for simple yes–no answers, examiners now ask questions that require detailed responses, demand that subjects remove their shoes, and even require them to sit on pressure-sensitive pads. These counter-countermeasures may effectively eliminate subjects' opportunity to beat the test. A recent study showed that providing information to subjects about countermeasures did not significantly increase false negatives on a variant of the CQT (Honts & Alloway, 2007).

What can we conclude about the validity of the polygraph? Reviewing research on the validity of polygraph examinations, a committee of the National Research Council found that only a handful met the standards necessary for National Science Foundation funding (National Research Council, 2003). The Council expressed concern over the quality of the research and the exaggerated claims of accuracy by some polygraph proponents.

But even the most vocal critics of the polygraph acknowledge that the technique has overall accuracy rates of 65% or better. The question is whether this figure is high enough to justify permitting polygraphic data as evidence at a trial or to use it as the primary evidence against a suspect. We think not. Polygraph tests are most valuable at the investigatory stages of a criminal prosecution and as a way to encourage confessions from suspects against whom other incriminating evidence has been gathered. A recent FBI report found that of 2,641 deceptive criminal polygraph reports, half resulted in the acquisition of information valuable to the investigations in other ways (Warner, 2005). This may be the best use for the polygraph.

Admissibility of Polygraph Records.   There are two ways in which polygraph results can be used in a lawsuit. In approximately half the states, a defendant takes a polygraph test with the understanding that the prosecutor will drop charges if the defendant passes the test but may use the results in court if the defendant does not pass.

The other way in which polygraph evidence is admitted is when a defendant has passed a polygraph

---

B o x 6.1   THE CASE OF BRIAN LEA AND HIS RIVAL'S CONTAMINATED ANIMALS

Brian Lea, an entrepreneur, was accused of dumping pesticides on a former business partner's dead farm animals being sold as food by the partner's company, National By-Products ("NBP") (*United States v. Lea*, 2001). Following notification that NBP had sold contaminated animal food, the business was ordered to close one of its plants and recall the contaminated food. Lea was indicted and charged with the offense. Lea maintained that a former employee of NBP, Barry Werch, was the actual culprit. In his defense, Lea provided results of a polygraph examination that Werch had "failed," as well as incriminating statements made by Werch. But the judge refused to admit this information into evidence. After being convicted of contaminating NBP's animal stock and sentenced to prison, Lea appealed. He asserted that by excluding Werch's polygraph examination, the judge deprived him of his Sixth Amendment right to present a defense. But the Court of Appeals affirmed the judge's decision to exclude the polygraph evidence because the polygrapher was unable to provide statistics on the accuracy rate of the test in this case.

---

exam and tries to have that evidence considered in an ongoing investigation. In 2006, embattled track coach Trevor Graham, former coach to Olympic star Marion Jones, claimed that he was not involved in providing performance-enhancing drugs to athletes. His attorney sent results of a polygraph test affirming his innocence to the grand jury investigating the Bay Area Laboratory Co-Operative (BALCO) scandal. Despite apparently "passing" the polygraph exam, Graham was indicted, tried, and convicted of making false statements to drug investigators.

In states that permit polygraph evidence to be used in trials, judges conduct pretrial hearings to determine whether polygraph results are admissible in particular cases according to the standards of admissibility established in *Daubert v. Merrell Dow Pharmaceuticals* (1993), the case we described in Chapter 1. Sometimes they allow polygraph evidence. But the United States Supreme Court declared that polygraph results and opinions shall not be admitted in court (*United States v. Scheffer*, 1998). Though binding only on military courts (because the case involved a Military Rule of Evidence), the Supreme Court's decision in *Scheffer* reinforces the general reluctance of judges to admit polygraph results and opinions. Another example is provided in Box 6.1.

How do juries react to polygraph evidence? Do they blindly accept it as proof of the defendant's guilt or alternately, of innocence? Professor Bryan Myers

and his colleagues conducted a simulation study of a sexual assault trial that included, for some mock jurors, results of a polygraph examination indicating that the defendant lied. Other mock jurors learned that the polygraph revealed the defendant had told the truth (Myers, Latter, & Abdollahi-Arena, 2006). Jurors put little stock in the results of the polygraph examination; knowing that the defendant had either passed or failed the polygraph affected neither their verdicts nor their estimates of the probability that the defendant committed the crime. Furthermore, they deemed polygraph evidence to be less trustworthy than DNA, fingerprint, eyewitness, and handwriting analysis evidence. According to these results, jurors have a healthy skepticism toward polygraph-based evidence.

Brain-Based Lie Detection

Recent developments in deception detection capitalize on scientific advances in neuroimaging and brain electrophysiology. Rather than relying on measures of physiological arousal as the polygraph does, these newer methods monitor changes in the brain's activity in response to stimuli. Two of the prominent brain-based methods of lie detection are functional magnetic resonance imaging, and brain-wave analysis.

Neuroimaging in Deception Detection.   Neuroimaging techniques such as **functional magnetic resonance imaging** (fMRI) use scanners fitted with powerful electromagnets to measure blood flow and oxygen utilization in selected parts of the brain. Increases in oxygen consumption and blood flow in a particular part of the brain indicate that that region of the brain is involved when a subject undertakes a certain task. The primary function of fMRI is to diagnose neurological disorders. But because it is highly sensitive to cognitive processes involved in memory recall (Burgess, Maguire, & O'Keefe, 2002) and motivation (Elliott, Friston, & Dolan, 2000), it holds promise as a way to monitor deception.

Early studies using fMRI to detect deception typically asked simple questions about one's past experiences or knowledge (e.g., "Who was your best friend at primary school?" "Does a bicycle have six wheels?"). Participants pressed buttons to answer "yes" or "no." Some were told to conceal information by lying in response to specific questions whereas others were told to respond truthfully. Scientists then compared brain activity in response to truthful answers and lies (Langleben et al., 2002)

These studies showed that different patterns of brain activation are associated with truth-telling and lying. Several brain regions, in particular, the prefrontal cortex and anterior cingulate cortex, respond more strongly during lies. These brain areas are associated with high-level executive function, suggesting that telling lies requires more cognitive effort than telling the truth (Spence et al., 2004). The prefrontal cortex seems to play a particularly large role in inhibiting truthful responses and generating falsehoods. Subsequent studies have examined the feasibility of using fMRI to distinguish lies from truths within a single subject. The accuracy of this method ranges from 76% to 90%.

Although fMRI holds some promise as a method of detecting deception, a number of issues have not yet been resolved. For example, most of the studies involve fairly benign questions and simplified experimental tasks that may not mimic the complexity of deception in the real world. Results obtained from the press of a button may not generalize to emotional responses associated with complex verbal communications. To increase the reality of experimental paradigms, some researchers have attempted to motivate participants by suggesting that their responses are being evaluated by external observers

(Phan et al., 2005) or by offering monetary rewards for successful deception (Mohamed et al., 2006). But whether these circumstances approximate real-life situations where people stand to lose their freedom, family, or livelihood if they cannot convince an investigator of their innocence, is unknown (Vrij & Mann, 2001).

It is also not clear whether fMRI technology can handle situations in which a subject's response cannot be neatly categorized as the truth or a lie. This occurs when a response is partly true and partly false, when people imagine that a fabricated memory is true, and when they consider the possibility of lying but ultimately decide to tell the truth (Appelbaum, 2007). Finally, questions remain about the use of fMRI for detecting deception in people with medical or psychiatric disorders, youth and the elderly, and those who take medications or use countermeasures. Despite these lingering concerns, fMRI techniques are being marketed commercially. Joel Huizenga, who founded a company called No Lie MRI, asserts confidently, "Once you jump behind the skull, there's no hiding." The test was recently used in a real-life criminal case, described in Box 6.2.

Brain-wave Analysis in Deception Detection. Imagine that a suspect denies that he or she was at the scene of a crime. Further imagine that he or she is confronted with pictures or verbal descriptions of the scene. New technology that measures brain-wave patterns that occur in response to familiar and unfamiliar images may eventually help investigators determine whether people are being deceptive when they claim "I wasn't there." This technique, termed **brain fingerprinting,** was the "brainchild" of Lawrence Farwell. It uses an electroencephalogram (EEG) to record electrical activity on the surface of the scalp, reflecting spontaneous activity from the underlying cerebral cortex.

The premise of brain fingerprinting is that the brain houses information about experienced events and emits electrical signals in response to stimuli. A unique brain-wave pattern—the P300 wave—is elicited by a stimulus that is meaningful to the subject. It derives its name from its positive polarity and occurrence approximately 300–900 milliseconds after

---

B o x 6.2   THE CASE OF CONTESTED POISONING: MUNCHAUSEN'S SYNDROME BY PROXY OR NOT? AND CAN FMRI TELL THE DIFFERENCE?

Munchausen syndrome by proxy is a psychiatric disorder in which parents, guardians, or other caregivers deliberately inflict pain and injury on vulnerable children in order to attract attention to themselves. Perpetrators are overwhelmingly female, often mothers of the victims. The disease is difficult to diagnose because many of the child's symptoms could result from organic causes or undiagnosed illnesses. The question posed in a recent case in England was whether a child's poisoning had been carried out by the mother. She was convicted of the charge and served four years in prison.

In a groundbreaking experiment, Professor Sean Spence, a pioneer of fMRI technology to detect deception, examined the woman's brain activity as she alternately repeated her protestations of innocence and her accusers' account of the poisoning (Spence, Kaylor-Hughes, Brook, Lankappa, & Wilkinson, 2008). The tests, repeated four times, showed that her prefrontal and anterior cingulate cortices were activated when she endorsed statements she believed to be false, namely her accusers' versions of the event. In short, the data suggested that she lied when she agreed with her accusers' statements. According to Professor Spence, "[A]t the present moment, this research doesn't prove that this woman is innocent. Instead, what it clearly demonstrates is that her brain responds as if she were innocent … If proved to be accurate, and these findings replicated, this technology could be used alongside other factors to address questions of guilt versus innocence."

---

the onset of a stimulus. Brain fingerprinting evaluates neural activity to assess how a suspect responds to crime scene details known only to the perpetrator. For example, after showing a suspect a series of common images while measuring P300 waves, investigators might show critical images of the crime scene and compare activation patterns. A guilty person, but not an innocent subject, would react differently to the critical details because they are meaningful. (You can probably see that this protocol borrows heavily from the Guilty Knowledge Test used with the polygraph.)

Researchers estimate the accuracy of brain fingerprinting by asking some participants to lie and others to tell the truth about a witnessed mock crime or autobiographical event when answering questions. They measure detection rates based on the resulting patterns of brain waves. Estimates range from 85% to 95% accuracy in distinguishing liars from truth-tellers under optimized laboratory conditions (Rosenfeld, Soskins, Bosh, & Ryan, 2004) though accuracy drops to near chance levels when tested in the field (Miyake, Mizutanti, & Yamahura, 1993). The technique's originator, Lawrence Farwell, has patented, developed, and promoted a commercial version of the tool that he claims is 100% accurate (Farwell & Smith, 2001) despite limited empirical support (Rosenfeld, 2005).

One might suspect that because the P300 response occurs a fraction of a second after the stimulus, it would be resistant to the kinds of countermeasures used to defeat the polygraph. But training guilty suspects to use mental or physical countermeasures (e.g., wiggling their toes) in response to *irrelevant* items increased the amplitude of the P300 wave, making detection worse (Rosenfeld et al., 2004). When subjects were instructed to use countermeasures in a study that involved a highly realistic crime scene in virtual reality, detection of guilty subjects was especially poor (Mertens & Allen, 2008).

Brain-based lie Detection in Court. Like the polygraph, brain-based technologies could be used in at least two different ways in legal contexts. Defendants and witnesses may try to introduce the results of these tests to demonstrate their innocence or bolster their credibility. In the only case in which brain-based evidence has been admitted in court, Terry Harrington's murder conviction was reversed by the Iowa Supreme Court in 2003 after Lawrence Farwell used brain fingerprinting to conclude that the "record of the night of the crime stored in Harrington's brain does not match the crime scene, and does match the alibi" (www.brainwavescience.com/HarringtonSummary.php). When confronted with this information, a key prosecution witness recanted his testimony and admitted that he accused Harrington to avoid being prosecuted himself (*Harrington v. Iowa*, 2003).

When defendants press to have this evidence used in court, judges must determine whether the testimony meets the standards for admissibility of scientific evidence set out in the *Daubert* case (*Daubert v. Merrell Dow Pharmaceuticals, Inc.*, 1993) (e.g., publication in peer-reviewed journals, general acceptance in the field). Although brain-based technologies may not meet these standards yet, with ongoing and carefully constructed field studies they are likely to pass the admissibility test in the future (Appelbaum, 2007).

Many people would agree that defendants and witnesses should be able to offer neuroscientific evidence to support their version of the facts, so long as that evidence is based on valid and reliable scientific testing procedures. But when we ponder the second use of this type of evidence—demanding that defendants and witnesses be screened for deception—some people will balk. This more controversial use of brain scans and brain-wave analysis could be used as part of the discovery process, for example, during interrogations.

A host of legal issues arise when brain-based techniques are conducted against the wishes of the subject being scanned. What happens if a person refuses to undergo an fMRI or brain-wave test? Can his or her credibility be questioned? Some have argued that these practices constitute a "search" of the brain that should be governed by the Fourth Amendment's prohibition against unreasonable search and seizure (Boire, 2005; Farah, 2005). A related question is whether brain-based tests conducted without the consent of the subject violate the protection against self-incrimination guaranteed by the Fifth Amendment. Alternatively, perhaps brain fingerprinting is just another form of physical evidence, similar to DNA or fingerprint evidence.

Although probing a person's brain to detect a lie may seem highly intrusive, the government's interests in crime control and public protection may offset these concerns. How far the law can extend into the realm of exposing (and protecting) private thoughts

is unclear. Many commentators urge judges to resist the temptation to admit this evidence until more conclusive data are available (e.g., Appelbaum, 2007) and one legal scholar has proposed legislation that would prohibit the use of brain-based lie detection techniques until regulatory systems can be put in place to evaluate and monitor their safety and effectiveness (Greely, 2005). Perhaps the only certainty is that the controversy over brain-based lie detection systems will continue for some time.

EVALUATING CONFESSIONS

Throughout history, confessions have been accorded enormous importance. Confession is valued as an indicator of truth and as an act that benefits confessors because it relieves them of guilt and earns them forgiveness. Many religions maintain that confession is the first step toward redemption and have evolved special rituals to encourage it. Interrogations and confessions play a role in military matters, also. People detained as terrorist threats in military jails in Afghanistan, Iraq, Guantanamo Bay, and elsewhere are interrogated by harsh methods including both physical and psychological torture (described in Box 6.3) that are unacceptable in U.S. criminal courts (McCoy, 2006). But some tactics used in criminal interrogations are applied in military interrogations as well (Redlich, 2007a).

Confessions play a prominent role in the criminal justice system; many consider them to be the most powerful weapon at the state's disposal (Kassin & Gudjonsson, 2004). When the police capture suspects, one of their first acts is to encourage them to confess. A confession will, of course, permit a district attorney or grand jury to bring charges. Even if the suspect later denies the confession and pleads not guilty, the confession can be introduced into evidence at the trial.

Although disputed "confessions" by defendants occur surprisingly often and observers have documented many false confessions (e.g., Drizin & Leo, 2004; Gross, Jacoby, Matheson, Montgomery, & Patil, 2005), the number of false confessions is actually

Box 6.3 THE CASE OF OMAR KHADR: INTERROGATION, THE WAR ON TERROR, AND TORTURE

In July 2002, an American Special Forces Unit in Afghanistan learned that Al Qaeda fighters were holed up in Ab Khail, a small enclave near the Pakistani border. When the fighters refused to surrender, the Americans laid siege to the compound. After the dust had settled, they found a wounded fighter who, according to some accounts, threw a hand grenade at one of the troops, killing him. American soldiers fired back, shooting the fighter three times in the chest. Incredibly, he survived the bullet holes in his chest and shrapnel wounds to his head.

The fighter turned out to be just 15 years old; his name was Omar Khadr, and in fluent English he pleaded with the soldiers to kill him. Khadr is a Canadian, born to a fundamentalist Muslim family, and the son of an Al Qaeda operative. He was airlifted to Bagram Air Force Base and into the custody of American intelligence officials who began interrogating him as soon as he regained consciousness (Tietz, 2006).

Most of us would never have known about Omar Khadr had his videotaped interrogations from Guantanamo Bay detention center (where he was sent after he recovered) not been splashed across the Internet six years after his capture. The taped interrogations provide the most extensive record yet of the nature of interrogations inside the infamous prison. Throughout the interrogations, Khadr's demeanor swings from calmed indifference to grief-filled despair (Austen, 2008). At one point, he sobs inconsolably; at another, he shows officials wounds on his chest and back and pleads with Canadian intelligent officials to help him.

According to some reports, Khadr has endured unimaginable treatment in captivity. Pain medications were withheld to induce his cooperation, and he was attacked by dogs, bolted to the floor, shackled and dragged, deprived of sleep, nearly suffocated, and beaten. A medical

Omar Khadr

expert who reviewed his file reported that Khadr has been "traumatized and tortured to a degree that is, in [his] considerable experience, remarkable" (Tietz, 2006).

This case and others raise questions about torture. The United Nations High Commissioner for Human Rights defines torture as any act that intentionally inflicts severe pain or suffering, whether physical or mental, to serve a state purpose such as gathering information or intimidating dissenters. The federal government issued a memo in 2002, since rescinded, stating that coercive interrogations constitute torture only if they intentionally cause suffering "equivalent in intensity to the pain accompanying serious physical injury, such as organ failure, impairment of bodily function, or even death." Although the Bush administration insisted that it did not condone torture in interrogations, it authorized interrogation of terror suspects using both physical and psychological tactics. But there is no evidence that reliable information is gleaned from interrogations that involve torture (Costanzo, Gerrity, & Lykes, 2007), and torture survivors report that they would have said anything to "make the torture stop" (McCoy, 2006). The moral question is whether and to what extent we as a society accept such methods in the name of national security.

---

a matter of contention. Prosecutors observe that defendants can easily recant confessions by alleging that police coerced them, but defense attorneys say that false confessions happen more often than prosecutors acknowledge. It is undisputed that false confessions led to the wrongful conviction and imprisonment of five people in Beatrice, Nebraska in a case known as the Beatrice Six described in Box 6.4.

Historical Background and Current Legal Standing

Many "confessions" do not come spontaneously from the defendant. Rather, they result from intense questioning by the police—interrogations that may involve promises, threats, harassment, or even brutality (Kassin & Gudjonsson, 2004). Until 1966, the

---

B o x 6.4   THE CASE OF THE BEATRICE SIX AND THE CONFESSIONS OF FIVE INNOCENT SUSPECTS

The Beatrice Six—five people who falsely confessed and one who was wrongly convicted of the 1985 rape and murder of 68-year-old Helen Wilson in Beatrice, Nebraska—set the record for the most people exonerated by DNA evidence in one case. Their exonerations and pardons in 2008 shed light on the way that interrogators were able to get detailed statements from the suspects about a crime they did not commit.

The murder investigation had grown cold by 1989 after the actual killer, an Oklahoma City man who drifted through Beatrice around the time of the murder, was cleared because of a blood test mistake. Looking for leads, a county sheriff heard from a confidential informant that the six were involved. The suspects—three men and three women—were all young people who were abusing alcohol or drugs at the time and who had psychological problems. All six were arrested and charged; all were eligible for the death penalty (Hammel, 2008a, 2008b).

The interrogations, conducted by a psychologist who had also acted as therapist to some of the defendants, involved leading questions, planted suggestions about the crime scene, assurances that it is natural to block memories of gruesome crimes, and threats about the death penalty. Suspect Joann Taylor confessed after interrogators told her they wanted her to be the first female on Nebraska's death row. In fact, five of the six suspects, easily influenced and probably confused, falsely confessed to escape the threat of a death penalty. All pled guilty or no contest to reduced charges of second-degree murder or accessory to second-degree murder. Only one—Joseph White—maintained his innocence and insisted on a jury trial. He was convicted. Altogether, the Beatrice Six spent 77 years in prison.

---

traditional test for admissibility of a confession was voluntariness. A voluntary confession was given without overt inducements, threats, promises, or physical harm. The trustworthiness of a confession was believed to be lost when it was obtained through one or more of those means (*Hopt v. Utah*, 1884).

Assessing the voluntariness of confessions proved difficult for many reasons. The task was highly subjective, and it resulted in countless "swearing contests" between police and suspects about what went on behind the closed door of interrogation rooms. Therefore, in *Miranda v. Arizona* (1966), the Supreme Court held that a confession resulting from in-custody interrogation was admissible only if, in addition to being voluntary, it had been obtained after the police had ensured the suspect's protection from self-incrimination by giving the so-called *Miranda* warnings (see Box 6.5).

The *Miranda* case did not solve all problems associated with the validity of confessions. Although the warnings add a new element to the interrogation, intense and secretive interrogations continue to this day, with the interrogator intent upon persuading the suspect to confess. Furthermore, many suspects waive their *Miranda* rights, and after a suspect voluntarily enters the interrogation room, investigators can use any number of tactics to obtain a confession. Some suspects, including those who are young or mentally disabled are especially vulnerable to the tactics of a skillful interrogator, though the Supreme Court has stated that a suspect's mental limitations or psychological problems do not necessarily lead to the conclusion that a confession was involuntary (*Colorado v. Connelly*, 1986).

A defendant often makes and then withdraws a confession. The Supreme Court, in *Jackson v. Denno* (1964), held that criminal defendants are entitled to a pretrial hearing that determines whether any confession they have made was given voluntarily and not the outcome of physical or psychological coercion, which the U.S. Constitution forbids. Only if the judge determines that the confession was voluntary can it be introduced during the trial. The *Jackson v. Denno* decision explicitly acknowledged the possibility of coerced confessions.

Whittling Away at Miranda

Miranda v. Arizona, (1966) was one of the most controversial decisions of the past century. The Chief Justice at the time, Earl Warren, was castigated in

---

B o x 6.5   THE CASE OF ERNEST MIRANDA AND THE RIGHT TO REMAIN SILENT: FOREVER CHANGING THE FACE OF POLICE WORK

One of the best-known U.S. Supreme Court cases decided during the last century, *Miranda v. Arizona* (1966), dealt with the problem of coerced confessions. Late on a Saturday in May of 1963, an 18-year-old woman left her job at a theater in downtown Phoenix. As she was walking home, a man grabbed her. He dragged her to his car, tied her hands, laid her down in the back seat, drove her to the desert, and raped her. Then, as he waited for her to get dressed, he demanded money. She gave him the four $1 bills in her purse.

A week after the rape, the victim's brother-in-law spotted a car like the one she had described. He remembered enough of the license plate for the police to trace the car to a woman who had a friend named Ernest Miranda. When police located the car, they saw a rope strung along the front seat, just as the victim had described. They put together a lineup, selecting three Mexican Americans to stand with Miranda. But he was the only person with eyeglasses and tattoos—features the victim remembered about her assailant. Still, she couldn't identify anyone.

Frustrated, the police then took Miranda to an interrogation room for what they thought was routine questioning. But the exchanges that occurred in that tiny chamber forever changed the way police interact with citizens. Miranda asked about the lineup: "How did I do?" "You flunked," a police officer replied, and began to question Miranda. No attorneys, witnesses, or tape recorders were present. The police later reported that Miranda voluntarily confessed. Miranda described the interrogation differently:

Once they get you in a little room and they start badgering you one way or the other, "You better tell us ... or we're going to throw the book at you. ... And

I haven't had any sleep since the day before. I'm tired. I just got off my work, and they have me and they are interrogating me. They mention first one crime, then another one; they are certain I am the person.... Knowing what a penitentiary is like, a person has to be frightened, scared. And not knowing if he'll be able to get back up and go home." (Quoted in Baker, 1983, p. 13)

Whichever story one believes, Ernest Miranda emerged from the questioning a confessed rapist.

In June of 1963, Miranda was convicted of rape and kidnapping, and was sentenced to 20 to 30 years for each charge. He appealed his conviction to the U.S. Supreme Court, and the Court—by a 5–4 vote—concluded that his right against self-incrimination had been violated. Henceforth, they stated, the police must warn suspects of certain rights before starting a custodial interrogation. If these procedures are not followed, any damaging admissions made by suspects cannot be used by the prosecution in a trial.

Ironically, on the night of January 31, 1976, Miranda was playing poker in a flophouse section of Phoenix. A drunken fight broke out and Miranda was stabbed. He was dead on arrival at the hospital. Miranda's killer fled, but his accomplice was caught. Before taking him to police headquarters, a police officer read to him from a card:

You have the right to remain silent. Anything you say can be used against you in a court of law. You have the right to the presence of an attorney to assist you prior to questioning and to be with you during questioning, if you so desire. If you cannot afford an attorney, you have the right to have an attorney appointed for you prior to questioning. Do you understand these rights? Will you voluntarily answer my questions?

---

congressional committees and on the floor of Congress (Warren, 1977), and "Impeach Earl Warren" billboards were widely seen. Although *Miranda* has survived for more than 40 years, the case remains controversial to this day. In fact, it faced a major challenge in 2000 when Professor Paul Cassell claimed that a law passed by Congress in 1968 overruled the *Miranda* requirements. That law directed judges to admit any voluntary confession, regardless of whether

warnings had been given. But in a 7–2 decision, the Supreme Court reaffirmed that *Miranda* was a constitutional ruling and that the warnings have become part of the national culture (*Dickerson v. United States*, 2000). This case is a good example of *stare decisis*—the court's preference for maintaining stability in its decisions whenever possible. Given *Miranda's* longtime acceptance in the United States, the Court opted against outright change in the law of confessions.

The U.S. Supreme Court has weakened the *Miranda* requirements through a series of other decisions, however. Among the changes:

1. *Confessions that violate Miranda may still be used at a trial.* Suppose a person confesses when arrested, and the confession is taken in violation of the *Miranda* warnings. If the defendant testifies to his or her innocence at trial, the prosecutor may use the confession to show that the defendant should not be believed (*Harris v. New York*, 1971).

2. *Confessions by defendants who don't fully understand the warnings may still be used at a trial.* There are suspects whose young age, intellectual disability, or psychological instability renders them especially vulnerable to certain tactics of interrogation (Owen-Kostelnik, Reppucci, & Meyer, 2006; Redlich, 2007b). These individuals may have difficulty understanding the warnings and the meaning of a waiver. Nonetheless, if the police give the warnings and the defendant responds affirmatively when asked whether he or she wishes to make a statement, that statement is usually admissible (*Fare v. Michael C.*, 1979).

3. *Miranda does not apply unless the suspect is in the custody of the police.* The Supreme Court has treated *custody* in various ways. For example, the Court held that roadside questioning of a motorist stopped for drunk driving is not "custody," even though the motorist is not free to go (*Berkemer v. McCarty*, 1984). Warnings are not required in this circumstance. "Stop and frisk" questioning is also usually viewed as noncustodial because such questioning merely accompanies temporary detentions in public places.

4. *Miranda does not apply unless the defendant is being interrogated.* A volunteered confession is always admissible. Suppose the police arrest a robbery suspect and decide, for whatever reason, not to interrogate him. On the way to the station, the accused person volunteers that he wouldn't have been caught if he'd kept his mask on. This confession is admissible because it was not in response to police questioning (*Rhode Island v. Innis*, 1980).

The Validity of Confession Evidence

How valid is confession evidence? In a perfect world, guilty people would always confess, and innocent people would never do so. Unfortunately, this is far from reality. We know that two kinds of erroneous outcomes are possible: *false negatives* (when guilty suspects falsely proclaim their innocence) and *false positives* (when innocent suspects confess). The latter, termed a **false confession,** occurs when a suspect provides an "I did it" statement and an accompanying description of how and why the crime occurred, and both are factually false. Although false negatives occur more often than false positives, the latter outcome has captured the attention of psychologists, lawyers, judges, and the public, reflecting widespread agreement that innocent people should not be convicted of crimes they did not commit.

Why, one might ask, would a truly innocent person falsely confess to a crime that he or she did not commit? How often does this really happen? What are the circumstances that would lead someone to confess falsely? Although it is difficult to gauge the frequency of false confessions because no agency or organization keeps track of the results of interrogations, we do know that they occur. To date, studies have documented approximately 250 false confessions since the *Miranda* decision (Leo, 2008). Kassin (2005) noted that 25% of people who were exonerated by DNA evidence after serving time in prison had falsely confessed. These numbers almost certainly understate the problem because false confessions often are not revealed, and thus go unacknowledged by police and prosecutors and unreported by the media (Leo, 2008). Interrogation-induced false confessions tend to occur in more serious cases like homicides and other high-stakes felonies when the police are under pressure to solve the crime, and thus use more psychologically coercive tactics to wear the suspect down (Gross et al., 2005). Lacking a victim or an eyewitness to describe the crime, the police may need a confession to secure a conviction.

We are now beginning to understand the circumstances that give rise to false confessions. But before we describe them, we must ask how we can know, for certain, that a confession is false. Do we simply take the suspect or defendant at his word when he alleges that his admission of guilt was wrong? Alternatively, do we need some kind of evidence that proves, unequivocally, that the defendant could not have committed the crime to which he confessed?

Proving that a Confession is False.   There are four ways in which we can be certain that a disputed confession is false (Drizin & Leo, 2004). First, a suspect could confess to a crime that never happened. For example, three mentally retarded defendants (including Victoria Banks) were convicted by an Alabama jury of killing Ms. Banks's newborn child. Only after the three had served time in prison was it determined that Ms. Banks was incapable of giving birth to a child because she had had a tubal ligation operation that prevented her from getting pregnant.

Confessions can be proved to be false in situations where it was physically impossible for a suspect to commit the crime, as, for example, when jail records show that the defendant was incarcerated at the time the crime was committed. Three men suspected of committing crimes in Chicago were actually in jail when those crimes were committed (Drizen & Leo, 2004).

A third way in which a disputed confession can be proved false is that the actual perpetrator is identified and his guilt is objectively established. This happened in the case of Christopher Ochoa, a high school honor student, who confessed to robbing, raping, and murdering a woman in an Austin, Texas, Pizza Hut in 1988. Ochoa, who served 12 years in prison, claims that he confessed in order to avoid the possibility of a death sentence. He was released and exonerated only after the real perpetrator confessed to killing the woman and led authorities to the weapon and the bag in which he had placed the money (Drizin & Leo, 2004).

Finally, we know that a confession is false when there is scientific evidence—most commonly DNA—that definitively establishes the defendant's innocence. For example, three teenagers (Michael Crowe, Joshua Treadway, and Aaron Houser) all falsely confessed to the 1998 murder of Michael's 12-year-old sister Stephanie in Escondido, California. Charges against the boys were dropped only after DNA testing proved

that blood found on the sweatshirt of a mentally ill drifter who had been in the neighborhood on the night of the murder was Stephanie's (Drizin & Colgan, 2004).

Few cases involving disputed confessions come with independent evidence that the suspect is innocent, however (Leo, 2008). Rarely will the actual perpetrator come forward to claim responsibility and remove the blame from an innocent confessor, and in most cases there is no DNA evidence to compare to the confessor's DNA. As a result, few confessors can prove definitively that their confessions were false. Even when DNA evidence exonerates a false confessor, prosecutors sometimes refuse to concede innocence (Kassin, 2005). Bruce Godschalk was exonerated after 15 years in prison when DNA testing proved that he was not a rapist. Still, the prosecutor refused to release him after the results were known, claiming that the test was inaccurate and that the tape-recorded confession taken by police detectives should be trusted.

What would cause a person to confess to a crime he or she did not commit? New studies document the role that psychologically oriented coercion can have in inducing suspects to confess, especially when those suspects are particularly vulnerable (e.g., children, adolescents, and those with mental limitations). In fact, these studies point to the compounding effects of an interrogator's coercive tactics and a suspect's vulnerable state at the time of questioning.

Inside the Interrogation Room: Common Interrogation Techniques

At earlier times in our history, torture and other "third-degree" tactics were employed to get suspects to incriminate themselves. Because many people consider these techniques to be morally offensive and the techniques often yield statements of questionable veracity, physical intimidation is virtually nonexistent today. In its place, interrogators now use psychologically oriented coercion that, because it is less blatant, may actually be more insidious.

Based on his own observations of more than 100 police interrogations and his review of recorded interrogations in several hundred other cases, Professor

Richard Leo noted a fundamental contradiction concerning the nature of interrogations: "On the one hand, police need incriminating statements and admissions to solve many crimes, especially serious ones; on the other hand, there is almost never a good reason for suspects to provide them. Police are under tremendous organizational and social pressure to obtain admissions and confessions. But it is rarely in a suspect's rational self-interest to say something that will likely lead to his prosecution and conviction" (Leo, 2008, pp. 5–6).

Leo (2008) documented a vast array of subtle and manipulative ploys that police use to induce confessions. Most of these techniques are detailed in interrogation training manuals; the most popular are *Criminal Interrogation and Confessions*, currently in its fourth edition (Inbau, Reid, Buckley, & Jayne, 2004) and *Practical Aspects of Interview and Interrogation* (Zulawski & Wicklander, 2001). To fully understand why someone would falsely confess, one must be aware of the techniques of social influence recommended by these manuals and put into practice in interrogation rooms across the country.

We can divide an interrogation into the preinterrogation, "softening up" stage and the interrogation itself. Throughout the encounter, police use well-crafted, deliberate strategies to secure incriminating evidence from suspects.

Preinterrogation, "Softening Up" the Suspect. Would you prefer to be "interviewed" or "interrogated?" (Probably the former.) When the police arrange to question a suspect, they may "invite" him to the station house because they "just want to ask a few questions" to "clear up a little matter." They may explicitly tell the suspect that they do not consider him a suspect. This all sounds innocuous enough. But the police have actually misrepresented the nature and purpose of the "discussion" to disarm the suspect and reduce his resistance (Leo, 2008).

When a suspect arrives at the police station for questioning, he is typically shuffled off to a small, soundproof room with armless, straight-backed chairs, lacking sensory stimulation and distractions. By physically and socially isolating the suspect, the police begin to subtly exert pressure on him to talk. The interrogator may then try to soften up the suspect by using flattery, ingratiation, and rapport-building— asking benign questions and engaging in pleasant small talk. According to one detective, "I don't care whether it is rape, robbery or homicide … the first thing you need to do is build rapport with that person … I think from that point on you can get anybody to talk about anything." (Leo, 2008, p. 123) All the while, the detective is concealing the fact that he has already determined that the suspect is guilty of a crime and is intent on extracting incriminating evidence from him.

Although the police are required by law to give the *Miranda* warnings prior to questioning, there are various ways they can circumvent these warnings. Their intent is to get the suspect to waive his rights and begin to talk, thereby increasing the chances of hearing incriminating information. Recall that the warnings are required only when the suspect is being interrogated while in custody. By telling the suspect that he is not under arrest and is free to go, there is no need to warn him that statements he makes may be used against him. Sometimes the police will minimize the importance of the *Miranda* warnings by describing them as a mere bureaucratic necessity or formality. Richard Leo observed a detective who stated, "Don't let this ruffle your feathers or anything like that, it's just a formality that we have to go through, okay. As I said this is a *Miranda* warning and what it says is …" On other occasions, police can persuade the suspect to talk in order to tell "his side of the story." Almost all suspects waive their *Miranda* rights and talk to interrogators (Leo, 2008). Psychologists have wondered why they do so, especially when they are innocent. We describe relevant research findings later in this chapter.

The Interrogation Itself. During the heart of the questioning, interrogators use a set of carefully orchestrated procedures with the goal to eventually overwhelm even the most reluctant suspect and get him to provide incriminating statements. These procedures can be reduced to a few basic strategies: the police use **negative incentives** to break down a suspect's defenses; lower his resistance; and instill feelings of fear, despair, and powerlessness. Negative incentives are tactics (like accusations, attacks on the suspect's denials, and evidence fabrications) that convey to the suspect that he has no choice but to confess. The police also use **positive inducements** to motivate him to see that an admission is in his best interest. All interrogators try, implicitly or explicitly, to send the message that the suspect will receive some benefit in exchange for his admission of wrongdoing (Leo, 2008).

After the suspect has either implicitly or explicitly agreed to talk, the interrogation becomes accusatorial, with the interrogator confronting the suspect with a statement indicating absolute certainty in his guilt. Accusations are one of the most basic tactics in interrogations; police use them routinely and repeatedly. One subtle effect of an accusation is shifting the burden of proof from the state to the suspect. In what may be one of the most "ingenious psychological aspects of American interrogation" (Leo, 2008, p. 135) the suspect must now work to convince the police of his innocence.

During questioning, interrogators also frequently interrupt any statements of innocence and challenge any denials the suspect makes, often by simply cutting him off or expressing disbelief in his version of events. One effect of this ploy is to undermine the suspect's confidence in his memory, which may cause inconsistencies in later retellings of his story—even if he is telling the truth.

The most powerful tool in the interrogator's arsenal is his opportunity, often exercised, to present **fabricated evidence.** Even if interrogators have no evidence of the suspect's wrongdoing, they can make him believe that they do (Torkildson & Kassin, 2008). They can point to "signs" of his nonverbal behavior that indicate guilt, tell him that other people including eyewitnesses and accomplices have implicated him, and make up stories about the existence of fraudulent fingerprint evidence and surveillance videos that capture his image. On occasion, suspects take a polygraph examination, presented to them as an opportunity to prove innocence, when all along investigators plan to confront the suspect with evidence that he failed the test and urge him to confess. The police claim that they need to fabricate evidence in order to get guilty suspects to confess, but this tactic undoubtedly also tricks some of the innocent.

Finally, police use positive inducements to persuade a suspect that he will benefit from complying with authorities and confessing. This can take the form of providing scenarios to explain or justify the suspect's actions (e.g., suggesting that he was probably acting in self-defense or in the "heat of the moment"), or of promising some sort of a deal for confessing. Sometimes detectives simply imply that the suspect can go home if he accepts interrogators' demands. In another famous case involving false confessions—the Central Park jogger case in which five young men confessed to brutally raping and beating a female jogger—each suspect confessed in a way that minimized his own involvement and each thought that after confessing he could go home (Kassin, 2005). A recent survey of more than 600 police investigators showed that they commonly practice many of the ploys that Leo describes, including physically isolating suspects, establishing rapport, finding contradictions in their accounts, confronting them with evidence of their guilt, and appealing to their self-interests (Kassin et al., 2007).

An Empirical look at Interrogation Tactics. Psychologists have examined some of these interrogation tactics empirically, with surprising results. Recent studies explain why innocent people waive their *Miranda* rights and how interrogators' presumption of guilt affects the nature of the questioning, which in turn, affects the suspect's responding.

It seems logical, given the highly coercive nature of police interrogations, that most suspects would exercise their right to remain silent and refuse to answer investigators' questions. But many suspects waive their rights and submit to questioning (Leo & White, 1999). We pointed out that police have become adept at obtaining waivers from suspects by using small talk and establishing rapport. But another factor—suspects' innocence—may also explain why they talk. Leo (1996) found that people who lack experience in the criminal justice system are more likely than those with felony records to waive their rights and submit to questioning. People who lack experience and especially those who are innocent may naively believe in the transparency of their innocence (Kassin, 2005).

To test of the possibility that innocent people are likely to waive their rights and submit to questioning, Kassin and Norwick (2004) conducted a mock study in which participants were instructed either to steal $100 from a drawer (guilty condition) or to open the drawer but not take any money (innocent condition). When questioned by a male "detective" who sought a waiver of their *Miranda* rights, innocent participants were considerably more likely to grant the waiver than those who were guilty, by a margin of 81% to 36%. When asked to explain the reasons for their decisions, a large percentage (72%) of innocent people explained that they waived their rights precisely because they were innocent. A typical comment: "I did not have anything to hide." Innocents may waive their rights and answer questions because they believe in a just world in which truth and justice will prevail. They assume, naively, that their innocence will set them free. But ironically, "innocence may put innocents at risk" (Kassin, 2005, p. 224).

Recall that many interrogations begin with the detective issuing a statement of belief in the suspect's guilt. This presumption of guilt can apparently influence the way a detective conducts the questioning, causing the suspect to become defensive or confused, and increasing the chances of a false confession. This phenomenon—referred to as a *self-fulfilling prophecy* or **behavioral confirmation** (Meissner & Kassin, 2004) has been demonstrated in a wide range of settings (McNatt, 2000; Rosenthal & Jacobson, 1968). After people form a particular belief (e.g., in the guilt of a suspect), they unwittingly seek out information that verifies that belief, overlook conflicting data, and behave in a manner that conforms to the belief. In turn, the target person (here, the suspect) behaves in ways that support the initial belief.

Social psychologists have examined the effects of an implicit assumption of guilt on the conduct of interrogators and suspects, and on judgments of the interrogation made by neutral observers (Kassin, Goldstein, & Savitsky, 2003). In the first phase of a two-part study, "suspects" were instructed either to steal $100 from a locked cabinet or to engage in a related but innocent act (approaching the locked cabinet but not stealing any money). Other participants acted as interrogators and were led to believe either that most suspects in the study were truly guilty of the mock theft or that most were truly innocent. These interviewing sessions were taped and then, in the second phase of the study, played for observers whose task was to judge whether the suspect was guilty or innocent.

Interrogators who assumed that suspects were guilty used more guilt-based interrogative techniques such as presenting false evidence, trying harder to elicit a confession, and making innocent suspects sound more defensive. Suspects toward whom these techniques were directed acted more defensively and were more likely to be identified as being guilty of the mock crime. In fact, the most pressure-filled interrogation sessions occurred when innocent suspects were questioned by interrogators who presumed guilt. The presumption of guilt apparently ushers in a process of behavioral confirmation by which the expectations of interrogators affect their questioning style, the suspects' behavior, and, ultimately, judgments of the guilt of the suspect. These findings may actually *underestimate* the risks of behavioral confirmation in actual interrogations, where the questioning can go on for hours rather than minutes, interrogators have years of experience in questioning suspects, and they have confidence in their ability to get a confession (Meissner & Kassin, 2004).

So far, we have considered the effects of interrogation on adults accused of committing crimes. Although most children who interact with the law are witnesses or victims, a substantial number of juveniles come into contact with the police and legal system as suspects. Like adults, these juvenile suspects are interrogated by police. The training manual (Inbau et al., 2004) suggests that the principles of adult interrogation "are just as applicable to the young ones" (p. 298), and analyses of juvenile interrogations showed that police used many of the same strategies with them, including the possibility that the suspect can go home if he tells the police what they want to hear (Owen-Kostelnik et al., 2006; Redlich, Silverman, Chen, & Steiner, 2004). But many juveniles have difficulty understanding the rights accorded to them by the *Miranda* warnings (Viljoen, Zapf, & Roesch, 2007) and defendants age 15 and younger are willing to waive their rights and plead guilty even when the evidence against them is not strong (Viljoen, Klaver, & Roesch, 2005). Some juveniles may be unaware that they are signing a confession because many "confessions" are written by interrogating officers, based on the suspects' verbal account and other evidence. Thus, like adults, juveniles sometimes confess falsely (as did the defendants in the Central Park jogger case). How often does this happen? Of the 125 proven false confession cases compiled by Drizin and Leo (2004), fully 33% involved juveniles.

False Confessions

Innocent people tend to waive their *Miranda* rights and answer questions. Police presume guilt and even believe that truthful suspects are deceptive. Interrogators use carefully scripted techniques to elicit confessions. Consequently, detectives draw out confessions from innocent people as well as from the guilty. Yet not all false confessions are alike; they occur for different reasons and can be explained by different situational and dispositional factors. Kassin and Wrightsman (1985) devised a taxonomy to describe different kinds of false confessions. Although it has been critiqued and refined over the years (Kassin & Gudjonnson, 2004), it still serves as a good framework for understanding why they happen.

Some innocent people confess to criminal acts with little prodding. When Charles Lindbergh's baby was kidnapped in 1932, more than 200 people came forward and claimed responsibility (Kassin & Gudjonsson, 2004). After the murder of child beauty-pageant contestant JonBenét Ramsey had gone unresolved for several years, prosecutors were eager to consider the confession of Mark Karr. But Karr's DNA did not match the sample found on the victim and he was never charged. These **voluntary false confessions** arise because people seek notoriety, desire to cleanse themselves of guilt feelings from previous wrongdoings, want to protect the real criminal, or have difficulty distinguishing fact from fiction (Kassin & Wrightsman, 1985; McCann, 1998).

Sometimes suspects confess in order to escape or avoid ongoing aversive interrogations or to gain some sort of promised reward. Legal history is full of examples dating as far back as the Salem Witch trials of 1692 during which approximately 50 women confessed to being witches, some after being "tyed … neck and heels till the blood was ready to come out of their noses" (Karlsen, 1989, p. 101, cited by Kassin & Gudjonsson, 2004). The false confessions in the Central Park jogger case were of this sort; each of the defendants said he confessed because he wanted to go home. These confessions are termed **compliant false confessions** because the suspect is induced to comply with the interrogator's demands to make an incriminating statement (Kassin & Wrightsman, 1985). They occur when a suspect knows that he is innocent but publicly acquiesces to the demand for a confession because the short-term benefit of confessing (e.g., being left along, being allowed to leave) outweigh the long-term costs (e.g., being charged with a crime, being convicted).

Some suspects confess because they actually come to believe that they have committed the crime. These so-called **internalized false confessions** can be directly related to the highly suggestive and manipulative techniques that interrogators sometimes use during questioning. An internalized false confession can result when, after hours of being questioned, badgered, and told stories about what "must have happened," the suspect begins to develop a profound distrust of his own memory. Being vulnerable, he is then easily influenced by external suggestions and comes to believe that he "must have done it" (Gudjonsson & MacKeith, 1982).

We previously described the case of 14-year-old Michael Crowe, who falsely confessed to killing his sister. Despite his initial vehement denials, Michael apparently came to believe, over the course of three grueling interrogations, that he had actually stabbed her: "I'm not sure how I did it. All I know is I did it" (Drizin & Colgan, 2004, p. 141). During the interrogations, detectives told Michael at least four lies: that his hair was found on his sister's body, that her blood was in his bedroom, that all of the doors to the house had been locked, and that he failed a lie detector test. With no memory of the killing but persuaded by these details, Michael was apparently convinced that he had a split personality and that the killing was accomplished by the "bad Michael" while the "good Michael" blocked out the crime (Drizin & Colgan, 2004).

Inside the Courtroom: How Confession Evidence Is Evaluated

The first source of error involving confession evidence stems from what happens in the interrogation room. A second source of error occurs when prosecutors, defense attorneys, judges, and especially juries fail to understand why the suspect might have confessed and uncritically accept a false confession as valid. The false confession then sets in motion a chain of events with adverse consequences for the suspect because attorneys, juries, and judges make decisions—about plea-bargaining, convicting, and sentencing—assuming that what the suspect said was true.

Many prosecutors assume that only guilty suspects confess. So when they secure a confession, they tend to treat the suspect harshly, charging him with the highest number and types of offenses possible, requesting higher bail, and being reluctant to accept a plea-bargain to a reduced charge (Leo & Ofshe, 1998). The confession becomes, in essence, the crux of the prosecution's case.

Even defense attorneys assume that people who confess are guilty, and urge them to accept plea-bargains rather than risk their chances in a trial with confession evidence (Nardulli, Eisenstein, & Fleming, 1988). The California Supreme Court stated, "The confession operates as a kind of evidentiary bombshell which shatters the defense" (*California v. Cahill*, 1993).

Judges are also likely to treat confessors harshly. In cases of disputed confessions, they almost always decide that confessions are voluntary and thus, admissible as evidence in a trial (Givelber, 2001). In some cases, a defendant who has confessed will nevertheless enter a plea of not guilty and go to trial. If the jury convicts this defendant, judges are likely to sentence him harshly because they tend to punish offenders who claim innocence, waste resources in a trial, and fail to show remorse or apologize (Leo, 2007).

Confessions are an especially potent form of evidence to jurors, even more influential than eyewitness and character testimony (Kassin & Neumann, 1997). Jurors are highly likely to convict defendants who have confessed even when the confession is false. Archival analyses of actual cases in which false confessors pled not guilty and proceeded to trial show that jury conviction rates ranged from 73% to 81% (Leo & Ofshe, 1998; Drizin & Leo, 2004).

Jurors accept confession evidence because they assume, like most of us, that people would not act against their own self-interests and confess to something they had not done (Kassin & Gudjonsson, 2004). Jurors fail to take the circumstances of an interrogation into account. In a number of studies, they failed to discount a confession elicited by high-pressure tactics of interrogators. When explaining the causes of others' behavior, people often commit the **fundamental attribution error:** They do not give sufficient importance to the external situation as a determinant of behavior; instead, they believe the behavior is caused by stable, internal factors unique to the actor (Jones, 1990). In essence, jurors take a confession at face value, fail to adjust or correct for situational forces on behavior, and assume that if a suspect confessed, he must be guilty (Wrightsman & Kassin, 1993).

There is another reason that people (including jurors) tend to believe confessions: They are not adept at distinguishing true from false confessions. Kassin, Meissner, and Norwick (2005) crafted a clever study to examine this issue. They enlisted male prison inmates for videotaped interviews and instructed them either to give a full confession to the crime for which they were incarcerated, or to concoct a false confession consistent with a skeletal, one-sentence description of a crime committed by another inmate. The researchers then created a video of 10 different inmates "confessing" to a variety of crimes, including breaking and entering, automobile theft, burglary, armed robbery and aggravated assault, and showed them to college students and police investigators. The question was whether observers could tell which confessions were true and which were false. Accuracy rates hovered just above chance levels (i.e., 57%) for students and slightly below chance level (i.e., 48%) for police investigators. Investigators tended to make more false-positive errors (assuming that a false confession was true) than students, especially if they had extensive law enforcement experience. This finding may be explained by the guilt-presumptive nature of interrogators.

Interrogators are not able to tell whether a confession is true or false and most people take a confession at face value as an admission of guilt. So it is not surprising that innocent suspects' claims of wrongful conviction have historically fallen on deaf ears. But the development of DNA testing has begun to change that, revealing hundreds of wrongful convictions resulting from false confessions. In addition, psychologists now intervene in cases of disputed confessions, functioning as consultants to defense attorneys and sometimes testifying as expert witnesses in pretrial admissibility hearings and during trials. The objective is to educate jurors and judges about the nature of police interrogations and the dispositional and situational factors that lead to false confessions. But might there be a more efficient way to prevent wrongful convictions based on false confessions? Wouldn't it be better to assess, early in the investigation of a case, whether a suspect's confession resulted from a coercive interrogation? Several commentators advocate reforming the system with this objective in mind.

Reforming the System to Prevent False Confessions

Recording all police interrogations can provide a complete, objective, and reviewable record of how the suspect was questioned (see, e.g., Drizin & Reich, 2004). Recording can improve the quality of interrogations by deterring manipulative tactics by investigators and frivolous claims of coercion by defendants (Kassin & Gudjonsson, 2004). It also preserves an objective record of the entire session and avoids "he said/she said" disputes. More than half of all law enforcement agencies now record at least some of their interrogations, and a handful of states mandate videotaping.

But recording may not be a surefire preventive against the conviction of innocent people. Daniel Lassiter and his colleagues have shown that when the camera is focused on the suspect (as is usually done to allow observers to see what the suspect said and did), observers are more likely to judge the confession as voluntary, compared with the same confession recorded from a different camera perspective (e.g., focused equally on the suspect and the interrogator or solely on the interrogator) (Lassiter & Geers, 2004). This is an example of **illusory causation,** the tendency to attribute causation to one stimulus because it is more conspicuous than others. Even legal professionals—police interrogators and judges—are influenced by the perspective of the camera (Lassiter, Diamond, Schmidt, & Elek, 2007). When the recording shows both the suspect and the interrogator, observers are more attuned to situational pressures exerted by the interrogator. Lassiter et al. concluded that filming can be an effective tool for recording interrogations, but must be used judiciously. In particular, an equal-focus perspective that allows observers to view both interrogator and suspect can reduce any bias inherent in recording interrogations.

SUMMARY

1. ***What are some psychological investigative techniques used by the police?*** The police use a variety of such techniques to increase the likelihood that suspects will be prosecuted and convicted. Among these are criminal profiling, unaided judgments of deception, the so-called lie detector (technically, the polygraph technique), brain-based techniques for gauging deception, and procedures to induce confessions.

2. ***What is criminal profiling?*** Criminal profiling is an attempt to use what is known about how a crime was committed to infer what type of person might have committed it. Preliminary evidence about profiling suggests that it may

have some validity as a means of narrowing police investigations to the most likely suspects.

3. *What cues do people use to detect deception and how accurate are these judgments?* People tend to focus on the wrong cues when determining whether another person is telling the truth. Bodily signs like fidgeting and gaze aversion are not generally associated with lying. Verbal cues, including length of utterance and the presence of memory lapses and speech errors are better indicators. In general, people are not very accurate in discriminating between liars and truth-tellers, even when they have professional experience doing so.

4. *Is the polygraph a valid instrument for lie detection? What are some problems associated with it?* No measure of physiological reactions can precisely distinguish between guilt and other negative emotions, such as fear, anger, or embarrassment. Nevertheless, polygraph examiners claim high rates of accuracy in distinguishing between subjects who are lying and those who are not. There are several problems with such claims, including the misleading nature of "accuracy rates," lack of consistency between the conclusions of different examiners, and suspects' use of countermeasures to "beat the test."

5. *What brain-based techniques are used to detect deception and how well do they work?* Two

techniques, brain scans and neuroimaging using fMRI, record brain activity while people are either lying or telling the truth. Studies show that different patterns of brain activation are associated with truth-telling and lying. Advocates of these procedures promote their effectiveness in detecting deception, but their validity under conditions that approximate real-life questioning has not been established.

6. *How valid is confession evidence? What kinds of interrogation procedures can lead to false confessions?* Two kinds of errors arise in the context of confessions: guilty suspects falsely proclaiming their innocence, and innocent suspects falsely confessing. Among the interrogation techniques that can lead to false confessions are prolonged social isolation, confronting a suspect and expressing a belief in his or her guilt, exaggerating or fabricating evidence against the suspect, and offering psychological and moral justification for the offense.

7. *What are some of the reforms proposed to prevent false confessions?* Critics of police interrogations suggest that these interrogations should be recorded in order to improve the quality of questioning and to deter police misconduct. In addition, filming of interrogations can preserve a record that can be evaluated at a later time to assess the possibility of coercive influences.

KEY TERMS

behavioral confirmation

brain fingerprinting

cognitive load interviews

compliant false confessions

Control Question Test

countermeasures

criminal profiling

diagnostic cues

fabricated evidence

false confession

functional magnetic resonance imaging

fundamental attribution error

Guilty Knowledge Test

illusory causation

internalized false confessions

mass murderer

negative incentives

polygraph

positive inducements

serial killers

spree killers

truth bias

voluntary false confessions

7

Between Arrest and Trial

ORIENTING QUESTIONS

1. What are the major legal proceedings between arrest and trial in the criminal justice system?
2. Why do defendants and prosecutors agree to plea-bargain?
3. What are settlement negotiations and why are most civil lawsuits resolved through settlement, rather than trial?
4. What is bail, and what factors influence the amount of bail set?
5. In what ways does pretrial publicity pose a danger to fair trials? How can these dangers be reduced?

Previous chapters presented psychological perspectives on the actions of law enforcement officials as they investigate crimes and make arrests. Between these events and any eventual trial of a suspect are several other steps with psychological implications.

The grand finale in our adversary system of justice is the trial, a public battle waged by two combatants (prosecution versus defense in a criminal trial, and plaintiff versus defendant in a civil trial), each fighting for a favorable outcome. Trials can be fiercely contested; prosecutors desire convictions, criminal defendants seek their freedom through an acquittal, civil plaintiffs want compensation for wrongs they have suffered, and civil defendants hope to be absolved of wrongdoing and not required to pay damages.

Although the trial may be the most visible and dramatic ritual in our system, many other factors play large—often decisive—roles in determining case outcomes. For example, in the weeks and months following arrest, many criminal cases are simply dismissed for lack of evidence or other difficulties that prosecutors perceive in the case. Of some 49,000 defendants charged with a felony from 1990 to 2002 in the 75 most populous counties in the United States, 24% had their cases dismissed prior to trial (Cohen & Reaves, 2006).

For the vast majority of people charged with crimes and not fortunate enough to have the charges dropped, **plea bargains,** not trials, resolve the case. Plea bargaining, described in more detail later in the chapter, is a process in which a defendant agrees to plead guilty in exchange for some concession from the prosecutor. Such concessions typically involve a reduction in the type of charge, the number of charges, or the recommended sentence. By pleading guilty, defendants give up their right to a trial, allowing attorneys and judges to move on to other cases. Even most civil cases are resolved without a formal trial in a process termed settlement negotiation, described in more detail in this chapter.

If most cases are settled without a trial, why is our society (and indeed, psychologists who work in the legal arena) so fascinated by trials and trial procedures? Without a doubt, there are theatrical aspects to many trials, especially those featured in media portrayals, films, novels, and on Court TV. Trials grab our attention because they vividly portray the raw emotions of sad, distraught, and angry people. Interest in trials is also related to their very public nature; most trials are conducted in open court for all to see. Some are televised or even available for online viewing.

In contrast, negotiations about plea bargains and settlements are largely hidden from public view. Prosecutors offer concessions to defense attorneys over the phone or in courthouse hallways. Defense attorneys convey these offers to their clients in offices or jail cells. Settlement negotiations in civil cases are also conducted in private. In fact, the eventual settlements in civil cases are often never made public.

Plea bargains and settlement negotiations are the most frequent means for resolving cases. But you may notice that we expend many more pages of this book on psychological issues before and during trials than we do on plea bargains or settlement negotiations.

This choice reflects the available data. Like the general public, psychologists are intrigued by the interpersonal dramas and behavioral complexities involved in trials. Thus, psychologists have conducted a great deal of research on trials and have much to say about them. We provide some of their findings in Chapter 12. But keep in mind that most cases are disposed of in a different and less public way—through plea bargains and settlement discussions that are core concepts of this chapter.

In addition to plea bargains and settlements, this chapter examines other pretrial proceedings in criminal cases including pretrial motions, bail setting, and requests to change venue to minimize the effects of pretrial publicity. All of these issues raise important psychological questions that have been addressed through experimentation, observation, or empirical analysis.

In Chapter 8, we discuss the legal concept of competence, emphasizing how it is assessed by psychiatrists and psychologists. In the criminal justice system, the term **adjudicative competence** (also called "competence to stand trial") refers to a defendant's capacity to understand and participate meaningfully in legal proceedings. It covers mental and psychological abilities that the criminal justice system requires of defendants in order for court actions to be applied to them. Like the topics we cover in this chapter, questions of adjudicative competence are usually raised between the time of arrest and disposition of the case.

Before we discuss pretrial motions, plea bargaining, bail, and change of venue in detail, it will be useful to provide a framework for these topics by describing the customary sequence of pretrial activities in the criminal justice system.

STEPS BETWEEN ARREST AND TRIAL

If the police believe that a suspect committed a crime, they will probably arrest the suspect. However, being arrested for a crime and being charged with a crime are two different events. A person may be arrested without being charged. For example, the police may arrest drunks to detain them and sober them up, but formal charges might never be filed. Charging implies a formal decision to continue with the prosecution, and that decision is made by the prosecuting attorney rather than the police.

The Initial Appearance

The **initial appearance** is a crucial step in the criminal process. The Fourth Amendment to the United States Constitution requires that any person arrested be brought before a judge within 48 hours of arrest. This is one of the most important protections of the Bill of Rights. In many countries the police arrest (or "detain," as arrest is euphemistically called) people and hold them without charge for extended periods— or indefinitely. In the United States, however, anyone who is arrested must be taken without delay before a judge, an important protection against abuse of power by the police. The primary purpose of the initial appearance is for the judge to review the evidence summarized by the prosecutor and determine whether there is reason to believe that the suspect committed the crimes charged. In addition, the judge will inform defendants of the charges against them, inform them of their constitutional rights, review the issue of bail, and appoint attorneys for those that cannot afford to hire their own.

The Preliminary Hearing

The next step is the **preliminary hearing.** One of its purposes is to filter out cases in which the prosecution has insufficient evidence. At a preliminary hearing, the prosecution must offer some evidence on every element of the crime charged and the judge must decide whether the evidence is sufficient to pursue the case further. No jury is present and defendants rarely testify or offer any evidence of their own. The judge will sometimes send the case to a grand jury (described next) or reduce the charges, either because he or she believes the evidence does not support the level of crime charged by the prosecutor or because of a plea bargain between the prosecutor and the defense attorney.

The Grand Jury

Consisting of citizens drawn from the community, the **grand jury** meets in private with the prosecutor to investigate criminal activity and return **indictments** (complaints prepared and signed by the prosecutor describing the crime charged). In about one-third of the states, a criminal defendant cannot be prosecuted unless a grand jury has found grounds to do so. The remaining states permit the prosecutor to proceed either by grand jury indictment or by a preliminary hearing. The grand jury may call witnesses on its own initiative if it is dissatisfied with the witnesses presented by the prosecutor. In some states the defendant has a right to testify.

If the grand jury decides there is sufficient evidence to justify the defendant being tried, it issues an indictment. For example, two Chinese companies and an American importer were indicted in 2008 for allegedly defrauding and misleading American manufacturers about poisonous ingredients used in pet food. The tainted food killed at least 16 dogs and cats, sickened thousands, and led to one of the largest pet food recalls in history.

Arraignment

A grand jury gives its indictments to a judge, who brings those indicted to court for arraignment. At the **arraignment**, the judge makes sure that the defendant has an attorney and appoints one if necessary. The indictment is then read to the defendant, and the defendant is asked to plead guilty or not guilty. It is customary for defendants to plead not guilty at this time, even those who ultimately plead guilty. The reason is to provide opportunities both for discovery (described next), meaning that the defendant's attorney can review some of the evidence against the defendant, and for plea bargaining.

Discovery and Pretrial Motions

Defendants and their attorneys want to be aware of the materials the prosecution will use to prove its case. In civil trials, each side is entitled to **discovery**—that is, each side has a right to depose (question) the witnesses on the opposing side, and to review and copy documents that the other side might use at trial. In criminal cases, however, just how much the prosecution must reveal to the defense varies widely. Some states require prosecutors to turn over all reports, statements by witnesses, and physical evidence to the defense. Most states, however, require only that the prosecutor share certain evidence (e.g., laboratory reports) and evidence that is **exculpatory** (i.e., that tends to show the defendant is not guilty or suggests that prosecution witnesses are not credible). In part because prosecutors failed to share exculpatory evidence, a Colorado man spent eight-and-a-half years in prison for a crime he didn't commit. We describe his case in Box 7.1.

Discovery is a two-way street. In general, states require the defense to turn over the same types of materials that the prosecution must turn over. If the prosecution is required to reveal laboratory reports, the defense will likewise be required to share such reports. In many states, the defense is required to notify the prosecution if it intends to rely on certain defenses, notably insanity and alibi defenses. The reason for requiring such pretrial notice is to give the state an opportunity to investigate the claim and avoid being surprised at trial.

During the discovery phase of the case, both sides file pretrial motions seeking favorable rulings on the admissibility of evidence. Motions commonly filed by the defense are:

1. *Motion for separate trials.* When two or more defendants are jointly indicted, one of them can be counted on to request a separate trial, claiming that to be tried together would be prejudicial. Such a motion was granted in the case of Timothy McVeigh and Terry Nichols, who were convicted in separate trials of bombing the federal building in Oklahoma City, killing 168 people. McVeigh was convicted of murder and sentenced to death, but Nichols was convicted of a lesser charge (conspiracy) and sentenced to life imprisonment.

2. *Motion to sever counts.* Suppose the indictment charges the defendant with robbing a convenience store on April 13 and burglarizing a

---

B o x 7.1   THE CASE OF TIM MASTERS, PROSECUTORS' FAILURE TO DISCLOSE EVIDENCE, AND EIGHT-AND-A-HALF YEARS IN PRISON FOR A CRIME HE DIDN'T COMMIT

In late January, 2008, Tim Masters became perhaps the first person in Colorado to walk up to a counter at the Department of Motor Vehicles and, without first taking a number and waiting in line, get a drivers' license. The crowds of people waiting their turns were only too happy to give Masters a break; after all, he had been released from prison just a few days before when his murder conviction and life sentence were wiped out by DNA evidence that pointed to another suspect. The DNA testing was the final chapter in a long saga of misplaced hunches, shoddy procedures, and prosecutors' failure to disclose crucial evidence.

In 1987, Masters—then only 15 years old—lived with his father in a trailer outside of Fort Collins, Colorado. A woman's body was found in a field about 100 feet from his home; she had been stabbed and sexually mutilated. Detectives interrogated Masters, who admitted to walking past the body on his way to catch a school bus and failing to report it. They also searched his home,

confiscating violent pictures he had drawn in his school notebooks. Over the next several years, prosecutors built a circumstantial case against Masters based on "psychological analysis" of his drawings, the fact that the murder coincided with the anniversary of his mother's death, and their suspicions. Masters was convicted of murder and sentenced to life imprisonment in 1999.

But several years later, a new team of investigators and attorneys began to glean clues that prosecutors knew more than they revealed in 1987. They learned that police had an alternate suspect back then, something not revealed to the defense. They learned that counter to the judge's orders, prosecutors had taken evidence from the case for their own examination. They alleged that prosecutors deliberately "stonewalled, delayed, and obstructed" in order to preserve the conviction. Eventually, DNA tests excluded Masters as a suspect. His conviction was set aside, he was released from prison, and he finally got the chance to drive.

---

house on April 15. The defendant may request separate trials on these offenses. A defendant may argue that it is prejudicial for the same jury to hear evidence about separate crimes because the jury will be tempted to combine the evidence introduced on the separate crimes to find the defendant guilty of each crime. There is good reason for defendants to be concerned about how a jury would react to multiple charges. Psychological research studies that simulate jury decision making have shown that jurors are more likely to convict a defendant on any charge (e.g., robbery) when it is combined with another (e.g., burglary) than when it is tried alone (e.g., Greene & Loftus, 1985). A review of nearly 20,000 federal criminal trials over a five-year period reached a similar conclusion (Leipold & Abbasi, 2006).

3. *Motion for change of venue.* The defendant may request a **change of venue** on the ground that community opinion, usually the product of prejudicial pretrial publicity, makes it impossible

to seat a fair-minded jury. We discuss the involvement of psychologists in such motions later in this chapter.

4. *Motion to suppress a confession or other statement by the defendant.* The Fifth Amendment protects against self-incrimination, and the Sixth Amendment forbids the use of a statement taken in violation of the right to counsel. One or both of these constitutional provisions may become relevant any time the prosecution offers a confession or other statement by a defendant as evidence of guilt. Typically, defense counsel files a motion alleging that the confession was obtained in violation of the defendant's constitutional rights, the prosecutor files a written response, and the court holds a hearing at which the defendant and police give their versions of the circumstances under which the confession was obtained. The judge decides the issue on the basis of what was said and the credibility of the witnesses. Questions of who is telling the truth are usually resolved in favor of the police. Criminal

defendants who believe that their confessions were coerced or made involuntarily have good reason to try to suppress them because juries tend to accept a defendant's confession without careful evaluation of the circumstances that led to the confession (see Chapter 6).

5. *Motions in limine.* Perhaps the most common pretrial motions are those that seek advance rulings on evidentiary issues that will arise at trial. A **motion in limine** is simply a request for a pretrial ruling. Suppose, for example, that the defendant was previously convicted of burglary; the judge must decide whether to allow the prosecution to introduce that conviction into evidence in order to discredit the defendant if he chooses to testify. The defendant obviously wants a pretrial ruling on this issue in order to plan the questioning of the jurors and to decide whether to testify. Similarly, the prosecutor may want a pretrial ruling on the admissibility of a certain piece of evidence in order to plan the opening statement.

PLEA BARGAINING IN CRIMINAL CASES

Plea bargaining has been practiced in the United States since the middle of the 19th century, although some states claim to forbid (Alaska) or restrict (California) the practice. The extensive use of plea bargaining in the criminal justice system illustrates the dilemma between truth and conflict resolution as goals of our legal system. Most criminal cases—by some accounts, 90% to 95%—end prior to trial when the defendant pleads guilty to some charge, usually in exchange for a concession by the prosecutor. Of the estimated 32,000 convictions between 1990 and 2002 in the 75 most populous U.S. counties, nearly 30,000 were reached through plea bargains (Cohen & Reaves, 2006). Interestingly, murder defendants were less likely to plead guilty than defendants charged with other violent felonies. Guilty pleas were offered by 88% of robbery suspects but by only 59% of murder suspects (Reaves, 2006). The harsh sentences imposed on most convicted murderers—often life in prison without parole—make it worthwhile for murder defendants to go to trial and hope for sympathetic judges or juries.

Both mundane and serious cases are resolved by plea bargains. In a routine case that would never have been publicized had the defendant not been a judge, Roger Hurley, a judge from Darke County, Ohio, pled guilty in a domestic violence case. He was accused of grabbing his estranged wife by the neck during an argument and threatening her with a bread knife. According to Hurley, he accepted a plea bargain in order to get on with his life and end the hurt and friction that this incident caused his family. In more notorious cases, Michael Vick, then the star quarterback of the Atlanta Falcons, accepted a plea bargain in a case stemming from a dog-fighting ring that was run from his property and James Earl Ray, the assassin of Martin Luther King, died in prison while serving a life sentence as a result of a plea bargain. In Vick's case, the plea bargain satisfactorily resolved the controversy. In exchange for a lighter sentence, he agreed to cooperate with the government's investigation, accepted responsibility for his actions, and apologized to those he had hurt. In the case of James Earl Ray, however, the plea bargain was not well received. Many thought Ray had not acted alone, and the plea bargain meant that the facts would never be aired in a public forum. Years after Dr. King's death, the King family was still searching for answers. After Ray's death in 1998, they released a statement expressing regret that Ray had never had his day in court and stating, "The American people have a right to the truth about this tragedy and we intend to do everything we can to bring it to light" (www.cnn.com, April 23, 1998).

The defendant's part of the bargain requires an admission of guilt. This admission relieves the prosecutor of any obligation to prove that the defendant committed the crimes charged. The prosecutor's part of the bargain may involve an agreement to reduce the number of charges or allow the defendant to plead guilty to a charge less serious than the evidence supports. For example, manslaughter is a lesser charge than murder, and many murder prosecutions are resolved by a plea of guilty to manslaughter.

In a common procedure known as **charge bargaining,** the prosecutor drops some charges in return for a plea of guilty. Charge bargaining may lead prosecutors initially to charge the defendant with more crimes or with a more serious crime than they could prove at trial as a strategy for motivating guilty pleas. Laboratory research using role-playing procedures (Gregory, Mowen, & Linder, 1978) indicates that "overcharging" is effective; subjects were more likely to accept a plea bargain when more charges had been filed against them. The defendants who engage in this type of bargaining may win only hollow victories. Cases in which prosecutors offer to drop charges are likely to be ones for which judges would have imposed concurrent sentences for the multiple convictions anyway.

Plea bargaining may also take the form of **sentence bargaining,** in which prosecutors recommend reduced sentences in return for guilty pleas. Sentencing is the judge's decision, and although judges vary in their willingness to follow prosecutors' recommendations, many simply rubber-stamp prosecutorial sentencing recommendations. In general, defendants can expect that judges will follow the sentences that have been recommended by a prosecutor, and prosecutors can earn the trust of judges by recommending sentences that are reasonable and fair.

Why do defendants plead guilty? Defendants have the final say in any decision or plea. In fact, before accepting a guilty plea, judges ask defendants if they made the decision freely and of their own accord. But defense attorneys have great influence in this process. Their recommendations interact with the defendant's wishes in complex ways to yield a decision. Defense attorneys gauge whether to recommend a plea offer based on the strength of the evidence against the defendant and the severity of the punishment (McAllister & Bregman, 1986). When the evidence points toward conviction and the defendant is facing a lengthy prison sentence, defense attorneys will recommend strongly that defendants accept plea offers. At least in some circumstances, defense attorneys also take their clients' preferences into account. Kramer, Wolbransky, and Heilbrun (2007) had attorneys read vignettes that varied the strength of the evidence against a hypothetical defendant, the potential sentence if convicted, and the defendant's wishes. When the probability of conviction was high and the likely prison sentence was long, attorneys strongly recommended the plea offer, regardless of the defendant's desires. But when the probability of conviction was low and the prison sentence was short, attorneys were willing to consider the defendant's wish to proceed to trial.

Defendants try to negotiate a plea to obtain less severe punishment than they would receive if they went to trial and were convicted. But why do prosecutors plea-bargain? What advantages do they seek, given that they hold the more powerful position in this bargaining situation? Prosecutors are motivated to plea-bargain for one or more of the following reasons: (1) to dispose of cases in which the evidence against the defendant is weak (one such case is described in Box 7.2) or the defense attorney is a formidable foe; (2) to ensure a "win" when their office keeps a record of the "wins" (convictions) and "losses" (acquittals) of each prosecuting attorney in the office; (3) to obtain the testimony of one defendant against a more culpable or infamous codefendant; (4) to expedite the flow of cases for an overworked staff and a clogged court docket; (5) to maintain a cordial working relationship with defense attorneys from whom the prosecutor may want certain favors in the future; or (6) to avoid trials that might be unpopular because the defendant is a well-liked figure in the community or the crime charged might be seen as morally justified.

B o x 7.2   THE CASE OF "AMERICAN TALIBAN" JOHN WALKER LINDH, AND HIS GUILTY PLEA

One morning in late November 2001, a few months after 9/11 and in the early days of the war on terror, Central Intelligence Agency (CIA) agent Mike Spann was sorting through approximately 300 Taliban prisoners held in a military garrison near Mazar-e Sharif, Afghanistan. One prisoner had been separated from the others; he gave his name as Abdul Hamil, but his real name was John Walker Lindh, and he was a 20-year-old American who, until 2000, had lived with his family in Marin County, California. After escaping during a violent uprising later that day, getting shot in the thigh, starving for a week in a basement bunker, and being flushed out of the basement, Lindh eventually talked to his captors. During extensive questioning, he explained how he had trained with the Taliban in Osama bin Laden's camps, and he signed confession documents acknowledging that he was not merely fighting for the Taliban but also was a member of al-Qaeda. In February 2002, he was indicted on 10 charges, including conspiracy to support terrorist organizations and conspiracy to murder American citizens.

The prosecution might have had an easier case had the conditions of Lindh's confession been different. During his interrogation, Lindh was stripped of his clothes, blindfolded, duct-taped to a stretcher, and placed in a metal shipping container for transportation. Despite several requests, he was denied the assistance of a lawyer, and he was threatened with denial of med-

John Walker Lindh

ical assistance if he opted not to cooperate. Fearing that the confession might be excluded from evidence as having been coerced, Michael Chertoff, then-head of the criminal division of the Department of Justice, authorized prosecutors to offer Walker a plea bargain: If he pled guilty to just two charges—serving with the Taliban and carrying illegal weapons—the remaining eight counts would be dropped. According to some commentators (e.g., Babb, 2003), the government would not have been able to sustain a treason charge against Lindh. John Walker Lindh pled guilty in July 2002 and was sentenced to 20 years without parole.

Plea bargaining serves the need of the defense attorney to appear to gain something for his or her client and the need of the prosecutor to appear fair and reasonable. Both prosecutors and defense attorneys believe they are making the "punishment fit the crime" by individualizing the law to fit the circumstances of the case, and both are comfortable with a system in which most cases are resolved without a clear winner or clear loser. Experienced prosecutors and defense attorneys teach plea bargaining to the rookies in their offices, and lawyers from both sides engage in a ritual of give and take, with changing facts and personalities but with the same posturing and rationalizations. In fact, the procedures are so well known that in some cases no formal bargaining

even takes place; everyone involved—prosecutor, defense attorney, defendant, and judge—knows the prevailing "rate" for a given crime, and if the defendant pleads guilty to that crime, the rate is the price that will be paid.

Psychological Influences on the Plea-Bargaining Process

Although there are only a few empirical studies of plea bargaining, we can generalize from other bargaining situations to understand the role of psychological factors in the process (McAllister, 2008). One factor concerns **framing effects.** Psychologists who study decision making have learned that the way decision alternatives are presented (or framed)—as either *gains* or *losses*—can have a significant impact on a person's choice. Individuals are more willing to take chances when the decision alternatives are presented in terms of gains than in terms of losses. Imagine that two defendants have been charged with the same crime, each has a 50% chance of being convicted at trial and, if convicted, each is likely to be sentenced to 20 years in prison. The prosecutor has offered both defendants a deal that would result in only 10 years imprisonment in exchange for a guilty plea. Now imagine that Defendant A's options are framed as a *gain* and Defendant B's options are framed as a *loss*. Defendant A is told that if he went to trial, there would be a 50% chance that he would be acquitted and *gain 10 years* outside of prison compared to the plea-bargain offer. Defendant B is told that if he went to trial, there would be a 50% chance that he would be convicted and *lose an additional 10 years* of life in prison compared to the plea-bargain offer. Although the two situations are identical except for the decision frame, Defendant A is more likely to take his chance at trial and Defendant B is more likely to take the plea bargain to avoid a loss.

Other psychological factors affect and sometimes distort offenders' decisions concerning plea bargains. In general, people tend to be too optimistic about their chances of securing favorable outcomes and are therefore overconfident. The **overconfidence bias** suggests that because defendants believe (incorrectly) that they have a chance to win at trial, they might reject reasonable offers from prosecutors. Defense attorneys then have to exert strong pressure to persuade their clients to accept these offers (Bibas, 2004).

Overconfidence skews beliefs about the likelihood of acquittal. Denial mechanisms affect thoughts about one's guilt and the chances for successful plea-bargain arrangements. Offenders often have difficulty acknowledging guilt to their attorneys; some cannot even admit it to themselves (Bibas, 2004). Thinking about one's immoral or illegal actions is painful and depressing, and denial mechanisms allow people to avoid dealing with those thoughts. But denial results in minimizing

the harm caused to others and an unwillingness to accept responsibility for wrongdoing. Defendants in denial are unlikely to take a plea bargain even when it is advantageous for them to do so.

Evaluations of Plea Bargaining

Although the U.S. Supreme Court has called plea bargaining "an essential component of the administration of justice" (*Santobello v. New York*, 1971), it remains a controversial procedure. It has been defended as a necessary and useful part of the criminal justice system (American Bar Association, 1993b), and it has been condemned as a practice that should be abolished from our courts (Lynch, 2003). Advocates cite the following justifications for the procedure: (1) The defendant's admission of guilt is an important first step in rehabilitation; (2) guilty pleas relieve the backlog of cases that would otherwise engulf the courts; (3) outcomes are reached promptly and with a sense of finality; (4) other criminal justice participants benefit from the process—from the police officer who doesn't have to spend hours in court testifying, to the victim who is spared the trauma of a trial; and (5) the defendant's cooperation may facilitate prosecution of others.

Critics urge the abolition of plea bargaining on the following grounds: (1) Improper sentences—sometimes too harsh but more often too lenient—are likely; (2) the process encourages defendants to surrender their constitutional rights; (3) prosecutors exert too much power in negotiating guilty pleas; (4) the process is private and encourages "shady" deals not available to all defendants; and (5) innocent defendants might feel coerced to plead guilty because they fear the more severe consequences of being convicted by a jury.

Data on these contentions are limited, but the limited available evidence suggests that plea bargaining is not as evil as its opponents claim or as essential as its defenders believe. Rates of plea bargaining are surprisingly consistent across rural and urban jurisdictions, as well as across understaffed and well-funded prosecutors' offices (Heumann, 1978; Silberman, 1978). After Alaska ended plea bargaining in 1975, defendants continued to plead guilty at about the same rate, court proceedings did not slow down, and a modest increase in the number of trials occurred—though not so great an increase as had been feared (Rubinstein, Clarke, & White, 1980). On the other hand, when El Paso, Texas, abolished plea bargaining in 1975, it experienced a serious backup of cases. This result occurred largely because defendants perceived no benefit of pleading in comparison to waiting for their trials and hoping that witnesses would not be available or other weaknesses in the prosecution's case would develop, making acquittal more likely (Greenberg & Ruback, 1984).

Of course, there is a "dark side" to plea bargaining. It is troubling that adolescent defendants, lacking sophistication about the legal system, are more likely to accept guilty pleas than adults (Grisso et al., 2003) and that, at least among adolescents aged 11–13, the decision to accept a plea bargain is unrelated to the strength of the evidence against them (Viljoen, Klaver, & Roesch, 2005).

Plea bargaining may work against the long-range goal of achieving justice. It may prevent the families of victims from seeing the defendants "get justice" or hearing them acknowledge full responsibility for their offenses. In 2000, a Missouri man, Terrance Wainright, was sentenced to life without parole plus 90 years for killing his wife and her 15-year-old daughter. The case seemed closed. But during the appeals process five years later, a prosecutor offered Wainright a deal to plead guilty to a lesser charge and a reduced sentence, infuriating family members of the victims. According to the father of the 15-year-old girl, the prosecutor proposed the deal without ever consulting him. To address this concern, victims' rights legislation increasingly ensures that the victim or his or her family has a say in plea bargaining and some states now involve victims in the plea-bargaining process.

Finally, it is troubling that cases are not always resolved in line with the gravity of the offense. When these "errors" are in the direction of sentencing leniency, they often are attributed to a perceived overload in the prosecutor's office or the courts. A defendant should not be able to plead to a greatly reduced charge simply because the criminal justice system lacks the resources to handle the case. However, the answer to problems of unwarranted leniency is not the abolition of plea bargaining; rather, adequate funding must be provided for the court system, as well as for the correctional system, so that when severe penalties are necessary, severe penalties can be given. In the long run, if plea bargaining serves primarily as a method for managing the underfunded budgets of our courts and correctional systems, it will cease to be a bargain in the larger sense and will become, instead, too great a price for our society to pay.

SETTLEMENTS IN CIVIL CASES

Just as most criminal cases are resolved through plea-bargaining procedures prior to trial, the vast majority of civil disputes are also resolved (or settled) without a trial, typically in private negotiations between attorneys representing the disputing parties. This process is known as settlement negotiation. (Attorneys also negotiate with insurers, regulators, and sometimes even with their own clients in an attempt to settle a dispute.) Most divorces, landlord–tenant disputes, claims of employment discrimination, and accident cases are resolved without a trial.

Lawyers spend considerable time negotiating settlements because they would almost always prefer the certainty of a negotiated compromise to the uncertainty of a jury trial. Because their caseload (or docket) is so large, judges would always prefer that the participants in a civil dispute resolve their differences themselves, without using the considerable resources necessary for a trial.

Disputing parties obviously have different objectives in settlement negotiations. Hence, the attorneys representing these parties will have very different roles to play in the negotiation. In a personal injury case, a common civil dispute, plaintiffs' lawyers will try to extract every dollar that a defendant will pay, whereas defendants' lawyers will try to avoid paying all but the minimal cost necessary to settle the case.

Some lawyers have become highly skilled at these tasks. Consider, for example, the case of Valerie Lackey who, at age 5, was disemboweled by the suction power of a pool drain pump produced by Sta-Rite Industries. Valerie sat on an open pool drain after other children removed the protective cover that a swim club had failed to install properly. Despite 12 prior suits with similar claims, Sta-Rite continued to make and sell drain covers lacking installation warnings. Former North Carolina senator and presidential hopeful John Edwards served as the attorney for the plaintiffs, Valerie Lackey and her family. After lengthy negotiations that continued "backstage" throughout the trial, Sta-Rite eventually settled and the Lackey family received $25 million, the largest personal injury award in North Carolina history.

What makes some lawyers so skilled at negotiating and winning such large damages? Do they have a knack for deciding whether a case is worth pursuing and an ability to assess accurately what it might be worth? Do they have a particular interpersonal style that facilitates compromise? Or do they have especially shiny crystal balls? In recent years, psychologists, economists, and game theorists (scientists who study behavior in strategic situations) have conducted studies of actual and simulated settlement negotiations (though they have yet to study the crystal-ball hypothesis!) to determine what factors predict settlement amounts.

Factors that Determine Settlement Amounts

The legal merits of the case matter most, of course. In an automobile accident case, plaintiffs with strong cases on liability—those with evidence of the defendant's reckless driving—and those with obvious and severe injuries will recover more money from a defendant than would plaintiffs whose cases are weak on liability or damages.

But other factors matter as well. Negotiation theory suggests that outcomes are also influenced by the negotiators' **reservation price,** or bottom line (Korobkin & Doherty, 2009). The defendant's reservation price is the *maximum* amount of money

that he or she would be willing to pay to reach an agreement, whereas the plaintiff's reservation price is the *minimum* amount of money that he or she would accept to settle the claim. Say that a plaintiff was injured when a piece of machinery malfunctioned, injuring him or her and resulting in medical and other costs of approximately $100,000. The defendant manufacturer may set a reservation price of $75,000, authorizing the defense attorney to negotiate a settlement that does not exceed that amount, while the plaintiff may set a reservation price of $25,000, meaning that he or she will accept nothing less. Though the parties are not initially aware of the other's reservation prices, they have a $50,000 "bargaining zone" in which to negotiate a compromise. If they fail to reach a compromise, negotiators walk away from the bargaining table and the case goes to trial. Various psychological factors influence reservation points, including perceptions of the likely outcome if the case goes to trial and negotiators' goals and views on the merits of the case.

In considering the merits of their case, plaintiffs, defendants, and attorneys alike are influenced by psychological biases, often referred to as **heuristics** (Greene & Ellis, 2007; Ross & Ward, 1995). One such heuristic, the **self-serving bias,** occurs when people interpret information or make decisions in ways that are consistent with their own interests, rather than in an objective fashion. When evaluating their cases, involved parties often have difficulty seeing the merits of the other side, believing that the evidence favors their position and that the fairest resolution is one that rewards them. For example, laypeople who were asked to play the role of either the plaintiff or defendant in a personal injury case involving an automobile–motorcycle collision and to assess the value of the case exhibited the self-serving bias: Although all participants had the same information, those who evaluated the case from the perspective of the plaintiff predicted that the judge would award approximately $14,500 more than the role-playing defendants predicted (Loewenstein, Issacharoff, Camerer, & Babcock, 1993). When asked what they believed to be a fair settlement in the case, the number suggested by the "plaintiffs" was, on average, nearly $18,000 more than the amount suggested by the "defense."

Another heuristic, termed the **anchoring and adjustment bias,** occurs when negotiators are strongly influenced ("anchored") by an initial starting value and when, in subsequent discussion, they do not sufficiently adjust their judgments away from this starting point. This bias is quite pervasive, and even wildly extreme anchors can influence judgments: people provided higher estimates of the average temperature in San Francisco when first asked whether it was higher or lower than 558 degrees, a number that may have induced people to consider the (unlikely) possibility that San Francisco temperatures are high (cited by Guthrie, Rachlinski, & Wistrich, 2001). In the context of settlement negotiations, the first offer can serve to anchor the final negotiated compromise; the higher the offer, the higher the ultimate settlement (Korobkin & Doherty, 2009).

Many legal disputes involve intense emotions that can also influence the likelihood of resolution. Imagine, for example, the despair and anguish that Rachel Barton must have experienced after being dragged 200 feet underneath a Chicago commuter train in 1995. The 21-year-old classical violinist and prodigy had her left leg severed above the knee, lost part of her right foot, and badly injured her right knee as terrified passengers tried to alert the engineer to halt the train. Barton sued the train company for $30 million. After several years of negotiations and 25 operations, she received nearly that amount and gave a sizeable portion to charity.

Emotions on the part of plaintiffs, defendants, and their attorneys all play a role in negotiation. The emotion most closely associated with disputes may be anger; parties involved in settlement discussions often feel resentment, antagonism, and sometimes outright fury. Presumably those expressions would harm the chances for concessions and compromise, and psychological data suggest that they do. Higher levels of anger on the part of negotiators is related to angry responses from the other party (Friedman et al., 2004), less regard for one's adversary (Allred, Mallozzi, Matsui, & Raia, 1997), and a higher incidence of impasse (Moore, Kurtzberg, Thompson, & Morris, 1999). Angry disputants have difficulty resolving their competing claims.

If anger tends to inhibit dispute resolution, do more positive emotions tend to enhance it? The answer is yes; positive emotions such as happiness foster cooperation and concession making (Kopelman, Rosette, & Thompson, 2006), stimulate creative problem solving (Isen, Daubman, & Nowicki, 1987), increase the use of cooperative negotiation strategies (Forgas, 1998), and positively influence negotiators' expectations (Carnevale, 2008). Experiencing positive emotions improves one's chances for successful settlement negotiations.

THE DECISION TO SET BAIL

Judges must decide whether to keep criminal defendants in custody during the lengthy process between arrest and trial or whether to release them into the community with a promise to reappear for subsequent hearings. Judges have many options. In some cases (capital cases and cases in which the defendant poses a serious risk to flee or commit other crimes), they can deny bail altogether. Short of denying bail, judges can require that money (or a bail bondsman's pledge) be deposited with the court or that a third person agrees to be responsible for the defendant's future appearances and to forfeit money if the defendant does not appear. When bail is higher than defendants can afford, they have no choice but to remain in jail. Studies of defendants who promised to reappear showed that most defendants did so (Ares, Rankin, & Sturz, 1963; Feeley, 1983). Whether bail bonds actually reduce the risk of nonappearance is not clear. Box 7.3 describes techniques that bail bond agents use to ensure that defendants who post bail will show up for court.

In addition to ensuring the defendant's return to court, bail has a secondary purpose, namely protecting public safety. In fact, bail evolved in the American legal system as an attempt to resolve the basic conflict (discussed in Chapter 1) between an individual's right to liberty on the one hand, and societal rights to be protected from criminal

---

Box 7.3   **THE CASE OF "LITTLE RANDY" WITHERS AND THE CYBERSEARCH**
FOR DEFENDANTS ON THE RUN

Bail bond agents like Duane Lee "Dog" Chapman (star of the reality television program *Dog the Bounty Hunter*) are renowned for their diligence in tracking down defendants who have skipped bail and failed to return to court as required. Bonding agents stand to lose the value of the bond posted if the defendant cannot be located, so their financial incentive for locating and returning the defendant to custody is considerable. Although bonding agents have been criticized in the past for strong-arm search-and-return tactics, they increasingly are turning to modern technology to catch defendants on the run. One of those fugitive defendants was "Little Randy" Withers, who was charged with possession of a firearm by a felon and whose picture was included on the Web site entitled "The World's Most Wanted—Bail Jumpers" (www.mostwanted.org). The 21st century's counterpart to the old "Wanted Dead or Alive" posters of the western frontier, this Web site describes Withers as a black male, born on April 28, 1975, 5 feet 7 inches tall,

Courtesy of the Alabama Department of Public Safety-Alabama Bureau of Investigation.

Cybersearch for a wanted suspect

175 pounds, black hair and brown eyes, residing in Charlotte, North Carolina. Warning that these defendants have "Nowhere to Run! Nowhere to Hide!" the subscribing companies typically offer $1000 and $2000 cash rewards for information that leads to the apprehension of the most wanted bail fugitives. They also caution would-be bounty hunters that most of the suspects are armed and should be considered dangerous.

---

behavior on the other. The Eighth Amendment to the U.S. Constitution says that excessive bail shall not be required, but the Supreme Court has ruled that this provision does not guarantee a right to bail; it simply requires that bail, if any, should not be excessive (*United States v. Salerno*, 1987). Although various laws govern the bail decision, they are typically vague and ill defined, allowing judges considerable leeway in the factors they consider and in the way they make the decision about bail.

What Considerations Affect the Decision to Set Bail?

Psychologists and other social scientists have examined how judges make bail-setting decisions (Allan, Allan, Giles, Drake, & Froyland, 2005; Dhami, 2003; Dhami & Ayton, 2001). In particular, they have evaluated the factors that judges consider and the cognitive processes by which judges weigh and combine these factors.

Bail decisions are influenced by both legal and extralegal factors. **Legal factors** are those variables related to the offense or the offender's legal history; research has shown that bail is likely to be denied or set very high when the offense was serious and when the defendant has prior convictions. **Extralegal factors** that influence the bail decision include the race and gender of the defendant. Data gathered on felony defendants from the 75 most populous counties in the United States between 1990 and 1996 showed that after controlling for prior record and nature of the offense, Hispanic and African American defendants were more likely to be detained than similarly situated White defendants (Demuth & Steffensmeier, 2004). A major factor in securing pretrial release is the ability to post bail, which minority defendants are less frequently able to do. Female defendants were more likely to be released than their male counterparts with similar records and charges.

Psychologists have assessed the cognitive processes that judges use in determining whether bail should be allowed. In some of these studies, judges respond to simulated cases presented as vignettes. In other studies, researchers observe them dealing with real cases in the courtroom (Dhami, 2003; Dhami & Ayton, 2001). In both settings, judges tend to use a mental shortcut called the **matching heuristic:** They search through a subset of available case information and then make a decision on the basis of only a small number of factors (for example, offense severity and prior record), often ignoring other seemingly relevant information. This is not especially surprising; judges' large case loads force them to make fast decisions and people often use shortcut reasoning strategies when forced to think quickly.

The opinions of police and prosecutors can also sway judges' decisions about bail. Dhami (2003) analyzed bail-setting decisions in two London courts and found that the prosecutor's request and the position of the police strongly influenced the judge's choices. Judges were less swayed by an offender's risk of committing further crimes while out of jail (Dhami, 2005), raising questions about whether judges are sufficiently concerned about society's right to be protected against the harm caused by defendants on bail. Finally, although judges were highly confident that they had made the appropriate decisions (the overconfidence bias in a new context), they tended to disagree with their colleagues who were responding to the same simulated fact patterns, raising troubling questions of fairness and equality.

Does Pretrial Release Affect Trial Outcome?

What if the defendant cannot provide bail and remains in jail until the time of trial? Does this pretrial incarceration affect the trial's outcome? Clearly, yes. Defendants who are detained in jail are more likely to plead guilty or be convicted and to receive longer sentences than those who can afford bail, even when the seriousness of their offenses and the evidence against them are the same (Goldfarb, 1965; Kellough & Wortley, 2002). Some data suggest that prosecutors use pretrial detention as a "resource" to

encourage (or coerce) guilty pleas. Pretrial detention is likely to cost defendants their jobs, making it harder for them to pay attorneys—so the threat of it may make them more likely to plead guilty. Among defendants who actually go to trial, an accused person who is free on bail finds it easier to gather witnesses and prepare a defense. Jailed defendants cannot meet with their attorneys in the latter's office, have less time with their attorneys to prepare for trial, and have less access to records and witnesses. Detention also corrodes family and community ties. Casper's (1972) interviews with convicted defendants who were serving prison sentences revealed that for many of them, the time spent in local jails prior to trial was worse than the time in prison; the conditions were terrible, there was nothing to do, and the guards were hostile.

Can High-Risk Defendants Be Identified?

Around 1970, a push began for legislation that would increase the use of **preventive detention**—the detention of accused persons who pose a risk of flight or dangerousness. Civil libertarians oppose preventive detention because it conflicts with our society's fundamental assumption that a defendant is innocent until proven guilty. But most citizens approve, valuing society's need to be protected from possible future harm over the rights of individual suspects to be free until proven guilty. Although the preventive detention of suspected terrorists is controversial, many people believe that the risk of a large-scale attack similar to 9/11 outweighs suspects' individual rights. The U.S. Supreme Court has taken the view that preventive detention is not a punishment but rather a regulation (like a quarantine) for the public's protection.

Preventive detention assumes that valid assessments of risk and accurate predictions of future dangerous conduct can be made, an assumption that is not always correct (Heilbrun, 2009). Thus, judges have difficulty knowing which defendants are dangerous and which can be trusted. In

Shepherd, Texas, Patrick Dale Walker tried to kill his girlfriend by putting a gun to her head and pulling the trigger. The loaded gun failed to fire. Walker's original bail was set at $1 million, but after he had been in jail for four days, the presiding judge lowered his bail to $25,000. This permitted Walker to be released; four months later, he fired three bullets at close range and killed the same woman. Afterward, the judge did not think he was wrong in lowering the bail, even though, since 1993, Texas has had a law that permits judges to consider the safety of the victim and of the community in determining the amount of bail. In fact, Patrick Walker had no previous record, was valedictorian of his class, and was a college graduate. Would a psychologist have done any better in predicting Walker's behavior?

Although mental health professionals now have some reasonable capacity to assess violence risk in some situations, particularly when using specialized tools (see, for example, Monahan et al., 2005), a few scholars have argued that mental health professionals should not make such specific numerical predictions because the associated scientific foundation is insufficient (e.g., Hart, Michie, & Cooke, 2007). We will return to this issue in Chapter 8 on forensic assessment, but for now we simply note that assessing risks and predicting violent behavior are difficult and complex tasks.

PRETRIAL PUBLICITY

Conflicting Rights

Two cherished rights guaranteed by the U.S. Constitution are freedom of speech (the First Amendment) and the right to a speedy, public trial before an impartial jury (the Sixth Amendment). The right to free speech applies to the written as well as the spoken word. It also applies to the institution of the press, not just to individuals. The press is expected to be the government watchdog, a role encouraged by constitutional protection. The right to an impartial jury and a fair trial is also a fundamental expectation of Americans. The fairness of our adversarial

system of justice rests in large part on the decision making of an unbiased group of jurors.

In the vast majority of cases, the liberties ensured by the First and Sixth Amendments are compatible and even complementary. The press informs the public about criminal investigations and trials, and the public not only learns the outcomes of these proceedings but often gains increased appreciation for both the justness and the foibles of our system of justice.

On occasion, however, the First and Sixth Amendments clash. The press publishes information that, when disseminated among the public, threatens a defendant's right to a trial by impartial jurors. These problem cases can involve defendants and/or victims who, because of their fame or infamous acts, gain a national reputation. In one case, an unknown fertilizer salesman named Scott Peterson, charged with killing his pregnant wife Laci, became a household name as the details of his case were splashed across the airwaves. Because of this intense publicity, his trial was moved to a new location (although one wonders how, in this age of 24-hour news networks, widespread access to cable and satellite programming, blogs, and specialized channels such as Court TV, *any* location was immune to the heavy coverage of this story.) Peterson's case is described in Box 7.4.

A more common problem occurs when local media and online postings, blogs, and Internet-based press releases disseminate prejudicial information. Once made public, this information can bias opinion about a defendant or a lawsuit. Examples include publication of details about a person's prior criminal record, a confession made by the accused, unfavorable statements regarding the defendant's character, and criticisms of the merits of pending cases. Indeed, it is exceedingly difficult to disregard previously acquired information. As Studebaker and Penrod (2005) point out,

> When making social judgments (such as those involved in deciding whether a defendant is guilty), it is natural for people to process information in an integrative manner. That is to say, people

---

B o x 7.4   THE CASE OF SCOTT PETERSON: THE "CLIFF-HANGER THAT HOOKED THE NATION"

The case against Scott Lee Peterson was the "stuff of crime novels," a "cliff-hanger that hooked the nation," a "whodunit with a torrid plot" (Finz & Walsh, 2004). The plot involved Peterson, a handsome, 30-something salesman and his beautiful, pregnant wife who disappeared on Christmas Eve, 2002 from their Modesto, California home. It also involved Peterson's girlfriend, a massage therapist who, unbeknownst to Peterson, was secretly taping their telephone conversations.

As Peterson's alibi began to unravel in the months following his wife's disappearance and the discovery of her body, as his affair became very public, and as it became clear that he lied to his girlfriend, to the police, and even to Diane Sawyer, who interviewed him on ABC's *Good Morning America*, the press had a field day. Reports of the ongoing investigation and of Peterson's alleged role in the murders were staple fare for news organizations, online message boards, and bloggers for months.

Because of this extensive pretrial publicity, the trial was moved from Stanislaus County, where Peterson had been charged with murder, to nearby San Mateo County. But that move was not enough to satisfy Peterson's attorney, who argued in the middle of jury selection that the sensational case should be moved

Laci and Scott Peterson, who married in 1997, in an undated family photo

again. Even though half of the prospective jurors who were questioned said they thought Peterson was guilty, a jury was eventually selected in San Mateo County. In late 2004, after months of testimony, jurors convicted Peterson on two counts of first-degree murder and sentenced him to death. He is now awaiting execution at San Quentin.

---

make connections between various pieces of information and base decisions on overall impressions rather than on specific pieces of information…. To set aside preconceived notions requires someone to identify previously received information as biasing, to know how that information was eventually processed and stored in memory, and to reverse or control for any biasing effects the information has had. The integrative nature of human information processing makes it very difficult for people to do this successfully (p. 257).

In cases with extensive pretrial publicity, the courts must answer two basic questions. First, does the publicity threaten the fairness of a defendant's trial? Second, if the answer to this question is yes, what steps should be taken to remedy the situation?

Psychologists have conducted research on both queries and can offer guidance to judges who are willing to listen. We describe that work later in this chapter.

Legal Rulings on Pretrial Publicity

The Supreme Court has considered several cases in which defendants claimed that their right to an impartial jury had been destroyed by inflammatory pretrial publicity. For example, in *Rideau v. Louisiana* (1963), the Court decided that exposure to news that included information strongly pointing to the defendant's guilt was a violation of due process. A local TV station broadcast at three different times a 20-minute clip of Rideau, surrounded by law enforcement officials, confessing in detail to charges of robbery, kidnapping, and murder. A request for a change of venue was denied, and Rideau was convicted and sentenced to death by a jury, of which at least three members had seen the televised confession. The Supreme Court reversed this decision, Rideau was granted a new trial, and he was eventually convicted of manslaughter, rather than murder. In the 43 years he spent in prison (he was released in 2005), Rideau transformed himself from an illiterate eighth-grade dropout to a national advocate for prison reform, a filmmaker, and an award-winning editor of Angola State Prison's renowned *Angolite* magazine. Perhaps most important, he acknowledged responsibility for his crime and apologized for the harm he caused (Green, 2005).

Judges have instituted various preventive or remedial techniques for negative pretrial publicity. One such measure involves a judge ordering the press not to publish pretrial information likely to be prejudicial, a procedure known as prior restraint or a **gag order.** The leading case is *Nebraska Press Association v. Stuart* (1976), in which the Supreme Court ruled that a trial judge could not order the press to refrain from publishing information likely to be prejudicial to a defendant unless the defendant would otherwise be denied a fair trial. In most cases, gag orders are quickly overturned on appeal.

Likewise, the press cannot be barred from attending and reporting a trial because the First Amendment guarantees public access to criminal trials (*Richmond Newspapers, Inc. v. Virginia*, 1980). However, the press can be excluded from pretrial hearings in which potentially prejudicial material might be at issue (*Gannett Co. v. De Pasquale*, 1979). The press can also volunteer to defer publishing incriminating information, and responsible members of the media often limit their disclosures, especially when the police are investigating possible suspects in unsolved crimes.

Defendants sometimes request that overwhelming pretrial publicity be remedied by a change of venue (moving the trial to a different location). In 1966, Jon Yount confessed that he had killed a high school student. His confession was published in two local papers and was admitted into evidence at trial. Prior to trial, Yount asked for a change of venue, citing continuing publicity

about the case. The motion was denied despite the fact that 77% of prospective jurors admitted they had an opinion about Yount's guilt. After his conviction, Yount appealed, claiming that the publicity had made a fair trial impossible. The Supreme Court ruled against Yount, reasoning that a "presumption of correctness" should be given to the trial judge's opinion because, being present at the trial, the judge was in a better position to evaluate the demeanor, credibility, and, ultimately, the competence of prospective jurors.

From a psychological standpoint, an obvious problem with this decision was the Court's willingness to accept, at face value, what jurors say about their own opinions. The problem is not that jurors lie about their beliefs (although some probably do). The issue is that there are many reasons why people might not admit the full measure of their prejudice in public. People might not recognize the extent of their biases; even if completely aware, they might not disclose them in an open courtroom before a judge who encourages them to be fair and open-minded. Finally, they might experience **evaluation apprehension,** whereby they provide the answers that they perceive the judge wants to hear, regardless of whether their responses are truthful (Vidmar, 2002).

Finally, in its most recent look at the potentially prejudicial effects of pretrial publicity (*Mu'Min v. Virginia*, 1991), the Supreme Court compounded the problem of jurors promising impartiality. In this case, the Court held that defendants do not have a constitutional right to ask prospective jurors about the specifics of their exposure to pretrial publicity. Under such circumstances, it is difficult to know how much trust to place in jurors' claims of impartiality, but the Supreme Court concluded that such assurances are all that the Constitution requires. (Frankly, we think there are better remedies for ensuring fair trials in light of heavy pretrial publicity; we discuss these remedies later in this chapter.)

Effects of Pretrial Publicity

Does pretrial publicity influence public opinion? Does adverse publicity produce negative opinions about defendants? If so, do these negative opinions continue despite efforts to control them? Several studies have measured the effects of various kinds of pretrial publicity presented in different media. Two types of studies—experimental and field studies—have addressed this issue. In experimental studies, participants are first exposed (or not exposed, in the control group) to some form of publicity and then are asked to assume the role of jurors in a simulated trial. Researchers measure the impact of the publicity on decision making. In field studies, respondents are surveyed to assess the effects of publicity about a particular real-life case. Taken together, these studies fairly convincingly point to the conclusion that jurors may be adversely affected by pretrial publicity and that the publicity can prejudice them in some surprising ways.

Experimental Studies of the Effects of Pretrial Publicity.

Experimental procedures, in which the researcher manipulates the presence of pretrial publicity and measures its impact on jurors' decisions, ensure that the only differences between the two sets of jurors (i.e., those who have seen pretrial publicity and those who have not) involve exposure to the publicity. Thus, researchers can be fairly confident that differences in responding are related to the impact of the pretrial information.

Some studies have looked at the effects of negative information in the pretrial publicity on perceptions of the defendant (Steblay, Besirevic, Fulero, & Jiminez-Lorente, 1999). These studies generally show that pretrial publicity affects jurors' evaluations of the defendant's character, the extent to which they like or sympathize with him, their pretrial sentiments about his guilt, and their final verdicts. Other studies have tried to explain *why*. Two explanations seem reasonable. Pretrial publicity may bias jurors' interpretations of the evidence to which they are exposed at trial; if the pretrial publicity about the defendant is negative, jurors evaluate trial testimony in a manner adverse to the defendant (Hope, Memon, & McGeorge, 2004). Jurors exposed to publicity also come to believe, wrongly, that the pretrial information was actually presented as part of the evidence at trial, a **source monitoring** error (Ruva, McEvoy, & Bryant, 2007).

An interesting question, given the pervasiveness of digital news sources and the declining readership of newspapers, is whether pretrial information conveyed on a screen has a different impact than information conveyed in print. In an experiment designed to test this question, participants were randomly assigned to one of three conditions that varied the format by which pretrial media information was presented about the Mount Cashel orphanage case, a highly publicized case in Canada concerning alleged sexual abuse by a group of Roman Catholic men who ran an orphanage in Newfoundland (Ogloff & Vidmar, 1994). The damaging pretrial material was presented to participants through (1) television, (2) newspaper articles, or (3) both TV and newspapers. Presentation of publicity via television had a greater biasing impact than the same information presented in print, but the combined effects of TV and newspaper publicity had the greatest impact of all. Of additional interest was the finding that participants were generally unaware that their opinions had been biased by this material; those who had formed opinions about the trial were just as likely to say that they could be fair as were those who had not formed opinions.

To this point, we have considered the effects of **specific pretrial publicity,** showing that case-specific information made available prior to trial can affect the sentiments of jurors in that trial. But other studies have shown that mock jurors can also be influenced by **generic prejudice**—that is, prejudice arising from media coverage of issues not specifically related to a particular case but thematically relevant to the issues at hand. Highly stigmatized conduct such as deviant sexual behavior or drug use in conservative communities can engender strong feelings among jurors that are unrelated to the facts of any particular case (Wiener, Arnot, Winter, & Redmond, 2006). In fact, Judge Abner Mikva of the Court of Appeals for the District of Columbia, suggested that generic prejudice may be more problematic than specific pretrial publicity:

> Pretrial publicity is not the big difficulty. It is generic prejudice. I do not think you can

get a fair child abuse trial before a jury any-where in the country. I really don't ... I do not care how sophisticated or how smart jurors are, when they hear that a child has been abused, a piece of their mind closes up, and this goes for the judge, the juror, and all of us. (cited by Doppelt, 1991, p. 821)

Psychological research seems to support Judge Mikva's assertion. For example, Wiener et al. (2006) found evidence of generic prejudice among mock jurors, and the effects of prejudice were greater in cases of sexual assault than homicide. Kovera (2002) showed that media exposure and preexisting attitudes interact: Exposure to a story about a rape case influenced participants' appraisals of the witnesses and verdicts in a different acquaintance rape case, but preexisting attitudes also moderated the influence of the media on mock jurors' judgments.

Generic prejudice probably works by transfer-ring preexisting beliefs and stereotypes about categories of people to a particular defendant in a trial setting (Vidmar, 2002). As a result, the facts of the case and the personal characteristics of the defendant go relatively unheeded. Racial and ethnic stereotypes are the most common forms of generic prejudice; for example, some people believe that an African American defendant is more likely to be guilty of a crime than a White defendant, all other things being equal. Any Arab Americans on trial in the United States in the aftermath of 9/11 were also likely to have experienced some form of generic prejudice.

Field Studies of the Effects of Naturally Occurring Publicity. Serious crimes attract extensive news coverage, typically from the prose-cutor's view of the case. A number of studies have examined the effects of such coverage by polling people exposed to reports of actual crimes. These studies, whether surveying opinions about notorious crimes (Studebaker et al., 2002) or cases of only local interest (Vidmar, 2002), consistently find that persons exposed to pretrial publicity possess more knowledge about the events in question, are more likely to have prejudged the case, and are more knowledgeable

of incriminating facts that would be inadmissible at the trial. On rare occasions, when a field study demonstrates that the volume of publicity has been overwhelming and when a crime has touched the lives of large numbers of local residents, a judge will have no option but to move the trial. The Oklahoma City bombing case described in Box 7.5 is a good example.

In field studies, participants are typically asked about their knowledge of the crime in question, their perceptions of the defendant's culpability, and their ability to be impartial in light of their knowledge. Surveys have revealed both specific prejudice stemming from media coverage of a particular case (as in the Oklahoma City bombing), and more generic prejudice that derives from mass media reports of social and cultural issues. Moran and Cutler (1991) showed that media descriptions of drug crimes influenced attitudes toward parti-cular defendants who were charged with drug distribution. Cases involving sexual abuse also engender strong sentiments, fed in part by media coverage. Sizeable percentages of Canadian jurors who were asked in court whether they could be impartial in a case involving sexual abuse of children said they could not be (Vidmar, 1997). Among the responses were these: "If I were to answer this question honestly, I do have a problem with this [given that I am] a teacher"; "I'm very prejudiced against child molesters, rapists and wife beaters and I think they should be lashed in my opinion."

Generic prejudices can also be engendered by publicity about jury damage awards and the controversy over tort reform in civil cases. Nearly half of prospective jurors awaiting jury selection in Seattle said that their attitudes about tort reform were informed by the media; the more these individuals supported tort reform, the more negatively disposed they were to civil plaintiffs (Greene, Goodman, & Loftus, 1991).

Survey studies have several strengths. For example, they use large and representative samples of prospective jurors, and they rely on naturally occurring publicity about actual cases. They also have a weakness: The data are correlational in

B o x 7.5   THE CASE OF TIMOTHY McVEIGH: DATA ON THE PREJUDICIAL EFFECTS OF MASSIVE PRETRIAL PUBLICITY

At 9:02 A.M. on April 19, 1995, a massive explosion destroyed the Murrah Federal Building in Oklahoma City. The bombing killed 163 people in the building (including 15 children in the building's day care center visible from the street) as well as 5 people outside. The explosion trapped hundreds of people in the rubble and spewed glass, chunks of concrete, and debris over several blocks of downtown Oklahoma City. It was the country's most deadly act of domestic terrorism.

Approximately 75 minutes after the blast, Timothy McVeigh was pulled over while driving north from Oklahoma City because his car lacked license tags. After the state trooper discovered a concealed, loaded gun in his car, McVeigh was arrested and incarcerated for transporting a firearm. Two days later, the federal government filed a complaint against McVeigh on federal bombing charges. By August 1995, McVeigh and codefendant Terry Nichols had been charged with conspiracy, use of a weapon of mass destruction, destruction by explosives, and eight counts of first-degree murder in connection with the deaths of eight federal law enforcement officials who had been killed in the blast.

The bombing, the heroic actions of rescue workers, and the arrest of McVeigh all generated a tremendous amount of publicity. Millions of Americans saw images of McVeigh wearing orange jail garb and a bulletproof vest, being led through an angry crowd outside the Noble County Jail in Perry, Oklahoma. One wondered, at that time, whether any location in the country was not saturated with news of the bombing. Predictably, McVeigh requested a change of venue from Oklahoma City to a more neutral (or at least a less emotionally charged) locale.

As part of a motion to change venue, McVeigh enlisted the help of a team of psychologists to provide information to the court about the extent and type of publicity in the Oklahoma City newspaper and in the papers from three other communities (Lawton, Oklahoma, a small town 90 miles from Oklahoma City; Tulsa; and Denver) (Studebaker & Penrod, 1997). The psychologists identified all articles pertaining to the bombing in these four papers between April 20, 1995, and January 8, 1996, and coded the content of the text including negative characterizations of the defendant, reports of a confession, and emotionally laden publicity.

Timothy McVeigh

They also measured the number of articles printed in each paper and the amount of space allotted to text and pictures (*United States v. McVeigh*, 1996).

The data were compelling: During the collection period, 939 articles about the bombing had appeared in the Oklahoma City newspaper and 174 in the *Denver Post*. By a whopping 6,312–558 margin, the *Daily Oklahoman* had printed more statements of an emotional nature (e.g., emotional suffering, goriness of the scene) than the *Denver Post* (Studebaker & Penrod, 1997). On the basis of this analysis and other evidence presented at the hearing, Judge Richard Matsch moved the trial to Denver. In June 1997, McVeigh was convicted on all 11 counts and sentenced to death. He was executed in June 2001.

Critics have long suggested that studies of pretrial publicity lack usefulness because they do not measure the public's reactions to naturally occurring publicity (as we pointed out, researchers often "expose" participants to news reports in the context of an experiment). To address these concerns, Christina Studebaker and her colleagues conducted a study using the Internet to examine how differences in naturally occurring exposure to pretrial publicity affected public attitudes, evidence evaluation, and verdict and sentencing preferences in the *McVeigh* case (Studebaker et al., 2002). They found, among other things, that the closer people were to the bombing site, the more they knew about it and the more they believed that McVeigh was guilty. This study employs a novel methodology to explore important real-world effects of pretrial information.

nature. As such, they cannot indicate the direction of the relationship between exposure to publicity and prejudice. For example, does exposure to publicity lead to prejudicial sentiments about the defendant, or, alternatively, are people with an antidefendant bias likely to expose themselves to such publicity? Reasoning from Kovera's study on the interactive effects of the media and preexisting attitudes in a rape case, we suspect that both alternatives are possible.

Some scholars (e.g., Carroll et al., 1986) have suggested another weakness in field surveys. They argue that courts should not conclude that pretrial publicity biases jurors just because it affects their attitudes; to be truly prejudicial, it must also affect their verdicts. According to this logic, we need to know whether pretrial publicity effects persist through the presentation of trial evidence. Some evidence suggests that antidefendant biases held at the beginning of the trial persist through the presentation of evidence and may even influence the way the evidence is interpreted (Hope et al., 2004).

Remedies for the Effects of Pretrial Publicity

Given that pretrial publicity adversely affects juror impartiality, what procedures should be used to restore the likelihood of a fair trial for the defendant? Four alternatives are available.

1. *Continuance.* The trial can be postponed until a later date, with the expectation that the passage of time will lessen the effects of the prejudicial material. This view remains in vogue with some judges. However, research indicates that although continuances may decrease jurors' reliance on factual pretrial publicity, they do not dampen jurors' recall or use of emotionally biasing information (Kramer, Kerr, & Carroll, 1990).

2. *Expanded voir dire.* The most popular method for identifying pretrial prejudice involves conducting a thorough **voir dire** (questioning) of potential jurors. But though expanded *voir dire* can be a valuable protection against partiality, it may not always be adequate. Jurors may not

recognize their own biases, and they can hide their true feelings from an examiner if they so choose. Jurors may also be hesitant to self-disclose in a public courtroom. Nietzel and Dillehay (1982) evaluated different types of questioning procedures in the jury selection process of 13 Kentucky death penalty trials. The questioning of jurors in these cases was directed either to an individual or to the entire group, and individual questioning was either in open court with other jurors present or in the judge's chambers. More jurors were excused in cases that involved individual questioning in seclusion than in cases that involved other procedures. Jurors probably feel more comfortable sharing their true feelings when they can do so privately.

3. *Judicial instructions.* A fairly simple remedy for the bias that can result from pretrial publicity involves an instruction from the judge to the jury, admonishing members to base their decision on the evidence rather than on nonevidentiary information. However, a judicial instruction may be insufficient to reduce the biasing effect of exposure to pretrial publicity (Nietzel, McCarthy, & Kern, 1999). In one study, participants read the transcript of a case in which the defendant was charged with killing his estranged wife and a neighbor (Fein, McCloskey, & Tomlinson, 1997). Before trial, half of the mock jurors read a series of articles about the murders and some also read an article in which the defense attorney complained about the negative publicity: "The coverage of this case serves as another fine example of how the media manipulates information to sell papers, and knowingly ignores acts which would point toward a defendant's innocence" (p. 1219). Despite judicial instructions to ignore the pretrial information, jurors' verdicts were significantly influenced by it, unless they had been made suspicious of the media's motives. Thus, mock jurors could follow the instruction only when they were given some reason to suspect the source of the pretrial information.

These three remedies appear, on the basis of existing research, to be largely ineffective. Why do the methods most commonly relied on tend to fail as safeguards? The answer probably lies in several basic features of the way that people remember and use information to form impressions and overall judgments (Studebaker & Penrod, 2005). Unless they have some reason to discount or ignore pretrial publicity when it is first encountered, most people will use it to help them interpret subsequent information and to make various pieces of information "fit" together in a coherent theme. Therefore, once the idea of a guilty perpetrator is established, it may become an organizing principle for the processing of additional information about the person. For these reasons, safeguards that attempt to remove an existing bias may never work as well as trying to seat jurors who never had a bias to start with. The value of achieving this goal is why most social scientists prefer changes of venue.

4. *Change of venue.* A change of venue is the most extreme remedy for pretrial prejudice. Changing venue requires that the trial be conducted in another geographic jurisdiction altogether and that jurors for the trial be drawn from this new jurisdiction. Because venue changes are expensive, inconvenient, and time-consuming, courts are reluctant to use them.

Venue changes can result in significant variations in characteristics of the communities involved, as was illustrated by the case of William Lozano, a Hispanic police officer who was convicted of killing an African American motorist in Miami. After his conviction was reversed because of pretrial publicity, the case was moved to Tallahassee (which has a much smaller Hispanic population than Miami) and finally to Orlando (where the Hispanic population is more sizeable). The Florida appellate court reasoned that in cases in which race may be a factor and changes of venue are appropriate, trials should be moved to locations where the demographic characteristics are similar to those of the original venue (*State v. Lozano*, 1993).

Psychologists can be enlisted to support a lawyer's motion for one or more of these protections against pretrial prejudices. When pretrial contamination is extensive, a professionally conducted public opinion survey is the technique of choice for evaluating the degree of prejudice in a community. Public opinion surveys gauge how many people have read or heard about a case, what they have read or heard, whether they have formed opinions, what these opinions are, and how their opinions influence perceptions of the case.

Public opinion surveys are time-consuming, hectic activities that often demand more resources than the typical client can afford. However, they usually yield valuable information. Obtaining a change of venue for a highly publicized case is probably the most effective procedure available for improving the chances for a fair trial. Moreover, even if the venue is not changed, the results of the survey can often be used in jury selection. Because of the multiple purposes for which they can be used, public opinion surveys are a popular tool among litigation consultants. We discuss some of these additional uses in Chapter 11.

SUMMARY

1. ***What are the major legal proceedings between arrest and trial in the criminal justice system?***
(1) An initial appearance, at which defendants are informed of the charges, of their constitutional rights, and of future proceedings; (2) a preliminary hearing, in which the judge determines whether there is enough evidence to hold the defendant for processing by the grand jury; (3) action by the grand jury, which decides whether sufficient evidence exists for the defendant to be tried; (4) an arraignment, involving a formal statement of charges and an initial plea by the defendant to these charges; (5) a process of discovery, requiring that the prosecutor reveal to the defense certain evidence, and pretrial motions, or attempts by both sides to win favorable ground rules for the subsequent trial.

2. **Why do defendants and prosecutors agree to plea-bargain?** Plea bargaining is an excellent example of the dilemma between truth and conflict resolution as goals of our legal system. The vast majority of criminal cases end between arrest and trial with the defendant pleading guilty to some (often reduced) charges. Plea bargaining benefits both defendants and prosecutors. Defendants who plead guilty often receive reductions in the charges or in their sentences; prosecutors secure a "conviction" without expending their time at trial.

3. **What are settlement negotiations and why are most civil lawsuits resolved through settlement, rather than trial?** Settlement negotiations are private discussions held between the attorneys representing disputing parties in a civil lawsuit. The objective of the negotiations is to resolve the dispute in a manner agreeable to both sides. Settlement negotiations are often preferable to trials because (1) a negotiated compromise is more appealing to most litigants than the uncertainty of a jury trial, and (2) judges have large caseloads (or dockets) and therefore prefer that participants in civil disputes resolve their differences themselves without using the considerable resources necessary to have a trial.

4. **What is bail, and what factors influence the amount of bail set?** Bail is the provision, by a defendant, of money or other assets that are forfeited if the defendant fails to appear at trial. In determining whether to release a defendant prior to trial, the judge should consider the risk that the defendant will not show up for his or her trial. Judges also consider the seriousness of the offense and the defendant's prior record as well as the defendant's race and gender.

5. **In what ways does pretrial publicity pose a danger to fair trials? How can these dangers be reduced?** The right to a free press and the right to a fair trial are usually complementary, but some criminal trials (and some civil trials) generate so much publicity that the defendant's right to an impartial jury is jeopardized. In addition, publicity about other cases or about social or cultural issues can create generic prejudice that can also influence jurors' reasoning in a particular case. Psychologists have studied the effects of pretrial publicity on potential fact finders and have also evaluated different mechanisms for curbing or curing the negative effects of pretrial publicity.

KEY TERMS

adjudicative competence

anchoring and adjustment bias

arraignment

change of venue

charge bargaining

discovery

evaluation apprehension

exculpatory

extralegal factors

framing effects

gag order

generic prejudice

grand jury

heuristics

indictments

initial appearance

legal factors

matching heuristic

motion *in limine*

overconfidence bias

plea bargains

preliminary hearing

preventive detention

reservation price

self-serving bias

sentence bargaining

source monitoring

specific pretrial publicity

voir dire

8

Forensic Assessment in Criminal and Juvenile Cases

ORIENTING QUESTIONS

1. What is the scope of forensic psychology?
2. What is meant by competence in the criminal justice process?
3. How do clinicians assess competence?
4. What are the consequences of being found incompetent to proceed in the criminal justice process?
5. What is the legal definition of insanity?
6. How frequently is the insanity defense used, and how successful is it?
7. What are the major criticisms of the insanity defense, and what attempts have been made to reform it?
8. What are the important criteria in deciding on juvenile transfer?

THE SCOPE OF FORENSIC PSYCHOLOGY

Forensic psychologists use knowledge and techniques from psychology, psychiatry, and other behavioral sciences to answer questions about individuals involved in legal proceedings. In most cases, forensic assessment activities are performed by clinical psychologists, and the field of forensic psychology has prospered and matured considerably in the last 30 years (Heilbrun, Grisso, & Goldstein, 2008; Nicholson, 1999; Nicholson & Norwood, 2000). For example, forensic psychology is officially recognized as a specialty by the American Board of Professional Psychology and the American Psychological Association, guidelines for the practice of forensic psychology have been approved (Committee on Ethical Guidelines for Forensic Psychologists, 1991) and are being revised, forensic psychology training programs have been developed, and the research and clinical literature on forensic practice has increased dramatically.

Despite both public concerns and professional skepticism about whether forensic psychology should be afforded as much credibility and stature as it now appears to enjoy, the field continues to expand. According to one survey, the use of expert witnesses increased from an average of three experts per case in 1991 to more than four in 1998. Of these expert witnesses called, about 40% were in the medical or mental health professions (Ivkovic & Hans, 2003). Other estimates suggest that psychologists and psychiatrists testify in about 8% of all federal civil trials, and mental health professionals participate as experts in as many as a million cases per year (O'Connor, Sales, & Shuman, 1996). If anything, this level of participation will continue to increase because of three forces at work that encourage forensic activities.

First, mental health experts may have expertise in a variety of areas relevant to litigation. As scientists learn more about human behavior, attorneys will find new ways to use this information in various legal proceedings; in this chapter and Chapter 9, we focus on several topics that mental health professionals are called on to assess for individuals involved in court proceedings.

Second, forensic psychology is flourishing because the law permits, and even encourages, the use of expert testimony in a host of areas, including psychology, anthropology, criminology, engineering, toxicology, genetics, and medicine. Expert testimony of all types is used increasingly often, but psychological topics have enjoyed an especially large increase in prominence.

Finally, expert testimony by forensic psychologists thrives because it can be very lucrative. At an hourly rate between $200 and $700, forensic experts can earn thousands of dollars per case. If one party in a lawsuit or criminal trial hires an expert, the other side usually feels compelled to match that expert. Consequently, the use of psychological experts feeds on itself, and it has become a significant source of income for many professionals.

In general, a qualified expert can testify about a topic if such testimony is relevant to an issue in dispute and if the usefulness of the testimony outweighs whatever prejudicial impact it might have. If these two conditions are satisfied—as they must be for any kind of testimony to be admitted—an expert will be permitted to give opinion testimony if the judge believes that "scientific, technical, or other specialized knowledge will assist the trier of fact to understand the evidence or to determine a fact in issue" (Federal Rule of Evidence 702). As we noted in Chapter 1, the U.S. Supreme Court ruled in the 1993 case of *Daubert v. Merrell Dow Pharmaceuticals* that federal judges are allowed to decide when expert testimony is based on sufficiently relevant and reliable scientific evidence to be admitted into evidence.

In the case of opinions offered by behavioral scientists and mental health experts, the *Daubert* standard suggests that admissible expert testimony should be based on methods and knowledge that are scientifically based (Penrod, Fulero, & Cutler, 1995; Rotgers & Barrett, 1996). The U.S. Supreme Court has also decided that this requirement also applies to *expert* opinions that are provided by those with technical or professional skills (such as clinicians) rather than primarily scientific expertise (*Kumho Tire Co. v. Carmichael*, 1999).

Insanity and Competence: Two Major Issues

The question of whether a criminal defendant was insane at the time of a criminal offense is one of the most controversial questions that forensic psychologists and psychiatrists are called upon to help the court decide. The question has attracted extensive research by forensic specialists, some of which we describe in this chapter. One of the most famous cases involving a defendant's mental state was that of Andrea Yates.

Andrea Yates with her family

In this chapter, we describe how insanity is defined, how claims of insanity are assessed by mental health professionals, and some of the implications of the insanity defense. Before that, however, we begin with competence to stand trial, which is often confused with insanity. We cover trial competence and insanity together in this chapter because these issues are raised together in some cases, because they occur fairly close to one another within the sequence of criminal adjudication, and because they are sometimes assessed at the same time and documented in the same report (Heilbrun & Collins, 1995). We also describe the process of transferring juveniles from juvenile to criminal (adult) court, and the criteria that are used to make this decision. In Chapter 9, we explore several other forensic questions that clinicians assess, including questions that arise in civil litigation, divorce and child custody disputes, commitment hearings, and many other types of legal proceedings.

B o x 8.1   THE CASE OF ANDREA YATES: TRAGEDY AND INSANITY

On the morning of June 20, 2001, Andrea Yates, a 37-year-old wife and mother of five, said goodbye to her husband as he left for work. Before her mother-in-law arrived to help care for the children, who ranged in age from 6 months to 7 years old, Yates filled the bathtub of her Texas home with water. Beginning with her middle son, Paul, she drowned each of her children in turn. She laid the four youngest children in the bed, covering them with a sheet. Her oldest boy was left floating lifelessly in the bathtub. She then called the police and her husband to tell them what she had done.

Prior to the killing of her children, Yates had a long psychiatric history. She reportedly suffered numerous psychotic episodes and had been diagnosed with schizophrenia and postpartum depression. These episodes resulted in several hospitalizations, including one just a month prior to the killings, and required psychotropic medications to help stabilize her.

Yates pled not guilty by reason of insanity (NGRI) to drowning three of her children; she was not charged in the other two deaths. Her insanity plea was based on her claim that she had no choice but to kill them because they would burn in hell if she did not kill them while they were still innocents (Wordsworth, 2005). No one disputed that Yates systematically killed each of her children, but the question remained: Was she so disturbed by the symptoms of her severe mental illness that she could not be held criminally responsible for the murders?

At the conclusion of her trial, Yates was found guilty and sentenced to life in prison. After she had served three years of her sentence, however, the court declared a mistrial and Yates's conviction was overturned. During the trial, one of the psychiatric experts testified that the television show *Law and Order* had aired an episode in which a defendant had been acquitted by reason of insanity after drowning her children in the bathtub. Although the expert himself did not link this observation to Yates's thinking or motivation, the prosecutor did so in closing arguments. In fact, there had never been an episode of *Law and Order* with this specific story line. Yates was found NGRI in a retrial, and is now hospitalized in the Texas state forensic hospital system.

COMPETENCE

The Andrea Yates case highlights the importance of evaluating a defendant's competence to stand trial. Did Yates understand the nature of her charges and the possible consequences of those charges? This question is particularly salient in light of an interview with Yates's mother, who recalled that Andrea Yates (while in prison for the murders of her children) asked her mother who would be watching them (Gibson, 2005). Questions were also raised about whether Yates was taking her antipsychotic medication at the time of the murders as well as during her trial.

Competence to Stand Trial and Adjudicative Competence

What do we mean by competence to stand trial? How do clinicians assess this kind of legal **competence**? What legal standards should be applied? The question of a defendant's competence is the clinical-legal issue most frequently assessed in the criminal justice system. **Competence to stand trial** refers to a defendant's capacity to function meaningfully and knowingly in a legal proceeding; defendants may be adjudicated (i.e., determined by a judge) to be incompetent if they are seriously deficient in one or more abilities, such as understanding the legal proceedings, communicating with their attorneys, appreciating their role in the proceedings, and making legally relevant decisions. Concerns about a defendant's competence are tied to one fundamental principle: Criminal proceedings should not continue against someone who cannot understand their nature and purpose, and assist in defending against prosecution on these charges. This rule applies at every stage of the criminal justice process, but it is raised most often at pretrial hearings concerned with two topics: pleading guilty and accepting a plea bargain, or pleading not guilty and proceeding to trial.

Competence is an important doctrine in our system and the law requires defendants to be competent for several reasons (Melton, Petrila, Poythress, &

Slobogin, 2007). First, defendants must be able to understand the charges against them so that they can participate in the criminal justice system in a meaningful way and make it more likely that legal proceedings will arrive at accurate and just results. Second, punishment of convicted defendants is morally acceptable only if they understand the reasons why they are being punished. Finally, the perceived fairness and dignity of our adversary system of justice requires participation by defendants who have the capacity to defend themselves against the charges of the state. As Grisso and Siegel (1986) observed, "there is no honor in entering a battle in full armor with the intention of striking down an adversary who is without shield or sword" (p. 146).

When defendants plead guilty, they waive several constitutional rights: the right to a jury trial, the right to confront their accusers, the right to call favorable witnesses, and the right to remain silent. The Supreme Court has held that waiving such important rights must be done knowingly, intelligently, and voluntarily (*Johnson v. Zerbst*, 1938), and trial judges are required to question defendants about their pleas in order to establish clearly that they understand that they are waiving their constitutional rights by pleading guilty. A knowing, intelligent, and voluntary guilty plea also includes understanding the charges and the possible penalties that can be imposed, and it requires the judge to examine any plea bargain to ensure that it is "voluntary" in the sense that it represents a considered choice between constitutionally permissible alternatives. For example, prosecutors can offer lighter sentences to a defendant in exchange for a guilty plea, but they cannot offer the defendant money to encourage a guilty plea.

The accepted national standard for competence to stand trial is a "sufficient present ability to consult with [one's] attorney with a reasonable degree of rational understanding, and … a rational, as well as factual understanding of the proceedings against [one]" (*Dusky v. United States*, 1960). With minor differences across jurisdictions, this is the standard for competence to stand trial in all American courts. It establishes the basic criteria for competence as the capacities for a factual and rational understanding of the court proceedings and for consulting with one's

attorney in a rational way. These criteria refer to *present* abilities rather than to the mental state of the defendant at the time of the alleged offense, which, as we will discuss later, is the focus of evaluations of a defendant's sanity.

The *Dusky* standard does not specify how the evaluator assessing competence should judge the sufficiency of rational understanding, ability to consult, or factual understanding. That is ultimately the job of the judge. However, a number of courts and mental health groups have expanded on *Dusky* by listing more specific criteria related to competence, to allow evaluators to provide courts with more detailed information in these areas. For example, evaluators may consider a number of factors elaborating on a defendant's competence-relevant capacities (Group for the Advancement of Psychiatry, 1974), including

- To understand the charges against him.
- To understand legal defenses available in his behalf.
- To understand the dispositions, pleas, and penalties possible.
- To appraise the likely outcomes.
- To appraise the roles of defense counsel, prosecutor, judge, jury, witnesses, and defendant.
- To trust and to communicate relevantly with his counsel.
- To comprehend instructions and advice.
- To make decisions after receiving advice.
- To maintain a collaborative relationship with his attorney and to help plan legal strategy.
- To follow testimony for contradictions or errors.
- To testify relevantly and be cross-examined if necessary.
- To refrain from irrational and unmanageable behavior during the trial.
- To disclose pertinent facts surrounding the alleged offense.

Logically, entering a plea of guilty would require that defendants understand the alternatives they face and have the ability to make a reasoned choice among them. In some respects, such capacities are more demanding than those necessary to stand trial. Defendants standing trial must be aware of the nature of the proceedings and be able to cooperate with counsel in presenting the defense, paying attention to the proceedings and controlling their behavior over the course of a trial. This creates a strong demand for *attention-concentration* and *behavioral control*. Defendants pleading guilty, on the other hand, must understand the possible consequences of pleading guilty instead of going to trial, and must be able to make a rational choice between the alternatives. This creates a particular demand for *cognitive awareness* and *reasoning*.

Despite this, the U.S. Supreme Court ruled that the standard for competence to stand trial will be used in federal courts for assessing other competence questions that arise in the criminal justice process (*Godinez v. Moran*, 1993). In doing so, it rejected the idea that pleading guilty involves a different standard than standing trial. As a result of this decision, some scholars are now suggesting that adjudicative competence is a clearer concept for describing the multiple abilities that criminal defendants are expected to exercise in different legal contexts (Bonnie, 1993; Hoge, Bonnie, et al., 1997). Nonetheless, the term *competence to stand trial* is still used frequently—although it has a broader meaning after the *Godinez* decision. In discussing adjudicative competence, we will do so with the understanding that it is synonymous with competence to stand trial, post-*Godinez*.

In evaluating adjudicative competence, the mental health professional focuses on two basic components. First, there is the *foundational* question of whether the defendant has the capacity to assist counsel. As Table 8.1 summarizes, this foundational component has three requirements: (1) the ability to understand the basic elements of the adversary system, (2) the ability to relate relevant information to one's attorney, and (3) the ability to understand one's situation as a criminal defendant. The second component of adjudicative competence is *decisional competence*, which consists of four interrelated abilities: (1) understanding the information relevant to decisions the defendant must make, (2) thinking rationally about the alternatives involved in these decisions, (3) appreciating the specific legal questions one must resolve as a defendant, and (4) making and expressing a choice about one's legal alternatives.

If an evaluator believes a defendant has the capacities to be competent, the evaluator will prepare a report that states this opinion and the reasons for it (see Table 8.1). However, if the evaluator believes the defendant does not have the relevant capacities to be competent, the report will also discuss possible treatments that might render the defendant

T A B L E 8.1 Foundational and Decisional Components of Adjudicative Competence

Foundational Competence
1. Can the defendant *understand* the basic elements (e.g., prosecutor, defense attorney, judge, jury, guilty plea) of the adversarial process?
2. Can the defendant use *reasoning* to relate relevant information to his or her attorney?
3. Can the defendant *appreciate* his or her legal predicament?

Decisional Competence
1. Can the defendant *understand* information that is relevant to decisions, such as pleading guilty or waiving a jury trial?
2. Can the defendant use *reasoning* about alternative courses of action in making decisions about his or her defense?
3. Can the defendant *appreciate* the decisions that need to be made in his or her own best interest?
4. Can the defendant make a *choice* among the alternative defense strategies available?

B o x   8.2   THE CASE OF JAMIE SULLIVAN: ASSESSING COMPETENCE

Jamie Sullivan was a 24-year-old clerk charged with arson, burglary, and murder in connection with a fire he had set at a small grocery store in Kentucky. The evidence in the case was that after closing hours, Sullivan had returned to the store where he worked and forced the night manager, Ricky Ford, to open the safe and hand over the $800 in cash it contained. Sullivan then locked Ford in a backroom office, doused the room in gasoline, and set the store on fire. Ford was killed in the blaze. On the basis of a lead from a motorist who saw Sullivan running from the scene, police arrested him at his grandmother's apartment a few hours later. If convicted on all charges, Sullivan faced a possible death sentence.

Jamie Sullivan was mentally retarded. (In 2002, the Supreme Court indicated that those with mental retardation cannot be executed [*Atkins v. Virginia*] so Jamie Sullivan might not have been charged with a capital crime after 2002.) He had dropped out of school in the eighth grade, and a psychologist's evaluation of him at that time reported his IQ to be 68. He could read and write his name and a few simple phrases, but nothing more. He had a history of drug abuse and had spent several months in a juvenile correctional camp at the age of 15 after vandalizing five homes in his neighborhood. The army rejected his attempt to volunteer for service because of his limited intelligence and drug habit. His attorney believed that Sullivan's mental problems might render him incompetent to stand trial (IST) and therefore asked a psychologist to evaluate him. After interviewing and testing Sullivan and reviewing the evidence the police had collected, the psychologist found the following: Sullivan's current IQ was 65, which fell in the mentally retarded range; he did not suffer any hallucinations or delusions, but he expressed strong religious beliefs that "God watches over his children and won't let nothing happen to them." The psychologist asked Sullivan a series of questions about his upcoming trial, to which he gave the following answers:

Q. *What are you charged with?*

A. Burning down that store and stealing from Ricky.

Q. *Anything else?*

A. They say I killed Ricky too.

Q. *What could happen to you if a jury found you guilty?*

A. Electric chair, but God will watch over me.

Q. *What does the judge do at a trial?*

A. He tells everybody what to do.

Q. *If somebody told a lie about you in court, what would you do?*

A. Get mad at him.

Q. *Anything else?*

A. Tell my lawyer the truth.

Q. *What does your lawyer do if you have a trial?*

A. Show the jury I'm innocent.

Q. *How could he do that best?*

A. Ask questions and have me tell them I wouldn't hurt Ricky. I liked Ricky.

Q. *What does the prosecutor do in your trial?*

A. Try to get me found guilty.

Q. *Who decides if you are guilty or not?*

A. That jury.

At a hearing to determine whether Jamie Sullivan was competent to stand trial, the psychologist testified that Sullivan was mentally retarded and that, as a result, his understanding of the proceedings was not as accurate or thorough as it might otherwise be. However, the psychologist also testified that Sullivan could assist his attorney and that he did understand the charges against him, as well as the general purpose and nature of his trial. The judge ruled that Jamie Sullivan was competent. A jury convicted him on all the charges and sentenced him to life in prison.

It is estimated that, much like Jamie Sullivan, as many as 60,000 defendants are evaluated annually to determine their competence (Poythress, Monahan, Bonnie, Otto, & Hoge, 2002). The single largest category is made up of defendants being evaluated for competence or already judged to be incompetent to stand trial (Steadman, Rosenstein, MacAskill, & Manderscheid, 1988).

competent. The evaluator's report should not be changed at the request of an attorney, although it may be supplemented in response to questions from an attorney. In the real world of the criminal justice system, attempts by attorneys to influence the content, style, or conclusions of these reports are not uncommon.

Raising the Issue of Competence

The question of a defendant's competence can be raised at any point in the criminal process, and it can be raised by the prosecutor, the defense attorney, or the presiding judge. Prior to the 1970s, defendants found incompetent were often confined in mental hospitals for excessive periods of time. (Sometimes such confinements were even longer than their sentences would have been had they stood trial and been convicted.) But the practice of providing long periods of hospitalization for defendants incompetent for trial was limited in 1972 when the U.S. Supreme Court decided the case of *Jackson v. Indiana*. This decision ordered that defendants who had been committed because they were IST could not be held "more than a reasonable period of time necessary to determine whether there is a substantial probability that [they] will attain that capacity in the foreseeable future." As a result of this decision, the length of time an incompetent defendant can be confined is now limited and many states have passed statutes that "limit" such hospitalization to a period not to exceed the maximum sentence that could have been imposed if the defendant were convicted of charges. In cases involving serious felony charges, such a period might well be 10 years or longer.

Once the question of incompetence is raised, the judge will order an evaluation of the defendant if a "bona fide doubt" exists that the defendant is competent. Judges consider the circumstances of each case and the behavior of each defendant when making this determination. However, if the question of competence is raised, an examination will usually be conducted. Because it is relatively easy to obtain such evaluations, attorneys often seek them for reasons other than a determination of competence. Competence evaluations are used for several tactical reasons: to discover information about a possible insanity

defense, to guarantee the temporary incarceration of a potentially dangerous person without going through the cumbersome procedures of involuntary civil commitment (see Chapter 9), to deny bail, and to delay the trial as one side tries to gain an advantage over the other (Berman & Osborne, 1987; Winick, 1996). Defense attorneys have questions about their clients' competence in up to 15% of felony cases (approximately twice the rate for defendants charged with misdemeanors); in many of these cases, however, the attorney does not seek a formal evaluation (Hoge, Poythress, et al., 1997; Poythress, Bonnie, Hoge, Monahan, & Oberlander, 1994).

Evaluating Competence

After a judge orders a competence examination, arrangements are made for the defendant to be evaluated by one or more mental health professionals. Although these evaluations were traditionally conducted in a special hospital or inpatient forensic facility, most evaluations are now conducted in the community on an outpatient basis (Grisso, Cocozza, Steadman, Fisher, & Greer, 1994; Nicholson & Norwood, 2000). The transition from inpatient to outpatient facility has occurred because inpatient exams are more costly and require more time and because local, outpatient evaluations are usually sufficient (Winick, 1985, 1996).

Physicians, psychiatrists, psychologists, and social workers are authorized by most states to conduct competence examinations, but psychologists are the professional group responsible for the largest number of reports (Nicholson & Norwood, 2000). Some data suggest that nonmedical professionals with relevant forensic specialty knowledge prepare reports of trial competence evaluations that are comparable in quality to those prepared by forensic psychiatrists (Petrella & Poythress, 1983; Sanschagrin, Stevens, Bove, & Heilbrun, 2006).

Under the *Dusky* standard, the presence of mental illness or mental retardation does not guarantee that a defendant will be found IST. The crucial question is whether the disorder impairs a defendant's ability to participate knowingly and meaningfully in the proceedings and to work with the defense attorney. A psychotic defendant might be competent to stand trial in a relatively straightforward case but incompetent to participate in a complex trial that would demand more skill and understanding. Consider the case of John Salvi, who, despite having an apparent psychotic disorder, was found competent to stand trial and was convicted of murdering two people and wounding five others during a shooting spree at two Massachusetts medical clinics that performed abortions. Salvi later committed suicide in prison. In addition, as we saw with Jamie Sullivan, his mental retardation did not substantially compromise his ability to understand the charges against him and the basic nature of his trial. Thus, he was found competent to stand trial. In contrast, Todd Hall was found IST on charges that he murdered nine people after starting a fire in an Ohio fireworks store. Hall displayed serious cognitive impairments as a result of severe brain damage that occurred earlier in his life, which rendered him unable to meet the *Dusky* standard required for a finding of competent to stand trial.

Current competence evaluations focus on the defendant's present ability to function adequately in the legal process. This focus has been sharpened by the development of several structured tests or instruments specifically aimed at assessing the capacities relevant to competence to stand trial. Psychological testing remains a common ingredient in competence evaluations, and although clinicians have begun to use one or more of these specially designed competence assessment instruments in their practice, their use is not as widespread as it should be (Lander & Heilbrun, 2009; Skeem, Golding, Cohn, & Berge, 1998). Examples of these instruments are described in the following paragraphs.

Competency Screening Test (CST). The CST is a 22-item sentence completion task designed as an initial screening test for incompetence (Lipsitt, Lelos, & McGarry, 1971). Because the majority of defendants referred for competence evaluations are later determined to be competent (Nicholson & Kugler, 1991; Roesch & Golding, 1987), an instrument that can quickly identify those referred defendants who *appear* competent is especially useful because it can save the time and expense of many unnecessary full evaluations. When taking the CST, the defendant answers the 22 sentence stems; each response is then scored as acceptable, questionable, or unacceptable.

The CST has several weaknesses. First, the scoring of the sentence completions reflects what some observers (Roesch & Golding, 1987) suggest is a naively positive view of the legal process. For example, on the item "Jack felt that the judge ...," the answer "would be fair to him" would be scored as an acceptable answer, whereas the response "would screw him over" would be scored as unacceptable. Yet some defendants have encountered judges for whom the second answer was more accurate than the first, so such a response should not necessarily be regarded as unacceptable.

A second difficulty is that the CST produces a large number of false positives (defendants called incompetent who, with fuller evaluations, appear to be competent). Although a false positive is less troubling than mistakenly forcing to trial a defendant who is incompetent (a false negative), too many false positives discredit the CST's claim to be an effective screening instrument.

Competency Assessment Instrument (CAI). Developed as a more in-depth instrument for assessing competence, the CAI is a structured, one-hour interview that covers 13 functions relevant to competent functioning at trial (Laboratory of Community Psychiatry, 1974) including appraisal of available legal defenses, unmanageable behavior, quality of relating to attorney, and planning of legal strategy.

Interdisciplinary Fitness Interview (IFI)/Fitness Interview Test-Revised (FIT-R). The IFI is a semistructured interview that evaluates a defendant's abilities in five specific legal areas. It also assesses 11 categories of psychopathological symptoms. Evaluators rate the weight they attached to each item in reaching their decision about competence. These weights vary depending on the nature of the defendant's case; for example, hallucinations might impair a defendant's ability to participate in some trials, but they would have minor effects in others and would therefore be given slight weight. Golding, Roesch, and Schreiber (1984) found that interviewers using the IFI agreed on final judgments of competence in 75 of 77 cases evaluated. These judgments agreed 76% of the time with independent decisions about competence made later at a state hospital. Research on the Fitness Interview Test-Revised (FIT-R) suggests that it is a promising screening tool (Roesch, Zapf, & Eaves, 2006).

Georgia Court Competency Test (GCCT). Consisting of 21 questions, the GCCT has been found to be a highly reliable instrument that taps three dimensions: general legal knowledge (e.g., the jobs of the judge, the lawyer, etc.), courtroom layout (e.g., where the judge or the jury is located in the courtroom), and specific legal knowledge (e.g., how to interact with defense counsel) (Bagby, Nicholson, Rogers, & Nussbaum, 1992). The GCCT does not do as good a job of measuring the less cognitive aspects of competence, such as defendants' ability to cooperate with counsel and assist in their own defense, but it shows significant correlations with a variety of independent criteria of competence (Nicholson, 1999).

The measures described thus far have been used in the past, but, the scientific rigor with which they were developed and validated is limited. We now turn to the MacArthur Measures of Competence and the Evaluation of Competency to Stand Trial-Revised (ECST-R), which were developed more recently and with much greater attention to empirical validation. Because these tools have a much more solid scientific grounding, they are preferable for contemporary forensic clinicians evaluating competence to stand trial.

Contemporary Measures of Competence. Growing out of the concept of adjudicative competence, which describes several interrelated components that need to be considered in the evaluation of competence, the *MacArthur Structured Assessment of the Competence of Criminal Defendants* (MacSAC-CD; Hoge, Bonnie, et al., 1997) is a highly regarded research instrument. Most of the 82 items in the MacSAC-CD rely on a hypothetical vignette about

which the defendant is asked questions that tap foundational and decisional abilities. Defendants are asked the questions in a sequence: Open-ended questions come first. If there is a wrong answer, correct information is provided to the defendant. Defendants are then asked additional open-ended questions to determine whether they now have the necessary understanding based on this disclosure; a series of true–false questions concludes each area of assessment. This format has several advantages. It offers a more standardized evaluation across different defendants, and it is possible to assess separately defendants' preexisting abilities as well as their capacity to learn and apply new information.

One major disadvantage of the MacSAC-CD is that it was developed as a research instrument and takes about two hours to complete, far too long to be used in clinical practice. To overcome this limitation, a 22-item clinical version of this measure, called the *MacArthur Competence Assessment Tool-Criminal Adjudication* (MacCAT-CA) was developed (Poythress et al., 1999). This instrument begins with a hypothetical vignette about a crime, upon which the first 16 items are based. These items assess the defendant's general understanding of the legal system and adjudicative process and his or her reasoning abilities in legal situations. The remaining six items are specific to the defendant's own legal situation.

The ECST-R (Rogers, Tillbrook, & Sewell, 2004) is a semi-structured interview that was developed using the *Dusky* criteria. Its three factors (factual understanding of proceedings, rational understanding of proceedings, and consultation with counsel) have been empirically tested using a statistical technique known as confirmatory factor analysis. It focuses on information that is specific to the case of the individual being evaluated (unlike the MacCAT-CA, which uses a general vignette involving two individuals who fight in a bar). It also addresses the question of whether the evaluee is trying to exaggerate or fake deficits that might make that person appear IST. Both the case specificity and the built-in measure of possible exaggeration are useful features of the ECST-R.

One specialized measure, the *Competence Assessment for Standing Trial for Defendants with Mental*

Retardation (CAST-MR; Everington & Luckasson, 1992), was developed specifically for assessing defendants with mild to moderate mental retardation. Two validations studies have been conducted; although the number of participants has been small, the results have been somewhat encouraging (Grisso, 2003). In addition, this is the only specialized tool developed specifically for assessing trial competence with individuals with developmental disabilities.

One important issue being studied by researchers is the extent to which defendants can successfully fake incompetence on these tests. Some research suggests that although offenders can simulate incompetence, they often take such simulations to extremes, scoring much more poorly on specialized measures of competence capacities than their truly incompetent counterparts (Gothard, Rogers, & Sewell, 1995; Gothard, Viglione, Meloy, & Sherman, 1995). Therefore, very low scores should make evaluators suspicious that a defendant might be exaggerating his or her deficiencies. As noted earlier, one specialized tool (the ECST-R) has a built-in measure to help the evaluator determine whether the defendant is exaggerating deficits.

This issue has gained a great deal of attention because estimates of malingering (faking or grossly exaggerating) mental illness in competence evaluations are close to 18% (Rogers, Salekin, Sewell, Goldstein, & Leonard, 1998). Therefore, screening tools have been developed to offer a more scientific method of detecting malingering in patients who are being evaluated for their competence to stand trial. One of these instruments is the Miller Forensic Assessment of Symptoms Test (M-FAST; Miller, 2001). The M-FAST is a brief, 25-item structured interview that can accurately identify individuals who are attempting to feign mental disorders (see Miller, 2004). Empirical evidence thus far supports the use of the M-FAST in detecting malingering (Jackson, Rogers, & Sewell, 2005), but it is a screening instrument and should be used in conjunction with a wider array of assessments to form a conclusive opinion about whether the defendant is actually malingering.

Following the collection of assessment data, evaluators communicate their findings to the judge. Often, they submit a written report that summarizes the evidence on competence to stand trial, as well as the likelihood that appropriate treatment will sufficiently improve competence-relevant deficits. In controversial or strongly contested cases, it is more likely that there will be a formal competence hearing where the evaluating experts testify and are questioned by attorneys from both sides.

In formal competence hearings, who bears the burden of proof? Must prosecutors prove that defendants are competent, or are defendants required to prove their incompetence? In the 1992 case of *Medina v. California*, the U.S. Supreme Court held that a state can require a criminal defendant to shoulder the burden of proving that he or she is incompetent. But how stringent should that burden be? Most states established the criterion to be a "preponderance of the evidence," meaning that the defendant had to show that it was more likely than not that he or she was incompetent. But four states—Oklahoma, Pennsylvania, Connecticut, and Rhode Island—required a higher standard of proof that was "clear and convincing." Yet in 1996, the Supreme Court held that this standard was too stringent (*Cooper v. Oklahoma*, 1966).

Results of Competence Evaluations

About 70% of the defendants referred for evaluation are ultimately found competent to stand trial (Nicholson & Kugler, 1991; Melton et al., 2007); when very rigorous examinations are conducted, the rate of defendants found competent approaches 90%. Judges seldom disagree with clinicians' decisions about competence (Steadman, 1979), and opposing attorneys often will **stipulate** (agree without further examination) to clinicians' findings (Melton et al., 2007). One study asked judges, prosecutors, and defense attorneys to rank in order of importance eight items typically offered by expert witnesses in competence evaluations (e.g., clinical diagnosis of the defendant, weighing different motives and explanations, providing an ultimate opinion on the legal issue) (Redding, Floyd, & Hawk,

2001). The results revealed that judges and prose-cutors agreed that the expert's ultimate opinion on the legal issue was in the top three most important pieces of information the expert could provide. Depending upon how such "ultimate opinions" are used, this may suggest that mental health professionals exert great—perhaps excessive—influence on this legal decision.

What sort of person is most often judged to be incompetent? In his study of more than 500 defendants found IST, Steadman (1979) described them as often "marginal" men who were undereducated and deficient in job skills, with long histories of involvement in both the legal and the mental health systems (see also Williams & Miller, 1981). Problems of substance abuse were common. Minorities were overrepresented. Others report relatively high percentages of psychosis, lower intelligence, and more problems with certain aspects of memory among incompetent defendants (Nestor, Daggett, Haycock, & Price, 1999; Nicholson, Briggs, & Robertson, 1988; Roesch & Golding, 1980; Ustad, Rogers, Sewell, & Guarnaccia, 1996). Another consistent finding is that defendants deemed IST are charged with more serious crimes than defendants in general. After an extensive review of competence research, Nicholson and Kugler (1991) described the typical defendant found IST to (1) have a history of psychosis for which previous treatment had been received; (2) exhibit symptoms of current serious mental disorder; (3) be single, unemployed, and poorly educated; and (4) score poorly on specific competence assessment instruments. Another study compared hospitalized incompetent defendants with two other groups: those receiving psychiatric treatment in jail, and jail inmates who had not been referred for treatment. Compared with these other two groups, hospitalized incompetent defendants were lower in verbal IQ, more likely to have been diagnosed with schizophrenia, older, and more likely to have a history of prior mental health treatment (Hoge, Poythress, et al., 1997).

If a defendant referred for a competence evaluation is adjudicated competent to stand trial, the legal process resumes, and the defendant again faces the possibility of trial or disposition of charges through plea bargaining. If the defendant is found IST, however, the picture becomes more complicated. For crimes that are not serious, the charges are occasionally dropped, sometimes in exchange for requiring the defendant to receive treatment. In other cases, however, the defendant is hospitalized to be treated for restoration of competence, which, if successful, will result in the defendant proceeding with disposition of charges. Outpatient treatment of incompetent defendants is used less often, even though it might sometimes be justified.

How successful are efforts to restore defendants' competence? One study evaluated an experimental group treatment for a sample of incompetent defendants sent to one of three Philadelphia facilities (Siegel & Elwork, 1990). In addition to receiving psychiatric medication, defendants assigned to these special treatment groups watched videotapes and received special instructions on courtroom procedures. They also discussed different ways of resolving problems that a defendant might face during a trial. A matched control group received treatment for their general psychiatric needs, but no specific treatment relevant to incompetence. Following their treatment, defendants participating in the special competence restoration group showed significant increases in their assessment scores compared to the controls. In addition, hospital staff judged 43% of the experimental subjects competent to stand trial after treatment compared to 15% of the control subjects. In general, most defendants have their adjudicative competence restored, usually with about six months of treatment (Melton et al., 2007).

The real dilemma for IST defendants occurs when treatment is not successful in restoring competence and holds little promise of success in the future. At this point, all options are problematic. Theoretically, the previously described *Jackson* ruling bars the indefinite confinement of an individual adjudicated IST. The law varies across states as to how long such involuntary hospitalization is allowed, but many states permit the defendant to be hospitalized for a period up to the maximum sentence that he or she could have received if convicted of the charges. When such defendants have been hospitalized for this period, however, they can be found "unrestorably incompetent."

Typically, unrestorably incompetent defendants are committed to a hospital through involuntary civil commitment proceedings (see Chapter 9). Standards for this type of commitment are narrower than for being found IST, however. The state must show that the person is mentally ill and either imminently dangerous to self or others or so gravely disabled as to be unable to care for himself or herself. Should an incompetent defendant not meet the criteria for involuntary hospitalization, what happens? Despite the ruling in the *Jackson* case, some states simply continue to confine incompetent defendants for indefinite periods. Although this "solution" might appease the public, we believe it jeopardizes defendants' due process rights and results in lengthy periods of punishment (disguised as treatment) without a conviction.

Several alternative procedures have been proposed to solve this catch-22, including proposals to abolish the IST concept altogether (Burt & Morris, 1972), to allow defendants to seek trial continuances without going through an elaborate evaluation, or to waive their right to be competent under certain circumstances (Fentiman, 1986; Winick, 1996). One additional proposal (American Bar Association, 1984) is that a provisional trial be held for a defendant who is likely to be found unrestorably incompetent. This hearing would decide the question of guilt or innocence. If the defendant is found not guilty, he or she is formally acquitted and could be further confined only through civil commitment. If proven guilty, the defendant would be subject to a special form of commitment that would recognize society's needs for secure handling of these persons.

Amnesia and Competence to Stand Trial

Defendants with amnesia are not necessarily IST. Loss of memory might render a defendant incompetent, but the law does not presume that amnesia per se is incapacitating. Most courts believe this question should be answered on a case-by-case basis, with consideration given to the severity of the amnesia and the extent to which it interferes with preparation of a defense.

Most judges are skeptical about claims of amnesia, believing that it can be easily faked. Consequently, claims of amnesia do not usually lead to a finding of incompetence, but they might result in the prosecution having to cooperate more with the defense attorney in reconstructing the facts and exploring possible defenses.

Competent with Medication, Incompetent without

For most defendants found IST, psychoactive medication has been the treatment of choice because it is assumed to be the best intervention for restoring defendants to competence in a reasonable period of time. Can incompetent defendants refuse this treatment? If medicated, will defendants be found competent to stand trial even though the medication, through its temporarily tranquilizing effects, might undercut a defense such as insanity? The case *Sell v. U.S.* (2003), concerns questions of competence and forced medication (Box 8.3).

Other Competence Issues

Because questions about competence can be raised at any point in the criminal process, several other competences are at issue in deciding whether a defendant can participate knowingly in different functions. Competence for any legal function involves (1) determining what functional abilities are necessary, (2) assessing the context where these abilities must be demonstrated, (3) evaluating the implication of any deficiencies in the required abilities, and (4) deciding whether the deficiencies warrant a conclusion that the defendant is incompetent (Grisso, 1986, 2003). Mental health professionals are sometimes asked to evaluate each of the following competences (see also Melton et al., 2007). Other questions about competencies arising in civil law are discussed in Chapter 9.

B o x 8.3   THE CASE OF CHARLES SELL: INVOLUNTARY MEDICATION TO RESTORE COMPETENCE?

Charles Sell, once a practicing dentist, suffered an extensive history of severe mental illness and several hospitalizations. He was accused of fraud after he allegedly submitted fictitious insurance claims for payment. His competence to stand trial was evaluated, and he was found competent and released on bail. Subsequently, a grand jury indicted Sell on 13 additional counts of fraud and, later, attempted murder. During his bail revocation hearing, Sell's mental illness was markedly worse, and his behavior was "totally out of control, including spitting in the judge's face" (*Sell v. U.S.*, 2003, p. 2). His competence was again evaluated, at which time he was adjudicated IST. He was hospitalized for treatment to help restore his competence. Hospital staff recommended antipsychotic medication, which Sell declined to take. The hospital administered these medications to him involuntarily.

Sell challenged this in court, arguing that involuntary medication violates the Fifth Amendment Constitutional right to "liberty to reject medical treatment" (p. 10). The lower court found that Sell was a danger to himself and others, that medication was the only way to render him less dangerous, that the benefits to Sell outweighed the risks, and that the drugs were substantially likely to return Sell to competence. The court further held that medication was the only viable hope of rendering Sell competent to stand trial and was necessary to serve the Government's interest in obtaining an adjudication of his guilt or innocence. Sell appealed and this case was granted *certiorari* by the United States Supreme Court.

At the heart of this case is the issue of whether it is a violation of a defendant's rights to be forcibly medicated in order to become competent to proceed to trial, with the associated possibility of conviction and incarceration in prison. But if the defendant cannot be restored to competence without medication, he or she may remain hospitalized, and thus also deprived of his or her liberty, for a period that may be longer than the prison sentence that could have been imposed upon conviction. In this decision, the Court weighed these considerations and outlined the conditions under which the government may forcibly administer psychotropic medication to render a mentally ill defendant competent to stand trial. The treatment must be (1) medically appropriate, (2) substantially unlikely to have side effects that may undermine the trial's fairness, and (3) necessary to significantly further important government trial-related interests.

Capacities to Waive Miranda Rights. The waiver of *Miranda* rights requires that defendants, once in police custody, make a confession after having waived the Fifth Amendment right to avoid self-incrimination in a knowing, intelligent, and voluntary fashion. A clinician's assessment of these abilities is challenging because, in most cases, the waiver and confession have occurred months before the professional's evaluation, requiring a reconstruction of the defendant's psychological condition at the time.

Another aspect of a defendant's rights guaranteed by *Miranda* involves the Sixth Amendment right to be represented by counsel when he or she is in police custody. The same standard to waive this right—knowing, intelligent, and voluntary—is applied to the question of whether an individual had the capacity to waive the right to counsel before providing police with a confession.

A slightly different twist on the right to be represented by counsel involves the question of whether defendants can decide that they do not want a lawyer to represent them at trial. The Supreme Court has held that defendants have a constitutional right to waive counsel and represent themselves at trial, providing that this decision is made competently (*Faretta v. California*, 1975). In addition, the presiding judge must be convinced that the waiver of counsel is both voluntary and intelligent. Defendants do not have to convince the court that they possess a high level of legal knowledge, although some legal knowledge is probably important.

Competence to waive the right to counsel was at issue in the trial of Colin Ferguson, who was charged with murdering 6 passengers and wounding 19 more when he went on a killing rampage aboard a Long Island Railroad train in December 1993. Ferguson insisted on serving as his own attorney, after rejecting the "black rage" defense suggested by his lawyers. At first, Ferguson proved effective enough to have several of his objections to the prosecutor's case sustained. But then, giving new meaning to the old saying that a defendant who argues his own case has a fool for a client, Ferguson opened his case by claiming that, "There were 93 counts to that indictment, 93 counts only because it matches the year 1993. If it had been 1925, it would be a 25-count indictment." This was a prelude to Ferguson's attempt at cross-examining a series of eyewitnesses, who, in response to his preposterous suggestion that someone else had been the murderer, answered time after time, "No, I saw the murderer clearly. It was you."

Competence to Refuse the Insanity Defense. In cases in which it is likely that the defendant was insane at the time of the offense, can the defendant refuse to plead insanity? If there is evidence that a defendant was not mentally responsible for criminal acts, do courts have a duty to require that the defendant plead insanity when the defendant does not want to do so? Courts are divided on this question. In some cases, they have suggested that society's stake in punishing only mentally responsible persons requires the imposition of an insanity plea even on unwilling defendants (*Whalen v. United States*, 1965). Other decisions (*Frendak v. United States*, 1979) use the framework of competence to answer this question—if the defendant understands the alternative pleas available and the consequences of those pleas, the defendant should be permitted to reject an insanity plea. This latter approach is followed in most courts.

This question was at the heart of the prosecution of Theodore Kaczynski, a reclusive mathematician who was dubbed the "Unabomber" for sending a series of mail bombs to universities and airlines between 1978 and 1995. Although the consensus of several experts was that Kaczynski suffered from paranoid schizophrenia, he adamantly refused to let his attorneys use an insanity defense, arguing that he did not want to be stigmatized, in his words, as a "sickie." Was Kaczynski competent to make this decision, or was Judge Garland E. Burrell, Jr. correct in ruling that Kaczynski's lawyers could control his defense, even over the defendant's persistent objections? It is doubtful that an insanity defense would have been successful—Kaczynski's own diary proved that he understood and intended to commit his crimes—but we will never know for sure. Ultimately, to avoid the possibility of the death penalty, Kaczynski pled guilty to murder and was sentenced to life in prison.

" Paying my fee will also help as evidence for our insanity defense. "

Competence to Be Sentenced. For legal and humanitarian reasons, convicted defendants are not to be sentenced to punishment unless they are competent. In general, the standard for this competence is that defendants can understand the punishment and the reasons why it is being imposed, and can meaningfully execute their right to address the court at sentencing. Competence to be sentenced is often a more straightforward question for the clinician to evaluate than adjudicative competence, which involves issues of whether the accused can interact effectively with counsel and appreciate alternative courses of action.

Competence to Be Executed. A particularly controversial aspect of this area is determining whether a defendant is competent to be executed. The U.S. Supreme Court decided, in the case of *Ford v. Wainwright* (1986), that the Eighth Amendment ban against cruel and unusual punishments prohibits the execution of defendants while they are incompetent. Therefore, mental health professionals are at times called on to evaluate inmates waiting to be executed to determine whether they are competent to be executed. The practical problems and ethical dilemmas involved in these evaluations are enormous (Heilbrun, 1987; Heilbrun & McClaren, 1988; Mossman, 1987; Susman, 1992) and have led some psychologists to recommend that clinicians not perform such evaluations.

Juvenile Competence

Are juveniles competent to stand trial? Does it make a difference whether they are being processed in juvenile court or tried as adults? Do adolescents differ from adults in their abilities to participate in trials, and if so, what are these differences? These are questions asked by investigators (Grisso et al., 2003) when they studied a group of 927 adolescents in juvenile detention facilities and community settings. Participants were administered a specialized measure of competence for adults (the MacCAT-CA) as well as the MacArthur Judgment Evaluation (MacJen), which was designed to examine immaturity of judgment. Their research goal was to provide data

on *competence to proceed* (comprehension of the purpose and nature of the trial process, ability to provide relevant information to counsel and to process information, and ability to apply information to oneself without distortion or irrationality) and *decisional competence* (ability to make important decisions about waiver of constitutional rights and maturity of judgment).

Results indicated that participants who were age 15 and younger were significantly impaired in ways that compromised their abilities to function as competent defendants in a criminal (adult) proceeding. More specifically, one-third of 11–13 year olds and one-fifth of 14–15 year olds were as impaired in their functional legal capacities as mentally ill adults who are IST. Below-average intelligence was also associated with deficits in these functional legal capacities. Since a large proportion of adolescents in the juvenile justice system have below-average IQ, the risk for incompetence is further increased when adolescents in this system are transferred into criminal court (Grisso et al., 2003).

These findings have fewer implications for adolescents in juvenile court. Since the expectations for competence in juvenile court are different—juveniles are being tried in a setting that is designed for adolescents—it is more likely that an adolescent with limited functional legal capacities to understand and assist would be adjudicated competent in juvenile court than if he or she were processed in adult criminal court.

THE INSANITY DEFENSE

The issue of insanity intensifies each of the dilemmas of Chapter 1. Any society that respects the rights of individuals recognizes the possibility that some of its citizens cannot comprehend the consequences or the wrongfulness of their actions. Yet the highly publicized "success" of defendants who claimed insanity as an explanation for their actions (e.g., John Hinckley, the would-be assassin of President Reagan) has spawned new legislation intended to make it more difficult for jurors to acquit defendants by reason of insanity.

The quest for equality is also threatened by discretion in how the insanity defense is used. It is much harder to find a defendant NGRI in some states than in others because of differing definitions of insanity held by different jurisdictions. Five states (Idaho, Kansas, Montana, North Dakota, and Utah) have abolished the insanity defense (Melton et al., 2007), even though they do allow defendants to introduce evidence about their mental condition at the time of an offense.

Likewise, it may be very difficult to accurately gauge a defendant's mental state at the time of the offense, as must be done when a defendant uses insanity as a defense. The jury or judge must answer the question "What was he experiencing when he fired the gun?" rather than "Did he fire the gun?" How can we determine whether a defendant is legally insane? Can we know a person's state of mind when he or she committed an antisocial act? This becomes even more difficult when the fact finders—juries and judges—must determine not whether the person is currently insane but whether he or she was insane at the time of the crime, possibly months or years before.

This problem is further complicated by the reality that there are far fewer specialized tools specifically designed to assess insanity than there are to assess competence. One brief screening instrument—the Mental Status Examination at the Time of the Offense (Slobogin, Melton, & Showalter, 1984)—has been developed, but research on its reliability and validity is limited to one study. More research has been conducted on the Rogers Criminal Responsibility Scales (RCRAS; Rogers, 1986), a set of 25 scales that organize the many factors and points of decision that clinicians need to consider when assessing criminal responsibility. Although the RCRAS has clear limitations, it is the only formal instrument with some proven reliability and validity for guiding clinicians' decision-making process in insanity evaluations (Nicholson, 1999).

Another reason why truth is so elusive in cases of alleged insanity stems from the conflict between law and behavioral sciences as alternative pathways to knowledge. Insanity is a legal concept, not a medical or psychological one. In many states, a defendant could be hallucinating, delusional, and diagnosed as schizophrenic, but if the individual knew the difference between right and wrong, he or she would be legally sane. Thus, psychiatrists and clinical psychologists are called on as forensic experts to provide information regarding a decision that is ultimately outside their professional/scientific framework. The therapeutic goals of psychiatry and clinical psychology (diagnosis and assessment that are probabilistic and complex) do not fit well with the legal system's demand for a straightforward "yes or no" answer (Heilbrun, 2001). Furthermore, although psychiatrists and other mental health experts can offer diagnoses, the particular diagnosis is less important than the specific symptoms and their impact on the functional legal demands associated with the insanity standard (whether the defendant "knew" the behavior was wrong; in some states, additionally, whether the defendant could conform his or her conduct to the requirements of the law).

Some mental health professionals even argue that the law and the behavioral sciences are incompatible (Winslade & Ross, 1983). Certainly they hold competing assumptions on the important question of personal responsibility for one's behavior. The law assumes that we are free agents (with a few exceptions) and that when we act illegally, we should be punished. The behavioral sciences assume that behavior is caused both by conditions within the person and by the environment acting on the person. Under the latter assumption, the concept of "responsibility" and the associated justification for punishment are both diluted.

Rationale for the Insanity Defense

Insanity refers to the defendant's mental state at the time the offense was committed (as contrasted with *competence to stand trial*, which refers exclusively to the defendant's relevant legal capacities at the time of the trial or plea bargain). Why do we have laws about insanity at all? Wouldn't it be simpler to do away with insanity in the legal system? Allowing a criminal defendant to plead NGRI reflects a fundamental belief that a civilized society should not punish people who do not know what they are doing or are incapable of controlling their conduct. Thus, the state must occasionally tell the victim's friends and family that even though it abhors the defendant's acts, some offenders do not deserve punishment. Before it can do that, however, a judgment about whether such persons were responsible for their actions must be made.

What is the legal standard for insanity? There is no single answer. The following sections describe several definitions currently in use. The legal standards that define criminal responsibility vary from state to state, but in all states, the defendant is initially presumed to be responsible for his or her alleged offense. Therefore, if pleading insanity, defendants have the duty to present evidence that would disprove the presumption of criminal responsibility in their case— a requirement known as an **affirmative defense.** A related legal issue is the assessment of *mens rea,* or the mental state of knowing the nature and quality of a forbidden act. To be a criminal offense, an act not only must be illegal but also must be accompanied by the necessary *mens rea*, or guilty mind.

The M'Naghten Rule: An Early Attempt to Define Insanity

In 1843, an Englishman named Daniel M'Naghten shot and killed the private secretary of the British prime minister. Plagued by paranoid delusions, M'Naghten believed that the Prime Minister, Sir Robert Peel, was part of a conspiracy hatched by the Tory party against him. At first, M'Naghten sought to escape his imagined tormentors by traveling through Europe. When that didn't work, he stalked the Prime Minister and, after waiting in front of his residence at No. 10 Downing Street, shot the man he thought was Peel.

M'Naghten was charged with murder, and his defense was to plead NGRI. Nine medical experts, including the American psychiatrist Isaac Ray, testified for two days about his mental state, and all agreed that he was insane. On instructions from the lord chief justice, the jury rendered a verdict of NGRI without even leaving the jury box to deliberate. M'Naghten was committed to the Broadmoor asylum for the insane, where he remained for the rest of his life.

The public was infuriated, as was Queen Victoria, who had been the target of several attempts on her life. She demanded a tougher test of insanity. Subsequent debate in the House of Lords led to what has come to be called the **M'Naghten rule,** which was announced in 1843, long before psychiatry became a household word. The M'Naghten rule defines insanity as follows:

> The jury ought to be told in all cases that every man is to be presumed to be sane, and to possess a sufficient degree of reason to be responsible for his crimes, until the contrary be proved to their satisfaction; and that to establish a defense on the grounds of insanity it must be clearly proved that, at the time of committing the act, the accused was laboring under such a defect of reason, from disease of the mind, as not to know the nature and quality of the act he was doing, or, if he did know it, that he did not know what he was doing was wrong. (quoted in Post, 1963, p. 113)

The M'Naghten rule, which became the standard for defining insanity in Great Britain and the United States, thus "excuses" criminal conduct if the defendant, as a result of a "disease of the mind": (1) did not know what he was doing (e.g., believed he was shooting an animal rather than a human) or (2) did not know that what he was doing was wrong (e.g., believed killing unarmed strangers was "right").

The M'Naghten rule (or a close variation) is now used in 28 states (Melton et al., 2007). However, it has been criticized by legal scholars and mental health professionals alike for a number of years, often on the basis that the cognitive focus ("knowing wrongfulness") is too limiting, and does not allow consideration of motivational and other influences affecting the control of behavior. As we will see, there have been a number of alternative legal tests of insanity since M'Naghten was first decided.

The Brawner Rule, Stemming from the Model Penal Code

A committee of legal scholars developed the Model Penal Code, which led to what is now called the **Brawner rule.** This rule states that a defendant is not responsible for criminal conduct if he, "at the time of such conduct as a result of mental disease or defect, [lacks] substantial capacity either to appreciate the criminality [wrongfulness] of his conduct or to conform his conduct to the requirements of the law." This standard, or a variation, allows judges and juries to consider whether mentally ill defendants have the capacity to understand the nature of their acts or to behave in a lawful way. As of 2006, it was used in 14 states (Melton et al., 2007). Federal courts once used the Brawner rule, but the federal insanity standard has now been drastically altered under the Insanity Defense Reform Act.

The Brawner test differs from the M'Naghten rule in three substantial respects. First, by using the term *appreciate*, it incorporates the emotional as well as the cognitive determinants of criminal actions. Second, it does not require that offenders exhibit a total lack of appreciation for the nature of their conduct, but only a lack of "substantial capacity." Finally, it includes both a cognitive element and a volitional element, making defendants' inability to control their actions a sufficient criterion by itself for insanity.

The Insanity Defense Reform Act

In the wake of the trial of John Hinckley, Jr., who attempted to assassinate President Ronald Reagan, the U.S. Congress enacted the Insanity Defense Reform Act (IDRA) in 1984. The law modified the existing insanity defense (eliminating the "volitional" prong and retaining the "cognitive" prong), with the expectation that fewer defendants would be able to use it successfully. The law did not abolish the insanity defense. However, it changed it substantially. In addition to eliminating the volitional prong, it also changed the insanity defense process as follows:

1. It prohibited experts from giving ultimate opinions about insanity. Although this prohibition may have little effect on jurors, reformers believed it would prevent expert witnesses from usurping the province of the jury.

2. It placed on the defendant the burden to prove insanity by clear and convincing evidence, replacing the previous requirement that the prosecution must prove a defendant's sanity beyond a reasonable doubt.

What little research has been conducted on the IDRA suggests that it does not accomplish either what its proponents envisioned or what its critics feared. At least in mock jury studies, verdicts do not significantly differ regardless of whether the jurors have heard IDRA instructions, Brawner instructions, or no instructions (Finkel, 1989). In addition, states with the broadest test of insanity (Brawner) do not show higher rates of insanity acquittals than states with the narrowest test (M'Naghten) (Melton et al., 2007).

Empirical Research Relevant to Varying Insanity Defense Rules

In theory, varying rules for insanity should influence jurors' understanding of the defense, but psychologists have questioned whether the typical juror can comprehend the legal language of these definitions and then apply them as intended by the courts. (Further evaluation of the effectiveness of the judge's instructions to the jury can be found in Chapter 12.) Elwork, Sales, and Suggs (1981) found jurors only 51% correct on a series of questions testing their comprehension of instructions regarding the M'Naghten rule. Ogloff (1991) obtained similar results: Regardless of what insanity rule was used, college students showed very low rates of recall and comprehension of crucial components in various insanity definitions. It may be that jurors (or mock jurors) do not understand the differences between these different tests very well, consistent with the broader conclusion that jurors do not understand the nuances of a variety of legal instructions that are provided to them (Lieberman & Sales, 1997).

The limited empirical evidence indicates that different standards of insanity also make little difference in verdicts. Simon (1967) presented mock juries with re-creations of two actual trials in which the insanity defense had been used; in one the charge was housebreaking, in the other it was incest. A third of the juries received the M'Naghten rule, a third received yet another rule, and a third no instructions about how to define insanity (although they knew the defendant was using this as his defense). In both trials, jurors operating with the M'Naghten rule were less likely to vote for acquittal (although the differences between conditions were not large). Interestingly, at least half of the uninstructed juries brought up the defendant's ability to distinguish between right and wrong—the M'Naghten standard—during their deliberations. This latter finding suggests that although instructions have some effect on jury decision making in insanity cases, they tell only part of the story—and perhaps a minor part at that (Finkel, 1989; Finkel & Slobogin, 1995; Ogloff, 1991; Roberts & Golding, 1991; Roberts, Golding, & Fincham, 1987).

Probably more important than formal instructions are jurors' own views through which they interpret and filter the evidence and then reach verdicts that are compatible with their personal sense of justice. This decision process is an example of how jurors are prone to interpret "facts" in the context of a personal story or narrative that "makes the most sense" to each of them subjectively. (We describe the "story model" of juror decision making in Chapter 12.)

Differences among jurors in the individual narratives they weave about the same set of trial "facts" may be related, in turn, to the different attitudes they hold about the morality of the insanity defense and the punishment of mentally ill offenders (Roberts & Golding, 1991). For instance, one study found that jurors conceptualized the prototypical insanity defendant in one of three ways: (1) severely mentally disordered (SMD), characterized by extreme, chronic, uncontrollable mental illness and retardation that impaired the defendant's ability to function in society; (2) morally insane (MI), typified by symptoms of psychosis and psychopathy, a categorization used to represent a malevolent, detached, and unpredictably violent offender; and (3) mental-state-centered (MSC), describing a defendant who suffered from varied, but clearly supported, impairments in his or her mental state at the time of his offense (Skeem & Golding, 2001). The MSC group emphasized the most legally relevant characteristics for a defendant pleading insanity. Jurors who held SMD- or MI-like prototypes made up the vast majority of the sample (79%), and they tended to believe that the insanity defense was frequently raised, was easily abused, and jeopardized public safety. By contrast, those jurors who held MSC-like prototypes (21%) were less likely to perceive the insanity defense as unjust and tended to believe that the constitutional rights ascribed to defendants were necessary components of the legal process.

Famous Trials and the Use of the Insanity Plea

Before reporting on the actual frequency and effectiveness of attempts to use the plea, we review the results of several highly publicized trials that have molded public opinion about insanity pleas.

Trials in Which the Insanity Plea Failed. Among murder defendants who have pleaded insanity as a defense were Jack Ruby, whom millions of television viewers saw kill Lee Harvey Oswald, President John F. Kennedy's alleged assassin; Sirhan Sirhan, charged with the assassination of Robert F. Kennedy; John Wayne Gacy, who was convicted of killing 33 boys in Chicago; and Andrea Yates, charged with drowning her children in the bathtub. All these defendants were convicted of murder despite their pleas of insanity, although Ms. Yates was found NGRI in a second trial granted after her appeal of her conviction in the first.

In the Jeffrey Dahmer case (described in Chapter 3), jurors rejected a plea of insanity as a defense against murder charges. Dahmer admitted killing and dismembering 15 young men over about a 10-year period, but his attorney, Gerald Boyle, argued that Dahmer was insane at the time—a sick man, not an evil one. Prosecutor Michael McCann disagreed, arguing that Dahmer knew that what he was doing was wrong. After listening to two weeks of evidence and expert testimony about Dahmer's mental condition, the jury ruled, by a 10–2 margin, that Jeffrey Dahmer was sane. He was subsequently sentenced to life in prison for his crimes, and was killed in prison by a fellow inmate.

Wisconsin defines insanity with the Brawner rule; consequently, to have found Dahmer insane, the jury would have had to conclude that he suffered a mental disorder or defect that made him unable either to appreciate the wrongfulness of his conduct or to control his conduct as required by the law. The jury rejected both conclusions, perhaps because of evidence that Dahmer was careful to kill his victims in a manner that minimized his chances of being caught. This cautiousness suggested that he appreciated the wrongfulness of his behavior *and* could control it when it was opportune to do so.

Several other famous defendants who might have attempted to escape conviction through use of the insanity plea did not do so. Among these are Son of Sam serial murderer David Berkowitz, cult leader Charles Manson, and Mark David Chapman, who killed John Lennon.

Trials in Which the Insanity Plea "Succeeded"
Occasionally, when a judge or jury concludes that the defendant is NGRI, the defendant spends only a short period of time in a treatment program. After being acquitted on charges of malicious wounding (for cutting off her husband's penis), Lorena Bobbitt was released from the mental hospital following only several weeks of evaluation to determine whether she met criteria for involuntary hospitalization as NGRI (she did not).

But sometimes when the insanity plea "works," the defendant spends more time in an institution than he or she would have spent in prison if found

guilty. In fact, this outcome has led defense attorneys to request that judges be required to instruct jurors that if the defendant is found NGRI, he or she will probably be committed to a secure psychiatric hospital (Whittemore & Ogloff, 1995). The Supreme Court, however, has refused to require such an instruction (*Shannon v. United States*, 1994).

The case of John W. Hinckley, Jr. has had the greatest influence of any of those discussed in this chapter, triggering much of the court reform and legislative revision regarding the insanity plea since 1982. Television replays show his March 30, 1981, attempt to kill President Ronald Reagan. When Hinckley came to trial 15 months later, his lawyers didn't dispute the evidence that he had planned the attack, bought special bullets, tracked the president, and fired from a shooter's crouch. But he couldn't help it, they claimed; he was only responding to the driving forces of a diseased mind. (Box 8.4 summarizes the key points of the defense's case.) Dr. William Carpenter, one of the defense psychiatrists, testified that Hinckley did not "appreciate" what he was doing; he had lost the ability to control himself.

Even though the Hinckley case is one in which the insanity defense was successful in the narrow sense of the word, that outcome was largely a result of a decision by the presiding judge regarding the burden of proof. Judge Barrington Parker instructed the jury in accordance with then-existing federal law, which required the prosecution to prove the defendant sane beyond a reasonable doubt, rather than with the law of the District of Columbia (which has its own penal code), which would have placed on the defendant the burden of proving his insanity. After listening to two months of testimony, the Hinckley jury deliberated for four days before finding the defendant NGRI. Afterward, several jurors said that given the instruction that it was up to the government prosecutors to prove Hinckley sane, the evidence was too conflicting for them to agree. They thought his travel meanderings raised a question about his sanity, and both sides' expert psychiatric witnesses had testified that he suffered from some form of mental disorder.

B o x 8.4   THE CASE OF JOHN W. HINCKLEY, JR. AND THE ATTEMPTED ASSASSINATION OF PRESIDENT REAGAN

The defense in John Hinckley's trial made several claims:

1. Hinckley's actions had reflected his pathological obsession with the movie *Taxi Driver*, in which Jodie Foster starred as a 12-year-old prostitute. The title character, Travis Bickle, is a loner who befriends Foster after he is rejected by the character played by Cybill Shepherd; he stalks a political candidate but eventually engages in a bloody shootout to rescue the Foster character. It was reported that Hinckley had seen the movie 15 times and that he so identified with the hero that he had been driven to reenact the fictional events in his own life (Winslade & Ross, 1983).
2. Although there appeared to be planning on Hinckley's part, it was really the movie script that provided the planning force. The defense argued, "A mind that is so influenced by the outside world is a mind out of control and beyond responsibility" (Winslade & Ross, 1983, p. 188).
3. The defense tried to introduce the results of a CAT scan—a "picture" of Hinckley's brain using computerized axial tomography—to support its contention that he was schizophrenic. The admissibility of this evidence became a controversy at the trial. The prosecution objected,

John W. Hinckley, Jr.

claiming that all the apparent scientific rigor of this procedure—the physical evidence and the numerical responses—would cause the jury to place undue importance on it. The prosecution also contended that there are no grounds for concluding that the presence of abnormal brain tissue necessarily denotes schizophrenia. Initially, the judge rejected the request to admit this testimony, but he later reversed the decision on the ground that it might be relevant.

Facts about the Insanity Plea

When the Insanity Defense Is Used. The insanity defense is not used only for murder or attempted murder charges (Pasewark & Pantle, 1981); one study noted that in Oregon and Missouri, only one of ten such pleas was for the crime of murder (Sales & Hafemeister, 1984). Usually, the charges do involve violent felonies, however. In the largest study to date of insanity acquittees, data from NGRI acquittees from four states ($N = 1,099$) were obtained (Steadman et al., 1993). These investigators found that 22.5% of the insanity acquittees had been charged with murder and that a total of 64% had been charged with crimes against persons (murder, rape, robbery, or aggravated assault).

Available research consistently suggests that the majority of defendants found NGRI have been diagnosed as psychotic, suggesting severe and probably chronic mental impairments (Melton et al., 2007). Steadman and colleagues (1993) reported that 67.4% of the insanity acquittees described in their study were diagnosed with a schizophrenic disorder and that another 14.9% were diagnosed with another major mental illness. One study revealed that defendants who were found NGRI had significantly lower IQ scores than men who pleaded insanity but were convicted (Boehnert, 1989).

How often do criminal defendants being assessed for insanity try to fake a mental disorder? On the basis of his research, Rogers (1986, 1988) estimated that about one of four or five defendants being assessed for insanity engages in at least moderate malingering of mental disorders. This figure suggests that crafty conning is not rampant but is frequent enough to cause concern. As a result, psychologists have developed a number of assessment methods to detect persons who are trying to fake a mental disorder. These methods include special structured interviews, psychological tests, and specialized measures (Rogers, 2008). In several laboratory studies, these techniques have shown promising results in distinguishing between subjects who were trying to simulate mental illness (to win monetary incentives for being the "best" fakers) and those who were reporting symptoms truthfully.

In a careful study that was limited to the court records of a single county, Steadman, Keitner, Braff, and Arvanites (1983) were able to compare defendants who were successful and those who were unsuccessful in their pleas of insanity. The factor most strongly associated with success was the outcome of a court-authorized mental examination conducted before the trial. When the conclusion of this evaluation was that the defendant was insane, in 83% of cases the charges were dismissed or the defendant was later found at a trial to be NGRI. If the mental examination concluded that the offender was sane, the insanity defense "worked" in only 2% of the trials. In their larger, four-state study, Steadman et al. (1993) observed that the decision to acquit by reason of insanity was most strongly influenced by clinical factors. They compared those who successfully employed the insanity defense with others who entered this plea but were nevertheless found guilty, and reported that 82% of the former group but only 38% of the latter group had been diagnosed with a major mental illness.

On the basis of research studies, we have learned more about defendants who are found NGRI. For instance:

1. Although most NGRI defendants have a record of prior arrests or convictions, this rate of previous criminality does not exceed that of other felons (Boehnert, 1989; Cohen, Spodak, Silver, & Williams, 1988).

2. Most NGRI defendants come from lower socioeconomic backgrounds (Nicholson, Norwood, & Enyart, 1991).

3. Most NGRI defendants have a prior history of psychiatric hospitalizations and have been diagnosed with serious forms of mental illness, usually psychoses (Nicholson et al., 1991; Steadman et al., 1993).

4. Most NGRI defendants have previously been found IST (Boehnert, 1989).

5. Although most studies have concentrated on males, female defendants found NGRI have similar socioeconomic, psychiatric, and criminal backgrounds to their male NGRI counterparts (Heilbrun, Heilbrun, & Griffin, 1988).

Public Perceptions of the Insanity Plea. The American public has repeatedly expressed its dissatisfaction with the insanity defense. Several surveys have concluded that most U.S. citizens view the insanity defense as a legal loophole through which many guilty people escape conviction (Bower, 1984; Hans & Slater, 1983; Skeem & Golding, 2001). After John Hinckley was found NGRI, a public opinion poll conducted by ABC News showed that 67% of Americans believed that justice had not been done in the case; 90% thought Hinckley should be confined for life, but 78% believed he would eventually be released back into society.

The public's disapproval of the insanity defense appears to be stimulated by trials such as Hinckley's that receive massive publicity. Melton et al. (2007) reported the following three beliefs to be prevalent among the public:

(1) A large number of criminal defendants use the insanity defense.

(2) Those defendants found NGRI are released back into society shortly after their NGRI acquittals.

(3) Persons found insane are extremely dangerous.

How accurate are these views? Are they myths or realities? Given the interest and debate surrounding the insanity defense, it is surprising that so few empirical studies have been conducted to investigate its actual outcomes. But we have some data concerning each of these questions.

How Often Is the Plea Used, and How Often Is It Successful?   The plea is used much less often than people assume. A study in Wyoming showed that people assumed that the insanity plea was used in nearly half of all criminal cases and that it was successful in one of five cases (Pasewark & Pantle, 1981). The actual figures: This plea was entered by only 102 of 22,102 felony defendants (about 1 in every 200 cases) in a one-year period and was successful only once in those 102 times. A survey of the use of the insanity defense in eight states between 1976 and 1985 found that although the public estimated that the insanity defense was used in 37% of the cases, the actual rate was only 0.9% (Silver, Cirincione, & Steadman, 1994). Consistent with these figures, the data reported from the states of California, Georgia, Montana, and New York (Steadman et al., 1993) indicate that defendants in those states, over a 10-year period, entered an insanity plea in 0.9% of felony cases and were successfully acquitted as NGRI in 22.7% of the cases in which this plea was entered.

Studies such as these are particularly valuable because few individual states keep complete records on the use of the insanity plea and its relative success. The findings reported in these studies suggest that of the nine insanity pleas raised in every 1,000 criminal felony cases, about two will be successful.

To answer the question of how many people are acquitted by reason of insanity each year, Cirincione and Jacobs (1999) contacted officials in all 50 states and asked for the number of insanity acquittals statewide between the years 1970 and 1995. After persistent attempts to collect these data from a variety of sources, they received at least partial data from 36 states. Few states could provide information for the entire 25-year period, but the results shown in Table 8.2 were obtained.

Of greatest interest is whether there has been any trend in the frequency of insanity acquittals. Are they becoming more common, or is the volume decreasing? Judging on the basis of these data, there appeared to be a steady increase from 1970 to 1981, followed by a gradual decline. Might this finding point to a "Hinckley effect"—a decrease in insanity acquittals that can be traced to reforms in insanity defense laws and the public outcry that followed John Hinckley's insanity acquittal in 1982? Whatever the interpretation, we can safely conclude that the number of insanity acquittals represents an extremely small percentage of the dispositions of criminal charges.

What Happens to Defendants Who Are Found Not Guilty by Reason of Insanity?   Many mistakenly assume that defendants who are found NGRI go free. Steadman and Braff (1983) found that defendants acquitted on the basis of the insanity plea in New York had an average hospital stay of three years in a secure hospital. During the period studied, the average length of hospitalization was increasing. These researchers also found a clear trend for longer detentions of defendants who had committed more serious offenses. Also, the average length of involuntary hospitalization was greater for those who had been charged with violent offenses

T A B L E 8.2   Insanity Acquittals per 100,000 People

- The median number of insanity acquittals per state per year was 17.7.
- California and Florida had the highest annual averages (134 and 111, respectively)
- New Mexico (0.0) and South Dakota (0.1) had the lowest annual averages.
- Most of the acquittals were for felonies rather than misdemeanors.

(34.1 months) than for individuals with other categories of offenses (Steadman et al., 1993). The average length of confinement for all NGRI individuals was 28.7 months. But this figure undoubtedly underestimates the "true" average period of confinement. Why? These data describe only individuals who were hospitalized and released—they cannot tell us about individuals who were hospitalized but not released (even if they were hospitalized for a long period of time). This points to one of the important differences between a criminal sentence, which is determinate (of fixed length), and the hospital commitment following acquittal by reason of insanity, which is indeterminate (depending on the individual's no longer meeting criteria for hospitalization).

Researchers have been particularly interested in learning whether defendants found NGRI are confined for shorter periods than defendants who are found guilty of similar crimes. The previously described survey of the use of the insanity defense across several states, covering nearly 1 million felony indictments between 1976 and 1985, sought answers to that question (Silver, 1995). On the basis of more than 8000 defendants who pleaded insanity during this period, Silver (1995) found that:

- compared to convicted defendants, insanity acquittees spent less time in confinement in four states and more time in confinement in three states.

- in all seven states, the more serious the crime, the longer the confinement for those found NGRI.

Some states use a procedure known as *conditional release*, in which persons found NGRI are released to the community (following a period of hospital confinement) and are monitored and supervised by mental health personnel. Conditional release is the mental health system's counterpart to parole; it functions essentially like a form of outpatient commitment. According to one four-state follow-up of 529 persons found NGRI, about 60% of these individuals were conditionally released within five years of their confinement (Callahan & Silver, 1998). Of those released, the median period of hospital confinement was 3.6 years for violent offenders and 1.3 years for those charged with less serious offenses.

How Dangerous Are Defendants Found Not Guilty by Reason of Insanity? Because most defendants who are found NGRI are quickly committed to an institution following their acquittal, it is difficult to assess the risk they pose to public safety at that time. In addition, they are likely to receive treatment in the hospital to which they are committed, further complicating the question of their risk of reoffending without this treatment. The limited evidence available on this question points either to no difference in recidivism rates between NGRI defendants and "regular" felons or to slightly lower recidivism rates among the NGRI group (Cohen et al., 1988; Melton et al., 1997). For instance, in a year-long study examining rehospitalization and criminal recidivism in 43 NGRI acquittees, nearly half (47%) were rehospitalized, a minority of the patients (19%) were rearrested or had committed a new crime, and nearly a fourth of the patients (24%) were reintegrated into the community without difficulty (Kravitz & Kelly, 1999).

Nicholson et al. (1991) collected data on 61 defendants found NGRI in Oklahoma; this group constituted the entire population of NGRI defendants over a five-year period who had been treated in the state forensic hospital. Follow-up of persons released from custody indicated that within two years, half of the discharged patients had been either rearrested or rehospitalized. Thus, insanity acquittees continue to have legal and/or psychiatric problems, but their overall rate of criminal recidivism falls in the range found for criminals in general.

Whether the period of hospital commitment and treatment following an acquittal has any benefits for persons found NGRI is not entirely clear. One study showed that individuals who complete a treatment program do better than those who go Absent without Leave (AWOL) from the institution (Nicholson et al., 1991), but another study reported no differences between regularly discharged acquittees and those who escaped from the institution (Pasewark, Bieber, Bosten, Kiser, & Steadman, 1982). It is certainly safe to say that individuals who escape from secure psychiatric hospitals will be perceived as a greater threat to public safety than those who are released with the authorization of the court. We would also note that there is such limited evidence on this question that it can do no more than raise an interesting possibility: Perhaps some individuals are hospitalized in a forensic facility longer than necessary for their safe and responsible functioning in the community.

Current Criticisms of the Insanity Defense

Even if the insanity defense is not successful as often as presumed, legitimate concerns remain about its continued use. We evaluate several of these.

It Sends Criminals and Troublemakers to Hospitals and then Frees Them. Psychopathic killers can try to capitalize on the insanity plea to escape prison and eventually get released from the hospital. How often this happens is unknown, but as we have already discussed, some data indicate that persons found NGRI are confined more frequently and for longer periods than defendants convicted of similar crimes (Perlin, 1996; but compare Steadman et al., 1993). Certainly the length of such confinement is indeterminate for NGRI acquittees, whereas sentences for criminal convictions are determinate in length. After confinement, acquittees may also undergo an additional period of conditional release. Furthermore, NGRI defendants tend not to differ from non-NGRI felons in their reoffense risk.

The biggest problem with such insanity acquittals is that they are sometimes highly publicized, contributing to the public's perception that they "happen all the time," and that the insanity defense is therefore a constant threat to justice. Such acquittals are relatively rare, in reality.

Furthermore, if in the interest of protecting society all NGRI defendants were kept hospitalized until they no longer showed symptoms of mental illness, then society would have to be willing to violate the rights of many mentally ill persons to protect against the violence of a few.

It Is a Defense Only for the Rich. The parents of John W. Hinckley, Jr. spent between $500,000 and $1,000,000 on psychiatric examinations and expert psychiatric testimony in their son's trial—an amount that contributes to the perception of the insanity defense as a jail dodge for the rich. Of all the criticisms leveled at the insanity defense, this one is perhaps the most clearly contradicted by the data. A long line of studies have failed to find socioeconomic or racial bias in the use or the success of the insanity defense (Boehnert, 1989; Howard & Clark, 1985; Nicholson et al., 1991; Pasewark & Pantle, 1981; Steadman et al., 1983).

In addition, this criticism is further weakened by the Supreme Court's 1985 ruling, in the case of *Ake v. Oklahoma*, that poor defendants who plead insanity are entitled to psychiatric assistance at state expense in pursuing this defense. Although defendants who can afford to hire their own experts might be more likely to benefit from raising the issue of insanity, this is not a problem unique to the insanity defense. Defendants who can afford ballistics experts, chemists, and their own private detectives also have an advantage over poor defendants, but no one suggests that a defense relying on ballistics evidence, blood analyses, or mistaken identity should be prohibited because of the expense.

It Relies too much on Psychiatric Experts. Several issues are pertinent here. One criticism is that testifying about insanity forces psychiatrists and clinical psychologists to give opinions about things they are not competent or trained to do— for example, to express "reasonable certainty" rather than probability about a person's mental condition, and to claim greater knowledge about the relationship between psychological knowledge and legal questions than is justified.

Within the field of psychology, there is debate on these matters. The debate centers on two related questions: (1) Can clinicians reliably and validly assess mental illness, mental retardation, neuropsychological disorders, and disorders occurring in childhood and adolescence? and (2) will this assessment permit the formulation of accurate opinions about a defendant's criminal responsibility for acts committed in the past? In a recent literature review, researchers found some support for the reliability and validity of psychologists' evaluations of criminal responsibility. Results from several studies revealed strong agreement (88% to 93%) between evaluators' recommendations and courts' decisions about defendants' criminal responsibility (see Viljoen, Roesch, Ogloff, & Zapf, 2003).

Additionally, critics are concerned over the intrusion of psychology and psychiatry into the decision-making process. They want to reserve the decision for the judge or jury, the fact finder in the trial. This criticism is an example of the general concern (discussed in Chapter 1 and earlier in this chapter) over the use and willingness of experts to answer legal questions for which they possess limited scientific evidence. One remedy proposed to solve this problem is to prevent experts from giving what is often called **ultimate opinion testimony**; that is, they could describe a defendant's mental condition and the effects it could have had on his or her thinking and behavioral control, but they could not state conclusions about whether the defendant was sane or insane. The federal courts, as part of their reforms of the insanity defense, now prohibit mental health experts from offering ultimate opinion testimony about a defendant's insanity. But does this prohibition solve any problems, or is it, in the words of Rogers and Ewing (1989), merely a "cosmetic fix" that has few effects?

In a study of whether prohibiting ultimate opinion testimony affects jury decisions (Fulero & Finkel, 1991), subjects were randomly assigned to read one of ten different versions of a trial, all of which involved a defendant charged with murdering his boss and pleading insanity as a defense. For our purposes, the comparisons among three different versions of the trial are of greatest interest. Some

subjects read transcripts in which the mental health experts for both sides gave only *diagnostic testimony* (that the defendant suffered a mental disorder at the time of the offense); a second group read a version in which the experts gave a diagnosis and then also offered differing *penultimate opinions* about the effects this disorder had on the defendant's understanding of the wrongfulness of his act; a final group read a transcript in which the experts offered differing diagnoses, penultimate opinions, and *ultimate opinion testimony* about whether the defendant was sane or insane at the time of the killing. Did ultimate opinion testimony affect the subjects' verdicts? Not in this study; subjects' verdicts were not significantly different regardless of the type of testimony they read. The lack of difference could be interpreted as evidence that the prohibition of ultimate opinion testimony is unnecessary, or it could indicate that the ban streamlines the trial process without sacrificing any essential information.

Finally, there is the feeling that the process of assessing sanity in criminal defendants holds mental health professionals up to ridicule. When the jury sees and the public reads about a parade of mental health experts representing one side and then the other, their confidence in the behavioral sciences is jeopardized (Slater & Hans, 1984). Further, some experts, in an effort to help the side that has retained them, offer explanations of such an untestable nature that their profession loses its credibility with jurors and the public. However, in many cases involving claims of insanity, the experts retained by each side basically agree on the question of insanity. These cases receive less publicity because they often end in a plea agreement.

Revisions and Reforms of the Insanity Defense

Several reforms in the rules and procedures for implementing the insanity defense have been introduced. Proposals have ranged from abolition of the insanity defense (as has already been done in five states), to provision of a "guilty but mentally ill" verdict, to reform of insanity statutes, to maintenance of the present procedures. We review three reforms in this section.

The Guilty but Mentally Ill Verdict. Since 1976, about a quarter of the states have passed laws allowing juries to reach a verdict of guilty but mentally ill (GBMI) in cases in which a defendant pleads insanity. These GBMI rules differ from state to state, but generally they give a jury the following verdict alternatives for a defendant who is pleading insanity: (1) guilty of the crime, (2) not guilty of the crime, (3) NGRI, or (4) GBMI. Typically, a judge will sentence a defendant found GBMI exactly as would he or she found guilty of the same offense, however, the prisoner would start his or her term in a hospital and then be transferred to prison after treatment is completed.

Proponents of GBMI verdicts hoped that this compromise verdict would decrease the number of defendants found NGRI. Whether insanity acquittals have actually decreased as a result of GBMI legislation is highly questionable. Mock jury research consistently suggests that adding the GBMI option decreases NGRI verdicts (Roberts & Golding, 1991; Roberts, Sargent, & Chan, 1993). Actual GBMI statutes, however, have not produced decreases in NGRI verdicts in South Carolina or Michigan. One possible explanation for the lack of change in NGRI verdicts in states with GBMI statutes is that jurors do not understand the diff-erences between the verdicts. One study examined jurors' knowledge about the two verdicts and found that only 4.2% of 101 potential jurors correctly identified meanings and outcomes of both NGRI and GMBI verdicts (Sloat & Frierson, 2005).

Other problems have provoked a "second look" at the GBMI reform, leading to skepticism about its value (Borum & Fulero, 1999). If regular insanity instructions are confusing to jurors, the GBMI verdict only adds to the confusion by introducing the very difficult distinction for juries to make between mental illness that results in insanity and mental illness that does not. One possible effect of

the GBMI verdict is that it raises jurors' threshold for what constitutes insanity, leading to a more stringent standard for acquitting defendants who use this defense (Roberts et al., 1993).

Also, the claim that the GBMI option will make it more likely that mentally ill offenders will receive treatment is largely a false promise. Overcrowding at hospitals in most states has impeded implementation of this part of the GBMI option. In one Michigan study, 75% of GBMI offenders went straight to prison with no treatment (Sales & Hafemeister, 1984).

In Kentucky, in spite of a statute that appears to promise treatment to those found GBMI, the chair of the parole board filed an affidavit in 1991 stating that "from psychological evaluations and treatment summaries, the Board can detect no difference in treatment or outcome for inmates who have been adjudicated as 'Guilty But Mentally Ill,' from those who have been adjudicated as simply 'guilty'" (Runda, 1991).

The Defense of Diminished Capacity

Several states allow a defense of **diminished capacity**, which is a legal doctrine that applies to defendants who lack the ability to commit a crime purposely and knowingly. Like the insanity defense, diminished capacity often involves evidence that the defendant suffers a mental disorder. It differs from insanity in that it focuses on whether defendants had the state of mind to act with the purpose and intent to commit a crime—that is, to think through the consequences of their contemplated actions—not on whether they knew the crime was wrong or whether they could control their behavior. Suppose M'Naghten knew that murder was wrong but, because of his mental condition, wasn't thinking clearly enough to intend to kill Peel's secretary. Under these conditions, he would not be insane, but he would lack the *mens rea* for first-degree murder, so he probably would have been convicted of second-degree murder or manslaughter.

The rationale for this defense is straightforward: Offenders should be convicted of the crime that matches their mental state, and expert testimony should be offered on the issue of their mental state. Even when the diminished capacity defense "works," it still usually leads to a prison sentence.

In June 1982, a proposition to abolish the diminished capacity defense was overwhelmingly passed by the voters of California (that state still permits defendants to use a M'Naghten-based insanity defense), and several other states either have outlawed the diminished capacity defense or do not allow expert testimony about it. In general, however, the majority of states permit expert testimony about a defendant's *mens rea*, thereby allowing clinicians to present testimony that could be used in support of a diminished-capacity defense (Melton et al., 2007). As long as proof of a defendant's *mens rea* is required, defendants are likely to put forward expert evidence about it, especially in those states that have abolished an affirmative insanity defense.

Elimination of the Insanity Plea

Winslade and Ross (1983) reviewed seven trials (mostly for murder) in which the insanity defense was used and psychiatric testimony was introduced to justify it. They conclude that the possibility of an insanity defense often leads to injustice for the following reasons:

1. Juries are asked to decide questions that predispose them to make arbitrary and emotional judgments because of either overidentification with or alienation from the defendant;

2. Psychiatrists and other mental health professionals are encouraged to offer opinions, guesses, and speculations under the banner of scientific expertise; and

3. Society's views about criminality and craziness are so intertwined that an insanity defense to a crime does not make much sense (p. 198).

On the basis of their analysis of the outcomes of these trials, Winslade and Ross recommend that the insanity defense be eliminated:

> A workable solution would require the elimination of the insanity plea; the elimination of any testimony by psychiatrists about the actual or theoretical state of the defendant's mind at the time of the crime; the elimination of psychiatric expert witnesses in the guilt phase of the trial; and the requirement of a two-phase trial that would, in its first phase, establish guilt or innocence of the commission of the crime with no concern for the individual's state of mind in terms of mental illness at the time the crime was committed. The second phase of the trial, if guilt were found, would address itself to the appropriate disposition of the defendant (p. 219).

In the second part of the trial, if a defendant claimed mental illness, he or she would be required to testify. Psychiatrists representing state institutions would also be required to testify about the likelihood of rehabilitating the defendant; they would be asked to specify at least a minimum duration of treatment. Combinations of hospitalization and incarceration, in Winslade and Ross's proposal, would be based on the defendant's amenability to treatment.

Arguments against Eliminating the Plea. Winslade and Ross (1983) advocate an initial phase of a trial to "establish guilt or innocence of the commission of the crime with no concern for the individual's state of mind" (p. 219).

James Kunen (1983), a former public defender, challenges this idea, noting that "Anglo-American legal tradition … has required that to convict someone of a crime, the prosecution must prove not only that he did a particular act—such as pulling a trigger—but that he did it with a particular state of mind" (p. 157). Kunen argues that we cannot talk about guilt without bringing in the person's state of mind. If a defendant slashes his victim's throat, thinking that he is slicing a cucumber, we say that he committed an act but not that he was guilty of the intent to commit a crime. This is why, even in those few states that have abolished the insanity defense, defendants may still introduce evidence that they lacked the mental state required for the crime.

Some offenders are truly "NGRI"; they do not know the "nature and quality of their acts"—they literally do not know what they are doing. Harvard law professor Alan Dershowitz has said, "I almost would be in favor of abolishing the insanity defense, except there really are a few genuinely crazy people who believe they're squeezing lemons when they're actually squeezing throats" (quoted in Footlick, 1978, p. 108). Of course, the actual number of such people is much smaller than the number of defendants who raise the NGRI defense.

We believe that the NGRI plea should be maintained as an option, and modifications of the system should be restricted to those that clarify the rule and later evaluate those for whom it is successful. For example, the U.S. Congress passed the Insanity Defense Reform Act, which changed the law that gave the prosecution the burden of proving beyond a reasonable doubt that John Hinckley was not insane. If an act similar to Hinckley's were committed today in a federal jurisdiction and in the vast majority of states, the defendant, not the prosecution, would bear the responsibility of proving his plea; otherwise, he would be found guilty. States should carefully monitor people committed after NGRI verdicts to ensure that they are not released while still mentally ill and dangerous. All indications are that this precaution is being taken.

CAPITAL SENTENCING
EVALUATIONS

Although mental health professionals are involved in many aspects of the legal process, none has more

implication for a defendant's life than capital sentencing evaluations, which have literally been described as "a life or death matter" (*Satterwhite v. Texas*, 1988, p. 1802). The U.S. Supreme Court, in *Eddings v. Oklahoma* (1982), held that a trial court must consider any potentially mitigating information—evidence that argues *against* a death sentence—which leaves the forensic clinician with a very broad focus for the evaluation. They must consider information about a defendant's physical, cognitive, social, and developmental history. Mitigating factors involve "... any aspect of a defendant's character or record, or any of the circumstances of the offense that the defendant proffered as a basis for a sentence less than death" (*Lockett v. Ohio*, 1978, p. 604).

One aspect of mitigation involves the concept of moral culpability (Cunningham & Reidy, 2001). Understanding, judgment, impulsivity, and values are influenced by developmental, cognitive, neuro-psychological, cultural, community, situational, and other life influences, and it is important to consider these dimensions as part of a capital sentencing evaluation. Some jurisdictions also consider the question of a defendant's future risk to society, and Texas incorporates this question specifically into one of three "special issues" that the jury must consider in weighing a sentence of death (Cunningham & Reidy, 2001).

JUVENILE TRANSFER

Forensic psychologists sometimes evaluate youths whose criminal cases are being considered for transfer to adult court. During the 1980s and 1990s, there was substantial reform in the juvenile and criminal justice systems in the United States to allow more frequent prosecution of juveniles in criminal (adult) court. Such reform was motivated largely by the perception that juvenile crime had increased—and become more serious. Some legal professionals adopted a "get tough" approach in the attempt to decrease the rate of juvenile offending. One aspect of this "do the crime, do the time" philosophy involved expansion of ways in which adolescent (under 18 years old) offenders could be **transferred** (also called certification or waiver) into criminal court.

A number of criteria are described in state laws on juvenile transfer. Two of the most important are (1) public safety and (2) treatment needs and amenability. Those evaluating juveniles for a possible transfer must focus on the risk of future offending, the interventions needed to reduce this risk, and the likelihood that the youth will respond favorably to such interventions. The risk/needs/responsivity (RNR) model (Andrews, Bonta, & Hoge, 1990) is useful in this respect, as it prompts the evaluator to consider risk of reoffending and risk-relevant deficits carefully. This consideration can be facilitated by using an empirically supported specialized tool, such as the Structured Assessment of Violence Risk in Youth (SAVRY; Borum, Bartels, & Forth, 2005), the Youth Level of Service/Case Management Inventory (YLS/CMI; Hoge & Andrews, 2002), or the Risk-Sophistication-Treatment Inventory (Salekin, 2004). These tools are discussed in detail in Chapter 15.

Evaluating a youth being considered for transfer is a forensic evaluation. It involves a legal question that will be answered by the judge with input from the evaluator, just as competence and insanity call for a forensic evaluation. With juveniles, this means that evaluators must pay particular attention to school and family functioning, often by obtaining school records and conducting interviews of family members. They should also obtain information in other important areas. Peers, for example, can have an important influence on an adolescent's behavior. Was the offense committed alone, or was the youth with peers who may have encouraged one another (or at least refused to back down) to offend? Substance abuse is another very important risk factor for offending; both using drugs and selling drugs are areas that should be targeted for intervention.

States vary in their specification of the age at which an adolescent is eligible for prosecution in the criminal system. Some states do not have any age limit; others have passed legislation decreasing the age of eligibility. Most still use the age of 14 or 15,

however. There are several justifications for transfer of an adolescent into the criminal system: (1) charged with homicide, (2) charged with other specific violent felonies (e.g., sexual assault, armed robbery, aggravated battery), or (3) a history of prior juvenile offending suggesting a failure to respond to interventions provided by the juvenile system. In addition, some states have a policy involving "once an adult, always an adult," under which any adolescent convicted (or even tried) in criminal court will be charged in criminal court for future offenses, regardless of their nature or that individual's age.

Juveniles can be transferred to criminal (adult) court in several different ways. The state legislature in a given jurisdiction can determine that certain offenses allegedly committed by an adolescent must be filed directly in adult court (Griffin, 2003). For example, a state legislature may pass a law dictating that certain serious felony charges (e.g., armed robbery, sexual battery) be prosecuted in criminal court if the defendant is over a certain age. This approach to transfer is called **statutory exclusion**. As of 2004, 29 states had statutory exclusion for certain offenses (Snyder & Sickmund, 2006).

A second approach to transferring juveniles to criminal court has been termed **judicial discretion**. When this procedure is used, the juvenile court decides whether the youth should be transferred to criminal court. Some 46 states provide for this type of transfer (Griffin, 2003). In making such a decision, the judge typically considers statutorily specified influences such as the youth's risk to public safety, amenability to treatment, and maturity (Brannen et. al., 2006). Such factors can be evaluated by mental health professionals and the results described in the report and possibly testimony, to help inform the judge in making this decision. Generally judicial discretion transfer laws authorize, but do not mandate, a move to adult court. However, as of 2004, 15 states had established circumstances that make such transfers mandatory (Snyder & Sickmund, 2006).

A third approach to juvenile transfer is called **prosecutorial discretion**. Prosecutorial discretion requires prosecutors to decide whether cases are filed initially in juvenile or adult court. As of 2004, 15 states had established the option of prosecutorial discretion for certain offenses (Snyder & Sickmund, 2006).

Is putting juveniles in the adult system effective in reducing reoffending? Common sense might suggest that adolescents would be less likely to offend if they knew that offending could result in more severe punishment. But research has actually not supported this: There has been no decline in juvenile crime after these transfer laws came into effect. One study found no differences in the juvenile homicide/manslaughter rates in the states with prosecutorial discretion policies in the first five years after transfer laws were enacted (Steiner & Wright, 2006). Housing juveniles with adult criminals may also promote criminal attitudes and motivations (Forst, Fagan, & Vivona, 1989). Juveniles detained in New York's adult system were 89% more likely to be rearrested for a violent offense and 44% more likely to be rearrested for a property offense than juveniles in the New York metropolitan area but detained within New Jersey's juvenile court system (Fagan, 1996). Higher rates of recidivism have also been observed in other studies with youth detained in the adult correctional system (Bishop, Frazier,

Lanza-Kaduce, & Winner, 1996; Mason & Cheng, 2001; Myers, 2001). Research also suggests that juveniles in adult facilities were more likely to be sexually assaulted and physically assaulted than were youth in the juvenile facilities (Beyer, 1997).

Juvenile transfer may also occur in the other direction (when juveniles placed in adult court are returned to juvenile court). This procedure has been called **reverse transfer**. Many states provide this option, allowing the criminal court judge to review the case and determine whether the youth should remain in adult court. Some 25 states currently have reverse transfer procedures that allow juveniles in adult court to petition for transfer back to juvenile court (Snyder & Sickmund, 2006). Fifteen states have a procedure in which a juvenile may not be tried as an adult without the opportunity to contest being in adult court (Griffin, 2003). In six states there are no reverse transfer procedures, but in those states no juvenile can be tried as an adult without the review of a juvenile court judge. Finally 14 states and the District of Columbia have no reverse transfer mechanism (Snyder & Sickmund, 2006).

SUMMARY

1. ***What is the scope of forensic psychology?*** Forensic psychology is a specialty that involves the application of knowledge and techniques from the behavioral sciences to answer questions about individuals involved in legal proceedings. The range of topics about which psychological and psychiatric experts are asked to testify continues to grow, despite some professional concerns and public skepticism about the validity of such testimony.

2. ***What is meant by competence in the criminal justice process?*** Adjudicative competence entails having a sufficient present ability to consult with one's attorney with a reasonable degree of rational understanding and with a rational, as

well as factual, understanding of the proceedings. This same standard is applied to the questions of whether a defendant is competent to plead guilty and whether a defendant is competent to stand trial, so the phrase "competence to stand trial" is often used to refer to the entire process of disposition of charges, not merely the trial.

3. ***How do clinicians assess competence?*** When mental health professionals assess a defendant's competence, they should use one of several special instruments designed specifically for the purpose of evaluating how well a defendant understands the charges and potential proceedings. These specific tests and structured

interviews have made competence assessments more reliable, valid, and useful. Competence evaluations are sometimes complicated by such factors as malingering, amnesia, and the problem of whether incompetent defendants can be treated against their will. Other competence issues (e.g., competence to refuse the insanity defense and competence to be sentenced) can arise at different points in the criminal process.

4. *What are the consequences of being found incompetent to proceed in the criminal justice process?* When defendants are found IST, they can be committed for a period of treatment designed to restore their competence. If later found competent, they will stand trial or dispose of their charges through the plea bargaining process. If treatment is not successful in restoring competence, the state will usually attempt to commit the person to a mental hospital for a period of time.

5. *What is the legal definition of insanity?* Three major definitions of insanity are used currently. The M'Naghten rule defines insanity as not knowing the difference between right and wrong: "To establish a defense on the grounds of insanity it must be clearly proved that, at the time of committing the act, the accused was laboring under such a defect of reason, from disease of the mind, as not to know the nature and quality of the act he was doing, or, if he did know it, that he did not know what he was doing was wrong." In some jurisdictions, an "irresistible impulse" test has been added to the M'Naghten rule.

The Brawner rule/American Law Institute test states that a person is not responsible for a criminal act if, as a result of mental disease or defect, the person lacked "substantial capacity either to appreciate the criminality of his or her conduct or to conform his or her conduct to the requirements of the law." This rule or a variation of it is the standard in fewer than half of the states. Until 1984, it was also the federal

standard, but the federal system now (under the Insanity Defense Reform Act) requires the defense to show that, as a result of a severe mental disease or defect, the defendant was unable to appreciate the nature and quality or the wrongfulness of his or her acts. Five states have outlawed insanity as a defense, although these states still allow the defendant to introduce evidence about his or her mental condition that is relevant to determining *mens rea.* Some highly publicized trials have led to "successful" use of the insanity defense. But many others who used this defense were found guilty.

6. *How frequently is the insanity defense used, and how successful is it?* The insanity plea is used much less frequently than people assume; it is tried in only about 9 of every 1,000 cases, and it succeeds in only about 23% of these cases. When it does succeed, there is no guarantee that the defendant will be released from the hospital any sooner than he or she would have been paroled from prison.

7. *What are the major criticisms of the insanity defense, and what reforms have been attempted?* Some examples of early release of NGRI defendants have led to justified criticism of the procedure. Other criticisms are that insanity cannot be reliably and validly assessed and that the insanity defense relies too much on psychiatric testimony. Reforms include the Insanity Defense Reform Act and the adoption in several states of a "guilty but mentally ill" verdict, resulting (at least in theory) in the defendant's being treated in a state hospital until releasable and then serving the rest of the sentence in prison. A number of states also allow the diminished capacity plea, a partial defense based on mental condition. But it also has been controversial, and at least one state (California) that formerly allowed the defense no longer does so.

KEY TERMS

affirmative defense

Brawner rule

competence

competence to stand
    trial

diminished capacity

insanity

judicial discretion

M'Naghten rule

mens rea

prosecutorial discretion

reverse transfer

statutory exclusion

stipulate

transferred

ultimate opinion
    testimony

9

Forensic Assessment in Civil Cases

ORIENTING QUESTIONS

1. What problems are associated with expert testimony, and what reforms have been proposed?
2. Under what conditions can a plaintiff be compensated for psychological damages?
3. What is workers' compensation, and how do mental health professionals participate in such cases?
4. What capacities are involved in civil competence?
5. What criteria are used for decisions about disputes involving child custody or parental fitness?
6. What steps are taken in civil commitment and how well can clinicians assess the risk of dangerousness, or violent behavior, a key criterion for civil commitment?

Whether a defendant is mentally competent to stand trial (often called *adjudicative competence*, because it refers to a defendant's capacities to dispose of charges either through a trial or via plea bargaining) and whether a defendant was insane at the time of an alleged criminal offense are perhaps the best-known legal questions that mental health professionals help courts decide. However, they are certainly not the only questions. Throughout earlier chapters, we examined other questions arising in the legal system that psychologists are often asked to consider. Is a given individual a good candidate for police work? Will a person who is suffering from mental illness be violent in the future? How accurate is one's memory for, and testimony about, highly traumatic events likely to be? These questions—like those of competence and insanity—are often asked of forensic psychologists and psychiatrists, and they are usually answered on the basis of a combination of research knowledge and the results of individual assessments performed by forensic clinicians.

Different kinds of litigation are making use of scientific knowledge and expert opinion. Psychology and psychiatry are two fields in which the use of experts has proliferated. Melton, Petrila, Poythress, and

Slobogin (2007) offer a comprehensive listing and description of the legal questions that are most often addressed in civil, juvenile/family, and criminal cases. In addition to the legal questions discussed in previous chapters, mental health experts are involved in hearings or trials in the areas of civil commitment, psychological damages in civil cases, psychological autopsies (i.e., to what extent psychological problems are attributable to a preexisting condition), negligence and product liability, trademark litigation, discrimination, guardianship and conservatorship (a guardianship-like arrangement for financial assets), child custody, adoption and termination of parental rights, professional malpractice, and other social issues such as sexual harassment in the workplace. Therefore, judges now often find themselves in the position of having to decide whether the expert testimony that an attorney seeks to introduce at trial meets the criteria that the *Daubert* and *Kumho* cases (discussed in Chapters 1 and 8) have established as the modern standard for admitting scientific evidence and expert testimony.

In this chapter, we introduce some points about expert testimony in civil cases, and describe six areas of forensic assessment in which psychologists and psychiatrists are involved: (1) psychological damages to civil plaintiffs, (2) workers' compensation claims, (3) the assessment of civil competence, (4) psychological autopsy, (5) child custody and parental fitness, and (6) civil commitment and risk assessment. Although these areas do not rival the publicity commanded by adjudicative competence or insanity at the time of the offense, which were discussed in Chapter 8, they illustrate several ways in which psychological expertise can be brought to bear on important legal questions. For each of the six areas, we will:

- Discuss the basic psycho–legal questions that experts are expected to address

- Describe the techniques typically used by forensic clinicians to evaluate these questions

- Summarize the empirical evidence and legal status associated with the forensic activity

EXPERTS IN THE ADVERSARIAL SYSTEM

In general, a qualified expert can testify about a topic if such testimony is relevant to an issue in dispute and if the usefulness of the testimony outweighs whatever prejudicial impact it might have. If these two conditions are met, an expert will be permitted to testify if the judge believes that the testimony is based on sufficiently relevant and reliable scientific evidence. In other words, under the *Daubert/Kumho* criteria, the judge serves as a "gatekeeper" who must determine whether the theory, methodology, and analysis that are the basis of the expert's opinion measure up to scientific standards. If they meet this standard, the judge will probably admit relevant expert testimony; if they do not, the judge should not allow the testimony.

Judges generally do not perform this gatekeeper function well (Gatowski et al., 2001). Many judges lack the scientific training that *Daubert/Kumho* appears to require. Even with such training, the range of expert topics about which judges will need to be informed is staggering. As a result, many critics, including experts and judges themselves, believe that the difficulty of distinguishing valid from invalid scientific evidence will result in jurors too often being exposed to "expert" testimony that is based on little more than "junk science" (Grove & Barden, 1999; see Box 9.1).

Some of the advantages of having mental health professionals provide expert testimony are clear. Mental health professionals have specialized knowledge and training that can provide the court with valuable information in a variety of cases. For example, some psychologists are trained to administer tests to determine malingering mental health or neuropsychological problems in workers' compensation cases or are experienced in conducting clinical interviews to assess parental fitness.

However, judges, lawyers, and mental health professionals themselves have expressed great concern about the reliability, validity, propriety, and usefulness of expert testimony and the forensic assessment on which it is based. Former federal appellate judge David T. Bazelon (1974) once complained that "psychiatry ... is the ultimate wizardry ... in no case is it more difficult to elicit productive and reliable testimony than in cases that call on the knowledge and practice of psychiatry." This view was echoed by Warren Burger (1975), a former chief justice of the United States Supreme Court, who chided experts for the "uncertainties of psychiatric diagnosis." Critiques of psychologists' expert testimony in this area can be found in several sources (Bonnie & Slobogin, 1980; Ennis & Litwack, 1974; Morse, 1978; Tillbrook, Mumley, & Grisso, 2003).

B o x 9.1 THE CASE OF COLUMBINE SHOOTER ERIC HARRIS, ANTIDEPRESSANT MEDICATION, AND VIOLENCE: EXPERT OPINION OR JUNK SCIENCE?

In 2002, Mark Taylor, a survivor of the Columbine High School shooting, sued the pharmaceutical company that manufactures the antidepressant drug (Luvox) that one of the shooters, Eric Harris, was taking. Is there scientific evidence that this drug caused Eric Harris to be violent? Peter Breggin, M.D., one of the experts involved in the litigation, thought so, yet was his testimony impartial and based on good science? Or was it an example of expert bias, poor science, or both?

Breggin opined in a preliminary report filed with the U.S. District Court in Denver that Luvox triggered Harris's rampage. "Absent persistent exposure to Luvox, Eric Harris would probably not have committed violence and suicide," noted Breggin.

Breggin is a Washington, D.C.-area psychiatrist who describes himself as a medical expert with 30 years of experience in product liability lawsuits involving psychiatric drugs. However, some of this history reflects the skepticism of legal fact finders about his impartiality. A Wisconsin judge in 1997 observed, "Dr. Breggin's observations are totally without credibility. I can almost declare him [to be a] fraud or at least approaching that. I cannot place any credence or credibility in

Eric Harris and Dylan Klebold, Columbine High shooters

what he has to recommend in this case." On the question of whether his opinion reflects good science, another court held in 1995 that "Dr. Breggin's opinions do not rise to the level of an opinion based on 'good science.' The motion to exclude his testimony as an expert witness should be granted." The question of Breggin's impartiality may be one reason that Taylor eventually dropped his lawsuit in exchange for a contribution from the pharmaceutical company to the American Cancer Society.

What are the main problems with or objections to testimony by psychological or psychiatric experts? Smith (1989) cites the following potential problems:

1. The scientific foundation for much of the testimony offered in court is often less than adequate, leading to unreliable information and therefore potentially incorrect verdicts.

2. Much of the testimony is of limited relevance, therefore wasting court time and burdening an already crowded docket.

3. Experts are too often permitted to testify about "ultimate issues" (Is the defendant insane? Was the plaintiff emotionally damaged?), which should be left to juries to decide.

4. Expert testimony is frequently used to introduce information that would otherwise be prohibited because it is hearsay. (Experts are permitted to share this information with juries if it is the kind of information they routinely rely on in reaching expert opinions.)

5. The adversarial system compromises experts' objectivity. Experts readily testify to opinions that favor the side that retained them.

6. Expert testimony is very expensive, and relying on experts gives an advantage to the side with more money.

7. Testing the reliability and validity of expert opinions through cross-examination is inadequate because attorneys are usually not well equipped to conduct such cross-examination, and juries often fail to understand the significance of the information that is uncovered during the cross-examination.

8. The spectacle of experts disagreeing with one another in trial after trial ultimately reduces the public's esteem for mental health professionals.

In response to these concerns, some of which are also supported by empirical research (which we discuss later in this chapter), several reforms of expert testimony have been proposed. Most of these

suggestions are aimed at reducing the undue influence or excessive partisanship that can adversely affect expert testimony. As a result, the federal courts do not permit testimony on the "ultimate issue" of insanity in forensic cases. As you will recall from Chapter 8, this change was part of the overall reform of federal law concerning insanity that occurred in 1984. Still, there is little evidence that limiting experts' testimony in this way has had much impact on the use or success of the insanity defense (Borum & Fulero, 1999) and it is even less likely to have an impact on the kinds of cases we will discuss in this chapter.

Other suggestions have involved reducing the overly adversarial nature of expert testimony by limiting the number of experts on a given topic, requiring that the experts be chosen from an approved panel of individuals reputed to be objective and highly competent, and allowing testimony only from experts who have been appointed by a judge rather than hired by one of the opposing attorneys. Although these changes would appear to reduce the "hired gun" problem, it is not clear that consensus could be easily reached on which experts belong on an approved list, or on whether being appointed by a judge ensures an expert's impartiality. Furthermore, some research suggests that jurors might already be inclined to discount the testimony of experts whom they perceive to be "hired guns" because of the high fees such experts are paid and their history of testifying frequently (Cooper & Neuhaus, 2000).

Several scholars have suggested that courts not permit clinical opinion testimony unless it can be shown that it satisfies standards of scientific reliability. The standard required by the *Daubert/Kumho* decisions has made this recommendation more feasible (Imwinkelried, 1994). Such a requirement might reduce the frequency of testimony by forensic psychologists and psychiatrists, but unless lawyers and judges are educated more thoroughly about scientific methodology, it is not clear that they can make informed distinctions between "good" and "bad" science (Gless, 1995).

A more modest reform would involve simply banning any reference to witnesses as providing *expert* testimony, a term that suggests that jurors should give it extra credence. Instead, judges would always refer—in the presence of juries—to *opinion* testimony or witnesses.

In addition to deleting any mention of expert testimony, federal judge Charles R. Richey (1994) recommended that juries be read a special instruction before hearing any opinion testimony in order to reduce its possible prejudicial impact. Here is an example of his recommended instruction:

> Ladies and Gentlemen, please note that the Rules of Evidence ordinarily do not permit witnesses to testify as to their opinions or conclusions. Two exceptions to this rule exist. The first exception allows an ordinary citizen to give his or her opinion as to matters that he or she observed or of which he or she has firsthand knowledge. The second exception allows witnesses who, by education, training and experience, have acquired a certain specialized knowledge in some art, science, profession or calling to state an opinion as to relevant and material matters. The purpose of opinion witness testimony is to assist you in understanding the evidence and deciding the facts in this case. You are not bound by this testimony and, in weighing it, you may consider his or her qualifications, opinions and reasons for

testifying, as well as all other considerations that apply when you evaluate the credibility of any witness. In other words, you should give it such weight as you think it fairly deserves and consider it in light of all the evidence in this case.

PSYCHOLOGICAL DAMAGES TO CIVIL PLAINTIFFS

When one party is injured by the actions of a second party, the injured individual can sue the second party to recover monetary damages as compensation for the injury. This action is covered by an area of civil law known as torts. A **tort** is a wrongful act that causes harm to an individual. The criminal law also exacts compensation for wrongful acts, but it does so on behalf of society as a whole; by punishing an offender, the criminal law attempts to maintain society's overall sense of justice. Tort law, on the other hand, provides a mechanism to remedy the harms that individuals have suffered from wrongful acts by another party.

As illustrated by the O. J. Simpson case, both criminal punishment and civil remedies can be sought for the same act. Simpson was prosecuted by the state, under the criminal law, for murder; he was also sued for money damages by the surviving relatives of the victims, who alleged that he caused the wrongful deaths of Nicole Brown Simpson and Ronald Goldman.

Many kinds of behavior can constitute a tort. Slander and libel are torts, as are cases of professional malpractice, invasion of privacy, the manufacture of defective products that result in a personal injury, and intentional or negligent behavior producing harm to another person.

Four elements are involved in proving a tort in a court of law and all involve behavioral issues. First, torts occur in situations in which one individual owes a **duty**, or has an obligation, to another; a physician has a duty to treat patients in accordance with accepted professional standards, and individuals have a duty not to harm others physically or psychologically.

Second, a tort typically requires proving that one party breached or violated a duty that was owed to other parties. The **breached duty** can be due to negligence or intentional wrongdoing. (**Negligence** is behavior that falls below a standard for protecting others from unreasonable risks; it is often measured by asking whether a "reasonable person" would have acted as the civil defendant acted in similar circumstances. **Intentional behavior** is conduct in which a person meant the outcome of a given act to occur.) Third, the violation of the duty must have been the proximate cause of the harm suffered by a plaintiff. A **proximate cause** is one that constitutes an obvious or substantial reason why a given harm occurred. It is sometimes equated with producing an outcome that is "foreseeable." So if a given event would be expected to cause a given outcome, it is a proximate cause. Fourth, a **harm**, or loss, must occur, and the harm has to involve a legally protected right or interest for which the person can seek to recover damages that have been suffered. If it can be established that (1) there was a duty that (2) was breached, which (3) proximally caused the (4) harm resulting, then a tort can be resolved in a civil lawsuit.

The damages a person suffers from a tort can involve destruction of personal property, physical injuries, and/or emotional distress (sometimes called "pain and suffering"). Historically, the law has always sought to compensate victims who are physically hurt or sustain property losses, but it was reluctant to allow compensation for emotional distress, largely out of concern that such damages are too easy to fake and too difficult to measure. In cases in which recovery for emotional damages was allowed, the courts often required that a physical injury has accompanied the psychological harm or that a plaintiff who was not physically injured was at least in a "zone of danger" (for example, even if the plaintiff was not injured by the attack of an escaped wild animal, he or she was standing next to his or her children when they were attacked) (Weissman, 1985).

One case that received extensive international coverage illustrates this historical approach to emotional damages. On the afternoon of March 22, 1990, the *Aleutian Enterprise*, a large fishing boat, capsized in the Bering Sea. Within 10 minutes, the boat sank, killing nine crew members. Twenty-two sailors survived the disaster; of these men, two returned to work in a short time, but the other 20 filed a lawsuit against the company that owned the ship. Of the 20 plaintiffs, 19 consulted a psychologist or psychiatrist, and every one of these 19 individuals was subsequently diagnosed with posttraumatic stress disorder (PTSD) by his mental health professional (Rosen, 1995). (The defendant company hired its own psychologist, who evaluated the plaintiffs and diagnosed PTSD in only five of them and some other postincident disorder in three others.) The surviving sailors were entitled to recover for their psychological injuries because they had been in the "zone of danger."

In recent years, the courts have progressed to a view in which psychological symptoms and mental distress are more likely to be compensated regardless of whether the plaintiff suffered physical injuries. Two types of "purely" psychological injuries are now claimed in civil lawsuits: those arising from "negligent" behavior and those arising from "extreme and outrageous" conduct that is intended to cause distress. In the former type of case, plaintiffs are often allowed to sue for psychological damages if they are bystanders to an incident in which a loved one is injured (for example, a parent sees her child crushed to death when a defective roller coaster—on which the child was riding—derails).

In the case of intentional torts causing psychological distress, a plaintiff must prove that a defendant intentionally or recklessly acted in an extreme and outrageous fashion (sometimes defined as "beyond all bounds of decency") to cause emotional distress. In addition, the plaintiff must prove that the distress is severe. In other words, the effects must be something more than merely annoying or temporarily upsetting (Merrick, 1985). What kinds of behavior might qualify? Courts have found that a debt collector who was trying to locate a debtor acted outrageously when he posed as a hospital employee and told the debtor's mother that her grandchildren had been seriously injured in a wreck and that he needed to find the debtor to inform him of this fact (*Ford Motor Credit Co. v. Sheehan*, 1979).

B o x 9.2   THE CASE OF ANTITERRORISM OFFICER "JOHN DOE": RACIAL/ETHNIC AND RELIGIOUS DISCRIMINATION IN THE WORKPLACE

Discrimination in the workplace can occur for different reasons. Consider the case of "John Doe," an undercover police officer in the New York City Police Department (NYPD). Egyptian-born and Muslim, he was subjected to treatment that may have been discriminatory for ethnic and religious reasons. The NPYD has contained an undercover unit of investigators, most of whom are of Middle Eastern or Asian backgrounds, who use their language and cultural skills to investigate potential terrorist threats against New York City. But one Egyptian-born analyst in the unit filed a suit charging that he was subjected to hundreds of anti-Muslim and anti-Arab e-mail messages sent out by a city contractor over the course of three years. In an interview, "Mr. Doe" (who was not named because he is still in the unit) said he complained repeatedly to supervisors but that no one took action.

The lawsuit cites e-mail briefing messages sent out several times a day to members of the unit by Bruce Tefft, a former Central Intelligence Agency (CIA) official who has identified himself in the past as the Police Department's counterterrorism adviser. The e-mail messages were sent to everyone in the division, according to the suit, which also alleges that the briefing messages were preceded by anti-Muslim and anti-Arab statements like, "Burning the hate-filled Koran should be viewed as a public service at the least" and "This is not a war against terrorism ... it is against Islam and we are not winning." In one, he asked, "Has the U.S. threatened to vaporize Mecca?" and responded, "Excellent idea, if

true." The lawsuit alleged that e-mails "ridiculed and disparaged the Muslim religion and Arab people, and stated that Muslim- and Arab-Americans were untrustworthy and could not reliably serve in law enforcement positions or handle sensitive data."

According to a Police Department spokesman, the police commissioner was not aware of the "offensive commentary" until the complaint was made. "As soon as the Police Department became aware of a complaint about the content of e-mail sent by an individual not employed by the Police Department, we took immediate action to block his e-mails, followed by a cease and desist letter to the individual and his employer, a consulting firm," he wrote.

Reportedly the department's contract with this advisor ended in 2003, but Tefft continued to send the e-mail messages on his own, circumventing attempts by the department to block them. Mr. Doe's lawyer commented, "It's incredible in this day and age that hundreds of racist e-mails could be sent to hundreds of NYPD officials over three years, and not one person did a thing to stop it."

This unit has been profiled on "60 Minutes" and in *The Wall Street Journal* and *The Daily News.* Mr. Doe said, "The NYPD was happy to introduce us to the press—'Here these guys are, the best of the best, they are doing a great job.' But then they failed to protect us under this smear, this constantly daily attack against my religion and against good Muslim Arab-Americans, and I will say good because the majority are good."

In recent years, an increasing number of cases have dealt with psychological injuries resulting from the tort of sexual harassment, usually in the workplace. (We discuss sexual harassment in more detail in Chapter 13.) A plaintiff who claims to have been sexually harassed at work can sue the workers responsible for the harassment and can also sue the company itself, if the plaintiff can show that the company knew (or should have known) about the harassment and failed to stop it. These cases can be filed either in state courts or in federal courts, where Title VII of the federal Civil Rights Act of 1991 applies to companies with at least 15 employees. Plaintiffs can seek both **compensatory damages** (payment for injuries suffered) and **punitive damages** (punishing

the company for its failure to respond properly to the misconduct).

Of course, the tort of harassment is not always based on gender. It may incorporate other characteristics—including racial/ethnic group or religious beliefs, as we see in the following case (Box 9.2).

Assessment of Psychological Damages

When a mental health professional assesses a plaintiff, the clinician will typically conduct an evaluation that, like most evaluations, includes a social history, a clinical interview, and a number of psychological tests and specialized forensic measures (Boccaccini & Brodsky, 1999; Melton et al., 2007). One major difference, however, between standard clinical evaluations and forensic assessments is the much greater use of third-party interviews and review of available records in forensic examinations. This practice is based on two basic considerations (Heilbrun, 2001; Melton et al., 2007). First, forensic experts must be sure that their opinions are based on accurate information, and self-reported information in the context of litigation is not necessarily accurate. Second, forensic experts are often asked to evaluate an individual's psychological condition at some specific moment or in some particular situation in the past. Therefore, clinicians are obligated to use independent sources of information, when possible, to verify their descriptions and judgments about such matters.

On the basis of the data gleaned from these sources, the clinician arrives at an opinion about the psychological condition of the person in question. With the exception of greater reliance on third-party interviews and records, this part of the evaluation is not much different from how a clinician would assess any client, regardless of whether the person was involved in a lawsuit. The more difficult question the clinician must answer in litigation is whether the psychological problems were caused by the tort, were aggravated by the tort, or existed before the tort. In fact, given that some research suggests that psychological problems make people more prone to accidents, the clinician even needs to consider whether certain psychological conditions might have contributed to the plaintiff's being injured in the first place.

There is no established procedure for answering these questions, although most clinicians will try to locate records and other sources of data that will help them date the development of any disorder that is diagnosed. In some situations, a plaintiff might allege that he or she was targeted for harassment precisely because the defendants knew of some prior difficulty that made the plaintiff vulnerable to a particular kind of harassment. In such cases, the clinician must factor in this additional piece of information before reaching a conclusion about the significance of the prior psychological problem.

Another complication affects many evaluations of individuals who claim to have suffered psychological harm: Plaintiffs may be motivated to exaggerate their claims in order to improve their chances of winning large awards. In some cases, the distortion is so large as to constitute outright lying. In other, more subtle instances of **malingering**, a real psychological disturbance is present, but the plaintiff exaggerates its seriousness. In some cases, no deception is intended at all; the plaintiff has simply become convinced that he or she is suffering from a disorder and responds to the evaluation in a way that is meant to convince the examiner to reach the same conclusion.

A meta-analysis found that the possibility for receiving compensation for an injury increased subjects' reports of pain (Rohling, Binder, & Langhinrichsen-Rohling, 1995). Another study examined the effects of compensation on self-reported changes in levels of pain after rehabilitative efforts (Rainville, Sobel, Hartigan, & Wright, 1997). Results revealed differences between patients who were seeking financial compensation through litigation and patients who were not. Individuals seeking compensation reported no changes in pain symptoms at the 12-month follow-up, whereas those not seeking compensation did report improvement. These findings are particularly interesting in that the groups did not differ on measures of treatment compliance and satisfaction with the rehabilitative efforts. They suggest that the experience of being involved in a lawsuit for damages may actually prolong suffering and emotional distress (Greene, 2008).

In a recent literature review exploring the ethics of attorneys "coaching" their clients on how to "beat" psychological tests in civil litigation cases, Victor and Abeles (2004) argued that these techniques are well within the ethical boundaries of legal practice and that attorneys often view such coaching as an important part of advocating for their clients. Another study found that some attorneys believe it to be malpractice *not* to coach their clients on the malingering scales of psychological assessments (e.g., the Minnesota Multiphasic Personality Inventory-2 [MMPI-2]) often used in civil litigation) (Youngjohn, 1995). These coaching strategies may be effective. One study revealed that the *F* scale on the MMPI-2 (one of the instrument's validity scales designed to detect possible malingering) was not as effective at identifying coached malingerers as at identifying noncoached malingerers

(Storm & Graham, 2000). Of course, forensic evaluators who suspect that coaching has occurred are likely to compensate by gathering additional information from sources other than self-report.

Spurred by results like these and by estimates of experienced clinicians that malingering and self-serving presentations are not at all uncommon in forensic evaluations (Rogers, 2008), some have recommended that clinicians be attentive in forensic contexts to consider the particular motivation of litigants and take extra steps to scrutinize their claims (Heilbrun, 2001; Williams, Lees-Haley, & Djanogly, 1999).

WORKERS' COMPENSATION

When a worker is injured in the course of his or her job, the law provides for the worker to be compensated through a streamlined system that avoids the necessity of proving a tort. This system is known as *workers' compensation law*. All 50 states and the federal government have some type of workers' compensation system in place. Prior to workers' compensation, a person who was injured at work had to prove that the employer was responsible for a tort in order to receive compensation. This was difficult because employers had several possible defenses to the worker's claim. They often blamed the employee's negligence or the negligence of another worker for the injury. In other cases, employers said that a worker's injuries were simply the unavoidable risks of particular jobs and that the worker was well aware of these risks at the time of employment. As a result, up to the early part of the 20th century, many seriously injured workers and their families were denied any compensation for their work-related injuries.

Workers' compensation systems were developed around the beginning of the 20th century to provide an alternative to the tort system. In workers' compensation systems, employers contribute to a large fund that insures workers who are injured at work, and employers also waive their right to blame the worker or some other individual for the injury. For their part, workers give up their right to pursue a tort case against their employers, and if they are compensated, the size of the award they receive is

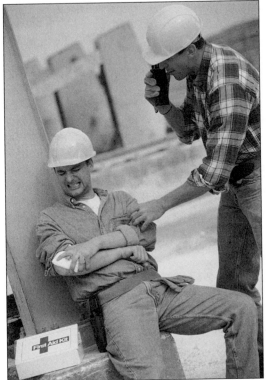

Injured on the job

determined by (1) the type and duration of the injury and (2) their salary at the time of the injury. Workers can seek compensation for

- physical and psychological injuries suffered at work,
- the cost of whatever treatment is given,
- lost wages, and
- the loss of future earning capacity.

Determining how much impairment in future earning capacity a given mental disorder or psychological condition might produce is very difficult. Physicians can assess the degree of impairment from a ruptured disc or a paralyzed arm, but how can we measure the degree or permanence of a mental disability? To bring some uniformity to these determinations, many states require evaluators to use the American Medical Association's *Guide to the Evaluation of Permanent Impairment*. The *Guide* provides five categories of impairment, ranging from "no impairment" to "extreme impairment," that clinicians can use to organize their descriptions of a claimant. In general, however, ratings of psychological impairments are hard to quantify reliably.

Both employers and employees should benefit from a process in which workers' claims can be resolved fairly quickly, which is a major goal of the workers' compensation system. Formal trials are not held, and juries do not resolve these cases; they are heard and decided by a hearing officer or commissioner. (These decisions can be appealed.) In theory, workers' compensation cases should be handled expeditiously, but they often drag on for years as both sides go through a process of hiring one or more experts to examine the worker and give opinions about the injuries and any disability suffered.

How do mental health professionals become involved in workers' compensation claims? Due to the fact that psychological injuries or mental disorders arising from employment can be compensated, clinicians are often asked to evaluate workers and render an opinion about the existence, cause, and implications of any mental disorders. Claims for mental disability usually arise in one of two ways. First, a physical injury can lead to a mental disorder and psychological disability. A common pattern in these *physical–mental* cases is for a worker to sustain a serious physical injury (e.g., a broken back or severe burns) that leaves the worker suffering chronic pain. As the pain and the disability associated with it continue, the worker also experiences associated psychological problems, usually depression and anxiety. These problems can worsen until they become full-fledged mental disorders, resulting in further impairments in the worker's overall functioning.

The second work-related pathway to mental disability is for an individual either to suffer a traumatic incident at work or to undergo a long period of continuing stress that leads to substantial psychological difficulties. A night clerk at a convenience store who is the victim of an armed robbery and subsequently develops posttraumatic stress disorder is an example of such *mental–mental* cases. Another example is the clerical worker who, following years of overwork and pressure from a boss, experiences an anxiety disorder.

In a third kind of case, known as *mental–physical*, work-related stress leads to the onset of a physical disorder such as high blood pressure. Many states have placed restrictions on these types of claims, and psychologists are seldom asked to evaluate them.

In recent years, the number of psychological claims in workers' compensation litigation has increased dramatically, and much of the increase can be attributed to a surge in mental–mental cases (Bonnie & Monahan, 1996). In the 1980s, stress-related mental disorders became the fastest-growing category of occupational disease in the United States (Hersch & Alexander, 1990). According to one study, these claims account for only about 2% of all nonfatal workplace violence claims, but their average cost is nearly three times higher than the average cost for other nonfatal workplace violence claims (Hashemi & Webster, 1998).

Although it is not clear what accounts for the increase in psychological claims, at least three explanations have been proposed. First, because more women have entered the workforce, and because women are more often diagnosed with anxiety and depression disorders than men, the rise in psychological claims might be due to the growing percentage of female workers (Sparr, 1995). A second possibility is that a shift in the job market from manufacturing and industrial jobs to service-oriented jobs has produced corresponding increases in job-related interpersonal stressors and decreases in physical injuries. A third possibility is that claims of psychological impairments are motivated primarily by financial incentives, generating a range of cases in which genuine impairments are mixed in with exaggerated or false claims of disability.

Assessment in Workers' Compensation Claims

Very few empirical studies have been conducted on the assessment of psychological damages in workers' compensation cases. The little research that does exist has usually addressed one of the following questions:

- How do workers' compensation claimants score on standard psychological tests such as the MMPI-2?

- Are certain injuries or stressors associated with a particular pattern of psychological test scores?

- Can psychological tests distinguish claimants who are suffering from a bona fide disorder from those who are faking or exaggerating their problems?

One study investigated the most common pattern of scores on the MMPI for 200 individuals who filed worker compensation claims (Repko & Cooper, 1983). Seventeen percent of the profiles did not show any significant elevations, but over one-third of the MMPIs involved elevated scores on one or more of the scales measuring depression, fatigue and physical complaints, worrying, and a general lack of insight into psychological symptoms. These results have been replicated in other studies that have found, in addition to these psychological test patterns, a tendency for claimants to receive elevated scores on the MMPI scale measuring feelings of disorientation, isolation, alienation, and confusion (Hersch & Alexander, 1990). Of course, these high scores do not prove that the psychological distress was caused by a work-related difficulty; it is possible that already-existing psychological problems make it more likely that a person will suffer stressful or harmful experiences at work.

The research does not suggest that particular injuries or claims are reliably linked with different patterns of test scores (Melton et al., 2007). One reason for the lack of distinguishing patterns might be that regardless of the injury or the stressor, most people manifest psychological distress through a mixture of physical complaints and negative emotions such as anxiety, depression, and feelings of isolation.

The objectivity of psychological evaluations performed in workers' compensation cases is threatened by several factors (Tsushima, Foote, Merrill, & Lehrke, 1996). Chief among these problems is that attorneys often retain the same expert to conduct evaluations over different cases. An expert who is repeatedly hired by the same attorney, whether a plaintiff's or defense attorney, may risk merely advocating the opinions the expert knows is desired by the attorney, rather than rendering impartial opinions about each case.

One study investigated this issue by examining whether psychological assessments of workers' compensation claimants were related to the side that had retained the expert. Hasemann (1997) collected and compared 385 reports that had been prepared by various mental health professionals. Of these reports, 194 had been conducted by defense-hired experts, 182 were completed by plaintiff-hired experts, and 9 evaluations could not be classified. Did plaintiff and defense experts differ in their opinions in these cases? Several results indicate that they did and that they might have been unduly influenced by the adversarial system.

Consider these three results:

- Plaintiff experts gave impairment ratings to claimants that were nearly four times larger than the impairment ratings assigned by defense experts.

- Defense experts concluded that MMPIs completed by claimants were invalid or malingered in 72% of their evaluations, whereas plaintiff experts reached this conclusion in 31% of their evaluations.

- Of the 19 experts who had conducted three or more evaluations, 17 tended to do so almost exclusively for one side. Ten showed partiality toward plaintiffs, conducting a total of 107 plaintiff evaluations and only 8 defense evaluations. Seven experts completed 147 assessments for the defense and only 36 for the plaintiffs.

Although these data do not prove that forensic experts cannot be impartial, they clearly raise concerns that experts are influenced by the adversarial nature of the legal process. It is conceivable that the experts were accurately describing claimants who behaved differently depending on the evaluator. One study suggests that plaintiffs who were referred for evaluations by their attorneys or who sought evaluations on their own tended to exaggerate their symptoms or respond inconsistently on the MMPI more often than did plaintiffs who were evaluated at the request of defense attorneys (Fox, Gerson, & Lees-Haley, 1995). Alternatively, it might be that the experts are reasonably impartial but the attorneys selectively introduce expert opinions depending on whether those opinions support their side. In order to consider the latter possibility, investigators such as Hasemann would need to acquire the results of evaluations requested by attorneys but not subsequently presented as evidence. This is comparable to the "file drawer problem" encountered by investigators performing meta-analysis: Because research reporting nonsignificant differences is often not accepted for publication, such results tend to languish, unpublished, in a file drawer, which limits the accuracy of the investigator's ability to determine an overall "effect" of a research phenomenon based on all the evidence. Even if forensic evaluators can be reasonably impartial, they still conduct such evaluations in the context of an adversarial system, and decisions about whether to introduce such reports as evidence are often made by attorneys who are advocates for their clients.

In addition, comparing the numbers of evaluations conducted for plaintiffs with the number conducted for defendants can be misleading, because these numbers depend on the number of referrals from each side. A better measure of evaluator impartiality involves the proportion of "useful" opinions (that is, opinions helpful to the referring attorney) relative to the overall number of referrals. For example, an evaluator who has conducted 90 evaluations for the defense and 10 for the plaintiffs might appear less impartial than the evaluator who has done 50 for the defense and another 50 for the plaintiffs. However, looking more closely at the "usefulness" proportion (termed the *contrary quotient* by Colbach, 1981) might reveal that the first evaluator has reached a conclusion favorable to the referring attorney in 50% of the defense cases and 45% of the plaintiff cases, whereas the second evaluator has favored the referring attorney in 98% and 100% of defense and plaintiff cases, respectively. Which evaluator appears less impartial?

Can psychological tests distinguish between claimants with bona fide disorders and those who are exaggerating? As we discussed in Chapter 4, the MMPI contains sets of items that are sometimes used to assess the test-taking attitudes of a respondent. These validity scales can be examined to determine whether respondents might have tried to fool the examiner by exaggerating or denying psychological problems. In workers' compensation cases, a main concern is that some plaintiffs might "fake bad" by exaggerating or inventing symptoms to improve their chances for an award.

A growing body of research focuses on whether existing or new validity scales on the MMPI-2 can distinguish respondents who have bona fide problems from those who are malingering. Tests such as the Validity Indicator Profile (Frederick, 1997, 2000; Frederick & Crosby, 2000) and the Test of Memory Malingering (Tombaugh, 1997) have been developed to detect malingering on cognitive and neuropsychological measures.

The typical case of a person trying to exaggerate or fake mental disorder involves the individual answering many items in the "bad" direction, thereby attempting to look as disturbed as possible. However, the strategy might be more complicated in the case of a person who is faking or exaggerating a disorder in a workers' compensation case. These individuals usually want to appear honest, virtuous, and free of any psychological problems that might have existed prior to the injury, while at the same time endorsing many symptoms and complaints that would establish that they had been harmed by a work-related incident. In other words, their motivation involves a combination of faking good and faking bad. A special validity scale composed of MMPI-2 items that tap this simultaneous fake-good/fake-bad strategy has been developed and has had some success in distinguishing between genuine and faked psychological injury claims (Lees-Haley, 1991, 1992).

CIVIL COMPETENCIES

The concept of legal competence extends to many kinds of decisions that individuals are called on to make throughout their lives. When we discussed competence to stand trial in Chapter 8, we focused on the knowledge that criminal defendants must have and the decisions they are required to make. However, the question of mental competence is raised in several noncriminal contexts as well; we refer to these other situations with the general term **civil competencies**.

The question of civil competence focuses on whether an individual has the capacity to understand information that is relevant to decision making in a given situation and then make an informed choice about what to do in that situation. Here are some questions that address issues of civil competence:

- Is a person competent to manage his or her financial affairs?

- Can an individual make competent decisions about his or her medical or psychiatric treatment?

- Is a person competent to execute a will and decide how to distribute property to heirs or other beneficiaries?

- Can a person make advance decisions about the kind of medical treatment he or she wants or does not want to receive if terminally ill or seriously injured?

The legal standards used to define competence have evolved over many years. Scholars who have studied this issue usually point to four abilities that contribute to competent decision making (Appelbaum & Grisso, 1995, Grisso, 2003). A competent individual is expected to be able to (1) understand basic information that is relevant to making a decision, (2) apply that information to a specific situation in order to anticipate the consequences of various choices, (3) use logical—or rational—thinking to evaluate the pros and cons of various strategies and decisions, and (4) communicate a personal decision or choice about the matter under consideration.

The specific abilities associated with each of these general criteria depend on the decision that a person must make. Deciding whether to have risky surgery demands different information and thinking processes than deciding whether to leave property to children or to a charitable organization.

Decisions about medical treatment that one might receive in the future, including the desire to

have life-sustaining medical treatments discontinued, involve a special level of planning that has been encouraged by a 1990 federal statute known as the Patient Self-Determination Act. Planning about future medical treatments is formalized through what are known as **advance medical directives**, in which patients indicate what kinds of treatment they want should they later become incapacitated and incompetent to make treatment decisions.

The most controversial of these advance directives is the "living will," in which a patient essentially asserts that he or she prefers to die rather than to be kept alive on a ventilator or feeding tubes. (In Chapter 2, we described the case of Terri Schiavo, the brain-damaged woman who died after her feeding tube was removed in 2005. Her case was controversial precisely because she had no living will; her husband vowed that she would have preferred death over life by artificial means. As a result of the intense publicity that surrounded that case, many more Americans now have advance medical directives.) The ethical and practical issues involved in determining patients' competence to issue advance medical directives are enormous, but the trend, revealed in Supreme Court decisions such as *Cruzan v. Director, Missouri Department of Health* (1990), is to recognize that patients have great autonomy in accepting or rejecting a variety of treatments and health care provisions (Cantor, 1998; Rich, 1998).

Advance medical directives seem like a simple and direct way to communicate end-of-life decisions. But for living wills to be effective, individuals must be able to generate preferences that are stable over time and across changes in health. Unfortunately, individuals' predictions about what kind of care they might want in the future vary from one occasion to the next and are affected by the status of their present health.

In studies that examined the stability of advance directives, participants were asked to record their preferences for various life-sustaining treatments (e.g., cardiopulmonary resuscitation [CPR]) in different medical scenarios (e.g., coma). After an interval ranging from one month to two years, these individuals recorded their preferences again. The average stability of preferences across all judgments was 71%, suggesting that over time periods as short as two years, nearly one-third of individuals' stated treatment preferences changed (Ditto et al., 2003). Of course, a person could change his or her preferences for good reason—perhaps as a result of some relevant, intervening life experience such as a health crisis or a relative's need for life-sustaining treatment. However most people are unaware that their preferences change; they mistakenly believe that the preferences they express at the second interview are identical to those they provided at the first interview (Gready et al., 2000).

Preferences are also dependent on the context in which they are made. For example, when patients recently discharged from hospitals are asked about their desire for life-sustaining treatment, they show a characteristic "hospital dip;" they report less desire for interventions than they did prior to hospitalization—and less than they report several months after their discharge (Ditto, Jacobson, Smucker, Danks, & Fagerlin, 2005). Apparently people have difficulty expressing stable preferences for medical care in the future.

Assessing Competence to Make Treatment Decisions

The question of competence to consent to treatment usually arises when a patient refuses treatment that seems to be medically and psychologically justified. Under these circumstances, the first step might be to break down the explanation of the treatment decisions facing the patient into smaller bits of information. (Research results have shown that patients are capable of significantly better understanding when treatment information is presented to them one element at a time.) Using this kind of presentation might facilitate a patient's appreciation of whether a recommended treatment would be in his or her best interest. Should an impasse between the patient and treating professionals still exist after such a presentation, it would be important to administer a clinical assessment instrument to determine whether a given patient lacks the necessary ability to reach a competent decision. Such an instrument—the MacArthur Competence Assessment Tool for Treatment Decisions (MacCAT-T)—is now commercially available (Grisso & Appelbaum, 1998a; 1998b).

The research for the MacCAT-T, conducted as part of a larger MacArthur Research Network on Mental Health and Law study on competencies, coercion, and risk assessment, focused on the capacities of individuals with severe mental disorders to make decisions and give informed consent about their own psychiatric treatment. Can persons with serious mental disorders make competent treatment decisions for themselves? Do their decision-making abilities differ from those of persons who do not suffer mental disorders?

Researchers in the MacArthur Treatment Competence Study developed a series of structured interview measures to assess the four basic abilities—understanding information, applying information, thinking rationally, and expressing a choice—involved in legal competence (Grisso, Appelbaum, Mulvey, & Fletcher, 1995). For example, here is an item that taps a person's ability to apply information to the question of whether he or she has a condition that could be effectively treated:

"Most people who have symptoms of a mental or emotional disorder like your doctor believes you have can be helped by treatment. The most common treatment is medication. Other treatments sometimes used for such disorders are having someone to talk to about problems, and participating in group therapy with other people with similar symptoms." "… [D]o you believe that you have the kind of condition for which some types of treatment might be helpful?" "All right, you believe that … (paraphrase of the patient's expressed opinion). Can you explain that to me? What makes you believe that … (again paraphrase as above)?" For a patient who believes that treatment will not work because he or she is "just too sick," the interviewer would ask: "Imagine that a doctor tells you that there is a treatment that has been shown in research to help 90% of people with problems just as serious as yours. Do you think this treatment might be of more benefit to you than getting no treatment at all?" (Grisso et al., 1995, p. 133)

Standardized interviews, using items of this type, were conducted with three groups of patients—those with schizophrenia, those with major depression, and those with heart disease—and with groups of people from the community who were *not* ill but were demographically matched to the patient groups (Grisso & Appelbaum, 1995). Only a minority of the persons in all the groups showed significant impairments in competent decision making about various treatment options. However, the patients with schizophrenia and major depression tended to have a poorer understanding of treatment information and used less adequate reasoning in thinking about the consequences of treatment than did the heart patients or the members of the community sample. These impairments were more pronounced and consistent across different competence abilities for patients with schizophrenia than for patients with depression, and the more serious the symptoms of mental disorder (especially those involving disturbed thinking), the poorer the understanding.

These results obviously have implications for social policies involving persons with mental disorders. First, contrary to popular impressions, the majority of patients suffering from severe disorders such as schizophrenia and major depression appear to be capable of competent decision making about their treatment. On the other hand, a significant number of patients—particularly those with schizophrenia—show impairments in their decision-making abilities.

Assessing Competence to Execute a Will

Clinicians may also be asked to evaluate whether a person (called a "testator") was competent to execute a will; such competence is a requirement for the provisions of the will to be valid. Typically, challenges to this capacity are raised when there is suspicion that the testator lacked the necessary mental capacity to execute a valid will (Frolik, 1999; Melton et al., 2007). Ronald Eisaman challenged his aunt's will in a Pennsylvania probate court, arguing that his aunt, Harriet Schott, lacked **testamentary capacity**. Schott executed a will in 1993, leaving the bulk of her estate to Eisaman. But she executed a second will in 1997, reducing his share to 50% and passing the remaining 50% to the corporation that owned the assisted-living facility where she resided prior to her death. The expert witnesses who testified about Schott's mental capacity were equivocal. Thus, the judge determined that Eisaman had not established that his aunt lacked testamentary capacity to change her will. The 1997 version was admitted to probate.

According to one study, situations that may raise concern about capacity to execute a will include the following: There is a radical change from a previous will (72%), undue influence is alleged (56%), the testator has no biological children (52%), the testator executed the will less than a year prior to death (48%), and the testator suffered from comorbid conditions such as dementia (40%), alcohol abuse (28%), and other neurological/psychiatric conditions (28%) (Shulman, Cohen, & Hull, 2004).

The legal standard for testators' competence to execute a will is derived from *Banks v. Goodfellow* (1870), in which the court held as follows:

1. Testators must know at the time of making their wills that they are making their wills.

2. They must know the nature and extent of their property.

3. They must know the "natural objects of [their] bounty."

4. They must know the manner in which the wills they are making distribute their property.

This type of competence has a lower threshold than other competencies because it requires only that persons making a will have a general understanding of the nature and extent of their property and of the effect of their will on members of their family or others who may naturally claim to benefit from the property cited in the will (Melton et al., 2007). A person cannot be deemed incompetent to execute a will simply on the basis of the presence of a mental illness, unless there is clear evidence that the mental illness specifically interfered with the individual's ability to meet the set standard at the time the will was written.

Assessment of this competence focuses on the individual's functional abilities at the time his or her will was written. Melton and colleagues (2007) outline some strategies used by mental health professionals in assessing competence to execute a will. First, they recommend structuring the evaluation to conform to the associated legal elements. They suggest using the sources available (e.g., the testator, family, friends, records) to first determine the purpose of the will and why it was written at that time. Second, they recommend gathering information about the testator's property holdings, which may include asking questions about occupation and salary, tangible property, and intangibles (e.g., bank accounts, investments). Third, the clinician should determine the testator's "values and preferences" (p. 361) to gain insight into the family dynamics (e.g., with whom the testator has a good relationship, with whom he or she does not get along). This information can shed light on the testator's rationale for bequeathing his or her belongings to specific individuals. Finally, Melton and colleagues recommend that clinicians assess the general consequences of the dispositions outlined in the will.

One of the obvious difficulties in these types of evaluations is that the testator, the subject of the evaluation, is often deceased at the time the question of competence to execute the will arises. Thus, the sources of information will be different. If the testator is alive, he or she will be a primary informational source—but if he or she is deceased, the evaluator must gather information from family, friends, acquaintances, medical records, and other available sources without the testator's specific input.

PSYCHOLOGICAL AUTOPSIES

Like most clinical assessments, the typical forensic assessment involves a clinician interviewing, observing, and testing a client to arrive at an understanding of the case. However, in a few unusual circumstances, clinicians may be called on to give an opinion about a deceased person's state of mind as it existed at a specific time before death. Obviously, in these cases, the clinician must conduct an evaluation without any participation by the individual whose prior condition is in question. These evaluations are termed **psychological autopsies** (Ogloff & Otto, 1993).

Psychological autopsies originated in the 1950s when a group of social scientists in the Los Angeles area began assisting the coroner's office in determining whether suicide, murder, or accident was the most likely mode of death in some equivocal cases. Their use has spread over the years, and now they are encountered most often in cases such as determining the cause of death in situations where an insurance company could deny death benefits if the policy holder committed suicide; assessing claims in workers' compensation cases that stressful working conditions or work trauma contributed to a worker's death or suicide; evaluating a deceased individual's mental capacity to execute or modify a will; and assessing the validity of an argument occasionally made by criminal defendants that a victim's mode of death was suicide rather than homicide.

Although there is no standard format for psychological autopsies, most of them rely on information from two sources: interviews with third parties who knew the decedent, and prior records. General guidelines for what should be included in psychological autopsies have been published (La Fon, 2008). Some investigators concentrate on more recent data, generated close in time to the person's death. What was the person's mood? How was the person doing at work? Were there any pronounced changes in the person's behavior? Others—especially those who take a developmental perspective on behavior—look for clues early in the person's life. As a child, how did the person interact with his or her parents and siblings? What was the individual's approach to school? Peers? Hobbies and other activities?

As with any assessment technique, the first question to be considered is the reliability of the psychological autopsy. There are several reasons to suspect that the reliability of psychological autopsies is low. For starters, the person in question is not available to be interviewed or tested. Also, the persons who are interviewed might not remember the past accurately, or they might have reasons to distort their answers.

We are aware of only one study that has addressed the question of reliability, and it did so in a very indirect fashion, using data from the investigation of the U.S.S. *Iowa* explosion (see Box 9.3).

Box 9.3   THE CASE OF THE U.S.S. *IOWA*

On April 19, 1989, 47 U.S. Navy sailors were killed when an explosion ripped through turret 2 of the U.S.S. *Iowa*. The Navy's investigation of this tragedy initially concluded that the explosion was caused by the suicidal acts of Gunner's Mate Clayton Hartwig, who was himself killed in the explosion. The major foundation for this conclusion was a psychological autopsy conducted by FBI agents working at the National Center for the Analysis of Violent Crime. The Navy's conclusions were later evaluated by a congressional committee, which commissioned its own panel of 14 psychological and psychiatric experts to review the FBI's analysis. Partly on the basis of this panel's input, the congressional committee rejected the FBI analysis as invalid. Ultimately, the U.S. Navy also concluded that the cause of the explosion could not be determined.

Forensic psychologist Randy Otto and his colleagues asked 24 psychologists and psychiatrists to rate the reports prepared by the 14 experts commissioned by the U.S. House of Representatives to review the FBI analysis of the U.S.S. *Iowa* explosion (Otto, Poythress,

The U.S.S. *Iowa*, damaged in an explosion

Starr, & Darkes, 1993). Three raters judged each of the 14 reports, and although they failed to show precise agreement in how they thought the reports should be interpreted, they did achieve a moderate amount of broad agreement in their ratings of the 14 reports. Note, however, that this agreement pertains only to how the raters interpreted the 14 panelists' reports, not to the contents or opinions in the reports themselves.

No empirical information exists concerning the validity of psychological autopsies—that is, whether they accurately portray a person's state of mind at the time of death. Obviously, a major problem is that the decedent's "true" state of mind is unknown; in fact, if it *were* known, the autopsy would be unnecessary. However, it might still be possible to examine the validity of psychological autopsies by giving reputed experts background information in cases that appear ambiguous (but in which the cause of death *is* actually known) and studying the opinions offered and the reasons for them.

How has testimony about psychological autopsies fared in court? In cases involving workers' compensation claims and questions of whether insurance benefits should be paid, the courts have usually admitted psychological autopsy testimony; in criminal cases or in cases involving the question of whether a person had the mental capacity to execute a will, the courts have been more reluctant to permit the testimony (Ogloff & Otto, 1993). Judges are more hesitant to allow expert testimony in criminal cases than in civil ones, perhaps because the risks of prejudicial

testimony are greater when one's liberties can be taken away. One reason for the courts' hesitancy in permitting psychological autopsy testimony in cases involving the validity of wills might be that, in such cases, the state of mind of the deceased is the critical question for the jury. Allowing expert testimony on this matter might therefore be viewed as invading the province of the jury, a perception that judges usually want to avoid.

CHILD CUSTODY AND PARENTAL FITNESS

The "Best Interests of the Child" in Custody Disputes

One of the growing areas of forensic psychology is the evaluation of families for the purpose of recommending the particular custodial arrangement that is in the best interests of a child whose parents are divorcing or separating. The increase in these cases is attributable to two facts. First, about 50% of marriages in the United States end in divorce. As of 2007, 29% of households with children in the United States were single-parent families, and more than 60% of children born since 1986 will spend some time in a single-parent household. Therefore, the issue of custody is a practical concern for millions of families. Second, from the end of the 19th century to about the middle of the 20th century, the prevailing assumption was that awarding custody of young children (sometimes called children of "tender years") to their mothers was usually in their best interests. This preference for maternal custody has diminished at the beginning of the 21st century; now many courts want to know about the parenting abilities of each parent before making a decision about custody (Liss & McKinley-Pace, 1999).

Currently, the prevailing standard for custody decisions is the **future best interests of the child**. Although the child's "best interests" must be assessed on a case-by-case basis, the Uniform Marriage and Divorce Act indicates that courts should consider the following criteria: (1) the wishes of the child; (2) the wishes of the child's parents; (3) the relationships between the child and the parents, siblings, and significant others who interact with the child; (4) the child's adjustment at home and school and in the community; and (5) the physical and mental health of the parties involved.

Child custody evaluations usually arise in situations in which divorcing parents disagree about which of them can better meet the needs of their children and should therefore have custody. Most states permit two kinds of custodial arrangements, each with two aspects (physical and legal). *Physical custody* refers to the living arrangement, whereas *legal custody* concerns the responsibility for decision making. In **sole custody**, the child will live only with one parent (although the other parent may be granted visitation rights), and/or all legal decision-making authority for that child will rest with one parent. In **joint custody**, both parents can retain parental rights concerning decisions about the child's general welfare, education, health care, and other matters (this is called joint legal custody), and the child can alternate living in the home of the mother and in the home of the father according to the schedule provided in the custody decision (this is called joint physical custody). Joint custody does not necessarily mean that the child spends equal time with each parent, however. Usually, one parent is designated the residential parent, and the child spends more time living at the home of that parent. In general, families that are functioning better at the time that custody is awarded are more likely to ask for joint custody than families that are experiencing ongoing difficulties (Gunnoe & Braver, 2001).

The three main differences between sole custody and joint custody are as follows:

1. Joint custody distributes the frequency of interaction more evenly between the children and each parent.

2. Joint custody requires more interactions between the divorced parents and generates more demands for cooperation concerning the children.

3. Joint custody results in more alterations in caregiving arrangements, along with more separations and reunions between children and parents (Clingempeel & Reppucci, 1982).

Psychologists have examined the effects of sole custody and joint custody on children and parents. Although the findings are not clear-cut, there appear to be several advantages to joint-custody arrangements. In a meta-analysis of 21 studies, Bauserman (1997) concluded that children in joint custody fared better than children in sole custody on a number of measures related to adjustment and interpersonal relations. Fathers benefited from joint custody because they had more frequent contact with their children. Joint custody was advantageous for mothers because it afforded them greater opportunity for courtship; as a result, these mothers repartnered more rapidly than mothers with sole responsibility for their children, a situation that may be beneficial for the children (Gunnoe & Braver, 2001).

Assessment in Custody Disputes

Many mental health professionals regard child custody cases to be the most ethically and clinically difficult forensic evaluations they perform. First, the emotional stakes are extremely high, and both parents are often willing to spare no expense or tactic in the battle over which of them will win custody. The children involved are usually forced to live— for months, if not years—in an emotional limbo in which they do not know in whose home they will be residing, where they will be going to school, or how often they will see each parent.

Second, a thorough custody evaluation requires that the clinician evaluate the children, both parents, and others who have interacted with the child, such as relatives, teachers, and family health care providers. Often, not all the parties agree to be evaluated or do so only under coercion, resulting in a lengthy and sometimes tense process. Such tension can be worsened if the evaluation is requested by the attorney for one of the two divorcing spouses, which may lead the other spouse to perceive the evaluator as unfairly biased in favor of the spouse who retained this evaluator. An alternative arrangement—having the court order the evaluation and designate a neutral expert, with both parties agreeing to this appointment—can help to reduce this perception of bias.

Third, to render a valuable expert opinion, a clinician must be quite knowledgeable—about the children and parents under evaluation, but also about child development, bonding and attachment, family systems, the effects of divorce on children, adult and childhood mental disorders, and several different kinds of testing. Added to these factors are variations in what we have traditionally defined as a family. With increasing acceptance of different lifestyles and family structures, clinicians must often confront questions about whether parents' sexual orientation or ethnicity should have any bearing on custody decisions.

Finally, child custody evaluations are often highly adversarial, with each parent trying to expose all the faults of the other and each side vigorously challenging any procedures or opinion by an expert with which it disagrees. Clinicians who conduct custody evaluations must be prepared for challenges to their clinical methods, scholarly competence, and professional ethics. Even evaluators who operate under court appointment may have their findings challenged in some cases.

There are actually three models under which custody evaluators can be appointed: (1) A judge can appoint one clinician to conduct a custody evaluation that is available to all the parties, (2) each side can retain its own expert to conduct independent evaluations, or (3) the sides can agree to share the expenses of hiring an expert to conduct one evaluation (Weissman, 1991). Most clinicians prefer either the first or the third option because they do not want to be subjected to the pressures that are brought to bear when separate experts are hired by each side (Keilin & Bloom, 1986). Attorneys tend to agree with this preference, believing that option 2 leads to greater bias (LaFortune & Carpenter, 1998).

Specific guidelines for conducting custody evaluations have been developed by the American Psychological Association (1994) and the Association of Family and Conciliation Courts (AFCC, 2006). Although the methods used in custody evaluations vary depending on the specific issues in each case, most evaluations include the following components: (1) clinical, social history, and mental status interviews of the parents and the children; (2) standardized testing of the parents and the children; (3) observation of interactions between each parent and the children, especially when the children are minors; (4) assessments or interviews with other people who have had opportunities to observe the family (adult children of the parents, grandparents, neighbors, the family physician, school teachers, and other observers); and (5) documents or records that might be relevant to the case (medical records of children and parents, report cards, and arrest records).

In any forensic psychological evaluation, it is useful to include a specialized tool that has been developed to measure capacities that are associated with the legal decision. In child custody evaluations, such capacities are associated with parenting skills and capacities (for the parents) and needs (for the children). Two of the specialized approaches that are available for child custody evaluations are the Ackerman–Schoendorf Scales for Parent Evaluation of Custody (ASPECT; Ackerman & Schoendorf, 1992) and the several scales developed by Bricklin (the Bricklin Perceptual Scales; Perception-of-Relationships Test, Parent Awareness Skills Survey, and Parent Perception of Child Profile; see Bricklin, 1995). However, these tests are of questionable validity (see Melton et al., 2007; Otto & Edens, 2003), so it remains for the field to develop a specialized measure that is consistent with the principles of scientific test development.

Custody evaluations are time-consuming. In a national survey of mental health professionals who conducted child custody evaluations, Ackerman and Ackerman (1997) found that experts spent an average of about 30 hours on each evaluation. Much of this time was devoted to interviewing and observing the parties in various combinations. In fact, more than two-thirds of the respondents indicated that they conducted individual interviews with each parent and each child, observed each parent interacting (separately) with each child, and conducted formal psychological testing of the parents and the children.

Experts also reported how often they recommended different kinds of custodial arrangements (Keilin & Bloom, 1986). Joint legal custody (parents share the decision making, but one parent maintains primary physical custody) was the most common recommendation (42.8%), and sole custody without visitation was the least often recommended alternative (4.6%). Sole custody with visitation (30.4%) and joint physical custody (21.7%) were among the other preferred recommendations.

One question addressed by several research studies is whether children raised in joint-custody arrangements function better than children in sole custody. One could predict that to the extent that joint custody allows the child to maintain close ties to both parents, better child adjustment would be promoted by joint-custody arrangements. Alternatively, one might argue that because sole custody simplifies custodial arrangements, minimizes the child's confusion over where his or her home is, and keeps still-angry parents away from each other, better adjustment will occur with sole custody.

A meta-analysis (Bauserman, 2002) considered the results of 33 studies (11 published and 22 unpublished, including 21 doctoral dissertations) addressing the question of whether there is a difference in the adjustment of children in joint-custody versus sole-custody arrangements. Children in joint physical or legal custody were better

adjusted than children in sole-custody on measures of general adjustment, family relationships, self-esteem, emotional and behavioral adjustment, and divorce-specific adjustment. Joint-custody parents reported less current and past conflict than did sole-custody parents. This did not explain the better adjustment of joint-custody children, but did suggest that joint custody can promote more positive involvement with both parents. Research (Crosbie-Burnett, 1991; Emery, 1982; Hetherington & Arasteh, 1988) also suggests that continuing hostility and conflicts between the parents—regardless of the type of custody arrangement—were associated with poorer adjustment on the part of the children.

In recent years, divorced couples have sometimes returned to court to ask judges to resolve both ongoing and novel disputes. For example, Pamela Peck, a divorced mother, went to family court in Dallas to seek an injunction that would ban her ex-husband's girlfriend from spending the night at his house when his son was there. A Texas judge ruled in her favor, enjoining both parties from having overnight guests of the opposite sex when "in possession of" their 9-year-old son. One of the thorniest custody issues is whether a custodial parent can relocate. An example of a "move-away case" is described in Box 9.4.

Because divorce is a potent stressor for children and because protracted custody battles tend to leave a trail of emotionally battered family members in their wake, increasing attention is being given to helping parents and children cope with these transitions or to finding alternatives to custody fights (Grych & Fincham, 1992; Kelly, 1996). Many judges require divorcing couples to attempt to settle issues of custody, visitation, and support through mediation, a form of alternative dispute resolution that minimizes the adversarial quality of the typical custody dispute. (We discussed mediation in Chapter 2.) If mediation fails, the couple can return to court and have the judge decide the issues. The benefits of custody mediation are that resolutions are reached more quickly, and with better compliance among the participants, than with adversarial procedures.

The Association of Family and Conciliation Courts (2006) has developed model standards for

---

B o x 9.4   THE CASE OF *CIESLUK V. CIESLUK*: CAN A CUSTODIAL PARENT MOVE AWAY?

When Michelle and Christopher Ciesluk were divorced in 2002, they arranged to share joint legal custody of their son, Connor, who lived primarily with his mother. But when Michelle Ciesluk lost her job with Sprint in early 2003 and the company offered to rehire her provided that she was willing to move from Colorado to Arizona, Christopher Ciesluk objected. He opposed the move, fearing he would lose any relationship with his son and would miss his son's school and athletic activities. Unfortunately for Ms. Ciesluk, neither the Colorado legislature nor the courts have made it easy for her. In 2001, the legislature abolished a legal presumption that a custodial parent has the right to move away,

and an appellate court ruled that a parent who wishes to move must demonstrate a *direct* beneficial effect on the child. (The more commonly used test requires the parent to show that the move would have an *indirect* effect on the child, typically by enhancing the custodial parent's job opportunities.) Michelle Ciesluk was not able to meet that test, so she remains in Colorado with her son, working for $10 an hour as an administrative assistant and feeling that her "whole life is on hold" (Eaton, 2004). In 2005 the Colorado Supreme Court reversed the decision by the appellate court and sent the case back to the trial court (*Ciesluk v. Ciesluk*, 2005).

---

the practice of family and divorce mediation, indicating that a mediator shall (among other things):

- recognize that mediation is based on the principle of self-determination by the participants;

- conduct the mediation process in an impartial manner ... disclose all actual and potential grounds of bias and conflicts of interest reasonable known to the mediator. Structure the mediation process so that participants make decisions based on sufficient information and knowledge;

- assist participants in determining how to promote the best interests of children;

- recognize a family situation involving child abuse or neglect or domestic violence and take appropriate steps to shape the mediation process accordingly;

- suspend or terminate the mediation process when the mediator reasonably believes that a participant is unable to effectively participate or for other compelling reasons.

Research generally supports the favorable adjustment of those who go through mediation. Two reviews of a decade of research (Hahn & Kleist, 2000; Kelly, 1996) indicate that families that go through mediation to determine custody have better adjustment than those going through the more traditional child custody litigation process.

Assessing Fitness to Be a Parent

Evaluations of parental fitness involve different questions from the typical custody dispute (Condie, 2003). In every state, the agency responsible for the protection of children will intervene if it receives a credible report that a child is being abused or neglected. After an investigation, the agency might file a petition asking a court to remove the child from the home and arrange placement with a relative or in foster care. In such cases, the issue before the court is whether the child should be left with the parents or removed from the home because of parental unfitness.

The issue for the evaluator is what arrangement protects the child's well-being, while properly respecting the rights of the parents. Although parental rights are important, the state must protect children from parents who cannot or will not provide adequate food, shelter, and supervision. The state must also protect children from parents who abuse them, physically or psychologically. A clinician might recommend that the child be placed temporarily in foster care and that the parents receive training in parenting skills as a condition of having the child returned to them. In extreme cases—those in which parents abandon a child or are clearly incapable of caring for a child—the state might seek to terminate parental rights. This is done most often when relatives or others wish to adopt the child (Heilbrun, Marczyk, & DeMatteo, 2002).

In an interesting twist on the usual circumstances of termination cases, 12-year-old Gregory Kingsley asked a Florida judge in 1992 to terminate his parents' right to function as parents on his behalf. Gregory had been removed from his home and placed in foster care, but when the state attempted to return him to his birth parents, Gregory objected and tried to sever his parents' ties to him. Courts had never before confronted the question of whether a 12-year-old can bring a termination petition, but both the trial judge and an appellate court ruled in Gregory's favor (Haugaard & Avery, 2002).

CIVIL COMMITMENT AND RISK ASSESSMENT

All 50 states and the District of Columbia have **civil commitment** laws that authorize the custody and restraint of persons who, as a result of mental illness, are a danger to themselves or others or who are so gravely disabled that they cannot care for themselves. This restraint is usually accomplished by compulsory commitment to a mental hospital. The courts also provide safeguards and rules for how these involuntary commitments are to be accomplished.

Many of these procedures were instituted in the 1970s in response to a concern that in the 1950s and 1960s, it was too easy to commit people to state psychiatric facilities. At that time, people who were mentally ill could be involuntarily committed whenever the state believed they needed treatment. Beginning around 1970, commitment proceedings began to be reformed, resulting in more legal rights for the mentally ill to resist compulsory commitment. A key case in this reform movement was *O'Connor v. Donaldson* (1975), in which the Supreme Court held that mental illness and a need for treatment were insufficient justifications for involuntarily committing mentally ill persons who were not dangerous.

Similar limits on involuntary hospitalizations have been upheld by the Supreme Court more recently (e.g., *Foucha v. Louisiana*, 1992). The standard for commitment changed from mental illness and in need of treatment to mental illness that was associated with dangerousness or a grave lack of ability to care for oneself. This narrowing of the commitment standard, along with other societal influences during the last 40 years (the community mental health movement, deinstitutionalization), has resulted in fewer public hospital beds for mental health treatment, and shorter hospital stays. Although the legislative changes of the 1970s were intended to protect the rights of the mentally ill, an exclusive concern with rights can sometimes leave patients without adequate care, housing, or the effective psychiatric treatment that can be provided in some hospitals (Turkheimer & Parry, 1992; Wexler, 1992).

Four Types of Commitment Procedures

The laws permit four types of civil commitment: (1) emergency detention, (2) voluntary inpatient commitment, (3) involuntary inpatient commitment, and (4) outpatient commitment. Emergency detention is the means by which most individuals are initially admitted to hospitals. A police officer, a mental health professional, or sometimes a private citizen can initiate involuntary detention of another person. Usually, the cause is actual or anticipated harmful behavior by the patient either against self (e.g., attempted suicide) or against others. An examination is performed by a physician or a qualified mental health professional. Patients committed on an emergency basis can be detained for only a specified length of time—usually two or three days—before a review takes place. Then a preliminary hearing must be held before the patient can be confined any longer.

A person may volunteer to enter a psychiatric hospital, although he or she still must meet the criteria for hospitalization (typically some version of "mentally ill and in need of treatment"), but even those who are being hospitalized "voluntarily" may feel pressure from family, mental health personnel, or the legal system to enter the hospital. Individuals who have been provided with more information and given the chance to express their views report feeling less coercion, regardless of whether they are voluntarily or involuntarily hospitalized (Dennis & Monahan, 1996). While voluntarily hospitalized, the patient may find that the hospital has instigated commitment proceedings to challenge or delay release.

The third type of commitment—involuntary inpatient commitment—requires a court order. The criteria for obtaining an involuntary civil commitment vary from state to state; in general, however, the person must be mentally ill and must also be dangerous to self and others, or so gravely disabled as to be unable to provide for his or her own basic needs. Although the criterion of "dangerousness" is the most often discussed standard and therefore is deemed the most important for involuntary hospitalization, grave disability is the standard that determines most commitments (Turkheimer & Parry, 1992).

To obtain an involuntary commitment, the concerned persons must petition the court for a professional examination of the individual in question. A formal court hearing usually follows the examination. In most states, the hearing is mandatory, and persons whose commitment is sought can call witnesses and have their lawyer cross-examine witnesses who testify against them.

A fourth type of commitment procedure, known as outpatient commitment, is available in nearly all states and allows a patient to be mandated to receive treatment in an outpatient setting, such as a community mental health center, rather than in a hospital (Hiday & Goodman, 1982). Outpatient commitment often involves conditional release from a hospital. That is, formerly hospitalized patients are ordered to continue treatment in the community. Several legal and clinical complications arise with this approach. For example, what should be done with patients who refuse medication? Are therapists who treat these patients liable for any dangerous acts the patients might commit? And, most important, is effective community-based treatment available?

Dangerousness and Risk Assessment

Dangerousness is one of the central constructs of mental health law. Whether a person is now or could in the future be dangerous is an issue that underlies many decisions in our system of justice, including questions of civil commitment. Although the law often uses the terms *dangerous* and *dangerousness*, these terms are difficult to define. They actually merge three distinct constructs: (1) risk factors (variables associated with the probability that violence or aggression will occur), (2) harm (the nature and severity of predicted and actual aggression), and (3) risk level (the probability that harm will occur) (National Research Council, 1989). In some combination, these factors provide a major justification for involuntarily committing the mentally ill to hospitals.

As we saw in Chapter 1 when we discussed the *Tarasoff* case, dangerousness is the basis for requiring therapists to protect third parties from possible acts of violence against them by the patients of these therapists. Chapter 7 identified dangerousness as a reason for denying bail to certain defendants. In Chapter 8, we learned that dangerousness is the justification for hospitalizing defendants after they have been found not guilty by reason of insanity. Some states also use future dangerousness as one factor a jury can consider when deciding whether to sentence a convicted murderer to life in prison or death by execution.

Difficulties in Assessing Dangerousness

Because dangerousness is hard to define, we prefer to use the term *violence risk* and will do so throughout the remainder of this chapter. Can mental health experts accurately assess a person's present violence risk and then predict whether that person will be violent in the future? Is mental illness a sign that a person is likely to be violent? Do certain types of mental illness make a person more prone to violent behavior? These questions have been examined extensively by researchers for more than three decades, and they are at the heart of many real-life cases. For example, should the mental health professionals who treated John Hinckley have predicted that he posed a danger to President Reagan? What about Jeffrey Dahmer? Was his brutal behavior predictable, given his early psychological problems?

Clinicians who attempt to answer these questions perform what are called **risk assessments;** using the best available data and research, they try to predict which persons are and which are not likely to behave violently in certain circumstances, give some estimate of the risk for violence, and offer suggestions on how to reduce the risks (Heilbrun, 2009; Monahan & Steadman, 1994).

Many factors make such predictions difficult. For example, the base rate of violence in some groups is low, so clinicians are being asked to predict a phenomenon that rarely occurs. The clinical assessments of persons assessed for violence risk are often conducted in hospitals or prisons, whereas the environment where violence is relevant for those being considered for release is the community. The predictions have often been for long-term risk, which is harder to predict than violence risk over a shorter time frame.

The original consensus of researchers was that clinicians could not predict with accuracy the risk of violence. Leading scholars such as John Monahan (1984) of the University of Virginia summarized the research this way: "In one study after another, the same conclusion emerges: For every correct prediction of violence, there are numerous incorrect predictions" (Pfohl, 1984). Another early summary of the research on clinicians' ability to predict violence was that their predictions were wrong in two of every three cases in which a "yes" prediction of future violence was made.

Subsequent research has modified the early pessimism about clinicians' ability to predict violence, however. Researchers have learned that these predictions can sometimes reach moderate to good levels of accuracy when certain conditions are present (Borum, 1996; Otto & Douglas, 2009). Specifically, clinicians who consider a set of factors that research has shown to be related to future violence can predict the risk for violence considerably better than was the case 30 years

ago (Heilbrun, 2009). Specifically, when clinicians have information about a range of historical, personal, and environmental variables related to violence, when they limit their predictions to specific kinds of violent behavior, and when they concentrate on appraising risks in certain settings rather than in all situations, they can do so with a fair degree of accuracy. Although they still make a large number of errors, they do significantly better than chance.

One of the most important advances in the area of risk assessment has involved the development and use of such specialized risk assessment tools (Heilbrun, 2009). A number of specialized tools are now available (Otto & Douglas, 2009), some of which are actuarial. An actuarial tool (such as the Violence Risk Appraisal Guide; Harris, Rice, & Quinsey, 1993) uses specified risk factors that are rated and scored, with scores being combined into a final score that is then applied to the prediction in a way that is specified by a formula (which in turn has been developed through empirical research). Other tools (such as the HCR-20 which measures historical, clinical, and risk management variables [Webster, Douglas, Eaves, & Hart, 1997]) employ a "structured professional judgment." They do not combine to yield a total score. Rather, the evaluator is asked to make a judgment about risk in light of the status of these risk factors. Present evidence indicates that good actuarial and structured professional judgment approaches to risk assessment are comparably accurate in predictions of violence (Heilbrun, Douglas, & Yasuhara, 2009).

SUMMARY

1. ***What problems are associated with expert testimony, and what reforms have been proposed?*** The main objections to expert testimony are that it invades the province of the jury, is too adversarial and thus not impartial, takes too much court time, introduces irrelevant information, and is often founded on an insufficient scientific base. Proposed reforms have focused on limiting the scope of expert testimony, reducing the partisanship involved in adversaries retaining their own experts, requiring judges to examine more strictly the scientific foundation

of expert testimony, and referring to it as *opinion testimony* rather than as expert testimony. The limitation in scope and having judges consider the scientific foundation more carefully are proposals that have been implemented.

2. ***Under what conditions can a plaintiff be compensated for psychological damages?*** Plaintiffs can seek damages in civil trials if they are a victim of a tort, which is a wrongful act that can be proved to have caused them harm. Although the law has historically been skeptical of claims for psychological harm and emotional distress

unless they are accompanied by physical injuries, the recent trend has been to allow plaintiffs to be compensated for emotional damages (without any physical injuries) resulting from intentionally outrageous or negligent conduct.

3. ***What is workers' compensation, and how do mental health professionals participate in such cases?*** Workers' compensation is a no-fault system now used by all states and in the federal system to provide a streamlined alternative for determining the compensation of workers who are injured in the course of their jobs. Formal trials are not held or juries used in workers' compensation cases. Psychologists may testify in workers' compensation hearings about the extent, cause, and likely prognosis for psychological problems that have developed following a physical injury and/or work-related stress.

4. ***What capacities are involved in civil competence?*** Questions of civil competence focus on whether an individual has the mental capacity to understand information that is relevant to decision making in a given situation and then make an informed choice about what to do. The issue of civil competence is raised when it is not clear that an individual is capable of managing his or her financial affairs, giving informed consent to current or future medical treatments, or executing a will.

5. ***What criteria are used for decisions about disputes involving child custody or parental fitness?*** The future best interest of the child is the main criterion applied to disputes about which parent should have custody of a child following divorce. Evaluations of parental fitness address a different question: Should a parent's custody of a child be terminated because of indications of parental unfitness? Many mental health professionals regard custody and parental fitness assessments as the most difficult evaluations they perform. For this reason, and in an attempt to reduce the stress of custody battles, custody mediation has been developed as a less adversarial means of resolving these disputes.

6. **What steps are taken in civil commitment and how well can clinicians assess the risk of dangerousness, or violent behavior, a key criterion for civil commitment?** Persons who are considered gravely disabled or dangerous to themselves or others may be committed to a state psychiatric hospital against their will, but they have the right to a hearing shortly thereafter to determine whether they should be retained. After being hospitalized, some patients may continue on outpatient commitment. Long-term predictions of violence risk are more difficult to make with accuracy, but there is a reliable association among historical, personal, and environmental factors and dangerous behavior that provides a basis for reasonably accurate short-term assessments of risk. The use of structured risk assessment, whether through the use of a specialized actuarial risk assessment measure or a tool using structured professional judgment, can increase predictive accuracy beyond what is possible with unstructured judgment.

KEY TERMS

advance medical directives	dangerousness	joint custody	punitive damages
breached duty	duty	malingering	risk assessments
civil commitment	future best interests of the child	negligence	sole custody
civil competencies	harm	proximate cause	testamentary capacity
compensatory damages	intentional behavior	psychological autopsies	tort

10

The Trial Process

ORIENTING QUESTIONS

1. What is the purpose of a trial?
2. What are the steps the legal system follows in bringing a case to trial?
3. What is the order of procedures in the trial itself?
4. How has the introduction of emerging technologies changed the way that trials are conducted?
5. How do juries' verdicts differ from those of judges?

Box 10.1   THE CASE OF BRUNO RICHARD HAUPTMANN: ARGUMENTS AND EVIDENCE

Even though the trial occurred more than 70 years ago, people still talk about it, books are still being published about it, and critics still speculate about whether the verdict was just (Behn, 1995; Berg, 1998). The offense has been termed one of the "crimes of the century" (Geis & Bienen, 1998).

Sometime during the night of March 1, 1932, the young son of Colonel Charles A. Lindbergh was kidnapped from a crib in the nursery of his parents' estate in Hopewell, New Jersey. Lindbergh, who ironically had been called "Lucky Lindy," was the first person to complete a solo flight from the United States to Europe.

A month after the baby's kidnapping, Col. Lindbergh, through a go-between, paid $50,000 to a shadowy figure he had arranged to meet in a Bronx, New York, cemetery; Lindbergh had been assured that the kidnapper would return the child unharmed. But two months after the kidnapping, the baby's body was found in a shallow grave about five miles from Lindbergh's home. His skull had been bashed in.

For more than two years, the police and the FBI sought the criminal. They found several physical clues, including ransom notes, footprints under a first-floor window, and a makeshift ladder apparently used to climb to the second-floor nursery, but it was not until September 19, 1934, that police arrested Bruno Hauptmann and charged him with the crime. Hauptmann, 34 at the time, was German-born and was in the United States illegally.

Lindberghs

The trial took place in Flemington, New Jersey, in 1935. Public interest was intense; hundreds of reporters crowded into the small courthouse to cover the trial. Radio stations retained well-known attorneys to broadcast their opinions about the progress of the case—commonplace now but unheard of at that time. The whole country seemed to harbor a deep-felt desire that the defendant be convicted and executed (and he was). But was Bruno Hauptmann actually guilty? Here are the arguments and evidence that each side used in his trial. What do you think?

WHAT IS THE PURPOSE OF A TRIAL?

Every trial, civil or criminal, presents two contrasting versions of the truth, just as the Hauptmann trial did. Both sides try to present the "facts" in question in such a way as to convince the judge or the jury that their claims are true. The judge or jury must render judgments on the probable truth or falsity of each side's statements and evidence.

The jury system evolved from an ancient ritual during which a defendant stood before a priest, surrounded by friends who swore that the defendant had not committed the crime. But the victim also brought friends who swore to just the opposite (Kadri, 2005). Because this arrangement was not especially satisfactory to anyone, the English monarchy began to have defendants appear in front of a panel of citizens whose task was to swear to the innocence or guilt of the defendant.

If we are asked about the purpose of a modern trial, our first response might be "to determine the truth, of course." But is this really the prime function of a trial? In fact, trials also serve other purposes: They provide a sense of stability and a way to resolve conflicts so that the disputants can receive satisfaction. Miller and Boster (1977) have identified three images of the trial that reflect these contrasting conceptions.

In the Lindbergh kidnapping trial, the prosecution presented the following evidence and arguments:

1. A thorough search of Hauptmann's garage revealed $14,600 of the Lindbergh ransom money secreted in an extraordinary hiding place.
2. In examining one of the ransom bills, the FBI discovered written on it an automobile license plate number—that of a car registered to Hauptmann.
3. Written on a strip of wood in a closet in Hauptmann's house was the telephone number of the man who served as an intermediary in the transport of the ransom money.
4. When the police dictated to Hauptmann the contents of the ransom notes and asked him to transcribe them, he misspelled certain words, just as the author of the notes had. (The wording of the notes—such as "The child is in gut care"—implied that they had been composed by a German-speaking person.)
5. Hauptmann stopped work on the very day the ransom was paid and never thereafter resumed steady employment. He bragged to friends that he could live without working because he knew how to beat the stock market, although in actuality he was losing money (Whipple, 1937).
6. Wood from the makeshift ladder could have come from a portion of the floorboards of Hauptmann's attic that had been removed.

The defense presented the following responses:

1. Several witnesses testified that they saw Hauptmann in the Bronx, New York, on the night of the kidnapping, implying that he could not have kidnapped the baby.
2. Expert witnesses claimed that the wood on the makeshift ladder did not match that from the attic.
3. The ransom money in his garage, Hauptmann said, had belonged to a friend who had returned to Germany and then died, so he had kept the money safely hidden.
4. Hauptmann claimed that when the police dictated the ransom notes to him, they insisted that he spell the words as they were spelled in the notes. He knew, for example, that *boat* was not spelled "boad," as it was on the notes.

Hauptmann proclaimed his innocence to the day he died. So did his wife, who for 60 years sought to reverse the decision. In 1985, the U.S. Third Circuit Court of Appeals rejected her request to reinstitute a lawsuit against the state of New Jersey for wrongfully trying and convicting her husband. In that same year, a book by Ludovic Kennedy (1985) concluded that the prosecution withheld evidence, perjured its witnesses, and capitalized on the public mood in order to frame Hauptmann. A more recent review of the case (Behn, 1995) reconsiders early speculation that Mrs. Lindbergh's sister was the real murderer.

The Trial as a Search for the Truth

Many people see a trial as a rule-governed event involving the parties' collective search for the truth (Miller & Boster, 1977). This view assumes that what really happened can be clearly ascertained—that witnesses are capable of knowing, remembering, and describing events completely and accurately. Although this image of the trial recognizes that the opposing attorneys present only those facts that buttress their positions, it assumes that the truth will emerge from the confrontation of conflicting facts. It also assumes that judges or jurors, in weighing these facts, can "lay aside their prejudices and preconceived views regarding the case and replace such biases with a dispassionate analysis of the arguments and evidence" (Miller & Boster, 1977, p. 25).

But this image of the trial as a rational, rule-governed event has been challenged on several grounds. Chapter 5 questioned the assumption that eyewitnesses are thorough and accurate reporters, as the legal system would like to believe. We saw in Chapter 6 that interrogations can sometimes result in false confessions and that jurors are not particularly good at distinguishing false confessions from true confessions. Sections of Chapters 11 and 12 review the limitations of jurors and judges as they seek to put aside their own experiences and prejudices.

Attorney questioning a witness during a trial

Although this image of the trial remains as an inspiring ideal, other images need to be considered as well.

The Trial as a Test of Credibility

A second conception—that the trial is a test of credibility—acknowledges that facts and evidence are always incomplete and biased. Hence the decision makers, whether judge or jury, must not only weigh the information and evidence but also evaluate the truthfulness of the opposing sources of evidence (Miller & Boster, 1977). They must focus on the way evidence is presented, the qualifications of witnesses, and the inconsistencies between witnesses. Competence and trustworthiness of witnesses take on added importance in this image.

The image of the trial as a test of credibility also has problems. Both judges and jurors can make unwarranted inferences about witnesses and attorneys on the basis of race, gender, mannerisms, or style of speech. Judges' and jurors' judgments of credibility may be based more on stereotypes, folklore, or "commonsense intuition" than on the facts.

The Trial as a Conflict-Resolving Ritual

The first two images share the belief that the primary function of a trial is to produce the most nearly valid judgment about the guilt of a criminal defendant or the responsibility of a civil defendant. The third image shifts the function of the trial from determining the truth to providing a mechanism to resolve controversies. Miller and Boster (1977) express it this way: "At the risk of oversimplification we suggest that it removes primary attention from the concept of doing justice and transfers it to the psychological realm of *creating a sense that justice is being done*" (p. 34). Truth remains a goal, but participants in the trial process also need both the opportunity to have their "day in court" and the reassurance that, whatever the outcome, "justice was done." In other words, they need closure that only a trial can provide.

A trial conducted in Oklahoma in 2004 exemplified this desire for closure. Several years before, Oklahoma City bombing suspect Terry Nichols was convicted on federal charges and sentenced to life in prison, rather than to death (his codefendant, Timothy McVeigh, was executed in 2001). An Oklahoma prosecutor, responding to some victims' families who were eager to see Nichols also put to death, charged him in state court with 161 counts of first-degree murder (for the 160 people and one fetus who were killed in the blast) and requested the death penalty. But Nichols was again spared execution when this second jury, despite convicting him, deadlocked over his sentence. By law, Nichols was sentenced (again) to life in prison—161 consecutive life sentences, to be exact—and those families hoping for closure were disappointed (again).

The stabilizing function of a trial is worthless, of course, if the public doubts that justice was done in the process. That sense of closure is sometimes missing after a trial; the widespread dissatisfaction in some segments of our society with the outcome of O. J. Simpson's criminal trial (Brigham & Wasserman, 1999) ensured continued media interest and public fascination with his actions and statements. The belief that "he got away with murder" even led to proposals to reform and restrict the jury system. Other segments of society were equally dissatisfied with the verdict in Simpson's civil trial, in which he was found liable for the deaths of his ex-wife and her friend Ronald Goldman. Perhaps together, the verdicts in the two trials converged on a reasonable outcome—Simpson probably was the killer, but this couldn't be proven **beyond a reasonable doubt**, the level of certainty required for a criminal conviction.

These three contrasting images are guideposts for interpreting the findings presented in this and the next two chapters. Truth is elusive, and in the legal system, all truth seekers are subject to human error, even though the system seems to assume that they approach infallibility. The failure to achieve perfection in our decision making will become evident as we review the steps in the trial process.

STEPS IN THE TRIAL PROCESS

The usual steps in a trial are sketched out here as a framework for issues to be evaluated in this and the next two chapters.

Preliminary Actions

In Chapter 7, we discussed **discovery**, the pretrial process by which each side tries to gain vital information about the case that will be presented by the other side. This information includes statements by witnesses, police records, documents, material possessions, experts' opinions, and anything else relevant to the case.

The U.S. Constitution provides criminal defendants with the right to have the charges against them judged by a jury of their peers. But a defendant could decide instead to have the case decided by a judge. Although most defendants opt for a jury trial, some choose to waive a jury trial and, if the prosecutor agrees, have a judge decide the case. Does it make any difference? We answer this important question in a later section of this chapter.

Civil lawsuits may also be decided by either a jury or a judge, depending on the preferences of the opposing parties. Many states have revised the size and **decision rule** from the traditional 12-person jury requiring a unanimous verdict. In some states, for some kinds of civil cases, juries as small as six persons or decision rules requiring only a three-fourths majority are in effect.

Jury Selection

If the trial is before a jury, the selection of jurors involves a two-step process. The first step is to draw a panel of prospective jurors, called a *venire*, from a large list (usually based on voter registration lists and lists of licensed drivers). Once the *venire* for a particular trial has been selected—this may be anywhere from 30 to 200 people, depending on the customary practices of that jurisdiction and the nature of the trial—a process known as *voir dire* is employed to question and select the eventual jurors. Prospective jurors who reveal biases and are unable to be open-minded about the case are dismissed from service, so the task of jury selection is really one of elimination. Prospective jurors who appear free of these limitations are thus "selected." *Voir dire* can have important effects on the outcome of the trial; we describe the process in detail in Chapter 11.

The Trial

All trials—whether related to criminal law or to civil law—include similar procedural steps. At the beginning of the trial itself, lawyers for each side are permitted to make **opening statements**. These are not part of the evidence, but they serve as overviews of the evidence to be presented. The prosecution or plaintiff usually goes first, because this side is the one that brought charges and bears the burden of proof. Attorneys for the defendant, in either a criminal or civil trial, can choose to present their opening statement immediately after the other side's or to wait until it is their turn to present evidence.

Some psychologists have wondered whether the timing of the opening statement matters. In other words, would it be preferable for the defense attorney (and more beneficial to the defendant) if the defense's opening statement immediately followed the prosecutor's opening statement or would it be better to wait until all of the prosecution witnesses had testified? Their study, using a mock jury simulation, varied the timing of the defense opening statement in an auto theft case (Wells, Wrightsman, & Miene, 1985). The results were striking: When the defense opening statement was given earlier rather than later, verdicts were more favorable to the defense, and the perceived effectiveness of the defense attorney was enhanced. Defense attorneys who take their first opportunity to make an opening statement can apparently counter the story told by the prosecutor or at least urge jurors to consider an alternative interpretation of the evidence.

After opening statements, the prosecution or plaintiff calls its witnesses. Each witness testifies under oath, with the threat of a charge of **perjury** if the witness fails to be truthful. That witness is then cross-examined by the opposing attorney, after which the original attorney has a chance for **redirect questioning**. Redirect questioning is likely if the original attorney feels the opposition has "impeached" his or her witness; **impeach** in this context refers to a cross-examination that has effectively called into question the credibility (or reliability) of the witness.

The purpose of redirect examination is to "rehabilitate" the witness, or to salvage his or her original testimony. The defense, however, has one more chance to question the witness, a process called **recross** (short for "re-cross-examination"). After the prosecution's or plaintiff's attorneys have presented all their witnesses, it is the defense's turn. The same procedure of direct examination, cross-examination, redirect, and recross is used. After both sides have presented their witnesses, one or both may decide to introduce additional evidence and witnesses and so asks the judge for permission to present **rebuttal evidence**, which attempts to counteract or disprove evidence given by an earlier witness.

Once all the evidence has been presented, each side is permitted to make a **closing argument**, also called a summation. Although jurisdictions vary, typically the prosecution or plaintiff gets the first summation, followed by the defense, after which the prosecution or plaintiff responds and has the final word.

The final step in the jury trial is for the judge to give instructions to the jury. (In some states, instructions precede the closing arguments.) The judge informs the jury of the relevant law. For example, a definition of the crime is given, as well as a statement of what elements must be present for it to have occurred—that is, whether the defendant had the motive and the opportunity to commit the crime. The judge also instructs jurors about the standard they should use to weigh the evidence. We discuss jury instructions in more detail in Chapter 12.

With criminal charges, the jurors must be convinced beyond a reasonable doubt that the defendant is guilty before they vote to convict. Although the concept of "reasonable doubt" is difficult to interpret, generally it means that jurors should be strongly convinced (but not necessarily convinced beyond *all* doubt). Each of us interprets such an instruction differently, and as Chapter 12 illustrates, this instruction is often a source of confusion and frustration among jurors.

In a civil trial, in which one party brings a claim against another, a different standard is used. The **preponderance of the evidence** is all that is necessary for a finding in favor of one side. Usually, judges and attorneys translate this to mean, "Even if you find the evidence favoring one side to be only slightly more convincing than the other side's, rule in favor of that side." Preponderance is sometimes interpreted as meaning at least 51% of the evidence, though it is difficult to quantify a concept that is expressed verbally.

The jury is sometimes given instructions on how to deliberate, but these are usually sparse. Jurors are excused to the deliberation room, and no one—not even the bailiff or the judge—can be present during or eavesdrop on their deliberations. When the jury has reached its verdict, its foreperson informs the bailiff, who informs the judge, who reconvenes the attorneys and defendants (and plaintiffs in a civil trial) for announcement of the verdict.

Now that we've detailed the steps involved in trials, we consider the advantages accorded by these procedures to the prosecution and the defense in criminal trials. You will notice that opposing sides have roughly offsetting advantages. For example, the prosecution gets the first and last chance to address the judge or jury, but it also has the burden of proving its case. The defense, on the other hand, is not given the opportunity to speak first or to speak last. But it has the advantage of not needing to prove anything to the judge or jury. If the prosecution is unable to meet its obligation to convince the judge or jury of the defendant's guilt, then the defendant prevails. What other advantages does each side have in a criminal case?

The prosecution, in its efforts to convict wrongdoers and bring justice to bear, has several advantages including these:

1. It has the full resources of the government at its disposal to carry out a prosecution. Detectives can locate witnesses and subpoena them. The prosecutor can request testimony from chemists, fingerprint examiners, medical examiners, psychiatrists, photographers, or whoever is an appropriate expert.

2. In the trial itself, the prosecution presents its evidence before the defense, getting "first crack" at the jury. In presenting opening statements, which are not evidence but do provide a structure for the entire trial, the prosecution always goes first. At the end of the trial, when both sides are permitted closing arguments (again, not part of the evidence), the prosecution again gets to go first and also gets the chance to offer a final rebuttal to the defense attorney's closing argument. Therefore, the prosecution has the advantages of both *primacy* and *recency* in its attempts at jury persuasion, and research shows that information presented first (primacy) and last (recency) has more persuasive influence than information presented in the middle of a discussion.

Trial procedures also provide defendants with certain benefits including the following:

1. The defense is entitled to "discovery"; the prosecution must turn over exculpatory evidence (evidence that would tend to absolve the defendant), but the defense does not have to turn over incriminating evidence.

2. If a trial is before a jury, the defense may have more opportunities than the prosecution to remove potential jurors without giving a reason. We describe this process in further detail in Chapter 11.

3. Defendants do not have to take the stand as witnesses on their own behalf. In fact, they do not have to put on any defense at all; the burden is on the prosecution to prove beyond a reasonable doubt that the defendant is guilty of the crime.

4. Defendants who are found not guilty can never be tried again for that specific crime. For example, National Basketball Association star Jayson Williams was acquitted on the charge of aggravated manslaughter in the death of a chauffeur at his mansion. (In a confusing

verdict, the jury did convict Williams of trying to cover up the man's death as a suicide, hindering apprehension, and fabricating evidence.) But even if clear evidence of Williams' guilt on the manslaughter charge comes to light at some time in the future, he can never be retried for that offense.

Sentencing

If the defendant in a criminal trial is judged guilty, a punishment must be decided. In the vast majority of jurisdictions, the trial judge makes this decision. In the past, judges have had wide discretion to impose sentences by taking into account all they knew about the defendant and his actions, regardless of whether those actions constituted a crime or were proven to a jury. But in a landmark 2004 decision, the U.S. Supreme Court ruled that judges may not increase defendants' sentences on the basis of what they perceive as aggravating factors (circumstances that seem to make the "crime" worse). In *Blakely v. Washington* (2004), the Court reserved those determinations for juries.

The ruling came from a case in which the defendant, Ralph Blakely, pled guilty to kidnapping his estranged wife, a crime that carried a penalty of 53 months. But the judge, after deciding that Blakely acted with "deliberate cruelty"—a circumstance that Blakely had not admitted and that no jury had decided—increased his sentence to 90 months. In overturning this sentence (and thereby striking down dozens of state sentencing laws and potentially affecting thousands of cases), the Court said the imposition of additional time violated Mr. Blakely's right to a jury trial.

In a handful of states, sentencing is determined by a jury. After the verdict is rendered, the jury is reconvened, and attorneys present evidence relevant to the sentencing decision. The jury then deliberates until it agrees on a recommended punishment. In cases involving the death penalty (described in Chapter 14), jurors, rather than judges, decide the sentence (*Ring v. Arizona*, 2002).

The Appellate Process

Treatment of guilty defendants within the legal system does not end when they are sentenced to a prison term or to probation. To protect the rights of those who may have been convicted unjustly, society grants any defendant the opportunity to appeal a verdict to a higher level of courts. Appeals are also possible in virtually every civil suit.

As in earlier steps in the legal process, a conflict of values occurs as appeals are pursued. One goal is equality before the law—that is, to administer justice consistently and fairly. But appellate courts also try to be sensitive to individual differences in what at first appear to be similar cases. Appellate courts recognize that judges and juries can make errors. The appellate process can correct mistakes that impair the fairness of trials; it also helps promote a level of consistency in trial procedures.

When a decision is appealed to a higher court, the appellate judges read the record (the transcript of the trial proceedings), the pleadings (motions and accompanying documents filed by the attorneys), and the briefs (written arguments, which are rarely brief, from both sides about the issues on appeal) and then decide whether to overturn the original trial decision or to let it stand. Appellate judges rarely reverse a verdict on the basis of the facts of the case or the apparent legitimacy of that verdict. When they do reverse, it is usually because they believe that the trial judge made a procedural error, such as allowing controversial evidence to be presented or failing to allow the jury to consider some evidence that should have been included.

If a verdict in a criminal trial is overturned or reversed, the appeals court will either order a retrial or order the charges thrown out. In reviewing the decision in a civil case, an appellate court can let the decision stand, reverse it (rule in favor of the side that lost rather than the side that won), or make some other changes in the decision and remand (return) the case to a lower court for reconsideration. One possible conclusion in either civil or criminal appeals is that certain evidence should not have been admitted or that certain instructions should not have been given; hence, a new trial may be ordered.

Courtroom of the Future

With only minor variations, courtroom trials and appeals have followed these procedures for much of our nation's history. The trials of Bruno Hauptmann, John Scopes (tried in 1925 for teaching the theory of evolution in a Tennessee public school science class), Julius and Ethel Rosenberg (tried in 1951 on espionage charges), and defendants facing charges across the United States today all follow essentially the same format. But recently, the introduction of emerging technologies in the legal system has begun to change the face of trials. Today, juries and judges expect attorneys to use more than yellow legal pads and grainy videos. Many jurors, especially younger jurors and those who are more tech-savvy, now expect to see and hear multimedia approaches (Griffin, 2008), and some judges want all documents presented during a trial to be scanned and displayed electronically. The courtroom of the future will look very different from that of the past; some contend that it is already here (Wiggins, 2006). We describe one case that incorporated some of these new technologies in Box 10.2.

New technologies being used in courts these days include:

- videoconferencing that permits live, two-way video and audio communication between hearings and trials in courtrooms and remote sites—useful when witnesses and defendants are medically incapacitated, incarcerated, or unavailable during the trial;

- electronic and digital evidence such as digital recordings, documents, and photographs that allow judges and jurors to easily observe the evidence themselves, rather than hear others' descriptions of it;

- computer animations and simulations that feature computer-generated depictions of complex physical events like accidents and crimes, often accompanied by voice-overs from participants in the event; and

- virtual environment technologies that allow observers to experience a re-creation of an event as if they were actually present when it occurred. Using video game technology,

---

B o x 10.2 THE CASE OF U.S. ARMY STAFF SERGEANT TERRENCE DILLON IN VIRTUAL REALITY

To treat his high cholesterol levels, U.S. Army Staff Sergeant Terrence Dillon underwent a surgical procedure in February 2002, in which doctors implanted a "new life stent." The stent was designed to cleanse blood of cholesterol and to dissolve cholesterol-forming plaque blocking the arteries. But for Dillon, the stent worked too well, loosening large amounts of plaque that clogged his circulatory system and causing a stroke. Dillon died in March, 2002. Shortly thereafter, the stent's manufacturer, NewLife MedTech, was criminally indicted for manslaughter (Horrigan, 2002).

In truth, none of this actually happened. But these facts served as the basis for a simulated trial, one feature of a legal technology program dubbed "Courtroom 21 Project" by the National Center for State Courts. The project provides technology information to lawyers and judges.

During the "trial," the defense argued that New-Life MedTech was not at fault and that blame lay with the surgeon who allegedly placed the stent in the wrong part of the artery. To bolster that argument, the defense offered the testimony of a nurse who donned a virtual reality headset and specialized goggles, giving him a three-dimensional view of the operating room and allowing him to describe the stent's placement. The prosecution countered by arguing that because the nurse's view of the surgery was obstructed, he was unable to see where the stent had been implanted. Because virtual environment technology allowed jurors themselves to watch a reenactment of the surgery on laptops, they could decide for themselves what the nurse was able to observe. Images were also projected to wide-screen monitors in the courtroom, allowing the judge, lawyers, trial-watchers, and even observers outside the courtroom to view the virtual operation and reach their own conclusions. Whether NewLife MedTech was convicted is largely irrelevant; the noteworthy fact is that the "trial" introduced many people to the courtroom of the future.

so-called "virtual reality" allows judges and jurors to "virtually" walk through a crime scene or accident site to gauge for themselves what could be seen from different points of view and under relevant lighting conditions.

Each of these high-tech methods raises interesting and complex psychological questions. What effect does remote viewing have on a judge's or juror's ability to determine whether a witness is credible and sincere? Are nuances of body language and verbal expression adequately captured in video-conferencing or are they missing? Does the person testifying at a remote site—a setting that lacks the trappings and formality of a courtroom—feel less obligated to show respect and tell the truth? Would courtroom participants with high-tech experience put more emphasis than others on digital media presented during a trial? Would their voices carry more weight in the deliberation room? Do computer animations, simulations, and virtual reality re-enactments make difficult or technical concepts easier to visualize and, hence, to understand? Might they also serve to cement one version of a contested event in observers' minds, making it harder to construe alternative explanations? In other words, might observers assume that animations, simulations, and virtual realities represent true and uncontroversial facts, rather than just one party's theory of the case (Wiggins, 2006)?

Psychologists have begun to address some of these questions. One study examined the effects of computer animations on jurors' verdicts (Dunn, Salovey, & Feigenson, 2006). In cases involving a plane crash and an automobile accident, mock jurors saw either a computer-animated display of the crash site or a diagram of the scene. Further, the use of animations and diagrams by the plaintiff and defendant was varied, resulting in four versions of the mock trial: (1) plaintiff animation/defendant animation, (2) plaintiff animation/defendant diagram, (3) plaintiff diagram/defendant animation, and (4) plaintiff diagram/defendant diagram.

The results of these variations on verdicts in the plane crash case were unambiguous: When the plaintiff presented an animation and the defendant

had only a diagram, 68% of jurors voted in favor of the plaintiff whereas when both plaintiff and defendant used diagrams, only 32% sided with the plaintiff. At least in this case, the animation increased the ease by which participants could visualize the events leading up to the crash, allowing the plaintiff to persuade them about the merits of his case (see Figure 10.1). (Interestingly, in the car accident case, the animations had far less impact on jurors' verdicts, probably because few of us need help in visualizing automobile accidents, unfortunately!)

Why do animations persuade people in ways that diagrams cannot? Basic psychological theorizing about the **vividness effect** suggests that information has a greater impact on judgments and decisions when it is vivid and attention-grabbing than when it is pallid and bland. Information presented in a highly imaginable way is more persuasive than simple verbal descriptions of the same material.

Virtual environments have also piqued psychologists' interests in the notion of **presence**, or the degree to which a user or observer has the

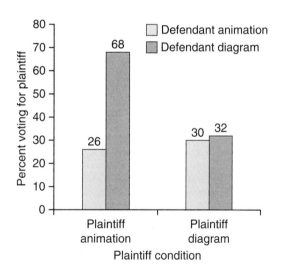

FIGURE 10.1 Percentage of participants in Experiment 1 who rendered a verdict in favor of the plaintiff

Source: Dunn, M., Salovey, P., & Feigenson, N. (2006). The jury persuaded (and not): Computer animation in the courtroom. *Law & Policy, 28,* 228–248 (Figure is on p. 233).

impression of actually "being in another world" and present in the virtual environment. For virtual environments to be effective, they should realistically create this alternate reality. But think for a moment about how to objectively measure whether someone is experiencing an alternative reality. It quickly becomes clear why, despite efforts to capture the subjective experience of being present in another world, objective measures are, at present, lacking (Bailenson, Blascovich, Beall, & Noveck, 2006).

A concern about the use of virtual environments in court is that people who witness them may be so swept up in the experience and persuaded by the lifelike nature of these scenes that they have difficulty imagining or visualizing a different point of view. This notion, termed **experiential inflammatory bias**, suggests that in the least, both sides in a trial should be able to manipulate and alter any virtual environment introduced into evidence (Bailenson et al., 2006).

Although virtual environment technology is not yet routinely used in actual trials, that day may arrive soon. Indeed, proponents believe that the technology is already mature enough to warrant its use in court: "If a picture is worth a thousand words, then a … virtual reality simulation should be worth at least ten thousand" (Bailenson et al., 2006, p. 265). The day has already arrived for animations, simulations, remote videoconferencing and other forms of digitally presented evidence. To what extent they will alter the way that trials are conducted is a question that will concern psychologists for some time to come.

JUDGES' DECISIONS VERSUS JURIES' DECISIONS

As noted earlier, defendants in criminal trials ordinarily opt for a jury to decide their guilt or innocence, but if the prosecutor consents, they can choose to have a judge decide. Such a proceeding is called a **bench trial**. Three New York City police officers charged with the shooting death of Sean Bell in November 2006 opted for a bench trial. Bell and two friends died in a barrage of police bullets while standing outside a Queens strip club just hours before Bell's wedding. Learning of the officers' request, Reverend Al Sharpton remarked "I think that it is stunning that these officers want to do everything but be accountable to the people they serve in Queens. [T]hey do not want to face a jury of their peers whom they serve and by whom they are paid." The police officers apparently gambled correctly: the New York judge who presided over their trial acquitted all three.

Why do some defendants (and, in civil cases, some plaintiffs) choose to have their case decided by a jury and others opt for a judge? A survey (MacCoun & Tyler, 1988) found that citizens believe a jury decision offers more procedural fairness (greater thoroughness, better representation of the community, fewer personal biases affecting decisions) than a decision by a judge.

Does it matter who decides? Do juries and judges generally agree with each other? When they disagree, can we say who made the better decision? Of course, jury verdicts are not systematically compared against some "correct," back-of-the-book answer—even if there were such a thing (which there is not!). Fortunately, we can rely on survey data to estimate how frequently judges and jurors agree and why they might disagree.

Harry Kalven and Hans Zeisel (1966), professors at the University of Chicago, carried out an extensive survey of the outcomes of jury trials. In a classic application of the methods of social science to understand legal decisions, Kalven and Zeisel asked each district court judge and federal judge in the United States to provide information about recent jury trials over which he or she had presided. Of approximately 3500 judges, only about 500 responded to a detailed questionnaire. But some judges provided information about a large number of trials—some, amazingly, about more than 50 trials—so the database for this analysis consisted of approximately 3500 trials.

Two questions are relevant to our discussion: (1) What was the jury's verdict? and (2) Did the judge agree? By considering the frequency of this agreement, we can get hints about the extent of juries' deviations from "correct" application of the law.

T A B L E 10.1 **Agreement of Judges' and Juries' Verdicts Based on 3576 Criminal Trials (in percentage of all trials)**

Judge's Verdict	Jury's Verdict		
	Acquit	Convict	Hung
Acquit	**13.4**	2.2	1.1
Convict	16.9	**62.0**	4.4

SOURCE: Adapted from Kalven and Zeisel (1966, p. 56). Figures in bold show cases in which judge and jury were in agreement on the verdict.

T A B L E 10.2 **Agreement of Judges' and Juries' Decisions in Civil Trials (in percentage of all trials)**

Judge Finds For:	Jury Finds for:	
	Plaintiff	Defendant
Plaintiff	**47**	10
Defendant	12	**31**

SOURCE: Adapted from Kalven and Zeisel (1966, p. 63). Figures in bold show cases in which judge and jury were in agreement on the verdict.

In criminal trials, the judges reported that their verdict would have been the same as the jury's actual verdict in 75% of the cases (see Table 10.1 for detailed results). Thus, in three-fourths of the trials, two independent fact-finding agents would have brought forth the same result. Similar consistency was found for civil trials, as illustrated in Table 10.2. Although each of us may have our own opinion about the desirability of this level of agreement, it does suggest that jurors are not deviating to a great extent from their mandate to follow the judge's instructions about the law and use only that information plus the actual evidence to reach their verdict.

We might speculate on what is an optimal level of agreement between judge and jury. What if they agreed 100% of the time? That undesirable outcome would indicate that the jury was a rubber stamp of the judge. But if judge and jury agreed only 50% of the time, given only two possible outcomes of guilty and not guilty (putting aside "hung" juries momentarily), it would reflect a level of agreement no better than that which would occur by chance. (Two independent agents, choosing yes or no at random, would agree 50% of the time by chance alone.) Appropriately

enough, the 75% level of agreement is halfway between chance and perfect agreement.

Among the 25% of the criminal cases in which there was disagreement, 5.5% resulted in hung juries; that is, the jury members could not agree on a verdict. Thus, it is more appropriate to say that in only 19.5% of the criminal cases did the jury return a guilty verdict where the judge would have ruled not guilty, or vice versa.

In most of these discrepant decisions, the jury was more lenient than the judge. The judge would have convicted the defendant in 83.3% of these cases, whereas the jury convicted in only 64.2% of them. For every trial in which the jury convicted and the judge would have acquitted, there were almost eight trials in which the reverse was true.

Determinants of Discrepancies

What accounts for the discrepancies between judge and jury? For their sample of cases, Kalven and Zeisel unfortunately had only one source to answer this question: the judge's opinion. On this basis, they offer a classification of cases.

A few of these discrepancies apparently resulted from facts that one party knew but the other did not. For example, in several cases, the judge was aware of the defendant's prior arrest record (a matter not introduced into evidence) and would have found him guilty, but the jury acquitted him. The reverse situation can also occur. Especially in a small community, a member of the jury might share with fellow jurors some information about a witness or the defendant that was not part of evidence and was not known to the judge at the time.

A second, smaller source of judge/jury discrepancies was the relative effectiveness of the two attorneys. In some trials, the jury was swayed by the apparent superiority of one lawyer over the other and produced a verdict that was, at least in the judge's opinion, contrary to the weight of the evidence. If this is a generalizable finding, it is a matter of some concern. At the same time, it is not surprising that some portion of jury verdicts would have such determinants because, as we describe in the next chapter, jurors are sometimes affected by information that is not truly "evidence."

An example of information that is not truly "evidence" but that may affect jurors differently than judges is the "CSI effect." Given the popularity of *CSI (Crime Scene Investigation)* and two spinoffs, *CSI: Miami* and *CSI: New York,* CBS shows that are consistently near the top of the Nielsen ratings, laypeople have apparently come to expect that forensic evidence will be provided in most criminal cases. (Many prosecutors now believe that they have lost cases in which the evidence was sufficient to sustain a conviction but in which forensic evidence—mitochondrial DNA, latent prints, and trace evidence—was unavailable.) This expectation of plentiful scientific evidence biases some jurors' perceptions of the evidence (Reardon & O'Neil, 2008). In one case, Arizona corrections officers found a syringe in a cell with the name "Jimbo" written on it. An inmate nicknamed Jimbo was nearby with a fresh mark on his arm consistent with syringe use and even admitted that the syringe was his. Still, jurors were unimpressed. They told the prosecutor that they wanted DNA or fingerprint analysis of the syringe and

handwriting analysis of the written label! Judges are much less likely to expect that forensic evidence will be produced and tend not to hold it against prosecutors when it is absent.

But judge/jury discrepancies may also arise when the two disagree about the evidence that *is* presented. In cases in which the evidence is evenly balanced, it is inevitable that the judge will occasionally disagree with the jury and it is often unclear whether the judge or the jury has reached the "correct" verdict (MacCoun, 1999).

Consider a case of theft in which there is a solitary eyewitness and the accused person claims mistaken identity. In a "bare-bones" case like this, the issue boils down to whom one really believes. The judge may trust the eyewitness more; the jurors may give the defendant the benefit of their collective doubt. In such cases, judge and jury may differ in their estimates of the probability that the defendant committed the crime. On such matters, there can be honest disagreement. (In fact, two judges could disagree over these issues.)

Jury Sentiments

Perhaps the most important explanation of judge/jury differences, accounting for roughly half of the disagreements, involves what Kalven and Zeisel called **jury sentiments**. They used this term to cover all trials in which, *in the judge's view,* the jury's verdict was detrimentally determined by factors beyond the evidence and the law. (There is an implicit assumption here that the judge's decision was free of sentiments—a dubious claim, given that judges are also all-too-human and subject to the same predispositions as the rest of us.)

In what situations do jurors' sentiments play a role? Sometimes, jurors feel that the "crime" is just too trivial for any punishment or at least for the expected punishment, and hence they find the defendant not guilty, thus making sure that he or she will not be punished. In one case, a man was brought to trial for stealing two frankfurters. Because this was his second crime, he would have been sentenced to prison. Whereas the judge would have found him guilty, the jury voted 10–2 for acquittal.

In other instances, jurors believe that the defendant had already been sufficiently sanctioned and that punishment by the legal system is therefore unnecessary. Here is an example: In a case of income tax evasion, the following series of misfortunes plagued the defendant between the crime and the trial: "His home burned, he was seriously injured, and his son was killed. Later he lost his leg, his wife became seriously ill, and several major operations were necessary.... his wife gave birth to a child who was both blind and spastic" (Kalven & Zeisel, 1966, p. 305). The jury found the defendant not guilty of income tax evasion, apparently concluding that he had already suffered divine retribution. The judge would have found him guilty.

Jurors sometime acquit because they believe that a law is unfair. In trials for the sale of beer and liquor to minors who were in the military, juries have concluded that there was minimal social harm. Apparently they felt that if a young man can be forced to die for his country, "he can buy and consume a bottle of beer" (Kalven & Zeisel, 1966, p. 273). We discuss this concept in more detail in Chapter 12.

In actuality, jury sentiments have surfaced in many types of cases involving "unpopular" crimes— for example, in small misdemeanors such as gambling and in so-called victimless crimes such as prostitution. Often the jurors' brusque announcement of a not-guilty verdict, when technically the defendant had committed a crime, was their way of expressing frustration. "Why waste our time over such minor affairs?" they might have been thinking.

As noted in Table 10.2, the level of agreement between the jury and the judge is also high in civil trials. Judges report that their verdict would have favored the side favored by the jury in 78% of the civil suits analyzed by Kalven and Zeisel. Also important is the nearly equal likelihood of finding for the plaintiff; the jury ruled for the plaintiff in 59% of the cases, whereas the judge did so in 57%.

These figures are a healthy empirical response to the critics (Huber, 1990; Olson, 1991) who conclude that in civil suits, especially those involving personal injury claims, juries are overly sympathetic to plaintiffs. In fact, in certain kinds of cases, plaintiffs who go to trial before juries win infrequently, a matter that we address further in Chapter 12.

Juries do occasionally make high awards to injured plaintiffs, sometimes higher than what judges would award (Hersch & Viscusi, 2004). These are the decisions that are publicized in our newspapers and on talk shows (Bailis & MacCoun, 1996). But in controlled studies, most juries make decisions— verdicts and awards—quite akin to those made by judges and experienced lawyers, and there is little evidence that juries are especially pro-plaintiff, as several critics have claimed. In fact, some would argue that because the jury can apply its sense of community standards to a case, its award of damages in a civil case might actually be more fitting than a judge's award: "The appreciation of pain and suffering, and the likely impact on an individual's life and his or her ability to earn a living, are not matters which judges are any more qualified to assess than is a member of the public applying his or her life experience" (Watson, 1996, p. 457). Any disagreement between judge and jury that *does* exist might be better attributed to the jury's interest in fairness, its consideration of a range of factors that might be broader than those considered by an individual judge, or its emotional closeness to the parties in the case, than to its lack of competence (Shuman & Champagne, 1997).

A Critique of the Kalven and Zeisel Study

The study by Kalven and Zeisel described in *The American Jury* (1966) was a massive undertaking supported by a $1.4 million grant from the Ford Foundation (Hans & Vidmar, 1991). But the actual data were collected between 1954 and 1961, and in the intervening decades, the methodological limitations of the study have become increasingly apparent:

1. Judges were permitted to choose which trial or trials they reported. Did they tend to pick those cases in which they disagreed with the jury, thus causing the sample's result to misrepresent the true extent of judge/jury disagreement? We do not know.

2. Only 555 judges out of 3500 provided responses to the survey; half of the cases in the study were provided by only 15% of the judges—an unrepresentative sampling of possible responses, leading us to question how well these results can be generalized to the entire population of judges and juries.

3. Juries have changed in many ways. In some jurisdictions, jury decisions no longer need be unanimous, and many states have shifted to smaller juries. Removing a requirement for unanimous verdicts would probably decrease the percentage of "hung" juries.

4. Furthermore, the membership of juries has changed; "juries are today more representative and heterogeneous than in the 1950's when Kalven and Zeisel conducted their research" (Hans & Vidmar, 1986, p. 142). The increased diversity in contemporary juries might increase their rate *of disagreement* with the judge's position because their broader experiences and cultural differences might give them insights or perspectives on the trial evidence to which judges do not have access (Hans & Vidmar, 1986). For example, a jury of African Americans may be less likely than a White judge to believe a White police officer's testimony that a drug dealer "dropped" a bag of cocaine.

5. As for *causes* of discrepancies between verdicts by the judge and jury, we have only the judge's attribution of what the jurors' feelings and sentiments were (Hans & Vidmar, 1991).

Some New Data on Judge/Jury Differences

Updating Criminal Case Comparisons. As Hans and Vidmar (1991) observed, replication of this classic study has been long overdue. Fortunately, an excellent replication now exists. To examine the applicability of these early findings to 21st-century juries, researchers at the National Center for State Courts collected data from jurors, judges, and attorneys in more than 350 trials in four jurisdictions: Los Angeles, Phoenix, the Bronx (in New York City), and the District of Columbia (Eisenberg et al., 2005). They researched some of the same issues that Kalven and Zeisel had explored, including how often judges and juries agreed on verdicts in criminal trials.

In a careful replication of earlier procedures, participants in noncapital felony trials completed questionnaires that asked about preferred verdicts and their evaluation of the evidence. There was a very high response rate (questionnaires were returned in 89% of cases, and 91% of judges responded—a very impressive number indeed, considering that many researchers are content with a 50% response rate!), so we can be fairly certain that the data are representative of most trials. As before, judges stated, prior to hearing the juries' verdicts, whether they would opt to acquit or convict and what they thought about the evidence. One obvious advantage of this study over its predecessor is that all groups (judges, attorneys, and jurors alike) gave their views of the evidence, thus reducing an important concern about Kalven and Zeisel's work, namely that all the information about a trial came from the judge.

Perhaps the most striking finding was how closely the new results mirrored those of the earlier study. The rate of jury/judge agreement was 70% (compared to Kalven and Zeisel's 75%), and when there was disagreement, it also mirrored the earlier asymmetry: Juries were more lenient. They were more likely to acquit when judges opted to convict than they were to convict when judges would acquit (see Table 10.3).

Further scrutiny of the data collected by the National Center for State Courts revealed the circumstances in which jurors were more likely than judges to return "not guilty" verdicts (Givelber & Farrell, 2008). Jurors were more impressed than judges by the presence of a third-party defense witness (someone other than the defendant). Thus, when the defendant *and* another defense witness testified, jurors were 50% more likely than judges to acquit. Jurors were also

TABLE 10.3   **Agreement of Judges' and Juries' Verdicts Based on 350 Trials (National Center for State Court data, in percentage of all trials)**

	Jury's Verdict		
Judge's Verdict	Acquit	Convict	Hung
Acquit	**11.6**	5.0	1.9
Convict	16.0	**58.5**	6.9

SOURCE: Adapted from Eisenberg et al. (2005). Figures in bold show cases in which judge and jury were in agreement on the verdict.

impressed by the absence of a prior criminal record. Thus, when the defendant and another defense witness both testified *and* when the defendant had no prior record, jurors were 90% more likely to acquit!

A reasonable explanation for these differences is that jurors and judges assume their roles differently; whereas jury duty is a unique experience for a juror, judges have probably heard it all (or most of it!) before. So jurors may take more seriously their instruction to acquit unless the prosecution can prove the case beyond a reasonable doubt, may feel sympathy for someone in the defendant's situation, and may possess a common-sense understanding that some judges lack of what motivates people to act impulsively.

Although there are limitations to these more recent studies—they did not assess jury/judge agreement in civil cases, and their sample was smaller—they support with additional rigor the important finding that judges and juries agree on the appropriate verdict most of the time, and when they do not, it is because judges tend to convict when jurors would acquit. It is satisfying to know

that Kalven and Zeisel's landmark study has withstood the test of time, even as the makeup of juries has changed in the intervening years.

Can we conclude then that jurors are generally more lenient than judges? Though the studies we described reached this conclusion, the answer may not be quite so simple. Whereas jurors *do* tend to be more lenient than judges when it comes to determining guilt, they can be harsh when it comes to sentencing decisions. (Recall that jurors in a few states also determine the defendant's punishment. In fact, it is estimated that about 4000 defendants are sentenced each year by juries.) Consider what happened to Donald Pease when he came up against a jury in Lubbock, Texas (Box 10.3).

A scientific comparison of juries' and judges' sentencing decisions in two states that authorize jury sentencing in noncapital cases—Arkansas and Virginia—examined patterns and trends in previously decided cases (King & Noble, 2005). At least for fairly serious offenses, jury sentences were more severe than sentences selected by judges in the same kind of case. For example, the average

Box 10.3   THE CASE OF DONALD PEASE AND HIS BUM LUCK WITH THE JURY

Donald Pease was charged with robbing a man at gunpoint and was tried by a Texas jury in 2008. Because he had no prior felony convictions, Pease would have been eligible for probation had he pleaded guilty. But Pease maintained his innocence and went to trial. Unfortunately for him, the jury disagreed and convicted

him of aggravated robbery. Next came the sentencing phase of the case where, instead of the probationary sentence he *could* have received, Pease was sentenced by the jury to 28 years in prison. His sentence was even 3 years longer than that of his accomplice who had already spent time in prison.

sentence imposed by Arkansas jurors in aggravated robbery cases was 221 months, yet the average sentence imposed by judges for this crime was only 169 months.

Why are judges apparently more lenient than jurors in sentencing convicted offenders? One explanation stems from the fact that because jury trials are very expensive—requiring a great deal of time and effort from the judge, courthouse staff, and the attorneys—judges want to encourage defendants to plead guilty and avoid those costs. Thus, they may deliberately choose more lenient sentences as an incentive to encourage plea bargaining and to send a message that those who accept plea bargains in the future will be rewarded. In essence, there is a "his-time-for-my-time" sentencing discount.

Updating Civil Case Comparisons.   In addition to new data comparing judges and juries in criminal cases, we also have updated findings on how judges compare to juries in civil cases. Neil Vidmar and his colleagues compared judges' and jurors' decisions in medical malpractice cases by asking the two groups to respond to the same trial evidence. A comparison of the damage awards of mock jurors with those of experienced legal professionals (primarily lawyers) showed no important differences. However, the awards by individual jurors were more variable than those of the lawyers; jurors awarded the plaintiff anywhere between $11,000 and $197,000, whereas the lawyers' awards ranged only from $22,000 to $82,000 (Vidmar & Rice, 1993).

There is much controversy about whether jurors are able to make competent decisions about punitive damages. These damage awards, which are described further in Chapter 12, are generally used to punish or to deter corporations that have engaged in serious wrongdoing. Indeed, some punitive damage awards have been very high; since 1989, the Supreme Court has ruled on five occasions about whether a punitive damage award was excessively so. Thus, a reasonable question is whether jury awards for punitive damages are different from awards assessed by judges, and

whether the two groups differ on the basis of those awards.

The most comprehensive study of jury/judge agreement on punitive damages, conducted by Theodore Eisenberg and his colleagues (Eisenberg, LaFountain, Ostrom, Rottman, & Wells, 2002), analyzed data from nearly 9000 trials that ended in 1996 from 45 of the nation's largest trial courts. The primary finding was that judges and juries did not differ substantially in these cases; they awarded punitive damages of about the same size, although the range of the jury awards was somewhat greater than that of the judicial awards. These results call into question the notion that juries are unable to set reasonable limits on punitive damages.

Do jurors do as well as judges in attending to the relevant evidence in these cases, setting aside any sympathy for the plaintiff and focusing only on the factors that *should* matter to the determination of punitive damages (i.e., the actions of the defendant)? The answer is a qualified yes. Jennifer Robbennolt (2002) asked judges and jury-eligible citizens to read a vignette about a patient who experienced harmful side effects of a medication prescribed for depression. The trial evidence included a memo demonstrating that employees of the defendant, an HMO (health maintenance organization), knew about the potential side effects of the drug—effects that were not communicated to the plaintiff. Research participants were told that the defendant's liability had already been determined and that they were to make awards for pain and suffering and, if appropriate, punitive damages.

As we've seen before, the decision making of judges and that of laypeople with regard to punitive damages were quite similar; their awards were of roughly the same magnitude and variability. Just as important, both groups used the evidence in appropriate ways, basing damages for pain and suffering on the severity of the plaintiff's injury, and basing punitive damages on the nature of the defendant's conduct.

Returning to the question we posed earlier—whether jurors perform as well as judges when deciding damage awards—we find little evidence that jurors' reasoning processes are inherently different from those of judges. Although some studies suggest that jurors render erratic and unpredictable awards, in part because their decision-making processes are influenced by various cognitive biases (see, for example, Sunstein, Hastie, Payne, Schkade, & Viscusi, 2002), judges are also human and apparently can fall prey to the same cognitive illusions as juries (Guthrie, Rachlinski, & Wistrich, 2001).

SUMMARY

1. ***What is the purpose of a trial?*** Every trial presents two contrasting views of the truth. Although at first glance, the purpose of a trial seems to be determining truth, conflict resolution may be an equally valid purpose. This debate is exemplified by three contrasting images of a trial: (1) as a search for the truth, (2) as a test of credibility, and (3) as a conflict-resolving ritual.

2. ***What are the steps the legal system follows in bringing a case to trial?*** When a case is brought to trial, the legal system employs a series of steps. Pretrial procedures include discovery, or the process of obtaining the information about the case held by the other side. Interviews of potential witnesses, called depositions, are a part of the discovery procedure. Before the trial, attorneys may make motions to exclude certain witnesses or testimony from the trial. The decision whether a judge or jury will render the verdict is also made at this point.

3. ***What is the order of procedures in the trial itself?*** After the jury, if any, is selected (a process called *voir dire*), the following sequence of steps unfolds in the trial itself:
   a. Opening statements by attorneys for the two sides (prosecution or plaintiff goes first)
   b. Direct examination, cross-examination, and redirect and recross of witnesses, with prosecution witnesses first, then defense witnesses
   c. Presentation of rebuttal witnesses and evidence
   d. Closing statements, or summations, by the two sides, usually in the order of

   prosecution, then defense, then prosecution again
   e. Judge's instructions to the jury (in some jurisdictions, these come before the closing statements)
   f. Jury deliberations and announcement of a verdict
   g. If the verdict is guilty, determination of the punishment

4. ***How has the introduction of emerging technologies changed the way that trials are conducted?*** Over time, the emergence of more sophisticated technologies into the legal system has begun to change the face of courtroom trials and appeals. With more tech-savvy judges and jurors taking their place in the courtroom, documentation and presentation methods of the past have been overshadowed by the use of newer technologies such as computer animations and simulations, videoconferencing, "virtual reality," and electronic and digital presentations of evidence. These high-tech methods have raised a number of interesting and complex psychological questions regarding the influence and effectiveness of technology in the courtroom.

5. ***How do juries' verdicts differ from those of judges?*** The question of whether juries' and judges' verdicts differ significantly was answered in a massive empirical study by Harry Kalven and Hans Zeisel. In actual trials, 75% of the time the jury came to the same verdict that the judge would have reached. In 19.5% of trials, the judge and jury disagreed. In the vast majority of these disagreements, especially those involving minor offenses, the jury was more lenient than the judge would have been.

Among the sources of the discrepancies were facts that the judge possessed and the jury did not (accounting for a small percentage of disagreements), the relative effectiveness of the two attorneys (also a small percentage), disagreements over the weight of the evidence, and what Kalven and Zeisel call "jury sentiments," or factors beyond the evidence and the law.

A recent replication of this classic study showed remarkably similar results: In criminal cases, the judge and jury agreed on a verdict in 70% of trials, and when there was disagreement, jurors were more likely than judges to acquit.

KEY TERMS

bench trial

beyond a reasonable
  doubt

closing argument

decision rule

discovery

experiential
  inflammatory bias

impeach

jury sentiments

opening statements

perjury

preponderance of the
  evidence

presence

rebuttal evidence

recross

redirect questioning

venire

vividness effect

11

Jury Representativeness and Selection

ORIENTING QUESTIONS

1. What does the legal system seek in trial juries?
2. What stands in the way of jury representativeness?
3. What procedures are used in voir dire?
4. What personality and attitudinal characteristics of jurors, if any, are related to their verdicts?
5. What role do jury consultants play in a trial?

THE ENRON TRIAL AS AN ILLUSTRATION OF JURY SELECTION

Though it may not be the "trial of the century" or even the most infamous trial to take place in Houston (dubbed by some the "murder trial capital of the world"), the 2006 trial of former Enron Corporation executives Kenneth Lay and Jeffrey Skilling focused the nation's attention on two of the most notorious high-profile businessmen to face criminal charges in our history. Thousands of Enron employees lost their jobs and their life savings in 2001 when Enron, one of the world's leading electricity and natural gas companies, was racked by accounting irregularities and plummeting stock and filed for bankruptcy. Prosecutors filed 35 charges against Skilling, the former Chief Operating Officer, including charges of conspiracy, wire fraud, securities fraud, and insider trading. Kenneth Lay, the former Enron CEO and Chairman, faced charges of conspiracy, wire fraud, and securities fraud.

Many observers believed that the outcome would hinge on the composition of the jury: "You can try the best case in the world, do the best cross-examination, have the best witnesses, but if you don't have a jury that's going to be open-minded...then you are going to fail," stated a prominent Houston trial lawyer. One hundred prospective jurors, prescreened via jury questionnaire, reported for jury selection. In cases involving corporate crimes, the prosecution generally wants jurors who will rally around the idea that the investing public was defrauded, whereas the defense prefers sophisticated jurors with business savvy. But in this case, those with business savvy were also most likely to know about the alleged scandal. In addition, there were strong antidefendant sentiments in the community prior to trial. According to Lay's jury consultant, Robert Hirschhorn, "That's why in my view it's going to take true artistry and intuition for picking this jury" (Jeffreys & Rosen, 2006).

Kenneth Lay

We will never know whether the defendants' jury consultants lacked artistry, or the prosecution simply had better facts, witnesses, and trial tactics. But the jury eventually convicted Skilling on 19 charges and Lay on 10 charges. Skilling is now serving a 24-year sentence; Lay died of a heart attack three months prior to sentencing. Was the selection process in the Enron trial fair? Was the outcome just? This trial highlights some of the challenges to the legal system's goal of forming juries that are both representative and fair.

JURY SELECTION BEGINS IN THE COMMUNITY: FORMING A PANEL, OR *VENIRE*

Jury selection begins before potential jurors arrive at the courthouse, as officials assemble a panel, or **venire**, of prospective jurors. Although each state— as well as the federal government—has its own procedures for determining how the panel of prospective jurors will be chosen, the general rules are the same: jury selection must neither systematically eliminate nor underrepresent any subgroups of the population.

To encourage representativeness, U.S. Supreme Court cases going back to 1880 (*Strauder v. West Virginia*, 1880) have forbidden systematic or intentional exclusion of religious, racial, and other **cognizable groups** (who, because of certain shared characteristics, might also hold unique perspectives on selected issues) from jury panels. But even as recently as 50 years ago, the rules were applied haphazardly. At that time, the composition of most *venires* was homogeneous, with middle-aged, well-educated White men generally overrepresented (Beiser, 1973; Kairys, 1972). In some cities and counties, juries were composed exclusively of White men. In small towns, it was customary to use as jurors retired or unemployed men who hung around the courthouse all day.

Judicial and Legislative Reforms

In a series of decisions and lawmaking, the U.S. Congress and Supreme Court established the requirement that the pool from which the jury is selected must be a representative cross-section of the community. These decisions were driven by two policy concerns, each of which includes psychological assumptions (Vidmar & Hans, 2007).

First, the government believed that if the pools from which juries were drawn represented a broad cross-section of the community, the resulting juries would be more heterogeneous. That is, they would be composed of people who were more diverse with respect to age, gender, ethnic background, occupation, and education. The courts assumed that this diversity would produce various benefits—for example, that juries composed of a diverse collection of people would be more likely to include minority group members, who might discourage majority group members from expressing prejudice. This assumption seems logical; casting a wider net will yield members of smaller religious and ethnic groups.

Another assumed benefit was that heterogeneous juries would be better fact finders and problem solvers. Extensive research on the dynamics of groups shows that, other things being equal, groups composed of people with differing abilities, personalities, and experiences are better problem solvers than groups made up of people who share the same background and perspectives (Baron, Kerr, & Miller, 1993). Heterogeneous groups are more likely to evaluate facts from different points of view and to have richer discussions.

Does this also happen in juries? Apparently so. Samuel Sommers (2006) used actual jury pool members to examine the effects of racial heterogeneity on jury deliberations in a rape trial. He asked the jurors to take part in simulated (mock) trials in which he varied the racial mix of jurors and recorded their deliberations. Sommers found that mixed-race groups had several advantages over juries composed of only White jurors. First, the mixed-race groups had longer, more thorough deliberations and were more likely to discuss racially charged topics such as racial profiling. Second, White jurors on racially mixed juries mentioned more factual information and were more aware of racial concerns than were their counterparts on all-White juries. A follow-up study suggested that

White jurors in diverse groups may actually process information differently than those in all-White groups (Sommers, Warp, & Mahoney, 2008). White jurors who expected to discuss a race-relevant topic in diverse groups showed better comprehension of relevant background information than did White jurors in all-White juries. On the basis of these studies, we can conclude that representative *venires* do, indeed, result in juries who undertake better, more thorough fact-finding.

The second policy reason for the Court's and Congress's decisions on representativeness is related to the *appearance* of legitimacy, rather than to the jury's actual fact-finding and problem-solving skills (Vidmar & Hans, 2007). Juries should reflect the standards of the community. When certain components of the community are systematically excluded from jury service, the community is likely to reject both the legal process and its outcomes as invalid.

We now know that the racial composition of a jury *can* affect public perceptions of the fairness and legitimacy of a trial and of the resulting verdict. To examine this issue, Leslie Ellis and Shari Diamond (2003) approached 320 adults in airports, bus and train stations, and parks, and asked them to participate in a short survey. These participants read a description of a shoplifting trial in which the racial makeup of the jury and the verdict were varied. Half of the respondents read that there were 12 Whites on the jury (racially homogeneous), and half read that there were 8 Whites and 4 African Americans (racially heterogeneous). In half of the descriptions, the jury's verdict was "guilty" and for the other half "not guilty." The researchers measured observers' perceptions of the fairness and legitimacy of the trial procedures. As shown in Figure 11.1, when the verdict was Not Guilty, racial composition of the jury had no effect on fairness ratings. But when the verdict was Guilty, a different picture emerged. Here, the racial composition of the jury *was* important: Observers considered a trial with a homogeneous jury less fair than a trial with a heterogeneous jury (Ellis & Diamond, 2003). Different elements of the community must see that they are well represented among those entrusted with doing justice—that they have a voice in the process of resolving disputes (Hans, 1992).

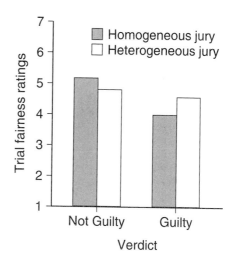

FIGURE 11.1 *Effect of verdict and racial composition of jury on fairness ratings*

The violent aftermath of the 1992 trial of four White Los Angeles police officers who were acquitted of assault for their role in beating Black motorist Rodney King illustrates this problem dramatically. The panel eventually selected for the trial of these officers contained no Black jurors (Box 11.1). After the jury found the police officers not guilty, the Black community rejected the verdict as invalid and angrily challenged the legitimacy of the entire criminal justice system for Black people. Shaken by the surprising verdicts and shocked by the ensuing riots, many Americans, regardless of their race, questioned the fairness of the jury's decision, in part because of the absence of Black citizens from its membership.

So, too, might defendants reject the fairness of decisions made by juries whose members share few social or cultural experiences with them. Consider, for example, the probable reaction of a college sophomore, on trial for possession of marijuana, who is found guilty by a jury composed entirely of people in their fifties and sixties.

Representative juries not only preserve the legitimacy of the legal process but also solidify participants' positive feelings toward the process. If members of underrepresented groups—the poor, the elderly, racial minorities, youth—do not serve

---

B o x 11.1   THE CASE OF RODNEY KING: DOES IT MATTER WHO SITS ON THE JURY?

When four White police officers were acquitted in 1992 of beating Rodney King, most people were surprised and appalled. Indeed, a *Los Angeles Times* poll reported that 92% of people who had seen the videotaped confrontation thought that excessive force was used against King. The jury was severely criticized, and observers sought to understand the outcome. Critics sometimes raise broader concerns (fairness and justice, for instance) but fail to consider the problem from the perspective of the jury, which must make a decision based only the evidence presented. Often a major cause of a surprising verdict by a jury (especially an acquittal) is that the prosecution was not effective in arguing its case or presenting its evidence. Or it may be that what the public hears or reads in the media is different from the evidence heard by the jury. Although the *evidence* is most important to trial

outcomes, the *composition of the jury* also contributes to the nature of verdicts.

The trial of the police officers in the King case was moved from urban Los Angeles to neighboring Ventura County as a result of pretrial publicity. The demographics of Ventura County favored the defense—suburban, White, a bedroom community with more than 2,000 police families, a place where people move to escape urban problems. It could be expected that jurors would empathize with the defendants—the "thin blue line" regarded by many as protecting the citizenry from drugs and gang violence—rather than with Rodney King, a large, Black, drunk driver. The six-man, six-woman jury, whose verdict of acquittal sparked one of the worst riots in this nation's history, consisted of ten Whites, one Hispanic, and one Asian American but included no African Americans.

---

on juries, they are more likely to become angry and impatient with the legal process. For some participants, at least, the net result of serving on a jury is an increased appreciation for the jury as a worthwhile institution (Rose, 2005).

Forming the *Venire*

Representativeness of jury pools is a worthwhile goal. But how should local courts go about forming the *venire* in order to reach this goal? (It is important to note that court decisions and legislation do not require any one pool to be representative; they require that a series of jury pools drawn over a period of several years be representative of the community's composition; Farmer, 1976.) A 1968 law—the Jury Selection and Service Act—required that voter registration lists be used as "the primary source" for jury pool selection. However, such lists risk underrepresenting certain segments of the community. Compared with the general population, young people are less likely to be registered to vote. Smaller percentages of the poor, Latinos, and other minorities register to vote. Thus, the pool of prospective jurors may be unrepresentative of the community in a number of important ways.

Various changes in selection procedures can increase representativeness. These include supplementing voters' lists with other sources, such as lists of licensed drivers, persons receiving public assistance, and unemployed people (Kairys, Kadane, & Lehoczky, 1977), and updating address lists to reduce the impact of greater mobility among lower-income citizens (Fukurai & Butler, 1994). Another option is to stratify the selection procedures so that historically underrepresented groups in a jurisdiction receive a larger number of jury summons, thereby increasing the ultimate yield of prospects from these groups (Diamond & Rose, 2005).

Exclusions, Nonresponses, and Exemptions: Threats to Representativeness?

Once a pool of potential jurors has been drawn, each individual in the pool receives a questionnaire to assess his or her qualifications and ability to serve. Some people may be excluded by law because their responses reveal personal limitations (e.g., blindness, mental incompetence), although these restrictions are changing.

Box 11.2   THE CASE OF ALEXANDER HARVEY AND HIS HARD-EARNED LESSON ABOUT JURY DUTY

During jury selection in a three-day civil trial in Fremont, Nebraska, prospective juror Alexander Harvey raised his hand and told the judge that he needed to use the restroom. When informed that he would have to wait, he bolted from the courtroom and disappeared. But officials tracked him down and subpoenaed him to appear in court a few days later when the judge—decidedly peeved by this vanishing act—offered Harvey the choice to write a letter of apology or spend 30 days in jail. He opted for the former. According to Harvey, "they take fulfilling your complete jury duty very seriously. It was my mistake and I shouldn't have done that, and I'm going to write the apology ... It's certainly not a landmark case but it was an education" (Associated Press, 2007).

The rationale for prohibiting the service of certain groups (for example, people who are visually impaired, mentally incompetent, non-English speakers, felons, and non-citizens) may be justified, but other issues that arise during this phase of jury selection further erode the representativeness of the eventual jury. A national survey of state court administrators showed that an average of 12% of juror questionnaires are returned by the post office as undeliverable, and many people who receive questionnaires simply do not respond (as many as 20% of Dallas residents!) (Boatright, 1999).

Without doubt, every jury commissioner (those courthouse employees responsible for securing jurors' participation) in the country could tell stories about the creative ways that people have tried to escape jury service. Hemorrhoids are a frequently used excuse. Vincent Homenick, the chief jury clerk of the courthouse in Manhattan, once received a summons that someone had returned with the word "deceased" written on it, along with a plastic bag supposedly containing the ashes of the prospective juror (Green, 2004)! Woody Allen scribbled a note on his jury summons complaining of the trauma he apparently suffered during a child custody battle with Mia Farrow. Unwavering, the jury commissioner insisted that he appear for jury duty. But when Allen showed up with his lawyer, agent, and bodyguard, and refused to have a seat in the jury waiting room, he was dismissed (Hartocollis, 2006). As Phoenix lawyer Patricia Lee Refo, chairwoman of the American Jury Project, put it aptly: "Everyone likes jury duty—just not this week."

From those persons who are eligible for jury service and who return the questionnaire, members of the *venire* are randomly selected and summoned to appear at the courthouse for jury service. But as many as half of qualified jurors ignore the jury duty summons, even though doing so constitutes a violation of law (Ellis & Diamond, 2003). In some jurisdictions, judges have begun to summon these "no-shows" to court, insisting that they explain why they were absent or face fines and jail time. A Nebraska man who skipped out on jury duty was offered the chance to apologize (see Box 11.2).

Until recently, all members of certain occupations were automatically exempted from jury service. For example, the state of New York gave automatic exemptions to physicians, firefighters, veterinarians, podiatrists, phone operators, and embalmers. Why? The rationale extends back a hundred years, to a time when each of these occupations played a vital role in small-town life, and the person (usually there was only one physician or one telephone operator) had to remain available to the community. In many jurisdictions, elected officials, lawyers, and judges were also exempted from jury duty. But those exemptions are less common nowadays. When presidential candidate John McCain showed up for jury duty in a Phoenix courtroom in January of 2005, he reminded some surprised fellow potential jurors that he too was a citizen. Most states, including New York, have now eliminated all exemptions from jury duty (Kaye, 2001).

Prospective jurors sometimes avoid jury service by claiming personal hardship. Some judges are sympathetic to claims of ill health, business necessity, vacation plans, and the like. But many other judges are unwilling to dismiss individual jurors because of perceived "hardships." Noted journalist H. L. Mencken famously defined a jury as "a group of twelve men who, having lied to the judge about their hearing, health, and business engagements, have failed to fool him." During the jury selection for the O. J. Simpson civil trial, Judge Hiroshi Fujisaki responded to one prospective juror who had requested dismissal because she suffered from claustrophobia, "How big is your living room? Is it as big as this courtroom?" She remained in the pool. Another prospective juror complained of the likelihood of getting stiff from sitting too long. "That's why we take breaks," replied the unsympathetic judge.

When some prospective jurors are excused for reasons of hardship, the result is a winnowing down of the pool. Thus, even before the formal jury selection begins in a courtroom—that is, before jurors are questioned by attorneys and the judge—some people have been removed from the panel of prospective jurors. These removals can distort the representativeness of juries. As Vidmar and Hans (2007) stated after reviewing the evidence, "The theory of the representative jury is solid. However, when we look closely at the process of assembling a jury pool, and the selection of those individuals who will serve on particular juries, we observe substantial deviations from the representative ideal. There are a number of reasons why American juries fall short, but fall short they do" (p. 76).

JURY SELECTION CONTINUES IN THE COURTROOM: THE *VOIR DIRE* PROCESS

Once the panel of prospective jurors has been assembled and summoned to the courthouse, selection issues change. The focus shifts from concerns about the representativeness of prospective jurors to questions about a given juror's ability and willingness to be fair and impartial (Diamond & Rose, 2005).

As part of the constitutional right to be tried by an "impartial" jury, a defendant is afforded the opportunity to screen prospective jurors to determine whether any of them are prejudiced. The forum in which the judge and/or the attorneys (both defense attorney and prosecutor) question prospective jurors is called *voir dire*, a French term meaning *to speak the truth*. But the ways in which *voir dire* is conducted are almost as numerous as the judges who hold trials (Hans & Jehle, 2003). Who asks the questions, what questions are asked and how they are phrased, how long the questioning goes on, and whether the questions are posed to individual jurors or to a group are all matters left to judges' discretion.

The most limited form of *voir dire* involves a small number of questions asked in yes-or-no format only by the judge and features group rather than individual questioning of prospective jurors. An example: "Do any of you have an opinion at this time as to the defendant's guilt or innocence?" Yes-or-no questions are effective in controlling the answers of witnesses and reducing the time spent in *voir dire*, but they offer little insight into jurors' beliefs and attitudes. Also note that this form of questioning requires jurors to self-identify any biases and report them to the judge. Many jurors may be unaware of their predispositions and/or hesitant to state them in public; thus, both of these obligations may be difficult for jurors to fulfill.

Several studies show that limited *voir dire* has drawbacks as a means of identifying biased jurors (Johnson & Haney, 1994). One of the most compelling demonstrations came from a project initiated by District of Columbia Superior Court Judge, Gregory Mize (1999). Prior to this study, Judge Mize, like many judges, conducted limited *voir dire* during which he asked questions in open court to a group of approximately 60 prospective jurors. He and the attorneys would then pose follow-up questions to those who responded affirmatively to the initial question. Judge Mize revised his procedures for the study; he interviewed all prospective jurors, regardless of whether they had responded affirmatively to the first question. In doing so, he determined that a number of jurors who were silent in response to a preliminary question actually had a great deal to say when prompted individually. Among the responses:

- "I was frightened to raise my hand. I have taken high blood pressure medications for twenty years. I am afraid I'll do what others tell me to do in the jury room."

- "My grandson was killed with a gun so the topic of guns makes my blood pressure go up."

- And remarkably, this one: "I'm the defendant's fiancée."

Why is limited *voir dire* so ineffective at uncovering juror bias? Obviously, some jurors will fail to disclose important information because of privacy concerns, embarrassment, or a failure to recognize their own biases. But an important psychological dynamic, termed the **social desirability effect**, is also a factor at this stage. Most people want to present themselves in a positive, socially desirable way. This desire to appear favorably, especially in the presence of a high-status person such as a judge, shapes how people answer questions and influences what they disclose about themselves. As Hans and Jehle (2003) point out, the questions asked during limited *voir dire* often elicit the socially desirable response. People might claim, for example, that they can set aside predispositions and biases when evaluating trial evidence, even if they would actually find that difficult or impossible to do.

At the other extreme is extended *voir dire*, in which both the judge and attorneys ask open-ended questions that require elaboration, cover a wide range of topics, and question jurors individually. Extended *voir dire* has several advantages in uncovering biases. Open-ended questions (for example, "What experiences have you had in your life that caused you to believe that a person was being discriminated against because of the color of his skin?") encourage jurors to talk more about their feelings and experiences. Individual questioning can result in disclosures that jurors might not otherwise offer, an advantage that prompted

Judge Mize to conclude that individual *voir dire* is "an indispensable way of ferreting out otherwise unknown jurors qualities" (Mize, 1999, pg. 12). But because extended *voir dire* can take a long time, most courts tend not to favor it.

The typical *voir dire* procedures involve a compromise between the limited and extended versions; both the attorneys and the judge pose questions to a group of prospective jurors, and then they ask brief follow-up questions of selected individuals. Judges usually impose severe time restrictions on questioning by attorneys (Rottman et al., 1998). The average length of *voir dire* in a felony case is 5.13 hours (Hans & Jehle, 2003). Remarkably, in the Enron fraud case, the judge delivered on his promise to select a jury in just one day.

Examination of jurors is typically conducted in open court, but if very sensitive topics are raised, the questioning may be done at the judge's bench or in the judge's chambers. This is likely to occur if, in the judge's opinion, issues that are ordinarily private (such as one's credit rating, health problems, religious beliefs, or history of victimization) may affect a juror's ability to be fair and impartial. Apparently, jurors consider many questions asked during jury selection to be either irrelevant or intrusive. Mary Rose interviewed 209 North Carolina jurors after they had served on juries. A total of 43% believed they had been asked irrelevant questions, 27% said the questions made them feel uncomfortable, and approximately the same number said the questions were overly personal (Rose, 2003). Aware that jurors are more likely to disclose personal and sensitive information in writing than orally, some judges use written questionnaires in place of, or in addition to, questions asked in open court. Jurors in the Enron trial answered a lengthy questionnaire before coming to the Houston courthouse. The "mother of all juror questionnaires" was the 294-item questionnaire used in the O. J. Simpson case.

Challenges for Cause and Peremptory Challenges

Technically, opposing attorneys do not select a jury; rather, the judge gives them the opportunity to exclude a number of potential jurors from the eventual jury. (For this reason, the procedure should perhaps be termed jury rejection rather than jury selection, although *rejection* is probably too strong a word!) There are two mechanisms—challenges for cause and peremptory challenges—by which panelists are excluded from serving on a jury. Both are explained in detail below. Here, we simply point out that after all the challenges have been made and ruled on, and some prospective jurors have been dismissed, the people who remain are sworn into service as the jury.

In any trial, each side can claim that particular jurors should be excluded because they are inflexibly biased or prejudiced or because they have a relationship to the parties or the issues that creates the appearance of bias. These exclusions are known as **challenges for cause**. For example, a relative or business associate of a defendant would be challenged, or excused, for cause. Additionally, the judge may excuse a panelist for cause without either attorney requesting it if the prospective juror is unfit to serve. In criminal cases, judges often inquire about whether prospective jurors have been crime victims and may excuse those who say that their own victimization experiences would affect their ability to be fair jurors. There is good reason to ask because mock jurors who had been victims of the crime for which the defendant was being tried were more likely than nonvictims to convict (Culhane, Hosch, & Weaver, 2004).

One juror was deemed unfit to serve for a different reason: body odor. Massachusetts Superior Court Judge Nancy Staffier-Holtz dismissed the unsworn juror, saying "Given the strength of the body odor, I'm satisfied that the other jurors would be put at a distinct disadvantage in their efforts to concentrate." As one blogger put it, "Justice may be blind, but it retains a healthy sense of smell" (http://legalblog watch.typepad.com/legal_blog_watch/2009/01/the-case-of-the-stinky-juror.html).

In theory, each side has an unlimited number of challenges for cause. In reality, few prospective jurors are excused for reasons of prejudice. In a survey of New Mexico courts over a three-year period, only about one of every 20 jurors was dismissed for cause (Hans & Vidmar, 1986).

Each side may also exclude a designated number of prospective jurors "without a reason stated, without inquiry, and without being subject to the court's control" (*Swain v. Alabama*, 1965). This procedure is known as a **peremptory challenge**. Peremptory challenges have multiple purposes. First, they allow attorneys to challenge potential jurors who they believe will not be sympathetic, for whatever reason, to their client. The number of peremptory challenges allocated to each side varies from one jurisdiction to another and also on the basis of the type of case (civil or criminal) and the seriousness of the charge.

The peremptory challenge is more than a simple mechanism for removing jurors thought to be unsympathetic. The peremptory challenge has a second, largely symbolic function: When the parties in a lawsuit play a role in selecting the people who decide the outcome, they may be more satisfied with that outcome (Saks, 1997).

The third function of peremptory challenges is to allow the attorney to begin to indoctrinate prospective jurors and influence those who ultimately will make up the jury. For example, Holdaway (cited in Blunk & Sales, 1977, p. 44) gives the following example of how an attorney can ask a question that will acquaint the juror with relevant law but also phrase it to make a point consistent with the attorney's position. The question is "Do you agree with the rule of law that requires acquittal in the event there is reasonable doubt?" The real purpose of this question is, of course, to alert the prospective juror from the beginning that reasonable doubt could exist in the case, and to make the juror aware of the rule in the hope that he or she will thus look for reasonable doubt and then vote to acquit.

As we shall see in the next section, the Supreme Court has imposed more and more limits on the exercise of peremptory challenges. As a result, the overall status of this jury selection tool is in doubt. Although opinions about the importance of the peremptory challenge remain divided—some experts favor its elimination altogether, and others argue that it is crucial for fair trials—only a few researchers have examined the use of peremptory challenges in real trials. Among the questions they asked were these: Are peremptory challenges used to remove minority jurors or other specific groups? Do the prosecution and defense repeatedly dismiss different types of jurors?

Some answers come from a study that tracked the fate of 764 prospective jurors questioned during jury selection in 28 cases (Clark, Boccaccini, Caillouet, & Chaplin, 2007). Of this number, 234 were dismissed by the prosecution and 202 by the defense. More importantly, jurors' race seemed to factor into the exercise of peremptory challenges: only 10% of jurors excused by the defense were African American, compared to 48% of those excused by the prosecution. Nevertheless, on most juries, the percentage of African American jurors mirrored their level of representation in the *venire*.

The Batson Decision: No Exclusion on Account of Race

As a result of a series of Supreme Court decisions, peremptory challenges may not be based *solely* on a juror's race or gender. Consequently, these challenges are "less peremptory" than they used to be. The decision regarding race was triggered by the case of James Batson, a Black man convicted of second-degree burglary by an all-White jury. During the *voir dire*, the prosecuting attorney used four of his six peremptory challenges to dismiss all the Black persons from the *venire*. In *Batson v. Kentucky*, decided in 1986, the Court held that Batson was denied his Fourteenth Amendment right to equal protection by the prosecution's dismissal of Black members of the panel (Pizzi, 1987). In *Holland v. Illinois* (1990), the Court held that a White defendant could also complain about the exclusion of Blacks because the principle of representativeness was violated by the arbitrary exclusion of *any* racial group. Finally, and most significantly, in 1991, the Court held that eliminating jurors solely on the basis of race violates the equal protection rights of the jurors (*Edmonson v. Leesville Concrete Co.*; *Powers v. Ohio*). The *Edmonson* decision makes it clear that race-based peremptory challenges are forbidden in *civil* cases, and in the 1992 case of *Georgia v. McCollum*, the Supreme Court prohibited race-based challenges *by the defense* in criminal cases (previous cases had

focused on the prosecution's peremptory challenges) (Bonora, 1995).

In the *Batson* case, the Supreme Court developed a procedure for determining whether a peremptory challenge was racially based. When a defense attorney believes that the prosecution's peremptory challenge was motivated by racial factors, he or she initiates a so-called "*Batson* challenge," and the judge then asks the prosecutor for an explanation. The prosecutor typically advances a race-neutral explanation for the challenge—for example, that the prospective juror has a brother in prison or has filed a lawsuit against the police. The judge then determines whether the explanation is genuine, taking into account the other jurors who were not challenged by the attorney. For example, if a prosecutor were to explain that she dismissed a Black juror because he had been robbed, the judge would want to know why she had not dismissed a White juror who also had been robbed.

It might appear that creative prosecutors can always find "race-neutral" reasons for excluding minorities from the jury. Indeed, attorneys are unlikely to cite a prospective juror's race as a factor in their dismissals. In an exhaustive analysis of every published decision of federal and state courts in the seven years after the *Batson* decision, Melilli (1996) found 2,994 *Batson* challenges but in only 1.8% of the sample did the attorney cite race as a factor.

Does a prospective juror's race really not matter, or are prosecutors simply unwilling to admit that it does? That question led to an experimental study in which college students, law students, and practicing attorneys played the role of a prosecutor trying a Black defendant (Sommers & Norton, 2007). They were given profiles of two prospective jurors, one Black and the other White, and had to use one remaining peremptory challenge. Although participants were more likely to challenge a Black juror than a White juror, they rarely cited race as a factor in their decision. Moreover, it was relatively easy for them to generate an ostensibly neutral explanation to justify their choice.

Psychological research on **social judgments** can help us understand why. People infrequently admit (even to themselves) that social category

---

Box 11.3 THE CASE OF THOMAS MILLER-EL AND THE DIFFICULTY OF PROVING RACIAL BIAS IN JURY SELECTION

Texas death row inmate Thomas Miller-El must have felt like a yo-yo, given the number of times his case bounced back and forth between the Fifth Circuit Court of Appeals and the Supreme Court. The issue was whether prosecutors engaged in purposeful discrimination during Miller-El's 1986 trial on charges that he robbed and murdered a hotel clerk in Irving, Texas. Probably no *voir dire* has been scrutinized as thoroughly as the one that occurred in this case.

Prosecutors in that trial used peremptory strikes to exclude 10 of the 11 Blacks who were eligible to serve on the jury, and Miller-El was convicted and sentenced to death. For years he contended that prosecutors used peremptory challenges in a biased way to keep African American jurors off his jury panel, but courts rejected this claim four times. Finally, when the Fifth Circuit refused to hear Miller-El's appeal, he appealed to the Supreme Court.

This time, with the support of some unusual allies (including numerous federal prosecutors and judges who, along with the former director of the FBI, filed a brief supporting Miller-El's position), he found a receptive audience. In an 8–1 ruling and a rare victory for Miller-El, the Supreme Court found that the lower courts had failed to fully consider the evidence he offered to show racial bias, and it ordered the Fifth Circuit to reconsider Miller-El's claim (*Miller-El v. Cockrell*, 2003). (That evidence included a history of discrimination by Dallas prosecutors and a training manual from the Dallas District Attorney's Office that instructed prosecutors to exercise their peremptory strikes against minorities.) But when the Fifth Circuit judges undertook such reconsideration and examined all the reasons prosecutors gave for

AP Images/Brett Coomer

Texas death row inmate, Thomas Miller-El, being told that he was granted a stay of execution in 2002. Miller-El challenged the prosecutor's use of peremptory challenges during his 1986 trial.

striking *venire* members, they concluded that Black and White jurors had been treated the same by prosecutors (*Miller-El v. Dretke*, 2004).

Miller-El again appealed to the Supreme Court, and again the high court ruled in his favor, overturning his conviction because of racial bias in jury selection. According to Justice Stephen Breyer, "[t]he right to a jury free of discriminatory taint is constitutionally protected. The right to use peremptory challenges is not." Justice David Souter was even more direct, writing that Miller-El's evidence of bias "is too powerful to conclude anything but discrimination" (*Miller-El v. Dretke*, 2005).

---

information such as race influences their decisions (Norton, Vandello, & Darley, 2004), often because they want to appear to be unprejudiced and to avoid the social consequences of showing racial bias (Norton, Sommers, Apfelbaum, Pura, & Ariely, 2006). These findings suggest that attorney self-reports are unlikely to encompass the real impact of racial considerations in jury selection.

Recall that the judge, after hearing the prosecutor's explanation, must ultimately decide whether the attorney dismissed a prospective juror because of race.

Easily concocted, plausible, and (above all) race-neutral justifications leave judges with little reason to reject them, and archival analyses of actual *voir dire* proceedings show that judges are unlikely to find that peremptory challenges violate the *Batson* rule (Melilli, 1996).

The case of Thomas Miller-El, detailed in Box 11.3, exemplifies the difficulty of proving racial bias in jury selection.

In the years since the Miller-El cases, the Supreme Court has looked more carefully at how

---

B o x 11.4 THE CASE OF *J. E. B. V. ALABAMA EX REL. T. B.*: WHOSE CHILD IS THIS AND WHO GETS TO DECIDE?

The facts of the case are simple: Teresia Bible gave birth to a child in May 1989; she named the child Phillip Rhett Bowman Bible, claimed that James E. Bowman, Sr. was the father, and filed a paternity suit against him to obtain child support. Even though a blood test showed that there was a 99.92% probability that he was the father, Mr. Bowman refused to settle, so a trial was held.

The jury pool was composed of 24 women and 12 men; after three prospective jurors were dismissed for cause, the plaintiff used nine of its ten peremptory challenges to remove males; the defendant used ten of his eleven to remove women (he also removed one man). Thus the resulting jury was composed of 12

women. (Note that in this case, it was men who were systematically excluded from the jury.) The jury concluded that Mr. Bowman was the child's father and ordered him to pay child support of $415.71 per month.

Bowman appealed and the U.S. Supreme Court eventually ruled that peremptory challenges that were used to eliminate one gender were, like those used to exclude a race, unacceptable. The Court's decision acknowledged that peremptory strikes against women hark back to stereotypes about their competence and predispositions, traced from a long history of sex discrimination in the United States (Babcock, 1993).

---

judges evaluate prosecutors' (theoretically) race-neutral explanations and decide whether they are genuine or a pretext for discrimination. In doing so, the Court overturned the murder conviction of a Black death row inmate because the prosecutor used tactics to pick an all-White jury that the judge should have disallowed (*Snyder v. Louisiana*, 2008).

Peremptory Challenges and Other Juror Characteristics

In 1994, the Supreme Court extended the logic of *Batson* to peremptory challenges based on another cognizable characteristic—gender. The case of *J. E. B. v. Alabama ex rel. T. B.* (1994) is described in Box 11.4.

How many different cognizable groups are there and could limitations on peremptory challenges eventually be extended to cover all of them? Dominic Massaro, a judge in the state of New York, decided that Italian Americans were entitled to *Batson*-type protection (Alden, 1996), and a California law bans attorneys from removing jurors simply because they are homosexual. But in other trials, attempts to apply the rule to obese jurors (*United States v. Santiago-Martinez*, 1995) and bilingual jurors (*Hernandez v. New York*, 1991; Restrepo, 1995) were denied.

Trial attorneys sometimes attempt to extend the principle of "a jury of your peers" to an extreme degree. In Houston, Texas, the attorney for accused murderer Jeffrey Leibengood asked to include only people less than five feet tall in the jury pool because his client's height was four feet six inches. The attorney told the judge, "We say a short person is subject to discrimination, and we hope to have two or three short people end up on the jury. *Batson* should be extended to include the little people" (quoted by Taylor, 1992, p. 43). The judge disagreed.

Some courts have held that peremptory challenges based on religious affiliation violate state constitutions (e.g., *State v. Fuller*, 2004), but the Supreme Court has yet to hold that it is unconstitutional to base peremptory challenges on religious persuasion (or on any other classification, for that matter). Attorneys' discretion in jury selection remains relatively unfettered, except that jurors cannot be challenged because of their race or their gender.

Lawyers' Theories: Stereotypes in Search of Success

Do the jury selection strategies of attorneys conflict with the goal of having unbiased fact finders? Before we answer this question, we need to answer a more basic one: How do lawyers go about selecting or excluding jurors, and do their strategies work?

In everyday life, our impressions about others are governed largely by what psychologists have termed implicit personality theories. An **implicit personality theory** is a person's organized network of preconceptions about how certain attributes are related to one another and to behavior. Trial lawyers often apply their implicit personality theories to jury selection. For example, William J. Bryan (1971) advised prosecutors to "never accept a juror whose occupation begins with a P. This includes pimps, prostitutes, preachers, plumbers, procurers, psychologists, physicians, psychiatrists, printers, painters, philosophers, professors, phonies, parachutists, pipe-smokers, or part-time anythings" (p. 28). Another attorney vowed always to use a peremptory strike against any prospect who wore a hat indoors. Famed criminal defense attorney, Clarence Darrow (1936), offered this advice:

> If a Presbyterian enters the jury box and carefully rolls up his umbrella, and calmly and critically sits down, let him go. He is cold as the grave; he knows right from wrong, although he seldom finds anything right. He believes in John Calvin and eternal punishment. Get rid of him with the fewest possible words before he contaminates the others; unless you and your clients are Presbyterians you probably are a bad lot, and even though you may be a Presbyterian, your client most likely is guilty.

Implicit personality theories lead to stereotypes, when a person believes that all members of a distinguishable group (e.g., a religious, racial, sexual, age, or occupational group) have the same attributes. They also produce assumptions that two qualities are associated—for example, when a lawyer assumes that slow-talking jurors are also unintelligent—when they actually may not be.

We tend to link qualities together and form our own implicit personality theories. Sometimes these judgments are rationally based; we may have had enough consistent experiences to draw a valid conclusion about the relationship. Other theories,

however, such as the examples just presented, are only intuitive or are based on limited experiences and purely coincidental relationships. Stereotypes are often formed on this basis. Former Supreme Court Chief Justice William Rehnquist recognized the possibility of stereotyping during *voir dire* when he stated that "[jury selection] is best based upon seat-of-the-pants instincts, which are undoubtedly crudely stereotypical and may in many cases be hopelessly mistaken."

But the emergence of implicit personality theories is almost inevitable when we form impressions of others and make interpersonal decisions. After all, human behavior is very complex. We must simplify it in some way. Richard "Racehorse" Haynes, a highly successful lawyer, once defended two White Houston police officers charged with beating a Black prisoner to death. Like all lawyers, Haynes had his ideas about the kind of juror who would be sympathetic to his police officer clients, but his candor was a surprise. After the trial was over, Haynes was quoted as saying, "I knew we had the case won when we seated the last bigot on the jury" (Phillips, 1979, p. 77).

The jury selection decisions in the trial of *J. E. B. v. T. B.* reflect the use of implicit personality theories and stereotypes. Ms. Bible's attorney dismissed male jurors, assuming they would be sympathetic to the man alleged to be the baby's father, whereas the defense dismissed female jurors because of similar beliefs that women would be biased in favor of another woman. But the courts are beginning to prohibit the use of such stereotypes. In his majority opinion in the *J. E. B.* case, Justice Harry Blackmun wrote, "Virtually no support [exists] for the conclusion that gender alone is an accurate predictor of [jurors'] attitudes," and if gender does not predict a juror's predisposition, then there is no legitimacy to dismissing jurors on this basis only (quoted by Greenhouse, 1994, p. A10).

Lawyers must choose which prospective jurors to challenge with their quota of peremptory challenges. Hence, their own implicit personality theories come into play. Typically, their decisions are based on little more than the juror's race, sex, street address, appearance, and occupation. Even if they are allowed to question jurors individually, lawyers cannot know for certain whether they are being told the truth. By necessity, they fall back on their own impressions. What attributes do lawyers find important? Textbooks and journal articles on trial advocacy provide a wealth of folklore about jurors' characteristics. Not surprisingly, characteristics that are visible or easily determined—age, gender, race, religion, occupation, country of origin—receive special attention.

In addition to applying their own theories of personality to juror selection, some attorneys use their understanding of group structure. For example, they play hunches about which jurors will be the most dominant during the deliberations. Who will be selected as foreperson if, as in most jurisdictions, that choice is left up to the jury? What cliques will form? Understanding group dynamics is more complicated than relying on simple stereotypes of individual jurors, so lawyers who try to forecast group behavior also make assumptions. Some lawyers maintain a simple "one-juror verdict" theory—that is, they believe that the final group decision is usually determined by the opinions of one strong-willed, verbal, and influential juror. Lawyers who adhere to this maxim look for one juror who is likely to be both sympathetic and influential and then, during the trial, concentrate their influence attempts on that individual. In pursuing this search for a "key juror," the typical attorney follows one basic rule of thumb: "In general, an individual's status and power within the jury group will mirror his status and power in the external world" (Christie, 1976, p. 270).

If jurors themselves are asked who among them was most influential during their deliberations, three characteristics tend to emerge: male gender, an extroverted personality style, and height greater than that of their fellow jurors (Marcus, Lyons, & Guyton, 2000). It should come as no surprise then that Massachusetts senator and former presidential candidate, John Kerry, was elected to serve as foreperson in a 2005 trial in Suffolk Superior Court. Fellow jurors described him as a "natural leader."

Another common attorney strategy is based on the assumption that jurors who are demographically or socially similar to a litigant will be predisposed to favor that litigant, a belief known as the **similarity–leniency hypothesis**. Does this rule of thumb hold true? Are jurors more likely to favor litigants with whom they share certain characteristics? One could make the opposite prediction in some cases—sharing similar qualities with another might make a juror more skeptical of that person's excuses or justifications for behavior that the juror dislikes. Here, the so-called **black sheep effect** may apply: Although people generally favor individuals who are part of their in-group, they may sometimes strongly sanction those fellow members who reflect negatively on and could embarrass the in-group.

The answer apparently depends on the strength of the evidence against the defendant. When the evidence against the defendant is weak or ambiguous, the similarity–leniency hypothesis seems apt: jurors tend to favor defendants who are like them in some way (Daudistel, Hosch, Holmes, & Graves, 1999). But when the defendant's culpability is clear, the black sheep effect is seen. Jurors are harsher on defendants with whom they share demographic features (Chadee, 1996). To complicate matters further, these effects seem to apply only to *individual* jurors' demographic closeness to the defendant and not to entire juries. When Taylor and Hosch (2004) tested the similarity–leniency hypothesis and black sheep effect using data from 418 actual felony cases in two Texas counties, they found that neither theory adequately captured the complex relationship between the ethnic composition of the jury and the defendant's ethnicity. As we've seen before, the strength of the evidence was the most important determinant of a jury's verdict.

Finally, some attorneys follow the "first 12 called" rule. Frustrated by past attempts to predict how jurors will behave, they simply accept the first prospects called to the jury box, sometimes deliberately drawing jurors' attention to their willingness to believe that everyone is fair and can be trusted to decide the case "correctly."

Demographic Characteristics of Jurors

Trial attorneys must make informed guesses about which prospective jurors will be more favorable to their side. To do so, they often rely on demographic features of jurors because many of these characteristics (e.g., age, race, gender, socioeconomic status [SES]) are easily observable (Kovera, Dickinson, & Cutler, 2002). Indeed, many attorneys actively select (or, rather, deselect) jurors on the basis of demographic information. When researchers (Olczak, Kaplan, & Penrod, 1991) gave attorneys mock juror profiles that varied along demographic lines (jurors' gender, age, marital status, and nationality) and asked them to rate the extent to which each profiled juror would be biased toward the defense or prosecution, they found that attorneys could do this task easily, focusing on one or two characteristics to the exclusion of others. Results of a separate study showed, however, that none of these juror characteristics actually predicted juror voting.

Demographic characteristics of jurors and juries *are* sometimes related to their verdicts, but the correlations are weak and inconsistent from one type of trial to another (Baldus, Woodworth, Zuckerman, Weiner, & Broffit, 2001; Devine et al., 2001). The relationships that emerge are usually small; they permit researchers to claim "there's something there" but offer no guarantee of success to the attorney who deals with only a few individuals and one trial at a time.

The relationship between demographic characteristics and verdicts may also depend on the type of case. For example, in trials that involve issues such as child sexual assault, domestic violence, and sexual harassment, jurors' gender may matter. In general, women are more likely than men to convict the perpetrators of these crimes (Golding, Bradshaw, Dunlap, & Hodell, 2007; Kovera, Gresham, Borgida, Gray, & Regan, 1997), and in civil trials, women are more inclined than men to perceive that sexual harassment has occurred in the workplace (Wiener, Hurt, Russell, Mannen, & Gasper, 1997). Even here, however, the gender effect is not particularly large (Blumenthal, 1998). Gender is not a reliable predictor of verdicts or punitive damages in high-stakes civil litigation (Vinson, Costanzo, & Berger, 2008). The most consistent gender difference involves social influence rather than content; men are

generally perceived by other jurors as more influential than women (Marcus et al., 2000).

Jurors' SES is related to their verdicts in only a very general way. In a survey of how jurors voted in 100 criminal trials, Adler (1973) found that jurors of higher SES (indicated by variables such as income, occupational level, and education) were more likely to vote for conviction than jurors of lower SES. Laboratory research showed that low SES mock jurors are also harsher on civil defendants (Bornstein & Rajki, 1994). Perhaps the most powerful effect of SES occurs at the deliberation table, where jurors of higher status are regarded as more influential because of what others believe about their competence (York & Cornwell, 2006).

Using jurors' race to predict their verdicts is complicated because few studies have examined the decision making of non-White jurors (Sommers, 2007), and the racial mix of the jury influences an individual juror's decision. Based on the existing data, we can tentatively conclude that Black jurors may be more lenient than Whites in the typical criminal case (Bothwell, 1999), but only if the defendant is also Black (Sommers & Ellsworth, 2000). In general, with regard to jurors' race as well as other demographic features, there is little evidence that these characteristics can consistently predict verdicts in criminal cases or damage awards in civil cases (Vinson et al., 2008).

Personality and Attitudinal Characteristics of Jurors

Given that demographic variables have only a weak relationship to verdicts, one might wonder whether jurors' personality and attitudinal characteristics are better predictors. A number of early studies concluded that enduring aspects of one's personality and belief system may influence courtroom decisions, though usually only to a modest degree. Using simulated juries, this research indicated that certain personality attributes of mock jurors such as authoritarianism and locus of control as well as attitudes such as belief in a just world may at times be related to jurors' verdicts.

Authoritarianism is one personality characteristic of jurors that is modestly correlated with their verdicts in criminal cases (Dillehay, 1999). People with an authoritarian personality adhere rigidly to traditional values, identify with and submit to powerful figures, and are punitive toward those who violate established norms. In terms of the legal system, authoritarian subjects are more likely to vote for conviction in mock jury experiments (Narby, Cutler, & Moran, 1993). However, when highly authoritarian jurors encounter a defendant who symbolizes authority, their usual tendency to punish the defendant is reversed (Nietzel & Dillehay, 1986). In fact, about the only time that authoritarian mock jurors are not more conviction-prone is in trials in which the defendant is a police officer. In such cases, the more authoritarian jurors tend to identify with the powerful and punitive image of the officer.

Beliefs about what determines our fate in life form another personality variable that sometimes affects jurors' verdicts in criminal cases. Clinical psychologist Julian Rotter (1966) proposed that people differ in their beliefs about whether their lives are controlled by internal factors, such as skill and effort, or by external factors, such as luck, fate, or the actions of others. Research has shown that this **internal/external locus of control** (or I-E, as it is abbreviated) is a potent influence on behavior in a variety of settings (Phares, 1976).

Jurors seem to project their own orientations onto the behavior of the litigants, so they may differ in whether they hold individuals or outside forces responsible for negative events (National Jury Project, 1990). Prospective jurors with an internal locus of control hold a "personal responsibility" viewpoint, believing that individuals are responsible for the adversities that beset them. Prosecutors tend to prefer these jurors. Prospective jurors with an external locus of control believe that social and environmental factors are key determinants of behavior. Criminal defendants may prefer jurors who are likely to attribute criminal acts to forces beyond the defendant's control (Phares & Wilson, 1972). Locus of control may be relevant in certain personal injury and medical malpractice cases—an older woman who slips on the ice in front of a grocery store or a hunter who accidentally shoots himself and then sues his emergency physician for improper treatment, for example. Jurors who have an internal locus of control take notice whenever the plaintiff has assumed a risk and has contributed in even a minor way to the harm he or she suffered (Hans, 1992).

Individuals differ in the extent to which they believe that people get what they deserve (and deserve what they get) in life. This attitudinal variable is called **belief in a just world** (Lerner, 1970). A person who believes in a just world needs explanation and justification; such a person is threatened by the possibility that events happen by chance. Imagine that someone is killed in what appears to be a completely coincidental accident, while walking along a sidewalk when a truck careens out of control and runs him down. Those who believe in a just world are so threatened by the idea that the victim died merely by chance that they will conclude that he must have deserved such a fate by having done something wrong to cause his misfortune. Relatives and friends of rape victims, instead of providing sympathy, may derogate them on the assumption that if they were raped, they must somehow have provoked, invited, or caused it. Consistent with this view, researchers have found that persons who believe in a just world will berate the victim of a crime or be tougher on the defendant in order to maintain their belief system (Gerbasi, Zuckerman, & Reis, 1977; Moran & Comfort, 1982).

In general, laboratory studies suggest that some personality and attitudinal variables may be modestly related to individual jurors' verdicts, at least in criminal cases. The relationships are less strong in civil cases and, in both contexts, probably depend upon the type of case (Vinson et al., 2008). But the trials used in these studies were "close calls." That is, the evidence for each side was manipulated to be about equally persuasive—in such cases, individual juror characteristics may have their greatest influence (Penrod, 1990). In the real world, the evidence is often so conclusive for one side that the jurors' personality dispositions may have less impact.

To test the impact of personality traits on attorneys' jury selection decisions and on jurors' verdicts in real cases, John Clark and his colleagues (2007) relied on the **Five Factor Model (FFM) of personality**, a generally accepted framework for describing personality characteristics (Costa & Widiger, 2002). The traits that form the model include (1) openness to experience, (2) neuroticism, (3) extraversion, (4) conscientiousness, and (5) agreeableness. According to this model, one's personality can be described by some combination of these traits.

Prior to *voir dire* in 28 real cases (11 criminal cases and 17 civil cases), the researchers asked prospective jurors to complete a questionnaire that measured these five traits. Court clerks provided information about which jurors were dismissed by the attorneys, which jurors remained to decide the case, and what the juries' verdicts were. Analyses revealed no differences in personality traits among those who were excused by the defense, those excused by the prosecution, and those who ultimately ended up on the jury. In real life, attorneys may pay little heed to prospective jurors' personality attributes, probably because these traits are largely hidden from view.

The second question addressed by this study was whether jurors' verdicts were related to their personality traits as measured by the FFM. The answer: only slightly. Jurors who opted for acquittals in criminal cases scored higher on measures of Extraversion and Conscientiousness than jurors who voted to convict, but none of the other personality traits were related to verdicts.

Attorney Effectiveness in *Voir Dire*

Attorneys take pride in their skill in selecting a proper jury. For example, a president of the Association of Trial Lawyers in America wrote, "Trial attorneys are acutely attuned to the nuances of human behavior, which enables them to detect the minutest traces of bias or inability to reach an appropriate decision" (Begam, 1977, p. 3). But findings from the study by Clark et al. (2007) are less encouraging on this point. Attorneys may overvalue the importance of demographic variables and undervalue the importance of personality variables when making peremptory challenges.

Some social scientists are indeed skeptical about how much lawyers can accomplish in *voir dire*. Broeder (1965) observed the jury selection process in 23 consecutive trials in a federal court in the Midwest and concluded that "the *voir dire* was grossly ineffective not only in weeding out 'unfavorable' jurors but even in eliciting the data which would have shown particular jurors as very likely to prove 'unfavorable'" (pp. 505–506).

In a study of attorney effectiveness, experienced trial attorneys were observed to use juror selection strategies that were not different from or better than those of inexperienced college and law students who were asked to evaluate mock jurors (Olczak et al., 1991). Trial attorneys did not appear to think any more accurately when making personality judgments than did nonprofessionals. Even when asked to perform a more realistic task—rating jurors from the videotapes of a previous *voir dire*—attorneys did no better than chance in detecting jurors who were biased against them (Kerr, Kramer, Carroll, & Alfini, 1991).

In another study evaluating the effectiveness of *voir dire*, Cathy Johnson and Craig Haney (1994) observed the full *voir dires* used in four felony trials in Santa Cruz, California. They collected information on the criminal justice attitudes of jurors by administering Boehm's (1968) Legal Attitudes Questionnaire. By comparing the attitudes of persons who were retained as jurors with those of persons who were challenged by the prosecutor or defense attorneys, they were able to gauge the effectiveness of each side's peremptory challenge strategy. Jurors who were peremptorily excused by prosecutors held stronger pro-defense attitudes than jurors excused by the defense. Jurors excused by the defense were more pro-prosecution than jurors excused by the prosecution. However, the overall score of the retained jurors was not significantly different from the average score of the first 12 jurors questioned or of a group of prospective jurors sampled at random. Apparently, although each side succeeded in getting rid of jurors most biased against it, the final result was a jury that would not have differed appreciably from a jury obtained by just accepting the first 12 people called or empanelling 12 jurors at random.

SCIENTIFIC JURY SELECTION: DOES IT WORK ANY BETTER?

For years, trial lawyers have been "picking" jurors on the basis of their own theories about how people behave. But recently, some attorneys (convinced of the importance of jury selection yet skeptical of their ability to do it well, or limited in the time they can devote to it) have hired social scientists as jury selection consultants. These consultants use empirically based procedures, including small group discussions called focus groups, shadow juries, systematic ratings of prospective jurors, and surveys of the community, to detect bias (Strier, 1999). This collection of techniques is known as **scientific jury selection**. Although these techniques were first used to aid defendants in several highly publicized "political" trials of the Vietnam War era (McConahay, Mullin, & Frederick, 1977; Schulman, Shaver, Colman, Emrich, & Christie, 1973), they are now frequently practiced in the full range of criminal and civil trials. They have been used in high profile cases including those involving Michael Jackson, Martha Stewart, and the Enron defendants. They have also been employed in less visible civil cases.

Scientific jury selection raises a number of complex issues and generates significant controversy. Some critics claim that it subverts the criminal justice system because it favors the wealthy and well-heeled over individuals of modest means (Strier, 1999) and creates a perception among the public that the system is rigged (Brown, 2003). Others claim that it is ineffective (Kressel & Kressel, 2002; Saks, 1997). Not surprisingly, consultants (and some attorneys) dispute these claims, pointing out that public defenders have benefitted from their services and touting the value of professional training and experience: "We've collected a lot of research and we can spot things a lawyer wouldn't normally be paying attention to.... Most attorneys do just one or two trials a year, if they're lucky. But a good consultant has studied hundreds of juries and knows which behaviors and characteristics to look out for" (quote by consultant Dan Wolfe, cited by McCann, 2004).

How effective *are* trial consultants at selecting juries? When attorneys in criminal trials first began to rely on empirically grounded scientific jury selection, they were often successful. Although the procedure seemed to work, the success rate may have been inflated by the following factors: (1) Many of the more widely discussed cases involved weak or controversial evidence against defendants and (2) attorneys who made the extra effort to enlist jury consultation resources may also have been more diligent and thorough in other areas of their case preparation.

The effectiveness of scientific jury selection depends on a number of variables including how many peremptory challenges are allowed, the extent to which questions delve into matters beyond superficial demographic details of prospective panel members, whether attorneys act on the guidance of the consultant, and perhaps most importantly, the extent to which jurors' attitudes and beliefs will determine the outcome of the case (Greene, 2002). The more freedom and flexibility inherent in the jury selection procedures and the more the case hinges on jurors' belief systems, the more room for consultants to ply their trade and the greater the chances they can succeed.

A few empirical studies have investigated the effectiveness of scientific jury selection. Horowitz (1980) compared scientific jury selection to traditional selection methods in four criminal cases. Traditional selection methods used by attorneys included relying on their past experience, interactions with similar jurors in prior trials, and conventional wisdom. Horowitz determined that neither approach was superior for all four trials. Scientific jury selection was more effective in cases in which there were clear-cut relationships between personality or demographic variables and jurors' votes. However, when these relationships were weak, scientific selection lacked accuracy and precision.

A study of scientific jury selection used in a series of actual capital murder trials provides more data on the effectiveness of jury consultants. Nietzel and Dillehay (1986) examined the outcomes of 31 capital trials, some of which used a jury consultant and others did not. Juries recommended the death sentence in 61% of the trials in which consultants were not employed by the defense but in only 33% of the trials in which they were used. Of course, these cases differed

---

B o x 11.5   THE CASE OF THOMAS BLANTON: A CHURCH BOMBING AND A JURY CONSULTANT

The 1963 bombing of the 16th Street Baptist Church in Birmingham, Alabama, is regarded by many as the most galvanizing moment of the civil rights era. Four African American girls were killed that Sunday morning as the bomb ripped through their church. The FBI investigated the murders and quickly identified four suspects. But the case was never prosecuted, presumably because the suspects—all White—would not have been convicted by a Birmingham jury, also presumably all White. Forty years later, one of those suspects, Thomas Blanton, a former member of the Ku Klux Klan, stood trial for the murders.

The prosecution was aided by a jury consultant, Andrew Sheldon, who conducted two focus groups and polled nearly 500 residents of the Birmingham area to measure their attitudes about racial issues in general and the church bombing in particular. According to Sheldon, this pretrial research convinced him that the prosecution should not focus on the Ku Klux Klan because the group had little relevance to most prospective jurors. Rather, Sheldon urged the prosecutor to question jurors and exercise challenges on the basis of whether

Aftermath of bombing of 16th Street Baptist Church in Birmingham, Alabama in 1963.

they had children and were churchgoers. Other relevant attitudes concerned school desegregation and racial conflict. After a three-week trial, the jury deliberated for barely two hours before convicting Blanton on four counts of murder. He was sentenced to life in prison.

---

on many variables besides the use of consultants, so it is not possible to conclude that different outcomes were due to their presence alone. But the results are consistent with claims that jury consultants might be effective in cases in which jurors' attitudes are particularly important, as they are when a jury is asked to choose between life and death. Reviewing a collection of studies that contrasted scientific jury selection with attorney methods, Fulero and Penrod (1990, p. 252) concluded, "If a defendant has his or her life... at stake, the jury selection advantages conferred by scientific jury selection techniques may well be worth the investment."

Still, trial-watchers and social scientists of the jury agree that in most cases the evidence is more important than jurors' attitudes or demographic characteristics (Jonakait, 2003; Kressel & Kressel, 2002) and that scientific jury selection may be of limited value in cases where the evidence is unambiguous. Richard Seltzer, a political scientist and jury consultant himself, acknowledged this indirectly: "Jurors cannot be predicted with the type of accuracy associated with experiments in physics" (2006).

Recognizing that jurors' demographic and personality characteristics do not correlate strongly with verdicts in general, many jury consultants have shifted their focus from advising lawyers about jury selection to providing services in realms other than jury selection (Seltzer, 2006). This new strategy emphasizes the following methods:

1. Conducting public opinion surveys, focus groups, and mock trials in which subjects hear abbreviated versions of the evidence, discuss it, and make individual and group decisions as the consultant watches and listens to their deliberations. Consultants can use respondent feedback to help attorneys present evidence so that it has the greatest possible appeal to actual jurors. In the realm of civil trials, this pretrial analysis can help determine the value that a jury would place on a plaintiff's injuries, thereby facilitating settlement negotiations. These procedures were used effectively by the prosecutor in a recent civil rights trial about an old crime (Box 11.5).

2. Analyzing how different jurors form a narrative or private story that summarizes the evidence into a coherent, compelling account (Pennington & Hastie, 1986, 1988). This analysis is followed by an attempt on the consultant's part to derive central themes that can serve to organize and explain the evidence. These themes are then reinforced by *voir dire* questions, evidence presentation, opening statements, and closing arguments so that the most salient psychological factors of the case are repeatedly presented to the jurors in a manner that best supports the attorney's desired interpretation of the facts (Kressel & Kressel, 2002; Lisnek, 2003).

ETHICAL ISSUES IN JURY SELECTION

The legal system idealistically assumes that all members of the community have an equal chance of serving on juries, but widespread practices prevent that. All segments of the community are not fairly represented in the jury pools of many jurisdictions across the nation. Furthermore, attorneys do not seek neutral jurors; they seek those favorable to their own side. Proponents of the current system acknowledge this tendency but assume that if both parties are successful in rejecting those who seem unfavorable to them, their respective challenges will balance out. In theory, both extremes will be eliminated, leaving those who are less biased and more open-minded.

This assumption is required by the logic of our adversarial system, which holds that fair process and just outcomes are achieved when two opponents work zealously to win outcomes favorable to themselves. But actual trials don't usually work out that way. Because some lawyers don't really care about jury selection ("Give me any 12 people and I'll convince 'em!") and others are inept in their selection of jurors—relying excessively on demographic

A juror being questioned during jury selection.

© Michael Kelley/Getty Images/Stone

features of jurors or on their own intuitive personality theories—this theoretical balance is seldom achieved. When one of the attorneys is more motivated or skilled in jury selection, this effectively gives that side a larger number of peremptory challenges.

Of course, this imbalance is not restricted to adversarial systems. Resources are not equally distributed in education, medicine, government, or any of our other social institutions. But the adversarial system may magnify the impact of unequally qualified participants; when opponents are not evenly matched, the superior one will win more often.

The practice of scientific jury selection presents other ethical concerns. Critics have condemned these techniques as "jury rigging" that undermine public confidence in the jury system and give wealthy litigants an unfair advantage over poor or average-income citizens (Kressel & Kressel, 2002). Though some commentators have advocated prohibiting the use of jury consultants or imposing greater limits on their work (Strier, 2001), these restrictions have not been seriously considered. Nor would they necessarily yield fairer outcomes. The American system of justice remains fundamentally adversarial. Because litigants are expected to present their version of the case as zealously as possible, they should be able to use every legal means available to sculpt and woo the jury to reach a favorable decision.

SUMMARY

1. *What does the legal system seek in trial juries?* The legal system seeks representative and unbiased juries. Both are hard to achieve. The jury selection process can, in some instances, create an unrepresentative jury.

2. *What stands in the way of jury representativeness?* The lists from which jurors' names were selected—originally only voter registration lists—underrepresent certain segments of society such as youth, older adults, and minorities. Many people fail to respond to their jury summons. Others seek dismissal by claiming personal hardship. To make jury pools representative, jurisdictions have (1) broadened the sources of names of prospective jurors by using lists of licensed drivers and those who receive federal assistance and (2) reduced automatic exemptions to persons in a limited number of occupations.

3. *What procedures are used in voir dire?* The process of selecting a jury from the panel of prospective jurors is called *voir dire*. Its goal is an unbiased jury. Prospective jurors who have biases or conflicts of interest can be challenged for cause and discharged. Each side may also discharge a certain number of prospective jurors without giving any reasons; these are called *peremptory challenges*. Questioning of the prospective jurors is done at the discretion of the judge. In most trials, there is some combination of questions from the judge and the attorneys. When questioning jurors, most attorneys also try to sway jurors to their viewpoint through various ingratiation and indoctrination techniques.

4. *What personality and attitudinal characteristics of jurors, if any, are related to their verdicts?* In choosing jurors, lawyers base their decisions on their implicit personality theories and stereotypes of what is a "good" juror. According to laboratory studies, a few personality and attitude-related characteristics—authoritarianism, locus of control, and belief in a just world—are weakly related to juror verdicts. These variables may be less important in real cases, however, and attorneys tend not to focus on jurors' personality characteristics when selecting jurors, probably because they are difficult to identify.

5. *What role do jury consultants play in a trial?* Initially, practitioners of scientific jury selection tried to determine which demographic characteristics of jurors were related to their sympathy for one side or the other in trials. More recently, trial consultants have broadened

their work to include (1) pretrial assessments of reactions to the evidence and (2) the development of themes that organize the evidence for specific jurors likely to be swayed by this approach. There is some evidence that science-oriented consultation may be useful in cases in which jurors' attitudes about the evidence are especially important.

KEY TERMS

authoritarianism

belief in a just world

black sheep effect

challenges for cause

cognizable groups

Five Factor Model (FFM) of personality

implicit personality theory

internal/external locus of control

peremptory challenges

scientific jury selection

similarity–leniency hypothesis

social desirability effect

social judgments

venire

voir dire

12

The Jury

Decision Processes and Reforms

ORIENTING QUESTIONS

1. Describe the issue of jury competence.
2. What is the impact of extralegal information on jurors?
3. Can jurors disregard inadmissible evidence?
4. How can jurors be helped to understand their instructions?
5. What is meant by the statement "Bias is inevitable in jurors"?
6. What reforms of the jury system do psychologists suggest?

The right to trial by jury is protected by state constitutions and by the Sixth (for criminal cases) and Seventh (for civil cases) Amendments to the U.S. Constitution. The U.S. Supreme Court underscored the importance of the jury by stating that "[t]he guarantees of jury trial in the state and federal constitutions reflect a profound judgment about the way in which the law should be enforced and justice administered" (*Duncan v. Louisiana*, 1968, p. 149). More recently, the Supreme Court acknowledged the preeminent role of juries in our legal system when it announced that nearly any contested fact that increases the penalty for a crime must be determined by a jury (*Blakely v. Washington*, 2004).

Trial by jury is an institution that routinely draws ordinary citizens into the apparatus of the justice system. Most legal disputes are resolved without a jury trial and the number of cases that are decided by juries has dropped recently (Galanter, 2004). However, there are still more than 150,000 jury trials conducted each year in the United States, and tens of thousands occur in other countries throughout the world. In fact, jury trials have recently been reintroduced in Russia and Spain, are being instituted in Japan, and form an integral part of the legal system in countries in Africa (e.g., Ghana, Malawi), Asia (e.g., Sri Lanka, Hong Kong), South America (e.g., Brazil), and Europe (e.g., England, Ireland, Denmark) (Vidmar, 2000). Jurors also decide many criminal cases in Canada.

Approximately two-thirds of Americans have been called to jury duty and approximately one-quarter have actually served as jurors (Harris Poll, 2008). For many jurors, their participation demands major sacrifices of income, time, and energy. In a massive class action lawsuit against the Ford Motor Corporation, one juror continued to attend the trial even after suffering injuries in a hit-and-run accident and in spite of requiring constant pain medication; another juror whose family moved out of the county opted to live in a hotel near the courthouse in order to continue hearing the case. On occasion, jury service can be extremely unpleasant: in 2009 a San Diego judge declared a mistrial in a kidnapping case after the defendant flung feces at the jury. Fortunately, he missed. Yet serving on a jury can also be educational and inspiring. Many jurors have a positive view of the court system after serving (Bornstein, Miller, Nemeth, Page, & Musil, 2005). Occasionally, jury service even brings great personal satisfaction, as it did for Erika Ozer and Jeremy Sperling, who met in a New York City jury box in 2001 and were married in 2005.

The jury system casts its shadow well beyond the steps of the courthouse, however, because predictions about jury verdicts influence decisions to settle civil lawsuits and to accept plea bargains in criminal cases. Thus the jury trial is an important and influential tradition; no other institution of government places power so directly in the hands of the people and allows average citizens the opportunity to judge the actions of their peers (Abramson, 1994).

Antecedents of the contemporary jury system may be seen in English law established 700 years ago and earlier. Even the ancient Greeks had a form of citizen jury. But throughout its history, the jury system has been under attack. One critic described the jury as, at best, 12 people of average

---

B o x 12.1   THE CASE OF THE *EXXON VALDEZ* AND THE "EXCESSIVE" DAMAGE AWARD

On the night of March 24, 1989, with the third mate at the helm, a 900-foot oil tanker was ripped open when it ran aground in Prince William Sound, Alaska. Eleven million gallons of oil spilled into the open sea and washed up onto shorelines. Aboard the tanker was an inebriated Captain Joseph Hazelwood, who had left the bridge to do paperwork in his cabin only moments before the accident.

In the years following the wreck, Exxon spent approximately $2.1 billion to remove oil from the water and surrounding shorelines, was fined $125 million for environmental crimes, was ordered to pay $900 million for restoration of the natural environment, and paid an additional $300 million to those parties who were financially affected by the oil spill.

Left out of the mix were commercial fishermen, who were not compensated for the losses they sustained when fishing habitats were destroyed. They sued in federal court in Alaska; a jury determined

U.S. Coast Guard Photo

Exxon Valdez

that Hazelwood's actions were reckless and that Exxon was to blame for giving command of an oil tanker to a known alcoholic. The jury assessed damages against Exxon at $5 billion, one of the largest damage awards in American history. But in 2008 the Supreme Court reduced the punitive damage award to $507 million, ruling that the massive award was unfair.

---

ignorance. Another critic, Judge Jerome Frank, who served on the federal appeals court, complained that juries apply law they don't understand to facts they can't get straight. Even Mark Twain took a swing at the jury system. In *Roughing It*, he called the jury "the most ingenious and infallible agency for defeating justice that wisdom could contrive." One anonymous commentator asked rhetorically, "How would you like to have your fate decided by twelve people who weren't smart enough to get out of jury duty?" (cited by Shuman & Champagne, 1997). Others have noted that when a judge makes an unpopular decision, that particular judge is criticized, but when a jury reaches an unpopular verdict, the entire jury system is indicted (Ellsworth & Mauro, 1998).

The civil jury, in particular, has been vilified. In fact, one prominent scholar of the civil jury points out that "so many writings, both scholarly and journalistic, have been devoted to criticizing the institution of the civil jury that it becomes boring to recite the claims" (Vidmar, 1998, p. 849). According to Vidmar, civil juries have been criticized as incompetent, capricious, unreliable, biased, sympathy-prone, confused,

gullible, hostile to corporate defendants, and excessively generous to plaintiffs. We examine some of these claims later in this chapter.

Much of the public outcry focuses on the seemingly excessive nature of jury damage awards. For example, Marc Bluestone of Sherman Oaks, California, received a jury award of $39,000 after his mixed-breed Labrador retriever, valued at $10, died a few days after returning home from a two-month stay at a pet clinic. Explains Steven Wise, a lawyer and animal rights activist: "The courts are beginning to realize that the bond between humans and animals is very powerful" (Hamilton, 2004).

Another large damage award came in the case against Exxon for its role in the 1989 *Exxon Valdez* oil spill (Box 12.1).

To be sure, the jury system also has its defenders. Many authors point out that claims about juries are often based on anecdotes that are unrepresentative or fabricated and on studies that lack scientific validity (see, for example, Greene & Bornstein, 2003; Hans, 2000). Indeed, most of us never hear about the hundreds of thousands of juries that each year toil out of the spotlight and, after careful deliberation, reach reasonable verdicts.

Proponents further argue that the notion of trial by jury epitomizes what is special about the justice system in that it ensures public participation in the process. Verdicts reached by representative juries can and often do increase the legitimacy of the process in the eyes of the public, particularly in controversial trials. Juries can serve as a check on the arbitrary or idiosyncratic nature of a judge. Because juries do not give a reason for their verdicts (as judges are required to do), they retain a flexibility that is denied to judges. Finally, participating on a jury can both educate jurors and enhance regard for the justice system. Alexis de Tocqueville (1900), a 19th-century French statesman, wrote, "I do not know whether the jury is useful to those who are in litigation, but I am certain it is highly beneficial to those who decide the litigation; and I look upon it as one of the most efficacious means for the education of the people which society can employ" (p. 290).

Who's right? Are juries capable of making fair and intelligent decisions, or is the jury system so flawed that its use should be restricted or possibly even eliminated? Are criticisms of the jury justified? If so, can the legal system do anything to improve the functioning of juries?

Over the past several decades, researchers have subjected the jury to careful scientific scrutiny by applying theories and principles of social psychology (e.g., social influence, conformity, and small-group behavior) and cognitive psychology (e.g., reasoning and decision making). In fact, studies of juror and jury decision making have become so plentiful that they occupy a center place in psychology and law research. From their findings, we have been able to obtain a better—though still somewhat incomplete—picture of how the jury system works.

In this chapter, we focus on what we have learned from these many studies. In particular, we focus on two broad questions: first, whether juries are competent to execute their duties properly, and, second, whether they are biased and prejudiced. Within each of these broad categories we examine several related issues and rely on research studies to

answer the questions. Finally, we consider various proposals to reform the institution of the jury.

ARE JURIES COMPETENT?

Some commentators have suggested that juries in criminal cases make more mistakes than the public should tolerate, in part because they are faced with tough cases—cases in which the evidence is neither flimsy enough to warrant dismissal nor compelling enough to induce a guilty plea (Arkes & Mellers, 2002). Reexamining the data on jury–judge comparisons first presented by Kalven and Zeisel (1966; described in Chapter 10), Northwestern University Professor Bruce Spencer estimates that jury verdicts are incorrect in at least one out of every eight cases (Spencer, 2007). He asks, "Can we be satisfied knowing that innocent people go to jail for many years for wrongful convictions?" (Northwestern University, 2007).

Psychologists have examined factors that affect the accuracy of jury verdicts. They have assessed the assumption that in reaching their verdicts, jurors rely only on the evidence and disregard information that is not evidence (e.g., preexisting beliefs; irrelevant facts about the defendant, victim, plaintiff, or witnesses; and any information that the judge asks them to disregard). They have determined whether jurors can listen attentively to expert testimony but not to give it undue weight. They have asked whether, as the legal system assumes, jurors understand and correctly apply the judge's instructions on the law and have the necessary reasoning skills to understand protracted and complex cases.

Some of what we know about the influences on jury verdicts comes from questioning jurors after trials; other data come from archival analyses of past verdicts and from jury simulation studies. In simulation studies, the researcher introduces and possibly manipulates some piece of information (e.g., the defendant's race, gender, or socioeconomic status) and then measures the extent to which that information, as well as the actual evidence, influence jurors' reasoning and their verdicts. Although simulation studies sometimes cast this information in a more prominent light than would be likely in real trials (e.g., a defendant's physical appearance might seem salient in an abbreviated and simulated trial but would lose its impact in a lengthy proceeding), they are nonetheless useful techniques for exploring how jurors reason and make decisions.

On the basis of such studies, we have learned that jurors in both criminal and civil cases pay considerable attention to the strength of the evidence. In fact, **evidentiary strength** is probably the most important determinant of jurors' verdicts (Devine, Clayton, Dunford, Seying, & Pryce, 2001; Greene & Bornstein, 2003, Taylor & Hosch, 2004). Differences in strength of the evidence can have profound effects on jury verdicts: Some studies have shown a 70% increase in conviction rates as the evidence against the accused becomes stronger (Devine et al., 2001).

Professor Stephen Garvey and his colleagues (2004) analyzed the verdicts of 3,000 jurors in felony trials in four metropolitan areas to find out what explained jurors' first votes. They measured (and controlled for) the strength of the evidence by asking the judge who presided in the case to estimate this evidentiary strength. They then determined that the judge's assessment of the strength of the evidence was powerfully associated with the jurors' first votes: The stronger the evidence against the defendant, the more likely the juror was to convict. In the realm of civil litigation, jurors also place considerable weight on the evidence and, in particular, on the severity of the plaintiff's injury. More seriously injured plaintiffs receive greater compensation than less seriously injured plaintiffs (Bovbjerg, Sloan, Dor, & Hsieh, 1991).

Effects of Extralegal Information

But studies document that jury decisions can also be influenced by irrelevant information about the defendant's background or appearance, by what jurors read in the newspaper, or by other sources of irrelevant information, all of which constitute **extralegal information**. For example, although conflicting findings exist, juror and jury decisions seem to be influenced by the defendant's race. In

particular, White jurors are harsher on Black defendants than on White defendants, and Black jurors are harsher on White defendants than on Black defendants (Mitchell, Haw, Pfeifer, & Meissner, 2005; Sommers, 2007). Some researchers suspect that jurors' unconscious associations and thoughts may be at the root of such biases (Krieger, 2004).

The defendant's race is particularly likely to influence White jurors when the crime is "blue-collar" as opposed to "white-collar" (Gordon, Walden, McNicholas, & Bindrim, 1988), the trial involves ambiguous evidence (van Prooijen, 2006), and no racially charged issues arise during the trial (Sommers & Ellsworth, 2000). Professor Samuel Sommers (2007) interprets these findings in the context of **aversive racism**, a social psychological framework that proposes that most White jurors are motivated to avoid showing racial bias and when cued about racial considerations (e.g., when the crime is racially charged or when jurors are instructed to avoid prejudice), they tend to render color-blind decisions. But without those explicit reminders to be objective, subtle racial biases can influence their decisions.

What accounts for the fact that although evidence strength is, in many cases, the primary influence on jurors' decisions, extralegal evidence exerts its impact in other cases? According to the **liberation hypothesis** (Kalven & Zeisel, 1966), when the evidence in a case clearly favors one side or the other, juries will decide the case in favor of the side with the stronger evidence. But when the evidence is ambiguous (i.e., the prosecution's case is weak), jurors are "liberated" and allowed to rely on their assumptions, sentiments, and biases—in short, on extralegal evidence—in reaching a verdict.

The mechanism by which juries reach these decisions is captured by the **dual-process theory of attitude change** (Eagly & Chaiken, 1993) that distinguishes two different kinds of information-processing strategies or "routes." When people are motivated to think systematically about some information and have ample time to do so, they take the **"central route"** and focus on the arguments or evidence provided. This way of thinking characterizes most jury trials and explains why the strength of the evidence is such a powerful predictor of verdicts. But when the evidence is conflicting or confusing, or when jurors are not motivated to think systematically, they are said to use a "**peripheral route**" that involves attention to tangential or extraneous details such as extralegal information.

Based on post-trial questionnaire data collected from jurors, judges, and attorneys in 179 criminal cases, Professor Dennis Devine and his colleagues determined that extralegal factors such as demographics of the foreperson and exposure to pretrial publicity were related to jury verdicts only when the prosecution's evidence was not strong (Devine, Buddenbaum, Houp, Studebaker, & Stolle, 2009). In these cases, jurors used the peripheral route to information processing. When the evidence was unambiguous, jurors used the central route and focused clearly on that evidence when determining their verdicts. Psychologists have now examined the impact of various kinds of extralegal information in both criminal and civil cases.

Impact of Extralegal Information in Criminal Cases

The Influence of Prior-Record Evidence. In 1993, Maria Ohler was convicted of possessing a small amount of methamphetamine and was sentenced to three years of probation. Four years later, customs inspectors found 84 pounds of marijuana behind a loose panel in the van that Ohler was driving into the United States from Mexico. When she was tried on the marijuana charge, evidence of her prior conviction was admitted at the trial in order to attack her credibility as a witness.

Once jurors have heard evidence about a defendant's prior criminal record, they may no longer be able to suspend judgment about that defendant and decide his or her fate solely on the basis of the evidence introduced at trial. Therefore, the prosecution is often not permitted to introduce evidence of a defendant's criminal record for fear that jurors would be prejudiced by it and judge the current offense in light of those past misdeeds. However, if defendants take the witness stand,

then prosecutors may be able to question them about certain types of past convictions in order to impeach their credibility as witnesses. In that circumstance, the judge may issue a **limiting instruction** to the effect that evidence of a defendant's prior record can be used for limited purposes only: to gauge the defendant's credibility but not to prove the defendant's propensity to commit the charged offense. Defense attorneys are decidedly suspicious of jurors' ability to follow this rule, as well they should be; limiting instructions are rarely effective (Shaw & Skolnick, 1995). Thus, attorneys often recommend to their clients with prior records that they not take the witness stand to testify on their own behalf.

An early study showed that attorneys' hunches were well founded. Mock jurors informed of a defendant's prior conviction were more likely than jurors who had no information about a prior record to convict the defendant on subsequent charges (Doob & Kirshenbaum, 1972). A subsequent study found that the similarity of the charges is an important variable: Conviction rates were higher when the prior conviction was for an offense similar to the one being decided (Wissler & Saks, 1985). Another study found that deliberating juries spend considerable time talking about a defendant's prior record, not for what it suggests about credibility, but rather to decide whether the defendant has a criminal disposition (Shaffer, 1985).

Why does evidence of a prior conviction increase the likelihood of conviction on a subsequent charge? For some jurors, the prior record, in combination with allegations related to the subsequent charge, may show a pattern of criminality; together they point to an individual who is prone to act in an illegal or felonious manner. Other jurors, upon hearing evidence of a prior conviction, may need less evidence to be convinced of the defendant's guilt beyond a reasonable doubt on the subsequent charge. Prior-record evidence may lead a juror to think that because the defendant already has a criminal record, an erroneous conviction would not be serious. This juror might therefore be satisfied with a slightly less compelling demonstration of guilt.

> **B o x   12.2**   THE CASE OF CHARLES FALSETTA AND HIS PROPENSITY TO COMMIT SEX CRIMES
>
> When Charles Falsetta was tried for rape and kidnapping in Alameda County Court, the prosecutor introduced evidence of two prior uncharged sexual assaults allegedly committed by Falsetta. In the first, the defendant was alleged to have begun jogging beside a woman, asked her where she was going, and then tackled and raped her. In the second incident, the defendant allegedly blocked the path of a woman as she walked to work and later jumped out from behind some bushes, grabbed her, threw her into the bushes, and sexually assaulted her. These incidents bore a striking resemblance to the Alameda County case in which the defendant was alleged to have stopped a 16-year-old girl as she was walking to her house from a convenience store. After initially refusing a ride, the girl eventually accepted and was
>
> driven to a darkened parking lot and raped. The defendant was convicted and appealed his conviction, contending that the admission of evidence of other uncharged rapes violated his rights.
>
> In an appeal to the California Supreme Court, Richard Rochman, the deputy attorney general who argued the case on behalf of the State of California, stated that because victims of sex offenses often hesitate to speak out and because the alleged crimes occur in private, prosecutors are often faced with a "he said, she said" credibility problem. Allowing prosecutors to present propensity evidence in these cases would give jurors the full picture of the defendant's past sexual misconduct, reasoned Rochman. The California Supreme Court agreed (*People v. Falsetta*, 1999).

The Impact of Evidence on Multiple Charges. Consider the case of Bryon Quinn, charged with 21 counts (including several for aggravated robbery) stemming from multiple robberies of office supply and pet stores in Colorado in 2003. Would jurors be able to keep the evidence straight on all of these charges?

Most courts permit a criminal defendant to be tried for two or more charges at the same time as long as the offenses are similar or are connected to the same act. This procedure, called **joinder**, exists primarily for purposes of efficiency: It is more efficient to try similar cases together than to stage separate trials. But does trying someone for two or more charges at the same time increase the likelihood that the jury will convict the defendant of at least one of these crimes? Was Quinn more likely to be convicted of any of those robberies because they were tried in conjunction with other robberies? A meta-analysis of simulation studies that have examined the effects of joinder (Nietzel, McCarthy, & Kern, 1999) concluded that such a procedure was clearly to the defendant's disadvantage. Criminal defendants are more likely to be convicted of any single charge when it is tried in combination with other charges than when it is tried alone. Some evidence indicates that jurors who hear multiple cases misremember and confuse evidence against the

defendant across charges and conclude that the defendant has a criminal disposition because of the multiplicity of charges (Nietzel et al., 1999).

The Impact of Character and Propensity Evidence. Evidence about a defendant's character is generally not admissible to prove that the defendant committed a crime. Likewise, evidence of other crimes or wrongdoing (so-called **propensity evidence**) is typically not admissible to suggest that because a defendant had the propensity to act in a criminal manner, he is guilty of the charge now at issue. There are exceptions, however. Character evidence can be used in federal court to provide evidence on guilt when it is relevant to the defendant, the alleged victim, or a witness (Federal Rule of Evidence 404). Also, sex crimes are treated differently in federal court and in some states. In 1994, Congress passed a law making evidence of other sex offenses admissible to show a defendant's propensity to commit the charged sex offense. (The promulgation of this law reflects a belief that some people have a propensity toward aggressive and sexual impulses.) The California legislature enacted a similar law in 1995, and the California Supreme Court upheld the law in the case described in Box 12.2.

What effect might propensity evidence have on jurors? In arguing in support of allowing propensity evidence in the *Falsetta* case, the California Attorney General assumed that jurors could properly use propensity evidence to gauge the defendant's disposition to commit sex crimes. Yet psychologists can point to a fundamental error in this assumption—the belief that this characteristic or trait is stable over time and that situational factors are irrelevant (Eads, Shuman, & DeLipsey, 2000). In short, making this assumption constitutes the fundamental attribution error.

At least one study raises questions about jurors' abilities to use propensity evidence properly. In their study of jury decision making in sexual assault cases, Bette Bottoms and Gail Goodman (1994) exposed some mock jurors to information about a defendant's past criminal acts and to other negative evidence bearing on the defendant's character. These jurors perceived the victim as more credible and the defendant as more likely to be guilty than did jurors not exposed to this character evidence.

Impact of Extralegal Information in Civil Cases

When individuals have a dispute with their landlord, their insurance company, or the manufacturer of a product that they allege to have caused them harm, they can attempt to resolve that dispute through the workings of the civil justice system. Although the vast majority of civil cases are resolved outside the courtroom, typically in settlement discussions between the opposing lawyers, thousands of civil cases are tried before juries each year. Juries in these cases typically make two fundamental decisions: whether the defendant (or, in some instances, the plaintiff) is **liable** or responsible for the alleged harm and whether the injured party (typically the plaintiff) should receive any money to compensate for his or her losses, and if so, in what amount. These monies are called **damages**.

Although the vast majority of scholarly research on juror and jury decision making has focused on criminal cases, in recent years psychologists have devoted considerable attention to the workings of civil juries. As a result, they are increasingly able to address the question of whether jurors are compe-

tent to decide civil cases fairly and rationally. Do jurors determine liability and assess damages in a rational way, or are they swayed by emotion and prejudice?

Determining Liability. An important decision that jurors must make in civil cases concerns the parties' respective responsibility for the harm that was suffered. When psychologists study juries' liability judgments, they are really asking how people assign responsibility for an injury. When a baby is stillborn, do jurors perceive the doctor to be at fault for not performing a cesarean section? Would the child have died anyway? When a smoker dies from lung cancer, do jurors blame the cigarette manufacturer for elevating the nicotine level in its product or the smoker who knowingly exposed himself or herself to a dangerous product over the course of many years? Or do they blame both?

Jurors should decide liability on the basis of the defendant's conduct. Were his actions reckless? Were they negligent? Were they malicious and evil? The severity of an injury or accident, sometimes referred to as **outcome severity**, though legally relevant to decisions about the damage award in a civil case, should be irrelevant to a judgment concerning liability or legal responsibility. The defendant should not be saddled with a liability judgment against him simply because the plaintiff was seriously injured. Are jurors able to use the evidence concerning outcome severity for the limited purposes for which it is intended—namely, to assess damages? Or do they factor it into their decision about responsibility as well?

To examine how the consequences of an accident affect judgments of responsibility, Walster (1966) presented participants with the facts of an accident and asked them to rate the responsibility of the actor who was potentially at fault. Some participants learned that the actor's conduct resulted in a dented fender (a low-severity outcome), and others learned that his actions resulted in major property damage or personal injury (a high-severity outcome). Walster found that participants assigned more responsibility to the actor in the high-severity condition than in the low-severity condition.

Why would we assign more responsibility to an individual as the consequences of his or her conduct become more serious? One explanation is **defensive attribution** (Fiske & Taylor, 1991), an explanation of behavior that defends us from feelings of vulnerability. As the consequences of one's actions become more severe and more unpleasant, we are likely to blame a person for their occurrence because doing so makes the incident somehow more controllable and avoidable.

Walster's study was conducted with college students who read a brief description of an accident and assigned responsibility judgments. One wonders whether similar results occur when information concerning injury severity is presented in combination with other testimony, and when this complex set of evidence is discussed during deliberations. Will jurors continue to focus inappropriately on the outcome of the incident? Will their liability judgments be improperly influenced?

This question was addressed by Greene and her colleagues (Greene, Johns, & Bowman, 1999; Greene, Johns, & Smith, 2001) in a reenactment of an automobile negligence case in which the defendant, a truck driver, crashed into a highway median and struck a small pickup truck being driven in the opposite direction by the plaintiff. These researchers manipulated evidence about the defendant's driving behavior and the severity of the injuries to the plaintiff. In theory, jurors' judgments of liability should be affected by evidence of the defendant's conduct but not by evidence related to the severity of the outcome.

As is legally appropriate, the defendant's conduct had a strong impact on citizen–jurors' judgments of the defendant's liability, but evidence about the severity of the plaintiff's injuries also mattered—the defendant was perceived to be more negligent when the plaintiff suffered more serious injuries. Perhaps most troubling, these effects were not erased during deliberation. (One might hope that jurors would correct each other's misuse of the evidence as they discussed it during deliberation.) Rather, individual jurors were more likely to rely on irrelevant

information regarding the plaintiff's injuries *after* deliberating than they had been *before* deliberations. These results are consistent with a meta-analysis (Robbennolt, 2000) showing that people attribute greater responsibility to a wrongdoer when the outcome of an incident is severe than when it is minor.

Although the legal system expects jurors to evaluate liability objectively, jurors' emotional reactions also influence their assessment of the facts and evidence. For example, jurors who are angered by evidence of wrongdoing and harm to others feel more sympathy for a plaintiff (Feigenson, Park, & Salovey, 2001) and less sympathy for a defendant (Bornstein, 1994). These experienced emotions are likely to interact with jurors' preexisting emotional states, implying that the legal assumption of strict objectivity in how jurors evaluate evidence is probably inaccurate (Wiener, Bornstein, & Voss, 2006).

Assessing Damages.   Pity the poor man. Michael Brennan, a St. Paul bank president, was simply responding to nature's call when he was sprayed with more than 200 gallons of raw sewage as he sat on the toilet in the bank's executive washroom. The geyser of water came "blasting up out of the toilet with such force that it stood him right up," leaving Brennan "immersed in human excrement." He sued a construction company working in the bank at the time, but the jury awarded Brennan nothing. Why, then, did a jury award $300,000 to a workman who slipped from a ladder and fell into a pile of manure (a story aired on CBS's "60 Minutes")?

One of the most perplexing issues related to juries is how they assess damages (Greene & Bornstein, 2003; Sunstein, Hastie, Payne, Schkade, & Viscusi, 2002). This complex decision seems especially subjective and unpredictable because people value money and injuries differently and because jurors are given scant guidance on how to award damages (Greene & Bornstein, 2000). The awards for punitive damages—intended to punish the defendant and deter future malicious conduct— are of special concern because the jury receives little instruction about how those awards should be determined. Consider the staggering $145 billion punitive damage award against the tobacco industry in 2000. Even the judge in the case was amazed. "A lot of zeros," he observed dryly, after reading the verdict.

Psychologists have conducted some research on this issue. What have they learned? First, few people get rich by suing for damages. In state court civil trials in 2005, the median damage award was $28,000 and only 4% of winning plaintiffs received more than $1 million (Langton & Cohen, 2008). Although the media are eager to tell us about multimillion-dollar damage awards, these colossal awards are very unusual. Second, in general, the more a plaintiff requests, the more that plaintiff receives. Jurors tend to adjust their awards toward "anchor points," the most obvious of which is the plaintiff's requested damages (Chapman & Bornstein, 1996).

What factors do jurors consider in their decisions about damages? Data from interviews with actual jurors, experimental studies, and videotapes of actual jury deliberations show that, as in criminal cases, jurors put most weight on the evidence they hear in court. But in addition, they sometimes consider attorneys' fees and whether any loss is covered by insurance—issues that are theoretically irrelevant to decisions about the amount of damages to award. According to psychologists Shari Diamond and Neil Vidmar (2001), discussions about insurance coverage are quite common in jury rooms. They examined the deliberations of 50 juries in Tucson, Arizona, as part of the landmark Arizona Jury Project (the research project evaluated a number of reforms in jury trials that we describe later in this chapter). They determined that conversations about insurance occurred in 85% of these cases; often, jurors expressed concern about overcompensating plaintiffs whose medical bills had already been covered by their own insurance.

Another common (but theoretically forbidden) topic of discussion is attorneys' fees. Attorneys who represent plaintiffs in personal injury cases (a kind of civil case that is sometimes tried before a jury) typically work on a contingent fee basis. Plaintiffs do not pay their attorneys in advance to represent them. Rather, if successful in securing a settlement or damage award for the client, the attorney takes some percentage (typically 25% to 35%) as a fee. If unsuccessful, the attorney (and the plaintiff as well) receive nothing. In their analysis of the Arizona jury deliberations, Diamond and Vidmar (2001) found that the topic of attorneys' fees came up in 83% of jury discussions. Other research has shown, though, that jury awards are not directly influenced by the frequency with which jurors talk about these topics (Greene, Hayman, & Motyl, 2008).

Can Jurors Disregard Inadmissible Evidence?

Anyone who has ever watched television shows depicting courtroom drama is familiar with the attorney's statement, "I object!" If the judge sustains an objection, then the opposing attorney's objectionable question or the witness's objectionable response will not be recorded, and the judge will instruct, or admonish, the jury to disregard the material. But are jurors able to do so?

Most of the empirical evidence indicates that they are not, and furthermore, that a judge's admonition to disregard **inadmissible evidence** is relatively ineffective (Steblay, Hosch, Culhane, & McWerthy, 2006). But jurors *are* more likely to comply with a judge's instruction to ignore inadmissible evidence if the judge also provides a reason for the inadmissibility ruling.

On occasion, instructions to ignore inadmissible evidence backfire and result in jurors being *more* likely to use the inadmissible evidence than if they had not been told to ignore it (Lieberman & Arndt, 2000). For example, Broeder (1959) presented a civil case in which mock jurors learned either that the defendant had insurance or that he did not. Half the subjects who were told that he had insurance were admonished by the judge to disregard that information. Juries who believed that the defendant lacked insurance awarded an average of $33,000 in damages. Juries who believed that he did have insurance awarded an average of $37,000. But those juries that were aware of the insurance but had been admonished to disregard it gave the highest average award, $46,000.

These findings imply that instructions to disregard certain testimony may heighten jurors' reliance on the inadmissible evidence. Psychologists have explained this phenomenon using **reactance theory** (Brehm, 1966; Brehm & Brehm, 1981) which suggests that instructions to disregard evidence may threaten jurors' freedom to consider all available evidence. When this happens, jurors may respond by acting in ways that restore their sense of decision-making freedom.

Jurors' overreliance on evidence they are admonished not to use may also reflect a cognitive process described in **thought suppression** studies. Wegner and his associates (Wegner & Erber, 1992; Wegner, Schneider, Carter, & White, 1987) found that asking people "not to think of a white bear" increased the tendency to do just that. In fact, the harder people try to suppress a thought, the less likely they are to succeed (Wegner, 1994). Jurors may think more about inadmissible evidence as a direct consequence of their attempts to follow the judge's request to suppress thoughts of it (Clavet, 1996).

But what happens when individual jurors come together to deliberate? Will the process, or even the expectation of discussion with other jurors, motivate jurors to follow the judge's instructions? Limited research on mock juries indicates that jury deliberations can indeed lessen the impact of inadmissible evidence (London & Nunez, 2000).

The jury's decision could also be influenced by many other irrelevant factors in the trial presentation, including the personal style and credibility of attorneys, the order of presentation of evidence, and the gender, race, age, physical appearance, and attractiveness of the litigants and other witnesses (Devine et al., 2001). In a sensational case stemming from the murder of wealthy fashion journalist Christa Worthington on Cape Cod in 2002 and the subsequent conviction of her African American garbage collector, Christopher McCowen, jurors were summoned back to court a year after the trial to describe racially based remarks made during deliberations. Two White female jurors apparently referred to the defendant's race and size in justifying

their verdict preferences. One juror, in the midst of a discussion about the physical evidence, allegedly pointed to a photograph of the bruising on the victim and "exclaimed that this is what happens 'when a 200-pound Black guy beats on a small woman'" (Sommers, 2009).

An early review by Gerbasi, Zuckerman, and Reis (1977) offered a summary that is, unfortunately, still relevant today: "It appears that extraevidential factors, such as defendant, victim, and juror characteristics, trial procedures, and so forth, can influence the severity of verdicts rendered by individual jurors" (p. 343). After reviewing a variety of extralegal influences ranging from speculative questions during cross-examination (Kassin, Williams, & Saunders, 1990) to hearsay as communicated by an expert witness (Schuller, 1995), two researchers concluded that "indeed, mock jury research has shown that verdicts can be influenced by a wide range of nonevidentiary factors presented both inside and outside the courtroom" (Kassin & Studebaker, 1998, p. 3). Yet judges implicitly assume that jurors are able to eliminate such irrelevant considerations from their decisions.

Psychologists emphasize that, in contrast to the stated view of the legal system, jurors are active information processors. Their goal is to make a decision based on what they believe is just, not necessarily one that reflects only the legally relevant information. Thus, for example, when mock jurors were told to disregard certain evidence because of a legal technicality, they still allowed that evidence to influence their verdicts when they thought that it enhanced the accuracy of their decisions (Sommers & Kassin, 2001). Because jurors want to be correct in their judgments, they may rely on information that *they* perceive to be relevant, regardless of whether that information meets the law's technical standards of admissibility.

Jurors are increasingly turning to the Internet to find information they perceive to be relevant, despite judge's admonitions not to seek information outside of the courtroom. But the technological landscape now allows jurors to use their cell phones to search for a defendant's or attorney's name on the Web, view a scene using Google Maps, get

B o x 12.3 THE CASE OF ALEXANDER PRING-WILSON, HIS EXPERT WITNESS, AND THE ISSUE OF A CONCUSSION

Had their paths not crossed on the night of April 12, 2003, Harvard graduate student Alexander Pring-Wilson might have gone on to a successful career as an environmental lawyer, and 18-year-old Michael Colono might have married the mother of his 3-year-old child (O'Connell, 2004). Instead, Pring-Wilson and Colono got into a late-night fight outside a pizza parlor, apparently after Colono made a wisecrack about Pring-Wilson's drunken demeanor. The Ivy Leaguer claimed that he had acted in self-defense as the victim and victim's cousin repeatedly punched and kicked him in the head, but in the end, Colono died as a result of five stab wounds inflicted by Pring-Wilson's 4½-inch pocket knife.

During the first of two trials, Pring-Wilson enlisted the testimony of expert witness Jeremy Schmahmann, a neurologist from Massachusetts General Hospital, who reviewed the defendant's medical history (including a concussion sustained during a rugby match) and suggested that Pring-Wilson's confusion and inconsistent

AP Images/Ted Fitzgerald

Alexander Pring-Wilson

answers to police in the hours after the stabbing incident could indicate that he sustained another concussion as he was being beaten by the victim. Pring-Wilson eventually pled guilty to involuntary manslaughter and was sentenced to two years and one day in a state prison.

explanations of complex technological concepts or medical conditions on Wikipedia, or send Twitter messages or blogs from the jury box. Some wonder whether jurors' use of Blackberrys and iPhones will wreak havoc in courtrooms around the country and some cases in which jurors searched the Web have already ended in mistrials (Schwartz, 2009).

Effects of Expert Testimony

As society has become increasingly specialized and technical knowledge has accumulated rapidly, the judicial system has come to rely on expert witnesses to inform jurors about these advances. Experts typically testify about scientific, technical, or other specialized knowledge with which most jurors are not familiar. In criminal cases, they may describe procedures used to gather and test evidence such as blood, fingerprints, DNA, and ballistics, or scientific findings relevant to victims' or perpetrators' conduct. In accident cases, they may describe the nature and causes of various claimed injuries. In commercial cases, they may detail complex financial transactions and contractual arrangements. An example is given in Box 12.3.

A concern that arises when experts testify about highly specialized or technical matters is that because jurors lack rigorous analytical skills, they may resort to unsystematic or peripheral processing. As we previously noted, peripheral processing involves attention to peripheral or superficial aspects of experts' testimony including their credentials, appearance, personality, or presentation style rather than to the content of the testimony (Eagly & Chaiken, 1993). But post-trial interviews, analysis of the questions asked by jurors, and observations of deliberations by the Arizona Jury Project showed that jurors spend considerable time focusing on the content of the expert's testimony (Vidmar & Diamond, 2001), suggesting that they are using central processing, rather than peripheral processing.

Another concern is that expert testimony will mesmerize jurors, causing them to discount their own commonsense and rely too heavily on the opinions of the experts. The "battle of the experts"—a situation that arises when both sides present their own experts—is thought to compound problems for the jury: "An especially perplexing task for lay jurors is to assimilate and select in some rational manner from the competing testimonies of expert witnesses." (Strier, 1996, p. 112). Do jurors place undue weight on testimony from experts? How are their verdicts affected by expert testimony? A number of studies show that expert testimony exerts a small but reliable effect on jurors' decisions (Greene et al., 2002). When prosecutors introduce expert testimony, convictions are more likely; when experts testify on behalf of the defense, the likelihood of conviction decreases. If jurors do not understand an expert's testimony, they simply tend to ignore it.

When questioned about their reliance on expert testimony, jurors have stated that they evaluated the testimony on the basis of the experts' qualifications, the quality of the experts' reasoning, and the experts' impartiality (Shuman & Champagne, 1997). So it is fair to say that they do not routinely defer to the experts' assessments. A meta-analysis (Nietzel et al., 1999) supports this notion: Examining the effects of psychological expert testimony in 22 studies, Nietzel and his colleagues found little support for the concern that expert testimony will dominate jurors' decision making. Nor is it an expensive waste of time. Jurors appear to give reasoned and balanced consideration to experts whom they perceive as fair and professional.

To this point, we have assumed that expert testimony is based on valid scientific methodologies. But judges, who ultimately decide what expert evidence is admitted into court (*Daubert v. Merrell Dow Pharmaceuticals, Inc.*, 1993), may not be accurate in assessing the quality of the scientific enterprise on which the expert relies and may allow unreliable expert testimony to be admitted into evidence (Kovera & McAuliff, 2000). Are jurors able to distinguish between reliable scientific evidence and "junk science?"

This question was addressed in the context of a hostile work environment trial (Kovera, Russano, & McAuliff, 2002). Mock jurors read a 15-page trial description that included variations in the validity of the plaintiff's expert testimony: The expert's research either was valid, contained a confounding variable, lacked a control group, or involved a confederate who was not blind to the experimental condition. In general, jurors were unable to distinguish the valid

from the flawed research. Even the introduction of opposing expert testimony fails to sensitize jurors to flaws in scientific methodology (Levett & Kovera, 2008). This suggests that jurors could benefit from clear and thorough explanations to assist them in understanding scientific expert testimony.

Jurors' Abilities to Understand Their Instructions

Jury instructions, provided by the judge to the jury near the end of a trial, play a crucial role in every case. They explain the laws that are applicable to the case and direct jurors to reach a verdict in accordance with those laws. Ironically, jurors are often treated like children during the evidence phase of the trial—they are expected to sit still, pay attention, and not ask questions—but like accomplished law students during the reading of the judge's instructions, when they are expected to understand the complicated legal terminology of the instructions. According to one set of commentators, this legal education is "remarkably awkward, frequently incomplete, and in some respects almost obstinately opaque" (Diamond & Rose, 2005, p. 272). Not surprisingly, the greatest weakness for many juries is their inability to understand their instructions (Ellsworth, 1999; Lieberman & Sales, 2000).

One source of confusion is the legal language itself. Often, the instructions simply repeat statutory language and therefore are full of legal terms that are unfamiliar to laypeople. (For example, in most civil cases, jurors are informed that the burden of proof is on the plaintiff to establish his case by a *preponderance* of the evidence; the word *preponderance* appears 0.26 times per million words in the English language!) In addition, consider this example of how jurors are instructed about the meaning of *proximate cause*, an important concept in civil trials: "a cause which, in a natural and continuous sequence, produced damage, and without which the damage would not have occurred." Do you think the average layperson would understand the meaning of that term? Despite the fact that juries work hard to understand their instructions, spending 20% or more of their deliberation time trying to decipher the meaning of the judge's instructions (Ellsworth, 1989), they sometimes get it wrong simply because they do not understand the legal jargon.

Another source of confusion lies in the way the instructions are conveyed to jurors. Typically, the jury listens passively as the judge reads the instructions aloud. Jurors may or may not be provided with a written copy of the instructions, and they are almost never given the opportunity to ask questions in the courtroom to clarify misunderstandings they may have about the law. When jurors ask for assistance with the instructions in the course of deliberating, the judge is often unwilling to help, reasoning that rewording or clarifying the instructions could be grounds for appeal. In one of the cases studied by a Special Committee of the American Bar Association (ABA, 1991), during deliberations the jury asked the judge to define the word *tortious*. His response: "Take away the *-ious*." Not exceedingly helpful, we suspect! (A *tort* is an injury to persons or to property.)

Judges generally assume that the instructions will have the intended effects of guiding jurors through the thicket of unfamiliar legal concepts. That was the sentiment of the U.S. Supreme Court in *Weeks v. Angelone* (2000). Lonnie Weeks confessed to killing a Virginia state trooper in 1993 and was tried for capital murder. During the deliberations, jurors sent the judge a note asking for clarification of their instructions. The judge simply repeated the instruction. Two hours later, the jurors, some in tears, sentenced Weeks to death. Weeks appealed, citing the jury's apparent confusion about the instructions. But the appeal fell on deaf ears. Chief Justice William Rehnquist, author of the opinion, wrote that there was only a "slight possibility" that jurors had been confused by the trial judge's instructions. Ironically, a study conducted by Cornell Law Professor Stephen Garvey and his colleagues challenges that assumption. Simulating the Weeks case, Garvey and his colleagues concluded that the jury might not have sentenced Weeks to death had they received clarification of their instructions (Garvey, Johnson, & Marcus, 2000).

Can this situation be rectified? Could the instructions be rewritten, or could their presentation be revised so that jurors have a better chance of understanding and implementing them properly? Probably so. Borrowing principles from the field of **psycholinguistics** (the study of how people understand and use language), psychologists have been able to simplify jury instructions by minimizing or eliminating the use of abstract terms, negatively modified sentences, and passive voice, and by reorganizing the instructions in a more logical manner. These simplified instructions are easier for jurors to understand and use (English & Sales, 1997; Steele & Thornburg, 1988).

But it is one thing to document that revisions can improve jurors' comprehension, and quite another to convince judges to provide simplified instructions in their courtrooms. Even though there has been a steady accumulation of research showing that jurors have difficulty understanding their instructions, judges, legislatures, and rule-making commissions have not been especially receptive to reforms suggested by social scientists (Tanford, 1991). Some judges fear that omission of traditional language is "an elevator giving ready access to the justices upstairs" (*Godwin v. LaTurco*, 1969)—that is, any decision to use simplified instructions will be appealed.

That sentiment may be changing, however. States have begun to adopt reforms that focus on how judges communicate the law to jurors and several states have revised portions of their civil jury instructions. California was the first state to finalize "plain-English" instructions for both civil and criminal trials (Post, 2004b). Consider these changes to the California civil jury instruction on "burden of proof":

Old: "Preponderance of the evidence means evidence that has more convincing force than that opposed to it. If the evidence is so evenly balanced that you are unable to say that the evidence on either side of an issue preponderates, your finding on that issue must be against the party who had the burden of proving it."

New: "When I tell you that a party must prove something, I mean that the party must persuade you, by the evidence presented in court, that what he or she is trying to prove is more likely to be true than not true. This is sometimes referred to as 'the burden of proof.'"

Not surprisingly, simplified instructions enhance jurors' comprehension of the law and result in far fewer questions to the judge about what the jury instructions mean (Post, 2004b).

Another method for improving jurors' understanding of the instructions is to restructure how they are presented. Although instructions are typically read at the close of the trial, after the evidence has been presented and just before the jury retires to deliberate, some states now require judges to provide preliminary instructions before any of the evidence is presented, and many individual judges do so of their own accord (Dann & Hans, 2004).

Instructing the jury at the conclusion of the trial reflects a belief in the **recency effect**: that the judge's instructions will have a more powerful impact on a jury's decision when they are given late in the trial, after the presentation of evidence. The recency effect suggests that recent events are generally remembered better than more remote ones. Presenting the instructions after the evidence should thus increase the salience of the instructions and make the judge's directives more available for recall during deliberations. Having just heard the judge's instructions, deliberating jurors would have them fresh in their minds and be more likely to make references to them.

Logical as it might seem, this idea has been questioned by a number of authorities. Roscoe Pound, former dean of the Harvard Law School, and others have proposed what is essentially a "**schema**" theory—that jurors should be instructed *before* the presentation of testimony because this gives them a mental framework to appreciate the relevance or irrelevance of testimony as it unfolds. This line of reasoning gains support from research in cognitive psychology showing (1) that people learn more effectively when they know in advance

what the specific task is and (2) that schematic frameworks facilitate comprehension and recall (Bartlett, 1932; Neisser, 1976). Also, a number of judges (e.g., Frank, 1949) have objected to the customary sequence on the ground that instructions at the end of the trial are given after the jurors have already made up their minds. Judge E. Barrett Prettyman's (1960) position reflects this concern:

> It makes no sense to have a juror listen to days of testimony only then to be told that he and his conferees are the sole judges of the facts, that the accused is presumed to be innocent, that the government must prove guilt beyond a reasonable doubt, etc. What manner of mind can go back over a stream of conflicting statements of alleged facts, recall the intonations, the demeanor, or even the existence of the witnesses, and retrospectively fit all these recollections into a pattern of evaluations and judgments given him for the first time after the events; the human mind cannot do so. (p. 1066)

The delivery of jury instructions at the beginning of the trial rests on the notion of a **primacy effect**—that instructions will have their most beneficial effect if they are presented first, because jurors can then compare the evidence they hear to the requirements of the law and apply the instructions to the evidence in order to reach a verdict. In this way, jurors know the rules of the trial and the requirements of the law before the trial commences.

At what point in the trial proceedings, then, *should* the judge instruct the jury? ForsterLee and Horowitz (2003) reported that mock jurors who received instructions at the beginning of the trial recalled and used more of the evidence than did jurors who were instructed after the evidence.

Preliminary instructions have other beneficial effects. In a study conducted in Los Angeles Superior Court, jurors who received pretrial instructions said that they were able to focus better during the trial (Judicial Council of California, 2004). Judges also believe that substantive preliminary instructions help jurors to follow the evidence (Dann & Hans, 2004).

What practical applications can we draw from these findings? We would argue that judicial pre-instructions are vastly underutilized. There is no reason why general instructions about the law (e.g., burden of proof, assessment of the credibility of witnesses) should not be given at both the beginning and the end of trials. Interim instructions can be given as needed to explain issues that come up during the trial, and instructions that depend on the specific evidence in a trial can be given at the end (Ellsworth & Reifman, 2000).

Jurors' Willingness to Apply Their Instructions

A different question with regard to jury instructions is whether jurors are obligated to follow the judge's legal instructions. Specifically, must they follow the letter of the law if doing so violates their sense of justice and results in an unfair verdict?

A 1998 survey conducted by the *National Law Journal* showed that the vast majority of potential jurors would disregard the judge and the law and do what they thought was right. For example, after hearing evidence of domestic violence, a California jury acquitted Cheryl Orange of killing her husband despite clear evidence of her guilt. Orange's husband had repeatedly locked her in the trunk of his car, threatened her with a knife, smothered her, and raped her. The acquittal in 2006 came 21 years after Orange was originally convicted and incarcerated for the murder. What changed? The original jury was never told of the abuse. But a 2001 law allowed victims of domestic violence who kill their partners to present evidence of abuse, and Orange was given a second chance. With knowledge of the abuse, the second jury acquitted.

Juries do, in fact, have the implicit power to acquit defendants despite evidence and judicial instructions to the contrary. This power, termed **jury nullification**, has permitted juries to acquit defendants who were legally guilty but morally upright (Horowitz & Willging, 1991). Jury nullification reflects acknowledgement that while we trust jurors to resolve the facts and apply the law in a given case, we also expect them to represent the

conscience of the community (Abramson, 1994). In this role, jurors bring their commonsense to bear on matters between the government and private individuals.

Throughout history juries have occasionally ignored the law rather than enforced it, particularly when they believed the law was unjust. In the mid-1800s, juries acquitted abolitionists of helping slaves escape from the South even though the abolitionists' actions violated the fugitive slave law. But in the aftermath of these controversial acquittals, the Supreme Court ruled that criminal juries were obligated to apply the law as set out by the judge; they had no right to deviate from that law (*Sparf and Hansen v. United States*, 1895). The controversy resurfaced in the turbulent Vietnam War period when the government began to prosecute antiwar activists, usually on charges of conspiracy. In one case, a defendant asked the judge to instruct jurors on their right to nullify the law, but the judge refused and that decision was upheld on appeal (*United States v. Dougherty*, 1972). Thus, courts have created a curious irony: Jurors can thumb their noses at the law, but ordinarily they aren't told that they can.

How would juries behave if they were informed that they have the option to disregard the law? Would we have "chaos in the courtroom," as opponents of nullification suggest, with jurors swayed by emotions and personal biases? Would jurors be less likely to convict? Possibly so; in two trials of Vietnam War protesters who broke into offices and destroyed records, the judge in one trial allowed a jury nullification defense and the jury acquitted all the defendants, whereas the judge in the other trial did not, and all nine defendants were convicted (Abramson, 1994).

Empirical Evidence Concerning Jury Nullification. One way to assess the effects of nullification instructions is to consider the empirical evidence on this topic. What effect does explicit instruction about the jury's right to nullify have on verdicts in criminal cases? Does it actually unleash "chaos in the courtroom?" That question was addressed by Horowitz, Kerr, Park, and Gockel (2006) in a study of the impact of judicial instructions concerning jury nullification on mock jurors. Evidence in the case concerned the death of a terminally ill hospital patient who died as a result of a drug overdose. Jurors learned that the defendant, the patient's doctor, had acted either out of greed (killing the patient in order to gain access to his finances) or compassion (administering an overdose to relieve the patient's suffering). Jurors were then given either standard jury instructions that included elements of the crime of murder and reminders to focus on the evidence, or the standard instructions with a nullification addendum that told jurors they were free to use their feelings based on their conscience to reach a verdict. Data showed that nullification instructions unleashed jurors' emotional biases only in the euthanasia case, not in the murder case. In other words, when there was no issue about the fairness of the prosecution (i.e., in the murder trial), jurors tended to follow the law and convicted the defendant even when they had nullification instructions. These findings suggest that any "chaos" resulting from nullification instructions is limited: Jurors tend to rely on their feelings and sentiments and to nullify the law only when that law seems unfair.

What, exactly, determines the verdicts of juries with nullification instructions? Nullification instructions seem to change the way the evidence is weighed (Horowitz & Willging, 1991). The presence of these instructions shifts the discussion away from the evidence, and in the direction of what is just and fair (Hill & Pfeifer, 1992; Niedermeier, Horowitz, & Kerr, 1999). However, the deliberation process diminishes the importance of any individual's sentiments about justice (Meissner, Brigham, & Pfeifer, 2003).

Jury Nullification and Racial Considerations.

The issue of race is a subtext to the nullification debate. There are notorious cases of nullification where White southern juries refused to convict members of the Ku Klux Klan and others who terrorized Blacks during the early years of the civil rights movement. One case concerns Byron de la Beckwith and the murder of civil rights leader Medgar Evers (Box 12.4).

Many people suspect that jurors in the early trials of Beckwith and other Ku Klux Klan members set aside the law and refused to convict these defendants because they supported the defendants' racist dogma. Because we can't talk to the jurors, we will never know for sure. But it is certainly telling that a racially mixed jury convicted Beckwith for the murder of Medgar Evers 30 years after two all-White juries were unable to agree on a verdict.

Jurors' Abilities to Decide Complex Cases

Judge John V. Singleton looked up as his law clerk leaned against his office door as though to brace it closed. "You won't believe this," she said breathlessly, "but there are 225 lawyers out there in the courtroom!" (Singleton & Kass, 1986, p. 11). Judge Singleton believed it. He was about to preside over the first pretrial conference in *In re Corrugated Container Antitrust Litigation* (1980), at that time one of the largest and most complicated class action cases ever tried by a jury. (A **class action case** involves many plaintiffs who collectively form a "class" and claim that they suffered similar injuries as a result of the defendants' actions. The plaintiffs portrayed in the movies *Erin Brockovich* and *North Country* constituted a class. In 2008, Facebook faced a class action lawsuit over its participation in a program that alerted users' friends to their activity on other Web sites. Ironically, one can join a Facebook group called "Join the Class Action Lawsuit. … Against Facebook!")

The case in Judge Singleton's court actually entailed three trials: a 15-week criminal trial that involved 4 major paper companies, 27 corporate officers, scores of witnesses, and hundreds of documents; a four-month-long class action trial with 113 witnesses and 5,000 exhibits; and a second class action trial involving plaintiffs who had opted out of the original class action lawsuit. Discovery and trials took five years. In the midst of this organizational nightmare, Judge Singleton worried about the "unsuspecting souls out there in the Southern District of Texas whose destiny was to

Box 12.4   THE CASE OF BYRON DE LA BECKWITH: JURY NULLIFICATION AND RACE

Eager to see his children after a long day at work, civil rights leader Medgar Evers stepped out of his car in Jackson, Mississippi on a hot June night in 1963 and, in the blink of an eye, was gunned down from behind by an assassin. The shooting ignited a firestorm of protest that ended in several more deaths and galvanized the civil rights movement.

The case against Byron de la Beckwith was strong but circumstantial. His rifle with his fingerprint was found at the scene, and a car similar to his was seen in the vicinity of Evers's home. But no one saw Beckwith pull the trigger, and his claim that he was 90 miles away at the time of the shooting was substantiated by two former police officers.

Beckwith was tried twice in 1964; both times the all-White, all-male jury deadlocked and failed to reach a verdict. This was an era of volatile race relations in which African Americans were excluded from jury service and in which attorneys for Ku Klux Klan members charged with killing civil rights leaders openly appealed to White jurors for racial solidarity. Beckwith's segregationist views were a common bond between himself and the juries that failed to convict him.

But things were different in 1994. Despite the obstacles presented by stale evidence, dead witnesses, and constitutional questions, prosecutors tried Beckwith for the third time. They presented several witnesses who testified that Beckwith suggested—and even bragged—that he had murdered Evers. Witnesses also described Beckwith's racist views, including his description of African Americans as "beasts of the field" and his belief that NAACP (National Association for the Advancement of Colored People) leaders should be exterminated.

This time, Beckwith's racist ideology was a liability. Despite pleas from defense attorneys that jurors not focus on Beckwith's sensational beliefs, a jury of eight Blacks

Byron De La Beckwith, convicted in the slaying of civil rights leader Medgar Evers

and four Whites convicted Beckwith of murder in February of 1994. He was immediately sentenced to life in prison. Darrell Evers, the slain civil rights leader's son, who was 9 years old at the time of the shooting, said he attended the trial to confront Beckwith: "He never saw my father's face. All he saw was his back. I wanted him to see the face, to see the ghost of my father come back to haunt him."

weigh the facts under the complex antitrust law" (Singleton & Kass, 1986, p. 11).

Some of the loudest and most vehement criticisms of the jury center on its role in complex cases. In product liability and medical malpractice cases, for example, there are difficult questions related to causation (i.e., who or what actually caused the claimed injuries), and in business cases there are intricate financial transactions that must be dissected and evaluated. These cases often require the jury to

render decisions on causation, liability, and damages for multiple plaintiffs, multiple defendants, or both (Vidmar, 1998). In criminal cases, the use of forensic evidence contributes to case complexity (Heise, 2004).

Many arguments have been made against the use of juries in complex cases. Some prominent examples include (1) the evidence is too difficult for a layperson to understand; (2) the general information load on juries is excessive because of the large number of witnesses, particularly expert witnesses who testify in these cases; and (3) because of *voir dire* procedures that result in the exclusion of jurors with some understanding of or interest in the case, less capable jurors are left to decide.

Data on juries in complex cases support some, but not all of these concerns. Interview studies (e.g., ABA Special Committee, 1991; Sanders, 1993) consistently point to a substantial range in the abilities of jurors to understand and summarize the evidence. Some jurors are willing and able to attend to the complicated nature of the testimony and the sometimes-arcane questions of law that they raise; others are overwhelmed from the beginning. Richard Lempert (1993), professor of law at the University of Michigan, systematically examined the reports of 12 complex trials. He concluded that in 2 of the 12 cases, the expert testimony was so complicated and esoteric that only professionals in the field could have understood it. On the other hand, Lempert found little evidence of jury befuddlement—and concluded that the juries' verdicts were largely defensible.

Irwin Horowitz and his colleagues conducted several sophisticated studies of mock juror decision making in complex cases. Horowitz and his team based their simulation studies on an actual toxic tort case involving manufacture of a chemical known as DBX, or dibenzodioxin. (The facts of their case resembled those described in the popular book and movie *A Civil Action*.) Residents adjacent to a chemical plant sued the chemical manufacturer for injuries alleged to have been caused when the company allowed DBX to leach from the plant into the surrounding drainage ditches and waterways, thus entering the plaintiffs' drinking water and contaminating the fish and wildlife the plaintiffs consumed. The studies involved multiple plaintiffs, all of whom complained, in varying degrees, of health problems such as skin rashes and elevated blood pressure, psychological distress, a fear of contracting cancer and future illnesses, and economic loss. Attorneys for the defendant chemical manufacturer presented evidence to refute these allegations.

Manipulating the structure of the trial and nature of the testimony, Horowitz and his colleagues examined the effects of the number and order of decisions required of jurors, the complexity of the language, the number of plaintiffs, and the role of preliminary instructions and group deliberations. The picture that emerges from this vast set of data is of a jury whose abilities and verdicts are significantly affected by nuances in trial procedure. For example, preinstructed jurors made more appropriate distinctions among plaintiffs who suffered different kinds of injuries (ForsterLee, Horowitz, & Bourgeois, 1993), complex language lessened jurors' ability to compensate plaintiffs who suffered injuries of varying severity (Horowitz, ForsterLee, & Brolly, 1996), and multiple plaintiffs increased the unpredictability of punitive damage awards (Horowitz & Bordens, 2002).

None of these findings suggests that jurors are inherently unable to decide complex matters, however. As psychologist Phoebe Ellsworth (1999) has noted, there is little support for the popular idea that bad jury decisions are caused by bad jurors. Rather, the findings point to the need for attention to how a complex case is presented to the jury. A judge has wide discretion to set the tone and pacing of the trial, to implement procedures to assist the jury, and, ultimately, to ensure equal justice under law. Jury aids such as written summary statements of expert testimony and the opportunity to take notes can enhance the quality of jurors' decision making (ForsterLee, Kent, & Horowitz, 2005), as can other reforms discussed later in the chapter.

We would not expect a college student to pass a course without taking notes, asking questions to seek clarification, or discussing an interesting concept with a professor or fellow student. Yet all too often, we handicap jurors by using trial procedures that discourage or even forbid these simple steps toward better understanding. We suspect that jurors would have an easier time—and their verdicts would be more reasoned—if judges were willing to structure jurors' tasks to be more conducive to their learning (e.g., preinstruction and simplifying the language of the instructions). Fortunately, as we point

---

B o x 12.5   THE CASE OF MICHAEL JORDAN: THE SEARCH FOR UNBIASED JURORS

When 36 prospective jurors filed into a drab, window-less courtroom in Chicago, a big surprise awaited them: Seated at the defense table was former basketball star Michael Jordan, undoubtedly one of the biggest sports heroes in American history. Jordan was being sued for allegedly reneging on a deal to star in the basketball film *Heaven Is a Playground*. The movie flopped without him. Dean Dickie, attorney for the plaintiff production company, anticipated difficulties in finding jurors who were not partial toward Jordan. Indeed, after five long hours of jury selection, only three jurors had been selected. Nearly all of the other prospective jurors stated that their admiration and adoration of Jordan would interfere with their neutrality in the case. In the end, the jury returned a judgment in Jordan's favor. In fact, jurors determined that the corporation that made the film owed Jordan $50,000 for failing to live up to its financial obligation to him.

© AFP/Getty Images

Michael Jordan

---

out later in the chapter, some judges have now begun that process.

ARE JURIES BIASED?

The Assumption of a Blank Slate

Courts assume that jurors can put aside any preconceptions about the guilt of a criminal defendant or the merits of civil defendants and plaintiffs when forming their judgments. In other words, jurors are assumed to enter a trial as "blank slates," free of overwhelming biases. (In criminal cases, the "blank slates" should be tinted at the outset by a presumption that the defendant is innocent of the charges.) If jurors cannot set aside their biases, they should be excused for cause.

As we noted in Chapter 11, the judge and the attorneys inquire about a prospective juror's biases during the jury selection process. A frequent question during *voir dire* takes the following form: "Do you believe that you, as a juror, can set aside any negative feelings you might have toward the

defendant because he is (from the Middle East or a police officer or a used-car salesman—whatever the group membership that possibly elicits prejudice) and make a judgment based on the law and the facts of this case?" If prospective jurors say yes, the judge usually believes them, and they are allowed to serve as jurors.

Less frequently, prospective jurors may have positive feelings about the defendant that could influence their ability to be impartial. Consider the lawsuit filed against basketball great Michael Jordan (see Box 12.5).

The courts assume that individual jurors can divest themselves of any improper "leaning" toward one side or the other, and that through detailed, sometimes time-consuming jury selection procedures the ideal of open-minded jurors can be achieved. Courts also assume that attorneys can identify and dismiss prospective jurors whose preconceptions would affect their verdicts, so the trial can begin with a fair and unbiased jury. For various reasons, this optimism may be misguided. First, attorneys are motivated to select jurors who are favorable to their own side, rather than those who are neutral and thus unpredictable. Second, it is impossible for anyone to be completely uninfluenced by past experiences and resulting prejudices.

Inevitability of Juror Bias

Bias is an inevitable human characteristic. In a society that respects all persons, some biases (e.g., age, race, or gender bias) are clearly prejudicial and should be shunned. But other biases—those based on expectations and experiences—may actually be inevitable. As we use the term here, **juror bias** is a juror's predisposition to interpret and understand information based on past experience—to try to fit new stimuli and concepts into one's already developed system for looking at the world. When we are exposed to a new event, we respond to it by relying on past experiences. When we view a traffic accident, for instance, we may make judgments that one car was going too fast or that another car was in the wrong lane. We may assume that a particular driver was at fault simply because we happen to have a negative stereotype about, for example, drivers from a particular state.

Bias in our responses to the actions of others is inevitable because people must make assumptions about the causes of behavior. Why was Emily so abrupt when she spoke to me this morning? Why did Juan decide to buy a new car? Why did the defendant refuse to take a lie detector test? Every day, we make decisions on the basis of our assumptions about other people. College admission officers decide who will be admitted on the basis of applicants' credentials and academic promise. Criminal defense lawyers make recommendations to their clients on how to plead on the basis of their expectations about the reactions of prosecuting attorneys, judges, and jurors. Choices are always necessary, and our expectations about the outcomes of our choices rest partly on our biases.

Why do we have expectations? We probably could not tolerate life if people were constantly surprising us. We need assumptions about people to help us predict what they will do. Our expectations often help simplify our explanations for people's behavior. Such processes also apply to the thoughts of jurors. When former Dallas Cowboys wide receiver Michael Irvin appeared before the grand jury with regard to a charge of cocaine possession, he was wearing a mink coat, a lavender suit, and a bowler hat. Jurors undoubtedly formed impressions of him on the basis of his attire and judged his behavior in light of those impressions.

Virtually all the legal and psychological conceptions of how a juror makes decisions in a criminal case propose that verdicts reflect the implicit operation of two judgments on the part of jurors. One judgment is an estimate of the probability of commission—that is, how likely it is that the defendant actually committed the crime. Most jurors base their estimates of this probability mainly on the strength of the specific evidence, but as we have noted, extralegal information and jurors' previous beliefs and experiences also have an impact on how they interpret the evidence (Finkel, 1995).

A second judgment by the criminal juror concerns reasonable doubt. Judges instruct jurors in criminal cases that they should bring back a verdict of not guilty if they have any reasonable doubt of the defendant's guilt. Yet the legal system has difficulty defining reasonable doubt (a common, but not very informative, definition is that it is a doubt for which a person can give a reason), so jurors apply their own standards for the threshold of certainty deemed necessary for conviction.

On the basis of these factors, many jurors can be classified as having a pro-prosecution bias or a pro-defense bias. Jurors with a pro-prosecution bias view the conflicting evidence through the filter of their own past experiences and beliefs which make them more likely to think that the defendant committed the crime. A pro-prosecution juror would tend to agree with the statement "Any suspect who runs from the police probably committed the crime." Persons with pro-defense biases filter the same evidence in light of *their* past experiences and reactions. Agreement with the statement "Too many innocent people are wrongfully imprisoned" reflects filters leading to biases sympathetic to the defense.

To determine how bias affects verdicts, Kassin and Wrightsman (1983) asked potential jurors to complete a 17-statement attitude inventory containing statements such as those given as examples. Later, these mock jurors watched videotapes of reenacted actual trials or read transcripts of simulated trials. After being exposed to the trial, each mock juror was asked to render an individual verdict about the defendant's guilt or innocence. Jurors voting guilty were then compared with those voting not guilty to see whether their preliminary biases differed. In most cases, they did. The average rate of conviction was 81% for the prosecution-biased jurors and only 52% for defense-biased ones. Thus, even though everyone was exposed to the same evidence, mock jurors holding a pro-prosecution bias were more likely to find the defendant guilty. It appears that, at least in some cases, personal beliefs and values may influence, and occasionally even overwhelm, the evidence presented in court.

Personal predispositions may also affect the very way the evidence is evaluated. Jane Goodman-Delahunty and her colleagues found that mock jurors' beliefs about the death penalty influenced more than the penalty they imposed in a capital murder case; they also influenced jurors' perceptions of the evidence (Goodman-Delahunty, Greene, & Hsiao, 1998). Mock jurors in this study watched the videotaped murder of a convenience store clerk that had been captured on film. When asked questions about the defendant's motive and intentions, jurors who favored the death penalty were more likely than those who opposed capital punishment to "read" criminal intent into the actions of the defendant. For example, pro-death-penalty jurors were more likely than those opposed to infer from the videotape that the defendant intended to murder the victim and that his specific actions indicated premeditation. These findings remind us of the common situation in which two people experience the same event—a movie or a play, for example—and interpret the actions in very different ways, partly because of the "mindset" with which they watched or experienced that event. These beliefs, or schemas, can apparently influence the way jurors make sense of the evidence in a trial.

We now know something about *how* those schemas manage to influence jurors' decision making. When jurors are exposed to a new piece of evidence, they evaluate the evidence in a way that is consistent with their current verdict preferences rather than in an objective fashion. Assume that two jurors hear the same evidence that favors the prosecution's case. Also assume that Juror A favors the prosecution and Juror B favors the defense at that point in the trial. According to the notion of **predecisional distortion** (Carlson & Russo, 2001), these jurors will distort their evaluation of the evidence in a direction that supports their verdict choice. Thus, Juror A would evaluate this evidence as favoring the prosecution, whereas Juror B might evaluate it as favoring neither party, actually distorting his or her interpretation of the evidence away from its objective value (i.e., in favor of the prosecution) and in the direction of the side favored. A powerful source of premature beliefs and judgments about a defendant is prejudicial pretrial publicity (described in detail in Chapter 7). Exposure to this kind of publicity can distort how jurors search for, use, and evaluate subsequent evidence at trial, usually in favor of the prosecution (Hope, Memon, & McGeorge, 2004).

Do jurors' biases predispose them to favor one side over another in a civil case? A common perception is that jurors are generally biased in favor of injured plaintiffs. Are they? Was the Miami jury's decision to award $37 million to the family of 12-year-old honor student Jill Goldberg, who was killed in a 1997 car accident, fueled by feelings of sympathy for her grieving family members? It seems natural for people to have feelings of compassion for injured persons and for these feelings to translate into favorable verdicts and lavish damage awards for plaintiffs. But do they?

Surprisingly, perhaps, a variety of studies using different methodologies suggest that the answer is no. From posttrial juror interviews, we have learned that although elements of sympathy play *some* role in deliberations (as do feelings of anger toward a defendant), this happens relatively infrequently. In her study of cases involving claims by individuals against corporate defendants, Professor Valerie Hans (1996) interviewed jurors who decided these cases, conducted surveys of jurors' attitudes, and ran experimental studies that manipulated variables related to this **sympathy**

hypothesis. All these sources of data pointed to the same conclusion: that the general public is "quite suspicious of, and sometimes downright hostile to, civil plaintiffs" (p. 244). A survey conducted by the consulting firm DecisionQuest yielded similar results: 84% of the 1012 people polled agreed with the statement "When people are injured, they often try to blame others for their carelessness." According to the same survey, potential jurors do not think highly of civil defendants, either. For example, more than 75% of respondents believe that corporate executives often try to cover up evidence of wrongdoing by their companies, and more respondents say that product warnings are intended to protect manufacturers than say they are intended to keep consumers safe.

These findings raise the next question: Do juries give larger awards when a defendant is wealthy? Some data would seem to support this so-called deep-pockets effect. Jury damage awards *are* consistently higher in products liability and medical malpractice cases than in automobile negligence cases. (The former group typically involves wealthy defendants, whereas the latter does not.) But a number of studies (e.g., Hans & Ermann, 1989; MacCoun, 1996) suggest that the wealth of the defendant alone is not the important variable. Rather, the public believes that businesses and corporations should be held to a higher standard of responsibility than individual defendants. Any inflation of awards against corporate defendants is apparently related to their status as a corporation and not to their wealth.

The jury that awarded $37 million to the family of Jill Goldberg clearly focused on the duties and responsibilities of the defendant, Florida Power and Light (FPL) Company. The victim was killed when a car driven by her mother, Rosalie, sailed through an intersection and was struck by a Ford Expedition on a rainy September afternoon. So, what exactly was the role of the defendant? Ten minutes before the accident occurred, an FPL lineman pulled a fuse from a transformer box about 100 feet away from the intersection, cutting power to the traffic light. At trial, FPL lawyers told the jury that the utility couldn't be obligated to ensure that every traffic light in the county worked when it terminated power. The lineman testified that he never looked to see whether the traffic light had been affected. Neither of these contentions sat well with jurors. Said jury foreman Juan Perez, "To them, power outages were a fact of life and they throw switches all the time. But to say that in front of a jury is almost suicidal to the defense." After a week-long trial, the jury deliberated for three hours and determined that FPL was entirely at fault. But for the power outage, they reasoned, the accident would never have happened. They awarded $17 million to Walter Goldberg, Jill's father, and $20 million to Rosalie Goldberg, Jill's mother—far more than the plaintiffs had requested.

JURORS' INFERENCES AND THE STORIES THEY TELL

We have seen that jurors' pretrial beliefs can affect their decisions in both criminal and civil trials (although the evidence is still the primary determinant of verdicts). But how do jurors make sense of the evidence that they hear *during* the trial? In many ways, the juror's task is like that of the reader of a mystery story. The joy of reading a mystery comes from savoring each clue, bouncing it off prior clues, and then evaluating its significance in the overall puzzle of who committed the crime. That is how most jurors operate. They form a schema, a mental structure that aids in the processing and interpretation of information. As indicated earlier, such schema can produce a skewed perception and recall of reality because they provide a cognitive framework. Just like mystery readers who remember those clues that fit their hypothesis and forget others that do not, jurors construct their own private stories about the evidence so that it makes sense to them; in the process, they pay inordinate attention to certain pieces of evidence while ignoring others.

Good lawyers know this. In fact, really great lawyers know that an important task for them at trial is to convince the jury that their story, and not their opponent's story, is the right one. Famed criminal defense attorney "Racehouse" Haynes once said, "The lawyer with the best story wins."

Psychologists Reid Hastie and Nancy Pennington developed the **story model** to describe inferences that individual jurors make when reaching a decision in a case (see, generally, Pennington & Hastie, 1993). Hastie and Pennington dubbed their theory the story model because they suspect that the core cognitive process involved in juror decision making is construction of a story or narrative summary of the events in dispute. To illustrate the role of narrative evidence summaries in juror decision making, Hastie and Pennington interpreted the dramatic differences between White Americans' and African Americans' reactions to the verdict in the 1995 murder trial of O. J. Simpson. They suspected that because of their life experiences and beliefs, African Americans can more easily construct a story about police misconduct and police brutality than can White Americans. Thus, African Americans were more likely than Whites to accept the "defense story" that a racist police detective planted incriminating evidence on Simpson's property (Hastie & Pennington, 1996).

In one of their early empirical studies, Pennington and Hastie (1986) interviewed mock jurors who had seen a filmed reenactment of a murder trial and who were asked to talk out loud while making a verdict decision. The evidence summaries constructed by jurors had a definite narrative story structure, and, importantly, jurors who reached different verdicts had constructed different stories.

In a later study, Pennington and Hastie (1988) assessed whether these stories were constructed spontaneously in the course of jurors' decision making and how jurors represented the evidence in memory. To answer these questions, they asked mock jurors to read a written description of the murder case that included sentences from different verdict stories gleaned from the previous interview study (e.g., sentences from stories that resulted in guilty verdicts as well as sentences from stories that led to not-guilty verdicts). All participants then determined a verdict and were asked to say whether various sentences had been included in the trial evidence or had not been presented before.

Mock jurors were more likely to "recognize" those sentences that were associated with their chosen verdict than sentences from stories associated with other, rejected verdicts.

Does the order in which evidence is presented influence jurors' judgments? Apparently so. In that same study, Pennington and Hastie (1988) found that stories were easy to construct when the evidence was presented in a temporal order that matched the occurrence of the original events ("story order") but harder to construct when the evidence was presented in an order that did not match the sequence of the original events ("witness order").

Prosecutors and defense attorneys might be wise to familiarize themselves with these findings because the study has significant implications for the practice of actual trials. When Pennington and Hastie manipulated the order of evidence, they affected the likelihood of a guilty verdict. For example, mock jurors were *most* likely to convict a criminal defendant when the prosecution evidence was presented in story order and the defense evidence in witness order. They were *least* likely to convict when the prosecution evidence was presented in witness order and the defense evidence in story order.

Is the story model a complete and accurate description of how jurors organize themselves to decide the verdict in a trial? No. For starters, it focuses only on *jurors* and does not address the complex nuances that come into focus when jurors deliberate as a jury. But as a framework for understanding the cognitive strategies employed by individuals to process trial information prior to deliberations, it is highly useful. Indeed, several other studies (e.g., Dunn, Salovey, & Feigenson, 2006; Huntley & Costanzo, 2003) have been inspired by its elegant theorizing.

JURY REFORM

The traditional legal model treats jurors as passive recipients of information who, like tape recorders, record a one-way stream of communication. Jurors were expected to process all incoming information passively, without interpretation, until finally instructed by the judge to decide something. As we pointed out earlier, this conception of juror-as-blank-slate is largely wrong; jurors actively evaluate the evidence through the lens of their personal experiences and frames of reference, pose questions to themselves, and construct narratives or stories to help them understand the evidence and make a judgment about it.

Acknowledging that most jurors are active "thought processors," psychologists and other social scientists began suggesting reforms to the jury system in the 1970s. For some time, however, few people listened. For example, in 1991, Alexander Tanford, a professor of law at Indiana University, reviewed the impact of research on pretrial and written instructions on state court judges, legislatures, and rule-making commissions and concluded that the research had very little impact: Lawmakers were not being persuaded about the need for reform on the basis of empirical research studies alone. (This finding raises some interesting and difficult questions about whether psychologists, armed with sophisticated theories and well-honed research techniques, can effectively influence the landscape of the law.)

Many observers of the jury (e.g., Ellsworth, 1999; Marder, 1999a) now suspect that intense media coverage of a series of dramatic trials and controversial verdicts has accomplished for jury reform what decades of social science research could not. As trials and tribulations of celebrities O. J. Simpson, Martha Stewart, Michael Jackson, and Kobe Bryant were broadcast and streamed across the country, and as the media splashed news of a $2.7-million award to an 81-year-old New Mexico grandmother who was burned by hot coffee at McDonald's (the award was reduced by the judge to $480,000, and the plaintiff eventually settled for even less—something that the media generally failed to report), the public grew increasingly dissatisfied and occasionally even outraged about the failure of the jury system. Calls for reform became more frequent and more urgent.

Convinced that the time was right for serious discussion of reform to the jury system, the University of Michigan sponsored a symposium that brought together judges, lawyers, legal academics, social scientists, and even a thoughtful and experienced juror to share their concerns and suggest solutions. Despite the diversity in intellectual backgrounds and practical experience, there was remarkable convergence of opinion among participants. For example, none of them subscribed to the "bad juror" theory—that bad jury decisions are caused by bad jurors. Rather, all shared the view, long advocated by psychologists, that the system is primarily to blame. According to the "bad system" theory, deficiencies in the performance of jurors reflect deficiencies in the jury system, and any jury reform should be directed at how the task is presented to jurors, rather than at how people are selected to serve. As Phoebe Ellsworth (1999), one of the participants at the Michigan forum, aptly noted, "Before deciding that jurors are governed by their hearts, we should consider the possibility that the system does very little to encourage the intelligent use of their minds."

Against the backdrop of increasing support for reform, many jury scholars, some creative court personnel, and a few courageous judges have proposed and implemented reforms that take advantage of jurors' natural inclinations and that provide tools to encourage jurors' active involvement in the trial process. Some of the reforms have been uncontroversial and benign: providing notebooks that list the witnesses and summarize their testimony in long or complex cases; giving preinstructions or interim instructions during the course of a lengthy trial; allowing jurors to take notes; designating alternate jurors only after the trial is completed; providing a written copy of the judge's instructions to each juror; and allowing jurors to examine the demonstrative evidence during their deliberations.

Two reforms have been more radical: allowing jurors to pose questions to witnesses (questions are screened by the judge, who decides whether they are appropriate) and to discuss the evidence in the midst of trial (traditionally, jurors were forbidden from talking about the case until they began deliberating.) Not only have these reforms been implemented in many jurisdictions, but research studies have now been conducted to chart their effectiveness. What have we learned about the effects of these new practices on jurors' sentiments and decision-making abilities?

Jurors questioned about the opportunity to submit written questions have been strongly supportive of that innovation. Fully 83% of jurors surveyed by the Seventh Circuit American Jury Project between 2005 and 2008 reported that the opportunity to ask questions enhanced their understanding of the facts (Seventh Circuit American Jury Project, 2008). Results of a mock jury study that tested the effects of question asking on jurors' understanding of contested DNA presentations lead to the same conclusion (Dann, Hans, & Kaye, 2004). An analysis of the content of more than 2,000 questions posed in 164 actual trials (both civil and criminal) characterized the nature of the questions. This study revealed that jurors questioned both lay and expert witnesses in order to clarify previous testimony and to ask about common practices in unfamiliar professions (Mott, 2003). Finally, although some judges have expressed concern that jurors would be offended by having a question disallowed or would speculate about the reasons why a submitted question could not be asked, jurors themselves tend to accept that decision and drop the issue (Diamond, Rose, & Murphy, 2004). Therefore, we see no serious drawbacks to allowing jurors to ask questions. Although the process can take more time, it can also clarify jurors' understanding of the evidence, enhance their involvement in the trial process, and create an environment more conducive to learning.

The most radical reform permits jurors to discuss the evidence during the trial, rather than having to wait until their formal deliberations began. The rules were simple: All jurors must be present in the deliberation room during these discussions, and jurors must keep an open mind and avoid debating verdict options. Psychologists have described a number of potential advantages of such mid-trial discussions based on fundamental principles of cognitive and social psychology. In theory, juror discussions about the evidence can

- improve juror comprehension by permitting jurors to sift through and organize the evidence into a coherent framework over the course of the trial;

- improve juror recollection of the evidence and testimony by emphasizing and clarifying points made during trial; and

- promote greater cohesion among jurors, thereby reducing the time needed for deliberations (Hans, Hannaford, & Munsterman, 1999).

But there are also several potential drawbacks to jury discussions during trial, and these are also based on well-established psychological principles. They include the possibility that jury discussions may

- facilitate the formation or expression of premature judgments about the evidence,

- diminish the quality of the deliberations as jurors become more familiar with each other's views, and

- produce more interpersonal conflicts prior to formal deliberations (Hans et al., 1999).

The first empirical test of this reform was a field experiment in which researchers randomly assigned approximately 100 civil jury trials to an experimental "trial discussion" condition and an equal number to a control "no discussion" condition (Hannaford, Hans, & Munsterman, 2000; Hans et al., 1999). For both conditions, questionnaires were distributed to jurors, judges, attorneys, and litigants to assess their impressions.

Perhaps surprisingly, given their general tendency to adhere to traditional courtroom procedures, judges were the most enthusiastic group. Three-quarters of the judges indicated that they supported the reform, and only 15% opposed it (others were neutral). Another large percentage (75%) agreed that juror discussions helped jurors understand the evidence; only 30% expressed concern that jurors who engaged in these discussions were likely to prejudge the evidence. Attorneys and litigants were more negative, however. About half of each group thought that trial discussions improved juror understanding of the evidence, and approximately half agreed that trial discussions might encourage premature decision making.

How did the innovation affect jurors' experiences and views? Of the 686 jurors who were permitted to discuss the evidence, approximately 70% reported that their jury had at least one such discussion, suggesting that even when permitted to talk about the case, a sizeable minority of juries did not. Experience with the reform apparently increases support for it. Jurors who reported having these discussions were quite positive about them. They said that trial evidence was remembered very accurately during these discussions, that discussions helped them understand the evidence in the case, and that all jurors' points of view were considered during the course of the discussions. The perceived drawbacks were mostly logistical: Jurors said that there were difficulties in getting all jurors together at the same time. (After all, these short breaks represent the only time in the course of several hours that jurors may use the rest rooms or smoke a cigarette. Some people's desire for these comforts undoubtedly outweighed their interest in talking about the evidence!)

The most useful data on the issue of jury discussions come from the analysis of videotapes of 50 civil jury trials in Arizona (the state that has been at the forefront of jury reform) (Diamond, Vidmar, Rose, Ellis, & Murphy, 2003). This study examined all mid-trial jury discussions, as well as the deliberations. These tapes make it clear that jurors seek information from one another, discuss questions they intend to ask, and talk about the as-yet-unpresented evidence they would like to hear. Such discussions led to modest enhancements in jurors' understanding of the evidence and did not result in premature judgments. These data provide a fascinating and previously unseen picture of the jury at work as it discusses the evidence in the midst of the trial and reaches a final verdict at the trial's conclusion. We see few negative effects of mid-trial discussion, and believe that allowing jurors the opportunity to talk about the case simply legitimizes what they are likely to do anyway.

THE JURY: SHOULD IT BE VENERATED OR VILIFIED? REVERED OR REVILED?

The jury system brings together multiple individuals with diverse backgrounds, experiences, and biases who pool their perceptions of the evidence to reach a verdict (Diamond, 2006). In this way, the trial jury is a remarkable institution and, in important respects, also a unique one. The use of average citizens to determine trial outcomes for rich or politically powerful figures such as Lewis (Scooter) Libby, assistant to former Vice President Dick Cheney, or the Microsoft Corporation underscores our country's commitment to egalitarian values. It is no exaggeration to say that the trial jury is sanctified as one of our fundamental democratic institutions. Political scientist Jeffrey Abramson (1994), author of *We, the Jury*, put it eloquently:

> [T]here are all the jurors we never read about, who toil out of the limelight every day, crossing all kinds of racial and ethnic lines to defend a shared sense of justice. These examples convince me that the jury, far from being obsolete, is more crucial than ever in a multiethnic society struggling to articulate a justice common to [all] citizens. Though the jury system is a grand phenomenon—putting justice in the hands of the people—we still have lessons to learn about how to design an institution that gathers persons from different walks of life to discuss and decide upon one justice for all. (p. 5)

Although there remains much to learn, we now know a good deal about how juries function. We know that juries don't always get it right; on occasion, jurors are overwhelmed by the sheer volume of evidence, misunderstand their instructions, and use evidence in inappropriate ways. We know that their biases and prejudices can rise to the surface and color their judgments. But by and large, we find little support for the extreme claims that charge juries with poor and irresponsible performance. On the contrary, we believe the institution of the jury is worth defending and worth improving.

SUMMARY

1. *Describe the issue of jury competence.* Some commentators have wondered whether jurors and juries are overly attentive to extralegal information that, in theory, is irrelevant to the guilt decision in criminal cases and to the liability judgment in civil cases. Others have asked whether jurors will be mesmerized by the testimony of an expert or, conversely, that they will not understand such testimony and dismiss it outright. Whether jurors and juries are able to understand and apply their instructions is another question. Finally, some have asked whether jurors can decide the complicated issues that arise in so-called complex cases.

2. *What is the impact of extralegal information on jurors?* Research studies suggest that occasionally jurors are influenced by evidence of a defendant's prior record, multiple charges, or character and propensity to commit crimes. In civil cases, evidence related to an accident victim's injury may influence the judgment of a defendant's liability.

3. *Can jurors disregard inadmissible evidence?* When a question posed or an answer offered during a trial is ruled inadmissible by the judge, jurors are instructed to disregard it. Psychological evidence indicates that it is difficult for jurors to disregard this testimony; in fact, the stronger the judge's admonition, the less effective it may be.

4. *How can jurors be helped to understand their instructions?* Jurors can be instructed before the trial begins about the relevant elements of the law that they will apply to the facts they hear. Judges can provide written copies of the instructions for all jurors. Unfortunately, judges rarely answer jurors' questions about their instructions.

5. *What is meant by the statement "Bias is inevitable in jurors"?* Bias, as used here, refers to the human predisposition to make interpretations on the basis of beliefs and past experiences. Bias is inevitable because it is inescapable human nature to make assumptions about human behavior.

6. *What reforms of the jury system do psychologists suggest?* The information-processing demands placed on jurors should be simplified. More clearly worded instructions, in written as well as oral form, delivered at the beginning and at the conclusion of the trial would be helpful. In complex trials in which multiple verdicts must be decided, preinstruction, access to a trial transcript, and simplifying complex language may be especially helpful. During the trial, jurors should be able to pose questions that the judge would then ask of the witnesses. Finally, mid-trial discussion of the evidence might have great value; such discussion might help jurors to organize the evidence in a thematic framework and thus improve their memory of the testimony.

KEY TERMS

aversive racism	evidentiary strength	liberation hypothesis	psycholinguistics
central route	extralegal information	limiting instruction	reactance theory
class action case	inadmissible evidence	outcome severity	recency effect
damages	joinder	peripheral route	schema
defensive attribution	juror bias	predecisional distortion	story model
dual-process theory of attitude change	jury nullification	primacy effect	sympathy hypothesis
	liable	propensity evidence	thought suppression

13

Psychology of Victims of Crime and Violence

ORIENTING QUESTIONS

1. What is the frequency of crime victimization?
2. What types of research have psychologists conducted on victimization?
3. What factors predict the development of PTSD after being a crime victim?
4. What are the components of the battered woman syndrome?
5. How have the laws about rape changed?
6. How can rape be prevented?
7. What are two types of sexual harassment recognized by the courts?

PERCEPTION OF THOSE WHO EXPERIENCE CRIME AND/OR VIOLENCE

One element of almost every crime is the presence of at least one victim. Even so-called victimless crimes—crimes such as prostitution, ticket scalping, and gambling—have victims, even if they do not immediately recognize it or would not describe themselves that way. The social burdens and psychological costs of these offenses—the squandering of a person's income as a consequence of the inevitable losses from habitual gambling or the physical abuse and underworld crimes that surround prostitution—are often delayed but ultimately, society and individuals are victimized by these crimes.

Society has conflicting feelings toward victims. At the same time that most individuals feel sympathy toward them, we also tend to question why they became victims, and sometimes we even blame them for their plight. One reason for this inclination is the need to believe in a "just world." The thought of becoming victims ourselves is so threatening that we feel compelled to find an explanation why other people are victimized (Lerner, 1980). These justifications often take the form of singling out victims as the primary cause of their own plight.

Such judgments are predicted by the perspective known as attribution theory, which originated with the work of Fritz Heider (1958). Heider stated that people operate as "naive psychologists"; they reach conclusions about what caused a given behavior by considering both personal and environmental factors.

Generally, when considering someone else's actions, we use *dispositional attributions* that focus on the person's ability level, personality, or even temporary states (such as fatigue or luck) as explanations for the conduct in question. To explain a person's misfortune on the basis of his or her physical disabilities, lack of effort, or loose morals reflects a kind of defensive attribution that puts the onus for bad outcomes on the person rather than on the environment. Such reactions help shape our responses to victims. The norms of our society demand that we help others if they deserve our help, but if people are responsible for their own suffering, we feel less obligated to help them (Mulford, Lee, & Sapp, 1996).

Since 1970, the phrase *blaming the victim* has been heard. The term was first popularized in a widely read book by William Ryan (1970), in which the author observed that people on welfare were often seen as lazy or shiftless and hence responsible for their fate. An extreme example of blaming the victim is offered by trial attorney Robert Baker, who represented O. J. Simpson in his civil trial for the wrongful deaths of Nicole Brown and Ronald Goldman. His opening statement for the defense included a scorching attack on Nicole Brown, whom he portrayed as a heavy-drinking party girl whose dangerous lifestyle often included companions who were prostitutes and drug dealers. Sometimes by implication and sometimes by direct comment, he communicated that she had many boyfriends and had had at least one abortion. As a trial observer noted, "it was as close to calling her a slut [as one could come] without using the word" (quoted by Reibstein & Foote, 1996, p. 64). Baker demeaned the victim for a reason, of course; he wanted to imply that a sordid lifestyle had led to her becoming involved with someone other than O. J. Simpson and that this supposed individual had killed her (Toobin, 1996a). Simpson himself has echoed this claim, stating that he feels angry at Nicole because he believes her careless lifestyle contributed to her being murdered.

TYPES OF VICTIMS

There is no shortage of victims in our society. Estimates of the numbers of children who are sexually abused, of adults who are battered by their partners, and of women and men who are assaulted, robbed, or raped run into the millions each year.

The primary source of information on crime victims in the United States is the Bureau of Justice Statistics' National Crime Victimization Survey, which can be found at www.ojp.usdoj.gov/bjs/. Each year, data are collected from a national sample of 50,000 households on the frequency and consequences of criminal victimization in the form of rape and other sexual assaults, robbery, theft, assault, household burglary, and car theft. From these figures, one can calculate the rate of victimization nationwide. For example, it is estimated that in 2006, approximately 25 million criminal victimizations occurred; more than 18.9 million involved property crimes (a rate of 160 incidents per 1,000 households), and over 6.1 million were crimes of violence (25 incidents per 1,000 persons). Additional statistics on the frequency, consequences, and prevention of criminal victimization can be found at the National Center for Victims of Crime Web site (www.ncvc.org).

For other offenses, it is difficult to assess the frequency of victimization, but what we do know is that they happen all too often. Included here, for example, are acts of racial or religious discrimination in which the recipient is denied rights that are accorded to others. Homophobic attitudes are frequently expressed (Herek, 1987; Larsen, Reed, & Hoffman, 1980); 90% of gay men report having been threatened or subjected to verbal abuse, and

Identify theft warning

more than 33% were victims of violence (Segell, 1997). Compared with gay adults, homosexual youth are at higher risk for violent victimization, and the psychological consequences of the victimization may be more severe for them (D'Augelli, 1998). We describe the story of one victim in Box 13.1.

One study examined data from self-report measures of victimization and found that gay students were significantly more likely than others to be victims of violent and property crimes while at school (Faulkner & Cranston, 1998). Specifically, homosexual students were more than twice as likely to report having been threatened or injured with a weapon at school, and they were more than three times as likely to report not going to school because they felt unsafe. In addition, these students were significantly more likely than others to report having their property damaged or stolen while they were at school. Gay students were also several times more likely to have been in 10 or more physical fights in the

---

B o x 13.1   THE CASE OF MATTHEW SHEPARD: VICTIM OF A HATE CRIME

On a chilly October evening in 1998, two bicyclists riding on Snowy Mountain View Road outside of Laramie, Wyoming saw what they thought was a scarecrow tied to a rough-hewn deer fence. Only after coming closer did the horror set in. This was no scarecrow. This was—or had been—a man. His head had been beaten, his face was cut and covered with blood and tears, and his limbs had been scorched with burn marks. Police believe that Matthew Shepard, a slightly built freshman at the University of Wyoming who was comfortable with his homosexuality (although he did not flaunt it), was lured into a pickup truck by two tall, muscular men who pretended that they too, were gay. All pretenses vanished as the pair began pounding Shepard on the head with a .357 Magnum revolver, then tied him to the post, beat him relentlessly, and left him to die. He was found 18 hours later, barely alive, and died within days of the beating.

As Shepard's case riveted the nation, state and federal legislators became increasingly concerned about the proliferation of **hate crimes**—criminal acts intended to harm or intimidate people because of their race, ethnicity, sexual orientation, religion, or other minority group status. To date, the federal government

© Sygma/CORBIS

Matthew Shepard

and 45 states have enacted laws that allow stiffer sentencing for defendants who choose their victims based on perceptions of the victim's race, religion, ethnicity, or sexual orientation. Wyoming is not among them.

---

previous year. In terms of the consequences of this increased victimization, homosexual students were significantly more likely to report substance abuse and suicidal ideation. Specifically, homosexual students were nine times as likely to report using alcohol on each of the 30 days preceding the survey, six times as likely to report recently using cocaine, and nearly 1.5 times as likely to report seriously considering or attempting suicide in the 12 months prior to the study.

Persons diagnosed with AIDS are also frequently stigmatized in our society (Crandall, Glor, & Britt, 1997); not only laypersons but even medical professionals rate people with AIDS more negatively than they rate people with cancer, diabetes, or heart disease (Katz et al., 1987). In fact, being threatened by the risk of illness can harden our attitudes toward seriously ill people and cause us to stigmatize them (Jones et al., 1984). We often come to believe that someone's disease is not just a consequence of his or

her behavior or physical predisposition but that the illness somehow reflects the afflicted person's intrinsic value (Sontag, 1978).

Technological advancements and cultural changes have brought new forms of victimization to the fore. "Identity theft," in which information about an individual's personal and financial life is stolen by computer hackers and then used fraudulently, has become a major fear of people in the 21st century. "Cyberstalking" is a recently emerged technique favored by some sexual predators as a way to target victims. "Cyber bullying" can occur through blogs, MySpace, Facebook, and other social networking sites. The first-ever cyber bullying trial involved a Missouri woman, Lori Drew, who perpetrated a "mean-spirited Internet hoax" (Risling, 2008). Drew created a fictitious 16-year-old boy on MySpace and sent flirtatious messages to her 13-year-old neighbor, Megan Meier, who had apparently been mean to Drew's daughter.

But after the "boy" dumped Meier, saying "The world would be a better place without you," Meier hanged herself in her bedroom closet. Drew was convicted on three misdemeanor charges.

Nationwide, 9% of all students in secondary schools report feeling afraid that they will be attacked at school and avoid certain places within their schools because they believe these places to be unsafe (Verlinden, Hersen, & Thomas, 2000); millions more are traumatized by bullying and other forms of peer victimization that cause them to dread going to school (Hanish & Guerra, 2000).

This chapter concentrates on three types of victims and the effects of victimization on them: targets of sexual harassment, battered women, and victims of violent crime—particularly rape, the violent crime that has been studied most often. For each of these, the field of psychology has generated theory and research relevant to the laws and court decisions instituted to protect such victims. The responses of the legal system reflect conflicting views in our society about the nature of victims, especially victims of sex-related offenses. For example, how extreme does a situation need to be before we conclude that sexual harassment exists, and how distressed does the response of the victim need to be? In the case of a battered woman who kills her batterer, will a claim of self-defense be accepted by a jury? Also, why do as many as two-thirds of rape victims never report the attack to the police?

VICTIMS OF VIOLENT CRIME

The dilemmas confronted throughout this book, especially the quest to preserve both the rights of suspects and the rights of victims, come into sharp focus when we consider the victims of crime, particularly victims of violent crimes such as rape. Until recently, society had not paid much attention to crime victims. Their trial testimony was necessary to obtain convictions, but most of the legal rights formally protected in the adversarial system are extended to defendants, not victims. As a result, the needs and rights of crime victims have often been ignored.

This imbalance began to change in the late 1970s and early 1980s as victim advocacy groups, mental health professionals, police, and court officials all began to acknowledge the need to better recognize and serve crime victims. Several developments reflect the growing stature and influence of the victims' rights movement:

- The emergence of the interdisciplinary field of **victimology**, which concentrates on studying the process and consequences of victimization experiences and how victims (or *survivors*, which is the term preferred by many) recover

- The increasing availability of services to crime victims, including compensation and restitution programs, victim assistance programs in the courts, self-help programs, and formal mental health services

- The expanded opportunity for victims to participate in the trials of their victimizers through mechanisms such as victim impact statements

- The heightened focus on victims brought about by new journals (one example is *Victimology*; another is *Violence and Victims*), organizations such as the National Organization for Victim Assistance, and commissions such as the President's Commission on Victims of Crime (1982) and the American Psychological Association's Task Force on the Victims of Crime and Violence

For their part, psychologists have conducted research on and delivered clinical services to a diverse array of crime victims. Three areas have received special attention: the consequences of physical/sexual abuse on child victims; the role of violent victimization as a cause of psychological disorders, particularly posttraumatic stress disorder; and the psychology of rape. We review the latter two topics in this chapter.

Consequences of Early Victimization

One might wonder whether early victimization experiences increase the likelihood of adolescent and adult criminality. Cathy Spatz Widom (1989,

1992) used court records to identify a group of 908 children in a Midwestern American city who had suffered abuse (i.e., sexual abuse or physical assault leading to injury) or severe neglect (i.e., inadequate food, clothing, shelter, or medical care) between 1967 and 1971. This "abuse/neglect" group was matched to a group of 667 children who had not been exposed to abuse or neglect but who were similar in gender, age, ethnicity, and family socioeconomic status. Matching the abused and nonabused groups on these variables was important, because it enabled Widom to assume that any differences between the groups in terms of violent behavior in adolescence or adulthood were not due to differences in demographic characteristics.

Widom's analysis of police and court records showed that, as earlier research had suggested, abused or neglected children were significantly more likely than the comparison group to have been arrested for violent crimes as juveniles or as adults. In addition, the abused or neglected individuals were, on average, a year younger than comparison subjects at the time of their first arrest and had committed twice as many total offenses over the 15- to 20-year period studied. These differences were seen in boys and girls and in European Americans and African Americans; however, the relationship between abuse and violence was particularly strong among African Americans.

As disturbing as these results are, they may actually *underestimate* the risks created by childhood abuse. For one thing, only offenses that resulted in arrest or trial were included in this study. Many undetected or unreported crimes may have been committed by the abused/neglected group. Furthermore, this aspect of the study did not assess group differences in mental disorders, substance abuse, educational and occupational difficulties, or other possible long-term consequences of childhood abuse.

Data on this sample were collected again 22 to 26 years after the abuse or neglect (Maxfield & Widom, 1996). The researchers found that by age 32, almost half of the abused/neglected group (49%) had been arrested for a nontraffic offense. This percentage was considerably greater than for the matched control sample (38%). Furthermore, victims of abuse and neglect were more likely than members of the control group to have been arrested for violent crimes, even after controlling for age, race, and gender.

More recently, Widom and her colleagues examined the impact of sexual abuse, physical abuse, and neglect in childhood on adult mental health outcomes (Horwitz, Widom, McLaughlin, & White, 2001). Findings suggested that both men and women with histories of childhood abuse and neglect displayed increased levels of mood disorders and antisocial personality characteristics when compared with matched controls. The abused and neglected women also reported more alcohol problems than both the men and the matched groups. Although this line of research has suggested a strong association between childhood experiences of abuse and neglect and elevated levels of mental health problems in adulthood, these differences dissipated after controlling for other stressful life events. These findings highlight the importance of including early child abuse and neglect as part of a broader constellation of life stressors rather than isolating them as independent predictors of adult outcomes.

VIOLENT VICTIMIZATION AND POSTTRAUMATIC STRESS DISORDER

Individuals who suffer a severe trauma and, weeks or months later, continue to experience intense, fear-related reactions when reminded of the trauma, may be experiencing **posttraumatic stress disorder** (PTSD). By definition, such trauma must involve a threat of serious injury or death. We saw an example of this trauma as we watched the victims of Hurricane Katrina try to reconstruct their homes and their lives. Most instances of violent crime qualify as trauma severe enough to trigger PTSD in at least some victims.

B o x 13.2   THE CASE OF JIM: A VICTIM OF POSTTRAUMATIC STRESS DISORDER

When Jim appeared for treatment at age 40, he had been suffering from anxiety and depressive symptoms for eight years. He dated his problems to the autumn day when he foiled a burglary attempt across the street from his workplace. A distance runner, Jim decided to pursue the fleeing burglar and to attract help along the way. After a chase, Jim slowed and looked around for help. Turning again to the burglar, he found himself staring down the barrel of a handgun. The burglar fired, hitting Jim in the legs with three bullets and immobilizing him. Jim begged the young man to spare his life. Instead, the assailant continued firing until the gun was empty. He then fled, leaving Jim to die.

Fortunately, Jim was found and rushed to surgery. After eight days in the hospital, he knew he would recover and felt elated just to be alive. Soon, however, the elation wore off, and Jim began thinking of what might have occurred had he not been found in time. With increasing frequency, everyday sights and sounds

in Jim's life began to evoke the memory of the shooting and the panic he had experienced. The sight of guns or depictions of violence on TV triggered waves of strong emotion. Sirens and the sight of ambulances would startle him, and then panic and despair would set in. By the following year, even the cool fall weather could reactivate the event in his mind. He had frequent nightmares involving looking into a gun barrel.

As time went on, Jim felt more on edge. He became wary of people, and he kept to himself. He no longer experienced life's joy and excitement. Due to injury-related leg pain, he had to stop running, giving up one of his major pleasures and outlets for stress. Leg pain also evoked images of the shooting that, in turn, brought fear, hyperventilation, and a racing heart. Episodes in which Jim felt deeply depressed and suicidal would sometimes follow exposure to various stimuli. After eight years of nightmares and daily reminders of the trauma, Jim sought treatment and was able to make substantial improvements in his condition.

The symptoms of PTSD fall into three broad classes (these symptoms must last longer than one month to qualify as PTSD):

1. Frequent reexperiencing of the event through intrusive thoughts, flashbacks, and repeated nightmares and dreams

2. Persistent avoidance of stimuli associated with the trauma and a general numbing or deadening of emotions (feeling detached or estranged from others)

3. Increased physiological arousal resulting in exaggerated startle responses or difficulty sleeping

The case of Jim (Box 13.2) reveals how these diagnostic criteria apply to a real-life case. Shot and left to die, Jim suffered an extremely traumatic event; guns and related stimuli would trigger a reexperiencing of the trauma. He avoided stimuli associated with the trauma and was hyperaroused and reactive. In some cases of PTSD, the symptoms may not emerge for months or even years following the actual event.

How common is PTSD? Heidi Resnick and her colleagues (Resnick, Kilpatrick, Dansky, Saunders, &

Best, 1993) conducted a diagnostic survey of 4,008 females and found that 12% of the sample had symptoms of PTSD at some time in their lives and that 4.6% were currently suffering PTSD symptoms. These percentages suggest that in the United States alone, 11,800,000 women have had PTSD at some time in their lives and that 4,400,000 currently suffer from it (Resnick et al., 1993). Recent estimates place the rate of PTSD among Iraq War veterans at between 12% and 20%, and Veterans Administration psychiatrists expect that the long-term effects will be significant.

The source of one's trauma is an important consideration. Resnick et al. (1993) found that 26% of women whose trauma was related to crime developed PTSD, whereas only 9% of women who had sustained a noncriminal trauma developed PTSD symptoms. The extent of injury during trauma also predicts whether PTSD symptoms will develop. Women who were injured by a trauma are more likely to develop PTSD symptoms than those who were not. Victims' perceptions of trauma are also important in determining the likelihood of PTSD. The belief that the victim's life is in danger and that he or she has no control over the trauma increases risk for PTSD (Foa & Kozak, 1986; Green, Grace, Lindy, Gleser, & Leonard, 1990; Kushner et al., 1992). One study suggests that cognitive processing during the trauma (such as persistent dissociation) and beliefs after the trauma (such as negative interpretations of trauma memories) predict PTSD symptoms to a greater degree than objective and subjective measures of the severity of the trauma (Halligan, Michael, Clark, & Ehlers, 2003).

Although traumas are unfortunate facts of life, there is reason to believe that PTSD—in some trauma victims, at least—can be prevented. For one thing, although many persons who experience severe trauma may develop **acute stress disorder** (trauma-related symptoms that last less than one month), most do not go on to develop PTSD. One reason may be that those experiencing trauma, but not PTSD, tend to receive high levels of social support from family, friends, or counselors immediately following the event (e.g., Sutker, Davis, Uddo, & Ditta, 1995). Thus, providing immediate social support for trauma victims may prevent their experiences from progressing into posttraumatic stress disorder.

Two other characteristics distinguish people who develop PTSD from those who do not. Individuals who suffer PTSD often perceive the world as a dangerous place from which they must retreat, and they come to view themselves as helpless to deal with stressors. If these two misconceptions could be eliminated, full-blown cases of PTSD might be prevented in many victims. Edna Foa has developed a four-session prevention course designed to attack these two misconceptions in women who have been raped or assaulted. Foa includes the following elements in her PTSD prevention course:

1. Education about the common psychological reactions to assault in order to help victims realize that their responses are normal

2. Training in skills such as relaxation so that the women are better prepared to cope with stress

3. Emotionally reliving the trauma through imagery-based exposure methods to allow victims to defuse their lingering fears of the trauma

4. Cognitive restructuring to help the women replace negative beliefs about their competence and adequacy with more realistic appraisals

Foa and her colleagues evaluated these procedures on 10 women who had recently been raped or assaulted and who completed the four-week course. Victims' PTSD symptoms were compared with those of 10 other women who had also been assaulted or raped but who did not take part in the course. At the times of two follow-up assessments (2 months and 5.5 months, respectively, after the assaults) victims who had completed the prevention course had fewer PTSD symptoms than control subjects who had not received treatment. Two months after their trauma, 70% of the untreated women, but only 10% of the treated women, met the criteria for PTSD (Foa, Hearst-Ikeda, & Perry, 1995). These results suggest that a brief program that facilitates emotionally reexperiencing trauma *and* correcting beliefs about personal inadequacy can reduce the incidence of PTSD.

Regardless of whether they result in PTSD, the frequency and consequences of traumatic and other adverse events may be greater than many have thought. The Adverse Childhood Experience (ACE) Study (Felitti et al., 1998) involving a collaboration between the Centers for Disease Control and Prevention and the Kaiser Health Plan's Department of Preventive Medicine, provided evidence from a survey of 13,934 adults that adverse childhood events were common, with over half the respondents reporting the experience of at least one. Investigators found a graded relationship between the number of categories of childhood exposure and each of the adult health risk behaviors and diseases that were studied (including alcoholism, drug abuse, depression, suicide attempts, smoking, poor health, multiple sexual partners and sexually transmitted disease, and severe obesity). Such traumatic events have particularly been linked to increased risk of PTSD (Breslau et al., 1998; Breslau, Chilcoat, Kessler, & Davis, 1999; Helzer, Robins, & McEvoy, 1987; Perkonigg, Kessler, Storz, & Wittchen, 2000) and mental health disorder more generally (Kessler, Davis & Kendler, 1997; Turner & Lloyd, 1995).

The question of how such traumatic events affect the risk of antisocial behavior toward others, in the form of juvenile delinquency and criminal offending, is a complex one. In addition to the Widom research described earlier, there is evidence of a relationship between trauma and posttraumatic symptoms in younger cohorts. When adolescents are studied, the evidence suggests that this relationship is similar to the adverse outcomes experienced by adults (Breslau, Davis, Andreski & Peterson, 1991; Cuffe et al., 1998; Giaconia et al., 1995), although adolescents may be particularly vulnerable because the context in which the trauma occurs (often the family) is where the individual continues to live in many instances.

High-risk youths have often been abused or neglected (Swahn et al., 2006). Consistent with this finding, Abram and colleagues (2004, 2007) have conducted large-scale studies of incarcerated youth and described a substantially elevated risk for traumatic history and psychiatric comorbidity (multiple diagnoses) among such youth. This suggests that early victimization experiences may be related to multiple psychiatric diagnoses and criminal conduct among adolescents.

BATTERED SPOUSES

Prevalence Rates

The extent of physical abuse directed toward spouses and romantic partners in American society is difficult to estimate, but many observe that it is extensive. It has been estimated that some form of physical aggression occurs in one-fourth to one-third of all couples (Straus & Gelles, 1988). More recent estimates suggest that 33% of men and 25% of women have been involved in a physically aggressive altercation, with the most severe episodes occurring in or near a bar for the men and in the home for the women (Leonard, Quigley, & Collins, 2002). One-year prevalence estimates for violence against women in the United States have been described as 0.3% to 4% for severe violence and 8% to 17% for total violence.

Lifetime prevalence for severe violence against women is estimated at 9% (Wilt & Olson, 1996).

Although relationship aggression by women against men is as frequent as male-to-female aggression (Magdol et al., 1997), male aggression is significantly more likely to result in serious injuries; 39% of female physical assault victims and 24.8% of male assault victims reported having been injured during the most recent assault upon them (Tjaden & Thoennes, 2000). About 30% of all the women murdered in the United States each year are killed by their male partners; in fact, women are 3.7 times more likely to be killed by their partner than by a stranger (Kellerman & Mercy, 1992). For this reason, most of the research on relationship aggression has concentrated on male aggression against female partners (Rosenbaum & Gearan, 1999); we echo that emphasis in this chapter.

Despite these disturbing statistics and the continuing research on relationship aggression, myths about battered women still abound. The mass media often pay little attention to this kind of violence (except in highly publicized cases, such as those of Rihanna and Whitney Houston). Some professionals, such as physicians and police, fail to ask appropriate questions when a battered woman reports an attack by her intimate partner. Arrest and prosecution of perpetrators of partner violence remain unpredictable, and protective restraining orders against batterers are often not consistently enforced.

Myths and Exaggerated Beliefs

Experts emphasize that many oversimplified beliefs, exaggerations, and myths about battered women exist. Follingstad (1994) identified the following misconceptions:

1. Battered women are masochists.
2. They provoke the assaults inflicted on them.
3. They get the treatment they deserve.
4. They are free to leave these violent relationships any time they want to.
5. Violence among intimate partners is not common.

6. Men who are nonviolent in their dealings with outsiders behave the same way in their dealings with their intimates.

7. Middle-class and upper-class men don't batter, and middle-class and upper-class women don't get beaten.

8. Battering is a lower-class, ethnic-minority phenomenon, and such women don't mind because this is a part of their culture.

9. "Good" battered women are passive and never try to defend themselves. (p. 15)

Research examining U.S. perceptions of domestic violence is nearly two decades old, so it may not reflect current attitudes in this area. A recent survey regarding attitudes and beliefs shows that most respondents think of domestic violence as stemming from individual problems, relationships, and families, but not from the nature of our society. Not many think that women cause their own abuse, but about 25% believe that some women want to be abused, and most believe that women can end abusive relationships (Worden & Carlson, 2005).

Research conducted in some other countries has yielded somewhat consistent results. For instance, a national study conducted in Singapore found that the overwhelming majority of the 510 participants disapproved of battery, and only about 6% agreed that under some circumstances it is acceptable for a husband to use physical force against his partner (Choi & Edleson, 1996). Another study conducted with Israeli husbands found that the majority of participants (58%) agreed that "there is no excuse for a man to beat his wife" (p. 199). However, investigators also found that nearly one-third believed that wife-beating is justified on certain occasions (e.g., unfaithful sexual behavior, disrespect of relatives) (Haj-Yahia, 2003). The attitudes of this latter group are consistent with the belief that women provoke domestic assaults and are treated in the way they deserve.

The misconceptions listed earlier obscure several truths about the plight of battered women: Battered women face many real obstacles that make it difficult for them to leave their abusers, and when they do attempt to leave abusive relationships—as many women do—they often suffer further threats, recriminations, and attacks.

The Causes of Battering

What are the main risk factors for battering? Researchers who have studied the causes of battering have focused on ecological factors, the characteristics of the battering victim, the nature of violent intimate relationships, and the psychological makeup of batterers.

One review of this literature points to several risk factors as important (Rosenbaum & Gearan, 1999). Although batterers come from all socioeconomic and ethnic backgrounds, they are more likely than nonbatterers to be unemployed, less well educated, members of minority groups, and of lower socioeconomic status. Batterers tend to have been raised in families in which they either suffered physical abuse as children or observed an abusive relationship between their parents. Adolescents who later become batterers have experienced a higher rate of conduct problems and are more likely to have engaged in early substance abuse; early experiences with coercive or aggressive behavior may set the stage for similar strategies in adult relationships (Magdol, Moffitt, Caspi, & Silva, 1998). In addition, batterers usually have poor self-concepts, are not very good problem solvers, and often have limited verbal skills. They are prone to extreme jealousy and fear of being abandoned by their partners. As a result, they monitor their partners' activities closely and exert excessive control over their partners' whereabouts and activities. They overreact to signs of rejection and alternate between rage and desperation.

Although research suggests that batterers have many characteristics in common, not all batterers share a common profile. For instance, one comprehensive study revealed three distinct types of batterers: generally violent, psychopathological, and family-only (Waltz, Babcock, Jacobson, & Gottman, 2000). These groups were distinguished by the degree of violence within the relationship and the degree of general violence reported, as well as by personality characteristics. For instance, generally violent batterers displayed the highest levels of aggressive-sadistic behavior, psychopathological batterers exhibited more passive-aggressive/dependant characteristics, and family-only batterers displayed violent behaviors but generally did not hold violence-supportive beliefs and attitudes.

Findings from this study further indicated that differences in life experiences accounted for some of the variations in each of the group's behavior. For instance, when the generally violent batterers and the family-only batterers were compared, both groups were found to have experienced physical abuse as children, but significant differences existed in the frequency and severity of interparental violence witnessed; the generally violent batterers had witnessed more frequent and severe parental violence. These findings suggest that understanding the risk factors associated with batterers may be more complex than once was believed.

The Cycle of Violence

Batterers are sometimes described as displaying a **cycle of violence** involving a Jekyll-and-Hyde pattern of emotional and behavioral instability that makes their victims all the more fearful of the battering they believe is inevitable. A man may be loving and attentive to a woman's needs early in their relationship as he cultivates her affection and relies on her to satisfy his dependency needs; however, when disappointments or disagreements occur in the relationship, as they invariably do, a *tension-building phase* begins, characterized by increased criticism of the partner and perhaps even minor physical assaults.

This phase leads to a second stage in the cycle, an *acute battering incident*. By the time this more serious form of aggression occurs, the woman has become too dependent on the man to break off the relationship easily. He has succeeded in controlling her behavior and curtailing her contact with friends who might have possibly helped extract her from her plight. The woman also tends to believe that if only she can find the right way to mollify the man's anger and reassure him of her faithfulness and obedience, he will change his behavior.

Following a battering incident, a third stage (called the *contrite phase*) occurs, in which the batterer apologizes for his attack, promises never to do it again, and persuades the woman that he is a changed man. Often this is an empty pledge. Indeed, sometimes the humiliation that the man feels over having apologized so profusely to his partner simply fuels more intense anger and violence, and the cycle repeats itself.

How pervasive is the cycle of violence? Even though Walker (1979) portrays it as a significant dynamic faced by battered women, she identified it in only about two-thirds of the 400 women she studied. What the *cycle of violence* may actually be describing is an underlying personality disorder that typifies a certain category of batterer.

According to Donald Dutton (1995, 2000), a psychologist at the University of British Columbia and one of the experts who testified for the prosecution in O. J. Simpson's murder trial, as many as 40% of batterers have the features of **borderline personality disorder**, a severe disturbance that is characterized by unstable moods and behavior. People with borderline personality disorder are drawn into intense relationships in which they are particularly unable to tolerate certain emotions. They are demandingly dependent, which causes them to feel easily slighted, which leads to jealousy, rage, aggression, and subsequently guilt. These emotional cycles repeat themselves, providing the underlying motivation for the cycle of violence. In addition to emotional instability, batterers are also prone to believing the worst about others; for example, they are quick to attribute hostile intentions to their partners (Eckhardt, Barbour, & Davison, 1998). Dutton traces the origin of this personality disorder to insecure attachments that batterers experienced with their parents, which later cause them to feel intense anger toward partners whenever things go awry in a relationship.

Responses to Victims of Battering

The prevalence of many myths about battered women reflects the negative feelings toward crime victims described earlier in this chapter. A deep uneasiness, even hostility, exists toward some victims of battering (Jones, 1994). They are often seen as pathological "doormats" or delusional alarmists "crying wolf" over minor disagreements. When victims retaliate against their abusers—when battered women kill their batterers—they may receive a greater punishment than men who commit acts with similar outcomes. The question of whether women receive harsher sentences than men for domestic homicide is difficult to answer because the circumstances may be quite different. Jenkins and Davidson (1990) analyzed the court records of 10 battered women charged with the murder of their abusive partners in Louisiana between 1975 and 1988; all pleaded guilty or were convicted at trial. Their sentences ranged from five years' probation to life in prison; with half receiving the latter sentence.

Ewing (1987) surveyed a larger number of women who had killed their batterers. All 100 were charged with murder, manslaughter, or some form of criminal homicide. The outcomes were as follows: 3 were found not guilty by reason of insanity, 3 had their charges dropped, 9 pleaded guilty, and 85 went to trial. Of these 85, a total of 63 were convicted. For those convicted, 12 were given life in prison, 1 was sentenced to 50 years without parole, and the others received anywhere from 4 years' probation to 25 years in prison, with 17 receiving prison sentences longer than 10 years.

Battered Woman Syndrome as a Defense. Only a very small minority of battered women kills their attackers, but these victims receive a great deal of public scrutiny, usually in connection with their trial for murder. When they go to trial, most battered women use either insanity or self-defense as a defense; in either instance, **battered woman syndrome** is likely to be part of the defense. Battered woman syndrome is defined as a collection of symptoms and reactions by a woman to a pattern of continued physical and psychological abuse inflicted on her by her mate. Lenore Walker (1984), the psychologist who is recognized for naming this syndrome, emphasizes the following elements:

1. As a result of chronic exposure to repeated incidents of battering, the woman develops a sense of learned helplessness, in which she comes to believe that there is nothing she can do to escape from the batterer or improve her life; finally, she gives up trying to make a change.

2. As a result of her social isolation and often her economic dependence on the batterer, the woman falls more and more under his domination. She believes that she has diminished alternatives for solving her problem.

3. As she restricts her outside activities and has less contact with friends or relatives, the woman grows increasingly fearful of the threats and attacks of the batterer. Most of the women Walker interviewed stated that they believed that their batterer would eventually kill them.

4. Trapped in this existence, the woman experiences several emotional and psychological reactions. Her self-esteem is diminished, she feels guilty and ashamed about what she sees as her multiple failures and shortcomings, and she also feels increasing rage and resentment toward her partner, whose control over her seems to grow over time.

5. After years of victimization, the woman grows hypervigilant; she notices subtle things—reactions by the batterer that others wouldn't recognize as a signal of upcoming violence (for example, her partner's words come faster, he assumes a specific posture, or his eyes get darker). This heightened sensitivity to danger cues often motivates the woman to kill her assailant and accounts for her belief that she acted in self-defense.

Evaluating Battered Woman Syndrome.   How have claims of battered woman syndrome fared in court? Does it advance the cause of victims who feel they are forced to retaliate after years of abuse? A battered woman's claim of self-defense often faces both legal hurdles and the skepticism of jurors (Dodge & Greene, 1991; Schuller, McKimmie, & Janz, 2004). These obstacles might account for the fact that the majority of battered women charged with murdering their abusive partner are convicted.

Historically, a claim of **self-defense** has applied to homicides in which, at the time of the killing, the individual reasonably believed that he or she was in imminent danger of death or great bodily harm from an attacker. The defense was usually invoked in cases in which a specific attack or fight put defendants in fear for their lives, however, the typical case in which a battered woman relies on a theory of self-defense to clear her from charges of murdering her partner is much different. The violence does not involve a specific episode; rather, it is ongoing. The woman's response may seem disproportionate to what a "reasonable" person believes was necessary; often she kills her abuser while he is unarmed or even is sleeping.

To help jurors understand how battered woman syndrome leads to a woman's perception that she is acting in self-defense, defendants often try to introduce expert testimony about the characteristics and consequences of the syndrome. Some mock jury research has explored the effect of expert testimony in a criminal homicide case in which the defendant was a battered woman (Schuller et al., 2004). Participants were more inclined to accept the woman's claim of self-defense when they heard from an expert testifying for the defense. In addition, compared to the no-expert control condition, those exposed to expert testimony on battered woman syndrome believed that the defendant's options were far more limited.

It is important to remember that no single set of reactions or characteristics can describe all victims of battering. One study (Dutton, Perrin, Chrestman, & Halle, 1990) that investigated the characteristics of battered women seeking help at a counseling program identified five distinct personality types, with different patterns of psychological functioning among them, including profiles that were "normal."

Although battered women share the experience of being victimized by a violent partner, their reaction to this aggression and how they cope with it takes many different forms. This variation has implications for developing the most effective types of intervention for these women. Rather than assuming that they need traditional services such as psychotherapy or couples counseling, it would be more effective to provide battered women with special advocates who would support these survivors and help them find the resources they need to improve their lives. Just such an intervention has proved very effective in helping bring about changes that allowed battered women to become violence-free (Sullivan & Bybee, 1999). After providing battered women with a personal advocate who helped them gain access to the resources that each needed to reduce her risk of partner abuse, Sullivan and Bybee found that the women who received advocacy services were twice as likely, during the two-year outcome period, to be free of any battering than were women without such a service.

THE PSYCHOLOGY OF RAPE

Until recently, rape victims were singled out for misunderstanding, harassment, and neglect. For example, if a rape victim did not resist her attacker, people might incorrectly assume that she wanted to be raped; in contrast, people never raise the question of whether victims wanted to be robbed, or struck by a hit-and-run driver, or have their identity stolen. Furthermore, society struggles over how to deal with convicted rapists. Is rape a sexual crime or an act of violence? Is it the act of a disordered mind or a result of extraordinary circumstances?

Among serious crimes, rape is perhaps the most appropriate for psychological analysis (Allison & Wrightsman, 1993). Myths abound about the nature of rapists and their relationship to their victims. Rape is a crime in which the interaction between the criminal and his prey is central to attributions of responsibility and blame (Stormo, Lang, & Stritzke, 1997). Since the 1970s, there has been a good deal of psychological research directed toward understanding sexual assaults (Beech, Fisher, & Thornton, 2003; Ellis, 1991; Hall & Hirschman, 1991; Jones,

Wynn, Kroeze, Dunnuck, & Rossman, 2004; Marshall, Fernandez, & Cortoni, 1999). For these reasons, we devote special attention to the crime of rape and its victims. We focus on female rape victims, although the fact that men are also raped should not be overlooked.

Myths and Stereotypes about Rape

Myths and misleading stereotypes about rape, rapists, and rape victims take three general forms: (1) Women cannot be raped against their will, (2) women secretly wish to be raped, and (3) most accusations of rape are faked. For example, we are told, "Only bad girls get raped." Yet, we are also told, "All women want to be raped" and "Women ask for it." We also learn that "any healthy woman can resist a rapist if she really wants to." These mistaken perceptions create a climate hostile to rape victims, often portraying them as willing participants in or even instigators of sexual encounters. In fact, these attitudes often function as self-serving rationalizations and excuses for blaming the victim.

Rape means different things to different people, and these differing attitudes and perceptions affect behaviors toward both offenders and their victims (Feild, 1978). Some respondents feel more empathy toward rape victims than others do; some feel empathy toward defendants charged with the crime of rape (Deitz, Russell, & Hammes, 1989; Weir & Wrightsman, 1990). Thus, the measurement of attitudes about rape can clarify what different people believe about this crime, its victims, and its perpetrators.

In his groundbreaking studies of attitudes toward rape, Herbert S. Feild (1978, 1979; Barnett & Feild, 1977; Feild & Barnett, 1978; Feild & Bienen, 1980) hypothesized that a person's view of rape cannot be summarized by one score on a single scale. After constructing a 75-item Attitudes Toward Rape questionnaire and analyzing responses to it, Feild concluded that seven different attitude clusters contribute to our overall perspective. Among these factors is the degree to which:

1. women are seen as responsible for preventing their own rape,

2. a desire for sex is seen as the main motive for rape,

3. severe punishment is advocated for rapists, and

4. a woman is seen as instigating rape through flirtatious behavior or provocative dress.

What Accounts for Stereotypes and Myths about Rape? Individuals who, on the basis of answers to Feild's questionnaire, are unsympathetic to victims and tolerant of rapists also tend to believe in many of the myths about rape described earlier. Such persons have developed a broad ideology that encourages the acceptance of myths about rape (Burt, 1980). This ideology embraces the following beliefs:

1. *Sexual conservatism.* This attitude emphasizes restrictions on the appropriateness of sexual partners, sexual acts, and circumstances under which sexual activity should occur. Burt (1980) observes, "Since many instances of rape violate one or more aspects of this conservative position, a sexually conservative individual might feel so strongly threatened by, and rejecting of, the specific circumstances of rape that he or she would overlook the coercion and force involved, and condemn the victim for participating" (p. 218).

2. *Adversarial sexual beliefs.* This component refers to the belief that sexual relationships are fundamentally exploitive—that participants in them are manipulative, unfaithful, and not to be trusted. To a person holding this ideology, "rape might seem the extreme on a continuum of exploitation, but not an unexpected or horrifying occurrence, or one justifying sympathy or support" (Burt, 1980, p. 218).

3. *Acceptance of interpersonal violence.* Another part of the ideology is the belief that force and coercion are legitimate behaviors in sexual relationships. This ideology approves of men dominating women and overpowering passive partners with violence and control.

4. *Sex-role stereotyping.* The last component of Burt's ideology casts each gender into the

traditional mold of behaviors associated with that gender.

Burt constructed a set of attitude statements and administered them to a sample of 598 Minnesota adults to determine whether each of these components contributed to acceptance of myths about rape. When subjects' responses on the ideology clusters were compared to their answers on a scale measuring beliefs in myths about rape, Burt found that three of the four clusters had an impact (sexual conservatism did not). The strongest predictor of believing the myths was the acceptance of interpersonal violence. The subjects, both men and women, who felt that force and coercion were acceptable in sexual relationships were the ones who agreed with items such as "Women who get raped while hitchhiking get what they deserve" and "Any healthy woman can successfully resist a rapist if she really wants to."

A review of more than 70 studies that employed a variety of measures of attitudes about rape supports Burt's conclusions (Anderson, Cooper, & Okamura, 1997). Those subjects who are more tolerant of rape are more likely to have traditional beliefs about gender roles, more adversarial sexual beliefs, greater needs for power and dominance, and heightened expressions of aggressiveness and anger.

Facts about Rape

As we have seen, mistaken beliefs about rape are related to general attitudes toward law and crime. Still, what are the facts about rape? The United States has one of the highest rates of forcible rape among the world's industrialized countries (Marshall et al., 1999). Between 75 and 85 forcible rapes are reported annually to the police for every 100,000 females (Butterfield, 1997). This rate is more than three times that of England and twice that of countries such as France, Norway, and Spain (Kutchinski, 1988; Quinsey, 1984; Russell, 1984).

A major study of rape, published in 2000, provided valuable data on the frequency of rape and on women's reactions to this crime. The National

Women's Study was organized and funded by several governmental agencies and crime victim organizations. A nationwide, stratified sample of 8,000 adult women and 8,005 adult men were interviewed over the telephone about their experiences as victims of sexual aggression. Due to the fact that children and adolescents were excluded from the sample, the figures underestimate the total number of rapes, but they do give us an idea of the magnitude of the problem with adults. Among the study's findings are the following:

1. In the sample surveyed, 17.6% of all women said they had been the victim of rape or attempted rape sometime in their lifetime, and 21.6% of these women reported that they were younger than 12 years old at the time of their first rape.

2. Among rape victims, 31.5% reported being physically injured during their most recent rape.

According to the National Violence Against Women Survey, almost 18 million women (and almost 3 million men) in the United States have been raped. In a single year, more than 300,000 women and almost 93,000 men are estimated to have been raped. Women who reported being raped as minors were twice as likely to report being raped as adults (Tjaden & Thoennes, 2006).

Women of all ages, social classes, and ethnic groups are vulnerable to rape. According to a study by the U.S. Bureau of Justice Statistics, the high-risk age groups are children and adolescents; victims younger than age 12 account for 15% of those raped and victims aged 12 to 17 account for an additional 29% (Butterfield, 1997). Other surveys report that between 1% and 12% of victims are over 50 years of age.

According to the National Violence against Women Study, however, only 19% of the women and 13% of the men who were raped after age 18 said their rape was reported to the police (Tjaden & Thoennes, 2006). Several factors account for the low report rates (Feldman-Summers & Ashworth, 1981): The woman may be convinced that reporting won't help, that she would suffer further embarrassment as a result of reporting, and/or that law enforcement officers would not believe her. Many victims are afraid that the attacker will retaliate if charges are made, and these expectations are sometimes fulfilled. According to FBI figures, only about half of reported rapes result in an arrest, and if a suspect is charged and the victim is a witness at his trial, his defense attorney may ridicule her testimony and impugn her character.

Motivations and Characteristics of Rapists

Not all rapists have the same motives. Rape involves diverse combinations of aggressive and sexual motivation and deviant lifestyles for different offenders (Barbaree & Marshall, 1991). Experts have developed typologies of rapists, some proposing as many as nine types (Prentky & Knight, 1991), others as few as two or three (Groth, 1979). Most typologies have emphasized four factors that distinguish different types of rapists: (1) the amount and type of aggression the rapist used, (2) when the level of aggression was high, whether it heightened sexual arousal in a sadistic manner, (3) whether the offender showed evidence of psychopathy or antisocial personality disorder, and (4) whether the offender relied on deviant sexual fantasies to produce sexual arousal. Theories of sexual aggression combine several causal factors into an integrated scheme that accounts for the different types of rapists (Sorenson & White, 1992).

From a somewhat different perspective, Ellis (1989) identified three theories of rape: the *feminist theory*, emphasizing rape as a pseudosexual act of male domination and exploitation of women (Donat & D'Emilio, 1992; White & Sorenson, 1992); the *social-learning approach*, suggesting that sexual aggression is learned through observation and imitation; and the *evolutionary theory*, holding that natural selection favors men who use forced sexual behavior (Buss & Malamuth, 1996). Ellis (1991) also suggests that high levels of testosterone increase the inclination to rape by increasing the man's sexual urges and decreasing his sensitivity to aversive outcomes such as a victim's suffering.

These different approaches illustrate that rape cannot be easily explained by any one theory, and yet every one of these classification systems fails to capture the full spectrum of behaviors and motivations that typify rapists. Some of these systems are also limited by the fact that they are based on studies of convicted rapists who have been sentenced to prison. The majority of rapists are never imprisoned for their offenses; fewer than 10% of rapes result in convictions or prison sentences (Frazier & Haney, 1996).

Acquaintance Rape and "Date Rape"

Over three-fourths of rapes are committed by acquaintances (Koss, 1992; Warshaw, 1988), and these are the assaults that women are least likely to report. Sometimes these actions are not even interpreted as rape. Kanin (1957, 1971) found that over a 20-year period, between one-fourth and one-fifth of college women he surveyed reported forceful attempts at sexual intercourse by their dates, during which the women resorted to such reactions as screaming, fighting, crying, and pleading, but usually they did not label the event as attempted rape.

More recent surveys draw similar conclusions; 22% of college females in Yegidis's (1986) survey reported being a victim at least once of an attempted or a completed acquaintance rape; 25.3% of a sample of undergraduates in New Zealand reported being raped or having a rape attempted against them (Gavey, 1991). Muehlenhard and Linton (1987) reported that 78% of females had experienced some kind of unwelcome sexual initiative during a date. Even among college males, 6% in one study reported having been sexually assaulted at least once (Lott, Reilly, & Howard, 1982). The 2000 National Women's Study reported that only 14.6% of rapes were committed by a stranger to the victim; 16.4% were committed by a nonrelative acquaintance; 6.4% by a relative; and 64% by an intimate partner.

In general, date rapes differ from sexual assaults by a stranger in several ways. They tend to occur on weekends, between 10:00 P.M. and 1:00 A.M., and they usually take place at the assailant's home or apartment. Date rapes tend to involve situations in

AP Images/Ed Andrieski

Kobe Bryant enters the courthouse

which both the attacker and the victim have been using alcohol or drugs but they are less likely to involve the use of weapons; instead, the date rapist employs verbal threats and physical prowess to overpower his victim.

Consequences of Being Raped

Rape victims suffer physical injuries, emotional pain and humiliation, and sometimes severe psychological after-effects. Recovery from the trauma of rape can be very slow, and victims often describe a sense that they will never be the same again. Providing psychological assistance to rape victims is of utmost importance.

The plight of rape victims has received increased attention through a number of highly publicized cases in which women have come forward to report their experiences. As these cases have unfolded in the public eye, sexual aggression has become a topic of increased discussion among men and women. The gang rape of the Central Park jogger during a "wilding" spree; Desiree Washington's rape charges that

resulted in the conviction of former heavyweight boxing champion Mike Tyson; the arrest of more than a dozen men for a string of daylight sexual assaults on scores of women in Central Park during Puerto Rican National Day celebrations; the Vail, Colorado, resort employee who accused Kobe Bryant of rape; and, most recently, rape charges brought against three Duke University lacrosse players have focused this nation's attention on matters of sexual conduct and on the plight of the victims of sexual aggression.

One part of this discussion has been a debate about whether the names of victims of sexual assault should be made public. The tradition in this country has been to protect the identity of rape victims by not using their names in media coverage. Still, in the case of Kobe Bryant, both television and online reporting broke with this tradition and published the name of Bryant's accuser, Katelyn Faber. Defenders of this decision argue that not naming rape victims perpetuates the stigma of having been raped, making it more difficult in the long run for victims to come forward and confront their attackers. Critics of the practice claim that publishing the victim's name invades her privacy and perhaps ruins her future because she would forever be branded as a rape victim. According to the National Women's Study, most rape victims prefer not to have their names published; over three-quarters of the respondents said they would be less likely to report a rape if they knew their names would be made public.

How Do Women React to Being Raped?

Burgess and Holmstrom (1974, 1979) describe a collection of symptoms experienced by many rape victims. This pattern—**rape trauma syndrome**—comprises three kinds of reactions: emotional responses, disturbances in functioning, and changes in lifestyle. The primary emotional response is fear, including fear of being left alone and fear of situations similar to the one in which the rape occurred (Calhoun, Atkeson, & Resick, 1982). Even the most general of associations with the rape or rapist may trigger an emotional response.

Judith Rowland (1985), a deputy district attorney, describes a reaction of a white rape victim, Terri Richardson, as the trial of her alleged attacker began. Her attacker was a black man.

> [T]he San Diego Municipal Court had one black judge among its numbers. As it happened ... his chambers were next door. As Terri and I stood ... while the bailiff scurried out to reassemble the jury, this lone black judge was also preparing to take the bench. I was aware of him standing in his doorway, wearing his ankle-length black robes. It was only when his bailiff held the courtroom door open for him and he was striding toward it that Terri saw him. In less than the time it took him to get through the door, Terri had bolted from the corridor, through the courtroom, and into the main hallway. By the time I got to the outside corridor, I found only a group of startled jurors. I located Terri in a nearby ladies' room, locked in a stall, crying. With a bit more comforting, she was able to regain her composure and get

through both my direct and the defense's cross-examination with only minor bouts of tears, particularly while describing the attack itself. (pp. 166–167)

Guilt and shame are also frequent emotional responses. Victims may blame themselves: "Why was I at a bus stop in a strange part of town?" "Did I check that the back door was locked that night?" They may worry that they didn't resist the attacker vigorously enough. The victim often feels a loss of autonomy and of control over her body. She may no longer trust others, a loss that may never be fully repaired throughout her lifetime. One victim describes the feeling this way: "I never feel safe. I couldn't stand the apartment where I lived, but I'm so afraid to be alone anywhere. I never was like that before. I carry things with me, like kitchen knives and sticks, when I go out" (quoted in Rowland, 1985, p. 146).

The second type of reaction, a disturbance in functioning, also frequently appears among rape victims. Specific disturbances include changes in sleep patterns (insomnia, nightmares, and early awakening), social withdrawal, changes in appetite, and problems in sexual functioning. Feldman-Summers, Gordon, and Meagher (1979) studied the impact of rape on victims' sexual satisfaction. Although the sample consisted of only 15 victims, the study did include a comparison group of women who had not been sexually assaulted. Compared with this group, the rape victims reported less satisfaction with most areas of sexual functioning one week after the rape than in the period before the rape. The level of dissatisfaction diminished somewhat over the next two months, but women who had been raped did not, during this period, approach the level of sexual satisfaction they had experienced before the attack. A study conducted by Bartoi and Kinder (1998) on 175 college students found that women who were sexually abused in adulthood were more sexually dissatisfied and nonsensual than women with no history of sexual abuse. Additionally, women with a history of sexual abuse as a child or as an adult were less satisfied with their most recent sexual relationship than women with no history of abuse. These women also tended to have a higher number of unsafe sexual partners.

Changes occur not only in emotions and general functioning but also in lifestyle. Some victims report obsessively checking doors to make sure they are double-locked; one of the victims whose attacker was prosecuted by Rowland (1985) took 45-minute showers two or three times daily, trying to remove the rapist's odor from her body. Other women make major changes in lifestyle, breaking up with their boyfriends, changing jobs, and moving to new residences. The overall socioeconomic impact of rape can be profound; victims of sexual assault are at greater risk of subsequently losing income, becoming unemployed, and going through a divorce (Byrne, Resnick, Kilpatrick, Best, & Saunders, 1999). Women who have been sexually assaulted in the past or who were sexually abused as children are two to three times more likely to suffer a subsequent sexual attack than women without prior sexual victimizations (Nishith, Mechanic, & Resick, 2000).

Although the reasons for the heightened risk are not clear, one possibility is that some women who have been victimized before are slower to recognize when they are at risk and therefore are more likely to remain in situations where they are vulnerable (Wilson, Calhoun, & Bernat, 1999). Women with more than one sexual victimization across their childhood and adult years are more likely to report unplanned and aborted pregnancies (Wyatt, Guthrie, & Notgrass, 1992).

The impact of rape trauma tends to change over time as well. In fact, observers (Burgess & Holmstrom, 1974; Ellison & Buckhout, 1981) have described the typical rape victim's response as a crisis reaction that unfolds in a series of discrete phases.

The *acute phase* begins with the attack and lasts a few hours or a day. During this acute phase, the primary needs of the victim are to understand what is happening, regain control over her life, predict what will happen next, and air her feelings to someone who will listen without passing judgment (Ellison & Buckhout, 1981). At this point, police officers investigating the crime can either help or hinder the victim. For example, a pelvic examination

and the collection of any semen samples are necessary at this point; it is unlikely that the suspect can be prosecuted in the absence of such evidence, but the examination may cause a resurgence of the initial feelings of disruption, helplessness, hostility, and violation—a reaction known as **secondary victimization**. In fact, negative experiences with legal and medical authorities have been shown to increase rape victims' symptoms of posttraumatic stress disorder (Campbell et al., 1999).

Within a few hours or days of the attack, many victims slip into a period of false recovery. Denial occurs: "I'm OK; everything is the same as before." Then a secondary crisis occurs—a sort of flashback— in which some of the symptoms of the acute crisis phase, particularly phobias and disturbances in eating and sleeping, return (Ellison & Buckhout, 1981, p. 59). This phase may last for hours or days before another "quiet period" emerges in which the victim feels a range of negative emotions such as loneliness, anger, and guilt.

Because of increased public awareness of the needs of rape victims, rape crisis centers have been established in many cities. These centers provide crisis counseling to victims. Most follow up with at least one further interview (usually by phone), and a third of their clients have from two to six follow-up interviews. The crisis center also checks for pregnancy and sexually transmitted disease.

Long-term counseling for rape victims is more difficult to provide because of the lack of staff at some rape crisis centers and, in some cases, because of a feeling that counseling is no longer needed. Burgess and Holmstrom (1979), in a follow-up of their earlier sample, found that 74% of rape victims felt that they had recovered and were "back to normal" four to six years after the rape. But 26% did not. A longitudinal study of 20 rape victims (Kilpatrick, Resick, & Veronen, 1981) measured the personality and mood of these victims and of a matched control group at three time intervals: one month, six months, and one year after the rape. Even at a one-year follow-up, many victims continued to suffer emotionally from the sexual assault. Among the major problems were fear and anxiety, often severe enough to constitute a diagnosis of posttraumatic stress disorder.

The long-term consequences of rape are also concerning. One study involved interviewing 35 rape victims between 2 and 46 years after their rape and compared their responses to 110 matched, nonabused participants to determine the long-term psychological effects of rape (Santiago, McCall-Perez, Gorcey, & Beigel, 1985). Findings showed that fear and anxiety were significantly higher in the rape victim population, compared to the nonabused sample, regardless of the length of time since their rape. Findings also indicated that the rape victims were significantly more depressed than those who had not been raped and that fear, anxiety, and depression were highest in women who had been raped more than once.

Providing social support is one of the most helpful interventions. The therapeutic power of social support may derive in part from the fact that women, in particular, tend to react to stress by seeking opportunities for attachment and caregiving—or what psychologist Shelley Taylor has termed the *tend-and-befriend* response (Taylor et al., 2000). (Men, on the other hand, are more likely to respond to stress with the well-known "fight-or-flight" strategy.) Therefore, it might be especially useful to female crime victims to have ample opportunities for social support so that their preference to be with others in times of need can be fully addressed.

Rape Trauma Syndrome in Court. Psychologists, along with psychiatrists and other physicians, often testify as expert witnesses in rape trials, especially about the nature and consequences of rape trauma syndrome (Fischer, 1989; Frazier & Borgida, 1985, 1988). This syndrome is usually thought of as an example of a posttraumatic stress disorder, similar to that experienced by veterans of combat, survivors of natural disasters, and victims of other violent crimes. The expert can be of special use to the prosecution in those trials in which the defendant admits that sexual intercourse took place but claims that the woman was a willing participant; evidence of rape trauma syndrome can be consistent with the complainant's version of the facts (Frazier & Borgida, 1985). In addition, jurors are often not familiar with the reactions that rape victims frequently experience (Borgida & Brekke, 1985), so psychological experts can educate the jury. Courts around the country are divided, however, on the admissibility of such testimony, and the resulting controversy has generated considerable debate.

The main argument against admitting expert testimony on rape trauma syndrome is as follows: The psychological responses of rape victims are not unique to rape and are not uniform, so it is impossible to say with certainty that a woman exhibiting any given set of responses has been raped. Therefore, a psychologist should not be allowed to testify that a woman is suffering from rape trauma syndrome because to do so is tantamount to telling the jury that she has been raped, which should remain a matter for the jury to decide. Many courts also reject expert testimony on rape trauma syndrome on the ground that the reliability of the syndrome has not been established.

Legislation and Court Decisions

Laws about rape in the United States, rooted in English common law, changed little throughout much of our country's history (Harper, 1984). The first American law about rape, created in Massachusetts, imposed the death penalty on the rapist except when the victim was unmarried, reflecting a view that women belonged to their husbands (Estrich, 1987). But beginning in the 1970s, legislation about rape began to undergo dramatic review and revision. These changes are correlated with our increased knowledge about rape generated by social science research and feminist groups. The revisions have usually involved replacing the term *rape* with the term *sexual assault*, reflecting the view that this crime primarily involves the sexual expression of violence (Harper, 1984). This term also eliminates any lingering requirements that the state provide corroborating evidence for the victim's testimony, and it devotes more attention to the extent of physical and psychological injury inflicted on the victim.

The basic definition of sexual assault is nonconsenting sexual contact (such as intercourse) that is obtained by using force or coercion against the victim; however, how do we distinguish between sexual assault and a consensual sexual act? No single standard defines what is meant by *nonconsent*, which is why, despite legal reforms, the nature of the victim's conduct in a sexual assault often remains an issue.

Shifts in Rape Laws.   How much does the victim's behavior contribute to the determination of nonconsent? Is resistance relevant or necessary? Until the 1980s, about four-fifths of the states still imposed a resistance standard—it had to be shown that the victim attempted to resist a sexual assault—in their definition of rape (Largen, 1988), but sexual assault statutes now concentrate more on the behavior of the assailant and have expanded their definition of force to include coercion or intimidation by the alleged assailant. The requirement of resistance has been diminished or eliminated.

A second shift in sexual assault laws has been to define several different crime levels. Previously, some states found that with only one degree of offense, which carried possibly severe penalties, juries saw the sentence (which could be life in prison) as too extreme for some cases; hence, they opted for not-guilty verdicts. Many of the newer laws divide sexual assault into degrees according to the extent of force or threat that was used. For example, a *first-degree* sexual assault would involve sexual intercourse by forcible compulsion under aggravated circumstances (e.g., using a deadly weapon or kidnapping the victim). A *second-degree* sexual assault would require sexual intercourse by forcible compulsion. A *third-degree* sexual assault would be defined as sexual intercourse without consent or with threat of substantial harm to property rights.

Another legislative change concerns **spousal rape**. Until approximately 1980, most states did not consider the sexual assault of a spouse to be rape. Now, all states have eliminated this exception and recognize spousal rape as a crime. In Florida in 1984, a 41-year-old man was found guilty of kidnapping and raping his wife. He was the first man to be convicted of a sexual assault that occurred while the couple was married and living together.

Even though spousal rape is now considered a crime in every state, it is not always treated the same as a sexual assault involving unmarried persons. For example, some states impose a shorter "reporting period" on victims of spousal rape than on victims of other violent crimes. If a victim does not report the assault within this period, the spouse cannot be prosecuted. Another difference between spousal rape and nonspousal rape is the requirement that force or threat of force by the spouse must be proved, rather than just the lack of consent by the victim, which is the requirement in many nonspousal sexual assault statutes.

The Rape Victim as a Trial Witness.   Shifts in the rape laws have addressed another persistent problem in the trials of alleged rapists. Before such laws were changed, a frequently used defense strategy involved attacking the victim's truthfulness and her general morality. Jurors can be influenced by testimony about the woman's character, reputation, and lifestyle (Lee, 1985), and this has led all states to adopt **rape shield laws** to provide victims with more protection as trial witnesses. In addition, the Privacy Protection for Rape Victims Act of 1978 amended the federal rules of evidence with regard to the admissibility of testimony on the victim's sexual history with parties other than the defendant. As a result, it is more difficult for defense attorneys to introduce evidence regarding a victim's sexual history, and today defense attorneys probably rely much more on the argument that the sexual contact was consensual.

Rape shield laws are designed to protect victims' rights to privacy during trial and to exclude evidence about past sexual behavior that might influence the jury's decision in the case. Findings from a study of jurors' use of sexual history evidence underscore the importance of this protection. Schuller and Hastings (2002) varied the evidence of prior sexual history of the complainant and defendant in a mock sexual assault trial. In the condition in which the complainant and defendant had a history of involvement including sexual intercourse, compared with the no-sexual-history control condition, the complainant was perceived

The importance of consent

as less credible, more likely to have consented, and more blameworthy. Prior sexual history also affected jurors' verdicts: The more intimate the prior contact between complainant and defendant, the less guilty the defendant was believed to be. Jurors apparently gauge the credibility of the complainant and the culpability of the defendant through the lens of the parties' prior sexual encounters.

Despite the frequent application of rape shield laws, there is some debate about whether they serve their intended purpose. Many jurisdictions have exceptions that allow the introduction of sexual history evidence at trial when the judge deems it relevant and helpful to the jury (Schuller & Klippenstine, 2004). For example, in the Kobe Bryant rape case, the judge decided, prior to trial, that evidence of the complainant's sexual forays in the three days prior to her encounter with Bryant could be admitted at trial. The rape shield law in Colorado allows evidence of prior sexual conduct when such evidence is relevant to determining the source of vaginal injuries or semen. (Bryant contended that the woman suffered injury during her earlier sexual encounters; the case against him was dismissed after his accuser opted not to testify.)

Yet even if stringent rape shield laws are in force, some jurors will continue to doubt the testimony of rape victims or will use the testimony to make attributions about the witnesses' honesty. For example, mock jurors who are relatively lacking in empathy for rape victims are less likely to see an attacker as responsible for a rape (Dietz, Littman, & Bentley, 1984).

One experience that increases empathy for rape victims is to be personally acquainted with a woman who has been raped. In a laboratory study in which subjects read summaries of witness testimony and then rated the responsibility of a man charged with rape, men and women who themselves knew a rape victim were twice as likely to find the accused guilty of rape as were men and women who did not personally know a rape victim (Wiener, Wiener, & Grisso, 1989).

Preventing Rape

As we learn more about the frequency and consequences of rape, a primary goal of concerned citizens, law enforcement officials, and social scientists has been to develop effective interventions for preventing rape. Two basic strategies have been emphasized: (1) training potential victims how best to protect themselves against rape, and (2) designing effective treatment for rapists so that they do not repeat their crimes.

Training Potential Victims to Reduce the Risk of Rape.   If a woman finds herself in a situation in which a man begins to sexually assault her, what should she do? Should she scream? Should she fight back? Should she try to reason with him? Or should she submit to the attack, especially if the assailant has a weapon? There is no uniformly correct response, just as there is no one type of rapist. However, on the issue of passive compliance, a Justice Department survey of over a million attacks (quoted in Meddis & Kelley, 1985) found that women who did not resist a rape attack were twice as likely to suffer a completed rape as women who tried to protect themselves.

As we have already seen, national surveys suggest that between one-fifth and one-quarter of college women have suffered a sexual assault and that the majority of victims were acquainted with their assailants before the assault. Research has also uncovered several risk factors associated with sexual assault. For example, individuals who were previously victimized are at an increased risk for subsequent victimization (Smith, White, & Holland, 2003; Tjaden & Thoennes, 2000). In addition, acquaintance rape is more frequent (1) when both the victim and the assailant have been drinking or using drugs, (2) on dates in which the man pays all the expenses, and (3) when the date is at an isolated location. Several colleges and universities have incorporated this information about risk factors into rape prevention programs aimed at changing attitudes about sexuality, challenging rape myths and sex-role stereotypes, and improving women's coping responses in potentially dangerous situations.

In the typical rape prevention program, participants discuss several facts and myths about rape, learn how to avoid situations involving heavy use of alcohol, practice resisting pressure for unwanted sexual activity, and role-play other strategies for protecting themselves. The programs try to help women change behaviors and to dispel the notion that victims cause sexual assault. They also strive to minimize the blaming of women that can occur following sexual victimization. A recent study (Orchowski, Gidycz, & Raffle, 2008) investigated the impact of a sexual assault risk reduction program with a self-defense component for 300 college women. Using a placebo-control group, the study indicated that this program was effective in increasing levels of self-protective behaviors, self-efficacy in resisting against potential attackers, and use of assertive sexual communication over a four-month period, as well as reducing the incidence of rape among participants over the two-month follow-up.

While data suggest that previous sexual assaults are a potent risk factor for future assaults, they do not explain why. Perhaps victimization lowers self-esteem so that a woman thinks she has already been so damaged that subsequent victimizations don't matter. Perhaps victimization convinces a woman that she will not be wanted for any reason other than sex, so she continues to place herself in sexually risky situations. Whatever the explanation, these results send a clear message for other prevention programs: The earlier the attempt at prevention, the better. If women participate in assault prevention services before they are ever victimized, it appears that the success of such services will be substantially greater.

Designing Effective Treatments for Rapists. Society is rightfully concerned about the likelihood of sex offenders repeating their crimes (Quinsey, Lalumiere, Rice, & Harris, 1995). In some states, men convicted of sex crimes are required to complete a sex-offender treatment program before being considered for parole. In such programs, the offender must acknowledge responsibility for his actions and participate in special treatment programs (Glamser, 1997).

The treatment of rapists can involve psychological, physical, and medical procedures; in many treatment programs, different interventions are often combined. On the international scene, neurosurgery and surgical castration have been used, but their effectiveness is unclear. Because of the ethical controversies that surround these procedures, few experts advocate their use in the United States (Marshall, Jones, Ward, Johnston, & Barbaree, 1991).

In the United States it is not uncommon for antiandrogen drugs to be prescribed to sex offenders in order to reduce their sex drive, a procedure sometimes referred to as *chemical castration*. The most common treatment involves giving offenders a synthetic female hormone, MPA, which has the trade name of Depo-Provera. MPA decreases the level of testosterone in the body, thereby decreasing sexual arousal in most men; however, the drug has also been associated with a number of negative side effects, including weight gain, hair loss, feminization of the body, and gall bladder problems.

In some cases, men convicted of sexual assault have been given the choice to go to prison or to submit to drug treatments. Feminists, on the one side, and defense attorneys, on the other, have raised a number of concerns and criticisms regarding this procedure. In addition, its use with sexually aggressive offenders has met with mixed success (Bund, 1997) even though its advocates claim a very high success rate.

Antiandrogen treatments have problems other than negative side effects. The rate of men dropping out of such treatment prematurely is very high, and failure to complete treatment is one of the strongest predictors of recidivism for sex offenders (Hanson & Bussiere, 1998). Of greater concern is the fact that the treatment does not always reduce sexual arousal and sexual offenses. In some men, arousal is not dependent on their level of testosterone, so the drugs have little effect on their sexual behavior. This point is related to the fact that rape is often an act of violence, not of inappropriate sexual arousal; consequently, drugs aimed at reducing sexual desire may be pointing at the wrong target. Even if the drugs inhibit sexual appetites, they may not control violent outbursts.

Hence, they would not meaningfully control these offenders.

Another major approach to treating aggressive sexual offenders involves combining several behavior therapy techniques into an integrated treatment package designed to increase offenders' self-control, improve their social skills, modify their sexual preferences, and teach them how to prevent relapses of their offenses. These programs are usually situated in prisons, but they have also been implemented in the community. Some programs are run in a group format; others rely on individual treatment (Hall, 1996).

These integrated programs employ a wide range of treatment techniques. Sex education and training in social skills are common ingredients because of the widespread belief that sex offenders are often socially incompetent. Biofeedback and aversive conditioning are often used to decrease inappropriate sexual arousal and replace it with arousal to nonaggressive sexual cues. Existing programs appear to be able to produce short-term decreases in recidivism, but long-term improvements have been difficult to achieve. As a result, relapse prevention techniques (which have proved useful in the treatment of drug addictions and cigarette smoking) have been added to some programs.

SEXUAL HARASSMENT

Even though *sexual harassment* has been a significant problem in educational and work environments for many years, the term itself was not used until 1974. At that time, a group of women at Cornell University, after becoming aware that several of their female colleagues had been forced to quit because of unwanted advances from their supervisors, began to speak out against such harassment (Brownmiller & Alexander, 1992). Also in the early 1970s, the United States Equal Employment Opportunity Commission (EEOC) emerged as a major tool for redressing sexual harassment by employers.

AP Images/Gregory Bull

Andrea Mackris, who accused Bill O'Reilly of sexual harassment

AP Images/Jennifer Graylock

Talk show host Bill O'Reilly

Prevalence Rates

Several cases involving sensational charges of sexual harassment have received widespread attention and focused awareness on the problem of sexual harassment. A well-known case involved the four-year legal battle in which Paula Jones, a former Arkansas state employee, charged that then-governor Bill Clinton pressured her to perform oral sex in a Little Rock hotel room. Although he admitted no wrongdoing and refused to apologize to Jones, President Clinton eventually paid her $850,000 to drop the lawsuit. The consequences of the case went well beyond this, however, in that Clinton's apparently deceitful testimony in the Paula Jones case was a primary impetus for his eventual impeachment.

Talk show host Bill O'Reilly was accused of subjecting the former producer of his television show, Andrea Mackris, to "unwanted sexual conduct" and "a hostile work environment" by detailing his sexual fantasies during multiple phone calls (Spilbor, 2004). About two weeks after the suit was filed and without acknowledging culpability, O'Reilly agreed to pay Mackris approximately $2 million to settle the case (Kurtz, 2004).

How frequent is sexual harassment? A survey of 20,000 federal employees found that 42% of the female workers reported having experienced sexual harassment on the job in the previous two years (Brownmiller & Alexander, 1992). Similarly, 43% of the women lawyers in large law firms reported that they had been recipients of deliberate touching, pinching, or cornering in the office (Slade,

1994). A nationwide survey of female psychologists revealed that over half of them had experienced sexual harassment from a psychotherapy client at some point in their careers (deMayo, 1997). A study examining sexual harassment in academic medicine indicated that about half of female faculty experienced some form of sexual harassment, compared to very few male faculty, and these experiences were prevalent across different institutions in the sample and across all regions of the United States (Carr et al., 2000). One study suggested that about a quarter of female medical students (27.5%) experienced at least one incident of sexual harassment or gender discrimination while enrolled in medical school (Stratton, McLaughlin, Witte, Fosson, & Nora, 2005). Another study (Phillips & Schneider, 1993) reported that more than 75% of female family physicians in Ontario indicated that they had been sexually harassed by a patient at least once in their careers.

Sexual harassment is typically assumed to involve a male perpetrator and a female victim, but men also experience sexual harassment. One survey of 480 nursing students and faculty found that although more women than men experienced mild or moderate forms of sexual harassment (e.g., teasing, attempts to initiate romantic relationships), men were more likely to experience severe types of sexual harassment (e.g., intimate touch, forcing the respondent to touch someone else in an intimate way) (Bronner, Peretz, & Ehrenfeld, 2003).

The Supreme Court ruled in the case of *Oncale v. Sundowner Offshore Services, Inc.*, (1998) that male-on-male and female-on-female harassment is prohibited. Although popular depictions of sexual harassment of males, such as Michael Crichton's novel *Disclosure* and the movie based on it, feature an aggressive female boss demanding sex from a male subordinate, men more often report that other men sexually harass them. A survey of over 2,000 male workers found that 37% had experienced sexual harassment in the workplace, with 53% of these experiences perpetrated by other men (Stockdale, Visio, & Batra, 1999). Although lewd sexual comments, negative comments about men, and unwanted sexual attention were the most common

types of harassment, the form of harassment that these men found most upsetting involved statements or actions that belittled them for acting too "feminine" or that pressured them to adopt stereotypical "masculine" behavior.

Defining Sexual Harassment

Some of the studies described in this section use the term *sexual harassment* to mean unwanted sexual attention. But sexual harassment also has a specific meaning under the law. Title VII of the Civil Rights Act of 1964 prohibits discrimination in the workplace because of a person's gender. It therefore provides the legal basis for banning sexual harassment, although there is continued confusion about the nature of sexual harassment. "Can I tell my assistant that she looks especially nice today?" "What kinds of jokes are okay at the office party?" Questions like this reflect the uncertainty that men in particular seem to have about the possibility that a comment will be viewed by a woman as sexually harassing if it attempts to reflect a compliment or to be humorous (Gutek, 1985; Terpstra & Baker, 1987).

U.S. federal law defines harassment as follows:

> Unwelcome sexual advances, requests for sexual favors, and other verbal or physical conduct of a sexual nature constitute sexual harassment when (1) submission to such conduct is made either explicitly or implicitly a term or condition of an individual's employment, (2) submission to or rejection of such conduct by an individual is used as the basis for employment decisions affecting such individual, or (3) such conduct has the purpose or effect of unreasonably interfering with an individual's work performance or creating an intimidating, hostile, or offensive working environment (16 Code of Federal Regulations Section 1604.11).

One problem with this definition is that it leaves key terms such as *unwelcome* and *unreasonably interfering* open to varying interpretations. When men and women differ in their evaluations of potentially harassing interactions, women are more likely than men to classify a specific act as harassing (Rotundo, Nguyen, & Sackett, 2001). Who, then, determines when an act is harassing—the alleged victim, the alleged perpetrator, or an outside, "neutral" observer?

One contribution of psychological research is to provide information about just what behaviors people consider sexually harassing (Frazier, Cochran, & Olson, 1995). When psychologists study the way individuals define sexual harassment, they usually do this by presenting participants with a set of facts and asking them whether they believe those facts indicate that sexual harassment occurred. In some studies, the subjects read a summary of the facts; in others they watch or listen to a taped description of the events. Some fact patterns are taken from cases that have previously been tried in court; others are hypothetical scenarios created for the purpose of the study. Some studies involve college student participants; others evaluate opinions of the general public. These methodological variations can affect the results. For example, undergraduates tend to define sexual harassment more leniently than older adults (Blumenthal, 1998). In general though, studies show a gender difference in assessment of what constitutes sexual harassment: Women are more likely than men to identify offending behavior as harassment.

Some studies consider the impact of characteristics other than, or in addition to, observers' gender. For example, Wiener and his colleagues conducted a complex experiment that simultaneously assessed the impact of observers' gender and sexist attitudes on perceptions of allegedly harassing behavior in two workplace situations (Wiener, Hurt, Russell, Mannen, & Gasper, 1997). They classified participants as being either high or low in *hostile sexism* and *benevolent sexism*. Hostile sexism involves antipathy toward women, reflecting a belief that males are superior to women and should be dominant over them. Benevolent sexism is an attitude of protection toward women; it reflects a belief that as the "weaker sex," women need to be shielded from the world's harshness.

In addition to replicating the finding that females were more likely than males to find that sexual harassment had occurred in these two situations, Wiener and colleagues (1997) examined the impact of participants' attitudes on their perceptions of sexual harassment. They predicted that those high in hostile sexism would be less inclined to conclude that sexual harassment had occurred. The results supported their prediction. Participants high in hostile sexism were less likely than those who scored low on this dimension to find that the defendant's behavior constituted sexual harassment.

The harasser's status relative to the victim is more influential than gender on perceptions of sexual harassment. In his meta-analysis of 111 empirical studies examining how sexual harassment is evaluated, Blumenthal (1998) found that both men and women were more likely to perceive behavior directed by someone of higher status at someone of equal or lesser rank in the workplace as harassment than if such behavior occurred between peers. This is a reassuring result, given that the law also tends to assign greater liability to a defendant in cases where harassment by a supervisor or manager, as opposed to a peer or coworker, is alleged (Goodman-Delahunty, 1998).

Sexually harassing behaviors can range from lewd and negative comments directed at a person, to more overt overtures for sexual contact such as flirting and uninvited touching, and finally, to offers of bribes or threats of retaliation in exchange for sexual contact (Fitzgerald, Gelfand, & Drasgow, 1995). As you would expect, reactions to these behaviors vary widely. Fewer than 10% of respondents consider staring, flirting, or nonsexual touching to be harassment, but almost 100% believe that pressure for sexual favors or sexual bribery constitutes harassment (Frazier et al., 1995).

The courts, following the EEOC guidelines, have recognized two types of sexual harassment. The *quid pro quo* type involves sexual demands that are made in exchange for employment benefits; it is essentially sexual coercion. **Quid pro quo harassment** is seen in an implicit or explicit bargain in which the harasser promises a reward or threatens punishment, depending on the victim's

Box **13.3** THE CASE OF TERESA HARRIS: SEXUAL HARASSMENT ON THE JOB

Teresa Harris was the rentals manager at Forklift Systems in Nashville. Her boss (the company president) made a number of suggestive and demeaning comments to her. At first she tried to ignore him, and then she confronted him. He promised to stop, but a month later, in public, he asked whether she had slept with a client to get his account. This was the last straw; after working there two years, Harris quit. She sought relief from the EEOC and the courts, claiming that the boss's behavior had created a hostile workplace. She asked for back wages as part of the litigation.

When she did not receive satisfaction from the lower courts, she brought her appeal to the U.S. Supreme Court, which agreed to hear the case because different circuit courts had been inconsistent in their decisions in such cases. Some courts had adopted a subjective approach, focusing on the impact of the alleged harassment on the plaintiff. Others, taking a more objective approach, had asked whether a reasonable person would have found the environment abusive. Also unclear was the question of degree of impact. Was it sufficient that the environment interfered with the complainant's work performance, or was it necessary for "psychological injury" to have occurred? Even though there is ample evidence that sexual harassment produces psychological damage (Fitzgerald, Buchanan, Collinsworth, Magley, & Ramos, 1999), should plaintiffs be forced to prove that they were psychologically harmed in order to persuade a jury that the sexual harassment has occurred?

The unanimous decision of the Court, announced by Justice O'Connor, ruled in favor of Harris and held that it was not necessary for plaintiffs to prove that they had suffered psychological injuries. The case was returned to the lower court, which was instructed to examine the ruling and decide how much back pay, if any, Harris deserved. (Several months later, Forklift Systems settled with Harris out of court, for an undisclosed amount.) The Supreme Court decision listed several criteria by which to decide whether an action constitutes sexual harassment, including the frequency and severity of the behavior, whether the behavior was physically threatening or humiliating, and whether it would unreasonably interfere with an employee's work performance.

Prior to this decision there was controversy about whether to assess potentially harassing behavior from the perspective of a "reasonable man," "reasonable person," or "reasonable victim" (Gutek & O'Connor, 1995; Wiener & Gutek, 1999). Justice O'Connor's opinion suggested that if conduct was not sufficiently severe and pervasive as to create an "objectively hostile" work environment as defined by a *reasonable person*, then it was not sexual harassment. The Court's decision reflected an intermediate position; harassment was no longer defined by responses of a man, but neither could the victim define what is hostile.

---

response (Hotelling, 1991). When a teacher says to a student, "Sleep with me or you fail this course," it qualifies as *quid pro quo* sexual harassment (McCandless & Sullivan, 1991).

The second, more common type of harassment, usually referred to as **hostile workplace harassment**, involves demeaning comments, acts of touching or attempted intimacy, or the display of provocative photographs or artwork. Under Title VII, it is illegal for employers to create or tolerate "an intimidating, hostile, or offensive working environment." In Paula Jones's lawsuit against former President Clinton, the plaintiff claimed that Clinton's behavior constituted hostile workplace

harassment. How is this defined? How disabling must the environment be for the victim? The courts have answered these questions in several relevant cases.

In the 1986 case of *Meritor Savings Bank v. Vinson*, the U.S. Supreme Court recognized for the first time that sexual harassment creating a hostile work environment violates Title VII. Although evidence of repeated offensive behavior or behavior of a severe nature is usually required for the plaintiff to prevail, the effects of such harassment need not "seriously affect [an employee's] psychological well being" or lead the plaintiff to "suffer injury" to constitute *hostile workplace* harassment (*Harris v. Forklift Systems, Inc.*, 1993; see Box 13.3).

Applying Psychological Knowledge to Detecting Harassment

Psychological approaches contribute to our understanding of sexual harassment in two other ways. First, some psychologists have attempted to predict when sexual harassment will occur. Other psychologists have tried to determine the likelihood of a favorable outcome in litigation when a person who alleges sexual harassment files a complaint. We consider these issues next.

When does sexual harassment occur? Pryor, Giedd, and Williams (1995) proposed that certain individuals are inclined toward behavior that would be sexual harassment and that the norms in specific organizations function to encourage the expression of harassment. For example, a factory that permits its workers to display *Playboy* centerfolds or nude calendars in their work areas may encourage harassment on the part of a worker who, in another environment, would not exhibit such behavior. Similarly, a company that provides sexually oriented entertainment at office parties or has work-related parties that exclude one gender is expressing a norm that gives tacit approval to at least some forms of harassment.

Men also differ in their likelihood to harass. Pryor (1987) asked men to imagine themselves in a series of scenarios in which they had power over an attractive woman. In one scenario, for example, the man is a college professor meeting with a female student who is seeking to raise her grade in the class. The subjects were asked to rate how likely they were to engage in an act of *quid pro quo* sexual harassment in each scenario, given that they could do so without being punished. Men who scored relatively high on the Likelihood to Sexually Harass (LSH) scale were more accepting of myths about rape, indulged in more coercive sexual fantasies, and endorsed more stereotypical beliefs about male sex roles (Pryor et al., 1995). They had strong needs to dominate women and to seek sex for the sake of their own gratification. In a series of laboratory experiments, Pryor and his colleagues found that men high in likelihood to sexually harass

engaged in harassment in social situations in which harassing behavior was convenient, and under conditions in which local norms encouraged such behavior.

Another study yielded findings consistent with these results using a similar assessment protocol (Begany & Milburn, 2002). This study also indicated that authoritarian personality characteristics (such as a belief in obeying authority above all else) predicted men's self-reported likelihood of engaging in sexual harassment; men who reported higher levels of authoritarian characteristics are more likely to engage in sexual harassment. Other personality characteristics have also been associated with higher scores on the LSH scale, including a less feminine personality, more traditional beliefs about women's roles, more negative attitudes toward women, and less concern with social desirability (Driscoll, Kelly, & Henderson, 1998).

To determine which types of harassment claims succeed, and which ones fail, Terpstra and Baker (1988) examined 81 sexual harassment charges filed with the Illinois State EEOC over a two-year period. About 31% of these cases were settled in favor of the complainant. The researchers identified three characteristics that were significantly related to EEOC decisions. Sexual harassment charges were more likely to be resolved in favor of the complainant when:

1. the harassing behaviors were serious,

2. the complainant had witnesses to support the charges, and

3. the complainant had given notice to management prior to filing formal charges.

This analysis was repeated for another sample of 133 court decisions between 1974 and 1989 (Terpstra & Baker, 1992). A total of 38% of these cases were decided in favor of the complainants—higher than the 31% of the EEOC cases—even though the complainants' cases were generally not as strong as those heard by the EEOC. In these cases, complainants were more likely to win their cases if:

1. the harassment was severe,

2. witnesses supported their claims,

3. documents supported their claims,

4. they had given notice to management prior to filing charges, and

5. their organization had taken no action.

If a complainant had none of these factors in his or her favor, the odds of winning the case were less than 1%; if he or she had all five, the odds of winning were almost 100% (Terpstra & Baker, 1992).

OFFENDERS' EXPERIENCE AS VICTIMS OF CRIME AND VIOLENCE

When offenders are at the same time victims, or claim to be victims, society's reaction becomes even more complex, and decisions made by the legal system become even more controversial. Consider the trials of Lorena Bobbitt, Lyle and Erik Menendez, and the late Michael Jackson. What do these trials have in common? In each case, the defendant or defendants, charged with serious crimes, claimed the role of victim and argued that they were retaliating against an unwanted act or trying to prevent a feared attack. Lorena Bobbitt was outraged over an act earlier that evening that she considered to be spousal rape by her husband John, so while he was sleeping, she cut off his penis. At their trials, the Menendez brothers described episodes of physical and sexual abuse from their father, with their mother as a passive accomplice; fearing the worst, they said,

they decided to kill their parents first. Michael Jackson was charged with sexually molesting a young boy and holding his family captive at his "Neverland" ranch. Jackson claimed that the boy and his family had fabricated these accounts in an attempt to obtain money from him.

How did the juries react to these defenses? Lorena Bobbitt was found not guilty by reason of insanity. Jurors' reactions in the Menendez brothers' trials were more complicated. In the first trials, the jurors could not agree, producing a hung jury. The jurors agreed that each brother was guilty of a crime, but they could not agree on whether each should be convicted of murder or manslaughter (Thornton, 1995). With each jury deadlocked over the appropriate charge for conviction, the result was a mistrial. At the second trial, both brothers were found guilty of murder and sentenced to life in prison. Michael Jackson was acquitted on all charges after arguing that family members of his alleged victim were essentially con artists trying to take advantage of his celebrity.

In cases like those of Bobbitt and the Menendez brothers, in which a defendant claims to be a victim, critics are concerned that jurors will be tempted to accept what has been called the **abuse excuse**—"the legal tactic by which criminal defendants claim a history of abuse as an excuse for violent retaliation" (Dershowitz, 1994, p. 3). Although Dershowitz concluded that an increasing number of defense lawyers are using the abuse excuse and that juries increasingly are accepting it, evidence in support of the latter claim is sparse at best. In fact, such defenses seem to be met with increasing skepticism and with a willingness to blame the offender.

SUMMARY

1. *What is the frequency of crime victimization?*
   According to the National Crime Victimization Survey, crime victimization in 2006 occurred for property crimes at a rate of 160 incidents per 1,000 households), and for crimes of violence at a rate of 25 incidents per 1,000 persons. But this figure underestimates the true extent of victimization that befalls an unknown number of individuals in homes, schools, and the workplace.

2. ***What types of research have psychologists conducted on victimization?*** Three areas of victimization have received special attention from psychologists: violent victimization and posttraumatic stress disorder, including the psychology of rape; domestic violence (particularly battered spouses); and sexual harassment.

3. ***What factors predict the development of PTSD after being a crime victim?*** The extent of injury suffered in the crime and the belief that the victim has no control over his or her life heightens the risk of developing PTSD. Treatments that help restore a sense of control and that help victims reexperience the trauma so that its emotional power is drained are the most effective interventions for preventing and reducing PTSD after a criminal victimization.

4. ***What are the components of battered woman syndrome?*** Battered woman syndrome consists of a collection of responses, many of which are displayed by individuals who are repeatedly physically abused by their intimate partners. These include learned helplessness, lowered self-esteem, impaired functioning, fear or terror, loss of the assumption of invulnerability, and anger or rage.

5. ***How have the laws about rape changed?*** Beginning in the 1970s, state legislatures and the courts began to modify long-standing laws about rape. One general type of shift was to de-emphasize resistance as a requirement in showing that a rape took place. A second shift was to divide rape into several degrees of offense, enabling juries to render guilty verdicts more frequently. Virtually all states now permit a husband to be charged with rape against his wife. Most states now have rape shield laws that restrict the defense attorney's questioning of the victim about her sexual history.

6. ***How can rape be prevented?*** Prevention of rape has taken two routes. One is to determine what responses by potential victims are most effective in warding off a sexual assault. The other is to use effective treatments for convicted rapists. Antiandrogen drugs, which reduce sex drive, and a combination of various behavior therapy techniques have shown some effectiveness as treatment for convicted rapists.

7. ***What are two types of sexual harassment recognized by the courts?*** The first type of harassment, *quid pro quo* harassment, consists of sexual demands made in conjunction with offers of benefits in exchange for complying or threats of punishment if the respondent does not comply. The second type is harassment that creates a hostile work environment; it often involves demeaning comments, acts of touching or attempted intimacy, or the display of provocative photographs or artwork.

KEY TERMS

abuse excuse

acute stress disorder

battered woman
  syndrome

borderline personality
  disorder

cycle of violence

hate crimes

hostile workplace
  harassment

posttraumatic stress
  disorder

quid pro quo harassment

rape shield laws

rape trauma syndrome

secondary victimization

self-defense

spousal rape

victimology

14

Psychology of Punishment and Sentencing

ORIENTING QUESTIONS

1. What are the purposes of punishment?
2. How are the values of discretion and fairness reflected in sentencing decisions?
3. What factors influence sentencing decisions?
4. What special factors are considered in the sentencing of juveniles? Of recidivist sex offenders?
5. How is the death penalty decided by juries?
6. In what ways has the Supreme Court recently limited the use of capital punishment and what role have psychologists played in these decisions?

A sentencing decision comes near the end of a criminal prosecution and is typically made by a judge or magistrate. Sentencing options include probation, restitution, compensation, a fine, community service, imprisonment, and others. The purpose of the sentence—punishment, deterrence, incapacitation, and rehabilitation, for example—depends on the nature of the crime, characteristics and experiences of the offender, temperament of the judge, and in some cases, public sentiment. As you might suspect, judges have considerable latitude or discretion in the sentences they impose in this system, and significant disparities in sentence length can result. **Sentencing disparities** occur whenever similar offenders who committed similar crimes receive different sentences. Various efforts to reduce disparity, including maximum and minimum sentences, sentencing guidelines, and even revisions in sentencing guidelines have been instituted, with somewhat mixed success.

Great numbers of offenders in the United States are sentenced to prison. In fact, no other industrialized country except Russia imprisons its citizens at the rate of the United States. This situation is a result of what Professor Craig Haney, a psychologist and a lawyer, calls America's "rage to punish" (Haney, 2006, p. 4). Haney points to a political mandate for punishment over the past few decades that is overriding and absolute. (The three-strikes laws we described in Chapter 1 are

just one example.) In fact, according to Haney, "hundreds of thousands of people have been locked up in American jails and prisons who would not have been incarcerated (for the same misdeeds) in any other modern Western society" or "if they had committed their crimes at almost any other time in American history" (Haney, 2006, p. 11). Among them are prisoners with mental illness, drug offenders whose crimes stem from untreated addictions, and petty criminals serving lengthy terms triggered by mandatory sentencing laws.

According to United States Department of Justice statistics, on December 31, 2007, there were approximately 2.3 million people in prisons and jails and more than 5.1 million people on probation or parole. The comparable figures for 1995 were 1.5 million in prisons and jails and 3.7 million on probation or parole. At the end of 2007, about 3.2% of the population—1 in 32 adults—was incarcerated or on probation or parole (Glaze & Bonczar, 2008). Federal offenders are especially likely to be sentenced to prison (as opposed to probation or community confinement): 85% of federal offenders sentenced in 2007 went to prison; approximately one-third were illegal aliens awaiting deportation (Coyle, 2009).

African Americans are much more likely to be sentenced to prison than Whites: Of 10,000 Black males, 314 were sentenced prisoners in 2007. Comparable figures for Hispanic males were 126 per 10,000 and for Whites, 48 per 10,000. It is predicted that one-third of Black boys born in 2001 will spend some time in prison (Tonry & Melewski, 2008).

Here is another troubling statistic: The number of female inmates has quadrupled over the past 20 years and women of color lead the way (54% of incarcerated females are African American or Latina; Alleyne, 2007). This increase is linked directly to problems of drug and alcohol addiction. In addition, female inmates in prison substance abuse programs are significantly more likely than men to report a lifetime psychiatric disorder (Zlotnick et al., 2008). Unfortunately, treatment for substance abuse and psychiatric problems in correctional facilities is grossly underfunded. We discuss correctional treatment in more detail in Chapter 15.

How should we respond to individual criminals? With an inmate population over 2 million, does it make sense to continue locking up more offenders every year? Incarceration comes at a price; every dollar spent on corrections means one less dollar for public schools, health care, parks, and higher education. Although philosophical questions about the costs and benefits of punishment and incarceration have been debated for many years, the financial crisis of 2009 forced criminal justice officials and legislators to seek new approaches to punishing criminals. For example, New Mexico lawmakers repealed the death penalty in 2009 in order to save the state "millions of dollars," according to a fiscal report. Kansas legislators voted to reduce the number of probationers sent to prison for violating conditions of their release. Several states are reexamining lengthy minimum sentences for nonviolent drug offenders. But according to Joshua Marquis, spokesman for the National District Attorneys Association, if states "wind back some of the most intelligent sentencing policy we have … we will pay a price. No question" (Johnson, 2009).

In this chapter, we address these issues by describing the multiple goals and purposes of punishment and sentencing, some of which aim to exact retribution from an offender and others that favor practical ends such as deterrence, incapacitation, and rehabilitation. We describe the factors that judges consider in their sentencing decisions, and the specific issues that arise in sentencing of juvenile and sex offenders. Finally, we examine psychological aspects of the ultimate punishment, the death penalty.

THE PURPOSES OF PUNISHMENT

We described two models of the criminal justice system in Chapter 1: the due process model and the crime control model. The latter has heavily influenced police, prosecutors, and many judges over the past 30 years. It interprets the primary aim of law enforcement as the apprehension and punishment of criminals. Its major purpose is to punish offenders so that they will not repeat their offenses, and others will be deterred from similar acts.

Punishment of criminals, whether by imprisonment, probation, community service, or fines, can have several purposes. Psychologists have identified at least seven different goals (see, for example, Greenberg & Ruback, 1984):

1. *General deterrence.* The punishment of an offender—and the subsequent publicity that comes with it—are assumed to discourage other potential lawbreakers. Some advocates of the death penalty, for example, believe that fear of death may be our strongest motivation; hence, they believe that the death penalty serves as a general deterrent to murder.

2. *Individual deterrence.* Punishment of the offender is presumed to keep that person from committing other crimes in the future. Some theories assume that many criminals lack adequate internal inhibitors; hence, punitive sanctions must be used to teach them that their behavior will be controlled—if not by them, then by society.

3. *Incapacitation.* If a convicted offender is sent to prison, society can feel safe from that felon while he or she is confined. One influential position (Wilson, 1975) sees a major function of incapacitation as simply to age the criminal—an understandable goal, given that the rate of offending declines with age.

4. *Retribution.* Society believes that offenders should not benefit from their crimes; rather, they should receive their "just deserts," or "that which is justly deserved." The moral cornerstone of

punishment is that it should be administered to people who deserve it as a consequence of their misdeeds.

5. *Moral outrage*. Punishment can give society a means of catharsis and relief from the feelings of frustration, hurt, loss, and anger that result from being victims of crime; it promotes a sense of satisfaction that offenders have paid for what they have done to others.

6. *Rehabilitation*. One hope in sentencing has always been that offenders will recognize the error of their ways and develop new skills, values, and lifestyles so that they can return to normal life and become law-abiding. We discuss rehabilitation in some detail in Chapter 15.

7. *Restitution*. Wrongdoers should compensate victims for their damages and losses. Typical statutes require judges, in imposing a criminal sentence, to make defendants pay for victims' out-of-pocket expenses, property damage, and other monetary losses. Restitution is often a condition of probation.

Utilitarian Approaches

Most of these goals are **utilitarian**: They are intended to accomplish a useful outcome, such as compensating the victim, deterring crime, or incapacitating or rehabilitating the defendant. Utilitarian goals have a practical objective; they right the wrongs of past misconduct and reduce the likelihood of future criminal behavior.

Rehabilitation as a utilitarian goal has been in and out of favor throughout history. The basic notion is that offenders who receive treatment for the underlying causes of criminality will be less likely to reoffend. Though the original purpose of prisons was to rehabilitate (many prisons are still called *correctional* institutions), we now have evidence that prisons are not very effective at rehabilitating offenders. The extreme version of this view, dubbed the "nothing works" position, first appeared in a review article about rehabilitation by Robert Martinson (1974). After reviewing a large number of outcome studies, Martinson concluded that most attempts at offender

rehabilitation fail. Although we now know that this conclusion was too pessimistic—Martinson (1979) himself revised his opinion and acknowledged that there is more evidence supporting rehabilitation than he originally believed—the "nothing works" view has prevailed among many politicians, policymakers, and the public at large (Haney, 1997b).

When rehabilitation was the dominant goal, criminal sentences were expected to accomplish something other than incarceration and punishment. But in the past few decades, rehabilitation as a goal of sentencing lost much of its popular appeal. As rehabilitation fell out of favor, criminal sentences became longer. Whereas just a few decades ago, a "life sentence" meant 10 to 20 years behind bars, until very recently, tougher laws and less concern about rehabilitation meant that there were thousands of people sentenced each year "whose only way out of prison is likely to be inside a coffin" (Liptak, 2005b). Growth in the number of "lifers" far outpaced overall growth in the prison population. As a result, the United States now houses the largest permanent population of aging prisoners in the world, with all the accompanying medical and psychological issues of old age. As we have noted, the recession of 2009 may change, at least temporarily, the way that states sentence offenders.

Retributive Approaches

Two of the punishment goals we described are **retributive**: they involve looking back at the offense and determining what the criminal "deserves" as a consequence of committing it. These goals are retribution (sometimes called "just deserts") and moral outrage, a close cousin of retribution (Kaplan, 1996). The notion of retribution implies that an offender deserves to be punished and that the punishment should be proportionate to the severity of the wrongdoing.

The stark contrast between utilitarian and retributive approaches raises the question of why we punish people. What are our motives for punishing others? Psychologists have taken different approaches to answering this question. Some have simply asked people which philosophy they prefer and have assumed that respondents can report their true beliefs. But in studies that measured people's agreement with various sentencing policies, people tended to agree with all of them (Anderson & MacCoun, 1999)! Furthermore, people are sometimes unaware of the factors that influence their preferences (Wilson, 2002). An alternative research design involves considering the length of sentences that judges actually order and working backward from these sentences to identify the underlying motives (i.e., just deserts/retribution, deterrence, incapacitation). But this method can be fallible, too. Finally, other researchers have presented vignettes to respondents, varying the nature of the crime and details about the offender, and then measuring respondents' sentencing preferences.

Public Preferences for Deterrence and Retribution. Using a research technique called **policy capturing**, Carlsmith, Darley, and Robinson (2002) assessed the punishment motives of ordinary people. The specific motives for punishment that they contrasted were deterrence and retribution. Using scenarios that described a variety of harmful actions, the researchers attempted to understand (or "capture") the policies underlying the punishments that people assigned. They varied different elements of the crimes described, elements that should or should not matter to respondents depending on which motive they preferred. For example, the magnitude of the harm should matter to people who are motivated by retribution, and the likelihood of reoffending should matter to those who are concerned with future deterrence. Carlsmith and his colleagues then measured the degree to which each respondent's sentence was influenced by these variables. The data showed a high sensitivity to factors associated with retribution and relative insensitivity to factors associated with deterrence. People's preferences for punishment apparently focus on their sense of what an offender deserves.

Interestingly, that's not what people *say* about their punishment beliefs (Carlsmith, 2008). Responding to opinion polls, people are more likely to indicate support for punishment that deters criminals than punishment that exacts retribution (Ellsworth & Ross, 1983). In fact, legislatures have enacted three-strikes laws (described in Chapter 1) and zero-tolerance policies largely in response to the public's apparent support for the utilitarian principle of deterrence.

So why do people say they support deterrence but act like they favor retribution? One possibility is that people have a limited awareness of their own reasons for their punishment preferences. As attribution theorists have pointed out, when it comes to introspecting about why we behave in a particular way, "we are all strangers to ourselves" (Wilson, 2002). It may also be less socially acceptable to say that we favor a penalty based on reprisal and revenge than one based on notions of future good. It would certainly be interesting to know whether judges' underlying motives in sentencing are comparable to laypeople's.

These findings appear to support the idea that the public wants to punish offenders, and at least some politicians are happy to respond. Joe Arpaio, the controversial sheriff of Maricopa County, Arizona (Phoenix), is a "get tough" icon. His philosophy, which has gained him national notoriety, is to make jail so unpleasant that no one would want to come back—while simultaneously saving money. When he took office, he put prisoners in "leaky, dilapidated military-surplus tents set on gravel fields surrounded by barbed wire" and fed them "bologna streaked with green and blue packaging dye" (Morrison, 1995). He put prisoners on chain gangs in black and white striped uniforms (as in the movie *Oh Brother, Where Art Thou?*) and established the first women's and juvenile's chain gangs (Maricopa County Sheriff's Office, 2005). Sheriff Arpaio said that he does not consider these chain gangs to be punishment but, rather, a form of rehabilitation and claims that chain gangs are a hit with inmates. The chain gangs do public service work, including burying indigents in the county cemetery.

Another retributive goal—moral outrage—allows society the satisfaction of knowing that offenders have been made to pay for the harms they caused. Professor Dan Kahan (1996) argues that for a sentence to be acceptable to the public, it

---

B o x 14.1   THE CASE OF CURTIS LEE ROBIN AND HIS 30 NIGHTS IN THE DOGHOUSE

After Curtis Lee Robin pled guilty to charges that he had whipped his 11-year-old stepson with a car antenna, forced him to chop wood, and made him sleep in a doghouse, Orange County, Texas, Judge Buddie Hahn offered Robin a choice: 30 days in jail or 30 nights in a doghouse. Robin chose the doghouse in order to continue to work as the foreman for a demolition company. Judge Hahn then asked the state to provide a 2-by-3-foot doghouse, about the same size as the one that the boy claimed he slept in. Robin's attorneys argued that their client needed a bigger doghouse, a sleeping bag, and some mosquito netting. But Judge Hahn wouldn't budge, claiming that what Robin did was horrible: "He had beaten this kid and left him out at night. The kid climbed in the doghouse to sleep, so yeah, it was pretty appropriate and probably got more attention than giving him 30 days in jail" (Baldas, 2004). (Judge Hahn did allow the defendant to sleep with either his head or his feet outside of the doghouse, however.) The deal also required Robin to serve eight years of probation and pay a $1,000 fine.

© Scott Houston/CORBIS

The only female chain gang in America

must reflect society's outrage. He maintains that the expressive dimension of punishment is not satisfied by "straight" probation, "mere" fines, or direct community service. According to Kahan, probation appears to be no punishment, a fine appears to be a means to "buy one's way out," and community service is something everyone ought to do. Kahan argues that imposing a **shaming penalty** will make punishment more acceptable to the public and more meaningful to offenders.

Shaming is a traditional means by which communities punished offenders. In colonial days, those who committed minor offenses were put in stocks in a public place for several hours for all to see and ridicule. Serious offenders were branded or otherwise marked so they would be "shamed" for life. In Williamsburg, Virginia, thieves were nailed to the stocks by the ear; after a period of time the sheriff would rip the offender from the stocks, thus "ear-marking" the offender for life (Book, 1999).

Increasingly employed in state courts, the modern counterpart to shaming (without mutilation) is to allow offenders to avoid all or part of a jail sentence by publicly renouncing their crimes in a humiliating way. Federal judge Vaughn Walker sentenced a young mail thief to two months in jail and three years supervised release, on the condition that he apologize to those whose mail he had stolen and stand in front of the post office for eight hours wearing a two-sided sandwich board stating, "I stole mail; this is my punishment" (*United States v. Gementra*, 2004). Innovative sentences like this one are being used with increasing frequency as judges grapple with problems of repeat offenders and the ever-mounting costs of incarceration. One innovative sentence is described in Box 14.1.

The impetus for these alternative sentences is twofold. First, judges have become frustrated with revolving-door justice: Approximately one-third of offenders who are released from prison eventually return, suggesting that their punishments had little long-term effectiveness. Second, judges are aware of the longstanding problem of prison overcrowding and the high costs of incarceration. (The average cost for incarceration of a federal inmate is more than $22,000 per year.) The American Bar Association has urged judges to provide alternatives to incarceration for offenders who might benefit from them.

Some judges have been happy to oblige, and many of the sentences they have imposed are truly ingenious. Consider the following:

1. The punishment that dentist Michael Koplik received for sexually abusing a heavily sedated female patient was to provide free treatment for six AIDS patients who had been rejected by other dentists (Sachs, 1989).

2. Houston Judge Ted Poe ordered a teenager who had stolen and damaged a woman's car to turn his car over to the woman while her car was being fixed (Reske, 1996).

3. Judge Michael Foellger regularly gives "Deadbeat Dads"—fathers owing more than $10,000 in child support to more than three women—a choice: jail or a vasectomy (McAree, 2004).

As you might expect, alternative sentences like these are highly controversial. Some lawyers, defense attorneys, and prosecutors alike, applaud them, acknowledging that judges have discretion in sentencing and that incarceration is costly and does not always work. But others worry that the shaming inherent in these sentences is sometimes extreme.

Shaming has intuitive appeal as a penal sanction because everyone has experienced shaming in childhood. Parents teach their children to "be good" by making them ashamed of their bad behavior. A child forced to confess to the store owner that he stole a piece of candy should associate theft with embarrassment from that time on (Book, 1999). However, the 21st century lacks the social cohesiveness of earlier societies in which shaming was effective in controlling behavior. For this reason, some perceive modern shaming as ineffective and unnecessarily cruel. Although shaming sanctions may satisfy society's need to condemn the offender, Professor Sharon Lamb argues that externally produced shame causes the offender to feel resentment rather than remorse—and therefore may be counterproductive (Lamb, 2003). An extreme

example of counterproductive shaming: A 19-year-old was ordered to publish his name, photo, and offense in the local paper after his third DUI conviction. His mother saw the paper and left it on the breakfast table with a note saying she was ashamed of him. He wrote her a letter of apology and shot himself in the head (Braudway, 2004).

Restorative Approaches

Over the years, many people have become disenchanted with the retributive justice system. For one thing, punishing offenders in proportion to the severity of their offenses, although cathartic, has apparently done little to curb crime or reduce suffering. For another, inflicting punishment on offenders who "deserve" to be punished provides little opportunity for victims to be involved in the process or to have their own needs met.

In recent decades, a new approach has emerged that attempts to repair the damage caused by criminal offenses. This approach, called **restorative justice** (Wenzel, Okimoto, Feather, & Platow, 2008), uses open dialogue to gain consensus about resolving disputes. The goals of restorative justice are to repair the harm and restore the losses caused by offensive activity, encourage offenders to assume responsibility for their actions, and empower victims and the community to move beyond feelings of vulnerability and loss to a sense of understanding and closure (Umbreit, Vos, Coates, & Lightfoot, 2005).

Restorative justice is based on the premise that those who are most affected by crime—victims and offenders—should have the most prominent role to play in resolving the conflict and that the community also has a stake in its outcome. So it expands the circle of participants in a dispute beyond the offender and the state, and includes victims and members of the community. Participants are encouraged to use some combination of apology, remorse, and forgiveness to move beyond the harms caused by crime.

Restorative justice policies are used throughout the world (e.g., the Truth and Reconciliation Commissions in South Africa and Rwanda are based on these principles) and are now embedded in various components of many justice systems in the United States, including the criminal justice system (Sullivan & Tifft, 2006). For example, misdemeanor criminal offenses and school-related disputes that arise in the small town in which one of the authors lives are almost invariably resolved in facilitated restorative justice conferences. The typical result is that victims and community members have an opportunity to be heard, offenders usually take responsibility for their wrongdoing, and the parties can often agree on a way to remedy the harm and move on. Coincidentally, resources of the criminal justice system (such as judges' and prosecutors' time) are not required, freeing them up for other purposes.

Of course, resolving disputes by attempting to restore justice will not work in all situations. Individual differences in responding to transgressions mean that some people prefer retributive over restorative principles. In the context of school bullying incidents, for example, parents' values influence their openness to restorative justice. Parents who are more concerned about security and status tend to favor a punitive, retributive approach to deal with bullying, whereas parents who endorse values of equality and mutual respect tend to favor the dialogue strategies that form the centerpiece of restorative justice (Braithwaite, 2000).

More serious incidents of wrongdoing will almost certainly require more severe sanctions than can be enacted by restorative justice practices (Drew & Greene, 2008). In fact, studies reveal widespread support for restorative sentencing options such as restitution, community service, and compensation but only for less serious offenses and younger offenders. For adult offenders, particularly those who have committed serious crimes, the public tends to favor a sentence that is proportionate to the severity of the crime (Roberts & Stalans, 2004).

Given the public's preference for retribution in some contexts and restoration in others, it is worthwhile examining how judges assign criminal punishments, to what extent their choices mirror public sentiment, and how psychological factors influence their decisions.

JUDICIAL DISCRETION IN SENTENCING

Criminal sentencing lies at the heart of society's efforts to ensure public order. Hoffman and Stone-Meierhoefer (1979) go so far as to state, "Next to the determination of guilt or innocence, a determination waived by a substantial proportion of defendants who plead guilty (around 90%), the sentencing decision is probably the most important decision made about the criminal defendant in the entire process" (p. 241).

Sentencing is a judicial function, but sentencing decisions are largely controlled by the legislative branch—Congress and state legislatures. The legislative branch dictates the extent of judges' discretion, and many legislators believe that judges should have little or no discretion. They emphasize retribution and argue that the punishment should fit the crime. Mandatory sentences, sentencing guidelines, and the abolition of parole are the primary ingredients in these "get tough" schemes.

On the other hand, some legislators maintain that the sentence should fit the offender—that judges should have discretion to make the sentence fit not only the crime but the criminal as well. Discretion allows judges to capitalize on their perceptions of the crime, the offender, and external circumstances so that their decisions can "serve, within limits set by law, that elusive concept of justice which the law in its wisdom refuses to define" (Gaylin, 1974, p. 67). Those who advocate individually tailored sentences note that each offender is different and deserves to be treated as an individual. As Tonry (1996) observes, "theories [that] place primary emphasis on linking deserved punishments to the severity of crimes, in the interest of treating cases alike ... lead to disregard of other ethically relevant differences between offenders—like their personal backgrounds and the effects of punishments on them and their families" (p. 15).

Sentencing Policies

Some states have **indeterminate sentencing** schemes in which judges impose a variable period of incarceration for a given offense (e.g., 6–20 years), and a parole board determines the actual date of release. Such policies have been both hailed and criticized: hailed because they provide incentives for good behavior and encourage offenders to take advantage of available treatment programs to enhance the chances of earlier release, and criticized because they allow parole boards wide discretion in determining when the conditions of the sentence have been satisfied.

In other states, the legislative branch has imposed a determinate sentencing system on the judiciary. In these systems, offenders are sentenced for a fixed length of time. Such sentences are determined (fixed) by statutes and guidelines, judges have little choice about the length of sentences, and there is no parole. In such systems, the primary goals are retribution and moral outrage. There is little concern for the offender's personal characteristics, apart from his or her criminal record.

In a further attempt to reduce discretion, some states impose **mandatory minimum sentences** for certain offenses, including drug crimes. These policies require judges to sentence offenders to a minimum number of years in prison regardless of any extenuating circumstances. They too have been criticized as unjust. For example, a Utah judge was forced to sentence a first-time offender who had sold marijuana on three occasions to 61½ years in custody with no parole. The reason: He carried a gun during the marijuana sales. The statute imposed a 5-year minimum term for the first gun count and a minimum of 25 years for each subsequent count in addition to 6½ years for the sale of the marijuana. The judge noted that on the very day he sentenced the marijuana dealer to 61½ years, using the same guidelines he sentenced a murderer to a 21-year term. He asked the president to commute the drug dealer's sentence and asked Congress to reconsider mandatory minimum sentencing (*United States v. Angelos*, 2004).

The American Psychological Association (APA) has spoken out against mandatory minimum sentences: "[T]hey have done nothing to reduce crime or put big-time drug dealers out of business. What they have done … is to fill prisons with young,

nonviolent, low-level drug offenders serving long sentences at enormous and growing cost to taxpayers" (Hansen, 1999, p. 14).

Current federal sentencing policy is based on the Sentencing Reform Act of 1984 that abolished parole and established a Sentencing Commission to develop mandatory sentencing guidelines. An overriding goal of the Sentencing Commission was to ensure uniformity of sentences. Federal judges were required to sentence offenders within a narrow range prescribed by a complicated analysis of the severity and circumstances of the crime, among other factors. But this scheme also proved to be controversial. In 2005, the U.S. Supreme Court decided that the mandatory nature of the guidelines was unconstitutional (*United States v. Booker*, 2005). Federal sentencing guidelines are now advisory rather than mandatory, meaning that they are among the factors that judges consider.

Further revision of federal sentencing guidelines occurred in 2007 when the Sentencing Commission narrowed the disparity between penalties for crack and powder cocaine. Approximately 20 years earlier, Congress opted to assign harsher penalties for crack cocaine crimes, reasoning that crack cocaine was especially addictive, tied to violence, and harmful to users' unborn children. As a result, offenders trafficking in crack cocaine received the same sentence as those selling 100 times the amount of powder cocaine. Importantly, racial concerns prompted the revision, as offenders sentenced on crack cocaine charges are predominately Black, whereas those sentenced on powder cocaine charges are mostly White (Leigey & Bachman, 2007). Providing further evidence of the expansion of judicial discretion, federal judges lowered more than 12,000 crack cocaine sentences between March and December of 2008 (Gallagher, 2008).

Brian Gall benefited from judges' increased discretion in sentencing. In the late 1990s while a student at the University of Iowa, Gall had been involved in a drug ring distributing Ecstasy. But he stopped using drugs, graduated from college, became a master carpenter, and started his own business in Arizona. After being tracked down by federal authorities, he turned himself in and pleaded guilty to conspiracy to distribute a controlled substance. The judge, taking Gall's circumstances into account, departed from the guidelines and imposed a sentence of 36 months of probation, and no prison time. In 2007, the Supreme Court upheld the sentence, stating that federal judges have the authority to set any reasonable sentence as long as they explain their reasoning (*Gall v. United States*, 2007). Greater discretion not only satisfies many judges (and people like Gall) but, according to one law professor, may have an unexpected silver lining: She contends that increased discretion may actually decrease the rates of both violent and property crimes (Shepherd, 2007).

DETERMINANTS OF SENTENCING: RELEVANT AND IRRELEVANT

Psychologists have conducted research to describe and explain the sentencing decision. Among the questions they have asked is whether, during sentencing, judges consider only factors relevant to the decision (e.g., seriousness of the crime committed) or whether they also consider seemingly irrelevant factors like race, ethnicity, or gender. To answer this question, researchers have used a variety of procedures including surveys, archival analyses of case records and sentencing statistics, interviews, and experiments in which they manipulate various facts in simulated cases or vignettes and ask sentencers to respond.

To be morally acceptable, punishment should be consistent with the seriousness of the crime. Punishment does correlate strongly with the severity of the crime; even in systems in which judges retain wide sentencing discretion, more serious crimes earn greater punishments.

But factors other than the seriousness of the crime also influence sentencing. Should they? For example, should an offender's past be taken into account? Should it matter that a convicted offender was deprived as a child, hungry, abused, and denied opportunities to go to school or look for work? An offender's criminal record is relevant in every jurisdiction. In fact, most states require those with prior offenses to serve longer terms. California's famous "three strikes and you're out" law, mentioned in Chapter 1, is an example. A third-time offender with two prior convictions for violent felonies can be sentenced to life imprisonment without parole, even if the third offense is minor (*Ewing v. California*, 2003), as the majority of them are.

Many people would agree that it shouldn't matter whether the defendant in any particular case is a man or woman; what should matter are the individual's criminal history and the seriousness of the offense. Indeed, determinate sentencing has evolved to ensure that extralegal factors such as the offender's race, social class, or gender do not result in variations in sentence length. But gender does have an impact (so does the offender's race, as we describe later). An examination of the sentences handed out to 77,236 federal offenders between 1991 and 1994 showed that after controlling for offense type, criminal history, and socioeconomic variables, males received 12% longer sentences than females (Mustard, 2001). This means that regardless of the type of offense, a woman who (1) has the same criminal history, (2) commits the same crime, and (3) is sentenced in the same court receives a more lenient sentence than a man.

What accounts for these gender disparities? There is some evidence that they arise because judges' presentence reports contain a great deal of detail which may be difficult to process. To manage the information overload, judges may rely on well-honed stereotypes and attributions about the case and the defendant's characteristics to aid their decisions (Steffensmeier & Demuth, 2006). According to the **focal concerns theory** of judicial decision making, judges focus on three main concerns in reaching sentencing decisions: (1) blameworthiness (i.e., the defendant's culpability), (2) protection of the community (emphasizing incapacitation and general deterrence), and (3) practical constraints and consequences of the sentence (including concerns about disrupting ties to children and other family members). Though it is not exactly clear how judges evaluate these focal concerns, evidence from field observations of sentencing hearings (Daly, 1994; Steffensmeier, Ulmer, & Kramer, 1998) suggests that judges may view women as less dangerous and less of a public safety risk than men, understand women's crimes in the context of their own victimization (e.g., by coercive men, alcohol or drug problems), and perceive the social costs of detaining women as higher. They attend to the fact that women generally have more child care responsibilities and maintain closer ties to the community than men—factors that would insulate women from future criminal activity.

Although most of the research on the influence of gender on sentencing has focused on the gender of the *offender*, crime victims' gender also has an impact on sentencing decisions. Relying on data on Texas offenders who were convicted of three violent crimes in 1991, Curry, Lee, and Rodriguez (2004) found that offenders who victimized females received substantially longer sentences than those who victimized males. Because this analysis controlled for the type and severity of crime, we cannot assume simply that the offenses perpetrated against women were more serious and hence more deserving of a longer sentence. Rather, this finding may reflect some subtle form of sexism, paternalism, or an implicit belief that a female crime victim would suffer more than a male victim.

Another important demographic characteristic that influences sentencing decisions is the race of the offender. Determinate sentencing and sentencing guidelines have been only minimally successful in reducing racial disparity. A representative study using data from Maryland showed that on average, African Americans receive 20% longer sentences than Whites (Bushway & Piehl, 2001). Of the felony drug offenders convicted in 2000 in a large urban jurisdiction in North Carolina, White offenders received the least severe sentences and Hispanic offenders were sentenced most harshly (Brennan & Spohn, 2008).

These differences cannot be fully explained by characteristics of the offenses committed by people of varying races, so observers have looked for alternative explanations. Again, attribution theory and stereotypic beliefs of judges may partly explain this apparent bias in sentencing decisions. According to attribution theory, people make assumptions about whether the cause of crime was a bad person or a bad environment and then convert their assumptions into sentencing decisions (Bridges & Steen, 1998). Judges may attribute the deviant behavior of minority offenders to negative attitudes and personality traits (rather than to environmental factors) and assume that these offenders are more likely to repeat their crimes, thus believing that a longer sentence is more appropriate. Judges may view minorities as more evil and threatening than Whites who commit similar crimes (Hagan & Peterson, 1995).

Another factor that influences judicial sentencing patterns is the way a conviction came about: whether by guilty plea, bench trial, or jury trial. In Chapter 7, we explained that defendants who plead guilty are often given a reduced sentence, partly to encourage them to plead guilty and thereby reduce costs for court time and personnel. But overlaying the guilty plea is the requirement that judges adhere to sentencing guidelines that have been established in most states. Few guidelines recognize "plea agreement" as an acceptable reason for judges to depart from rigid application of the sentencing guidelines. But analysis of differences in sentences imposed for the same offense in five states with sentencing guidelines showed significant discounts for guilty pleas (King, Soule, Steen, & Weidner, 2005). Defendants who were convicted by a jury received the longest sentences. Judges apparently factor the cost savings of a guilty plea into their sentencing decisions.

Some judges give more severe sentences in order to punish the offender for lying on the stand as well as for committing the initial crime. Paul A. Bilzerian, a Florida investor who was one of the most successful corporate raiders of the 1980s, was sentenced to four years in prison and fined $1.5 million for conspiracy to violate securities laws. Federal Judge Robert Ward stated that the sentence was stiff in part because he believed that Bilzerian had perjured himself when he testified in his own defense: "I do believe that if Mr. Bilzerian had not testified at all at the trial, his sentence would not be what it was" (quoted in Eichenwald, 1989, p. 29).

Judges are human. When they have latitude in the punishments they can give, their backgrounds and personal characteristics may influence their decisions (Hogarth, 1971). They may be prejudiced for or against certain groups—immigrants, antiwar protestors, or homosexuals. They may simply be uninformed. A Dallas judge told a reporter that he was giving a lighter sentence to a murderer because the victims were "queers." He was censured by the Texas State Commission on Judicial Conduct. A Maryland judge acquitted an alleged assailant on domestic violence charges after the victim failed to testify. He stated that one can't simply assume that a woman who is being hit didn't consent to the attack. "Sadomasochists sometimes like to get beat up," he said (Houppert, 2007).

THE SENTENCING PROCESS

The procedure used in most courts for sentencing has several components. The judge receives a file on the offender that contains information about the offender's personal history and prior convictions (if any), and a number of documents describing various procedures (e.g., the date of the arraignment, the formal indictment). The judge reviews the file before the sentencing hearing.

At the hearing, recommendations for a sentence are presented to the judge first by the prosecutor and second, by the attorney representing the defendant. Statements are arranged in this order to give the defendant the final word before the judge makes his or her sentencing decision. But there may be an unexpected consequence of this arrangement: It grants the prosecution the opportunity to set an initial sentencing recommendation. A large body of research has shown that initial numeric requests serve as powerful standards or "anchors" on subsequent judgments (Tversky & Kahneman, 1974). In fact, judges' sentencing decisions are highly influenced by the prosecutor's request for a lengthy sentence (Englich & Mussweiler, 2001), a finding that

can be explained by a judgment process called anchoring.

Defense attorneys' sentencing recommendations are *also* influenced by the prosecutors' demands. When researchers asked lawyers to assume the role of defense attorneys in a simulated rape case, they found that though defense attorneys requested a lower punishment than prosecutors, they were still influenced by the level of the prosecutors' recommendation, and **assimilated** their own sentencing demands to those of the prosecutor (Englich, Mussweiler, & Strack, 2005). This, in turn, will affect judges' decisions. So rather than being aided by going last, the defense may be hindered by having to follow, and counter, the prosecution's demand—its "anchor."

In addition to demands from the prosecutor and defense attorney, the sentencing judge also has a probation officer's report and recommendation. The judge may ask the offender questions and will usually permit the offender to make a statement. In some cases, a forensic mental health professional may provide input on issues such as diminished capacity or coercion and duress (Krauss & Goldstein, 2007). On the basis of these sources of information and taking sentencing options into account, the judge then sentences the offender.

SENTENCING JUVENILE OFFENDERS

The juvenile justice system differs from the adult system in some crucial ways. Not all juveniles come into the system via arrests. Some are referred by school officials, social service agencies, and even by parents. Early in the case, juvenile justice officials must decide whether to send it into the court system or divert the offender to alternative programs such as drug treatment, educational and recreational programs, or individual and group counseling. If the decision is to involve the courts, then prosecutors determine whether the case should be handled by a juvenile court or transferred to criminal court. (We described the transfer process in Chapter 8.) Sentencing procedures and options vary depending on whether the child is adjudicated in juvenile court or transferred to adult criminal court.

Juvenile Court Dispositions

Approximately 60% of young people whose cases are adjudicated in juvenile court are found to be delinquent (Stahl, 1999) and moved to the sentencing, or **dispositional phase** of the case. Dispositional hearings typically combine adversarial procedures and attention to the particular needs—social, psychological, physical—of the child. They include "recommendations by probation and social workers; reports of social and academic histories; and interactions within the court among … the offender and his or her family, probation staff, and perhaps, psychologists and social workers" (Binder, Geis, & Bruce, 2001, p. 286). Issues of substance abuse, family dysfunction, mental health needs, peer relationships, and school problems may be addressed.

The goals of juvenile court dispositions—ensuring public safety and addressing children's needs—are reflected in the options available to juvenile court judges. These include (1) probation at home; (2) probation in the home of a relative or foster home; (3) probation in combination with restitution to the victims or community; (4) house arrest; (5) detention followed by probation; (6) placement in a group home, drug treatment program, or boot camp; and (7) placement in a correctional facility (Elrod & Ryder, 1999). More than half of all juvenile offenders are sentenced to probation although placement in group homes, drug treatment programs, and boot camps are becoming more popular (Snyder & Sickmund, 1999).

When determining the appropriate disposition for a juvenile, judges may consider whether the parents are able to supervise the offender at home, assist in rehabilitation efforts, and insist on school attendance. They may also consider the family's financial resources and the availability of community-based treatment programs and facilities (Campbell & Schmidt, 2000).

Juvenile court judges are also expected to assess offenders' rehabilitative needs and personal circumstances. Thus, one might expect that they would put

considerable weight on offenders' unique characteristics including their psychosocial functioning, developmental maturity, responsibility taking, and gang involvement. But researchers who have examined the effects of demographic, legal, and psychological factors on dispositional outcomes (i.e., probation and confinement) in a sample of 1,355 offenders 14 to 18 year old found that legal factors (e.g., seriousness of the offense, whether the offender had prior court referrals) had the strongest influence on dispositions. Individual factors were not strongly linked to dispositional decisions (Cauffman et al., 2007). When judges adopt clinicians' recommendations for placement, however, they tend to put less weight on offense-related factors (O'Donnell & Lurigio, 2008).

Blended Sentencing

Juveniles who meet the criteria for transfer to adult criminal court are typically sentenced under **blended sentencing** statutes that combine the options available in juvenile court with those used in criminal court. These sentencing laws attempt to simultaneously address rehabilitation concerns and impose a "get tough" accountability (Redding & Mrozoski, 2005). In practice, this means that serious and violent young offenders can stay under juvenile court jurisdiction and receive more lenient sentences than if they were transferred to adult court. But they can also be subjected to harsh sentences if they commit new offenses, violate probation, or fail to respond to rehabilitation efforts (Torbet et al., 1996). Blended sentencing schemes provide incentives to offenders to avoid the more serious consequences of an adult sentence. Prosecutors often use the threat of transfer to adult criminal court to persuade juvenile offenders to plead guilty and accept a particular blended sentence (Podkopacz & Feld, 2001).

Life Sentences for Juvenile Offenders

Judges can also impose adult sanctions—sometimes very lengthy prison sentences—on offenders who were under 18 when they committed a serious crime. These sentences are often mandatory, an automatic consequence of being tried as adults and convicted of murder, attempted murder, or felony murder (meaning they participated in a crime involving a murder but did not do the killing themselves). According to a report from the human rights organization Equal Justice Initiative, over 2,225 juveniles age 17 or younger have been sentenced to life imprisonment without parole in the United States; 73 of them were 13 or 14 when they committed their crimes (Equal Justice Initiative, 2007).

These cases pit human rights and judicial reform advocates on the one hand, against prosecutors and victims' rights groups on the other. Human rights groups argue that applying life-without-parole sentences to juveniles constitutes cruel and unusual punishment. Stephen Bright, director of the Southern Center for Human Rights, said, "It goes against human inclinations to give up completely on a young teenager. It's impossible for a court to say that any 14-year-old never has the possibility to live in society." Prosecutors and victims groups say that such statutes are popular with voters, comforting to victims, and make sense in their "adult-crime, adult-time" approach.

The complexity of these issues is apparent in the case of Ashley Jones who, in 1999 at the age of 14, helped her 16-year-old boyfriend kill her grandfather and aunt, stab her 10-year-old sister, and set her mother on fire. Jones' life had never been easy: She was abandoned by her mother (a crack cocaine addict), sexually assaulted by her stepfather, physically abused by other family members, and abducted by a gang shortly before the crimes. Jones was sentenced to life in prison in Alabama. But even her grandmother and sister think the sentence was too extreme. "I believe she should have gotten 15 or 20 years," her grandmother said. "If children are under age, sometimes they're not responsible for what they do" (Liptak, 2007).

SENTENCING SEX OFFENDERS

Many people believe that sex offenders are especially likely to reoffend sexually and therefore require different kinds of punishment than other offenders. But the truth is not so clear. A meta-analysis of 82 studies that traced the recidivism rates of 29,450 sex offenders up to six years postrelease (Hanson & Morton-Bourgnon, 2005) showed that only 13.7% of sex offenders were arrested for another sexual offense in that period. Sexual deviancy and antisocial orientations (e.g., psychopathy, antisocial traits) were the best predictors of sexual recidivism. The vast majority of convicted sex offenders were *not* rearrested for another sex crime within six years.

A 25-year follow-up study of sex offenders in Canada provides a more nuanced picture of sex offending patterns over many years. It found that the typical sex offender's criminal career spanned two decades, which suggests that recidivism can remain a problem over much of a sex offender's adult life (Langevin et al., 2004). Indeed, many sex offenders have committed more sex crimes than those for which they were arrested, so recidivism rates may underestimate actual rates of sexual offending. The public fears sexual offenders, and legislatures have adopted special measures to protect the public from them.

There are three ways in which judges and corrections professionals treat sex offenders differently than other offenders, based on the belief that they are particularly likely to reoffend: (1) Upon release from prison, sex offenders in many jurisdictions are required to register with state officials who then publicly notify the community about the location of the offender's residence; (2) sex offenders can be involuntarily committed to a mental health facility following the completion of their sentence; and (3) sex offenders can be subjected to extraordinary sanctions, including enhanced sentences, mandatory treatments, and chemical or surgical castration.

Sentencing for sex crimes, particularly those against children, has been singled out for special attention by the states. Probation for serious sex offenses is no longer an option in most states; in fact, sentences for sex offenses against children can be as severe as sentences for murder. Until recently, the rape of a child was punishable by death in six states. This kind of sentence was deemed unconstitutional by the U.S. Supreme Court in 2008 (*Kennedy v. Louisiana*, 2008).

Registration and Notification

Convicted sex offenders are required to register with local law enforcement after they are released from prison and to notify authorities of subsequent changes of address. The period of required registration depends on the classification of the offender, which is a product of a formal risk assessment. In Kentucky, for example, high-risk offenders are required to register for life, whereas moderate- or low-risk offenders are required to register for 10 years after their formal sentence is completed.

Notification is more controversial than registration. Community notification laws allow states to disseminate information about convicted sex offenders to the public. In some states (New Jersey, for example), police go door-to-door to notify neighbors that a high-risk sex offender has moved into the neighborhood (Witt & Barone, 2004). Most states and the federal government rely on the Internet as a means of notification. (The federal government Web site is a compilation of data on an estimated 500,000 sex offenders listed on separate Web sites maintained by the states.) Typically, offenders' names are placed on the Web for the period of their required registration, and law enforcement officials take no further steps to notify the community.

Web site notification appears to be plagued by the worst of two extremes. On the one hand, it is overinclusive; the entire world can learn about the offender, even though only one or a few communities really need to know. On the other hand, Web notification is underinclusive; persons who cannot or do not regularly access the sex offender Web site will not be made aware of a sex offender living in the neighborhood. Not surprisingly, most Web site hits appear to involve idle browsers rather than citizens who are concerned that an offender might be living nearby.

Web site posting also raises serious concerns about invasion of privacy. No matter how minor the offense, most states and the federal government post offenders' personal information (including their photos) on the Web for all to see during the period of required registration. Other information is also available. On the federal sex offender registry (URL/www.nsopr.gov), for example, one can search by offender's name, city, county, or zip code. An offender posted on the Web will live under the shadow of his conviction in a way that no other type of offender must endure. A murderer could move to a new community, safe in the knowledge that his past, although a matter of public record, is not readily accessible to friends and neighbors. But a sex offender will know that his past is available to anyone in the world at the click of a mouse.

When someone learns that an offender is living nearby, the result may be public hysteria. In Danville, Kentucky, a released parolee classified as a "high-risk offender" was taken in by a middle-class couple who wanted to put their newfound Christian faith to work. The couple wasn't prepared for their neighbors' reaction when they were notified that there was a high-risk sex offender in their suburban neighborhood. Fliers appeared in mailboxes and on light poles, anonymous letters were written, children were kept in their homes and off the streets, and the couple was shunned by the neighbors. When a crew from the television program *Extra* showed up, the ex-offender packed his bags and left without a word (Breed, 1999). After the community was notified about a released offender in Waterloo, Iowa, children started carrying bats and sticks as they walked to school; the recently released offender was threatened and was ultimately hounded out of the community (VanDuyn, 1999). Research shows that community notification has led to harassment and vigilantism directed at sex offenders, and has interfered with offenders' ability to find stable work and housing, important factors in reintegration into the community (Levenson & D'Amora, 2007).

Involuntary Commitment

A second form of sanction on repeat sex offenders is involuntary commitment to a mental health facility after the prison term has been completed. The leading case on this topic is *Kansas v. Hendricks* (1997). Leroy Hendricks was "every parent's nightmare" (Kolebuck, 1998, p. 537). He was in his 60s at the time he was scheduled to be released from a Kansas prison where he had served 10 years for child molestation. But Kansas had recently

---

B o x 14.2   THE CASE OF LEROY HENDRICKS: LOCK 'EM UP AND THROW AWAY THE KEY?

Leroy Hendricks had done his time—or so he thought. By August 1994, he had served 10 years for taking indecent liberties with two 13-year-old boys. Unfortunately for Hendricks, his reputation preceded him. In fact, he had a long history of sexually abusing children, beginning in 1955 and including five convictions for sex crimes involving children. Hendricks readily admitted to having difficulty controlling his urges. In fact, he told a Kansas judge that only his death would guarantee that he would never commit another sexual offense on a child. In 1994, shortly before Hendricks was to be released, the state invoked the SVP Act and sought his involuntary commitment.

Hendricks challenged the constitutionality of the act, claiming, among other things, that it violated the double-jeopardy and *ex post facto* clauses of the Constitution. (The double-jeopardy clause prevents the government from punishing people twice for the same crime, and the *ex post facto* clause forbids the enactment of new laws that extend punishment for past crimes.) Resolution of the issue turned on whether Hendricks' continued confinement was considered "punishment."

Writing for the 5–4 majority of the Supreme Court, Justice Clarence Thomas concluded that it was not (*Kansas v. Hendricks*, 1997). Thomas reasoned that Hendricks' confinement could not be considered "punishment" because, in constitutional terms, punishment derives from criminal proceedings, not civil ones. He also pointed to the indefinite duration of the confinement (theoretically, individuals can be released when their "abnormality" is no longer threatening) as proof of its nonpunitive nature. In a bit of irony, Thomas dismissed the fact that the state failed to provide treatment for Hendricks. By analogy to cases upholding quarantine of persons with communicable

Leroy Hendricks

diseases, Thomas held that the state could lock up those for whom no treatment was available but who posed a danger to others.

Professor Stephen Morse has raised concerns about the role of the *Hendricks* case in striking a balance between the due process and crime control models of criminal justice (Morse, 1998). He asserted that in its quest for public safety, society is now willing to punish people who are merely *at risk for* reoffending, in essence punishing them more severely than they deserve.

There are also concerns about the costs and consequences of indeterminate civil commitment. Hendricks' confinement costs $185,000 per year, more than eight times the cost of housing a prisoner in Kansas. And Hendricks, who has had a stroke and suffers from diabetes and circulatory problems, is largely confined to a wheelchair and may not live long enough to "graduate" from treatment (Davey & Goodnough, 2007).

---

passed a Sexually Violent Predator (SVP) Act, allowing for the involuntary commitment of offenders suffering from a "mental abnormality" that would make them likely to commit predatory acts of sexual violence. A Kansas judge determined that Hendricks was a SVP and committed him to a mental hospital. His case is described more fully in Box 14.2.

Predictably, other states passed statutes similar to the Kansas statute. As of 2007, 20 states had enacted some form of civil proceedings for the involuntary commitment of sex offenders. Once such an individual

is committed, release is rare. By 2007, almost 2,700 persons had been committed as SVPs, but only about 250 had been released, half on technical or legal grounds unrelated to treatment (Davey & Goodnough, 2007).

The Supreme Court's rulings on the SVP Act make clear that selected individuals must have a "mental abnormality" or personality disorder that predisposes them to sexual violence. In making assessments of "mental abnormality," evaluators typically use the diagnostic criteria for pedophilia, paraphilia, or antisocial personality disorder set out in the *Diagnostic and Statistical Manual-IV* (Becker, Stinson, Tromp, & Messer, 2003).

The U.S. Supreme Court has also said that individuals subjected to SVP laws must be unable to control their behavior and thus, likely to commit future sexually violent crimes (*Kansas v. Crane*, 2002). How does one assess the likelihood of some possible event in the future? The risk of sexual reoffending is typically determined via actuarial risk assessment instruments that include measures of deviant sexual preferences and persistent antisocial behaviors. These tests compare a given individual to individuals who have similar characteristics and for whom the rates of recidivism are known. Obviously, these instruments cannot predict with certainty that a given individual will behave in any particular way, but they can be quite useful in gauging the likelihood of future behavior (Levenson, 2004).

Civil commitment evaluations are conducted around the time the offender is scheduled to be released from prison and typically rely on such actuarial instruments as the Sex Offender Risk Appraisal Guide (SORAG; Quinsey, Harris, Rice, & Cormier, 1998), the Violence Risk Appraisal Guide (VRAG; Harris, Rice, & Quinsey, 1993), the Rapid Risk Assessment for Sex Offense Recidivism (RRA-SOR; Hanson, 1997), and the Static-99 (Hanson & Thornton, 2000). Studies of the predictive accuracy of these instruments (the ability of the tests to predict violent and sexual recidivism, or the absence of such recidivism) in a sample of approximately 400 sex offenders showed high accuracy rates when the VRAG and SORAG were used (Harris & Rice, 2003; Harris et al., 2003).

Actuarial assessments are, in general, more accurate than unstructured clinical judgments in making a prediction. In evaluations made for the purposes of involuntary commitments, examining clinicians may offer their opinion about whether the defendant is suffering from a mental abnormality (or illness) that will render him a substantial risk to reoffend. Compared to actuarial prediction schemes, such unstructured clinical predictions are less accurate (Falk, 1999) and should not be used as the sole basis for risk-based decisions concerning involuntary commitment. Janus and Prentky (2003)

argue that psychologists should use one of the standard instruments as part of any evaluation of propensity to reoffend.

Mandated Treatments for Sex Offenders

Unlike other offenders, sex offenders are often required to undergo treatment designed to "cure" them of their antisocial tendencies. Offenders sentenced to prison are required to participate in offender treatment programs or give up hope of parole; offenders offered probation are required to participate in counseling sessions. These typically involve cognitive-behavioral interventions that require offenders to acknowledge wrongdoing and that challenge their rationalizations, minimizations (e.g., "no one was hurt"), and other erroneous beliefs that support the commission of the offense. Treatment may also include an assortment of behavior modification techniques, including aversive conditioning that pairs aversive stimuli such as mild electric shock with deviant sexual responses. Over time, the deviant behavior is expected to decrease. Pure behavioral therapy has fallen out of favor, with preference for more integrative and comprehensive treatment plans (Marshall, Fernandez, Marshall, & Serran, 2006).

Some treatment programs have effectively reduced sexual offending by suppressing offenders' sex drive. This pharmacological approach, sometimes called **chemical castration**, involves administering hormones to reduce testosterone levels and thereby lower sex drive, sexual arousal, and sexual fantasizing. Therapists have also had some success using selective serotonin reuptake inhibitors (SSRIs) to reduce deviant sexual behavior. This class of drugs may reduce intrusive or obsessive thoughts associated with sexual offending (Marshall et al., 2006).

In the past, judges have sometimes given convicted sex offenders a choice: prison or hormone treatment. It is not surprising that some men have opted for the drugs, even though the possible side effects include lethargy, hot flashes, nightmares, hypertension, and shortness of breath (Keene, 1997).

California was the first state to pass a law requiring repeat child molesters (**pedophiles**) to be treated with hormones as a condition of parole. The California statute requires that clinicians assess offenders to determine whether they suffer from a condition (e.g., pedophilia) that creates a substantial risk of reoffending. If so, the California legislature reasoned, it makes sense to deny parole unless the offender agrees to the treatment. At the time the California Chemical Castration Bill was being considered, Assemblyman Bill Hoge, one of its sponsors, reasoned as follows:

> What we're up against is the kind of criminal who, just as soon as he gets out of jail, will immediately commit this crime again at least 90% of the time. So why not give these people a shot to calm them down and bring them under control? (Ayres, 1996, p. A1)

Although Assemblyman Hoge clearly overstated the probability of reoffending, there may be a certain logic in requiring sex offenders to take a drug that diminishes their sex drive.

The most controversial form of treatment is **surgical castration**. It involves removal of the testes (termed *orchiectomy*). Although rarely used, surgical castration is effective in reducing sexual recidivism; sexual desires are diminished in men who have been castrated, even though these men are still able to develop an erection in response to sexual stimuli (Weinberger, Sreenivasan, Garrick, & Osran, 2005).

Since 1996, nine states have followed California's lead and passed laws authorizing the use of either chemical or surgical castration. In most of these states, repeat offenders are eligible for probation or parole only if they accept mandated chemical castration (though Texas offers only surgical castration) (Scott & Holmberg, 2003).

THE DEATH PENALTY: THE ULTIMATE PUNISHMENT

The ultimate punishment, of course, is death. Citizens of the United States can be executed by the federal government and by the governments of 35 states.

But capital punishment has had a controversial and volatile history in this country. Although a majority of Americans apparently favor capital punishment, and politicians and appellate judges have tended to make decisions that reflect that belief (Ogloff & Chopra, 2004), support for capital punishment may be waning. The American Bar Association has called for a nationwide moratorium on capital punishment, citing concerns about the way the death penalty is administered. In 2003, during his last few days as governor of Illinois, George Ryan effectively closed down Illinois's death row, commuting (or canceling) the death sentences of 156 condemned prisoners. Most of them are now serving life sentences. In recent years, three states—New Jersey, New Mexico, and New York—have abolished the death penalty, and legislatures in several other states are considering that option. Polls show that many people would be willing to abandon capital punishment if the alternative sanction was life without parole in combination with victim restitution (Bowers, Vandiver, & Dugan, 1994).

The modern history of capital punishment in the United States began in 1972 when the U.S. Supreme Court effectively abolished the death penalty on the grounds that it constituted "cruel and unusual punishment" (*Furman v. Georgia*, 1972). After the *Furman* case, state legislatures revised their death penalty laws to address the Court's concern that capital punishment was being applied in an arbitrary and discriminatory fashion as a consequence of the "unbridled discretion" in sentencing given to juries.

To remedy this problem, states passed statutes that guided the sentencing discretion of juries in death penalty cases. First, they made only certain crimes eligible for the death penalty. Second, they changed the structure of capital trials. Now, if a defendant is charged with one of these crimes, the trial is conducted in two phases. The jury decides the guilt or innocence of the defendant in the first phase (the "guilt phase"). If the defendant is found guilty, then the second phase, or "sentencing phase," of the trial is held. During this phase, the jury hears evidence of **aggravating factors** (elements of the crime, such as killing in an especially brutal or heinous manner, that make the defendant more likely to receive a death sentence) and **mitigating factors**

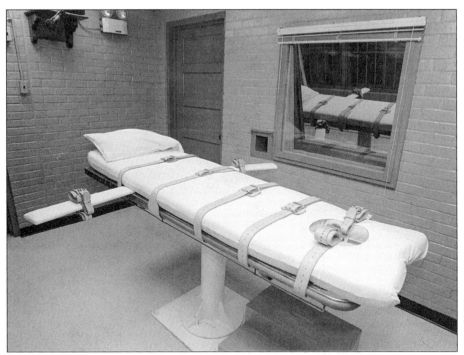

Gurney on which the prisoner is executed by lethal injection

(elements of the defendant's background or the crime, such as experiencing mental illness or acting under duress at the time of the offense, that make life imprisonment the more appropriate verdict). Specific aggravating and mitigating factors are listed in the statutes, but a jury is not required to consider only those factors in its deliberations. Before reaching a sentencing decision, jurors hear instructions from the judge on how to weigh the aggravating and mitigating factors. Generally, a jury cannot vote for a death sentence unless it determines that the prosecution has proven at least one aggravating factor. However, even if it decides that one or more aggravating factors were present, it may still, after considering the mitigating factors, return a sentence of life imprisonment.

In 1976, in the case of *Gregg v. Georgia*, and in response to these newly enacted laws and procedures, the Supreme Court reinstituted the possibility of the death penalty. Since that time, the Court has issued many death penalty opinions, focusing

often on the behavior of juries in death penalty cases (Haney & Wiener, 2004).

Following the *Gregg* decision, state after state began to execute those convicts who had been sentenced to die. The first to be executed, on January 17, 1977, was Gary Gilmore, in Utah, who gave up his right to challenge his conviction and resisted the efforts of his relatives to save him from the firing squad. (Since the death penalty was reinstituted in the United States, he is the only person to have been executed by firing squad. His life and case are described in great detail in Norman Mailer's *The Executioner's Song*.) Since the death penalty was reinstated in 1976, nearly 7,500 people have been sentenced to death and more than 1,150 people have been executed. The greatest number (98) was executed in 1999, and the rate of execution has declined since then. In 2008, 37 inmates were executed (Bureau of Justice Statistics, 2009). More than 80% of these executions have occurred in southern states, and Texas alone accounts for more than one-third of them.

Concerns about Innocence

We do not know exactly how many innocent people have been sentenced to death. One estimate is that 2.3% of those sentenced to death may actually be innocent (Gross & O'Brien, 2007). Another estimate puts the figure at 5% (Risinger, 2007). We also do not know exactly how many innocent people have been executed, though some have. David Protess, a Northwestern University journalism professor, drew attention to the possibility of "executing the innocent" when students under his supervision tracked down and obtained confessions from true killers, thereby exonerating two men on death row. Professor Protess's student investigators uncovered other instances of conviction of the innocent, and 13 inmates were ultimately exonerated from death row in Illinois. This led to Governor George Ryan's decision to commute the death sentences of all remaining death row inmates in Illinois (Marshall, 2002). In a speech delivered at Northwestern University at the time, Ryan was quoted as saying, "Our capital system is haunted by the demon of error: error in determining guilt and error in determining who among the guilty deserves to die."

The moratorium on executions gained further momentum from a large-scale Columbia University Law School study, "A Broken System: Error Rates in Capital Cases" (Liebman, 2000). This study analyzed every capital conviction in the United States between 1973 and 1995 and revealed that serious mistakes had been made in two-thirds of the cases, a startling indictment of the criminal justice system. The most common problems included incompetent defense attorneys (37%), faulty jury instructions (20%), and misconduct on the part of prosecutors (19%). Of those defendants whose capital sentence was overturned because of an error, 82% received a sentence less than death at their retrials, including 7% who were found not guilty of the capital crime with which they had originally been charged.

According to a report of the House Judiciary Subcommittee on Civil and Constitutional Rights,

since executions resumed after the *Gregg* case, 130 people have been freed from death rows upon proof of their innocence (Death Penalty Information Center, 2009). Some of these condemned convicts were cleared when new evidence came to light or when witnesses changed their stories. DNA evidence is credited with proving the innocence of scores of death row inmates in the United States (Gross, Jacoby, Matheson, Montgomery, & Patil, 2005). Many of these cases involved defendants who had originally been convicted on the basis of faulty eyewitness identifications or false confessions.

As a result of these widely publicized errors, a number of states have passed laws that give death row inmates the right to postconviction DNA testing. In 2004, Congress established a grant program to help states defray the costs of such testing. The grant program bears the name of Kirk Bloodsworth, the first death row inmate exonerated by DNA testing. We tell his story in Box 14.3.

Not all cases end as satisfactorily as Bloodsworth's did. Consider the case of Gary Graham, executed by the state of Texas in 2000 for the murder of a man during a holdup in a grocery store parking lot. Protesting his innocence to the end, Graham was forcibly hauled to the execution chamber and strapped to the gurney with extra restraints. The only evidence against Graham was an eyewitness who said she saw the killer through her car windshield. Two eyewitnesses who would have testified that Graham was not the killer did not testify, and three jurors, after watching the videotaped statements of the two potential witnesses, signed affidavits that they would have acquitted if the witnesses had been called. The Texas Board of Pardons wasn't convinced that an injustice had been done and voted not to recommend clemency.

Is the death penalty still justified if we know that innocent people have been executed? Some proponents insist that it is, invoking the analogy that administering a vaccine is justified even though a child might have an adverse—even lethal—reaction to it. Proponents of capital punishment suggest that even though innocent people are occasionally and mistakenly put to death, other compelling reasons justify maintaining this system of punishment.

B o x 14.3 THE CASE OF KIRK BLOODSWORTH: THE WORTH OF HIS BLOOD AND HIS EXONERATION ON DEATH ROW

Kirk Bloodsworth was the first death row inmate to be exonerated by DNA testing. A Marine veteran, Bloodsworth had never been in trouble with the law when, in 1985, he was convicted of the rape and murder of a 9-year-old girl who had been strangled, raped, and beaten with a rock. Bloodsworth was sentenced to die in Maryland's gas chamber. Bloodsworth's arrest was based in part on an identification by an eyewitness from a police sketch that was compiled from the recollections of five other eyewitnesses. At trial, all five eyewitnesses testified that they had seen Bloodsworth with the victim. All were wrong.

In 1992, prosecutors in the case agreed to DNA testing in which blood found on the victim's clothing was compared to her own blood and to Bloodsworth's; testing excluded Bloodsworth as the perpetrator, and he was released from prison in 1993. DNA evidence ultimately led police to the true killer, Kimberly Ruffner,

AP/Wide World Photos

Kirk Bloodsworth (at left), the first death row inmate exonerated by DNA testing, being introduced at a rally

who was arrested in 2003. In an ironic twist to the story, Bloodsworth had known Ruffner in prison. When Ruffner was arrested, Bloodsworth was quoted as saying, "My God, I know him. He lifted weights for us. I spotted weights for him." (Levine, 2003, A01)

Justifications for the Death Penalty

Many reasons have been advanced for endorsing the irrevocable penalty of death. While he was the mayor of New York City, Ed Koch contended that the death penalty "affirms life." By failing to execute murderers, he said, we "signal a lessened regard for the value of the victim's life" (quoted in Bruck, 1985, p. 20).

Most justifications for the death penalty reflect moral perspectives (e.g., "an eye for an eye") and thus extend beyond the capacity of empirical research to prove or disprove. But a testable argument for capital punishment is the expectation that it will act as a deterrent to criminal activity. Proponents of this position suggest that (1) the death penalty accomplishes general, as well as specific, deterrence; (2) highly publicized executions have at least a short-term deterrent effect; and (3) murderers are such dangerous people that allowing them to live increases the risk of injury or death to other inmates and prison guards.

Using a variety of empirical approaches, social scientists have evaluated the deterrent effects of the death penalty, and their studies consistently lead

to the conclusion that the death penalty does not affect the rate of crimes of violence (e.g., Peterson & Bailey, 2003). Evidence also contradicts the view that murderers are especially dangerous inmates. Some data indicate that capital murderers tend to commit fewer violent offenses and prison infractions than parole eligible inmates (Cunningham, Reidy, & Sorensen, 2005).

Not only is there little support for the deterrent effects of capital punishment, but some researchers contend that capital punishment actually *increases* crime, an effect known as **brutalization**. Brutalization theorists argue that executions increase violent crime by sending the message that it is acceptable to kill those who have wronged us. However, the evidence in support of brutalization effects is no stronger than the data in favor of deterrence (Radelet & Akers, 1996).

Equality versus Discretion in Application of the Death Penalty

Does the death penalty further the goal of equal treatment before the law? About a third of the states, plus the District of Columbia, do not permit it, and vastly different rates of executions occur in states that do. For example, even though the state of New Hampshire has the death penalty, no one has been executed or even sent to death row in that state since the penalty was reestablished. As we have noted, more than a third of all executions in the United States since 1977 have taken place in one state—Texas. So if equal treatment is the goal, it is safe to say that capital punishment has not furthered that goal. The death penalty is administered in only a minority of states and within those states, only in a subset of eligible cases. Furthermore, its determinants often seem inconsistent and unpredictable.

One concern is the issue of race. The victims of intentional homicide are equally divided between Blacks and Whites, yet the chance of a death sentence is much greater for criminals who kill Whites than those who kill Blacks (U.S. General Accounting Office, 1990). In fact, data from governmental and capital defense organizations show that between the late 1970s and the early 2000s, there was tremendous racial disparity in death sentences. So, for example, between 1990 and 1999, California offenders who killed Whites were more than three times more likely to receive the death penalty than offenders who killed Blacks, and more than four times more likely than offenders who killed Latinos (Pierce & Radelet, 2005).

The leading Supreme Court case on the issue of race and application of the death penalty, *McCleskey v. Kemp* (1987), considered this issue. The question was whether the death penalty discriminated against persons who murdered Whites. We describe McClesky's case in Box 14.4.

Psychologists have determined that not all Black offenders are equally likely to be sentenced to death for killing a White person. Jennifer Eberhardt and her colleagues showed to Stanford undergraduates the photographs of 44 Black offenders whose trials advanced to the penalty phase in Philadelphia between 1979 and 1999, and asked them to rate the stereotypicality of each offender's appearance. Controlling for various other factors that influence sentencing such as the severity of the murder and the defendant's and victim's socioeconomic status, researchers found that offenders whose appearance was rated as more stereotypically Black were more likely to have received the death penalty than offenders whose appearance was less stereotypical (Eberhardt, Davies, Purdie-Vaughns, & Johnson, 2006).

Capital Jury Decision Making

The *Furman* and *Gregg* cases, two pivotal challenges to the constitutionality of the death penalty, focused attention on the role of the jury in capital cases. For this reason, it is not surprising that there has been intense public and scientific scrutiny of two important aspects of capital jury decision making: the process of selecting jurors in capital cases, and the ability of those jurors to understand and apply the sentencing instructions they receive from the judge.

The Selection of Jurors in Capital Cases: "Death Qualification". In most cases, sentencing decisions are made by the trial judge. But capital cases are different because juries usually decide the sentence, essentially choosing either life imprisonment or death for the defendant. When jurors are empanelled to serve on cases in which the death penalty is being sought, they are required to answer *voir dire* questions about their attitudes toward capital punishment in a procedure called **death qualification**. If, in response to those questions, jurors indicate extreme beliefs about the death penalty, they may be excused "for cause"— that is, dismissed from that case. More precisely, prospective jurors are excluded if their opposition to capital punishment would "prevent or substantially impair the performance of [their] duties as juror[s] in accordance with [their] instructions and [their] oath" (*Wainwright v. Witt*, 1985, p. 424). Prospective jurors dismissed for this reason are termed *excludables*, and those who remain are termed *death qualified*. (Another group of prospective jurors—those who would automatically impose the death penalty at every opportunity—so-called "automatic death penalty" jurors—are also dismissed for cause, although they are fewer in number

---

Box 14.4   THE CASE OF WARREN MCCLESKY: DOES RACE MATTER?

Warren McCleskey, a Black man, was convicted in 1978 of armed robbery and the murder of a White police officer who had responded to an alarm while the robbery was in progress. McCleskey was sentenced to die in Georgia's electric chair. He challenged the constitutionality of the death penalty on the ground that it was administered in a racially discriminatory manner in Georgia. In the words of one of his attorneys, "When you kill the organist at the Methodist Church, who is White, you're going to get the death penalty, but if you kill the Black Baptist organist, the likelihood is that it will be plea bargained down to a life sentence" (quoted in Noble, 1987, p. 7).

The foundation for McCleskey's appeal was a comprehensive study of race and capital sentencing in the state of Georgia conducted by David Baldus, a law professor at the University of Iowa, and his colleagues. They analyzed the race of the offender and the race of the victim for about 2,000 murder and manslaughter convictions from 1973 to 1979 and concluded that those who killed Whites were 11 times more likely to

receive the death penalty than those who killed Blacks (Baldus, Pulaski, & Woodworth, 1983). Anticipating the argument that the heinousness of the murders may explain this finding, Baldus and colleagues eliminated cases in which extreme violence or other aggravating circumstances virtually ensured the death penalty and cases in which overwhelming mitigating circumstances almost guaranteed a life sentence. For the remaining cases—which permitted the greatest jury discretion—they found that defendants were about four times more likely to be sentenced to death if their victims were White. Similar patterns have been reported for capital sentencing in Arkansas, North Carolina, Illinois, Ohio, Texas, Mississippi, and several other states (Nietzel, Hasemann, & McCarthy, 1998).

Despite the mass of statistical evidence, the Supreme Court upheld McCleskey's death sentence. Because there was no evidence that individual jurors in his trial were biased, the Court was unwilling to assume that McClesky's jury valued a White life more than a Black life.

---

than "excludables.") Death-qualified jurors are qualified to impose the death penalty because they do not hold strong scruples or reservations about its use.

Death qualification raises some important constitutional questions. Recall that capital cases involve two phases but only one jury to decide both guilt and punishment. Although excludable jurors might be unwilling to impose the death penalty, many could fairly determine the guilt or innocence of the defendant. Yet death qualification procedures deny them the opportunity to make a decision. They also raise concerns about the leanings of jurors who *do* assess guilt.

Intuitively, one might expect that death-qualified juries (those made up of people who are not opposed to the death penalty) would be somewhat more conviction-prone than the general population. This was the argument made in the case of *Witherspoon v. Illinois*, decided by the U.S. Supreme Court in 1968. In his argument to the Supreme Court, Witherspoon presented

evidence from three social science research studies that death-qualified jurors were more conviction-prone than excludable jurors. The Court stated that the findings were too tentative to support Witherspoon's contention but left the door open for future consideration. In a rare statement of encouragement to social scientists to conduct further research (Ogloff & Chopra, 2004), the Court stated that "a defendant convicted by such a jury in some future case might still attempt to establish that the jury was less than neutral with respect to guilt" (p. 520).

The question that the *Witherspoon* decision left open was whether a death-qualified jury is more disposed toward conviction than a jury that is broadly representative of the entire community. Responding to this implicit "invitation" to undertake further studies, psychologists and other social scientists readily obliged. In particular, Professor Phoebe Ellsworth and her colleagues conducted a set of empirical studies that demonstrated the conviction-proneness of death-qualified juries.

In their first study, Fitzgerald and Ellsworth (1984) surveyed a random sample of 811 eligible jurors in Alameda County, California. A total of 64% favored the death penalty (37% did so "strongly"). Another 17% said they could never vote to impose the death penalty and thus were excludable under the *Witherspoon* criterion. In response to questions about the criminal justice system, death-qualified jurors were more inclined to favor the prosecutor's viewpoint, more likely to mistrust criminal defendants and their counsel, more in sympathy with a punitive approach toward offenders, and more concerned with crime control than with due process (a dilemma we discussed in Chapter 1).

A follow-up study by Cowan, Thompson, and Ellsworth (1984) involved showing a two-hour videotape of a murder trial reenactment to 288 mock jurors who were either death qualified or excludable, using the *Witherspoon* criterion. (Of the 288 mock jurors, 30 were excludable.) These adults were divided into juries. About half of the juries were composed entirely of death-qualified jurors; the others contained from two to four excludables, although the majority of jurors were death qualified. Three-fourths of the death-qualified juries found the defendant guilty; however, only 53% of the juries with excludable jurors did. These "mixed" juries took a more serious approach to their deliberation task; they were more critical of witnesses and better able to remember the evidence.

In a third study, Thompson, Cowan, Ellsworth, and Harrington (1984) examined why death-qualified jurors voted guilty more often than excludable jurors. The researchers found that the death-qualified jurors tend "to interpret evidence in a way more favorable to the prosecution and less favorable to the defense" (p. 104). The two groups also expressed different kinds of regret over making a mistake: Death-qualified jurors were more upset about acquitting a guilty defendant, whereas excludables were more disturbed about convicting an innocent one.

Death-qualified jurors may differ from the general population in other important ways. By questioning 200 venirepersons in Florida, Professor Brooke Butler determined that as support for the death penalty increased, so too did negative attitudes toward women, homophobic sentiments, and racist beliefs (Butler, 2007). Although these attitudes may not *overtly* affect jurors' judgments in capital cases, they could exert subtle and unconscious influences on the way that jurors process evidence and assess witness credibility.

Death qualification studies have consistently indicated that death-qualified juries are more disposed toward conviction than juries that include jurors with scruples against the death penalty (Bersoff, 1987). Ardia McCree made that point in appealing his conviction. At his trial in Arkansas, McCree had asked for two juries—one to decide guilt or innocence, and a second, death-qualified jury to decide the penalty if the first jury convicted. The judge denied his request and excluded eight prospective jurors who said that they could not, under any circumstances, impose a death sentence (Taylor, 1986). McCree was convicted and sentenced to death. He appealed his conviction to the U.S. Supreme Court, and the APA submitted an *amicus curiae* ("friend of the court") brief in support of his position. It summarized three decades of social science research showing that the process of death qualification produced juries that were likely to be conviction-prone and that were unrepresentative of the larger community (Bersoff, 1987).

In spite of this concerted effort and the substantial body of empirical support for McCree's position, the Supreme Court, in a 6–3 vote, held that the jury in McCree's trial was not an improper one (*Lockhart v. McCree*, 1986). Former Chief Justice Rehnquist wrote the majority opinion. On the issue of representativeness of death-qualified juries, he noted that the only requirement was to have representative *venires*, not necessarily to have representative juries. Exclusion of groups who were "defined solely in terms of shared attitudes" was not improper.

The majority opinion also rejected the claim that death-qualified juries were less than neutral in determining guilt and innocence. An impartial jury, Justice Rehnquist wrote, "consists of nothing more than jurors who will conscientiously apply the law and find the facts." He noted that McCree conceded that each of the jurors who convicted him met that test. Accordingly, the Supreme Court upheld the state's use of a death-qualified jury for the decision at the guilt-or-innocence phase.

Comprehension of Jury Instructions in Capital Cases. Jurors in capital cases receive a set of complex instructions that outline their duties and explain how to evaluate and weigh aggravating and mitigating circumstances to reach a sentencing decision. Several studies indicate that jurors do not adequately comprehend the instructions they receive about mitigating factors because, much like other types of judicial instructions, mitigation instructions are often couched in legal jargon and are unusually lengthy and grammatically complex (Haney & Lynch, 1994, 1997; Lynch & Haney, 2000).

If jurors do not understand a judge's instructions about mitigation, they are more likely to rely on other, more familiar factors to guide their verdicts, such as the heinousness of the crime or extralegal considerations such as racial stereotypes, sympathy for victims, or the expertise of the lawyers. The race of the defendant and that of the victim also appear to affect sentences to a significantly greater extent when comprehension of instructions is low than when it is high. In a study by Lynch and Haney (2000), jury-eligible participants who scored low on their comprehension of instructions recommended death 68% of the time for Black-defendant/White-victim cases versus 36% of the time for White-defendant/Black-victim cases. Among participants who comprehended the sentencing instructions well, neither the race of the defendant nor that of the victim affected the sentences.

Jurors have difficulty knowing how to evaluate mitigating evidence presented during the sentencing phase of a capital case. Margaret Stevenson and colleagues analyzed the content of jury deliberations in a mock capital trial in which there was mitigating evidence that the defendant had been abused as a child. Approximately 40% of jurors relied on evidence of childhood maltreatment to argue for a life sentence and approximately 60% either ignored it as a mitigating factor or used it as an aggravating factor to argue for a death sentence. They reasoned that being abused as a child increases the likelihood of violent behavior as an adult (Stevenson, Bottoms, Diamond, Stec, & Pimentel, 2008).

Would jurors fare better if these all-important instructions were presented in a different format? Richard Wiener and his colleagues posed this question. They tested various methods of improving jurors' **declarative knowledge** (their understanding of legal concepts) and **procedural knowledge** (their ability to know what to do in order to reach a sentencing decision) in a highly realistic trial simulation (Wiener et al., 2004). Their study involved both the guilt and sentencing phases of a capital murder trial based on an actual case, used death-qualified community members as jurors, and included jury deliberations. The modifications to the instructions involved (1) simplifying the language of the instructions, (2) presenting the instructions in a flowchart format so that jurors could understand the progression of decisions they were expected to make, (3) giving jurors the chance to review and practice using the instructions in a mock case so that they would gain some experience prior to the real trial, and (4) offering corrections to common misconceptions that jurors have about aggravating and mitigating circumstances. For example:

> [Some] people believe that an aggravating circumstance is a factor that aggravated or provoked the defendant to kill the victim. This definition is based on the common use of the word aggravation. However, this in an incorrect definition of aggravating circumstance and should not be used in imposing a sentence upon the defendant.

Each of these modifications was helpful in enhancing some aspect of jurors' declarative and procedural knowledge in capital cases.

Limiting Use of the Death Penalty

Another highly controversial aspect of the death penalty concerns its use in cases where the defendant, for reasons of mental illness, youth, or limited mental abilities, may not be fully culpable. In recent years, the Supreme Court has deemed the death penalty unconstitutional in cases involving defendants who are mentally retarded, mentally ill, or were under 18 years of age at the time of the murder. Psychologists often play a significant role in cases involving these defendants, evaluating and rendering expert opinions on questions concerning defendants' cognitive abilities and whether they meet diagnostic criteria for various psychiatric disorders.

Mental Retardation. In 1996, Daryl Atkins abducted and killed an airman from the Langley Air Force Base in Virginia. He was convicted and sentenced to death. His appeal to the U.S. Supreme Court focused on his limited mental abilities. In its opinion in the *Atkins* case (*Atkins v. Virginia*, 2002), the Supreme Court referred to definitions of *mental retardation* of the American Association of Mental Retardation and the American Psychiatric Association (*DSM-IV*). These definitions are based on three criteria: (1) manifestation prior to age 18; (2) below-average functioning in at least two adaptive skill areas such as communication, use of community resources, or work; and (3) an IQ level below 70–75. (Atkins's IQ was measured at different times as 59, 67, 74, and 76.)

Noting that many states prohibit the execution of the mentally retarded, the Supreme Court acknowledged that applying the death penalty to people with mental retardation does not further the legitimate goals of deterrence and retribution. The Court therefore declared that it was cruel and unusual punishment, in violation of the Eighth Amendment, to execute mentally retarded individuals (*Atkins v. Virginia*, 2002). This landmark ruling reflects awareness that those with mental retardation often cannot understand the consequences or their actions, the complex and abstract

Daryl Atkins, defendant in Supreme Court case on execution of the mentally retarded

concepts involved in criminal law, or the finality of a death sentence.

Although the Court deemed such executions unconstitutional, it deferred judgment about whether Atkins fit Virginia's definition of mental retardation. Thus, Atkins became one of the first death row inmates to have a jury trial on the question of whether he had mental retardation. If a jury were to deem him retarded, he would be spared the death penalty and sentenced to life imprisonment. Some of the evidence at Atkins's trial focused on his IQ.

One problem associated with reliance on IQ scores to assess mental retardation is that they are known to fluctuate over time (Ceci, Scullin, & Kanaya, 2003), just as Atkins's scores did. In fact, Evan Nelson, a clinical psychologist who tested

Atkins in 1998 and 2004, surmised that his scores rose "as the result of a forced march towards increased mental stimulation provided by the case itself" (Liptak, 2005a). According to Dr. Nelson, "Oddly enough, because of his constant contact with the many lawyers that worked on his case, Mr. Atkins received more intellectual stimulation in prison than he did during his late adolescence and early adulthood." (Indeed, Atkins dropped out of school after failing in his third attempt to pass 10th grade.)

In a 2005 trial in which the defense portrayed Atkins's capabilities as so limited that he was cut from the football team because he could not understand the plays, and the prosecution blamed his poor performance on alcohol and drugs, the jury decided that Atkins was *not* mentally retarded. But in the end, despite years of litigation, Atkins's sentence was commuted to life imprisonment in 2008 because of prosecutorial misconduct.

Youthful Offenders. In the 18th and 19th centuries, death sentences were rarely carried out on children who were under 14 years of age at the time of the crime, but there was little reluctance to execute those who were 16 or 17 when the crime was committed. Of 287 juveniles executed in the United States prior to 1982, 248 were either 16 or 17 when they committed the offense for which they were executed (Streib, 1983).

In 1988, the Supreme Court drew the line at age 16, reasoning that contemporary standards of decency bar the execution of a child who was under age 16 at the time of the offense (*Thompson v. Oklahoma*, 1988). This ruling effectively allowed executions of those who were 16 or 17 when they committed their crimes. But even this standard was relatively short-lived as the Court determined, in 2005, that it was cruel and unusual to execute any person who was younger than 18 at the time of the crime (*Roper v. Simmons*, 2005).

In his majority opinion in the *Roper* case, Justice Anthony Kennedy looked to the "evolving standards of decency that mark the progress of a maturing society." By that measure, the practice of executing juveniles had become outdated and even rare. In 2005, only 19 states allowed executions of convicted murderers who were under 18 at the time of the crime, and the United States was one of only a handful of countries in the world that condoned this practice.

Justice Kennedy also referred to psychological research findings concerning differences between juveniles and adults (e.g., Steinberg & Scott, 2003). He noted that "as any parent knows and as the scientific ... studies ... tend to confirm," young people lack maturity and the sense of responsibility of most adults, act in impetuous ways, and make ill-considered decisions. He commented on juveniles' vulnerability or susceptibility to negative influences and outside pressures, including peer pressure, and the fact that their characters are less well formed than those of adults. He concluded that "from a moral standpoint, it would be misguided to equate the failings of a minor with those of an adult, for a greater possibility exists that a minor's character deficiencies will be reformed" (*Roper v. Simmons*, 2005). The practical effect of sparing a youthful offender from execution is a life sentence without parole—potentially a very lengthy period of incarceration with little chance for redemption or release.

Mental Illness and Execution. Is it cruel and unusual punishment to execute an inmate who, due to mental illness, lacks a rational understanding of why he is being put to death? That was the question posed to the U.S. Supreme Court in the case of *Panetti v. Quarterman* (2007). (Earlier, in *Ford v. Wainwright* [1986], the Supreme Court held that it was unconstitutional to execute those who are incompetent for execution, but did not define the test for competence for execution.) Scott Panetti was convicted of killing his estranged wife's parents, with whom his wife had been living, in Fredericksburg, Texas in 1992. Panetti then held his wife and 3-year-old daughter hostage in the lengthy police standoff that followed. Panetti had a history of psychiatric problems prior to his conviction including 14 hospital stays over 11 years. During earlier stages of the case, four mental health professionals agreed that Panetti suffered from impaired cognitive processes and delusions consistent with schizoaffective disorder.

Scott Panetti believed that the government was executing him to prevent him from preaching the Gospel, not because he murdered his in-laws. Thus, the question for the Supreme Court was whether a person with serious mental illness who may not understand the reason for his execution, can still be put to death.

The APA teamed with the National Alliance on Mental Illness to assist the Court in developing standards for determining what level of mental illness should exempt an offender from execution. In its *amicus curiae* brief to the Supreme Court, the APA distinguished factual understanding from rational understanding. According to one of the authors of this book who consulted on the APA brief (Heilbrun), "factual understanding is about information. Rational understanding allows us to place that information in a meaningful context, without gross interference caused by certain symptoms of severe mental illness, or very serious impairment of intellectual functioning" (Medical News Today, 2007). The APA brief explained that some individuals who suffer from psychotic disorders have bizarre delusions that disrupt their understanding of reality and make it difficult or impossible for them to connect their criminal acts to punishment. The Supreme Court ruled that Panetti's delusions may have prevented him from understanding the reason for his punishment. That decision effectively means that defendants may not be executed if they do not understand *why* they are being put to death.

SUMMARY

1. ***What are the purposes of punishment?*** Punishment is associated with seven purposes: general deterrence, individual deterrence, incapacitation, retribution, expression of moral outrage, rehabilitation, and restitution. Although rehabilitation formerly played a greater role as a justification for punishment, deterrence, incapacitation, and retribution are now advocated as the major justifications for punishment, and the public claims to prefer deterrence over retribution.

2. ***How are the values of discretion and fairness reflected in sentencing decisions?*** The allocation of punishments is second only to the determination of guilt or innocence in importance to the criminal defendant. The sentencing process reflects many of the conflicts that permeate a psychological approach to the legal system. Historically, judges were given broad discretion in sentencing. Some judges are much more severe than the norm; others are more lenient. In recent years, concern over sentencing disparity led to greater use of determinate sentencing and tighter controls over judicial discretion in sentencing. Now, sentencing guidelines are sometimes merely advisory.

3. ***What factors influence sentencing decisions?*** Determinants of sentencing can be divided into relevant and irrelevant factors. For example, seriousness of the crime is a relevant factor, and there is a general relationship between it and the severity of the punishment. An offender's criminal history is another important determinant of the sentence. But a number of other, less relevant factors also are related to severity of sentence, such as race and gender of the offender and race and gender of the victim.

4. ***What special factors are considered in the sentencing of juveniles? Of recidivist sex offenders?*** Sentences for juvenile offenders are influenced by the jurisdiction in which the minor is sentenced (juvenile court, criminal court), the seriousness of the offense, the offender's rehabilitative needs, and professionals' recommendations. Because they are believed to be at high risk for reoffending, sex offenders have been singled out for three types of special punishment: (1) mandatory registration and community notification, (2) involuntary commitment, and (3) extreme sanctions such as

enhanced sentences and treatments such as castration.

5. ***How is the death penalty decided by juries?***
Jurors who oppose the death penalty regardless of the nature of the crime or the circumstances of the case are excluded from both the guilt phase and the sentencing phase of capital trials. Social science research has shown that the remaining so-called death-qualified jurors are conviction-prone. But the Supreme Court has not been responsive to these findings.

6. ***In what ways has the Supreme Court recently limited the use of capital punishment and what role have psychologists played in these decisions?***

In recent years, the Supreme Court has deemed the death penalty unconstitutional in cases in which the defendant is mentally retarded or younger than 18 at the time of the crime. The Supreme Court has also indicated that executing those with mental illness may be limited if such defendants do not understand the reasons for their execution. Psychologists have been involved in these cases to assess offenders' cognitive abilities, diagnose mental illness, and provide data to the court about juveniles' decision making and judgment.

KEY TERMS

aggravating factors

assimilated

blended sentencing

brutalization

chemical castration

death qualification

declarative knowledge

dispositional phase

focal concerns theory

indeterminate
   sentencing

mandatory minimum
   sentences

mitigating factors

pedophiles

policy capturing

procedural knowledge

restorative justice

retributive

shaming penalty

surgical castration

utilitarian

15

Juvenile and Adult Corrections

ORIENTING QUESTIONS

1. What are the important considerations in assessing juveniles prior to placement decisions?
2. What is the evidence for the effectiveness of interventions with juveniles in the community?
3. What are some characteristics of an effective treatment program?
4. What are the priorities in preparing individuals for the transition from incarceration to community living (the reentry process)?
5. How do specialized problem-solving courts compare to other correctional interventions?

6. What are the differences between jails and prisons and what roles do psychologists play in these settings?

7. What are some of the psychological consequences of imprisonment?

8. How can risk/need/responsivity help to provide effective rehabilitative services for adults?

In this final chapter, we discuss the process following a defendant's conviction for a criminal offense. This discussion will include both **adjudication of delinquency** (for adolescents) and **criminal conviction** (for adults). It will address the traditional aspects of corrections—probation, commitment to juvenile programs, incarceration in jail and prison for adults, and parole following release. But there have been some important innovations in correctional practice during the last decade which will also be discussed. In particular, there is now more emphasis on **diversion**, specialization in the nature of rehabilitative services delivered, and reentry (returning from incarceration to the community).

Four major justifications for correctional intervention have been traditionally cited: incapacitation, deterrence (both general, as it applies to others, and specific to the individual convicted), retribution, and rehabilitation. (You'll notice that these mirror the goals of punishment that we described in Chapter 14.) The role of psychology in addressing these goals is focused largely on deterrence and rehabilitation. The question of whether individuals undergoing juvenile or correctional intervention are deterred from committing further offenses is an important topic which psychological research can help address. It is related to the goal of rehabilitation. However, the rehabilitative question is broader: Has the individual gained skills, changed patterns of thinking, and diminished deficits that facilitate living a responsible life? Much of the discussion in this chapter, both for juveniles and adults, will address how psychology contributes to addressing the broad goals of deterring future crime to enhance public safety and rehabilitation.

JUVENILE CORRECTIONS

Interventions for adjudicated delinquents involve delivering services designed to reduce the risk of future offending, and improve or eliminate deficits that are relevant to such risk. This can be done in different settings, ranging from the community to secure residential programs (in some states, simply called juvenile prisons).

It is useful to consider what such interventions might have in common. In 2004, the National Institutes of Health assembled a "state of the science" conference entitled *Preventing Violence and Related Health-Risking Social Behaviors in Adolescents*. Summarizing the evidence presented at this conference, the organizers concluded that there are certain characteristics shared by programs that are successful in reducing the rates of violence, antisocial behavior, and risky health behavior in adolescents:

- They are derived from sound theoretical rationales

- They address strong risk factors (such as substance abuse, family problems, and educational problems)

- They involve long-term treatments, often lasting a year and sometimes much longer

- They work intensively with those targeted for treatment and often use a clinical approach

- They follow a cognitive/behavioral strategy

- They are multimodal and multicontextual (they use different kinds of interventions, and deliver them in different contexts such as home and school)

- They focus on improving social competency and other skill development strategies for targeted youth and/or their families

- They are developmentally appropriate
- They are not delivered in coercive institutional settings
- They have the capacity for delivery with fidelity (meaning that services are delivered as intended)

Likewise, there are common elements of programs that appear to be ineffective:

- They fail to address strong risk factors
- They are of limited duration
- They aggregate high-risk youth in ways that facilitate contagion (i.e., the intervention itself is likely to have harmful effects)
- Their implementation protocols are not clearly articulated
- Their staff are not well supervised or held accountable for outcomes
- They are limited to scare tactics (e.g., Scared Straight) or toughness strategies (e.g., classic boot camps)
- They consist largely of adults lecturing at youth (e.g., the classic drug abuse resistance education program, D.A.R.E.)

These are elements of interventions, both pro and con, that have a good deal of applicability to juvenile corrections. Keep them in mind as we discuss strategies, procedures, and outcomes, and try to distinguish between what will be effective and what will not.

Assessing Risk and Needs in Juveniles

There are two important considerations that recur in juvenile forensic assessment: public safety and treatment needs/amenability. The former means that courts, the juvenile system, and the larger society are rightly concerned with the question of whether the juvenile will reoffend following completion of the intervention. The second refers to the youth's deficits, problems, and symptoms, particularly those related to reoffense risk—and whether they can be improved or eliminated through intervention and within the time that is available until the youth "ages out" of eligibility for treatment as a juvenile (Grisso, 1998).

Social scientists have recognized that a number of influences are related to the risk of juvenile offending. For example, the Office of Juvenile Justice and Delinquency Prevention (OJJDP), in their 1995 *Guide for Implementing the Comprehensive Strategy for Serious, Violent, and Chronic Juvenile Offenders*, compared the factors used in eight different states to classify the risk for future offending in arrested juveniles. At least four of the states used factors that included age at first referral, number of prior referrals, and current offense (taken together, these provide an estimate of how long, how much, and how seriously the juvenile has offended). Other commonly used factors were drug/alcohol problems, school difficulties, negative peers, and family problems. These factors can be either historical and static (with no potential to change through intervention) or dynamic (with the potential to change through intervention).

Focusing on both risk and risk-relevant needs is an approach that was formally conceptualized in the late 1980s. Andrews, Bonta, and Hoge (1990) described three separate considerations, which they termed **risk, need, and responsivity** (RNR). Risk means that the likelihood of committing future offenses should be evaluated, and those at highest risk should receive the most intensive interventions. Needs are the deficits (such as substance abuse, family problems, educational problems, and procriminal attitudes) that increase the risk of reoffending. These are sometimes called **criminogenic needs**. Responsivity involves the likelihood of a favorable response to the interventions, and the influences that may affect such responding. It is easy to see the conceptual relationship between the juvenile priorities of public safety, treatment needs, and treatment amenability—and the Andrews, Bonta, and Hoge concepts of risk, need, and responsivity. Accordingly, the RNR model is a very useful foundation for the evaluation of juveniles (Andrews & Hoge, in press).

As we mentioned in Chapter 8, there are two specialized tools in particular that focus on the measurement of juvenile risk and needs: the Structured

Assessment of Violence Risk in Youth (SAVRY) (Borum, Bartels, & Forth, 2005) and the Youth Level of Service/Case Management Inventory (Hoge & Andrews, 2002). Both prompt the user to consider historical factors, such as the nature of current and previous offending, as well as contextual factors (e.g., family, school, peers), personal factors (e.g., substance abuse, anger, impulsivity, callousness, attitudes toward intervention, offending, and authority), and (for the SAVRY) protective influences such as social support, attachment, resilience, and commitment to positive activities. A similar tool, the Risk–Sophistication–Treatment Inventory (Salekin, 2004), also prompts the evaluator to focus on influences related to risk and risk-relevant treatment needs. It also includes "sophistication" (referring to the youth's adeptness and adult-like attitudes regarding offending), another factor that often appears in the law for decisions on juveniles.

Evaluating youth on the dimensions of risk and needs provides valuable information for several reasons. First, it structures the evaluation to require the psychologist to consider the influences that theory and research indicate are most strongly related to risk and needs. Second, it provides useful information for intervention planning. A specialized risk–needs tool could be used to help the court make a decision about placement, but could also be used by a program once the youth is placed to help determine what interventions should be provided to that individual. Third, it offers one approach to measuring progress and current status. A youth with deficits in certain areas who begins a program should be reevaluated at different times throughout the program to gauge whether he or she is making progress in important areas. This in turn can affect the assessment of current risk, and the needs for additional interventions following completion of the program. A careful evaluation of youth risk and needs is important for planning and future interventions at various levels in the juvenile system (Borum & Verhaagen, 2006).

Community-Based Interventions

There are a number of approaches to the rehabilitation and management of adjudicated delinquent youth in the community. As we mentioned in Chapter 14, youth may be placed on **probation**, involving a specified set of conditions for which compliance is monitored by the probation officer assigned to the case. A variation on the standard conditions of probation involves **school-based probation,** in which the youth's attendance, performance, and behavior in school are monitored through the probation officer's personal visits to the school. Probation conditions may also include drug use monitoring (through testing blood or urine), substance abuse treatment, mental health treatment, and skills-based training in particular areas (e.g., anger management, decision making). Probation may also vary with respect to intensity, with **intensive probation** involving more frequent monitoring contact.

Youth who are placed on probation typically live at home. Alternatively, a youth in a community-based placement might participate in a specific program or alternative school during the day but return home at night.

There is a wide range of specific interventions and broader programs available in the community to youth adjudicated as delinquent. Rather than attempting to describe them all, we focus on three particular community-based interventions for delinquent youth that have been heavily researched: Multisystemic Therapy, Oregon Treatment Foster Care, and Functional Family Therapy. On the basis of this research, these interventions can be described as empirically supported, cost-effective, risk-reducing, and amenable to quality assurance monitoring (Sheidow & Henggeler, 2005).

Multisystemic Therapy (MST). As the name implies, **Multisystemic Therapy** (Henggeler, Schoenwald, Borduin, Rowland, & Cunningham, 1998) focuses on multiple "systems": the individual, family, peer, school, and social networks as they relate to identified problems and risk factors for offending. It delivers services based in the home, school, or elsewhere in the community, with three to four therapists working in a team. This increases the frequency of participation well beyond what would be expected from having juveniles and their families come to the program or individual therapist's office. The training of therapists and supervisors in MST is highly standardized (Henggeler & Schoenwald, 1999), and the MST procedures are very clearly specified (Henggeler et al., 1998), so those receiving MST services are likely to receive them as they were intended to be delivered. (Researchers call this "treatment integrity.") Therapists are available 24/7, working to prevent problems or crises in the youth's life from having a major impact. Consequently, the rate of engaging and retaining families in treatment is very high; over the three to six months of direct service usually needed for MST, the retention rates are as high as 98% (Henggeler, Pickrel, Brondino, & Crouch, 1996; Henggeler et al., 1999).

As MST has become more popular, the amount of research on it has increased. This focus on treatment integrity has been important—particularly since studies have supported the link between adherence to MST treatment principles and favorable outcomes (Schoenwald, Henggeler, Brondino, & Rowland, 2000; Schoenwald, Sheidow, & Letourneau, 2003). In other words, there is a substantial "quality assurance" component built into MST, which was being provided in more than 30 states and 8 nations as of early 2003 (Sheidow & Henggeler, 2005).

MST is one of the best validated interventions for juveniles. Henggeler et al. (1986) reported that MST was more effective than usual diversion services on two outcomes: (1) improving both self-reported and observed family relations, and (2) decreasing youth behavior problems and time spent with deviant peers. It has also been shown to reduce recidivism and decrease placements outside the home over a 59-week period among juveniles charged with serious offenses (Henggeler, Melton, & Smith, 1992). The percentage of this MST group arrested over a longer outcome period (2.4 years) was about half that of the comparison group (Henggeler, Melton, Smith, Schoenwald, & Hanley, 1993).

A study in which participants were randomly assigned to either MST or individual counseling (the strongest kind of research design, with the random assignment to treatment versus control groups allowing the researcher to draw conclusions about the causal relationship between treatment and outcome) involved 176 chronic juvenile offenders (Borduin et al., 1995). It showed that MST produced better family functioning, better symptoms reduction, and a 69% reduction in recidivism over a period of four years. Another randomized assignment study (Henggeler, Melton, Brondino, Scherer, & Hanley, 1997) with juveniles who had chronic histories of offending and were charged with a violent offense ($N = 155$) yielded similarly favorable results, including a reduction in mental health symptoms, a 26% reduction in recidivism, and a 50% reduction in incarceration over 1.7 years.

There is also evidence that MST is effective with juveniles with substance abuse or dependence. Another study using random assignment to MST versus "treatment as usual" for substance abusing juveniles ($N = 118$) (Henggeler, Pickrel, & Brondino, 1999) showed a decrease in drug use, a 50% decrease in time in out-of-home placement, and a 26% decrease in recidivism over a one-year period, while a longer follow-up (four years) yielded significantly reduced violent offending and significantly increased drug use abstinence in the MST group (Henggeler, Clingempeel, Brondino, & Pickrel, 2002). Finally, a study conducted by the Washington State Institute for Public Policy (Aos, Phipps, Barnoski, & Lieb, 2001) concluded that the MST intervention costs an average of $4,743 per family. Considering that cost, the evidence of its effectiveness, and the savings from not placing the juvenile outside the home, the study estimated cost savings of nearly $32,000 per youth and about $132,000 in additional savings from decreased costs to victims. We provide a case example in Box 15.1.

Oregon Treatment Foster Care (OTFC). **Oregon Treatment Foster Care** is another treatment intervention based in the community, developed in the 1980s as an alternative to "treatment as usual" (typically out-of-home placement) for juveniles charged with serious offenses. The procedures for delivering this intervention are described in a treatment manual (Chamberlain & Mihalic, 1998),

---

B o x 15.1   THE CASE OF MARCUS: A YOUTH TREATED IN THE COMMUNITY WITH MULTISYSTEMIC THERAPY

Marcus was 15 years old when he was arrested for stealing a bicycle from a classmate. This was his second arrest. A year earlier he was arrested for possession of marijuana and received a disposition of six months of school-based probation, which required him to attend school (his probation officer periodically came to his school and checked whether he was there) and undergo urine tests for drug use.

Marcus completed his six-month probation without violating any of his conditions. However, despite this, he continued to have a number of difficulties in his life that increased the risk that he would continue to offend. His father had been absent from the family since Marcus was very young. He and his four siblings lived with his mother and grandmother. Because his mother had serious substance abuse problems herself, she was often unemployed and sometimes absent. The burden for supervising the children and supporting the family financially fell mainly to his grandmother. As she became older, she began to develop significant medical problems, and could not be as attentive to all the children as she had previously.

Marcus's grades and behavior in school improved during the first six months of the ninth grade, but after the probation was finished, he began missing a number of school days and falling behind in his work. Marcus was measured in the Average range on a standard IQ test (higher than most juveniles who are arrested), but he found it hard to pay attention to written materials and when his teacher was talking. He tended to avoid doing his homework as a result. He preferred playing basketball with his friends, talking with girls from his neighborhood, and hanging out with older boys who sold drugs.

After he was arrested for his present offense, Marcus was evaluated by a psychologist appointed by the juvenile court judge. The psychologist concluded that Marcus had potentially serious problems with family, school, substance abuse, and negative peers, and experienced Attention Deficit Disorder (ADD). However, he also had some strengths including his grandmother who was a strong role model (and to whom he felt close), average intelligence, and an interest in sports. He was recommended for a community disposition that involved treatment with MST.

The judge adjudicated Marcus delinquent on the charge of stealing the bicycle and sentenced him to one year of juvenile probation. One condition of probation involved treatment with MST. Marcus's MST team included a case manager, family therapist, substance abuse counselor, and two other staff members responsible for working with Marcus in school and in the neighborhood. The case manager immediately made an appointment with a child psychiatrist, who confirmed that Marcus had ADD and prescribed medication to help with the symptoms. One of his MST team members helped Marcus to join a community basketball league; his team practiced every day after school, and the gym was open for casual play (with adult supervision) after the season ended. His family therapist met with Marcus twice a week in his home to begin addressing the problems of helping his grandmother schedule her medical appointments more effectively, providing access to job training and substance abuse support for his mother, and arranging for a regular supervision schedule involving Marcus's grandmother, mother, and all the children. During the second week of scheduled appointments, the family therapist and case manager found nobody at home at the time of each appointment. Therefore, they came to the home at 6:00 A.M. on Sunday and held a make-up meeting at that time.

By the end of their six-month MST sessions, Marcus was doing much better. His school attendance and behavior were consistently improved, his after-school hours were almost always spent in playing basketball, his mother and grandmother were much more attentive to the children, and he was able to concentrate on his homework more easily. Much of this improvement was due to the fact that the MST was administered in the home, school, and gym rather than the office of a therapist or probation officer. In addition, those administering the MST were careful to do it precisely as intended, and were very good about making sure the appointments were kept.

---

which increases OTFC's treatment integrity. It involves placing juveniles with specially trained foster parents rather than in residential placement. Like MST, this intervention uses a team approach.

The OTFC team includes a case manager, therapists, and the foster parents who are available 24/7 over the 6–12 months usually needed. OTFC is designed to provide close supervision (including supportive relationships with adult mentors and reduced exposure to negative peers) within consistent limits. A variety of treatment modalities (including individual and group counseling, family therapy, and interventions to improve specific skills such as anger control and decision making) may be used. These are often conducted with the family, using both the foster parents and the biological parent(s), and in the school.

OTFC has been identified as a model treatment program by the U.S. Surgeon General (U.S. Public Health Service, 1999) and the *Blueprints for Violence Prevention* initiative (Mihalic, Irwin, Elliott, Fagan, & Hansen, 2001). One study involving OTFC (Chamberlain, 1990) treated 13- to 18-year-olds ($N = 16$) matched with a comparison group of 16 other juveniles treated in community residential treatment. Those in the OTFC group were less likely to be incarcerated and more likely to complete treatment over a two-year follow-up period. A second OTFC study (Chamberlain & Reid, 1998) involved random placement of youth ($N = 79$) between the ages of 12 and 17 into OTFC or treatment as usual. Youth treated with OTFC were more likely to complete treatment, spent more time with biological relatives and less time in detention over the next year, and were arrested less often during this period. OTFC is also a relatively cost-effective intervention. An analysis conducted by the Washington State Institute for Public Policy (Aos et al., 2001) estimated the cost per youth of about $2,000 (plus foster placement costs), which represents a savings of about $22,000 per youth relative to placement in group homes, and further savings of more than $87,000 in victim costs for each individual in OTFC.

Functional Family Therapy (FFT). Functional Family Therapy is a third community-based intervention for juvenile offenders. It is somewhat older than either MST or OTFC, having been used for almost 30 years. It is provided by a single therapist, who has a caseload of 12–15 cases, with weekly sessions over an average period of three months. As the name implies, it is family focused, and is often

delivered in the home (Alexander et al., 1998). Quality assurance/treatment integrity is addressed by careful training of therapists, yearly on-site consultation, ongoing telephone consultation, feedback from families, and weekly supervision. As we have seen, such quality assurance is a component that is common to FFT, MST, and OTFC—all take steps to ensure that services are delivered as intended.

The OJJDP identified FFT as a model treatment program (Mihalic et al., 2001). An early study of FFT (Alexander & Parsons, 1973) involved a randomized trial of FFT delivered to 13- to 16-year-old status offenders (those committing offenses such as truancy or running away from home that would not be illegal if committed by an adult), with 46 families receiving FFT and another 40 receiving family-centered "treatment as usual." The recidivism rate for those receiving FFT was 50% lower than it was in the comparison group. A second study (Gordon, Arbuthnot, Gustafson, & McGreen, 1988) involved 54 youths who had committed more serious offenses. The comparison group was composed of randomly selected youth who had not been referred for family therapy, which is termed a *no treatment control group*. The recidivism rate for those receiving FFT (11%) was substantially lower than for those in the group that did not receive treatment (80%).

These and other studies indicate that FFT is associated with a significant reduction in recidivism when compared with those receiving "treatment as usual" and others receiving no treatment (Alexander et al., 1998). The same Washington State Institute for Public Policy report (Aos et al., 2001) noted earlier, which described the cost and savings associated with MST and OTFC, also indicated that FFT had an average cost of $2,161 per participant, saved an average of $14,149 in costs for intervention compared with standard treatment in the juvenile justice system, and saved another $45,000 in victim costs per participant.

How would Marcus (Box 15.1) have done with OTFC or FFT? Consider the similarities between these two approaches and MST on the dimensions described earlier in this chapter. All three directly target important influences such as substance abuse, family problems, and educational deficits. All three involve intensive work, including clinical interventions, and are careful to ensure that the planned interventions are actually delivered. (Remember the unscheduled 6:00 A.M. Sunday meeting with Marcus's family after missed appointments? This kind of extreme but effective response is sometimes necessary.) All three approaches use different interventions delivered in more than one setting, such as at home and in the school. They are delivered in the community rather than an institution, and set goals that are developmentally appropriate. Finally, they are carefully planned and monitored for consistency with the plan. Marcus probably would have responded favorably to any of these three empirically supported interventions.

Secure, Residential Interventions

The previous section described three interventions that appear effective, both in terms of reducing the risk of reoffending and in saving money. So why not deliver most or all of juvenile interventions in the community, using MST, OTFC, or FFT? There are two answers to this question. First, not all communities offer these interventions. We cannot assume that because an effective intervention *could* be delivered in the community, it *will* be. Second, many judges would be inclined to place a youth in a secure residential facility as a consequence of a delinquency adjudication for a serious offense, even if that youth could possibly be treated in the community. Why? Community values (which judges represent) may support such a placement. The *publicly perceived* risk to society is lower when a youth is placed in a secure residential program, even though the actual risk (gauged through outcome research) may not be. Unfortunately, the impact of different placements for juveniles who commit serious offenses is a very difficult issue to answer through research. The ideal study to help understand the impact of a given program or placement involves random assignment to such a program, comparing the outcomes to those from the "treatment as usual" group. Very few judges,

juvenile system leaders, or legislators would be likely to support research that involved randomly placing very serious offenders in the community (versus in residential placement) to determine the impact of each on subsequent reoffense risk.

Accordingly, we must describe residential placements and their effectiveness without the best kind of evidence. We might add that while this is inconvenient for researchers, it is probably appropriate for those who represent our society and are responsible for promoting its safety. It would be very helpful to have good evidence about program effectiveness, but certainly a tragedy if citizens were victimized by offending as a result of such research. This is the main reason why research with random assignment is difficult to do in the juvenile and criminal justice systems—and why researchers must be satisfied with comparing a given intervention to "treatment as usual" rather than "no treatment." In a study like this, no citizen is put at additional risk, which could be the case when "no treatment" is provided to a group of serious offenders.

A meta-analysis of the predictors of general recidivism in juveniles (Cottle, Lee, & Heilbrun, 2001) suggested a number of "treatment targets" that may be addressed at any stage of the intervention process. However, since residential placement is typically longer and more intensive, these issues may be particularly relevant for residential placement. The predictors (and treatment targets) include, in order of their strength, nonsevere pathology (such as conduct disorder, for example), family problems, ineffective use of leisure time, delinquent peers, and substance abuse. A smaller meta-analysis, focusing on predictors of recidivism in violent juvenile offenders (Heilbrun, Lee, and Cottle, 2005), identified cognitive and family therapies as more effective in reducing recidivism rates than usual services. This underscores an important weakness in residential interventions: If the juvenile is isolated from his or her family because of the location of the program, it is much more difficult to involve the families in a meaningful way. Conversely, one of the common features of the effective community-based interventions discussed earlier in this chapter is the close involvement of families in the intervention.

One meta-analysis of 32 studies of juvenile and adult treatment programs, many of them residential, found a reduction in recidivism in 75% of the studies (Redondo, Sanchez-Meca & Garrido, 1999). Behavioral and cognitive-behavioral treatments appear to be most effective in reducing recidivism. Lipsey's (1992) meta-analysis of the impact of intervention on general recidivism risk in juveniles included a large number of studies (443) and estimated a 10% decrease in delinquency rates for juveniles receiving some kind of intervention. More frequent contact and longer periods of treatment were associated with more favorable outcomes—but only to a certain extent. This suggests that there is a "drop-off" in effectiveness of the intervention beyond a certain duration. More structured and multimodal treatments also had a stronger impact. Lipsey and Wilson's (1998) meta-analysis of 83 treatment programs for institutionalized juvenile offenders found that the most effective treatments reduced violent recidivism risk by 15–20%. The most effective of the residential treatments involved interpersonal skills training and family-centered interventions. As was true for MST, OTFC, and FFT, the most effective treatment programs were attentive to quality assurance, making them consistent with the treatment model. Individual characteristics of the juveniles being treated had little effect on these outcomes.

This research tells us that residential placements for juveniles can be effective, particularly when they focus on skills training (in areas like anger control and decision making), vocational training, educational and mental health needs, and also employ a treatment model that is "checked" through quality assurance. They should also be safe. If residents do not feel safe, it is very unlikely that rehabilitation efforts will be effective.

No comprehensive programs in juvenile residential settings have been studied through empirical research regarding their effectiveness. However, there have been studies of specific kinds of facilities, where youth are placed for mental health or substance abuse treatment—sometimes through court order (OJJDP, 2008). The OJJDP identified three residential programs supported by research. Two programs which focused on the treatment of substance abuse

included some juveniles, as well as other youths who were not involved in the juvenile justice system. In both programs, participation resulted in reduced levels of drug and alcohol abuse, although one program did not show a reduced rate of offending after one year (Morral, McCaffrey, & Ridgeway, 2004), and the second did not even look at reoffending as an outcome in the study (Morehouse & Tobler, 2000). The third effective residential program—the Mendota Juvenile Treatment Center (Caldwell & Van Rybroek, 2005)—combines security with mental health treatment for adolescents who have not responded well to "treatment as usual" in Wisconsin's juvenile justice system. The goal is to interrupt the escalation of defiance and legal consequences. Individualized therapy, behavioral control, and motivational interviewing are among the approaches used in this program. Those treated in this program were significantly less likely to recidivate within two years when compared with other juveniles with similar offenses who had been assessed (but not treated) in this program. This may be a particularly useful approach for serious offenders who also have substantial mental health problems.

A primary goal of residential treatment for juveniles is to reduce the deficits that are associated with reoffending risk. One approach to addressing anger problems (Anger Replacement Training; Goldstein, 2004) can be delivered either in a residential or community setting. It involves meeting with a therapist three times weekly for 10 weeks, and focuses on the development of specific skills such as impulse control, anger control, and thinking ahead, as well as reasoning. Research has demonstrated reductions in anger problems in secure residential settings (Goldstein, 2004), although the impact on recidivism risk has not yet been studied (Heilbrun et al., in press).

Another anger management program has been developed for girls in residential juvenile facilities. The Juvenile Justice Anger Management (JJAM) Treatment for Girls is an 8-week, 16-session group intervention that is delivered with careful attention to treatment integrity (through manuals and careful training of therapists) and intended to teach self-control, problem solving, and anger management

---

B o x 15.2   THE CASE OF THOMAS HARRIS: IMPRISONED, VIOLENT, AND SKEPTICAL

In the spring of 2008, 18-year-old Thomas Harris sat in a locked cell in an Ohio juvenile prison, a place he'd been for 2½ years. (This is longer than most juveniles are incarcerated, even for serious offenses.) In that time, he'd had group therapy approximately twice a month, had been beaten up 12 times, and had sustained a fractured leg and cut lip.

So when the agency that runs Ohio's juvenile prison agreed to improve the conditions for juvenile offenders—including offering better mental health and medical treatment and reducing violence—Harris was understandably skeptical. He said in a telephone interview from prison, "They tell us 'We're going to hire more staff to make you feel safer and hire more social workers so we can get you on the road to success.' It never happens" (DeMartini, 2008).

Violence in the Ohio juvenile prison system has been escalating in recent years. At the Marion County juvenile prison, juveniles attacked one another or a guard 504 times in 2007, up one-third from 2006. Violence may result from incarcerated juveniles' perceptions that they must fight to protect themselves. Violent acts may also be a means by which juveniles establish themselves in the hierarchy or get what they want. Violent behavior may also stem from a feeling of being disrespected. Whatever the reasons why Thomas Harris and others are involved in violence, such behavior must be controlled and minimized for rehabilitation to be effective.

But perhaps things are about to change. The agreement settled a class-action lawsuit filed against the Ohio prison system by a group of child-advocacy lawyers who claimed that the system was violent and ineffective. The new plan restricts how often and when prison staff can put juvenile offenders in solitary confinement, provides more medical and mental health services, and addresses overcrowding issues by releasing inmates who have served their minimum sentence and progressed in therapy.

(Goldstein, Dovidio, Kalbeitzer, Weil, & Strachan, 2007). A randomized controlled trial demonstrated significant reductions in anger, general aggression, verbal aggression, and indirect (relational) aggression for girls who completed the JJAM treatment in addition to treatment as usual, when compared with other girls receiving only treatment as usual.

When should juveniles be placed in the community, and when should they be assigned to secure residential placements? This decision depends on several considerations. Higher risk juveniles, often those who have a history of prior offenses, may need more secure placement. A judge may decide that a single offense, if it is very serious, merits a secure placement. Sometimes it can be important to remove a juvenile from extremely problematic circumstances (involving family, peers, gangs, and the like) that would continue with a community placement. However, there are substantial costs (both to the individual adolescent and to society) associated with secure placements. Juveniles very often respond better to correctional interventions when they are delivered in the community and can involve important influences such as family

and school. The case described in Box 15.2 highlights some of the complexities of secure placement.

This story raises some important questions about where juvenile correctional interventions should be made. When there are not proper resources and procedures in the community, interventions can be ineffective and put the public at continued risk. When there are not proper resources and procedures in secure settings, interventions are also ineffective and conditions can be brutal and dangerous. How can the necessary resources be obtained? (Lawsuits are one approach, as this story demonstrates.) How can they be most efficiently invested, so that interventions are as effective as possible? Much of the discussion in this chapter centers on the most efficient ways to use resources to provide effective interventions.

Reentry

Behavioral treatments for delinquent youth provided in residential facilities frequently do not generalize to the community after discharge (Quinsey, Harris, Rice, & Cormier, 2006). The process of **reentry** into the community should include planning for aftercare services (in some states, called juvenile **parole**) that are important to ensure ongoing treatment in the community and reduced recidivism risk. There are six areas in particular that are important in the reentry planning process: family functioning, housing (if not living with the family), school or job, mental health and/or substance abuse services, monitoring, and social support. Addressing each of these areas can help provide a smoother, safer transition from the youth's placement back to the community. Promising approaches to such relevant aftercare include the intensive aftercare program (IAP), wraparound services, and several of the community interventions already discussed (MST, FFT).

Intensive aftercare was developed to address the needs of chronic and serious juvenile offenders who are returning from residential placement. It used a graduated sanctions approach involving three steps: (1) prerelease planning; (2) a structured transition involving institutional and aftercare staff prior to, and following, release; and (3) long-term reintegrative activities to facilitate service delivery and social control (Altschuler & Armstrong, 1997). Studies addressing the impact of intensive aftercare (Altschuler, 1998) have produced mixed results. However, it also appears that many of the intensive aftercare interventions have not been consistent in providing appropriate and adequate treatment services. Accordingly, intensive aftercare remains an approach that appears promising and is consistent with both the emphasis on reentry planning and the "risk" principle of the RNR model ("treat the highest risk individuals most intensely"). But the empirical evidence about its effectiveness has been limited.

"Wraparound services" involve the delivery of individualized services in the context of collaboration between agencies such as those responsible for mental health care, educational services, and juvenile corrections. In this approach, funding follows the adolescent's treatment, rather than being allocated to particular programs (Brown, Borduin, & Henggeler, 2001). Such services are useful particularly for youths with serious mental or emotional problems.

One example of wraparound services designed to serve emotionally disturbed youths in the juvenile justice system is Wraparound Milwaukee. Families are involved in these services, which use "care coordinators" to assist in obtaining needed services from the available providers. Research on the functioning of Wraparound Milwaukee has indicated that it improves functioning, reduces recidivism, and improves the coordination of service delivery between the juvenile justice, mental health, and child welfare systems (Goldman & Faw, 1999; Kamradt, 2000). It is also less costly than residential treatment (by about $5,000 per month) or inpatient psychiatric care (by about $15,000 per month) (Goldman & Faw, 1999).

ADULT CORRECTIONS

The justifications for sentencing and intervening with adult offenders are somewhat different than for those with juveniles. Retribution, in particular, has been strongly emphasized during the last three decades—and particularly since 9/11, with concerns about terrorism being added to societal attention to criminal offending. One commentator has referred to this era of harsh punishment as an *imprisonment binge* (Ayre, 1995); another calls it *the mean season of corrections* (Haney, 2006). Indeed, as we pointed out in Chapter 14, there have never been as many Americans in the correctional system as there are at this very moment. We describe some of the psychological consequences to them, their families, and their communities in this chapter.

In many respects, though, the role of psychology in adult corrections incorporates the same correctional priorities that we saw with juveniles. Deterrence and rehabilitation as broad goals translate into the need to assess risks and structure interventions to reduce risk-relevant deficits.

Assessing and Diverting Offenders

The risk–need–responsivity (RNR) model, discussed earlier in this chapter, applies as well to adult corrections as it does with juveniles. Offenders who are convicted of criminal offenses (or charged with offenses but diverted from standard prosecution) will be assessed at some time, either as part of the legal proceeding or postsentencing, to gauge their risk and rehabilitation needs. In the prison system, this is called **classification.** Following the offender's commitment to the state department of corrections, he or she typically is evaluated at a classification center before being placed in a particular prison. The "risk" assessed at that stage is typically the risk of escape or misconduct within the prison, as these have direct implications for the security level of the prison to which this individual is assigned.

The risk of reoffending—and the needs relevant to such risk—are important for the vast majority of offenders who will be released from prison and return to the community following completion of their sentences, or upon the granting of parole. Risk–needs assessment can be facilitated by using a specialized measure. One example of such a measure is the Level of Service/Case Management Inventory (LS/CMI; Andrews, Bonta, & Wormith, 2004).

The LS/CMI is composed of 58 items in the following areas: Criminal History, Education/Employment, Family/Marital, Leisure/Recreation, Companions, Alcohol/Drug Problem, Procriminal Attitude/Orientation, and Antisocial Pattern (Andrews et al., 2004). It has been validated on both males and females. The males ($N = 956$), drawn from three Canadian correctional facilities, had a mean age of 26.9 years, mean sentence length of 325.6 days, and mean number of convictions of 3.7. The females ($N = 1,414$) were from the medium security institution for adult women operated by Ontario Ministry of Correctional Services; they had a mean age of 30.2 years and a mean sentence length of 322 days. LS/CMI total scores have been associated with (1) propensity for rules violations and assigned levels of supervision, (2) outcomes such as program outcome status, recidivism, and self-reported criminal activity in probation settings, (3) parole outcome, (4) the success of halfway house placements, and (5) maladjustment (Andrews & Bonta, 1995). This tool is useful in appraising risk for a variety of outcomes, including prison, various community settings, and under parole supervision.

A vitally important question may arise even before an offender is convicted, assessed, and classified,

however. In fact, one of the earliest questions concerning prosecution for criminal offending is whether the alleged offender should actually be prosecuted. There are a growing number of viable alternatives to the standard course of prosecution, conviction, and incarceration, particularly for individuals with serious mental illness or substance abuse.

One recent innovative development for diverting those with serious mental illness from prosecution is the **Sequential Intercept Model** (Munetz & Griffin, 2006). The model describes a number of points of "interception" at which an intervention can be made to prevent further progress along the conventional criminal justice track. These interception points are (1) law enforcement and emergency services; (2) initial detention and initial hearings; (3) jail, courts, forensic evaluations, and forensic commitments; (4) reentry from jails, state prisons, and forensic hospitalization; and (5) community corrections and community support. The model anticipates that most of these diversions will occur at early points (e.g., initial detention), although there is still a role for diversion into more specialized mental health services as late in the process as reentry and parole in the community.

Community-Based Interventions

Probation for adult offenders remains a frequent form of disposition of criminal charges, with the court placing the convicted offender on community supervision in lieu of incarceration. At the end of 2007, over 5.1 million adult men and women were supervised in the community. Most of these (over 80%) were on probation. The total population of offenders under supervision in the community grew by 103,100 (about 2%) during 2007. Offenses for those on probation included misdemeanors (51%), felonies (47%), and "other" (3%). The most frequent offenses of those on probation were drug charges (27%); this was also the most frequent offense for those on parole (37%). A total of 23% of those on probation were women; 55% were White, 29% African American, and 19% Hispanic (Bureau of Justice Statistics, 2008c).

Correctional supervision in the community involves monitoring the adherence to specified conditions. This is true for both probation and parole. The number of conditions and the nature of the monitoring can vary, depending on the individual's needs. Standard conditions involve specifying how often individuals must meet with a parole officer, where they will live, whether they will work (or receive another kind of financial support, such as Social Security Disability), and certain activities that must be avoided (e.g., drinking or drug use, weapon possession). Additional conditions can be added as needed. For example, if the individual had a serious drug abuse problem, he or she might be required to undergo urine screens and attend substance abuse treatment and Narcotics Anonymous meetings. An individual with a severe mental illness might be required to attend mental health treatment, take prescribed medication, and meet with a case manager. Requiring adherence to specified conditions and monitoring whether the individual actually does comply with these conditions mean that some individuals will violate the requirements of their probation or parole. If they do, there may be serious consequences, including the possibility of returning to a correctional facility. But those who do comply with the conditions of their probation or parole are more likely to be successful in returning, crime-free, to society. We describe a typical defendant on probation in Box 15.3.

Some people are required to undergo mental health treatment as a condition of community supervision. To what extent are probation and parole effective interventions for these individuals? This question was considered in some detail by Skeem and Louden (2006), who reviewed articles published between 1975 and 2005 on adults with mental illness on probation or parole. They concluded that the link between mental illness and supervision failure is complex and indirect (Dauphinot, 1996; Solomon & Draine, 1995; Solomon, Draine, & Marcus, 2002). However, they also noted that specialty agencies, in which offenders are assigned to officers with smaller caseloads, are more effective than traditional caseloads. They are also more effective in linking probationers with treatment services and reducing the risk of probation violation, and possibly reducing the short-term risk of parole violation. The

use of specialized probation and parole services for these purposes is consistent with a larger trend, discussed throughout this chapter, of providing specialized rehabilitation services for individuals in particular clinical categories (e.g., severe mental illness, substance abuse). On that note, we now turn to specialized interventions in the community—drug courts and mental health courts—that are also outside the standard stream of prosecution and incarceration of criminal offenders.

Drug Courts in Corrections.   Since 1980, in part because of the "War on Drugs" that began in the United States in the 1970s and expanded into the 1980s, the number of those charged with and convicted of drug offenses has expanded dramatically. Jail and prison admissions more than tripled during this period (Harrison & Karberg, 2003), with drug offenses involved in about 60% of federal cases and 30% of state-level cases contributing to this increase (Harrison & Beck, 2002). Neither punishing drug offenders by incarcerating them for long periods (the *public safety* approach) nor providing treatment while conceptualizing drug addiction as a disease (the *public health* approach) has been particularly effective in reducing the prevalence of drug abuse and drug-related crime. About 70% of drug offenders reoffend within three years of release from prison (Martin, Butzin, Saum, & Inciardi, 1999), while prison drug rehabilitation programs have shown little reoffense risk-reduction impact and even less impact on reducing the rate of drug use relapse (Marlowe, 2002).

As we discussed in Chapter 2, a community intervention that is both more effective and less costly than incarceration and prison rehabilitation would be welcome. Drug courts appear to be such an alternative. They are a kind of relatively new intervention known as "problem-solving courts," which have been influenced both by public safety and public health considerations. Consistent with the legal philosophy of therapeutic jurisprudence (Wexler & Winick, 1996), such courts consider how laws and legal decision makers can improve lives and solve problems and are designed to promote rehabilitation. Like the effective juvenile

---

B o x 15.3   THE CASE OF LOUISE FRANKLIN: A DEFENDANT ON PROBATION

Louise Franklin was a 24-year-old mother of three who was arrested for assault following an argument with a neighbor who she thought was stealing from her. Prior to the disposition of her case, Ms. Franklin was evaluated by a probation officer with respect to her criminal history (she had no prior arrests), vocational status and financial circumstances (she was the sole source of support for her children), home and family circumstances, drug and alcohol use, and medical/mental health history. Based on this evaluation (called a "presentence investigation"), and also using the results of a short, actuarial tool to inform the court about reoffense risk level, Ms. Franklin was recommended for probation as a low-risk offender. The judge considered this recommendation and assigned a one-year period of probation following a plea bargain in which Ms. Franklin pled guilty to assault.

There were several "standard" conditions of probation imposed: having monthly meetings with her probation officer, obtaining permission from her probation officer prior to leaving the city, paying $250 in restitution to cover her victim's medical costs, and maintaining continued employment and her current residence. There was one additional condition specific to her probation involving completing anger management group therapy. This condition was imposed because the judge observed that Ms. Franklin had been in two arguments (although not physical altercations) with other neighbors during the past year that resulted in police being contacted.

Ms. Franklin was glad that she was not incarcerated. She was also diligent about keeping her scheduled appointments with her probation officer. However, she insisted for the first three months that she had been unfairly treated, that her neighbor had started their dispute, and she responded by slapping her neighbor (resulting in a fall and a trip to the emergency room) only to protect herself. She also had not paid the $250

in restitution by the six-month mark in her probationary year, when she was required to have done so. Her probation officer indicated to her in their sixth monthly meeting that she must do so, or he would inform the court that she was in violation of the conditions of her probation. (This would result in a violation hearing and possible incarceration.) After this meeting, Ms. Franklin made arrangements to make this restitution payment within one week.

She attended weekly meetings of her anger management group for a total of 20 sessions, the scheduled duration of the group. She did not miss a meeting, and actively participated in the group. Her contributions reflected her initial feeling that she did not have a temper problem—others often provoked her, and she was justified in her reactions to such provocations. As the group progressed, however, Ms. Franklin began to see that others with similar perspectives did appear harsh and impulsive in their responses during the group sessions. She learned and practiced alternatives to angry dispute resolution, including identifying her own feelings better, avoiding confrontation when she was already angry, avoiding "high-risk" situations but dealing more openly and assertively with conflict, and "pausing and counting" before responding in situations in which unexpected confrontation occurred. She reported a noticeable decrease in the number of times she lost her temper after four months of being involved in this group. She also described the additional benefit of feeling more patient with her children. Her therapist reported to her probation officer that Ms. Franklin had satisfactorily completed anger management group therapy after six months. Ms. Franklin had satisfied all conditions of her probation after one year, so she was discharged from the supervision of the Department of Parole and Probation at that time.

---

interventions described earlier in this chapter, drug courts are intended to provide an intensive and specific intervention targeting a very strong risk factor (substance abuse) for reoffending. Theoretically, for offenders with a serious substance abuse problem and a history of offending related directly to this problem, treating this risk factor (and ensuring that the right kind of treatment is delivered) should substantially reduce the risk of criminal reoffending.

Drug courts provide judicially supervised drug abuse treatment and case management services to nonviolent drug-involved offenders, taking them out of the standard "prosecution/conviction/ incarceration" process. Participation is voluntary, and whether a defendant is eligible may be at the discretion of the prosecutor. Diversion in drug courts comes in two forms. First, those charged with a crime may be diverted entirely from prosecution with the stipulation that they successfully complete the requirements imposed in drug court or face reinstatement of prosecution. Second, those who are convicted of a crime may be diverted to drug court to avoid prison or modify their probation conditions.

How well do they work? As we explained in Chapter 2, the research conducted during the last 15 years gives reason for optimism about this particular intervention. In essence, drug courts are more effective than virtually any other approach with substance abusing offenders (Marlowe, DeMatteo, & Festinger, 2003). They seem particularly good at reducing drug use and criminal recidivism (e.g., Belenko, 2001, 2002; Belenko, DeMatteo, & Patapis, 2007; Government Accountability Office, 2005). Belenko (1998, 1999, 2001) described nearly 100 drug courts, concluding that about 60% of drug court clients attended at least one year of treatment, and approximately 50% graduated from the drug court program. These figures compare favorably to probation, where very few individuals (less than 10%) attend one year of treatment (Goldkamp, 2000). Belenko (1999, 2001) also reported that the frequency of positive urine screens for drug court clients (less than 10%) is lower than for those on probation, and that criminal recidivism rates for drug court clients are also lower than for similar offenders under other kinds of supervision in the community.

Two randomized controlled trials (the strongest kind of research design) indicate that drug court effectiveness is greater than standard criminal justice approaches to offenders with substance abuse. Drug court clients in one study (Turner, Greenwood, Fain, & Deschenes, 1999) were rearrested within three years at a rate of 33%, compared with 47% of those with drug problems on other probation conditions. A second study using random assignment to drug court (Gottfredson & Exum, 2002) reported that 48% of drug court clients, as compared with 64% of "treatment as usual" adjudicated control clients, were rearrested within one year, although the percentages of those arrested from each group were about the same by the end of the second year (Gottfredson, Najaka, & Kearley, 2003). In addition, a meta-analysis (Wilson, Mitchell, & Mackenzie, 2006) of 50 studies representing 55 drug court program evaluations found that the majority of studies reported lower rates of reoffending among drug court participants, with the average difference being 26% across all studies. Taken together, this research provides strong evidence that drug courts are more effective at reducing the rates of both substance abuse and reoffending over outcome periods of one year and perhaps longer, compared with more traditional forms of community supervision such as parole and probation.

Mental Health Courts in Corrections.   We also described mental health courts in Chapter 2. They handle both felony and misdemeanor offenders (Redlich, Steadman, Monahan, Petrila, & Griffin, 2005). Juvenile mental health courts have also been developed (Cocozza & Shufelt, 2006). Mental health services that include psychotropic medication, case management, and individual and group therapy are among those delivered through such specialized courts, with progress monitored by the court. Despite local differences, most mental health courts feature (1) a specialized docket for selected offenders, (2) judicial supervision of clients, (3) regularly scheduled hearings, and (4) specific criteria that must be met to remain in, and complete, the program (Thompson, Osher, & Tomasini-Joshi, 2007).

Mental health courts provide adjudication and monitoring for a particular group of defendants. In the context of corrections, how well do they work? As we noted in Chapter 2, there is less empirical evidence for the effectiveness of mental health courts than for drug courts. There are also fewer well-designed studies (particularly randomized controlled trials), and the operation of mental health courts varies more widely across different courts. Consequently, it is more difficult to draw conclusions about the operation of mental health courts (Heilbrun et al., in press).

But there is some relevant research. Boothroyd, Poythress, McGaha, and Petrila (2003) compared mental health court offenders ($N = 121$) and criminal court offenders ($N = 101$). They reported that the percentage of individuals under mental health court jurisdiction who received behavioral health services increased from 36% to 53% after coming under mental health court jurisdiction, while only 28% of criminal court offenders received behavioral treatment. Another study compared mental health court clients charged with misdemeanors ($N = 368$) before and after coming under mental health court jurisdiction. It reported an increase in the hours of case management and medication management, and the days of outpatient service, as well as fewer crisis intervention services and inpatient days (Herinckx, Swart, Ama, Dolezal, & King, 2005).

Several other studies have focused on whether greater access to clinical services actually results in improved clinical functioning. In one study using random assignment of offenders ($N = 235$) to mental health court versus "treatment as usual" (criminal court), investigators found that participants in both conditions improved in satisfaction and independent functioning, but mental health court individuals reduced their drug use more and developed more independent living skills (Cosden, Ellens, Schnell, Yamini-Diouf, & Wolfe, 2003).

By contrast, another study comparing mental health court offenders ($N = 97$) with criminal court offenders ($N = 77$) did not find differences between the mental health functioning of these two groups, or the nature of the mental health services available to both groups (Boothroyd, Mercado, Poythress, Christy, & Petrila, 2005). The investigators suggested that one explanation for these results might be the fact that the mental health court judges did not have much control over whether the mental health services were actually delivered. If their explanation is correct, it underscores the importance of control over service delivery. It would not be particularly useful to develop a specialized mental health court and divert those with particular mental health needs into this court, unless there is some assurance that additional specialized mental health services are available to those under the jurisdiction of this specialized court.

Other research has focused on criminal recidivism as an outcome variable in studying the impact of mental health courts. There is also mixed evidence on

this question. One study (Trupin & Richards, 2003) reported that mental health court clients had fewer arrests postdischarge than did criminal court clients, while another study (Christy, Poythress, Boothroyd, Petrila, & Mehra, 2005) reported that the number of arrests decreased for mental health court clients—but not significantly more than it did for those in criminal court. A third study (Cosden et al., 2003) used random assignment of offenders ($N = 235$) to either assertive community treatment (a particular form of mental health case management involving additional services and small caseloads, sometimes used as part of mental health court) or the standard case management services associated with criminal court. After one year, mental health court clients had significantly fewer arrests and convictions. By two years, however, these differences were much smaller, and both groups showed an increased number of arrests when compared with the first year (Cosden, Ellens, Schnell, & Yamini-Diouf, 2005).

One of the most important considerations in whether mental health court participation reduces criminal recidivism is whether the client actually completes the treatment required by the court; participants completing mental health court in one study were nearly four times less likely to reoffend than were those who did not graduate (Herinckx et al., 2005). Indeed, participants in mental health court who do not complete the program may not differ from those who are processed through traditional criminal court. For instance, Moore and Hiday (2006) reported that those who completed mental health court were rearrested at a rate about one-fourth that of those in criminal court after one year—and those who did *not* complete mental health court were rearrested at about the same rate as the criminal court clients. Other investigators (McNiel & Binder, 2007) also noted both the risk reduction impact of mental health court and the importance of successfully completing mental health court.

A principle of effective intervention discussed earlier in this chapter is treatment integrity. In order to be effective, interventions need to be delivered the way they were intended, and need to be completed. The data from completers versus noncompleters in mental health courts are consistent with this principle.

If a defendant is processed through a mental health court and does not participate in the services required by the court, then we should not expect his or her outcome to be better than it would have been through standard prosecution and disposition.

This research suggests that mental health courts, like drug courts, can have a favorable impact on both symptoms amelioration and reoffense risk reduction—when services are delivered and clients participate. Mental health courts vary more than drug courts in how they are administered across sites, however, and the supporting research is not quite as strong methodologically. Several studies indicate that the value of participation in mental health court is greatly limited when participants do not complete the program required by the court.

Institutional Interventions

There are several important differences between jails and prisons, even though both are secure institutional facilities which incarcerate individuals who have been convicted of criminal offenses. A jail is a community-based facility that houses both individuals who are pretrial (those who have been charged with offenses, but not yet convicted) and others who have been convicted of relatively minor offenses, usually with sentences no longer than a year. By contrast, a prison is part of a correctional system that is either operated by the state (usually a state department of corrections will include a number of prisons) or the federal government (which operates the Federal Bureau of Prisons within the Department of Justice). Those who are incarcerated in prison have all been convicted of criminal offenses. They have also received sentences that are longer than the relatively short sentences associated with jail inmates. Prison sentences can range from slightly over one year to life, and prisons also house those who have received a death sentence.

The functions carried out by psychologists also differ between jails and prisons. There are four broad purposes served by mental health professionals, particularly psychologists, in both jails and prisons: classification, consultation/crisis intervention, rehabilitation, and reentry planning. Because the nature of each function varies according to the facility, each will be discussed in terms of whether it is carried out in a jail or a prison.

The Role of Psychologists in Jails.   There has been a very substantial increase in the number of jail beds between the years 2000 and 2007. According to the Bureau of Justice Statistics (2008b), the total number of jail beds in the United States as of midyear 2007 was 813,502, an increase from an estimated 677,787 beds as of the same time in 2000. In 2007, nearly 30% of these beds were contained in the 50 largest jails in the country, and about half of all jail inmates were incarcerated in the 173 jails (6% of the total number) with a daily census of 1,000 or more inmates.

There is a much higher rate of severe mental illness in jail than in the general population (Bureau of Justice Statistics, 2006). For example, using inmate self-report of experiencing symptoms of severe mental illness such as hallucinations or delusions during the last 12 months, 17.5% of jail inmates reported the former and 13.7% the latter. These percentages are substantially higher than the percentage of adults over the age of 18 who report having experienced *either* symptom (3.1%).

Given these numbers, we might expect that many of the psychological services provided to jail inmates would focus on those with mental disorders. Such services, described in a national survey of U.S. jails (Steadman & Veysey, 1997), include

- Screening, evaluation, classification
- Diversion (helping to determine whether a pretrial inmate might meet criteria for a community-based program such as drug court or mental health court)
- Suicide prevention
- Crisis intervention
- Case management services/reentry (liaison with community treatment providers, planning for release, assistance with housing and transportation)
- Coordinating volunteers (teaching, mentoring, tutoring, guiding release)

Aerial view of Pelican Bay prison

- Teaching life skills
- Group therapy for inmates and their families

Larger jails with more resources might be able to offer most or all of these services, so a psychologist's role in such jails would be more varied. Smaller jails, by contrast, might be limited to screening, suicide prevention, and crisis intervention.

The Role of Psychologists in Prisons. The contemporary prison can trace its roots to London in the 19th century, when Jeremy Bentham developed the notion that incarceration could be considered part of punishment rather than just a means of holding an individual until trial (as jails do) or carrying out of a death sentence. Facilities at that time were sometimes called "penitentiaries," with the goal of invoking penance from those who were confined in them.

Imprisoning offenders is not necessarily the most effective approach to reducing the risk of future offending. This is perhaps not a surprise. Among the goals of criminal sentencing and incarceration discussed earlier in this chapter and in Chapter 14, are retribution, incapacitation, and general deterrence. Although lengthy sentences and punitive prison conditions may be consistent with these goals, such conditions are not necessarily consistent with the goal of rehabilitation. A meta-analysis of over 100 studies (Smith, Goggin, & Gendreau, 2002) indicated that the rate of reoffending following release from prison was 7% higher than following the completion of nonresidential sanctions.

Some approaches to prison-based rehabilitation are more effective than others, however. Bonta (1997) classified rehabilitation programs as either "appropriate" or "inappropriate" by determining their consistency with risk/need/responsivity principles discussed earlier in the chapter. Appropriate (RNR-consistent) treatments reduced criminal reoffending by an average of 50% when compared with inappropriate approaches. Appropriate treatment approaches were those that systematically assessed offender risk and needs with specialized tools (e.g., the Level of Service/Case Management Inventory; Andrews et al., 2004), targeted the criminogenic needs of offenders in treatment, and used cognitive-behavioral approaches to change deficits and increase strengths. By contrast, programs classified as inappropriate might provide intensive services for low-risk offenders and target noncriminogenic needs such as self-esteem. Such interventions were associated with slight *increases* in recidivism. Bonta (1997) concluded that RNR-consistent interventions, whether provided in prison or in the community, reduce recidivism risk and protect the public in the process. The exclusive application of punitive approaches, by contrast, does not reduce reoffending risk and is therefore less useful for public safety—at least via the rehabilitation of offenders.

One other approach that shows promise, particularly in treating drug offenders in prison, is the **therapeutic community** (TC). This involves an approach in which the staff, other clients, and physical setting are all part of the therapeutic environment. Group therapy, individual counseling, "community meetings" involving all residents, and specialized interventions to build skills in areas such as anger control, decision making, and recognizing high-risk situations are all used in the TC. Staff functions are not divided into those responsible for "security" versus those responsible for "treatment" (as is often the case in a secure hospital or correctional setting). Instead, all staff members are considered to be part of the rehabilitation process. All residents are likewise involved in maintaining an environment in which therapeutic goals are clear and important.

In correctional settings, the TC has most often been used to treat those with substance abuse problems. One quasi-experimental study (Welsh, 2007) focused on prison TC drug treatment program participants ($N = 217$) and comparison group participants ($N = 491$) for two-year outcomes following release. Prison TC was effective even without mandatory community aftercare, although effects varied somewhat across different outcome measures and sites. TC interventions significantly reduced rearrest and reincarceration

rates, but not drug relapse rates. Postrelease employment predicted a reduction in drug relapse and reincarceration.

One of the questions concerning the impact of rehabilitation in prison concerns "how much is enough?" Criminal sentences are imposed for a specific amount of time, not necessarily with rehabilitation as a primary determinant. But one interesting study (Bourgon & Armstrong, 2005) asked precisely this question: How much treatment is needed to reduce criminal reoffending? Researchers considered the recidivism rates of offenders in a Canadian prison ($N = 620$) who were followed up for one year after their release. While incarcerated, they had received (1) no treatment, (2) 100 hours of treatment over 5 weeks, (3) 200 hours of treatment over 10 weeks, or (4) 300 hours of treatment over 15 weeks. Treatment programs were cognitive-behavioral, and focused on substance abuse, criminal attitudes, aggression, and criminal peers. Offenders' risk and needs had also been assessed as part of their incarceration. A total of 31% of offenders who received treatment in any dosage recidivated, compared with 41% who received no treatment. Offenders with different risk–needs levels required different amounts of treatment for an effective "dosage." In high-risk offenders with many criminogenic needs, for example, 300 hours of treatment reduced the observed rate of recidivism from 59% to 38%. By contrast, for medium-risk offenders with few criminogenic needs, 100 hours of treatment was sufficient to reduce recidivism from 28% to 12%—but more treatment was not associated with a further reduction in recidivism. For high- and medium-risk offenders with a moderate number of criminogenic needs, 200 hours of treatment was associated with a recidivism rate of 30%, as compared to 44% for similar offenders who received no treatment.

These results have several implications for rehabilitation in prison. First, just as in correctional interventions with juveniles, it is useful to employ a formal, structured approach to assessing relevant needs and intervening according to those needs. Second, it is possible to identify a "dosage effect" for relevant treatment, and to administer such treatment according to who is likely to receive the most benefit. Third, it is feasible to have a favorable impact over a relatively short period of time. Long sentences are not necessary to rehabilitate many of those who are sentenced to prison—so the justification for keeping inmates in prison for a lengthy period must come from other reasons, such as retribution and deterrence. Box 15.4 concerns the incarceration and prospects for rehabilitation of a former professional athlete.

Psychological Consequences of Imprisonment

The psychological effects of institutional confinement are complex. Vast differences in prison conditions are undoubtedly important: Incarceration in a well-run, minimum-security prison with adequate programming and treatment options will have different effects than imprisonment in an overcrowded, mismanaged facility where staff use highly punitive practices such as excessive surveillance and isolation to control inmates. The psychological vulnerability and resilience of inmates and the length of their confinement matter as well. One prison expert who summarized the literature concluded that:

> imprisonment is not generally or uniformly devastating … Imprisonment, in and of itself, does not seem inevitably to damage individuals. [Yet] relationships with family and friends can be severed … particular vulnerabilities and inabilities to cope and adapt can come to the fore in the prison setting, [and] the behavior patterns and attitudes that emerge can take many forms, from deepening social and emotional withdrawal to extremes of aggression and violence. (Porporino, 1990, p. 35–36)

For a number of reasons, high-quality empirical studies of the psychological consequences of imprisonment are limited. First, it has been difficult to develop a standard measure to quantify the effects of long-term incarceration because they are so variable and subjective. Second, most studies have assessed the effects of incarceration among inmates still imprisoned (e.g., Bonta & Gendreau, 1990), and because prisoners can adapt and attempt to achieve a tolerable existence *inside* the prison, the full psychological implications of long-term confinement may be apparent only after release (Haney, 2006).

But social scientists have gleaned some generalities about the consequences of long-term incarceration. Many inmates show a particular pattern of coping mechanisms in response to high levels of prison stress. They may become hypervigilant in order to deal with the significant risks to their personal safety, learn to project a "tough guy veneer," socially isolate themselves and suppress any signs of emotion, and become generally distrustful of others (d'Arti, 1981; Jose-Kampfner, 1990; McCorkle, 1992). None of these characteristics will facilitate their reintegration into society, of course.

Inmates report that their initial period of confinement is the most difficult (Harding & Zimmerman, 1989). Over time, a gradual process takes place in which prisoners adjust to their environment. Sociologist Donald Clemmer called this process **prisonization** and defined it as "the taking on in greater or less degree of the folkways, mores, customs, and general culture of the penitentiary" (Clemmer, 1958). This tends to happen without conscious awareness by inmates as they gradually learn to give up control of choices and decisions, and to depend on institutional rulemakers to provide structure and routine to their lives. One commentator likened it to a kind of "behavioral deep freeze" (Zamble, 1992) from which it is difficult to emerge, especially into the unstructured and unpredictable world that awaits an inmate upon release.

Psychologists have identified a number of other consequences of imprisonment. Impoverished conditions and arbitrary and abusive treatment diminish inmates' sense of identity and self-worth, causing some to project a reputation for toughness and others to appear distant and aloof. Still others externalize their rage and adopt aggressive and violent survival strategies (Toch, 1985). Although estimates of the frequency of prison rapes vary, there is little doubt that their consequences can be severe (King, 1992).

B o x 15.4   THE CASE OF MICHAEL VICK: WAS HE REHABILITATED IN PRISON?

Michael Vick was the star quarterback for the Atlanta Falcons until he and his codefendants were arrested and charged with running a dogfighting kennel in Virginia. In September, 2007, while he was awaiting trial, Vick tested positive for marijuana. He was convicted of these charges in federal court, and received a sentence of 23 months in the federal system. He left Virginia in January 2008 to serve his sentence at a U.S. Bureau of Prisons facility in Leavenworth, Kansas.

How would the Bureau of Prisons have attempted to rehabilitate Michael Vick? First, he would have gone through "classification" (a period of assessment and individualized information gathering) to decide where he would be assigned. If he had a long sentence for a very serious charge, presented a substantial risk to harm others, or appeared to be an escape risk, he would probably have been assigned to a high-security facility. Apparently he did not meet these criteria, however, as Leavenworth is a minimum security prison. Then, prison staff would have needed to decide what particular deficits contributed to his involvement in the dogfighting charges for which he was convicted.

Another issue is drug use. Given that Vick tested positive for marijuana three months before he was sentenced, he might be referred for substance abuse treatment by prison staff. Bureau of Prisons policy on treating drug abuse involves having those in treatment (lasting at least 500 hours over a period of 6–12 months) set apart from the general prison population.

Would it help Vick to be involved in treatment to increase his empathy for animals? At least one person thinks so. The president of the group People for the Ethical Treatment of Animals wrote this to the editor of the online news service BasehorInfo.com:

> To the editor:
> Shortly after Michael Vick was indicted on federal dogfighting charges, he attended an empathy class at PETA's headquarters in Norfolk, Va. He learned a lot from the class that his friends had never taught him, including that dogs have feelings and deserve better than being treated like fighting machines.
> I believe that having time to reflect in prison, being brought to the brink of bankruptcy and being encouraged to do right might have made a new man of Michael Vick. I would be willing to bet he now knows that a man should be a dog's best friend—not his worst nightmare.
> Perhaps I am naïve, but I hope not. There is never any worth in hating; the only thing that

Michael Vick

makes life worth living is holding out hope that people will examine the bad things they do and change. I hope that Michael Vick has changed, and I hope that the people who were guided by his example will change too.
> Ingrid E. Newkirk,
> President, People for the Ethical Treatment of Animals
> Norfolk, Va.

Of course, it would also be helpful for Vick to be involved in planning to return to the community—the reentry process for adult inmates. Where will he live? How will he be employed? An individual like Michael Vick has strengths that most people in prison do not have. However, rehabilitating anyone in prison involves assessing their risk of reoffending, addressing their deficits that make such reoffending more likely, and strengthening their characteristics that help them live a responsible life without criminal offending. Some of these questions were answered when Vick signed with the Philadelphia Eagles in 2009, resuming his career as a professional football player. Other questions remain, however. Is he genuinely remorseful for his offending? Can he live his life without future offending? Can he avoid people and situations that elevate his risk for reoffending?

Obviously, inmates with both diagnosed and un-identified psychiatric disorders are at heightened risk and some inmates experience prison-related maladies in response to their harsh conditions. The secondary effects of incarceration extend to blameless spouses and the children of inmates. Having a parent in prison is a strong predictor of behavioral problems including future lawbreaking (Mumula, 2000).

One scholar of correctional systems raised the intriguing possibility that prisons themselves serve to further the maladaptive and dysfunctional behavioral patterns that resulted in confinement in the first place:

> [T]he long-term effects of exposure to powerful and destructive situations, contexts, and structures mean that prisons themselves also can act as criminogenic agents—in both their primary effects on prisoners and secondary effects on the lives of the persons who are connected to them ... Programs of prisoner change cannot ignore the situations and social conditions that prisoners encounter after they are released if there is to be any real chance of sustaining whatever positive growth or personal gains were achieved during imprisonment. (Haney, 2006, p. 8)

We discuss the problems associated with reentry into society later in this chapter.

Confinement at Guantanamo Bay

Any discussion of modern prison conditions must include the U.S. government's confinement of prisoners at Guantanamo Bay, Cuba. In the aftermath of the 2001 battle with the Taliban in Afghanistan, the United States shipped some of the battlefield prisoners to the naval base at Guantanamo Bay, Cuba, to be held as "unlawful combatants." The U.S. government contended that the prisoners were not entitled to the protections provided to prisoners of war by the Geneva Convention because they had not fought as conventional troops are supposed to fight— uniformed, in regular units, and with a command structure. Those sent to Guantanamo were suspected

of having some involvement in terrorist activities, though not necessarily in the 9/11 attack on the World Trade Center and the Pentagon.

In subsequent years, Guantanamo has served as a holding station for persons suspected of involvement in terrorism. Those incarcerated were questioned, sometimes returned to their home countries, but rarely charged with a crime. As some prisoners were sent home, others were brought in from Iraq, Afghanistan, or elsewhere, keeping the population between 500 and 600 for several years. In June 2003, 20 children were among the prisoners from 42 countries held in conditions more restrictive than those of a "super-max" prison (Conover, 2003). As of early 2009, approximately 250 detainees remained at Guantanamo Bay.

As the years have passed, the world press focused on the strange circumstances at the tip of Cuba, a sliver of land occupied by the United States under an ancient treaty but not part of the United States. In fact, the U.S. government had sent the prisoners to Guantanamo precisely because the naval station that served as the prison is not on American soil. The government believed that U.S. courts could not consider detainees' complaints because they were not being held in the United States. However, detainees filed lawsuits in federal courts, claiming they were being held illegally, were not "unlawful combatants," and were entitled to release, or at least to the protections afforded to prisoners of war. (The Geneva Convention requires a hearing by a "competent tribunal" if there is any doubt about a whether a prisoner is an "unlawful combatant" or a "prisoner of war.") Some of the detainees claimed that they were innocent civilians and were entitled to release, and others claimed that they should be treated as "lawful combatants" and hence entitled to the full protection of the Geneva Convention.

In June of 2004, the Supreme Court held that Guantanamo was effectively part of the United States and that the federal courts therefore could hear the detainees' claims. The Court opined that the detainees were entitled to hearings and that they could not be held indefinitely without charge, but it did not decide what kinds of hearings were necessary (*Rasul v. Bush*, 2004).

In June 2005, *Time* magazine's cover story exposed the Guantanamo interrogation log of "Detainee 063," Mohammed al-Qahtani, who may have been the 20th hijacker—the person who was supposed to be a member of the team that hijacked United Airlines Flight 93 that crashed in Pennsylvania on September 11. Some of the recorded interrogation methods used on al-Qahtani border on torture. He was forced to urinate in his clothes, go without sleep, and bark like a dog. The revelations of the al-Qahtani log prompted commentator Anthony Lewis to write, "We Americans have a sense of ourselves as a moral people. We have led the way in the fight for human rights in the world. Mistreating prisoners makes the world see our moral claims as hypocrisy" (Lewis, 2005, p. A23). In the article, Lewis referred to FBI reports of abuse similar to that reported in the al-Qahtani log, including prisoners chained in the fetal position for lengthy periods, deprived of food and water, and forced to defecate and urinate in their clothes.

The conditions at Guantanamo Bay raise many issues, including the definition of torture as a legal and moral matter, whether combatant hearings may be held by military tribunals, what due process rights detainees are accorded, whether those detained as "unlawful combatants" may be held for the duration of the "war against terror" (and how the end of such a war is declared), and whether those charged with a crime against the United States may be tried by a military commission as opposed to a civilian court. Although President Obama vowed, as one of his first acts in office, to close Guantanamo Bay, many of these questions linger.

The role that psychologists can and should play in interrogating detainees at Guantanamo Bay has been a very controversial issue. The American Psychological Association (APA) adopted a policy, effective in 2008, stating that psychologists cannot ethically participate in activities that involve torture. It reads (in part):

> BE IT RESOLVED that this unequivocal condemnation includes all techniques considered torture or cruel, inhuman or degrading treatment or punishment under

Guantanamo Bay detainees

the United Nations Convention Against Torture and Other Cruel, Inhuman, or Degrading Treatment or Punishment; the Geneva Conventions; the Principles of Medical Ethics Relevant to the Role of Health Personnel, Particularly Physicians, in the Protection of Prisoners and Detainees against Torture and Other Cruel, Inhuman, or Degrading Treatment or Punishment; the Basic Principles for the Treatment of Prisoners; or the World Medical Association Declaration of Tokyo. An absolute prohibition against the following techniques therefore arises from, is understood in the context of, and is interpreted according to these texts: mock executions; water-boarding or any other form of simulated drowning or suffocation; sexual humiliation; rape; cultural or religious humiliation; exploitation of fears, phobias or psychopathology; induced hypothermia; the use of psychotropic drugs or mind-altering substances; hooding; forced nakedness; stress positions; the use of dogs to threaten or intimidate; physical assault including slapping or shaking; exposure to extreme heat or cold; threats of harm or death; isolation; sensory deprivation and over-stimulation; sleep deprivation; or the threatened use of any of the above techniques to an individual or to members of an individual's family. Psychologists are absolutely prohibited from knowingly planning, designing, participating in or assisting in the use of all condemned techniques at any time and may not enlist others to employ these techniques in order to circumvent this resolution's prohibition. (APA, 2008)

Reentry

The process of reentry focuses on preparing inmates to move from incarceration back into the community and face a world that is fundamentally different from the one to which they adapted while in prison. To be successful, they must adjust quickly. Fortunately, there has been more emphasis on this transition during recent years, which is appropriate. In this chapter, we have seen the importance of services delivered in the community—and planning so that services are delivered as needed and intended. Partly because of the relatively recent nature of the emphasis on reentry in corrections, there is little empirical research regarding the effectiveness of reentry programs.

The priorities for reentry begin with the goal of reducing the risk of reoffending. There are a number of ways to pursue this goal. Just as drug courts and mental health courts target specific constellations of clinical symptoms with the expectation that providing relevant services in these areas will reduce the symptoms, promote better adjustment, *and* reduce recidivism risk, the reentry process aims to target risk-relevant needs as the individual returns to the community. Released inmates account for a

large proportion of the population with communicable health problems, for instance, including HIV/AIDS and hepatitis B and C (Mellow, Mukamal, LoBuglio, Solomon, Osborne, 2008). Reentry services can promote the provision of necessary health care services. They can also yield significant cost savings when done effectively, always an important consideration for local and state governments dealing with crime, especially during a recession.

Reentry can actually be considered broadly, to include services provided during custody, in preparation for release, and during the period of community supervision and eventual discharge. The custody phase involves measuring offenders' risks, needs, and strengths upon entry to the correctional facility and providing interventions designed to reduce risk, address needs, and build strengths. The release phase includes *inmate release preparation*, with a parole plan for supervision, housing, employment, drug testing, and other considerations, and *release decision making*, regarding the parole decision. The community supervision/discharge phase involves *supervision and services*, *revocation decision making* (including graduated sanctions in response to infractions), and *discharge and aftercare*, when community correctional supervision is terminated. This section of the chapter focuses on the community supervision/discharge phase of reentry.

Approximately 200 state parole officials are responsible for making decisions concerning release conditions for the offenders who are eligible for parole each year (Hughes, Wilson, & Beck, 2001), and for returning over 220,000 individuals to incarceration due to parole revocation (Harrison & Beck, 2005). About 400,000 of the 600,000 offenders released on parole each year are rearrested within three years (Petersilia, 2001), underscoring the importance of the reentry process and its potential to reduce new offending.

The "community classification center" is part of the trend toward greater structure in reentry. Such facilities accept inmates who are released from prison and returning to the community. However, rather than place them directly in the community, or send them home, the community classification centers provide assessment for a limited period of time, and structure the reentry process so that individuals receive housing and services that are consistent with their needs. Some limited evidence suggests that such centers do a good job in both providing treatment services and managing the risk of reoffending during the first 6–12 months in the community following prison (Wilkinson, 2001). Programs that target specific offender needs have also been associated with lower recidivism rates (Seiter & Kadela, 2003).

There have been other changes in practice consistent with contemporary approaches to reentry (Lowenkamp & Latessa, 2005). The *Second Chance Act of 2007: Community Safety through Recidivism Prevention*, which was signed into law by President Bush in April 2008, provides funding for improving reentry using approaches consistent with evidence-based policy (Burke & Tonry, 2006; Center for Effective Public Policy, 2007). Guidelines to assist in the reentry process have been published (Aos, Miller, & Drake, 2006; International Association of Chiefs of Police, 2006). The interest in using empirical evidence to guide the practice of reentry is strong, as it is in contemporary medicine and mental health under the rubric "evidence-based practice."

There has been a limited amount of empirical research on parole services provided in the reentry process. In the early 1990s, California started a community-based program to facilitate parolee success for reintegration into society (Zhang, Roberts, & Callanan, 2006). The investigators reported that those not participating in this program were 1.4 times more likely to be rearrested within 12 months on parole, and that meeting goals in four specified domains (which this program facilitated) was associated with the lowest risk for reincarceration. A second study (Martin, Lurigio, & Olson, 2003) focused on a community-based supervision facility providing relevant services (e.g., life skills training, violence prevention, literacy classes, job skills training, job placement services, and GED preparation) during the day. The findings of this study reflect the importance of sufficient time in a program. More clients remained arrest-free after a longer period in the program (70+ days) than a shorter period (less than 10 days). This difference in the recidivism reduction between the two groups (25% reduction for the first versus 10% for the second) provides an estimate of the potential "dosage" impact of this program.

Reentry as applied to parole is growing in popularity. In fiscal year 2004–2005, for example, nearly 44,000 paroled offenders were required to attend a reentry program (National Offender Management Service, 2005). As yet, however, there is very limited information on the effectiveness of such programs. One study suggested that offenders who "fit" well with the reentry program (in terms of their risk and needs) were more likely to be recommended for placement (McGuire et al., 2008). This is good as far as it goes, but it would be even better if we had more information on the impact of the program on the services delivered, and whether the delivery of such services was related to rearrest.

Several studies have addressed the results of specific programs, although none has been designed with random assignment to the program versus "treatment as usual." Accordingly, we cannot be confident that these reentry programs actually work as intended. One study, focusing on those with a history of violent offending, indicated that participants were less likely to test positive for drugs and also less likely to be arrested than were those from a comparison group (Bouffard & Bergeron, 2006). Several other studies noted various problems with noncompliance, however, including difficulty contacting participants following release from prison (Schram & Morash, 2002), having only a small percentage of participants actually receive an aftercare plan and even fewer actually seeking post-release services (Haas & Hamilton, 2007), and less participation in referred services than the comparison group (Bouffard & Bergeron, 2006).

If community reentry programs are to be effective, it is very important that they be committed to the "quality assurance" process described for effective juvenile programs—ensuring that intended services are actually delivered as planned. One consideration is whether such services are voluntary or required as part of parole. One would expect that required participation would increase the overall compliance rate. However, there is some evidence for a self-selection process when reentry services are voluntary, with the more motivated individuals seeking out and receiving services—and benefiting more. In one California program, for example, services to parolees were provided on a voluntary basis and included employment, substance abuse recovery, math and literacy skills, and housing services. Participants in at least one of these areas had a recidivism rate of 33.6%, compared to a recidivism rate of 52.8% among those not participating in this program (Zhang et al., 2006). These findings raise some complicated questions about whether parolees should be required to avail themselves of reentry services.

SUMMARY

1. ***What are the important considerations in assessing juveniles prior to placement decisions?*** The considerations that are most often considered by courts making juvenile placements are public safety and offenders' treatment needs and amenability to treatment. These factors, often cited in the law, overlap considerably with components of risk/need/responsivity, a well-supported approach to assessing and treating both juveniles and adults who have committed criminal offenses.

2. ***What is the evidence for the effectiveness of interventions with juveniles in the community?*** There is strong evidence for the effectiveness of three particular approaches to the community-based treatment of juveniles: Multisystemic Therapy, Oregon Treatment Foster Care, and Functional Family Therapy. These approaches are successful in both providing needed services for and reducing the risk of reoffending in those who receive them.

3. ***What are some characteristics of an effective treatment program?*** Research has identified a number of common elements in programs that are effective. They tend to use different treatment modalities, carefully train those who deliver services, use a team approach, monitor service delivery to ensure that services are actually being provided as intended and individuals do not drop out or miss appointments, and deliver services in family and school settings.

4. ***What are the priorities in preparing individuals for the transition from incarceration to community living (the reentry process)?*** There are six areas in particular that are important in the reentry planning process. How is the family functioning, and will the individual live with them; if not, where will he or she be housed? Will the individual return to school, have a job, or be actively receiving any kind of job training? What mental health and/or substance abuse services are needed, and how will they be delivered? How will the individual be monitored for adherence to conditions specified in the plan? Will there be particular intensity to this monitoring, or specialized aspects (e.g., case management)? Finally, what kind of social support is available, and what peers will the individual be around?

5. ***How do specialized problem-solving courts compare to other correctional interventions?*** These courts serve specific populations—individuals with particular problems (such as substance abuse or mental illness), for whom the provision of treatment services would both rehabilitate the individual and reduce the risk of reoffending. Service delivery and treatment participation are monitored by the court, giving participants a strong incentive to complete the planned course of treatment. These courts can either serve to divert defendants from standard prosecution (unlike more conventional correctional dispositions), or they can function as a specialized form of community corrections similar to probation. In some jurisdictions, if a defendant does not satisfy the required conditions of the specialized problem-solving court, he or she may be returned to the traditional prosecution process.

6. *What are the differences between jails and prisons and what role do psychologists play in these settings?* A jail is a community-based setting that houses both pretrial defendants and inmates who have been convicted of minor offenses and sentenced for terms of less than a year. A prison is part of a state- or federal-level correctional system, housing only inmates who have been convicted of more serious offenses. There are four particular functions served by psychologists who work in either a jail or a prison: classification, consultation/crisis intervention, rehabilitation, and reentry planning. The nature, scope, and distribution of these tasks vary according to whether the facility is a jail or a prison; they can also vary according to the size and resources of the facility.

7. *What are some of the psychological consequences of imprisonment?* Responses to imprisonment vary significantly as a function of the conditions of incarceration and inmates' psychological resilience and mental health. Many inmates experience adjustment problems early in their imprisonment; they may become hypervigilant, socially isolated, and emotionally suppressed. Over time, as they adapt to confinement, they may relinquish control to institutional rulemakers. Exposure to prison violence and sexual offending can have a serious impact on psychological well-being.

8. *How can risk/need/responsivity help to provide effective rehabilitative services for adults?* Assessment of risk helps determine who should be treated at a particular intensity (frequency of service) and dosage (total amount of service received). Assessment of needs helps to target the particular interventions that may be provided to individuals. Assessing responsivity helps a program to decide on the most applicable kinds of interventions, to which inmates are likely to respond best.

KEY TERMS

adjudication of
  delinquency

classification

criminal conviction

criminogenic needs

diversion

Functional Family
  Therapy

intensive probation

Multisystemic Therapy

Oregon Treatment
  Foster Care

parole

prisonization

probation

reentry

risk, needs, and
  responsivity

school-based probation

Sequential Intercept
  Model

therapeutic community

Glossary

absolute judgment An eyewitness's process of deciding, when looking at a sequential lineup, whether any of the people shown in the lineup match the perpetrator.

abuse excuse A legal tactic by which a person charged with a crime claims that past victimization justified his or her retaliation.

acute stress disorder The development of anxiety, dissociative, and other symptoms that occurs within 1 month after exposure to an extreme traumatic event and whose duration is between 2 days and 4 weeks.

adjudication of delinquency This process generally refers to decision making that involves a neutral third party with the authority to resolve or accept a plea agreement of some kind.

adjudicative competence The set of abilities necessary for a criminal defendant to understand the proceedings in which he or she is participating and make rational decisions about the alternative courses of action that are available to be pursued.

advance medical directives Legal documents in which patients indicate the kinds of future medical treatments they will agree to should they later become incapacitated and therefore be incompetent to make treatment decisions for themselves at the time.

adversarial system A system of resolving disputes in which the parties, usually represented by counsel, argue and present evidence to a neutral fact finder, who makes a decision based on the evidence and arguments presented by the parties; as distinguished from an inquisitorial system, in which the fact finder takes an active part in determining what occurred.

affirmative defense In a trial, a position by the defendant that places the burden on the defendant to prove his or her claim. Insanity or self-defense is an example of an affirmative defense.

aggravating circumstances Conditions that make a criminal act more serious—for example, to knowingly create a risk of death or serious injury to other persons as well as to the victim.

alternative dispute resolution Any legal mechanism used to settle a conflict without going to trial.

amicus curiae **brief** A "friend-of-the-court" brief filed in state and federal courts by a person or organization that is not a party to the litigation, but that has a strong view on the subject matter in the case.

anchoring A cognitive bias that describes the common human tendency of judges to rely too heavily, or "anchor," on a suggested piece of information (e.g., a dollar value in the context of damage awards) when making decisions.

anchoring and adjustment bias This occurs when individuals are strongly influenced or "anchored" by an initial starting value and when, in subsequent decisions, they do not sufficiently adjust their judgments away from this starting point.

anomie A sense of alienation or meaninglessness.

antisocial personality disorder A pervasive pattern of disregard for, and violation of, the rights of others that begins in childhood or early adolescence and continues into adulthood.

applied scientist An applied scientist applies knowledge to solve practical problems of the modern world, rather than to acquire knowledge for knowledge's sake.

arbitration A form of dispute resolution in which a neutral third party makes a decision that is binding on the two disputants.

archival analysis In psychology and law, a method of data collection that involves examination of previously-decided issues and cases.

arraignment A formal statement of charges and an initial plea by the defendant to these charges.

assimilation The mental process in which an individual internalizes a current perception or conception into their preexisting representation.

attitudinal model of decision making A description of decision making that focuses on judgments about the facts or disposition of a case in light of one's ideological attitudes and values.

attribution theory A theory in social psychology that deals with the explanations people make for the causes of their behavior and the behavior of others.

authoritarianism A set of beliefs and characteristics that include submissiveness to authorities, demands for obedience from subordinates, intolerance of minorities and other outgroups, and endorsement of the use of power and punishment to ensure conformity to conventional norms.

autobiographical memory Memory for one's own life experiences.

aversive racism When people believe in racial equality and view themselves as nonprejudiced, but have unconscious, negative beliefs about people of other races; in situations that make those negative beliefs salient, aversive racists try to avoid acting on them or express them in subtle ways.

basic scientist A scientist who pursues knowledge motivated by scientific curiosity or interest in a scientific question. They study a phenomenon to expand understanding in order to contribute to scientific advances in the area, not to solve a problem.

battered woman syndrome A collection of symptoms many of which are manifest in women who have suffered prolonged and extensive abuse from their spouses.

behavioral confirmation A situation in which people's expectations causes them to act in ways that confirm those expectations.

belief in a just world A belief that the world is orderly, predictable, and just, and that people get what they deserve and deserve what they get.

bench trial A trial in which the judge, rather than the jury, makes the decision.

beyond a reasonable doubt The standard of proof required in a criminal trial; generally means that jurors (or the judge) should be strongly convinced (but not necessarily convinced beyond all doubt) that the defendant is guilty before they convict.

biological theory of crime An explanation for the causes of criminal behavior that uses heredity and constitutional characteristics of the lawbreaker.

bioterrorism A form of terrorism that uses biological "weapons," such as viruses and bacteria, to harm or threaten to harm others.

black letter law Basic principles of law generally accepted by courts and embodied in statutes.

black sheep effect The tendency to be more punitive toward those members of one's group who violate the norms of the group.

blended sentencing Criminal blended sentencing schemes allow judges, in sentencing juveniles tried as adults, to combine sanctions available in juvenile court with those used in criminal court.

borderline personality disorder A personality disorder characterized by impulsivity and instability in moods, behavior, self-image, and interpersonal relationships.

brain fingerprinting A procedure that involves the measurement of brainwaves in response to a stimulus to assess whether the brain recognizes that stimulus.

Brawner rule This rule states that a defendant is not responsible for criminal conduct when, because of a mental disease or defect, he or she lacks substantial capacity either to appreciate the criminality (wrongfulness) of the conduct or to conform his or her conduct to the requirements of the law. (Also known as the ALI rule.)

breached duty The violation, through either negligence or intentional wrongdoing, of a duty that one party legally owes to another party.

brutalization The proposition that the use of capital punishment actually increases the crime rate by sending a message that it is acceptable to kill those who have wronged us.

burnout A syndrome that occurs in people who work with other people; symptoms include emotional exhaustion, depersonalization, and reduced personal accomplishment.

case law The body of previous legal decisions and legal principles developed from these earlier decisions, as contrasted with statutory laws (passed by the legislative branch and approved by the executive branch). Case law develops through the courts over time, based upon precedent, and tends to change slowly because of the legal principle of *stare decisis*.

central route When people carefully and effortfully think about all of the information relevant to the merits of the situation.

challenge for cause Occurs when individuals are interviewed during any jury selection. If the judge agrees that there is a justification for the attorney's claim of bias, a juror may be excused for cause. In addition, a judge may excuse a prospective juror for cause without a request to do so from either attorney.

change of venue A decision by a trial judge to move a trial to another locality, usually done because extensive pretrial publicity has prevented the paneling of an open-minded jury.

charge bargaining A form of plea bargaining in which a prosecutor reduces the number or severity of charges against a criminal defendant in exchange for a guilty plea.

chemical castration The use of injections of a female hormone into male rapists as a method of lowering their sex drive.

civil competence This term applies to civil (noncriminal) legal contexts in which the question of mental competence is raised for a specific task (e.g., making a will).

class action case A case that involves many plaintiffs who collectively form a "class" and who claim that they suffered similar injuries because of a defendant's actions.

classical conditioning A procedure in which one learns to associate a new response with a stimulus.

classical school of criminology The point of view that evolved in the 1700s and 1800s, emphasizing the role of free will and cost-benefit analysis in determining criminal behavior.

classification The evaluation of convicted offenders by a correctional facility or parole office to assess the level of risk of criminal recidivism, institutional misconduct, and escape or noncompliance.

closing argument A summation of evidence, made by an attorney at the end of a trial.

cognitive interview A procedure used to assist victims to recall aspects of a crime or other traumatic event.

cognitive load interviews Interviews that are designed to mentally tax a person due to high cognitive demand. In such interviews it becomes difficult to simultaneously answer a question and maintain a lie.

cognizable group A group of persons, usually defined by demographic characteristics such as race or gender.

commonsense justice Ordinary citizens' basic notions of what is just and fair in contrast to the dictates of formal, statutory law.

community-based policing A policy that increases direct police/citizen contacts within a neighborhood.

compensatory damages The payment or restitution owed to a plaintiff for the damages and harm that have been determined to be caused by a civil defendant.

competence The ability to understand implications of making legal decisions.

competence to plead guilty The ability of a defendant to understand the possible consequences of pleading guilty to criminal charges instead of going to trial and to make a rational choice between the alternatives.

competence to stand trial Sufficient ability to understand the legal proceedings in which one is involved and to consult with one's attorney.

compliant false confession The suspect is induced to comply with the interrogator's demands to make an incriminating statement.

concordance rate The extent of similarity in a behavior or characteristic between two twins.

conditioned stimulus An act that, through association, comes to elicit a learned response.

confirmation bias A tendency to search for information that confirms one's preconceptions.

confrontation clause The 6th Amendment guarantees defendants the right to confront their accusers.

containment theory The proposition that societal pressure controls the rate of crime.

content analysis Scientific analysis of the content of a conversation or discussion.

control question test A polygraph technique in which the subject is asked a question that elicits an emotional response.

control theory The proposition that people will act in an antisocial way unless they are prevented from doing so.

countermeasures Techniques employed by a deceptive subject to "beat" the polygraph test in order to avoid detection (e.g., breathing strategies, complex mental calculations, thinking about something exciting or dangerous, and self-inflicting pain).

crime control model The model which emphasizes the reduction of crime rates and vindicating victims' rights by the efficient detection of suspects and the effective prosecution of defendants, to help ensure that criminal activity is being contained or reduced.

criminal conviction The outcome of a criminal prosecution that concludes in a judgment that the defendant is guilty of the crime charged.

criminal profiling The use of psychological principles as a crime investigation technique to guide police toward suspects who possess certain personal characteristics as revealed by the way a crime was committed.

criminogenic needs The deficits (such as substance abuse, family problems, educational problems, and pro-criminal attitudes) that increase the risk of reoffending.

criminology The study of crime and criminal behavior.

crisis intervention team (CIT) This program was designed by the Memphis police department (also known as the Memphis Model) to increase officer and public safety while attempting to redirect those with mental illness from the judicial system to the mental health system.

cycle of violence Involving a pattern of periodic violence in a domestic context, often exhibited by batterers, that makes their victims even more fearful of the battering they believe is inevitable.

damages Money awarded to a person injured by the unlawful act or negligence of another.

dangerousness Behavior that involves acts of physical violence or aggression by one person against another.

death-qualified jury A jury panel that excludes persons whose attitudes about capital punishment would prevent them from performing their sworn duty as jurors.

decision rule The requirement whether a jury must reach a unanimous verdict or whether a majority vote will suffice for a verdict.

declarative knowledge In the context of jury behavior, jurors' understanding of legal concepts.

defensive attribution An explanation for behavior that enables people to deal with perceived inequities in others' lives and to avoid feelings of vulnerability.

deinstitutionalization The long-term trend of closing mental hospitals and transferring care to community-based mental health treatment facilities.

deliberative processes Thought processes that involve mental effort, concentration, motivation, and the application of learned rules.

determinate sentencing A sentence of confinement or probation for a fixed period of time specified by statute, as contrasted with an indeterminate sentence whose duration is determined by the offender's behavior.

diagnostic cues Cues that enable professionals to accurately diagnose or distinguish among available alternatives (e.g., between psychopaths and non-psychopaths, between truth-tellers and liars).

differential association approach Criminal behavior requires socialization into a system of values conducive to violating the law; thus, the potential criminal develops definitions of behavior that make deviant conduct seem acceptable.

differential association reinforcement theory A learning-theory approach that asserts that criminal behavior is the result of socialization into a system of values that is conducive to violations of the law.

diminished capacity A variation of the insanity defense that is applicable if the defendant (in the words of the law) lacks the ability to "meaningfully premeditate the crime."

discovery A procedure in which the attorney for one side seeks to become aware of the materials used by the other side to form its case.

discretion The ability to act according to one's own judgment and conscience. In judicial decisions, refers to a judge's consideration of factors that may lead to appropriate *variations* in how the system responds to offenses, as opposed to a decision based on predefined legal guidelines or rules.

dispositional phase The sentencing phase of the case in which hearings typically combine adversarial procedures and attention to the particular needs—social, psychological, physical—of the child.

dissociation The act of a person "escaping" from a traumatic event by detaching himself or herself from it.

distributive justice Concerns about what is right or just with respect to the allocation of goods within a society.

diversion The practice of officially stopping or suspending a case prior to court adjudication (without a formal trial) and referring the defendant to a community education, treatment, or work program in lieu of adjudication or incarceration.

dizygotic twins (DZ) Commonly called fraternal twins, occurs when two eggs are fertilized.

double-blind testing procedures Experimental procedures in which both the participant and experimenter are unaware of the particular conditions being tested.

dual-process theory of attitude change The theory that there are two different kinds of information-processing strategies or "routes" (central route and peripheral route) that people use to reach decisions.

due process model A perspective that emphasizes due process or procedural justice (fairness) under the law. In contrast to the crime control model, this model places stronger emphasis on defendants' rights than victims' rights.

duty The obligation that one party legally owes to another party.

ecological validity For a study to be ecologically valid, the methods, materials, and setting of the study must approximate the real-life phenomena being investigated. For example, mock-jury research that utilizes transcripts rather than re-enactments may low ecological validity.

encoding The process of entering a perception into memory.

equality This principle means that all people who commit the same crime or misdeed should receive the same consequences.

estimator variable The factors that are beyond the control of the justice system and whose impact on the reliability of the eyewitness can only be estimated (e.g., the lighting conditions at the time of the crime and whether the culprit was wearing a disguise).

euthanasia The act of killing an individual for reasons that are considered merciful.

evaluation apprehension Concern about the ways that others evaluate us.

evidentiary strength Refers to the nature of the evidence regarding guilt in a legal proceeding, and is probably the most important determinant of jurors' verdicts.

exculpatory Evidence that clears a defendant of fault or guilt.

executive function The cognitive ability to plan and regulate behavior carefully.

experiential inflammatory bias The notion that people who witness the use of virtual environments may be so swept up in the experience and persuaded by the lifelike nature of these scenes that they have difficulty imagining or visualizing a different point of view.

experimental methodology Experimental research studies involve manipulation of one or more factors (termed "independent variables"), observation of the effects of these factors on some behavior (termed "dependent variables"), and control of other relevant factors.

experimenter bias An experimenter's influence on the results of a research study.

expert witness A witness who has special knowledge beyond that of the ordinary lay person (juror) about a subject enabling him or her to give testimony regarding an issue that requires expertise to understand. Experts are permitted to give opinion testimony, while a non-expert witness is typically limited to testimony about which he or she has direct knowledge through first-hand observation.

extralegal information Irrelevant information about a particular case that is not presented in a legal context (e.g., age, race, gender, and socioeconomic status).

extrinsic motivation Involves pursuing goals that would please and impress others.

extroversion The personality cluster characterized by outgoing orientation, enthusiasm, and optimism.

fabricated evidence False or made up evidence presented by interrogators in order to elicit information from suspects.

false confession An admission of guilt to a crime in which the confessor is not culpable. False confessions occur for different reasons and they can be explained by different situational and dispositional factors.

fitness–for–duty evaluation The psychological assessment of an employee conducted to determine whether that individual is mentally, emotionally, or behaviorally impaired to continue his or her workplace duties. It is often used with those in dangerous occupations, such as police work, firefighters, and the military.

five-factor model (FFM) of personality This descriptive model assesses five broad factors or dimensions of personality. The personality dimensions (OCEAN) include Openness (intellect), Conscientiousness, Extraversion, Agreeableness, and Neuroticism (or emotional stability). The factors are stable dimensions and people generally fall between the extremes.

focal concerns A theory that explains the criminal activities of lower-class adolescent gangs as an attempt to achieve the ends that are most valued in their culture through behaviors that appear best suited to obtain those ends.

forensic evaluator These psychologists and psychiatrists provide forensic mental health assessments and expert court testimony on a variety of topics related to legal questions involving mental and emotional disorder, intellectual functioning, substance abuse, and other clinical disorders, as well as capacities that are directly related to the legal question.

forensic mental health assessment This includes evaluations conducted by a variety of disciplines including psychiatrists, psychologists, and social workers. The assessments address a wide range of questions in civil, criminal, and family law (e.g., competency to stand trial, child-custody, malingering, substance abuse, risk of future violence).

forensic psychologists These psychologists apply science and psychology to questions and issues related to the legal system. Their work may include conducting forensic mental health assessments for courts and attorneys, providing treatment to those under the supervision of the legal system, offering consultation to law enforcement, and other related tasks.

framing effects The way decision alternatives are presented (or framed)—as either gains or losses—can have a significant impact on a person's choice. Individuals are more willing to take chances when the decision alternatives are presented in terms of gains than in terms of losses.

Functional Family Therapy A community-based intervention for juvenile offenders. It is provided weekly by a single therapist, over an average period of three months. It is family-focused, and is often delivered in the home.

functional magnetic resonance imaging A type of specialized neuroimaging that registers blood flow related to neural activity in the brain or spinal cord.

fundamental attribution error The belief that behavior is caused by stable factors internal to a person rather than by situational factors external to a person.

future best interests of the child The legal standard by which most child custody decisions are made in the United States.

gag order A trial judge's order to the press not to print or broadcast certain information; gag orders of this type are usually found to violate the First Amendment. More common are court orders to attorneys and witnesses not to talk to the press about an upcoming trial; gag orders are entered to prevent pretrial publicity from affecting prospective jurors.

generic prejudice Prejudice arising from media coverage of issues not specifically related to a particular case but thematically relevant to the issues at hand.

grand jury A group of citizens who receive evidence in closed proceedings and decide whether to issue an indictment.

ground truth A clear-cut criterion of accuracy.

guilty knowledge test A polygraph technique in which the subject is asked a series of questions whose answers would only be known by the perpetrator.

harm The losses or adversities suffered by a person who is the victim of wrongdoing.

hate crimes Criminal acts intended to harm or intimidate people because of their race, ethnicity, sexual orientation, religion or other minority group status.

heuristic A mental shortcut, "rule-of-thumb," or educated guess used to help solve a problem. These methods typically utilize experimentation and trial-and-error techniques.

hostile workplace harassment A form of workplace harassment that does not involve a specific response (see "*quid pro quo* harassment"), but instead involves gender harassment and unwanted sexual attention, resulting in an intimidating, hostile, or offensive working environment.

illusory causation The belief in a causal relationship where none exists or the false impression that two variables are causally related.

impeach To cross-examine a witness with the purpose of calling into question his or her credibility or reliability.

implicit personality theory A person's preconceptions about how certain attributes are related to one another and to behavior.

inadmissible evidence That testimony, which the judge rules are not proper and, hence, instructs the jury to disregard.

indeterminate sentencing Sentencing schemes in which judges impose an indefinite period of incarceration for a given offense (e.g., 6-20 years) and the actual length of stay depends on whether the individual is released on parole or serves the full sentence.

indictment An accusation issued by a grand jury charging the defendant with criminal conduct.

in-group/out-group differences An in-group shares a common identity and sense of belonging, an out-group lacks these things. Eyewitness identifications are easier among in-group members.

initial appearance The constitutional right to be brought before a judge within 48 hours of arrest. The primary purpose is for the judge to review the evidence summarized by the prosecutor and determine whether there is reason to believe that the suspect committed the crimes charged.

inquisitorial approach The procedure used in Europe, in which questioning is the responsibility solely of the judge.

insanity The principal legal doctrine permitting consideration of mental abnormality in assessing criminal liability. Those acquitted of criminal charges as Not Guilty by Reason of Insanity are typically are required to spend an indeterminate period of treatment in a secure mental health facility until they are no longer dangerous to self or others.

intensive probation Probation involving more frequent monitoring and contact.

intention The offender's frame of mind in committing a criminal act.

intentional behavior The purposeful conduct in which a person meant the outcome of a given act to occur.

internal/external locus of control The tendency for people to believe that their lives are controlled by internal factors such as skill and effort or external factors such as luck or the actions of others.

internalized false confession An internalized false confession can result when, after hours of being questioned, badgered, and told stories about what "must have happened," the suspect begins to develop a profound distrust of his own memory.

interviewer bias Bias sometimes exhibited by an interviewer who has some knowledge or preconceived ideas about the topic in question.

intrinsic motivation Involves pursuing goals that involve internal or personal desires rather than external incentives.

intuitive processes Incidents of spontaneous mental processing which are often acted on but not thought through with careful thought or effort.

joinder The combining of multiple defendants or multiple charges in one trial.

joint custody A legal outcome in which divorcing parents share or divide various decision-making and control responsibilities for their children.

judicial discretion A judge's ability to make decisions guided by personal values and beliefs (e.g., juvenile court judges use discretion to decide whether a youth should be transferred to criminal court.

juror bias The tendency of any juror to evaluate the facts of the case such that the juror favors one side or the other.

jury nullification An option for the jury that allows it to disregard both the law and the evidence and acquit the defendant if the jury believes that an acquittal is justified.

jury sentiments Factors beyond the evidence and the law that jurors may rely on to decide a case.

learned helplessness A condition in which people come to believe that they have no personal influence over what happens to them and consequently they passively endure aversive treatment rather than to try to control it.

learning theory A form of criminological theory that emphasizes how specific criminal behaviors are learned directly from reinforcement and modeling influences.

legal factors Those variables related to the offense or the offender's legal history.

legal model of decision making This model suggests that legal decision makers dispassionately consider the relevant laws, precedents, and constitutional principles and that personal bias has no part in decision-making.

liable Responsible or answerable for some action.

liberation hypothesis This hypothesis implies that when the strength of the evidence against a defendant is weak, jurors are free to rely on nonlegal information to inform their decisions

limiting instruction A jury instruction that allows a prior record to be used only to gauge the defendant's credibility.

M'Naghten rule One test for the insanity defense. Under this rule, a defendant may be deemed insane by the court if, because of a "disease of the mind," he or she (1) did not know what he was doing, or (2) did not know that what he was doing was wrong.

malingering The intentional fabrication or exaggeration of physical or psychological symptoms in order to gain an incentive or advantage.

mandatory minimum sentences Sentencing schemes in which judges sentence offenders to a minimum number of years in prison for a given offense regardless of any extenuating circumstances.

mass murderer A person who kills four or more victims in one location during a period of time that lasts anywhere from a few minutes to several hours.

matching heuristic A process in which decision makers search through a subset of available case information and then make a decision based on only a small number of factors (e.g., offense severity and prior record), often ignoring other seemingly relevant information.

mediation A form of alternative dispute resolution in which a neutral third party helps the disputing parties agree on a resolution to their conflict.

mens rea A guilty mind; the mental state accompanying a forbidden act.

mitigating circumstances Factors such as age, mental capacity, motivations, or duress that lessen the degree of guilt in a criminal offense and thus the nature of the punishment.

monozygotic twins (MZ) Commonly called identical twins, occur when a single egg is fertilized to form one zygote, which then divides into two embryos.

motion *in limine* A legal request for a judge to make a pretrial ruling on some matter of law expected to arise at the trial.

Multisystemic Therapy An empirically-supported intervention for juvenile offenders implemented in multiple domains (e.g., family, school, structured activity) to reduce serious antisocial behavior and strengthen dysfunctional families.

negative incentives In the context of interrogations, tactics (such as accusations, attacks on the suspect's denials, and evidence fabrications) that interrogators use to convey that the suspect has no choice but to confess.

negligence Behavior that falls below a legal standard for protecting others from unreasonable risks; it is often measured by asking whether a "reasonable person" would have acted as the civil defendant acted in similar circumstances.

negotiation The process of conferring with another to attempt to settle a legal matter.

neuroticism A major dimension of personality involving the tendency to experience negative emotions such as anxiety, anger, and depression, often accompanied by distressed thinking and behavior.

open-ended questions This type of question does not specify or restrict the answers to be given; rather, respondents are being prompted to suggest their own ideas for answers.

opening statements Not part of the evidence, these orations made by the lawyers on each side give an overview of the evidence that will be presented.

operant learning A form of learning in which the consequences of a behavior influence the likelihood of it being performed in the future.

Oregon Treatment Foster Care An empirically-supported juvenile intervention that involves placing juveniles with specially trained foster parents rather than in residential placement.

other race effect The tendency for people to less accurately recognizes faces of other races.

outcome severity The severity of an accident or injury.

overconfidence bias Generally refers to one's overconfidence in various decision making contexts. It applies to defendants who believe (incorrectly) that they have a chance to win at trial, sometimes leading to rejection of reasonable plea offers from prosecutors.

parole The conditional release from prison of a person convicted of a crime prior to the expiration of that person's term of imprisonment, subject to both the supervision of the correctional authorities during the remainder of the term and a resumption of the imprisonment upon violation of the conditions imposed.

pedophile A person who takes sexual gratification from children.

peremptory challenge The opportunity to exclude a certain number of potential jurors from the eventual jury without having to give any reasons. Their number, determined by the judge, varies from one jurisdiction to another.

peripheral route When people utilize simple cues such as the mere presence of an expert or extraneous details (e.g., extralegal information) to influence their judgments.

perjury Lying while under oath.

photographic lineup A display of photographs of potential suspects that police often ask an eyewitness to examine to identify a suspect (also called a photospread).

photospread A display of photographs of potential suspects that police often ask an eyewitness to examine to identify a suspect (also called a photographic lineup).

physiognomic variability Perceived differences based on physical features.

plea bargaining In exchange for the defendant's promise to forgo a trial, the government may promise to charge the defendant with a lesser crime or ask the judge for a reduced sentence. When the "bargain" is reached, the defendant pleads guilty and no trial is held.

policy capturing Research to determine (capture) policy preferences and inclinations (e.g., the punishment motives of ordinary people).

policy evaluator A role in which psychologists who have methodological skills in assessing how well a policy has worked provide data regarding the effects of the policy (e.g., degree of change, degree of effectiveness, design recommendations, expected outcomes, etc.).

polygraph (sometimes called "lie detector") An instrument for recording variations in several physiological functions that may indicate whether a person is telling the truth or lying.

positive inducements Tactics used by interrogators to motivate suspects to see that an admission of guilt is in their best interest. All interrogators try, implicitly or explicitly, to send the message that the suspect will receive some benefit in exchange for his admission of wrongdoing.

positivist school of criminology A point of view that emphasized that criminal behavior by a person was determined, rather than a product of free will.

postdiction variable In the context of eyewitness memory, a variable (such as the speed of an identification) that does not directly affect the reliability of identification, but is a measure of some process that correlates with reliability.

postevent information Details about an event to which an eyewitness is exposed after the event has occurred.

posttraumatic stress disorder (PTSD) An anxiety disorder in which the victim experiences a pattern of intense fear reactions after being exposed to a highly stressful event.

precedents The ruling (or opinion) announced in a previous case that provides a framework in which to decide a current case. The expectation that a court must follow a precedent is called *stare decisis*.

predecisional distortion A phenomenon by which jurors' initial inclinations influence the way they interpret evidence presented during a trial.

predictive validity One form of psychometric validity, involving the accuracy with which a measure can predict something it should theoretically be able to predict.

preliminary hearing The step between arrest and trial. At a preliminary hearing, the prosecution must offer some evidence on every element of the crime charged and the judge must decide whether the evidence is sufficient to pursue the case further.

preponderance of the evidence The standard for a verdict in a civil suit; the evidence for one side outweighs that of the other by even a slight margin.

presence The degree to which a user or observer has the impression of actually "being in another world" due to the presentation in the virtual environment.

preventive detention The detention of accused persons who pose a risk of flight or dangerousness.

primacy effect The influence of information that is presented first in series.

primary deviance Behavior that violates a law or norm for socially acceptable conduct.

principle of proportionality The principle that the punishment should be consistently related to the magnitude of the offense.

prisonization The gradual process in which prisoners adjust to their environment (i.e., assimilate to the customs and culture of the penitentiary).

probation The conditional freedom from incarceration following criminal conviction. It involves a specified set of conditions of behavior for which compliance is monitored by the probation officer assigned to the case. Probation conditions may include drug use monitoring, substance abuse treatment, mental health treatment, and skills-based training in particular areas (e.g., anger management, decision-making).

procedural justice A sense that the methods for resolving a dispute have been fair.

procedural knowledge In the context of jury behavior, jurors' ability to know what to do to reach a decision.

propensity evidence Evidence of a defendant's past wrongdoings that suggest the defendant had the propensity, or inclination, to commit a crime.

prosecutorial discretion The autonomy of prosecutors to make decisions about criminal incidents. In the context of juvenile offenders, it involves deciding whether cases involving certain kinds of serious charges are filed initially in juvenile or adult court.

proximate cause A cause that constitutes an obvious or substantial reason why a given harm occurred.

psycholinguistics The psychological study of how people use and understand language.

psychological autopsy An attempt to determine the mode of death (whether an accident, suicide, homicide, or natural causes) by an examination of what was known about the deceased.

psychological theories Scientific principles that are formulated and applied to the analysis and understanding of cognitive and behavioral phenomena. For example, psychological theories of crime emphasize individual differences in behavior and the approaches to thinking, feeling, and decision-making that make some people predisposed to committing criminal acts.

psychopathy A personality disorder characterized by a long-term pattern of antisocial behavior and personal characteristics such as shallow emotion, limited capacities for guilt and empathy, and failure to learn from experience.

psychoticism A major element in Eysenck's theory of personality, characterized by insensitivity, trouble-making, and lack of empathy.

punitive damages Financial compensation as a form of punishment for failure to respond to a misconduct.

quid pro quo **harassment** An implicit or explicit bargain in which the harasser promises a reward or threatens punishment in exchange for a specific response (often sexual in nature) from a workplace supervisee.

racial bias When police officers, prosecutors, jurors, and judges use an individual's race as the primary determinant for discretionary decisions or judgments of his or her behavior.

racial profiling The police practice of using race as a factor in determining actions such as traffic stops, arrests, and questioning of suspects.

rape shield laws Laws that prevent or restrict the questioning of an alleged rape victim during that person's time on the witness stand; specifically, questioning about the alleged victim's past sexual activities is prohibited or limited.

rape trauma syndrome A collection of behaviors or symptoms that are frequent aftereffects of having been raped.

reactance theory A theory proposing that, if something is denied or withheld from a person, the person's desire for it will increase.

rebuttal evidence Evidence presented to counter or disprove facts previously introduced by the adverse party.

recency effect The influence of information that is presented last in a series.

recross To cross-examine a witness a second time, after redirect examination.

redirect questioning Questioning by the original attorney that follows the opposing counsel's cross-examination.

reentry The process of returning from incarceration to the community.

relative judgment An eyewitness's process of deciding, when looking at a simultaneous lineup, which of the people shown in the lineup looks most like the perpetrator.

repression The removal of certain unpleasant thoughts or memories into the unconscious.

reservation price In negotiations, a negotiator's bottom line. Defendants in settlement negotiations typically have maximum amounts they are willing to pay and plaintiffs have minimum amounts they are willing to accept.

restorative justice Programs to reconcile offenders with their victims; are designed to cause the offender to realize the victim's pain and the victim to understand why the offender committed the crime.

retention interval The period of time between viewing an event and being questioned about it.

retributive approach The notion that punishment should be exacted on a person who has taken something from another.

retrieval The process in which a memory is returned to a conscious state.

reverse transfer When juveniles placed in adult court are returned to juvenile court.

risk assessment The assessment of the probability that a person will behave violently in certain circumstances, often accompanied by suggestions for how to reduce the likelihood of violent conduct.

risk averse Unwilling to take a chance.

risk/need/responsivity (RNR) A theory that describes three separate considerations (risk, need, and responsivity) involving interventions for criminal offenders. Risk means that the likelihood of committing future offenses should be evaluated; those at highest risk should receive the most intensive interventions. Needs are the deficits (such as substance abuse, family problems, educational problems, and procriminal attitudes) that increase the risk of reoffending. Responsivity involves the likelihood of a favorable response to the interventions, and the influences that may affect such responding.

schema An individual's cognitive framework or set of preconceptions that helps that person attend to, organize, and interpret relevant information.

school-based probation A variation on the standard conditions of probation in which the youth's attendance, performance, and behavior in school are monitored through the probation officer's personal visits to the school.

scientific jury selection The process by which lawyers use social scientists as jury selection consultants. These consultants use empirically based procedures, including small group discussions called focus groups, shadow juries, systematic ratings of prospective jurors, and surveys of the community.

secondary deviance Creating or increasing the deviant identity of a person using official labels or formal legal sanctions.

secondary victimization A process in which post-event negative experiences with legal and medical authorities increase a victims' symptoms.

self-defense A legal defense relied upon by criminal defendants typically charged with homicide; it asserts that the defendant's actions were justified by a reasonable belief that he or she was in imminent danger of death or bodily harm from an attacker.

self-determination rights The right to make independent choices about one's own well-being.

self-serving bias The tendency to interpret information or make decisions in ways that are consistent with one's own interests, rather than in an objective fashion.

sentence bargaining A form of plea bargaining in which a prosecutor recommends a reduced sentence in exchange for a guilty plea.

sentencing disparity The tendency of different judges to administer a variety of penalties for the same crime.

Sequential Intercept Model The model assesses diversion needs for individuals with serious mental illness. It describes a number of points at which an intervention can be made to prevent further progress along the conventional criminal track. These points are (a) law enforcement and emergency services; (b) initial detention and initial hearings; (c) jail, courts, forensic evaluations, and forensic commitments; (d) reentry from jails, state prisons, and forensic hospitalization; and (e) community corrections and community support.

sequential presentation A lineup presentation in which the choices are shown one at a time.

serial killer A person who kills four or more victims on separate occasions, usually in different locations.

settlement negotiation In civil cases, the pretrial process whereby plaintiffs and defendants agree to an outcome that ends their legal disagreement.

shaming penalty A criminal sanction designed to embarrass an offender by publicizing the offense; shaming penalties are thought to express the community's moral outrage and to deter others from committing this type of crime.

similarity-leniency hypothesis The proposal that fact finders will treat those like themselves differently from those they perceive as different.

simultaneous presentation A lineup presentation in which all choices are shown at the same time.

social desirability effect People's wishes to present themselves in a socially appropriate and favorable way.

social framework testimony Expert witness testimony that is based on knowledge of scientific evidence on a particular for the purpose of helping a judge or jury better understand that issue.

social influence The influence of other people and the social context on behavior.

social labeling theory The theory that the stigma of being branded deviant by society can influence an individual's belief about himself or herself.

social learning theory A theory that states that learning occurs within a social context. It argues that behavior in a given situation is adaptive and depends on the consequences associated with actions (rewards, punishments).

social-psychological theory This group of theories propose that crime is learned in a social context, but they differ about what is learned and how it is learned.

sociological theories This group of theories maintains that crime results from social or cultural contexts (e.g., family, school/workplace, peer groups, community, and society). The various theories emphasize different social features and differ on the social causes of crime.

sole custody Awarding custody of a child to one parent, with the other parent being granted rights of visitation and other types of contact with the child.

source confusion Confusion about the origin of a memory.

source monitoring The ability to accurately identify the source of one's memory.

specific pretrial publicity Media coverage concerning the details of one specific case prior to trial.

spousal rape Sexual assault (rape) against a spouse. One form of intimate partner abuse.

spree killer A person who kills victims at two or more different locations with no "cooling-off" interval between the murders.

stare decisis The legal principle emphasizing the importance of decision-making that is consistent with precedent; literally, "let the decision stand."

statutory exclusion A statute stipulating that certain serious offenses allegedly committed by an adolescent must be filed directly in adult court.

stimulation-seeking theory A theory that claims that the thrill seeking and disruptive behavior of a psychopath serves to increase sensory input and arousal to a more tolerable level.

stipulate To agree about a fact in a legal proceeding without further argument or examination.

Stockholm syndrome Feelings of dependency and emotional closeness that hostages sometimes develop toward their kidnappers in prolonged hostage situations.

storage That phase of the memory process referring to the retention of information.

story model The notion that people construct a story or narrative summary of the events in a dispute.

structural explanations A key concept of structural approaches is that certain groups of people suffer fundamental inequalities in opportunities that impair their ability to achieve the goals valued by society.

structured interviews Interviews in which the wording, order, and content of the questions are standardized in order to improve the reliability of the information an interviewer obtains.

subcultural explanations The subcultural version of sociological theory maintains that a conflict of norms held by different groups causes criminal behavior. This conflict arises when various groups endorse subcultural norms, pressuring their members to deviate from the norms underlying the criminal law.

suggestive questioning Questioning that suggests an answer.

suicide by cop A crisis situation in which a citizen precipitates his or her own death by behaving in such a fashion that a police officer is forced to use lethal force.

summary jury trial A brief presentation of both sides of the case, usually lasting only one day, in which a jury renders a verdict that is only advisory to a judge.

surgical and chemical castration Surgical castration is the removal of the testes; chemical castration is the administration of hormones to lower the male sex drive.

sympathy hypothesis The assumption that jurors' decisions will be influenced by feelings of sympathy.

system variable In eyewitness identifications, a variable whose impact on an identification can be controlled by criminal justice system officials. Examples include the way a lineup is presented and the way a witness is questioned.

team policing A policy of less centralized decision making within police organizations.

terrorism The use of threat of violence to achieve certain organizational goals.

testamentary capacity Having the mental capacity to execute a will when the will is signed and witnessed, including the capacity to resist the pressures or domination of any person who might try to use undue influence on the distribution of the estate of the person writing the will.

therapeutic community A community-based approach in which all staff and participants are considered to be part of the treatment process. It has generally been used for drug offenders and domestic violence offenders. This approach may include group therapy, individual counseling, and drug testing with the objective of building skills in anger control, decision-making, and recognizing high-risk situations.

therapeutic jurisprudence A position that one aspect of the study of the law should be a consideration of the mental health impact of the legal system upon its participants and clients.

thought suppression The attempt to avoid thinking about something.

threat assessment A process which involves carefully considering the nature of the threat, the risk posed by the individual, and the indicated response to reduce the risk of harmful action.

three-strikes laws (also called habitual offender laws) A category of statutes that require state courts to hand down mandatory and long periods of imprisonment for persons convicted of three or more felonies on separate occasions, no matter how minor the offenses.

tort A tort is a civil suit that does not involve a contract; thus, tort litigation would be illustrated by a suit by one automobile driver against another, most medical malpractice cases, and other personal injury suits.

transfer laws Laws that allow juveniles who are charged with committing serious crimes to be tried as adults.

trial consultants Social scientists who work as jury selection consultants, conduct community attitude surveys, prepare witnesses to testify, advise lawyers on their presentation strategies, and conduct mock trials.

truth bias In the context of interrogations, people are better at detecting truthful denials than accurately judging deceptive elaborations. Thus, people tend to assume most assertions are honest unless their authenticity is called into question.

ultimate opinion testimony Testimony that offers a conclusion about the specific defendant or a specific witness, in contrast to testimony about a general phenomenon.

unconditioned stimulus An original stimulus not associated with a new or conditioned response.

unconscious transference Generation of a memory that is based on the recall of several past occurrences, so that an innocent person may be confused with an offender.

utilitarian approach The notion that criminal sentences should be designed to accomplish a useful outcome, such as compensating the victim or rehabilitating the offender.

validity scales Those measures whose goal is to access whether the test taker is telling the truth.

venire A panel of prospective jurors drawn from a large list.

vicarious learning Learning by observing the actions of another person and their outcomes.

victimology The study of the process and consequences of victim's experiences, including recovery.

vividness effect Information has a greater impact on judgments and decisions when it is vivid and attention-grabbing than when it is pallid and bland. Information presented in a highly imaginable way is more persuasive than simple verbal descriptions of the same material.

voir dire The process by which the judge and/or attorneys ask potential jurors questions and attempt to uncover any biases.

voluntary false confession False confessions that arise because people seek notoriety, desire to cleanse themselves of guilt feelings from previous wrongdoings, want to protect the real criminal, or have difficulty distinguishing fact from fiction.

weapon focus effect When confronted by an armed attacker, the victim's tendency to focus attention on the weapon and fails to notice other stimuli.

writ of certiorari An order by an appellate court allowing an appeal from a lower court; used in cases when the appellate court may, but is not required to, allow the appeal.

zero tolerance An approach to law enforcement in which the police attempt to arrest all lawbreakers, even those who have committed what are traditionally viewed as petty or nuisance crimes.

References

Abram, K. M., & Teplin, L. A. (1991). Co-occurring disorders among mentally ill jail detainees: Implications for public policy. *American Psychologist, 46,* 1036–1045.

Abram, K. M., Teplin, L. A., Charles, D. R., Longworth, S. L., McClelland, G. M., & Dulcan, M. K. (2004). Posttraumatic stress disorder and trauma in youth in juvenile detention. *Archives of General Psychiatry, 61,* 403–410.

Abram, K. M., Washburn, J. J., Teplin, L. A., Emanuel, K. M., Romero, E. G., & McClelland, G. M. (2007). Posttraumatic stress disorder and psychiatric comorbidity among detained youths. *Psychiatric Services, 58,* 1311–1316.

Abramson, J. (1994). *We, the jury.* New York: Basic Books.

Ackerman, M. J., & Ackerman, M. C. (1997). Child custody evaluation practices: A survey of experienced professionals (revisited). *Professional Psychology: Research and Practice, 28,* 137–145.

Ackerman, M., & Schoendorf, M. (1992). *Ackerman-Schoendorf Scales for Parent Evaluation of Custody.* Lutz, FL: PAR.

Adams, R. E., Rohe, W. M., & Arcury, T. A. (2005). Awareness of community-oriented policing and neighborhood perceptions in five small to midsize cities. *Journal of Criminal Justice, 33,* 43–54.

Adler, F. (1973). Socioeconomic factors influencing jury verdicts. *New York University Review of Law and Social Change, 3,* 110.

Adorno, T., Frenkel-Brunswik, E., Levinson, D., & Sanford, N. (1950). *The authoritarian personality.* New York: Harper & Row.

Ake v. Oklahoma, 105 S.Ct. 977 (1985).

Akers, R. L., Krohn, M. D., Lanz-Kaduce, L., & Radosevich, M. (1996). Social learning and deviant behavior: A specific test of a general theory. In D. G. Rojek & G. F. Jensen (Eds.), *Exploring delinquency: Causes and control* (pp. 109–119). Los Angeles: Roxbury.

Alden, B. (1996, September 9). Italian-Americans win "Batson" shield. *National Law Journal,* p. A8.

Alexander, J., Barton, C., Gordon, D., Grotpeter, J., Hansson, K., Harrison, R., et al. (1998). *Blueprints for violence prevention: Book three. Functional family therapy.* Boulder, CO: Center for the Study and Prevention of Violence.

Alexander, J., & Parsons, B. (1973). Short-term behavioral intervention with delinquent families: Impact on family process and recidivism. *Journal of Abnormal Psychology, 81,* 219–225.

Alexander, K., Quas, J., Goodman, G., Ghetti, S., Edelstein, R., Redlich, A., et al. (2005). Traumatic impact predicts long-term memory for documented child sexual abuse. *Psychological Science, 16,* 33–40.

Alison, L., Smith, M. D., & Morgan, K. (2003). Interpreting the accuracy of offender profiles. *Psychology, Crime and Law, 9*(2), 185–195.

Allan, A., Allan, M., Giles, M., Drake, D., & Froyland, I. (2005). An observational study of bail decision-making. *Psychiatry, Psychology and Law, 12,* 319–333.

Alleyne, V. (2007). Locked up means locked out: Women, addiction, and incarceration. *Women and Therapy, 29,* 181–194.

Allison, J. A., & Wrightsman, L. S. (1993). *Rape: The misunderstood crime.* Thousand Oaks, CA: Sage.

Allred, K., Mallozzi, J., Matsui, F., & Raia, C. (1997). The influence on anger and compassion on negotiation performance. *Organizational Behavior and Human Decision Processes, 70,* 175–187.

Almerigogna, J., Ost, J., Bull, R., & Akehurst, L. (2007). A state of high anxiety: How non-supportive interviewers can increase the suggestibility of child witnesses. *Applied Cognitive Psychology, 21,* 963–974.

Alpert, J. L., Brown, L. S., & Courtois, C. A. (1998). Symptomatic clients and memories of childhood abuse: What the trauma and child sexual abuse literature tells us. *Psychology, Public Policy, and Law, 4,* 941–995.

Altschuler, D. (1998). Intermediate sanctions and community treatment for serious and violent juvenile offenders. In R. Loeber & D. Farrington (Eds.), *Serious and violent juvenile offenders: Risk factors and successful interventions* (pp. 367–388). Thousand Oaks, CA: Sage Publications, Inc.

Altschuler, D., & Armstrong, T. (1997). Aftercare not afterthought: Testing the IAP model. *Juvenile Justice, 3,* 115–122.

American Bar Association. (1984). *ABA criminal justice mental health standards.* Washington, DC: Author.

American Bar Association. (1992). *Narrowing the gap.* St. Paul, MN: West.

American Bar Association. (1993). *ABA formal opinion 93–379.* Chicago: Author.

American Bar Association Commission on Racial and Ethnic Diversity in the Profession. (2006). *Goal IX Report 2005–2006: The status of racial and ethnic diversity in the American Bar Association.* Retrieved December 8, 2009, from http://www.abanet.org/minorities/publications/g9/GoalIX_0506.pdf

American Bar Association Special Committee. (1991). *Jury comprehension in complex cases.* Washington, DC: American Bar Association.

American Psychological Association. (1994). Guidelines for child custody evaluations in divorce proceedings. *American Psychologist, 49,* 677–680.

American Psychological Association. (2002). Ethical principles of psychologists and code of conduct. *American Psychologist, 57,* 1060–1073.

American Psychological Association (2008). *Amendment to the reaffirmation of the American Psychological Association position against torture and other cruel, inhuman, or degrading treatment or punishment and its application to individuals defined in the United States Code as "enemy combatants."* Retrieved April 15, 2009, from http://www.apa.org/governance/resolutions/amend022208.html

Anderson, K. B., Cooper, H., & Okamura, L. (1997). Individual differences and attitudes toward rape: A meta-analytic review. *Personality and Social Psychology Bulletin, 23,* 295–315.

Anderson, M., & MacCoun, R. (1999). Goal conflict in juror assessments of compensatory and punitive damages. *Law and Human Behavior, 23,* 313–330.

The Andrea Yates' case: Chronology of the Yates' case. (2005, January 7). *Houston Chronicle,* p. A10.

Andrews, D. A., & Bonta, J. (1995). *LSI-R: The Level of Service Inventory-Revised.* Toronto, Ontario, Canada: Multi-Health Systems, Inc.

Andrews, D. A., & Bonta, J. (2006). *The psychology of criminal conduct* (4th ed.). Newark, NJ: Lexis Nexis/Mathew Bender.

Andrews, D. A., Bonta, J., & Hoge, R. D. (1990). Classification for effective rehabilitation: Rediscovering psychology. *Criminal Justice and Behavior, 17,* 19–52.

Andrews, D. A., Bonta, J., & Wormith, J. (2004). *The Level of Service/Case Management Inventory user's manual.* North Tonawanda, NY: Multi-Health Systems.

Andrews, D. A., & Hoge, R. (in press). *Evaluation for risk of violence in juveniles.* New York: Oxford University Press.

Andrews, J. A., Foster, S. L., Capaldi, D., & Hops, H. (2000). Adolescent and family predictors of physical aggression, communication, and satisfaction among young adult couples. *Journal of Consulting and Clinical Psychology, 68,* 195–208.

Aos, S., Miller, M., & Drake, E. (2006). *Evidence-based adult corrections programs: What works and what does not.*

Olympia, WA: Washington State Institute for Public Policy.

Aos, S., Phipps, P., Barnoski, R., & Lieb, R. (2001). *The comparative costs and benefits of programs to reduce crime*. Olympia, WA: Washington State Institute for Public Policy. (Document No. 01-05-1201)

Appelbaum, P. (2005). Law & psychiatry: Behavioral genetics and the punishment of crime. *Psychiatric Services, 56*, 25–27.

Appelbaum, P. (2007). The new lie detectors: Neuroscience, deception, and the courts. *Psychiatric Services, 58*, 460–462.

Appelbaum, P. S., & Grisso, T. (1995). The MacArthur Treatment Competence Study. I: Mental illness and competence to consent to treatment. *Law and Human Behavior, 19*, 105–126.

Archer, J. (1991). The influence of testosterone on human aggression. *British Journal of Psychology, 82*, 128.

Ares, C. E., Rankin, A., & Sturz, H. (1963). The Manhattan bail project: An interim report on the use of pre-trial parole. *New York University Law Review, 38*, 67–95.

Arkes, H., & Mellers, B. (2002). Do juries meet our expectations? *Law and Human Behavior, 26*, 625–639.

Arrigo, B. A., & Claussen, N. (2003). Police corruption and psychological testing: A strategy for preemployment screening. *International Journal of Offender Therapy & Comparative Criminology, 47*, 272–290.

Aspin, L., & Hall, W. (1994). Retention elections and judicial behavior. *Judicature, 77*, 306–315.

Associated Press. (1988, January 13). Former Kansas woman identifies man in attack. *Kansas City Times*, p. B5.

Associated Press. (2000, July 14). *Analysis of Philadelphia arrest: 59 blows in 28 seconds*. Retrieved July 18, 2005, from http://archives.cnn.com/2000/US/07/14/police.beating.02/index.html

Associated Press. (2007, April 26). *Man could face 30 days in jail for skipping out on jury duty*. Retrieved June 25, 2009, from http://abclocal.go.com/ktrk/story?section=news/bizarre&id=5248553

Association of Family and Conciliation Courts. (2000). *Model standards of practice for family and divorce mediation*. Retrieved January 25, 2009, from http://www.afccnet.org/resources/resources_model_mediation.asp

Association of Family and Conciliation Courts. (2006). *Model standards of practice for child custody evaluation*. Retrieved January 25, 2009, from http://www.afccnet.org/pdfs/Model%20Stds%20Child%20Custody%20Eval%20Sept%202006.pdf

Atkins v. Virginia, 536 U.S. 304 (2002).

Austen, I. (2008, July 16). *Blurry peek at questioning of a Guantanamo inmate*. Retrieved July 18, 2008, from http://www.nytimes.com/2008/07/16/world/16khadr.html?scp=1&sq=khadr&st=cse

Ayre, R. (1995). The prison crisis: An essay on the social and political foundations of criminal justice police. *Public Administration Quarterly, 19*, 42.

Ayres, B. D., (1996, August 27). California child molesters face "chemical castration." *The New York Times*, p. A1.

Babb, S. (2003). Fear and loathing in America: Application of treason law in times of national crisis and the case of John Walker Lindh. *Hastings Law Journal, 54*, 1721–1744.

Babcock, B. (1993). A place in the palladium: Women's rights and jury service. *University of Cincinnati Law Review, 61*, 1139–1180.

Baer, R., Wetter, M., Nichols, J., Greene, R., & Berry, D. (1995). Sensitivity of MMPI-2 validity scales to underreporting of symptoms. *Psychological Assessment, 7*, 419–423.

Bagby, R. M., Nicholson, R. A., Rogers, R., & Nussbaum, D. (1992). Domains of competency to stand trial: A factor analytic study. *Law and Human Behavior, 16*, 491–508.

Bailenson, J., Blascovich, J., Beall, A., & Noveck, B. (2006). Courtroom applications of virtual environments, immersive virtual environments, and collaborative virtual environments. *Law & Policy, 28*, 249–270.

Bailey, D. (2003). Who is learning disabled? Psychologists and educators debate over how to identify students with learning disabilities. *APA Monitor, 34*, 58.

Bailis, D., & MacCoun, R. (1996). Estimating liability risks with the media as your guide: A content analysis of media coverage of tort litigation. *Law and Human Behavior, 20*, 419–429.

Baker, L. (1983). *Miranda: Crime, law, and politics*. New York: Atheneum.

Baldas, T. (2004, November 15). Considering the alternatives. *National Law Journal*, p. 18.

Baldus, D. C., Pulaski, C., & Woodworth, G. (1983). Comparative review of death sentences: An empirical study of the Georgia experience. *Journal of Criminal Law and Criminology, 74*, 661–753.

Baldus, D. C., Woodworth, G., Zuckerman, D., Weiner, N. A., & Broffitt, B. (1998). Race discrimination and the death penalty in the post-Furman era: An empirical and legal overview with recent findings from Philadelphia. *Cornell Law Review, 83*, 1638–1770.

Baldus, D. C., Woodworth, G., Zuckerman, D., Weiner, N. A., & Broffit, B. (2001). The use of peremptory challenges in capital murder trials: A legal and empirical analysis. *University of Pennsylvania Journal of Constitutional Law, 3*, 3–10.

Bandura, A. (1973). *Aggression: A social learning analysis.* Englewood Cliffs, NJ: Prentice Hall.

Bandura, A. (1976). Social learning analysis of aggression. In E. Ribes-Inesta & A. Bandura (Eds.), *Analysis of delinquency and aggression* (pp. 203–232). Hillsdale, NJ: Erlbaum.

Bandura, A. (1986). *Social foundations of thought and action: A social cognitive theory.* Englewood Cliffs, NJ: Prentice Hall.

Banks v. Goodfellow, L.R. 5 Q.B. 549 (1870).

Barbaree, H. E., & Marshall, W. L. (1991). The role of male sexual arousal in rape: Six models. *Journal of Consulting and Clinical Psychology, 59*, 621–630.

Bard, M. (1969). Family intervention police teams as a community mental health resource. *Journal of Criminal Law, Criminology, and Police Science, 60*, 24.

Bard, M., & Berkowitz, B. (1967). Training police as specialists in family crisis intervention: A community psychology action program. *Community Mental Health Journal, 3*, 209–215.

Barnett, N., & Feild, H. S. (1977). Sex differences in attitudes toward rape. *Journal of College Student Personnel, 18*, 93–96.

Barnett, O., Miller-Perrin, C., & Perrin, R. (2005). *Family violence across the lifespan: An introduction* (2nd ed.). Thousand Oaks, CA: Sage.

Baron, R. S., Kerr, N., & Miller, N. (1993). *Group process, group decision, group action.* Buckingham, UK: Open University Press.

Barovick, H. (1998, June). DWB: Driving while black. *Time,* p. 35.

Barr, W. (1992, March). *Comments by the attorney general of the United States.* Speech delivered at the University of Kansas, Lawrence.

Barrick, M., & Mount, M. (1991). The big five personality dimensions and job performance: A meta-analysis. *Personnel Psychology, 44*, 1–26.

Bartlett, F. C. (1932). *Remembering: A study of experimental and social psychology.* New York: Cambridge University Press.

Bartoi, M. G., & Kinder, B. N. (1998). Effects of child and adult sexual abuse on adult sexuality. *Journal of Sex & Marital Therapy, 24*, 75–90.

Bartol, C. R. (1983). *Psychology and American law.* Belmont, CA: Wadsworth.

Bartol, C. R. (1991). Predictive validation of the MMPI for small-town police officers who fail. *Professional Psychology: Research and Practice, 22*, 127–132.

Bartol, C. R. (1996). Police psychology: Then, now, and beyond. *Criminal Justice and Behavior, 23*, 70–89.

Bartol, C. R., & Bartol, A. (2006). *Current perspectives in forensic psychology and criminal justice.* Thousand Oaks, CA: Sage.

Batson v. Kentucky, 476 U.S. 79 (1986).

Bauserman, R. (1997, October). *Child adjustment in joint custody versus sole custody arrangements: A meta-analytic review.* Paper presented at the 11th Annual Conference of the Children's Rights Council, Arlington, VA.

Bauserman, R. (2002). Child adjustment in joint-custody versus sole-custody arrangements: A meta-analytic review. *Journal of Family Psychology, 16*, 91–102.

Bazelon, D. (1974). Psychiatrists and the adversary process. *Scientific American, 230*, 18–23.

Bechara, A., Damasio, H., Tranel, D., & Damasio, A. R. (1997). Deciding advantageously before knowing the advantageous strategy. *Science, 275*, 1293–1294.

Beck, A. (1987, July 25). Recruits graduate to police duties. *Lawrence Journal-World,* p. 3A.

Becker, J. V., Stinson, J., Tromp, S., & Messer, G. (2003). Characteristics of individuals petitioned for civil commitment. *International Journal of Offender Therapy and Comparative Criminology, 47*, 185–195.

Beech, A. R., Fisher, D. D., & Thornton, D. (2003). Risk assessment of sex offenders. *Professional Psychology: Research and Practice, 34*, 339–352.

Begam, R. (1977). Voir dire: The attorney's job. *Trial, 13*, 3.

Begany, J. J., & Milburn, M. A. (2002). Psychological predictors of sexual harassment: Authoritarianism, hostile sexism, and rape myths. *Psychology of Men and Masculinity, 3,* 119–126.

Behn, N. (1995). *Lindbergh: The crime.* New York: Onyx.

Beiser, E. N. (1973). Are juries representative? *Judicature, 57,* 194–199.

Belenko, S. (1998). Research on drug courts: A critical review. *National Drug Court Institute Review, 1,* 1–42.

Belenko, S. (1999). Research on drug courts: A critical review: 1999 update. *National Drug Court Institute Review, 2,* 1–58.

Belenko, S. (2001). *Research on drug courts: A critical review: 2001 update.* New York: National Center on Addiction and Substance Abuse at Columbia University.

Belenko, S. (2002). Drug courts. In C. Leukefeld, F. Tims, & D. Farabee (Eds.), *Treatment of drug offenders: Policies and issues* (pp. 301–318). New York: Springer Publishing Company.

Belenko, S., DeMatteo, D., & Patapis, N. (2007). Drug courts. In D. Springer & A. Roberts (Eds.), *Handbook of forensic mental health with victims and offenders: Assessment, treatment, and research* (pp. 385–423). New York: Springer Publishing Company.

Benner, A. W. (1986). Psychological screening of police applicants. In J. T. Reese & H. A. Goldstein (Eds.), *Psychological services for law enforcement* (pp. 11–20). Washington, DC: U.S. Government Printing Office.

Ben-Shakhar, G. (2002). A critical review of the Control Questions Test (CQT). In M. Kleiner (Ed.), *Handbook of polygraph testing.* London: Academic Press.

Benton, T., Ross, D., Bradshaw, E., Thomas, W., & Bradshaw, G. (2006). Eyewitness memory is still not common sense: Comparing jurors, judges and law enforcement to eyewitness experts. *Applied Cognitive Psychology, 20,* 115–129.

Berg, A. S. (1998). *Lindbergh.* New York: G. P. Putnam.

Berkemer v. McCarty, 468 U.S. 420 (1984).

Berman, L. M., & Osborne, Y. H. (1987). Attorneys' referrals for competency to stand trial evaluations: Comparisons of referred and nonreferred clients. *Behavioral Sciences & the Law, 5,* 373–380.

Berman, M. E. (1997). Biopsychosocial approaches to understanding human aggression: The first 30 years. *Clinical Psychology Review, 15,* 585–588.

Berman, M. E., Tracy, J. I., & Coccaro, E. F. (1997). The serotonin hypothesis of aggression revisited. *Clinical Psychology Review, 17,* 651–665.

Bersoff, D. N. (1987). Social science data and the Supreme Court: Lockhart as a case in point. *American Psychologist, 42,* 52–58.

Betts v. Brady, 316 U.S. 455 (1942).

Beutler, L. E., Storm, A., Kirkish, P., Scogin, F., & Gaines, J. A. (1985). Parameters in the prediction of police officer performance. *Professional Psychology: Research and Practice, 16,* 324–335.

Beyer, M. (1997). Experts for juveniles at risk of adult sentences. In P. Puritz, A. Capozello, & W. Shang (Eds.), *More than meets the eye: Rethinking assessment, competency, and sentencing for a harsher era of juvenile justice* (pp. 1–22). Washington, DC: American Bar Association, Juvenile Justice Center.

Bibas, S. (2004). Plea bargaining outside the shadow of trial. *Harvard Law Review, 117,* 2463–2547.

Binder, A. (1988). Juvenile delinquency. In M. R. Rosenzweig & L. W. Porter (Eds.), *Annual review of psychology* (pp. 253–282). Palo Alto, CA: Annual Reviews.

Binder, A., Geis, G., & Bruce, D. D. (2001). *Juvenile delinquency: Historical, cultural & legal perspectives.* Cincinnati, OH: Anderson Publishing.

Bishop, D. M., Frazier, C. E., Lanza-Kaduce, L., & Winner, L. (1996). The transfer of juveniles to criminal court: Does it make a difference? *Crime and Delinquency, 42,* 171–191.

Bittner, E. (1967). Police discretion in emergency apprehension of mentally ill persons. *Social Problems, 14,* 278–292.

Blair, I., Judd, C., & Chapleau, K. (2004). The influence of Afrocentric facial features in criminal sentencing. *Psychological Science, 15,* 674–679.

Blakely v. Washington, 124 S. Ct. 2348 (2004).

Blau, T. H. (1986). Deadly force: Psychosocial factors and objective evaluation. A preliminary effort. In J. T. Reese & H. A. Goldstein (Eds.), *Psychological services for law enforcement* (pp. 315–334). Washington, DC: U.S. Government Printing Office.

Blau, T. H. (1994). *Psychological services for law enforcement.* New York: Wiley.

Blume, E. S. (1990). *Secret survivors: Uncovering incest and its aftereffects in women.* New York: Ballantine.

Blumenthal, J. A. (1998). The reasonable woman standard: A meta-analytic review of gender differences in perceptions of sexual harassment. *Law and Human Behavior, 22*, 33–58.

Blunk, R., & Sales, B. (1977). Persuasion during the voir dire. In B. Sales (Ed.), *Psychology in the legal process* (pp. 39–58). New York: Spectrum.

BMW of North America v. Gore, 517 U.S. 599 (1996).

Boatright, R. (1999). Why citizens don't respond to jury summonses, and what courts can do about it. *Judicature, 82*, 156–157.

Boccaccini, M. T., & Brodsky, S. L. (1999). Diagnostic test usage by forensic psychologists in emotional injury cases. *Professional Psychology: Research and Practice, 30*, 253–259.

Boccaccini, M., Murrie, D., Clark, J., & Cornell, D. (2008). Describing, diagnosing, and naming psychopathy: How do youth psychopathy labels influence jurors? *Behavioral Sciences & the Law, 26*, 487–510.

Boehm, V. (1968). Mr. Prejudice, Miss Sympathy, and the authoritarian personality: An application of psychological measuring techniques to the problem of jury bias. *Wisconsin Law Review, 1968*, 734–750.

Boehnert, C. (1989). Characteristics of successful and unsuccessful insanity pleas. *Law and Human Behavior, 13*, 31–40.

Boersema, C., Hanson, R., & Keilitz, S. (1991). State court-annexed arbitration: What do attorneys think? *Judicature, 75*, 28–33.

Boire, R. (2005). Searching the brain: The Fourth Amendment implications of brain-based deception detection devices. *American Journal of Bioethics, 5*, 62–63.

Bond, C., & DePaulo, B. (2006). Accuracy of deception judgments. *Personality and Social Psychology Review, 10*, 214–234.

Bonnie, R. J. (1993). The competence of criminal defendants: Beyond *Dusky* and *Drope*. *University of Miami Law Review, 47*, 539–601.

Bonnie, R. J., & Monahan, J. (1996). *Mental disorder, work disability, and the law.* Chicago: The University of Chicago Press.

Bonnie, R. J., & Slobogin, C. (1980). The role of mental health professionals in the criminal process: The case for informed speculation. *Virginia Law Review, 66*, 427–522.

Bonora, B. (1995, February 27). Bias in jury selection continues. *National Law Journal*, pp. B8–B9.

Bonta, J. (1997). *Offender rehabilitation: From research to practice.* Ottawa: Department of the Solicitor General of Canada. (User Report No. 1997-01)

Bonta, J., & Gendreau, P. (1990). Reexamining the cruel and unusual punishment of prison life. *Law and Human Behavior, 14*, 347–372.

Book, A. S. (1999). Shame on you: An analysis of modern shame punishment as an alternative to incarceration. *William and Mary Law Review, 40*, 653–686.

Boothroyd, R., Mercado, C., Poythress, N., Christy, A., & Petrila, J. (2005). Clinical outcomes of defendants in mental health court. *Psychiatric Services, 56*, 829–834.

Boothroyd, R., Poythress, N., McGaha, A., & Petrila, J. (2003). The Broward mental health court: Process, outcomes, and service utilization. *International Journal of Law & Psychiatry, 26*, 55–71.

Borduin, C., Mann, B., Cone, L., Henggeler, S., Fucci, B., & Blaske, D. (1995). Multisystemic treatment of serious juvenile offenders: Long-term prevention of criminality and violence. *Journal of Consulting and Clinical Psychology, 63*, 569–578.

Borgida, E., & Brekke, N. (1985). Psycholegal research on rape trials. In A. Burgess (Ed.), *Research handbook on rape and sexual assault* (pp. 313–342). New York: Garland.

Bornstein, B. (1994). David, Goliath, and Reverend Bayes: Prior beliefs about defendants' status in personal injury cases. *Applied Cognitive Psychology, 8*, 232–258.

Bornstein, B., Miller, M., Nemeth, R., Page, G., & Musil, S. (2005). Juror reactions to jury duty: Perceptions of the system and potential stressors. *Behavioral Sciences & the Law, 23*, 321–346.

Bornstein, B. H., & Rajki, M. (1994). Extra-legal factors and product liability: The influence of mock jurors' demographic characteristics and intuitions about the cause of an injury. *Behavioral Sciences & the Law, 12*, 137–147.

Bornstein, B., Rung, L., & Miller, M. (2002). The effects of defendant remorse on mock juror decisions in a malpractice case. *Behavioral Sciences & the Law, 20*, 393–409.

Borum, R. (1996). Improving the clinical practice of violence risk assessment: Technology, guidelines, and training. *American Psychologist, 51*, 945–956.

Borum, R., Bartels, P., & Forth, A. (2005). *Structured assessment of violence risk in youth.* Lutz, FL: PAR.

Borum, R., Deane, M. W., Steadman, H. J., & Morrissey, J. (1998). Police perspectives on responding to mentally ill people in crisis: Perceptions of program effectiveness. *Behavioral Sciences & the Law, 16,* 393–406.

Borum, R., & Fulero, S. M. (1999). Empirical research and the insanity defense and attempted reforms: Evidence toward informed policy. *Law and Human Behavior, 23,* 375–394.

Borum, R., & Stock, H. V. (1993). Detection of deception in law enforcement applicants: A preliminary investigation. *Law and Human Behavior, 17,* 157–166.

Borum, R., & Verhaagen, D. (2006). *Assessing and managing violence risk in youth.* New York: Guilford.

Bothwell, R. K. (1999). The ethnic factor in voir dire. In W. F. Abbott & J. Batt (Eds.), *A handbook of jury research* (pp. 10.1–10.11). Philadelphia, PA: ALI-ABA.

Bottoms, B., & Goodman, G. (1994). Perceptions of children's credibility in sexual assault cases. *Journal of Applied Social Psychology, 24,* 702–732.

Bottoms, B. L., Shaver, P. R., & Goodman, G. S. (1996). An analysis of ritualistic and religion-related child abuse allegations. *Law and Human Behavior, 20,* 1–34.

Bouffard, J., & Bergeron, L. (2006). Reentry works: The implementation and effectiveness of a serious and violent offender reentry initiative. *Journal of Offender Rehabilitation, 44,* 1–29.

Bourgon, G., & Armstrong, B. (2005). Transferring the principles of effective treatment into a "Real World" prison setting. *Criminal Justice and Behavior, 32,* 3–25.

Bovbjerg, R., Sloan, F., Dor, A., & Hsieh, C. (1991). Juries and justice: Are malpractice and other personal injuries created equal? *Law and Contemporary Problems, 54,* 5–42.

Bower, B. (1984). Not popular by reason of insanity. *Science News, 126,* 218–219.

Bowers, W., Vandiver, M., & Dugan, P. (1994). A new look at public opinion on capital punishment: What citizens and legislators prefer. *American Journal of Criminal Law, 22,* 77–150.

Bowlby, J. (1949). *Why delinquency? Report of the conference on the scientific study of juvenile delinquency.* London: National Association for Mental Health.

Bowlby, J. (1953). *Child care and the growth of love.* Baltimore, MD: Penguin.

Bowlby, J., & Salter-Ainsworth, M. D. (1965). *Child care and the growth of love.* London: Penguin.

Boyer, P. J. (2000, January 17). DNA on trial. *The New Yorker,* pp. 42–53.

Bradfield, A., Wells, G., & Olson, E. (2002). The damaging effect of confirming feedback on the relation between eyewitness certainty and identification accuracy. *Journal of Applied Psychology, 87,* 112–120.

Braithwaite, V. (2000). Values and restorative justice in schools. In H. Strang & J. Braithwaite (Eds.), *Restorative justice: Philosophy to practice* (pp. 121–144). Aldershot, UK: Ashgate.

Brame, R. (2000). Investigating treatment effects in a domestic violence experiment with partially missing outcome data. *Journal of Quantitative Criminology, 16*(3), 283–314.

Brannen, D., Salekin, R., Zapf, P., Salekin, K., Kubak, F., & DeCoster, J. (2006). Transfer to adult court: A national study of how juvenile court judges weight pertinent Kent criteria. *Psychology, Public Policy, and Law, 12,* 332–355.

Braudway, B. (2004). Scarlet letter punishments. *Campbell Law Review, 27,* 63–90.

Braun, K., Ellis, R., & Loftus, E. (2002). Make my memory: How advertising can change our memories of the past. *Psychology and Marketing, 19,* 1–23.

Breed, A. G. (1999, September 2). "Love thy neighbor" tested in Danville. *Lexington Herald-Leader, 1,* 13.

Brehm, J. W. (1966). *A theory of psychological reactance.* Orlando, FL: Academic Press.

Brehm, S. S., & Brehm, J. (1981). *Psychological reactance.* New York: Academic Press.

Bremer, C., & Todd, S. (2004). Reducing judicial stress through mentoring. *Judicature, 87,* 244–251.

Brennan, P. A., & Raine, A. (1997). Biosocial bases of antisocial behavior: Psychophysiological, neurological, and cognitive factors. *Clinical Psychology Review, 17,* 589–604.

Brennan, P., & Spohn, C. (2008). Race/ethnicity and sentencing outcomes among drug offenders in North Carolina. *Journal of Contemporary Criminal Justice, 24,* 371–398.

Breslau, N., Chilcoat, H. D., Kessler, R. C., & Davis, G. C. (1999). Previous exposure to trauma and PTSD effects of subsequent trauma: Results from the Detroit Area Survey of Trauma. *American Journal of Psychiatry, 156*, 902–907.

Breslau, N., Davis, G. C., Andreski, P., & Peterson, E. (1991). Traumatic events and posttraumatic stress disorder in an urban population of young adults. *Archives of General Psychiatry, 48*, 216–222.

Breslau, N., Kessler, R. C., Chilcoat, H. D., Schultz, L. R., Davis, G. C., & Andreski, P. (1998). Trauma and posttraumatic stress disorder in the community: The 1996 Detroit Area Survey of Trauma. *Archives of General Psychiatry, 55*, 626–632.

Brewer, N., & Burke, A. (2002). Effects of testimonial inconsistencies and eyewitness confidence on mock-juror judgments. *Law and Human Behavior, 26*, 353–364.

Brewster, J., & Stoloff, M. (2003). Relationship between IQ and first-year overall performance as a police officer. *Applied H.R.M. Research, 8*, 49–50.

Bricklin, B. (1995). *The custody evaluation handbook: Research-based solutions and applications.* Levittown, PA: Brunner/Mazel.

Bridges, G., & Steen, S. (1998). Racial disparities in official assessments of juvenile offenders: Attribution stereotypes as mediating mechanisms. *American Sociological Review, 63*, 554–570.

Brigham, J., & Wasserman, A. (1999). The impact of race, racial attitude, and gender on reactions to the criminal trial of O. J. Simpson. *Journal of Applied Social Psychology, 29*, 1333–1370.

Broder, J. (2004). Starting over, 24 years after a wrongful conviction. *The New York Times.* Retrieved June 27, 2004, from http://www.nytimes/com/2004/06/21/national/

Broeder, D. W. (1959). The University of Chicago jury project. *Nebraska Law Review, 38*, 744–760.

Broeder, D. W. (1965). Voir dire examinations: An empirical study. *Southern California Law Review, 38*, 503–528.

Bronner, G., Peretz, C., & Ehrenfeld, M. (2003). Sexual harassment of nurses and nursing students. *Journal of Advanced Nursing, 42*, 637–644.

Brown v. Board of Education, 347 U.S. 483 (1954).

Brown, L. T. (2003). Racial discrimination in jury selection: Professional misconduct, not legitimate advocacy. *Review of Litigation, 22*, 209–317.

Brown, T., Borduin, C., & Henggeler, S. (2001). Treating juvenile offenders in community settings. In J. Ashford, B. Sales, & W. Reid (Eds.), *Treating adult and juvenile offenders with special needs* (pp. 445–464). Washington, DC: American Psychological Association.

Brownmiller, S., & Alexander, D. (1992, January/February). From Carmita Wood to Anita Hill. *Ms.,* pp. 70–71.

Bruck, D. (1985, May 20). The death penalty: An exchange. *New Republic,* pp. 20–21.

Bruck, M., Ceci, S., & Hembrooke, H. (1998). Reliability and credibility in young children's reports: From research to policy and practice. *American Psychologist, 53*, 136–151.

Bruck, M., Ceci, S., & Hembrooke, H. (2002). The nature of children's true and false narratives. *Developmental Review, 22*, 520–554.

Brunner, H., Nelen, M., Breakefield, X., Ropers, H., & van Oost, B. (1993). Abnormal behavior associated with a point mutation in the structural gene for monoamine oxidase A. *Science, 262*, 578–580.

Bryan, W. J. (1971). *The chosen ones.* New York: Vantage Press.

Buchan, L. (May 19, 2003) Jail diversion for mentally ill top priority in Miami-Dade. *County News Online, 37*, 12. Retrieved July 5, 2005, from http://www.naco.org/CountyNewsTemplate.cfm?template=/ContentManagement/ContentDisplay.cfm&ContentID=8091

Bund, J. M. (1997). Did you say chemical castration? *University of Pittsburgh Law Review, 59*(1), 157–192.

Bureau of Justice Statistics. (2005a). *State and local law enforcement statistics.* Retrieved July 18, 2005, from http://www.ojp.usdoj.gov/bjs/sandlle.htm#education

Bureau of Justice Statistics. (2005b). *National crime victimization survey.* Washington, DC: U.S. Department of Justice, Office of Justice Programs, Bureau of Justice.

Bureau of Justice Statistics. (2006). *Special report: Mental health problems of prison and jail inmates.* Retrieved January 26, 2009, from http://www.ojp.usdoj.gov/bjs/pub/pdf/mhppji.pdf

Bureau of Justice Statistics. (2008a). *Criminal victimization, 2007.* Retrieved January 26, 2009, from http://www.ojp.usdoj.gov/bjs/pub/pdf/cv07.pdf

Bureau of Justice Statistics. (2008b). *Jail inmates at midyear 2007*. Retrieved February 9, 2009, from http://www.ojp.usdoj.gov/bjs/abstract/jim07.htm

Bureau of Justice Statistics. (2008c). *Probation and parole statistics*. Retrieved January 29, 2009, from http://www.ojp.usdoj.gov/bjs/pandp.htm

Bureau of Justice Statistics. (2009). *Capital punishment statistics*. Retrieved March 26, 2009, from http://www.ojp.usdoj.gov/bjs/cp.htm

Burger, W. E. (1975). Dissenting opinion in *O'Connor v. Donaldson*. *U. S. Law Week, 42*, 4929–4936.

Burgess, A. W., & Holmstrom, L. L. (1974). *Rape: Victims of crisis*. Bowie, MA: Robert J. Brady.

Burgess, A. W., & Holmstrom, L. L. (1979). Rape: Sexual disruption and recovery. *American Journal of Ortho-psychiatry, 49*, 648–657.

Burgess, N., Maguire, E., & O'Keefe, J. (2002). The human hippocampus and spatial and episodic memory. *Neuron, 35*, 625–641.

Burgess, R. L., & Akers, R. L. (1966). A differential-reinforcement theory of criminal behavior. *Social Problems, 14*, 128–147.

Burke, P., & Tonry, M. (2006). *Successful transition and reentry for safer communities: A call to action for parole*. Silver Spring, MD: Center for Effective Public Policy.

Burnet v. Coronado Oil and Gas Co., 52 S.Ct. 443, 447 (1932).

Burt, M. R. (1980). Cultural myths and supports for rape. *Journal of Personality and Social Psychology, 38*, 217–230.

Burt, R., & Morris, N. (1972). A proposal for the abolition of the incompetency plea. *University of Chicago Law Review, 40*, 66–95.

Bush v. Schiavo, 885 So.2d 321 (Fla. 2004).

Bushway, S., & Piehl, A. (2001). Judging judicial discretion: Legal factors and racial discrimination in sentencing. *Law and Society Review, 35*, 733–764.

Buss, A. H. (1966). *Psychopathology*. New York: Wiley.

Buss, D. M., & Malamuth, N. M. (Eds.). (1996). *Sex, power, conflict: Evolutionary and feminist perspectives*. New York: Oxford University Press.

Butler, B. (2007). Death qualification and prejudice: The effect of implicit racism, sexism, and homophobia on capital defendants' right to due process. *Behavioral Sciences & the Law, 25*, 857–867.

Butler, W. M., Leitenberg, H., & Fuselier, D. G. (1993). The use of mental health consultants to police hostage negotiation teams. *Behavioral Sciences & the Law, 11*, 213–221.

Butterfield, F. (1996, March 8). Tough law on sentences is criticized. *The New York Times*, p. A8.

Butterfield, F. (1997, February 3). '95 data show sharp drop in reported rapes. *The New York Times*, pp. A1, A14.

Byrne, C. A., Resnick, H. S., Kilpatrick, D. G., Best, C. L., & Saunders, B. E. (1999). The socioeconomic impact of interpersonal violence on women. *Journal of Consulting and Clinical Psychology, 67*, 362–366.

Caetano, R., McGrath, C., Ramisetty-Mikler, S., & Field, C. A. (2005). Drinking, alcohol problems and the five-year recurrence and incidence of male to female and female to male partner violence. *Alcoholism: Clinical & Experimental Research, 29*, 98–106.

Caldwell, M., & Van Rybroek, G. (2005). Reducing violence in serious juvenile offenders using intensive treatment. *International Journal of Psychiatry and Law, 28*, 622–636.

Calhoun, K., Atkeson, B., & Resick, P. (1982). A longitudinal examination of fear reactions in victims of rape. *Journal of Counseling Psychology, 29*, 656–661.

California v. Cahill, 5 Cal.4th 497 (1993).

Callahan, L. A., & Silver, E. (1998). Factors associated with the conditional release of persons acquitted by reason of insanity: A decision tree approach. *Law and Human Behavior, 22*(2), 147–163.

Campbell, M. A., & Schmidt, F. (2000). Comparison of mental health & legal factors in the disposition outcome of young offenders. *Criminal Justice & Behavior, 27*, 688–715.

Campbell, R., Sefl, T., Barnes, H. E., Ahrens, C. E., Wasco, S. M., & Zaragoza-Diesfeld, Y. (1999). Community services for rape survivors: Enhancing psychological well-being or increasing trauma? *Journal of Consulting and Clinical Psychology, 67*, 847–858.

Canter, D., Alison, L., Alison, E., & Wentink, N. (2004). The organized/disorganized typology of serial murder: Myth or model? *Psychology, Public Policy and Law, 10*, 293–320.

Cantor, N. L. (1998). Making advance directives meaningful. *Psychology, Public Policy, and Law, 4*, 629–652.

Caperton v. A.T. Massey Coal, 555 U.S. ___ (2009).

Cardozo, M. (1993). Racial discrimination in legal education. *Journal of Legal Education, 43*, 79–84.

Carlsmith, K., Darley, J., & Robinson, P. (2002). Why do we punish: Deterrence and just deserts as motives for punishment. *Journal of Personality and Social Psychology, 83*, 284–299.

Carlsmith, K. M. (2008). On justifying punishment: The discrepancy between words and actions. *Social Justice Research, 21*, 119–137.

Carlson, C., Gronlund, S., & Clark, S. (2008). Lineup composition, suspect position, and the sequential lineup advantage. *Journal of Experimental Psychology: Applied, 14*, 118–128.

Carlson, H., Thayer, R. E., & Germann, A. C. (1971). Social attitudes and personality differences among members of two kinds of police departments (innovative vs. traditional) and students. *Journal of Criminal Law, Criminology, and Police Science, 62*, 564–567.

Carlson, K., & Russo, J. (2001). Biased interpretation of evidence by mock jurors. *Journal of Experimental Psychology: Applied, 7*, 91–103.

Carnevale, P. (2008). Positive affect and decision frame in negotiation. *Group Decision and Negotiation, 17*, 51–63.

Carr, P. L., Ash, A. S., Friedman, R. H., Szalacha, L., Barnett, R. C., Palepu, A., et al. (2000). Faculty perceptions of gender discrimination and sexual harassment in academic medicine. *Annals of Internal Medicine, 132*, 889–896.

Carroll, J. S., Kerr, N. L., Alfini, J. J., Weaver, F. M., MacCoun, R. J., & Feldman, V. (1986). Free press and fair trial: The role of behavioral research. *Law and Human Behavior, 10*, 187–201.

Carter, T. (1998, November), Terms of embitterment. *American Bar Association Journal, 84*, 42.

Carter, T. (2004, June). Red Hook experiment. *American Bar Association Journal, 90*, 37–42.

Carter, T. (2005, February). Mud and money. *American Bar Association Journal, 91*, 40–45.

Casey, P., & Rottman, D. (2005). Problem-solving courts: Models and trends. *The Justice System Journal, 26*, 35–56.

Casey, T. (2004). When good intentions are not enough: Problem-solving courts and the impending crisis of legitimacy. *Southern Methodist University Law Review, 57*, 1459–1519.

Casper, J. D. (1972). *American criminal justice: The defendant's perspective*. Englewood Cliffs, NJ: Prentice Hall.

Caspi, A., McClay, J., Moffitt, T., Mill, J., Martin, J., Craig, I., et al. (2002). Role of genotype in the cycle of violence by maltreated children. *Science, 297*, 851–854.

Castelli, P., Goodman, G., & Ghetti, S. (2005). Effects of interview style and witness age on perceptions of children's credibility in sexual abuse cases. *Journal of Applied Social Psychology, 35*, 297–319.

Catton, B. (1965). Foreword to *Twenty Days* by D. Kunhardt & P. Kunhardt. New York: Harper & Row.

Cauffman, E., Piquero, A., Kimonis, E., Steinberg, L., Chassin, L., & Fagan, J. (2007). Legal, individual, and environmental predictors of court disposition in a sample of serious adolescent offenders. *Law and Human Behavior, 31*, 519–535.

Ceci, S., Huffman, M., Smith, E., & Loftus, E. (1994). Repeatedly thinking about a non-event: Source misattribution among preschoolers. *Consciousness and Cognition, 3*, 388–407.

Ceci, S. J., Kulkofsky, S., Klemfuss, J. Z., Sweeney, C. D., & Bruck, M. (2007). Unwarranted assumptions about children's testimonial accuracy. *Annual Review of Clinical Psychology, 3*, 307–324.

Ceci, S., Scullin, M., & Kanaya, T. (2003). The difficulty of basing death penalty eligibility on IQ cutoff scores for mental retardation. *Ethics & Behavior, 13*, 11–17.

Cecil, J. (2005). Ten years of judicial gatekeeping under *Daubert. American Journal of Public Health, 95*(S1), S74–S80.

Center for Effective Public Policy. (2007). *Increasing public safety through successful offender reentry: Evidence-based and emerging practices in corrections*. Washington, DC: Author.

Cernkovich, S. A., & Giordano, P. C. (1996). School bonding, race, and delinquency. In D. G. Rojek & G. F. Jensen (Eds.), *Exploring delinquency: Causes and control* (pp. 210–218). Los Angeles: Roxbury.

Chadee, D. (1996). Race, trial evidence and jury decision making. *Caribbean Journal of Criminology and Social Psychology, 1*, 59–86.

Chamberlain, P. (1990). Comparative evaluation of specialized foster care for seriously delinquent youths: A first step. *Community Alternatives: International Journal of Family Care, 2*, 21–36.

Chamberlain, P., & Mihalic, S. (1998). *Blueprints for violence prevention: Book eight. Multidimensional treatment foster care*. Boulder, CO: Center for the Study and Prevention of Violence.

Chamberlain, P., & Reid, J. (1998). Comparison of two community alternatives to incarceration for chronic juvenile offenders. *Journal of Consulting and Clinical Psychology, 66*, 624–633.

Chandler, M., & Moran, T. (1990). Psychopathy and moral development: A comparative study of delinquent and nondelinquent youth. *Development & Psychopathology, 2*, 227–246.

Chapman, G., & Bornstein, B. (1996). The more you ask for, the more you get: Anchoring in personal injury verdict. *Applied Cognitive Psychology, 10*, 519–540.

Charles, M. T. (1986). *Policing the streets*. Springfield, IL: Thomas.

Chermack, S. T., & Giancola, P. R. (1997). The relation between alcohol and aggression: An integrated biopsychosocial conceptualization. *Clinical Psychology Review, 17*, 621–649.

Choi, A., & Edleson, J. L. (1996). Social disapproval of wife assaults: A national survey of Singapore. *Journal of Comparative Family Studies, 27*(1), 73–88.

Christie, R. (1976). Probability v. precedence: The social psychology of jury selection. In G. Bermant, C. Nemeth, & N. Vidmar (Eds.), *Psychology and the law: Research frontiers* (pp. 265–281). Lexington, MA: Lexington Books.

Christy, A., Poythress, N., Boothroyd, R., Petrila, J., & Mehra, S. (2005). Evaluating the efficiency and community safety goals of the Broward County mental health court. *Behavioral Sciences & the Law, 23*, 1–17.

Ciesluk v. Ciesluk, 113 P.3d 135 (2005).

Cirincione, C., & Jacobs, C. (1999). Identifying insanity acquittals: Is it any easier? *Law and Human Behavior, 23*, 487–497.

CIT National Advisory Board. (2006). *Crisis intervention team core elements*. Memphis, TN: University of Memphis CIT Center.

Clancy, P. (1987, July 22). Cops battle stress: "I'm hurting … ." *USA Today*, pp. 1A–2A.

Clark, J., Boccaccini, M. T., Caillouet, B., & Chaplin, W. F. (2007). Five factor model personality traits, jury selection, and case outcomes in criminal and civil case. *Criminal Justice and Behavior, 34*, 641–660.

Clark, S. (2005). A re-examination of the effects of biased lineup instructions in eyewitness identification. *Law and Human Behavior, 29*, 395–424.

Clark, S., & Davey, S. (2005). The target-to-fillers shift in simultaneous and sequential lineups. *Law and Human Behavior, 29*, 151–172.

Clavet, G. J. (1996, August). *Ironic effects of juror attempts to suppress inadmissible evidence*. Paper presented at the meeting of the American Psychological Association, Toronto, Canada.

Clemmer, D. (1958). *The prison community*. New York: Rinehart.

Clingempeel, W. G., & Reppucci, N. D. (1982). Joint custody after divorce: Major issues and goals for research. *Psychological Bulletin, 92*, 102–127.

Cloninger, C., Sigvardsson, S., Bohman, M., & vonKnorring, A. (1982). Predisposition to petty criminality in Swedish adoptees. II: Cross-fostering analysis of gene–environment interaction. *Archives of General Psychiatry, 39*, 1242–1249.

Cloud, J. (1998). Of arms and the boy. *Time, 152*.

Cloward, R. A., & Ohlin, L. E. (1960). *Delinquency and opportunity: A theory of delinquent gangs*. New York: Free Press.

CNN. (1998, April 23). Ray's death won't end assassination controversy. Retrieved June 10, 2009, from http://www.cnn.com/US/9804/23/james.earl.ray.reax/

CNN. (2004, June 25). No charges against man beaten during arrest. Retrieved June 20, 2005, from http://www.cnn.com/2004/US/West/06/25/lapd.video/index.html

Coccaro, E., Kavoussi, R., & Lesser, J. (1992). Self- and other-directed human aggression: The role of the central serotonergic system. *International Clinical Psychopharmacology, 6*, 70–83.

Cochrane, R., Tett, R., & Vandecreek, L. (2003). Psychological testing and the selection of police officers. *Criminal Justice and Behavior, 30*, 511–537.

Cocozza, J., & Shufelt, J. (2006, June). *Juvenile mental health courts: An emerging strategy*. Retrieved July 3, 2008, from http://www.ncmhjj.com/pdfs/publications/JuvenileMentalHealthCourts.pdf

Cohen, M. I., Spodak, M. K., Silver, S. B., & Williams, K. (1988). Predicting outcome of insanity acquittees released to the community. *Behavioral Sciences & the Law, 6*, 515–530.

Cohen, T., & Reaves, B. (2006). *Felony defendants in large urban counties, 2002*. Washington, DC: U.S. Department of Justice, Bureau of Justice Statistics.

Colbach, E. (1981). Integrity checks on the witness stand. *Bulletin of the American Academy of Psychiatry and the Law, 9*, 285–288.

Colorado v. Connelly, 107 S.Ct. 515 (1986).

Committee on Ethical Guidelines for Forensic Psychologists. (1991). Specialty guidelines for forensic psychologists. *Law and Human Behavior, 15*, 655–665.

Compton, M., Bahara, M., Watson, A., & Oliva, J. (2008). A comprehensive review of extant research on Crisis Intervention Team (CIT) programs. *Journal of the American Academy of Psychiatry and Law, 36*, 47–55.

Condie, L. O. (2003). *Parenting evaluations for the court: Care and protection matters.* New York: Springer.

Conger, R. (1980). Juvenile delinquency: Behavior restraint or behavior facilitation? In T. Hirschi & M. Gottfredson (Eds.), *Understanding crime: Current theory and research* (pp. 131–142). Newbury Park, CA: Sage.

Conover, T. (2003, June 29). In the land of Guantanamo. *The New York Times Sunday Magazine,* p. 40.

Cooper v. Oklahoma, 116 S.Ct. 1373 (1996).

Cooper, J., & Neuhaus, I. M. (2000). The hired gun effect: Assessing the effect of pay, frequency of testifying, and credentials on the perception of expert testimony. *Law and Human Behavior, 24*, 149–172.

Copes, J., & Forsyth, C. (1994). Behaviors and attitudes of police officers. *Journal of Police and Criminal Psychology, 10*, 38–45.

Copson, G., Badcock, R., Boon, J., and Britton, P. (1997). Articulating a systematic approach to clinical crime profiling. *Criminal Behaviour and Mental Health, 7*, 13–17.

Cordon, I., Saetermoe, C., & Goodman, G. (2005). Facilitating children's accurate responses: Conversational rules and interview style. *Applied Cognitive Psychology, 19*, 249–266.

Cornell, D. (2003). Guidelines for responding to student threats of violence. *Journal of Educational Administration, 41*, 705–719.

Cornell, D. (2006). *School violence: Fears versus facts.* New York: Routledge.

Cosden, M., Ellens, J., Schnell, J., & Yamini-Diouf, Y. (2005). Efficacy of a mental health treatment court with assertive community treatment. *Behavioral Sciences & the Law, 23*, 199–214.

Cosden, M., Ellens, J., Schnell, J., Yamini-Diouf, Y., & Wolfe, M. (2003). Evaluation of a mental health

court with assertive community treatment. *Behavioral Sciences & the Law, 21*, 415–427.

Costa, P. T., Jr., & Widiger, T. A. (2002). *Personality disorders and the five-factor model of personality* (2nd ed.). Washington, DC: American Psychological Association.

Costanzo, M., Gerrity, E., & Lykes, M. (2007). Psychologists and the use of terror in interrogations. *Analyses of Social Issues and Public Policy, 7*, 7–20.

Cottle, C., Lee, R., & Heilbrun, K. (2001). The prediction of criminal recidivism in juveniles: A meta-analysis. *Criminal Justice and Behavior, 28*, 367–394.

Cowan, C. L., Thompson, W. C., & Ellsworth, P. C. (1984). The effects of death qualification on jurors' predispositions to convict and on the quality of deliberation. *Law and Human Behavior, 8*, 53–79.

Cox, D. (1999, June 28). Arbitration is no simple matter. *National Law Journal,* p. 1.

Coy v. Iowa, 487 U.S. 1012 (1988).

Coyle, M. (2009). *New report shows sharp rise in prison time for federal offenders.* Retrieved February 13, 2009, from www.law.com

Crandall, C. S., Glor, J., & Britt, T. W. (1997). AIDS-related stigmatization: Instrumental and symbolic attitudes. *Journal of Applied Social Psychology, 27*, 95–123.

Crosbie-Burnett, M. (1991). Impact of joint versus sole custody and quality of coparental relationship on adjustment of adolescents in remarried families. *Behavioral Sciences & the Law, 9*, 439–449.

Cruzan v. Director, Missouri Department of Health, 497 U.S. 261 (1990).

Cuffe, S. P., Addy, C. L., Garrison, C. Z., Waller, J. L., Jackson, K. L., McKeown, R. E., et al. (1998). Prevalence of PTSD in a community sample of older adolescents. *Journal of the American Academy of Child & Adolescent Psychiatry, 37*, 147–154.

Culhane, C. E., Hosch, H. M., & Weaver, W. G. (2004). Crime victims serving as jurors: Is there bias present? *Law and Human Behavior, 28*, 649–659.

Cunningham, M., & Reidy, T. (2001). A matter of life or death: Special considerations and heightened practice standards in capital sentencing evaluations. *Behavioral Sciences & the Law, 19*, 473–490.

Cunningham, M., Reidy, T., & Sorensen, J. (2005). Is death row obsolete? A decade of mainstreaming death-sentenced inmates in Missouri. *Behavioral Sciences & the Law, 23*, 307–320.

Curry, T., Lee, G., & Rodriguez, S. (2004). Does victim gender increase sentence severity? Further explorations of gender dynamics and sentencing outcomes. *Crime and Delinquency, 50,* 319–343.

Cutler, B. L., & Penrod, S. D. (1988). Improving the reliability of eyewitness identification: Lineup construction and presentation. *Journal of Applied Psychology, 73,* 281–290.

D'Agostino, C. (1986). Police psychological services: Ethical issues. In J. T. Reese & H. A. Goldstein (Eds.), *Psychological services for law enforcement* (pp. 241–248). Washington, DC: U.S. Government Printing Office.

Daicoff, S. (1999). Making law therapeutic for lawyers: Therapeutic jurisprudence, preventive law, and the psychology of lawyers. *Psychology, Public Policy, and Law, 5,* 811–848.

Daly, K. (1994). *Gender, crime, and punishment.* New Haven, CT: Yale University Press.

Dann, B., & Hans, V. (2004). Recent evaluative research on jury trial innovations. *Court Review, 41,* 12–19.

Dann, B., Hans, V., & Kaye, D. (2004). *Testing the effects of selected jury trial innovations on juror comprehension of contested DNA evidence. Final technical report.* Washington, DC: National Institute of Justice.

Darley, J., Fulero, S., Haney, C., & Tyler, T. (2002). Psychological jurisprudence. In J. Ogloff (Ed.), *Taking psychology and law into the twenty-first century* (pp. 37–39). New York: Kluwer Academic/Plenum Publishers.

Darley, J., Sanderson, C., & LaMantha, P. (1996). Community standards for defining attempt: Inconsistencies with the Model Penal Code. *American Behavioral Scientist, 39,* 405–420.

Darrow, C. (1936, May). How to pick a jury. *Esquire,* p. 14.

d'Arti, D. (1981). Measuring prison stress. In D. Ward & K. Schoen (Eds.), *Confinement in maximum custody: Last resort prisons in the United States and Western Europe.* Lexington, MA: D.C. Heath.

Daubert v. Merrell Dow Pharmaceuticals, Inc., 113 S.Ct. 2786 (1993).

D'Augelli, A. R. (1998). Developmental implications of victimization of lesbian, gay, and bisexual youths. In G. M. Herek (Ed.), *Stigma and sexual orientation: Understanding prejudice against lesbians, gay men and bisexuals (Psychological perspectives on lesbian and gay issues)* (4th ed., pp. 187–210). Thousand Oaks, CA: Sage Publications.

Daudistel, H. C., Hosch, H. M., Holmes, M. D., & Graves, J. B. (1999). Effects of defendant ethnicity on juries' dispositions of felony cases. *Journal of Applied Social Psychology, 29,* 317–336.

Dauphinot, L. (1996). *The efficacy of community correctional supervision for offenders with severe mental illness.* Unpublished doctoral dissertation, University of Texas at Austin, Austin, TX.

Davey, M., & Goodnough, A. (2007). *Doubts rise as states hold sex offenders after prison.* Retrieved March 24, 2009, from http://www.nytimes.com/2007/03/04/us/04civil.html

Davis, S., & Bottoms, B. (2002). Effects of social support on children's eyewitness reports: A test of the underlying mechanism. *Law and Human Behavior, 26,* 185–215.

Death Penalty Information Center. (2009). *Facts about the death penalty.* Retrieved March 26, 2009, from http://www.deathpenaltyinfo.org/FactSheet.pdf

Deckel, A. W., Hesselbrock, V., & Bauer, L. (1996). Antisocial personality disorder, childhood delinquency, and frontal brain functioning: EEG and neuropsychological findings. *Journal of Clinical Psychology, 52,* 639–650.

Deci, E. L., & Ryan, R. M. (2000). The "what" and "why" of goal pursuits: Human needs and the self-determination of behavior. *Psychological Inquiry, 11,* 227–268.

Deffenbacher, K. A., Bornstein, B. H., & Penrod, S. D. (2006). Mugshot exposure effects: Retroactive interference, mugshot commitment, source confusion, and unconscious transference. *Law and Human Behavior, 30,* 287–307.

Deffenbacher, K., Bornstein, B., Penrod, S., & McGorty, E. (2004). A meta-analytic review of the effects of high stress on eyewitness memory. *Law and Human Behavior, 28,* 687–706.

Deffenbacher, K., Bornstein, B., McGorty, E., & Penrod, S. (2008). Forgetting the once-seen face: Estimating the strength of an eyewitness's memory representation. *Journal of Experimental Psychology: Applied, 14,* 139–150.

Deitz, S. R., Russell, S. A., & Hammes, K. M. (1989, August). *Who's on trial? Information processing by jurors in rape cases.* Paper presented at the meeting of the American Psychological Association, New Orleans.

DeMartini, A. (2008). *Juvenile prisons to make changes*. Retrieved April 15, 2009, from http://www.dispatch.com/live/content/local_news/stories/2008/04/04/Prisons_will_change.ART_ART_04-04-08_A1_579R1G7.html?sid=101

deMayo, R. A. (1997). Patient sexual behavior and sexual harassment: A national survey of female psychologists. *Professional Psychology: Research and Practice, 28*, 58–62.

Demuth, S., & Steffensmeier, D. (2004). The impact of gender and race-ethnicity in the pretrial release process. *Social Problems, 51*, 222–242.

Dennis, D., & Monahan, J. (Eds.). (1996). *Coercion and aggressive community treatment: A new frontier in mental health law*. New York: Plenum Publishing Corporation.

Department of Justice. (1999). *Postconviction DNA testing: Recommendations for handling requests*. Retrieved from http://www.ncjrs.org/pdffiles1/nij/177626.pdf

DePaulo, B. M., Lindsay, J. J., Malone, B. E., Muhlenbruck, L., Charlton, K., & Cooper, H. (2003). Cues to deception. *Psychological Bulletin, 129*, 74–118.

Dershowitz, A. M. (1994). *The abuse excuse*. Boston, MA: Little, Brown.

De Tocqueville, A. (1900). *Democracy in America* (Vol. 1) (Henry Reeve, Trans.). New York: Colonial Press.

Detrick, P., & Chibnall, J. T. (2002). Prediction of police officer performance with the Inwald Personality Inventory. *Journal of Police and Criminal Psychology, 17*, 9–17.

Devenport, J., Stinson, V., Cutler, B., & Kravitz, D. (2002). How effective are the cross-examination and expert testimony safeguards? Jurors' perceptions of the suggestiveness and fairness of biased lineup procedures. *Journal of Applied Psychology, 87*, 1042–1054.

Devine, D., Buddenbaum, J., Houp, S., Studebaker, N., & Stolle, D. (2009). Strength of evidence, extraevidentiary influence, and the liberation hypotheses: Data from the field. *Law and Human Behavior, 33*, 136–148.

Devine, D., Clayton, L., Dunford, B., Seying, R., & Pryce, J. (2001). Jury decision making: 45 years of empirical research on deliberating groups. *Psychology, Public Policy, and Law, 7*, 622–727.

Dewolf, C., Duron, B., & Loas, G. (2002). Electroencephalographic abnormalities in psychopaths: A controlled study. *Annales Médico-psychologiques, revue psychiatrique, 160*(5–6), 451–455.

Dhami, M. (2003). Psychological models of professional decision making. *Psychological Science, 14*, 175–180.

Dhami, M. (2005). From discretion to disagreement: Explaining disparities in judges' pretrial decisions. *Behavioral Sciences & the Law, 23*, 367–386.

Dhami, M., & Ayton, P. (2001). Bailing and jailing the fast and frugal way. *Journal of Behavioral Decision Making, 14*, 141–168.

Diamond, S. (2006). Beyond fantasy and nightmare: A portrait of the jury. *Buffalo Law Review, 54*, 717–763.

Diamond, S., & Rose, M. (2005). Real juries. *Annual Review of Law and Social Sciences, 1*, 255–284.

Diamond, S., Rose, M., & Murphy, B. (2004). Jurors' unanswered questions. *Court Review, 41*, 20–29.

Diamond, S., & Vidmar, N. (2001). Jury room ruminations on forbidden topics. *Virginia Law Review, 87*, 1857–1915.

Diamond, S., Vidmar, N., Rose, M., Ellis, L., & Murphy, B. (2003). *Civil juror discussions during trial: A study of Arizona's rule 39(f) from videotaped discussions and deliberations*. Retrieved October 5, 2005, from http://www.law.northwestern.edu/diamond/papers/arizona_civil_discussions.pdf

Dickerson v. United States, 2000 U.S. Lexis 5911 (2000).

Dickinson, J., Poole, D., & Laimon, R. (2005). Children's recall and testimony. In N. Brewer & K. Williams (Eds.), *Psychology and Law: An empirical perspective* (pp. 151–175). New York: Guilford Press.

Dietz, S. R., Littman, M., & Bentley, B. J. (1984). Attribution of responsibility for rape: The influence of observer empathy, victim resistance, and victim attractiveness. *Sex Roles, 10*, 267–280.

DiLalla, L. F., & Gottesman, I. (1991). Biological and genetic contributors to violence: Widom's untold tale. *Psychological Bulletin, 109*, 125–129.

Dillehay, R. C. (1999). Authoritarianism and jurors. In W. F. Abbott & J. Batt (Eds.), *A handbook of jury research* (pp. 13.1–13.18). Philadelphia: ALI-ABA.

Ditto, P., Jacobson, J., Smucker, W., Danks, J., & Fagerlin, A. (2005). *Context changes choices: A prospective study of the effects of hospitalization on life-sustaining treatment preferences.* Unpublished manuscript, University of California–Irvine.

Ditto, P., Smucker, W., Danks, J., Jacobson, J., Houts, R., Fagerlin, A., et al. (2003). Stability of older adults' preferences for life-sustaining medical treatment. *Health Psychology, 22,* 605–615.

Ditton, P. M. (1999, July), *Mental health treatment of inmates and probationers.* Washington, DC: U.S. Department of Justice. Retrieved September 20, 2005, from http://www.ojp.usdoj.gov/bjs/pub/pdf/mhtip.pdf

Dodge, M., & Greene, E. (1991). Jurors and expert conceptions of battered women. *Violence and Victims, 6,* 271–282.

Donat, P. L. N., & D'Emilio, J. (1992). A feminist redefinition of rape and sexual assault: Historical foundations and change. *Journal of Social Issues, 48,* 9–22.

Doob, A., & Kirschenbaum, H. (1972). Some empirical evidence on the effect of S. 12 of the Canada Evidence Act upon the accused. *Criminal Justice Quarterly, 15,* 88–96.

Doppelt, J. (1991). Generic prejudice: How drug war fervor threatens the right to a fair trial. *American University Law Review, 40,* 821–836.

Doren, D. M. (1987). *Understanding and treating the psychopath.* New York: Wiley.

Dougall, A. L., Hayward, M. C., & Baum, A. (2005). Media exposure to bioterrorism: Stress and the anthrax attacks. *Psychiatry, 68*(1), 28–43.

Douglas, J., Burgess, A. W., Burgess, A. G., & Ressler, R. (2006). *Crime classification manual: A standard system for investigating and classifying violent crimes* (2nd ed.). New York: Wiley.

Douglas, J. E., Ressler, R. K., Burgess, A. W., & Hartman, C. R. (1986). Criminal profiling from crime scene analysis. *Behavioral Sciences & the Law, 4,* 401–421.

Douglass, A., & Steblay, N. (2006). Memory distortion in eyewitnesses: A meta-analysis of the post-identification feedback effect. *Applied Cognitive Psychology, 20,* 859–869.

Drew, E., & Greene, E. (2008, March). *The effects of apology on legal reasoning in civil cases.* Paper presented at the annual conference of American Psychology-Law Society, Jacksonville, FL.

Driscoll, D. M., Kelly, J. R., & Henderson, W. L. (1998). Can perceivers identify likelihood to sexually harass? *Sex Roles, 38,* 557–588.

Drizin, S., & Colgan, B. (2004). Tales from the juvenile confession front: A guide to how standard police interrogation tactics can produce coerced and false confessions from juvenile suspects. In G. D. Lassiter (Ed.), *Interrogations, confessions, and entrapment* (pp. 127–162). New York: Kluwer Academic/Plenum.

Drizin, S., & Leo, R. (2004). The problem of false confessions in the post-DNA world. *North Carolina Law Review, 82,* 891–1007.

Drizin, S., & Reich, M. (2004). Heeding the lessons of history: The need for mandatory recording of police interrogations to accurately assess the reliability and voluntariness of confessions. *Drake Law Review, 62,* 619–646.

Duncan v. Louisiana, 391 U.S. 145 (1968).

Duning, C., & Hanchette, J. (1985, March 28). Don't shoot, Court tells police. *USA Today,* p. 2A.

Dunn, M., Salovey, P., & Feigenson, N. (2006). The jury persuaded (and not): Computer animation in the courtroom. *Law & Policy, 28,* 228–248.

Dusky v. United States, 362 U.S. 402 (1960).

Dutton, D. G. (1987). The criminal justice response to wife assault. *Law and Human Behavior, 11,* 189–206.

Dutton, D. G. (1995). Male abusiveness in intimate relationships. *Clinical Psychology Review, 15,* 567–582.

Dutton, D. G. (2000). *The domestic assault of women* (3rd ed.). Vancouver: University of British Columbia Press.

Dutton, M. A., Perrin, S. G., Chrestman, K. R., & Halle, P. M. (1990, August). *MMPI trauma profiles for battered women.* Paper presented at the annual convention of the American Psychological Association, Boston, MA.

Eads, L., Shuman, D., & DeLipsey, J. (2000). Getting it right: The trial of sexual assault and child molestation cases under Federal Rules of Evidence 413–415. *Behavioral Sciences & the Law, 18,* 169–216.

Eagly, A., & Chaiken, S. (1993). *The psychology of attitudes.* New York: Harcourt Brace.

Eaton, L. (2004, August 8). Divorced parents move, and custody gets trickier. *The New York Times,* p. 1. Retrieved June 25, 2009, from http://www.nytimes.com/2004/08/08/nyregion/divorced-parents-move-and-custody-gets-trickier.html?pagewanted=all

Eaton, L., & Kaufman, L. (2005, April 26). In problem-solving courts, judges turn therapist. *The New York Times,* p. A1.

Eberhardt, J., Davies, P., Purdie-Vaughns, V., & Johnson, S. (2006). Looking deathworthy: Perceived stereotypicality of Black defendants predicts capital-sentencing outcomes. *Psychological Science, 17*, 383–386.

Ebreo, A., Linn, N., & Vining, J. (1996). The impact of procedural justice on opinions of public policy: Solid waste management as an example. *Journal of Applied Social Psychology, 26*, 1259–1285.

Eckhardt, C. L., Barbour, K. A., & Davison, G. C. (1998). Articulated thoughts of maritally violent and nonviolent men during anger arousal. *Journal of Consulting and Clinical Psychology, 66*, 259–269.

Eckholm, E. (1985, July 4). Stockholm syndrome: Hostages' reactions. *Lawrence Journal-World,* p. 6.

Eckholm, E. (2008, October 14). Courts give addicts a chance to straighten out. *The New York Times.* Retrieved October 15, 2008, from www.nytimes.com/2008/10/15/us/15drugs.html

Eddings v. Oklahoma, 436 U.S. 921 (1982).

Edelstein, R., Luten, T., Ekman, P., & Goodman, G. (2006). Detecting lies in children and adults. *Law and Human Behavior, 30*, 1–10.

Edmonson v. Leesville Concrete Co., 111 S.Ct. 2077 (1991).

Eichenwald, K. (1989, September 28). Bilzerian gets four years in jail, stiffest in stock crackdown. *The New York Times,* pp. 29, 36.

Eisele, G. T. (1991), The case against mandatory court-annexed ADR programs. *Judicature, 75*, 34–40.

Eisenberg, T., Hannaford-Agor, P., Hans, V., Waters, N., Munsterman, T., Schwab, S., et al. (2005). Judge–jury agreement in criminal cases: A partial replication of Kalven and Zeisel's *The American Jury. Journal of Empirical Legal Studies, 2*, 171–207.

Eisenberg, T., LaFountain, N., Ostrom, B., Rottman, D., & Wells, M. (2002). Juries, judges, and punitive damages: An empirical study. *Cornell Law Review, 87*, 743–782.

Eley, T. C. (1997). General genes: A new theme in developmental psychopathology. *Current Directions in Psychological Science, 6*, 90–95.

Elliott, D. S., Huizinga, D., & Ageton, S. S. (1985). *Explaining delinquency and drug use.* Thousand Oaks, CA: Sage.

Elliott, R., Friston, K., & Dolan, R. (2000). Dissociable neural responses in human reward systems. *Journal of Neuroscience, 20*, 6159–6165.

Ellis, L. (1989). *Theories of rape: Inquiries into the causes of sexual aggression.* New York: Hemisphere.

Ellis, L. (1991). A synthesized (biosocial) theory of rape. *Journal of Consulting and Clinical Psychology, 59*, 631–642.

Ellis, L., & Diamond, S. (2003). Race, diversity, and jury composition: Battering and bolstering legitimacy. *Chicago-Kent Law Review, 78*, 1033–1058.

Ellison, K., & Buckhout, R. (1981). *Psychology and criminal justice.* New York: Harper & Row.

Ellsworth, P. C. (1989). Are twelve heads better than one? *Law and Contemporary Problems, 52*, 205–224.

Ellsworth, P. C. (1999). Jury reform at the end of the century: Real agreement, real changes. *University of Michigan Journal of Law Reform, 32*, 213–225.

Ellsworth, P. C., & Mauro, R. (1998). Psychology and law. In D. Gilbert, S. Fiske, & G. Lindzey (Eds.), *The handbook of social psychology* (Vol. 2, pp. 684–732). Boston, MA: McGraw-Hill.

Ellsworth, P. C., & Reifman, A. (2000). Juror comprehension and public policy: Perceived problems and proposed solutions. *Psychology, Public Policy, and Law, 6*, 788–821.

Ellsworth, P., & Ross, L. (1983). Public opinion and capital punishment: A close examination of the views of abolitionists and retentionists. *Crime and Delinquency, 29*, 116–169.

Elrod, P., & Ryder, R. S. (1999). *Juvenile justice: A social, historical, and legal perspective.* Gaithersburg, MD: Aspen Publishers, Inc.

Elwork, A., Sales, B. D., & Suggs, D. (1981). The trial: A research review. In B. D. Sales (Ed.), *The trial process* (pp. 1–68). New York: Plenum.

Emery, R. E. (1982). Interparental conflict and the children of discord and divorce. *Psychological Bulletin, 92*, 310–330.

Emery, R., Laumann-Billings, L., Waldron, M., Sbarra, D., & Dillon, P. (2001). Child custody mediation and litigation: Custody, contact, and coparenting 12 years after initial dispute resolution. *Journal of Consulting and Clinical Psychology, 69*, 323–332.

Englich, B., & Mussweiler, T. (2001). Sentencing under uncertainty: Anchoring effects in the courtroom. *Journal of Applied Social Psychology, 31*, 1535–1551.

Englich, B., Mussweiler, T., & Strack, F. (2005). The last word in court—A hidden disadvantage for the defense. *Law and Human Behavior, 29*, 705–722.

English, P. W., & Sales, B. D. (1997). A ceiling or consistency effect for the comprehension of jury instructions. *Psychology, Public Policy, and Law, 3,* 381–401.

Ennis, B. J., & Litwack, T. R. (1974). Psychiatry and the presumption of expertise: Flipping coins in the courtroom. *California Law Review, 62,* 693–752.

Equal Justice Initiative. (2007). *Cruel and unusual: Sentencing 13- and 14-year-old children to die in prison.* Montgomery, AL: Author.

Eron, L. (1990). Understanding aggression. *Bulletin of the International Society for Research on Aggression, 12,* 59.

Estrich, S. (1987). *Real rape.* Cambridge, MA: Harvard University Press.

Everington, C. T., & Luckasson, R. (1992). *Competence assessment for standing trial for defendants with mental retardation (CASTMR) test manual.* Columbus, OH: International Diagnostic Systems, Inc.

Ewing v. California, 538 U.S. 11 (2003).

Ewing, C. (1987). *Battered women who kill: Psychological self-defense as legal justification.* Lexington, MA: Lexington Books.

Eysenck, H. J. (1964). *Crime and personality.* Boston, MA: Houghton Mifflin.

Eysenck, H. J., & Gudjonsson, G. H. (1989). *The causes and cures of criminality.* New York: Plenum.

Fagan, J. (1996). The comparative advantage of juvenile versus criminal court sanctions on recidivism among adolescent felony offenders. *Law & Policy, 18,* 79–113.

Falk, A. J. (1999). Sex offenders, mental illness and criminal responsibility: The constitutional boundaries of civil commitment after *Kansas v. Hendricks. American Journal of Law and Medicine, 25,* 117–147.

Farah, M. (2005). Neuroethics: The practical and the philosophical. *Trends in Cognitive Science, 9,* 34–40.

Fare v. Michael C., 442 U.S. 707 (1979).

Faretta v. California, 422 U.S. 806 (1975).

Farmer, M. W. (1976). Jury composition challenges. *Law and Psychology Review, 2,* 45–74.

Farrington, D. P. (1995). The development of offending and antisocial behavior from childhood: Key findings from the Cambridge Study in Delinquent Development. *Journal of Child Psychology and Psychiatry, 360,* 929–964.

Farwell, L. A., & Smith, S. S. (2001). Using brain MERMER testing to detect knowledge despite efforts to conceal. *Journal of Forensic Sciences, 46,* 135–143.

Faulkner, A. H., & Cranston, K. (1998). Correlates of same-sex sexual behavior in a random sample of Massachusetts high school students. *American Journal of Public Health, 88,* 262–266.

FBI Academy. (2002). *Countering terrorism: Integration of practice and theory.* Retrieved July 22, 2005, from http://www.apa.org/releases/countering_terrorism.pdf

Feeley, M. M. (1983). *Court reform on trial.* New York: Basic Books.

Feige, D. (2006, June 7). *Witnessing guilt, ignoring innocence?* Retrieved July 28, 2008, from http://www.nytimes.com/2006/06/06/opinion/06feige.html?_r=1&scp=11&sq=david%20feige&st=cse&oref=slogin

Feigenson, N., Park, J., & Salovey, P. (2001). The role of emotions in comparative negligence judgments. *Journal of Applied Social Psychology, 31,* 576–603.

Feild, H. S. (1978). Attitudes toward rape: A comparative analysis of police, rapists, crisis counselors, and citizens. *Journal of Personality and Social Psychology, 36,* 156–179.

Feild, H. S. (1979). Rape trials and jurors' decisions: A psycholegal analysis of the effects of victim, defendant, and case characteristics. *Law and Human Behavior, 3,* 261–284.

Feild, H. S., & Barnett, N. J. (1978). Simulated jury trials: Students vs. "real" people as jurors. *Journal of Social Psychology, 104,* 287–293.

Feild, H. S., & Bienen, L. B. (1980). *Jurors and rape: A study in psychology and law.* Lexington, MA: Heath.

Fein, S., McCloskey, A. L., & Tomlinson, T. M. (1997). Can the jury disregard that information? The use of suspicion to reduce the prejudicial effects of pretrial publicity and inadmissible testimony. *Personality and Social Psychology Bulletin, 23,* 1215–1226.

Feinblatt, J., & Berman, G. (2001). *Responding to the community: Principles for planning and creating a community court.* Washington, DC: U.S. Department of Justice.

Feldman, M. P. (1977). *Criminal behavior: A psychological analysis.* New York: Wiley.

Feldmann, T. B. (2001). Characteristics of hostage and barricade incidents: Implications for negotiation strategies and training. *Journal of Police Crisis Negotiations, 1*, 3–33.

Feldman-Summers, S., & Ashworth, C. D. (1981). Factors related to intentions to report rape. *Journal of Social Issues, 37*, 71–92.

Feldman-Summers, S., Gordon, P. E., & Meagher, J. R. (1979). The impact of rape on sexual satisfaction. *Journal of Abnormal Psychology, 88*, 101–105.

Felitti, V. J., Anda, R. F., Nordenberg, D., Williamson, D. F., Spitz, A. M., Edwards, V., et al. (1998). Relationship of childhood abuse and household dysfunction to many of the leading causes of death in adults: The adverse childhood experiences (ACE) study. *American Journal of Preventive Medicine, 14*, 245–258.

Fenster, G. A., & Locke, B. (1973). Neuroticism among policemen: An examination of police personality. *Journal of Applied Psychology, 57*, 358–359.

Fentiman, L. (1986). Whose right is it anyway? Rethinking competency to stand trial in light of the synthetically sane insanity defendant. *University of Miami Law Review, 40*, 1109–1169.

Finkel, N. (1989). The Insanity Defense Reform Act of 1984: Much ado about nothing. *Behavioral Sciences & the Law, 7*, 403–419.

Finkel, N. (1995). *Commonsense justice: Jurors' notions of the law.* Cambridge, MA: Harvard University Press.

Finkel, N., & Groscup, J. L. (1997). When mistakes happen: Commonsense rules of culpability. *Psychology, Public Policy, and Law, 3*, 65–125.

Finkel, N., & Slobogin, C. (1995). Insanity, justification, and culpability toward a unifying theme. *Law and Human Behavior, 19*, 447–464.

Finnila, K., Mahlberga, N., Santtilaa, P., Sandnabbaa, K., & Niemib, P. (2003). Validity of a test of children's suggestibility for predicting responses to two interview situations differing in their degree of suggestiveness. *Journal of Experimental Child Psychology, 85*, 32–49.

Finz, S., & Walsh, D. (2004, December 15). *The stuff of crime novels finally has an end.* Retrieved September 1, 2005, from www.sfgate.com

Fischer, K. (1989). Defining the boundaries of admissible expert psychological testimony on rape trauma syndrome. *University of Illinois Law Review, 3*, 691–734.

Fischer, P. J., & Breakey, W. R. (1991). The epidemiology of alcohol, drug, and mental disorders among homeless persons. *American Psychologist, 46*, 1115–1128.

Fisher, R. P., & Geiselman, R. E. (1992). *Memory enhancing techniques for investigative interviewing: The cognitive interview.* Springfield, IL: Thomas.

Fisher, R. P., & Schreiber, N. (2007). Interviewing protocols to improve eyewitness memory. In M. Toglia, R. Lindsay, D. Ross, & J. Read (Eds.), *The handbook of eyewitness psychology: Memory for events* (Vol. 1, pp. 53–79). Mahwah, NJ: Erlbaum.

Fiske, S., & Taylor, S. (1991). *Social cognition* (2nd ed.). New York: McGraw-Hill.

Fitzgerald, L. F., Buchanan, N. T., Collinsworth, L. L., Magley, V. J., & Romos, A. M. (1999). Junk logic: The abuse defense in sexual harassment litigation. *Psychology, Public Policy, and Law, 5*, 730–759.

Fitzgerald, L. F., Gelfand, M., & Drasgow, F. (1995). Measuring sexual harassment: Theoretical and psychometric advances. *Basic and Applied Social Psychology, 17*, 425–445.

Fitzgerald, R., & Ellsworth, P. C. (1984). Due process vs. crime control: Death qualification and jury attitudes. *Law and Human Behavior, 8*, 31–51.

Fivush, R., & Shukat, J. (1995). Content, consistency, and coherence of early autobiographical recall. In M. Zaragoza, J. Graham, G. Hall, R. Hirschman, & Y. Ben-Porath (Eds.), *Memory and testimony in the child witness* (pp. 5–23). Thousand Oaks, CA: Sage.

Flynn, C., & Heitzmann, D. (2008). Tragedy at Virginia Tech: Trauma and its aftermath. *The Counseling Psychologist, 36*, 479–489.

Foa, E. B., Hearst-Ikeda, D., & Perry, K. J. (1995). Evaluation of a brief cognitive behavioral program for the prevention of chronic PTSD in recent assault victims. *Journal of Consulting and Clinical Psychology, 63*, 948–955.

Foa, E. B., & Kozak, M. J. (1986). Emotional processing of fear: Exposure to corrective information. *Psychological Bulletin, 99*, 20–35.

Follingstad, D. R. (1994, March 10). *The use of battered woman syndrome in court.* Workshop for the American Academy of Forensic Psychology, Santa Fe, NM.

Footlick, J. (1978, May 8). Insanity on trial. *Newsweek*, pp. 108–112.

Ford v. Wainwright, 477 U.S. 399 (1986).

Ford Motor Credit Co. v. Sheehan, 373 So.2d 956 (Fla. App. 1979).

Ford, W. (1998). *Managing police stress*. Walnut Creek, CA: The Management Advantage.

Forgas, J. P. (1998). On feeling good and getting your way: Mood effects on negotiator cognition and behaviour. *Journal of Personality and Social Psychology, 74*, 565–577.

Forst, M., Fagan, J., & Vivona, T. S. (1989). Youth in prisons and training schools: Perceptions and consequences of the treatment-custody dichotomy. *Juvenile and Family Court Journal, 40*, 1–14.

ForsterLee, L., & Horowitz, I. (2003). The effects of jury-aid innovations on juror performance in complex civil trials. *Judicature, 86*, 184–190.

Forsterlee, L., Horowitz, I. A., & Bourgeois, M. J. (1993). Juror competence in civil trials: Effects of preinstruction and evidence technicality. *Journal of Applied Psychology, 78*, 14–21.

Forsterlee, L., Kent, L., & Horowitz, I. (2005). The cognitive effects of jury aids on decision-making in complex civil litigation. *Applied Cognitive Psychology, 19*, 867–884.

Forth, A. (1995). *Psychopathy and young offenders: Prevalence, family background, and violence*. Canada: Ministry of the Solicitor General of Canada.

Forth, A. E., & Burke, H. C. (1998). Psychopathy in adolescence: Assessment, violence, and developmental precursors. In D. Cooke, A. E. Forth, & R. D. Hare (Eds.), *Psychopathy: Theory, research, and implications for society* (pp. 205–229). Dordrecht, The Netherlands: Kluwer.

Forth, A. E., Hart, S. D., & Hare, R. D. (1990). Assessment of psychopathy in male young offenders. *Psychological Assessment, 2*, 342–344.

Foucha v. Louisiana, 112 S.Ct. 1780 (1992).

Fox, D., Gerson, A., & Lees-Haley, P. (1995). Interrelationship of MMPI-2 validity scales in personal injury claims. *Journal of Clinical Psychology, 51*, 42–47.

Fox, J. A., & Levin, J. (1998). Multiple homicide: Patterns of serial and mass murder. *Crime and Justice, 23*, 407–455.

Fox, J., & Levin, J. (2005). *Extreme killing: Understanding serial and mass murder*. Beverly Hills, CA: Sage Publications.

Frank, J. (1949). *Courts on trial*. Princeton, NJ: Princeton University Press.

Frazier, P., & Borgida, E. (1985). Rape trauma syndrome evidence in court. *American Psychologist, 40*, 984–993.

Frazier, P., & Borgida, E. (1988). Juror common understanding and the admissibility of rape trauma syndrome evidence in court. *Law and Human Behavior, 12*, 101–122.

Frazier, P. A., Cochran, C. C., & Olson, A. M. (1995). Social science research on lay definitions of sexual harassment. *Journal of Social Issues, 51*, 21–37.

Frazier, P. A., & Haney, B. (1996). Sexual assault cases in the legal system: Police, prosecutor, and victim perspectives. *Law and Human Behavior, 20*, 607–628.

Frederick, R. (1997). *Validity Indicator Profile manual*. Minnetonka, MN: NSC Assessments.

Frederick, R. (2000). Mixed group validation: A method to address the limitations of criterion group validation in research on malingering detection. *Behavioral Sciences & the Law, 18*, 693–718.

Frederick, R. I., & Crosby, R. D. (2000). Development and validation of the Validity Indicator Profile. *Law and Human Behavior, 24*, 59–82.

Frederick, S. (2005). Cognitive reflection and decision making. *Journal of Economic Perspectives, 19*, 25–42.

Frendak v. United States, 408 A.2d 364 (D.C. 1979).

Freud, S. (1961). *The complete psychological works of Sigmund Freud* (Vol. 19). London: Hogarth.

Friedman, R., Anderson, C., Brett, J., Olekalns, M., Goates, N., & Lisco, C. (2004). The positive and negative effects of anger on dispute resolution: Evidence from electronically mediated disputes. *Journal of Applied Psychology, 89*, 369–376.

Frolik, L. A. (1999). Science, common sense, and the determination of mental capacity. *Psychology, Public Policy, and Law, 5*, 41–58.

Fukurai, H., & Butler, E. (1994, Fall). Sources of racial disenfranchisement in the jury and jury selection system. *National Black Lawyers Journal, 13*, 238–275.

Fulero, S. M., & Finkel, N. J. (1991). Barring ultimate issue testimony: An "insane" rule? *Law and Human Behavior, 15*, 495–508.

Fulero, S. M., & Penrod, S. D. (1990). Attorney jury selection folklore: What do they think and how can psychologists help? *Forensic Reports, 3*, 233–259.

Furman v. Georgia, 408 U.S. 238 (1972).

Fyfe, J. J. (1982). Blind justice: Police shootings in Memphis. *Journal of Criminal Law and Criminology, 73*, 707–722.

Gaines, L. K., & Falkenberg, S. (1998). An evaluation of the written selection test: Effectiveness and alternatives. *Journal of Criminal Justice, 26*, 175–183.

Galanter, M. (2004). The vanishing trial: An examination of trials and related matters in state and federal courts. *Journal of Empirical Legal Studies, 1*, 459–570.

Gall v. United States, 552 U.S. 38 (2007).

Gallagher, M. (2008). *Thousands of resentencings narrow gap between crack, powder cocaine penalties.* Retrieved December 23, 2008, from www.law.com

Gallagher, W. (1996). *I.D.: How heredity and experience make you who you are.* New York: Random House.

Gannett Co. v. DePasquale, 443 U.S. 368 (1979).

Gardner, J., Scogin, F., Vipperman, R., & Varela, J. G. (1998). The predictive validity of peer assessment in law enforcement: A 6-year follow-up. *Behavioral Sciences & the Law, 16*, 473–478.

Garner, J., Fagan, J., & Maxwell, C. (1995). Published findings from the spouse assault replication program: A critical review. *Journal of Quantitative Criminology, 11*, 3–28.

Garofalo, R. (1914). *Criminology* (R. W. Millar, Trans.). Boston, MA: Little, Brown.

Garvey, S., Hannaford-Agor, P., Hans, V., Mott, N., Munsterman, G. T., & Wells, M. (2004). Juror first votes in criminal trials. *Journal of Empirical Legal Studies, 1*, 371–399.

Garvey, S. P., Johnson, S. L., & Marcus, P. (2000). Correcting deadly confusion: Responding to jury inquiries in capital cases. *Cornell Law Review, 85*, 627.

Gatowski, S. I., Dobbin, S. A., Richardson, J. T., Ginsburg, G. P., Merlino, M. L., & Dahir, V. (2001). Asking the gatekeepers: A national survey of judges of judging expert evidence in a post-Daubert world. *Law and Human Behavior, 25*, 433–458.

Gavey, N. (1991). Sexual victimization prevalence among New Zealand University students. *Journal of Consulting and Clinical Psychology, 59*, 464–466.

Gaylin, W. (1974). *Partial justice: A study of bias in sentencing.* New York: Vintage Books.

Geis, G., & Bienen, L. B. (1998). *Crimes of the century.* Boston, MA: Northeastern University Press.

Gelles, R. J., & Cornell, C. P. (1985). *Intimate violence in families.* Newbury Park, CA: Sage.

Gellhorn, E. (1968). The law schools and the Negro. *Duke Law Journal, 6*, 1069–1099.

George, J. A. (2008). Offender profiling and expert testimony: Scientifically valid or glorified results? *Vanderbilt Law Review, 61*, 221–260.

Georgia v. McCollum, 112 S.Ct. 2348 (1992).

Geraerts, E., Schooler, J., Merckelbach, H., Jelicic, M., Hauer, B., & Ambadar, Z. (2007). The reality of recovered memories: Corroborating continuous and discontinuous memories of childhood sexual abuse. *Psychological Science, 18*, 564–568.

Gerbasi, K. C., Zuckerman, M., & Reis, H. T. (1977). Justice needs a new blindfold: A review of mock jury research. *Psychological Bulletin, 84*, 323–345.

Gerber, M. R., Ganz, M. L., Lichter, E., Williams, C. M., & McCloskey, L. A. (2005). Adverse health behaviors and the detection of partner violence by clinicians. *Archives of Internal Medicine, 165*, 1016–1021.

Gergen, K. J. (1994). Exploring the postmodern: Perils or potentials? *American Psychologist, 49*, 412–416.

Gerry, M., Garry, M., & Loftus, E. (2005). False memories. In N. Brewer & K. Williams (Eds.), *Psychology and law: An empirical perspective* (pp. 222–252). New York: Guilford Publications.

Giaconia, R. M., Reinherz, H. Z., Silverman, A. B., Pakiz, B., Frost, A. K., & Cohen, E. (1995). Traumas and posttraumatic stress disorder in a community population of older adolescents. *Journal of the American Academy of Child & Adolescent Psychiatry, 34*, 1369–1380.

Gibson, C. (2005, January 7). *Andrea Yates case interview with Andrea Yates' mother* [ABC News Transcript, Good Morning America]. Retrieved August 7, 2005, from http://www.lexisnexis.com/us/lnacademic/results/docview/docview.do?docLinkInd=true&risb=21_T8239962496&format=GNBFI&sort=RELEVANCE&startDocNo=1&resultsUrlKey=29_T8239962499&cisb=22_T8239962498&treeMax=true&treeWidth=0&csi=8277&docNo=7

Gideon v. Wainwright, 372 U.S. 335 (1963).

Gist, R. M., & Perry, J. D. (1985). Perspectives on negotiation in local jurisdictions. Part 1: A different typology of situations. *FBI Law Enforcement Bulletin, 54*, 21.

Givelber, D. (2001). The adversary system and historical accuracy: Can we do better? In S. Westervelt & J. Humphrey (Eds.), *Wrongly convicted: Perspectives on failed justice* (pp. 253–268). New Brunswick, NJ: Rutgers University Press.

Givelber, D., & Farrell, A. (2008). Judges and juries: The defense case and differences in acquittal rates. *Law and Social Inquiry, 33*, 31–52.

Glamser, D. (1997, January 27). Washington State testing therapy for sex felons. *USA Today*, p. 3A.

Glaze, L., & Bonczar, T. (2008). *Probation and parole in the United States, 2007.* Washington, DC: U.S. Department of Justice. (Bureau of Justice Statistics Report No. NCJ 224707)

Gless, A. G. (1995). Some post-*Daubert* trial tribulations of a simple county judge: Behavioral science evidence in trial courts. *Behavioral Science & the Law, 13*, 261–291.

Glymour, B., Glymour, C., & Glymour, M. (2008). Watching social science: The debate about the effects of exposure to televised violence on aggressive behavior. *American Behavioral Scientist, 51*, 1231–1259.

Godinez v. Moran, 113 S.Ct. 2680 (1993).

Godwin v. LaTurco, 272 Cal. App.2d 475 (1969).

Goldfarb, R. L. (1965). *Ransom.* New York: Harper & Row.

Golding, J. M., Bradshaw, G. S., Dunlap, E. E., & Hodell, E. C. (2007). The impact of mock jury gender composition on deliberations and conviction rates in a child sexual assault trial. *Child Maltreatment, 12*(2), 182–190.

Golding, S. L., Roesch, R., & Schreiber, J. (1984). Assessment and conceptualization of competency to stand trial: Preliminary data on the Interdisciplinary Fitness Interview. *Law and Human Behavior, 8*, 321–334.

Goldkamp, J. (2000). The drug court response: Issues and implications for justice change. *Albany Law Review, 63*, 923–961.

Goldman, S., & Faw, L. (1999). Three wraparound models as promising approaches. In B. Burns & S. Goldman (Eds.), *Promising practices in wraparound for children with serious emotional disturbance and their families. Systems of care: Promising practices in children's mental health, 1998 series* (Vol. 4, pp. 35–78). Washington, DC: American Institutes for Research Center for Effective Collaboration and Practice.

Goldstein, A. P. (2004). Evaluations of effectiveness. In A. P. Goldstein, R. Nensen, B. Daleflod, & M. Kalt (Eds.), *New perspectives on aggression replacement training* (pp. 230–244). Chichester, UK: Wiley.

Goldstein, N. E. S., Dovidio, A., Kalbeitzer, R., Weil, J., & Strachan, M. (2007). An anger management

intervention for female juvenile offenders: Results of a pilot study. *Journal of Forensic Psychology Practice, 7*, 1–28.

Goodman, G. S., Golding, J., Helgeson, V., Haith, M., & Michelli, J. (1987). When a child takes the stand: Jurors' perceptions of children's eyewitness testimony. *Law and Human Behavior, 11*, 27–40.

Goodman, G. S., Pyle-Taub, E., Jones, D., England, P., Port, L., Rudy, L., et al. (1992). Testifying in criminal court: Emotional effects of criminal court testimony on child sexual assault victims. *Monographs of the Society for Research in Child Development, 57*(5, Serial No. 229), i, ii, v, 1–159.

Goodman, G. S., Tobey, A., Batterman-Faunce, J., Orcutt, H., Thomas, S., & Shapiro, C. (1998). Face-to-face confrontation: Effects of closed-circuit technology on children's eyewitness testimony and jurors' decisions. *Law and Human Behavior, 22*, 265–203.

Goodman-Delahunty, J. (1998). Approaches to gender and the law: Research and applications. *Law and Human Behavior, 22*, 129–143.

Goodman-Delahunty, J., Greene, E., & Hsiao, W. (1998). Construing motive in videotaped killings: The role of jurors' attitudes toward the death penalty. *Law and Human Behavior, 22*, 257–271.

Gordon, D., Arbuthnot, J., Gustafson, K., & McGreen, P. (1988). Home-based behavioral-systems family therapy with disadvantaged juvenile delinquents. *American Journal of Family Therapy, 16*, 243–255.

Gordon, R. A. (1986, August). *IQ commensurability of black–white differences in crime and delinquency.* Paper presented at the meeting of the American Psychological Association, Washington, DC.

Gordon, R. A., Walden, T. L., McNicholas, M. L., & Bindrim, T. A. (1988). Perceptions of blue-collar and white-collar crime: The effect of defendant race on simulated juror decisions. *Journal of Social Psychology, 128*, 191–197.

Gothard, S., Rogers, R., & Sewell, K. W. (1995). Feigning incompetency to stand trial: An investigation of the Georgia Court Competency Test. *Law and Human Behavior, 19*, 363–374.

Gothard, S., Viglione, D. J., Meloy, J. R., & Sherman, M. (1995). Detection of malingering in competency to stand trial evaluations. *Law and Human Behavior, 19*, 493–506.

Gottfredson, D., & Exum, M. (2002). The Baltimore city drug treatment court: One-year results from a randomized study. *Journal of Research in Crime and Delinquency, 39,* 337–356.

Gottfredson, D., Najaka, S., & Kearley, B. (2003). Effectiveness of drug courts: Evidence from a randomized trial. *Criminology & Public Policy, 2,* 171–196.

Gottfredson, L. (1986, August). *IQ versus training: Job performance and black–white occupational inequality.* Paper presented at the meeting of the American Psychological Association, Washington, DC.

Government Accountability Office. (2005). *Adult drug courts: Evidence indicates recidivism reductions and mixed results for other outcomes.* Washington, DC: Author.

Gowan, M. A., & Gatewood, R. D. (1995). Personnel selection. In N. Brewer & C. Wilson (Eds.), *Psychology and policing* (pp. 177–204). Mahwah, NJ: Lawrence Erlbaum Associates.

Gray, E. (1993). *Unequal justice: The prosecution of child sexual abuse.* New York: Macmillan.

Gready, R., Ditto, P., Danks, J., Coppola, K., Lockhart, L., & Smucker, W. (2000). Actual and perceived stability of preferences for life-sustaining treatment. *Journal of Clinical Ethics, 11,* 334–346.

Greely, H. (2005). Premarket approval for lie detections: An idea whose time may be coming. *American Journal of Bioethics, 5,* 50–52.

Green, A. (2004, August 30). The waiting room: August. *The New Yorker,* pp. 37–38.

Green, B., Grace, M., Lindy, J., Gleser, G., & Leonard, A. C. (1990). Risk factors for PTSD and other diagnoses in a general sample of Vietnam veterans. *American Journal of Psychiatry, 147,* 729–733.

Green, S. (2005, January 31). When justice is delayed. *National Law Journal,* p. 22.

Greenberg, M. S., & Ruback, R. B. (1982). *Social psychology of the criminal justice system.* Pacific Grove, CA: Brooks/Cole.

Greenberg, M. S., & Ruback, R. B. (1984). Criminal victimization: Introduction and overview. *Journal of Social Issues, 40,* 1–8.

Greene, E. (2002). How effective? Review of Stack and sway: The new science of jury consulting. *Judicature, 85,* 1–3.

Greene, E. (2008). "Can we talk?" Therapeutic jurisprudence, restorative justice, and tort litigation. In B. Bornstein & R. Wiener (Eds.), *Civil juries and civil justice: Empirical perspectives* (pp. 235–258). New York: Springer.

Greene, E., & Bornstein, B. (2000). Precious little guidance: Jury instructions on damage awards. *Psychology, Public Policy, and Law, 6,* 743–768.

Greene, E., & Bornstein, B. (2003). *Determining damages: The psychology of jury awards.* Washington, DC: American Psychological Association.

Greene, E., Chopra, S., Kovera, M., Penrod, S., Rose, V., Schuller, R., et al. (2002). Jurors and juries: A review of the field. In J. Ogloff (Ed.), *Taking psychology and law into the twenty-first century* (pp. 225–285). New York: Kluwer Academic/Plenum.

Greene, E., & Ellis, L. (2007). Decision making in criminal justice. In D. Carson, B. Milne, F. Pakes, K. Shalev, & A. Shawyer (Eds.), *Applying psychology to criminal justice* (pp. 183–200). Chichester: Wiley.

Greene, E., Goodman, J., & Loftus, E. (1991). Jurors' attitudes about civil litigation and the size of damage awards. *American University Law Review, 40,* 805–820.

Greene, E., Hayman, K., & Motyl, M. (2008). "Shouldn't we consider …?" Jury discussions of forbidden topics and effects on damage awards. *Psychology, Public Policy, and Law, 14,* 194–222.

Greene, E., Johns, M., & Bowman, J. (1999). The effects of injury severity on jury negligence decisions. *Law and Human Behavior, 23,* 675–693.

Greene, E., Johns, M., & Smith, A. (2001). The effects of defendant conduct on jury damage awards. *Journal of Applied Psychology, 86,* 228–237.

Greene, E., & Loftus, E. (1985). When crimes are joined at trial. *Law and Human Behavior, 9,* 193–207.

Greene, J. A. (1999). Zero tolerance: A case study of police policies and practices in New York City. *Crime and Delinquency, 45,* 171–187.

Greenhouse, L. (1994, April 20). High court bars sex as standard of picking jurors. *The New York Times,* pp. A1, A10.

Gregg v. Georgia, 428 U.S. 153 (1976).

Gregory, W. L., Mowen, J. C., & Linder, D. E. (1978). Social psychology and plea bargaining: Applications, methodology, and theory. *Journal of Personality and Social Psychology, 36,* 1521–1530.

Griffin, M. (2008, March). *Old dogs and new tricks: Demographic variables and interest in technology implementation in the courtroom.* Paper presented at the annual conference of American Psychology-Law Society, Jacksonville, FL.

Griffin, P. (2003). *Trying and sentencing juveniles as adults: An analysis of state transfer and blended sentencing laws.* Pittsburgh, PA: National Center for Juvenile Justice.

Grisso, T. (1986). *Evaluating competencies: Forensic assessments and instruments.* New York: Plenum.

Grisso, T. (1998). *Forensic assessment of juveniles.* Sarasota, FL: Professional Resource Press.

Grisso, T. (2003). *Evaluating competencies: Forensic assessments and instruments* (2nd ed.). New York: Kluwer/Plenum.

Grisso, T., & Appelbaum, P. S. (1995). The MacArthur Treatment Competence Study. III: Abilities of patients to consent to psychiatric and medical treatments. *Law and Human Behavior, 19,* 149–174.

Grisso, T., & Appelbaum, P. (1998a). *Assessing competence to consent to treatment: A guide for physicians and other health professionals.* New York: Oxford University Press.

Grisso, T., & Appelbaum, P. (1998b). *MacArthur competence assessment tool for treatment (MacCAT-T).* Sarasota, FL: Professional Resource Press.

Grisso, T., Appelbaum, P. S., Mulvey, E. P., & Fletcher, K. (1995). The MacArthur Treatment Competence Study. II: Measures of abilities related to competence to consent to treatment. *Law and Human Behavior, 19,* 127–148.

Grisso, T., Cocozza, J. J., Steadman, H. J., Fisher, W. H., & Greer, A. (1994). The organization of pretrial forensic evaluation services: A national profile. *Law and Human Behavior, 18,* 377–394.

Grisso, T., & Saks, M. J. (1991). Psychology's influence on constitutional interpretation: A comment on how to succeed. *Law and Human Behavior, 15,* 205–211.

Grisso, T., & Siegel, S. K. (1986). Assessment of competency to stand criminal trial. In W. J. Curran, A. L. McGarry, & S. A. Shah (Eds.), *Forensic psychiatry and psychology* (pp. 145–165). Philadelphia: F. A. Davis.

Grisso, T., Steinberg, L., Woolard, J., Cauffman, E., Scott, E., Graham, S., et al. (2003). Juveniles' competence to stand trial: A comparison of adolescents' and adults' capacities as trial defendants. *Law and Human Behavior, 27,* 333–363.

Gross, J., & Hayne, H. (1996). Eyewitness identification by 5- to 6-year-old children. *Law and Human Behavior, 20,* 359–373.

Gross, S., Jacoby, K., Matheson, D., Montgomery, N., & Patil, S. (2005). Exonerations in the United States 1989 through 2003. *Journal of Criminal Law and Criminology, 95,* 523–560.

Gross, S., & O'Brien, B. (2008). Frequency and predictors of false conviction: Why we know so little, and new data on capital cases. *Journal of Empirical Legal Studies, 5,* 927–962.

Groth, A. N. (with Birnbaum, H. J.). (1979). *Men who rape.* New York: Plenum.

Group for the Advancement of Psychiatry. (1974). *Misuse of psychiatry in the criminal courts: Competency to stand trial. The Committee on Psychiatry and Law, Report 89* (Vol. 8, pp. 896–897). New York: GAP Publications.

Grove, W. M., & Barden, R. C. (1999). Protecting the integrity of the legal system: The admissibility of testimony from mental health experts under *Daubert/Kumho* analyses. *Psychology, Public Policy, and Law, 5,* 224–242.

Grutter v. Bollinger, 137 F. Supp. 2d 821 (2001); 123 S. Ct. 2325 (2003).

Grych, J. H., & Fincham, F. D. (1992). Interventions for children of divorce: Toward greater integration of research and action. *Psychological Bulletin, 111,* 434–454.

Gudjonsson, G., & MacKeith, J. (1982). False confessions: Psychological effects of interrogation. In A. Trankell (Ed.), *Reconstructing the past: The role of psychologists in criminal trials.* Deventer, The Netherlands: Kluwer.

Gudjonsson, G. H., & Copson, G. (1997). The role of the expert in criminal investigation. In J. L. Jackson & D. A. Bekerian (Eds.), *Offender profiling: Theory, research, and practice* (pp. 61–76). Chichester, England: Wiley.

Gunnoe, M. L., & Braver, S. L. (2001). The effects of joint legal custody on mothers, fathers, and children, controlling for factors that predispose a sole maternal vs. joint legal award. *Law and Human Behavior, 25,* 25–43.

Gunter, G. (1985, January 25). Voices across the USA. *USA Today,* p. 12A.

Gutek, B. A. (1985). *Sex and the workplace: Impact of sexual behavior and harassment on women, men, and organizations.* San Francisco: Jossey-Bass.

Gutek, B. A., & O'Connor, M. (1995). The empirical basis for the reasonable woman standard. *Journal of Social Issues, 51*, 151–166.

Guthrie, C., Rachlinski, J., & Wistrich, A. (2001). Inside the judicial mind. *Cornell Law Review, 86*, 777–830.

Guthrie, C., Rachlinski, J., & Wistrich, A. (2007). Blinking on the bench: How judges decide cases. *Cornell Law Review, 93*, 1–43.

Haas, S., & Hamilton, C. (2007, May). *The use of core correctional practices in offender reentry: The delivery of service delivery and prisoner preparedness for release.* Charleston, WV: Mountain State Criminal Justice Research Services.

Hagan, J., & Peterson, R. (1995). *Crime and inequality.* Stanford, CA: Stanford University Press.

Hahn, R., & Kleist, D. (2000). Divorce mediation: Research and implications for family and couples counseling. *The Family Journal, 8*, 165–171.

Haj-Yahia, M. M. (2003). Beliefs about wife-beating among Arab men in Israel: The influence of their patriarchal ideology. *Journal of Family Violence, 18*, 193–206.

Hall, G. C. (1996). *Theory-based assessment, treatment, and prevention of sexual aggression.* New York: Oxford University Press.

Hall, G. C., & Hirschman, R. (1991). Toward a theory of sexual aggression: A quadripartite model. *Journal of Consulting and Clinical Psychology, 59*, 662–669.

Halligan, S. L., Michael, T., Clark, D. M., & Ehlers, A. (2003). Posttraumatic stress disorder following assault: The role of cognitive processing, trauma memory, and appraisals. *Journal of Consulting and Clinical Psychology, 71*, 419–431.

Hamilton, A. (2004, December 13). Woof, woof, your honor. *Time*, p. 46.

Hammel, P. (2008a). *Psychologist had dual role in confessions of Beatrice 6.* Retrieved March 29, 2009, from http://www.omaha.com/index.php?u_page=2798&u_sid=10500550

Hammel, P. (2008b). *Pardons granted to five in murder they didn't commit.* Retrieved March 29, 2009, from http://www.omaha.com/index.php?u_page=2798&u_sid=10548085

Haney, C. (1997a). Commonsense justice and capital punishment: Problematizing the "will of the people." *Psychology, Public Policy, and Law, 3*, 303–337.

Haney, C. (1997b). Psychology and the limits to prison pain: Confronting the coming crisis in Eighth Amendment law. *Psychology, Public Policy, and Law, 3*, 499–588.

Haney, C. (2006). *Reforming punishment: Psychological limits to the pains of imprisonment.* Washington, DC: American Psychological Association.

Haney, C., & Lynch, M. (1994). Comprehending life and death matters: A preliminary study of California's capital penalty instructions. *Law and Human Behavior, 18*, 411–436.

Haney, C., & Lynch, M. (1997). Clarifying life and death matters: An analysis of instructional comprehension and penalty phase closing arguments. *Law and Human Behavior, 21*, 575–596.

Haney, C., & Wiener, R. (2004). Death is different: An editorial introduction to the theme issue. *Psychology, Public Policy, and Law, 10*, 373–378.

Hanish, L. D., & Guerra, N. G. (2000). The roles of ethnicity and school context in predicting children's victimization by peers. *American Journal of Community Psychology, 28*, 201–224.

Hannaford, P., Hans, V., & Munsterman, G. T. (2000). Permitting jury discussions during trial: Impact of the Arizona reform. *Law and Human Behavior, 24*, 359–382.

Hans, V. P. (1992). Judgments of justice. *Psychological Science, 3*, 218–220.

Hans, V. P. (1996). The contested role of the civil jury in business litigation. *Judicature, 79*, 242–248.

Hans, V. P. (2000). *Business on trial: The civil jury and corporate responsibility.* New Haven, CT: Yale University Press.

Hans, V. P., & Ermann, M. D. (1989). Responses to corporate versus individual wrongdoing. *Law and Human Behavior, 13*, 151–166.

Hans, V. P., Hannaford, P. L., & Munsterman, G. T. (1999). The Arizona jury reform permitting civil jury trial discussions: The views of trial participants, judges, and jurors. *University of Michigan Journal of Law Reform, 32*, 349–377.

Hans, V. P., & Jehle, A. (2003). Avoid bald men and people with green socks. Other ways to improve the voir dire process in jury selection. *Chicago-Kent Law Review, 78*, 1179–1201.

Hans, V. P., & Slater, D. (1983). John Hinckley, Jr., and the insanity defense: The public's verdict. *Public Opinion Quarterly, 47*, 202–212.

Hans, V. P., & Vidmar, N. (1986). *Judging the jury.* New York: Plenum.

Hans, V. P., & Vidmar, N. (1991). The American jury at twenty-five years. *Law and Social Inquiry, 16*, 323–351.

Hansen, M. (1999, April). Mandatories going, going, … going. *American Bar Association Journal, 85*, 14.

Hanson, R. K. (1997). *The development of a brief actuarial risk scale for sexual offense recidivism*. Ottawa: Department of the Solicitor General of Canada. (User Report No. 97–04).

Hanson, R. K., & Bussiere, M. T. (1998). Predicting relapse: A meta-analysis of sexual offender recidivism studies. *Journal of Consulting and Clinical Psychology, 66*, 348–362.

Hanson, R., & Morton-Bourgnon, K. (2005). The characteristics of persistent sexual offenders: A meta-analysis of recidivism studies. *Journal of Consulting and Clinical Psychology, 73*, 1154–1163.

Hanson, R. K., & Thornton, D. (2000). Improving risk assessments for sex offenders: A comparison of three actuarial scales. *Law and Human Behavior, 24*, 119–136.

Harding, T., & Zimmerman, E. (1989). Psychiatric symptoms, cognitive stress and vulnerability factors: A study in a remand prison. *British Journal of Psychiatry, 155*, 36–43.

Hare, R. D. (1991). *The Hare Psychopathy Checklist—Revised*. North Tonawanda, NY: Multi-Health Systems.

Hare, R. D. (2003). *The Hare Psychopathy Checklist—Revised (PCL-R)* (2nd ed.). Toronto, Ontario: Multi-Health Systems.

Hare, R. D., Hart, S. D., & Harpur, T. J. (1991). Psychopathy and the DSM-IV criteria for antisocial personality disorder. *Journal of Abnormal Psychology, 100*, 391–398.

Hare, R. D., & McPherson, L. M. (1984). Violent and aggressive behavior by criminal psychopaths. *International Journal of Law and Psychiatry, 7*, 35–50.

Harper, T. (1984, April 29). State rape laws see decade of change. *Lawrence Journal-World*, p. 1B.

Harpold, J. A., & Feemster, S. L. (2002). Negative influences of police stress. *FBI Law Enforcement Bulletin, 71*(9), 1–7. Retrieved July 18, 2005, from http://www.fbi.gov/publications/leb/2002/sept2002/sept02leb.htm#page_2

Harrington v. Iowa, 659 NW 2d 509 (Iowa, 2003).

Harris v. Forklift Systems, Inc., 510 U.S. 17 (1993).

Harris v. New York, 401 U.S. 222 (1971).

Harris, G., & Rice, M. (2003). Actuarial assessment of risk among sex offenders. *Annals of the New York Academy of Sciences, 989*, 198–210.

Harris, G. T., Rice, M. E., & Quinsey, V. L. (1993). Violent recidivism of mentally disordered offenders: The development of a statistical prediction instrument. *Criminal Justice and Behavior, 20*, 315–335.

Harris, G., Rice, M., Quinsey, V., Lalumiere, M., Boer, D., & Lang, C. (2003). A multisite comparison of actuarial risk instruments for sex offenders. *Psychological Assessment, 15*, 413–425.

Harris Poll. (2008). Just under three in five Americans believe juries can be fair and impartial all or most of the time. *Harris Poll #9*, January 21. Retrieved January 16, 2009, from http://www.harrisinteractive.com/harris_poll/index.asp?PID=861

Harrison, P., & Beck, A. J. (2002). *Prisoners in 2001. Bureau of Justice Statistics Bulletin*. Washington, DC: U.S. Department of Justice.

Harrison, P., & Beck, A. (2005). *Prison and jail inmates at midyear 2004*. Washington, DC: U.S. Department of Justice, Bureau of Justice Statistics.

Harrison, P., & Beck, A. (2006). *Prisoners in 2005*. Washington, DC: U.S. Department of Justice, Office of Justice Programs, Bureau of Justice Statistics.

Harrison, P. M., & Karberg, J. C. (2003, April). *Prison and jail inmates at midyear 2002. Bureau of Justice Statistics Bulletin*. Washington, DC: U.S. Department of Justice.

Hart, P. M., Wearing, A., & Headey, B. (1995). Police stress and well-being: Integrating personality, coping, and daily work experiences. *Journal of Occupational and Organizational Psychology, 68*, 133–156.

Hart, S., Michie, C., & Cooke, D. (2007). The precision of actuarial risk assessment instruments: Evaluating the "margins of error" of group versus individual predictions of violence. *British Journal of Psychiatry, 190*, s60–s65.

Hartcollis, A. (2006, April 13). Excuses from jury pool? He's heard them all. *The New York Times*.

Hartley, R. (2008). Dedication for the special issue on problem solving courts. *Criminal Justice Review, 33*, 289–290.

Hasemann, D. (1997). *Practices and findings of mental health professionals conducting workers' compensation evaluations*. Unpublished doctoral dissertation, University of Kentucky, Lexington, KY.

Hashemi, L., & Webster, B. S. (1998). Non-fatal workplace violence workers' compensation claims (1993–1996). *Journal of Occupational & Environmental Medicine, 40*(6), 561–567.

Hastie, R., & Pennington, N. (1996). The O. J. Simpson stories: Behavioral scientists' reflections on *The People of the State of California v. Orenthal James Simpson*. *University of Colorado Law Review, 67*, 957–975.

Hatch, D. E. (2002). *Officer-involved shootings and use of force: Practical investigative techniques*. Boca Raton, FL: CRC Press.

Hatcher, C., Mohandie, K., Turner, J., & Gelles, M. G. (1998). The role of the psychologist in crisis/hostage negotiations. *Behavioral Sciences & the Law, 16*, 455–472.

Haugaard, J. J., & Avery, R. J. (2002). Termination of parental rights to free children for adoption: Conflicts between parents, children, and the state. In B. Bottoms, M. Kovera, & B. D. McAuliff (Eds.), *Children, social policy, and U.S. law* (pp. 131–152). Boston, MA: Cambridge University Press.

Haw, R., & Fisher, R. (2004). Effects of administrator–witness contact on eyewitness identification accuracy. *Journal of Applied Psychology, 89*, 1106–1112.

Hawkins, H. C. (2001). Police officer burnout: A partial replication of Maslach's burnout inventory. *Police Quarterly, 4*, 343–360.

Hazelwood, R. R., & Douglas, J. E. (1980). The lust murderer. *FBI Law Enforcement Bulletin, 49*, 18–22.

Hazelwood, R., & Michaund, S. (2001). *Dark dreams*. New York: Macmillan.

Hazelwood, R. R., Ressler, R. K., Depue, R. L., & Douglas, J. C. (1995). Criminal investigative analysis: An overview. In A. W. Burgess & R. R. Hazelwood (Eds.), *Practical aspects of rape investigation: A multidisciplinary approach* (2nd ed., pp. 115–126). Boca Raton, FL: CRC.

Heide, K. M. (1997). Juvenile homicide in America: How can we stop the killing? *Behavioral Sciences & the Law, 15*, 203–220.

Heider, F. (1958). *The psychology of interpersonal relations*. New York: Wiley.

Heilbrun, K. (1987). The assessment of competency for execution: An overview. *Behavioral Sciences & the Law, 5*, 383–396.

Heilbrun, K. (2001). *Principles of forensic mental health assessment*. New York: Kluwer Academic/Plenum Press.

Heilbrun, K. (2009). *Evaluation for risk of violence in adults*. New York: Oxford University Press.

Heilbrun, K., & Collins, S. (1995). Evaluation of trial competency and mental state at the time of offense: Report characteristics. *Professional Psychology: Research and Practice, 26*, 61–67.

Heilbrun, K., Douglas, K., & Yasuhara, K. (2009). Violence risk assessment: Core controversies. In J. Skeem, K. Douglas, & S. Lilienfeld (Eds.), *Psychological science in the courtroom: Controversies and consensus* (pp. 333–357). New York: Guilford.

Heilbrun, K., Dvoskin, J., & Heilbrun, A. (2009). Mass killings on college campuses: Public health, threat/risk assessment, and preventing future tragedies. *Psychological Injury and Law, 2*, 93–99.

Heilbrun, K., Goldstein, N., DeMatteo, D., Hart, A., Riggs Romaine, C., & Shah, S. (in press). Interventions in forensic settings: Juveniles in residential placement, defendants in drug courts or mental health courts, and defendants in forensic hospitals as Incompetent to Stand Trial. In D. Barlow (Ed.), *Oxford handbook of clinical psychology*. New York: Oxford University Press.

Heilbrun, K., Grisso, T., & Goldstein, A. (2008). *Foundations of forensic mental health assessment*. New York: Oxford University Press.

Heilbrun, K., Heilbrun, P., & Griffin, N. (1988). Comparing females acquitted by reason of insanity, convicted, and civilly committed in Florida: 1977–1984. *Law and Human Behavior, 12*, 295–312.

Heilbrun, K., Lee, R., & Cottle, C. (2005). Risk factors and intervention outcomes: Meta-analyses of juvenile offending. In K. Heilbrun, N. Sevin-Goldstein, & R. Redding (Eds.), *Juvenile delinquency: Prevention, assessment, and intervention* (pp. 111–133). New York: Oxford University Press.

Heilbrun, K., Marczyk, G., & DeMatteo, D. (2002). *Forensic mental health assessment: A casebook*. New York: Oxford University Press.

Heilbrun, K., & McClaren, H. (1988). Assessment of competency for execution? A guide for mental health professionals. *Bulletin of the American Academy of Psychiatry and the Law, 16*, 206–216.

Heise, M. (2004). Criminal case complexity: An empirical perspective. *Journal of Empirical Legal Studies, 1*, 331–369.

Helzer, J. E., Robins, L. N., & McEvoy, L. (1987). Post-traumatic stress disorder in the general population. Findings of the Epidemiologic Catchment Area survey. *New England Journal of Medicine, 317,* 1630–1634.

Henggeler, S., Clingempeel, W., Brondino, M., & Pickrel, S. (2002). Four-year follow-up of multisystemic therapy with substance-abusing and substance-dependent juvenile offenders. *Journal of the American Academy of Child and Adolescent Psychiatry, 41,* 868–874.

Henggeler, S., Melton, G., Brondino, M., Scherer, D., & Hanley, J. (1997). Multisystemic therapy with violent and chronic juvenile offenders and their families: The role of treatment fidelity in successful dissemination. *Journal of Consulting and Clinical Psychology, 65,* 821–833.

Henggeler, S., Melton, G., & Smith, L. (1992). Family preservation using multisystemic therapy: An effective alternative to incarcerating serious juvenile offenders. *Journal of Consulting and Clinical Psychology, 60,* 953–961.

Henggeler, S., Melton, G., Smith, L., Schoenwald, S., & Hanley, J. (1993). Family preservation using multisystemic treatment: Long-term follow-up to a clinical trial with serious juvenile offenders. *Journal of Child and Family Studies, 2,* 283–293.

Henggeler, S. W., Pickrel, S. G., & Brondino, M. J. (1999). Multisystemic treatment of substance abusing and dependent delinquents: Outcomes, treatment fidelity, and transportability. *Mental Health Services Research, 1,* 171–184.

Henggeler, S., Pickrel, S., Brondino, M., & Crouch, J. (1996). Eliminating (almost) treatment dropout of substance abusing or dependent delinquents through home-based multisystemic therapy. *American Journal of Psychiatry, 153,* 427–428.

Henggeler, S., Rodick, J., Borduin, C., Hanson, C., Watson, S., & Urey, J. (1986). Multisystemic treatment of juvenile offenders: Effects on adolescent behavior and family interaction. *Developmental Psychology, 22,* 132–141.

Henggeler, S., Rowland, M., Randall, J., Ward, D., Pickrel, S., Cunningham, P., et al. (1999). Home-based multisystemic therapy as an alternative to the hospitalization of youths in psychiatric crisis: Clinical outcomes. *Journal of the American Academy of Child and Adolescent Psychiatry, 38,* 1331–1339.

Henggeler, S. W., & Schoenwald, S. K. (1999). The role of quality assurance in achieving outcomes in MST programs. *Journal of Juvenile Justice and Detention Services, 14,* 1–17.

Henggeler, S. W., Schoenwald, S. K., Borduin, C. M., Rowland, M. D., & Cunningham, P. B. (1998). *Multisystemic treatment of antisocial behavior in children and adolescents.* New York: Guilford Press.

Henry, M., & Rafilson, F. (1997). The temporal stability of the National Police Officer Selection Test. *Psychological Reports, 81,* 1259–1265.

Herek, G. M. (1987). Can functions be measured? A new perspective on the functional approach to attitudes. *Social Psychology Quarterly, 50,* 285–303.

Herinckx, H., Swart, S., Ama, S., Dolezal, C., & King, S. (2005). Rearrest and linkage to mental health services among clients of the Clark County Mental Health Court Program. *Psychiatric Services, 56,* 853–857.

Hernandez v. New York, 111 S.Ct. 1859 (1991).

Hersch, J., & Viscusi, W. (2004). Punitive damages: How judges and juries perform. *Journal of Legal Studies, 33,* 1–36.

Hersch, P. D., & Alexander, R. W. (1990). MMPI profile patterns of emotional disability claimants. *Journal of Clinical Psychology, 46,* 795–799.

Hetherington, E. M., & Arasteh, J. D. (Eds.). (1988). *Impact of divorce, single parenting, and step-parenting on children.* Hillsdale, NJ: Lawrence Erlbaum.

Heuer, L., & Penrod, S. (1988). Increasing jurors' participation in trials: A field experiment with jury notetaking and question asking. *Law and Human Behavior, 12,* 231–262.

Heumann, M. (1978). *Plea bargaining.* Chicago: University of Chicago Press.

Heussanstamm, F. K. (1975). Bumper stickers and the cops. In D. J. Steffensmeier & R. M. Terry (Eds.), *Examining deviance experimentally: Selected readings* (pp. 251–255). Port Washington, NY: Alfred.

Hiday, V. A., & Goodman, R. R. (1982). The least restrictive alternative to involuntary hospitalization, outpatient commitment: Its use and effectiveness. *Journal of Psychiatry and Law, 10,* 81–96.

Higgins, M. (1999, March). Tough luck for the innocent man. *ABA Journal, 85,* 46–52.

Hill, E., & Pfeifer, J. (1992). Nullification instructions and juror guilt ratings: An examination of modern racism. *Contemporary Social Psychology, 16,* 6–10.

Ho, T. (2001). The interrelationships of psychological testing, psychologists' recommendations, and police departments' recruitment decisions. *Police Quarterly, 4*, 318–342.

Hoffman, P. B., & Stone-Meierhoefer, B. (1979). Application of guidelines to sentencing. In L. E. Abt & I. R. Stuart (Eds.), *Social psychology and discretionary law* (pp. 241–258). New York: Van Nostrand Reinhold.

Hogarth, J. (1971). *Sentencing as a human process.* Toronto: University of Toronto Press.

Hoge, R., & Andrews, D. (2002). *The Youth Level of Service/Case Management Inventory (YLS/CMI) user's manual.* North Tonawanda, NY: Multi-Health Systems, Inc.

Hoge, S. K., Bonnie, R. J., Poythress, N., Monahan, J., Eisenberg, M., & Feucht-Haviar, T. (1997). The MacArthur adjudicative competence study: Development and validation of a research instrument. *Law and Human Behavior, 21*, 141–179.

Hoge, S., Poythress, N., Bonnie, R., Monahan, J., Eisenberg, M., & Feucht-Haviar, T. (1997). The MacArthur adjudicative competence study: Diagnosis, psychopathology, and competence-related abilities. *Behavioral Sciences & the Law, 15*, 329–345.

Hogg, A., & Wilson, C. (1995). *Is the psychological screening of police applicants a realistic goal? The successes and failures of psychological screening.* Payneham, Australia: National Police Research Unit. (National Police Research Unit Report Series No. 124).

Holland v. Illinois, 493 U.S. 474 (1990).

Holander-Blumoff, R., & Tyler, T. (2008). Procedural justice in negotiation: Procedural fairness, outcome acceptance, and integrative potential. *Law and Social Inquiry, 33*, 473–500.

Holmes, M. D., & Smith, B. W. (2008). *Race and police brutality.* Albany, NY: SUNY Press.

Holmes, O. (1881). *The common law.* Boston, MA: Little, Brown.

Holmes, R. M., & DeBurger, J. (1988). *Serial murder.* Newbury Park, CA: Sage.

Homant, R. J., & Kennedy, D. B. (1998). Psychological aspects of crime scene profiling. *Criminal Justice and Behavior, 25*, 319–343.

Honts, C. (2004). The psychophysiological detection of deception. In P. Granhag & L. Stromwell (Eds.), *Detection of deception in forensic contexts* (pp. 103–123). London: Cambridge University Press.

Honts, C., & Alloway, W. (2007). Information does not affect the validity of a comparison question test. *Legal and Criminological Psychology, 12*, 311–320.

Honts, C., Raskin, D., & Kircher, J. (1994). Mental and physical countermeasures reduce the accuracy of polygraph tests. *Journal of Applied Psychology, 79*, 252–259.

Hope, L., Memon, A., & McGeorge, P. (2004). Understanding pretrial publicity: Predecisional distortion of evidence by mock jurors. *Journal of Experimental Psychology: Applied, 10*, 111–119.

Hope, L., & Wright, D. (2007). Beyond unusual? Examining the role of attention in the weapon focus effect. *Applied Cognitive Psychology, 21*, 951–961.

Hopt v. Utah, 110 U.S. 574 (1884).

Horgan, D. D. (1988, August). *The ethics of unexpected advocacy.* Paper presented at the annual convention of the American Psychological Association, Atlanta, GA.

Horowitz, I. A. (1980). Juror selection: A comparison of two methods in several criminal cases. *Journal of Applied Social Psychology, 10*, 86–99.

Horowitz, I., & Bordens, K. (2002). The effects of jury size, evidence complexity, and note taking on jury process and performance in a civil trial. *Journal of Applied Psychology, 87*, 121–130.

Horowitz, I. A., Forsterlee, L., & Brolly, I. (1996). Effects of trial complexity on decision making. *Journal of Applied Psychology, 81*, 757–768.

Horowitz, I., Kerr, N., Park, E., & Gockel, C. (2006). Chaos in the courtroom reconsidered: Emotional bias and juror nullification. *Law and Human Behavior, 30*, 163–181.

Horowitz, I., & Willging, T. (1991). Changing views of jury power: The nullification debate, 1787–1988. *Law and Human Behavior, 15*, 165–182.

Horrigan, D. (2002, May). Technology on trial: Operating in virtual reality. *Law Technology News.* Retrieved June 25, 2009, from http://ltn-archive.hotresponse.com/may02/technology_on_trial_p21.html

Horwitz, A., Widom, C., McLaughlin, J., & White, H. (2001). The impact of childhood abuse and neglect on adult mental health: A prospective study. *Journal of Health and Social Behavior, 42*, 184–201.

Hotelling, K. (1991). Sexual harassment: A problem shielded by silence. *Journal of Counseling and Development, 69*, 497–501.

Houppert, K. (2007). *Deluded judge suggests domestic violence victim wanted to be hit.* Retrieved February 21, 2009, from http://www.alternet.org/blogs/peek/66153/

Houston, C. (1935). The need for Negro lawyers. *Journal of Negro Education, 4,* 49–52.

Howard, R. C., & Clark, C. R. (1985). When courts and experts disagree: Discordance between insanity recommendations and adjudications. *Law and Human Behavior, 9,* 385–395.

Huber, G., & Gordon, S. (2004). Accountability and coercion: Is justice blind when it runs for office? *American Journal of Political Science, 48,* 247–263.

Huber, P. (1990). *Liability: The legal revolution and its consequences.* New York: Basic Books.

Huesmann, L. R., Eron, L. D., Lefkowitz, M. M., & Walder, L. O. (1984). Stability of aggression over time and generations. *Developmental Psychology, 20,* 1120–1134.

Huesmann, L. R., Eron, L. D., & Yarmel, P. W. (1987). Intellectual functioning and aggression. *Journal of Personality and Social Psychology, 52,* 232–240.

Huesmann, L., Moise-Titus, J., Podolski, C., & Eron, L. D. (2003). Longitudinal relations between children's exposure to TV violence and their aggressive and violent behavior in young adulthood: 1977–1992. *Developmental Psychology, 39,* 201–221.

Hughes, T. A., Wilson, D. J., & Beck, A. J. (2001). *Trends in state parole, 1990–2000.* Washington, DC: U.S. Department of Justice, Bureau of Justice Statistics.

Hunter, J., & Hunter, R. (1984). Validity and utility of alternative predictors of job performance. *Psychological Bulletin, 96,* 72–98.

Huntley, J., & Costanzo, M. (2003). Sexual harassment stories: Testing a story-mediated model of juror decision-making in civil litigation. *Law and Human Behavior, 27,* 29–51.

Imwinkelried, E. J. (1994). The next step after *Daubert*: Developing a similarly epistemological approach to ensuring the reliability of nonscientific expert testimony. *Cardozo Law Review, 15,* 2271–2294.

In re Corrugated Container Antitrust Litigation, 614 F2d 958 (5th Circuit, 1980).

Inbau, F., Reid, J., Buckley, J., & Jayne, B. (2004). *Criminal interrogation and confessions* (4th ed.). Gaithersburg, MD: Aspen.

Innocence Project. (2008). *Understand the causes: Eyewitness misidentification.* Retrieved July 23, 2008, from http://www.innocenceproject.org/understand/Eyewitness-Misidentification.php

International Association of Chiefs of Police. (2006). *Building an offender reentry program: A guide for law enforcement.* Washington, DC: U.S. Bureau of Justice Assistance.

Inwald, R. E. (1986). Issues and guidelines for mental health professionals conducting pre-employment psychological screening programs in law enforcement agencies. In J. T. Reese & H. A. Goldstein (Eds.), *Psychological services for law enforcement* (pp. 47–50). Washington, DC: U.S. Government Printing Office.

Inwald, R. E. (1992). *Inwald Personality Inventory technical manual* (Rev. ed.). Kew Gardens, NY: Hilson Research.

Inwald, R. E., Knatz, H., & Shusman, E. (1983). *Inwald Personality Inventory manual.* New York: Hilson Research.

Irwin, J. (1970). *The felon.* Englewood Cliffs, NJ: Prentice Hall.

Isen, A. M., Daubman, K. A., & Nowicki, G. P. (1987). Positive affect facilitates creative problem solving. *Journal of Personality and Social Psychology, 52,* 1122–1131.

Ivkovic, S. K., & Hans, V. P. (2003). Jurors' evaluation of expert testimony. *Law & Social Inquiry, 28*(2), 441.

J.E.B. v. Alabama ex rel. T.B., 511 U.S. 127 (1994).

Jackson v. Denno, 378 U.S. 368 (1964).

Jackson v. Indiana, 406 U.S. 715 (1972).

Jackson, S. E., & Maslach, C. (1982). After-effects of job-related stress: Families as victims. *Journal of Occupational Behavior, 3,* 63–77.

Jackson, S. E., & Schuler, R. S. (1983, March–April). Preventing employee burnout. *Personnel, 60*(2), 58–68.

Jackson, R. L., Rogers, R., & Sewell, K. W. (2005). Forensic applications of the Miller Forensic Assessment of Symptoms Test (MFAST): Screening for feigned disorders in competency to stand trial evaluations. *Law and Human Behavior, 29*(2), 199–210.

James, D. J. (2004). *Bureau of Justice Statistics special report: Profile of jail inmates, 2002.* Washington, DC: U.S. Department of Justice.

Janus, E., & Prentky, R. (2003). Forensic use of actuarial risk assessment with sex offenders: Accuracy, admissibility and accountability. *American Criminal Law Review, 40*, 1443–1499.

Jeffers, H. P. (1991). *Who killed Precious?* New York: Pharos Books.

Jeffreys, B., & Rozen, M. (2006, January 30). The big show: Jury selection crucial element in imminent Lay-Skilling trial. *Texas Lawyer.*

Jenkins, P., & Davidson, B. (1990). Battered women in the criminal justice system: An analysis of gender stereotypes. *Behavioral Sciences & the Law, 8*, 161– 170.

Joe Arpaio 2004. (2004). Retrieved September 1, 2005, from http://www.reelectjoe.com

Johnson v. Zerbst, 304 U.S. 458 (1938).

Johnson, C., & Haney, C. (1994). Felony voir dire: An explanatory study of its content and effect. *Law and Human Behavior, 18*, 487–506.

Johnson, K. (2009). *To save money on prisons, states take a softer stance.* Retrieved March 23, 2009, from http://www.usatoday.com/news/nation/2009-03-17-prison-economy_N.htm

Jonakait, R. N. (2003). *The American jury system.* New Haven, CT: Yale University Press.

Jones, A. (1994). *Next time, she'll be dead: Battering and how to stop it.* Boston, MA: Beacon Press.

Jones, E. E. (1990). *Interpersonal perception.* New York: Freeman.

Jones, E. E., Farina, A., Hastorf, A. H., Markus, H., Miller, D. T., & Scott, R. A. (1984). *Social stigma: The psychology of marked relationships.* New York: Freeman.

Jones, E., Williams, K., & Brewer, N. (2008). "I had a confidence epiphany!" Obstacles to combating post-identification confidence inflation. *Law and Human Behavior, 32*, 164–176.

Jones, J. S., Wynn, B. N., Kroeze, B., Dunnuck, C., & Rossman, L. (2004). Comparison of sexual assaults by strangers versus known assailants in a community-based population. *American Journal of Emergency Medicine, 22*, 454–459.

Jose-Kampfner, C. (1990). Coming to terms with existential death: An analysis of women's adaptation to life in prison. *Social Justice, 17*, 110–125.

Judicial Council of California. (2004). *Final report: Task force on jury system improvements.* San Francisco, CA: Author.

Kadri, S. (2005). *The trial: A history, from Socrates to O. J. Simpson.* New York: Random House.

Kahan, D. (1996). What do alternative sanctions mean? *University of Chicago Law Review, 63*, 591–653.

Kairys, D. (1972). Juror selection: The law, a mathematical method of analysis, and a case study. *American Criminal Law Review, 10*, 771–806.

Kairys, D., Kadane, B., & Lehoczky, P. (1977). Jury representativeness: A mandate for multiple source lists. *California Law Review, 65*, 776–827.

Kalven, H., & Zeisel, H. (1966). *The American jury.* Boston, MA: Little, Brown.

Kamisar, Y., LaFave, W. R., & Israel, J. (1999). *Basic criminal procedure: Cases, comments and questions.* St. Paul, MN: West.

Kamradt, B. J. (2000). Wraparound Milwaukee: Aiding youth with mental health needs. *Juvenile Justice Journal, 7*, 14–23.

Kanin, E. (1957). Male aggression in dating-courtship situations. *American Journal of Sociology, 63*, 197–204.

Kanin, E. (1971). Sexually aggressive college males. *Journal of College Student Personnel, 12*(2), 107–110.

Kansas v. Crane, 534 U.S. 407 (2002).

Kansas v. Hendricks, 117 S.Ct. 2013 (1997).

Kaplan, J. (1996). *Criminal law.* Boston, MA: Little, Brown.

Kassin, S. (2005). On the psychology of confessions: Does innocence put innocents at risk? *American Psychologist, 60*, 215–228.

Kassin, S., Goldstein, C., & Savitsky, K. (2003). Behavioral confirmation in the interrogation room: On the dangers of presuming guilt. *Law and Human Behavior, 27*, 187–203.

Kassin, S., & Gudjonsson, G. (2004). The psychology of confessions: A review of the literature and issues. *Psychological Science in the Public Interest, 5*, 33–67.

Kassin, S. M., & Kiechel, K. L. (1996). The social psychology of false confessions: Compliance, internalization, and confabulation. *Psychological Science, 7*, 125–128.

Kassin, S., Leo, R., Meissner, C., Richman, K., Colwell, L., Leach, A., et al. (2007). Police interviewing and interrogation: A self-report survey of police practices and beliefs. *Law and Human Behavior, 31*, 381–400.

Kassin, S., Meissner, C., & Norwick, R. (2005). "I'd know a false confession if I saw one": A comparative study of college students and police investigators. *Law and Human Behavior, 29,* 211–227.

Kassin, S., & Neumann, K. (1997). On the power of confession evidence: An experimental test of the "fundamental difference" hypothesis. *Law and Human Behavior, 21,* 469–484.

Kassin, S., & Norwick, R. (2004). Why suspects waive their *Miranda* rights: The power of innocence. *Law and Human Behavior, 28,* 211–221.

Kassin, S. M., & Studebaker, C. A. (1998). Instructions to disregard and the jury: Curative and paradoxical effects. In J. M. Golding & C. M. MacLeod (Eds.), *Intentional forgetting: Interdisciplinary approaches* (pp. 413–434). Hillsdale, NJ: Erlbaum.

Kassin, S. M., Williams, L. N., & Saunders, C. L. (1990). Dirty tricks of cross-examination: The influence of conjectural evidence on the jury. *Law and Human Behavior, 14,* 373–384.

Kassin, S. M., & Wrightsman, L. S. (1983). The construction and validation of a juror bias scale. *Journal of Research in Personality, 17,* 423–441.

Kassin, S. M., & Wrightsman, L. S. (1985). Confession evidence. In S. M. Kassin & L. S. Wrightsman (Eds.), *The psychology of evidence and trial procedure* (pp. 67–94). Newbury Park, CA: Sage.

Katz, I., Hass, R. G., Parisi, N., Astone, J., Wackenhut, G., & Gray, L. (1987). Lay people's and health care personnel's perceptions of cancer, AIDS, cardiac and diabetic patients. *Psychological Reports, 60,* 615–629.

Katz, J. (1988). *Seductions of crime.* New York: Basic Books.

Kay, F., & Hagan, J. (2004) *Contemporary lawyers: Diversity and change in Ontario's legal profession.* Report submitted to the Law Society of Upper Canada. Toronto, Ontario: The Law Society of Upper Canada.

Kaye, J. (2001). *State of the judiciary address.* Delivered by New York Chief Judge Judith Kaye.

Kebbell, M., & Milne, R. (1998). Police officers' perception of eyewitness factors in forensic investigations. *Journal of Social Psychology, 138,* 323–330.

Kebbell, M., & Wagstaff, G. (1998). Hypnotic interviewing: The best way to interview eyewitnesses? *Behavioral Sciences & the Law, 16,* 115–129.

Keene, B. (1997). Chemical castration: An analysis of Florida's new "cutting-edge" policy towards sex criminals. *Florida Law Review, 49,* 803–820.

Keilin, W. G., & Bloom, L. J. (1986). Child custody evaluation practices: A survey of experienced

professionals. *Professional Psychology, Research and Practice, 17,* 338–346.

Kellerman, A. L., & Mercy, J. M. (1992). Men, women, and murder: Gender-specific differences in rates of fatal violence and victimization. *Journal of Trauma, 33,* 1–5.

Kellough, G., & Wortley, S. (2002). Remand for plea: Bail decisions and plea bargaining as commensurate decisions. *British Journal of Criminology, 42,* 186–210.

Kelly, J. (1996). A decade of divorce mediation research. *Family Court Review, 34,* 373–385.

Kennedy v. Louisiana, 554 U.S. _____(2008).

Kennedy, L. (1985). *The airman and the carpenter: The Lindbergh kidnapping and the framing of Richard Hauptmann.* New York: Viking Press.

Kerr, N., Kramer, G. P., Carroll, J. S., & Alfini, J. J. (1991). On the effectiveness of voir dire in criminal cases with prejudicial pretrial publicity: An empirical study. *American Law Review, 40,* 665–701.

Kessler, R. C., Davis, C. G., & Kendler, K. S. (1997). Childhood adversity and adult psychiatric disorder in the U.S. National Comorbidity Survey. *Psychological Medicine, 27,* 1101–1119.

Kiesler, C. A. (1982). Public and professional myths about mental hospitalization: An empirical reassessment of policy-related beliefs. *American Psychologist, 37,* 1323–1339.

Kilpatrick, D. G., Resick, P., & Veronen, L. (1981). Effects of a rape experience: A longitudinal study. *Journal of Social Issues, 37,* 105–112.

Kimonis, E., Frick, P., & Barry, C. (2004). Callous-unemotional traits and delinquent peer affiliation. *Journal of Consulting and Clinical Psychology, 72,* 956–966.

King, M. (1992). Male rape in institutional settings. In G. Mezey & M. King (Eds.), *Male victims of sexual assault.* Oxford: Oxford University Press.

King, N., & Noble, R. (2005). Jury sentencing in non-capital cases: Comparing severity and variance with judicial sentences in two states. *Journal of Empirical Legal Studies, 2,* 331–367.

King, N., Soule, D., Steen, S., & Weidner, R. (2005). When process affects punishment: Differences in sentences after guilty plea, bench trial, and jury trial in five guidelines states. *Columbia Law Review, 105,* 959–1009.

King, R., & Mauer, M. (2001). *Aging behind bars: "Three strikes" seven years later.* Retrieved June 16,

2006, from http://www.sentencingproject.org/pdfs/9087.pdf

Klein, C. (1996, May 6). Women's progress slows at top firms. *National Law Journal*, p. 1.

Kleinberg, H. (1989, January 29). It's tough to have sympathy for Bundy. *Lawrence Journal-World*, p. 5A.

Kleiner, M. (2002). *Handbook of polygraph testing.* New York: Academic Press.

Kleinmuntz, B., & Szucko, J. J. (1984). Lie detection in ancient and modern times: A call for contemporary scientific study. *American Psychologist, 39,* 766–776.

Klockars, C. (1985). *The idea of police.* Thousand Oaks, CA: Sage.

Knight, R. A., Warren, J. I., Reboussin, R., & Soley, B. J. (1998). Predicting rapist type from crime-scene variables. *Criminal Justice and Behavior, 25,* 30–45.

Koch, K. (2000). Zero tolerance. *CQ Researcher, 10,* 185.

Kohnken, G., Milne, R., Memon, A., & Bull, R. (1999). A meta-analysis on the effects of the cognitive interview. *Psychology, Crime and Law, 5,* 3–27.

Kolebuck, M. D. (1998). *Kansas v. Henricks*: Is it time to lock the door and throw away the key for sexual predators? *Journal of Contemporary Health and Law Policy, 14,* 537–561.

Kopelman, S., Rosette A. S., & Thompson, L. (2006). The three faces of Eve: An examination of the strategic display of positive, negative, and neutral emotions in negotiations. *Organizational Behavior and Human Decision Processes, 99,* 81–101.

Korobkin, R., & Doherty, J. (2009). Who wins in settlement negotiations? *American Law and Economics Review, 11,* 162–209.

Koss, M. P. (1992). The underdetection of rape: Methodological choices influence incidence estimates. *Journal of Social Issues, 48,* 61–75.

Kovera, M. (2002). The effects of general pretrial publicity on juror decisions: An examination of moderators and mediating mechanisms. *Law and Human Behavior, 26,* 43–72.

Kovera, M., Dickinson, J., & Cutler, B. (2002). Voir dire and jury selection. In A. Goldstein (Ed.), *Comprehensive handbook of psychology: Forensic psychology* (Vol. 11, pp. 161–175). New York: Wiley.

Kovera, M., Gresham, A., Borgida, E., Gray, E., & Regan, P. (1997). Does expert testimony inform or influence decision-making? A social cognitive analysis. *Journal of Applied Psychology, 82,* 178–191.

Kovera, M., & McAuliff, B. (2000). The effects of peer review and evidence quality on judge evaluations of psychological science: Are judges effective gatekeepers? *Journal of Applied Psychology, 85,* 574–586.

Kovera, M., Russano, M., & McAuliff, B. (2002). Assessment of the commonsense psychology underlying *Daubert*: Legal decision makers' abilities to evaluate expert evidence in hostile work environment cases. *Psychology, Public Policy, and Law, 8,* 180–200.

Kraemer, G. W., Lord, W. D., & Heilbrun, K. (2004). Comparing single and serial homicide offenses. *Behavioral Sciences & the Law, 22,* 325–343.

Kramer, G. P., Kerr, N. L., & Carroll, J. S. (1990). Pretrial publicity, judicial remedies, and jury bias. *Law and Human Behavior, 14,* 409–438.

Kramer, G., Wolbransky, M., & Heilbrun, K. (2007). Plea bargaining recommendations by criminal defense attorneys: Evidence strength, potential sentence, and defendant preference. *Behavioral Sciences & the Law, 25,* 573–585.

Krauss, D., & Goldstein, A. (2007). The role of forensic mental health experts in federal sentencing proceedings. In A. Goldstein (Ed.), *Forensic psychology: Emerging topics and expanding roles* (pp. 359–384). Hoboken, NJ: John Wiley & Sons.

Kravitz, H. M., & Kelly, J. (1999). An outpatient psychiatry program for offenders with mental disorders found Not Guilty by Reason of Insanity. *Psychiatric Services, 50,* 1597–1605.

Kressel, N., & Kressel, D. (2002). *Stack and sway: The new science of jury consulting.* Boulder, CO: Westview Press.

Krieger, L. H. (2004). The intuitive psychologist behind the bench: Models of gender bias in social psychology and employment discrimination law. *Journal of Social Issues, 60,* 835–848.

Kulik, C., Perry, E., & Pepper, M. (2003). Here comes the judge: The influence of judge personal characteristics on federal sexual harassment case outcomes. *Law and Human Behavior, 27,* 69–86.

Kumho Tire Co. v. Carmichael, 526 U.S. 137 (1999).

Kunen, J. (1983). *"How can you defend those people?" The making of a criminal lawyer.* New York: Random House.

Kurtz, H. (2004, October 29). Bill O'Reilly, producer settle harassment suit: Fox host agrees to drop extortion claim. *The Washington Post.* Retrieved September 1, 2005, from http://www.washingtonpost.com/wp-dyn/articles/A7578–2004Oct28.html

Kushner, M., Riggs, D., Foa, E., & Miller, S. (1992). Perceived controllability and the development of posttraumatic stress disorder (PTSD) in crime victims. *Behavior Research & Therapy, 31,* 105–110.

Kutchinski, B. (1988, June). *Pornography and sexual violence: The criminological evidence from aggregated data in several countries.* Paper presented at the Fourteenth International Congress on Law and Mental Health, Montreal.

Laboratory of Community Psychiatry. (1974). *Competency to stand trial & mental illness.* New York: Jason Aronson.

LaFave, W. (1965). *Arrest: The decision to take a suspect into custody.* Boston, MA: Little, Brown.

La Fon, D. (2008). *Psychological autopsies: Science and practice.* Boca Raton, FL: CRC Press.

Lafortune, K. A., & Carpenter, B. N. (1998). Custody evaluations: A survey of mental health professionals. *Behavioral Sciences & the Law, 16,* 207–224.

Lake, D. A. (2002, Spring). Rational extremism: Understanding terrorism in the twenty-first century. *Dialog-IQ, 15–29.* Retrieved June 23, 2005, from http://journals.cambridge.org/bin/bladerunner?30REQEVENT=&REQAUTH=0&500001REQSUB=&REQSTR1=S777777770200002X

Lamar, J. V. (1989, February 6). "I deserve punishment." *Time,* p. 34.

Lamb, H. R., Weinberger, L. E., & DeCuir, W. J. (2002). The police and mental health. *Psychiatric Services, 53,* 1266–1271.

Lamb, M., Sternberg, K., Orbach, Y., Esplin, P., Stewart, H., & Mitchell, S. (2003). Age differences in children's responses to open-ended invitations in the course of forensic interviews. *Journal of Consulting and Clinical Psychology, 71,* 926–934.

Lamb, S. (2003). The psychology of condemnation: Underlying emotions and their symbolic expression in condemning and shaming. *Brooklyn Law Review, 68,* 929–958.

Lambros, T. (1993). The summary jury trial: An effective aid to settlement. *Judicature, 77,* 6–8.

Lampinen, J., Judges, D., Odegard, T., & Hamilton, S. (2005). The reactions of mock jurors to the department of justice guidelines for the collection and preservation of eyewitness evidence. *Basic and Applied Social Psychology, 27,* 155–162.

Lander, T., & Heilbrun, K. (2009). The content and quality of forensic mental health assessment: Validation of a principles-based approach. *International Journal of Forensic Mental Health, 8,* 115–121.

Lane, S. (2006). Dividing attention during a witnessed event increases eyewitness suggestibility. *Applied Cognitive Psychology, 20,* 199–212.

Lange, J. (1929). *Verbrechen als Schiskal.* Leipzig: Georg Thieme.

Langevin, R., Curnoe, S., Federoff, P., Bennett, R., Langevin, M., Peever, C., et al. (2004). Lifetime sex offender recidivism: A 25-year-follow-up study. *Canadian Journal of Criminology and Criminal Justice, 46,* 531–552.

Langleben, D., Schroeder, L., Maldjian, J., Gur, R., McDonald, S., Ragland, J., et al. (2002). Brain activity during simulated deception: An event-related functional magnetic resonance study. *Neuroimage, 15,* 727–732.

Langton, L., & Cohen, T. (2008). *Civil bench and jury trials in state courts, 2005.* Washington, DC: U.S. Department of Justice. (Bureau of Justice Statistics Special Report No. NCJ 223851)

Largen, M. A. (1988). Rape-law reform: An analysis. In A. W. Burgess (Ed.), *Rape and sexual assault* (Vol. 2, pp. 271–292). New York: Garland.

Larsen, K. S., Reed, M., & Hoffman, S. (1980). Attitudes of heterosexuals toward homosexuality: A Likert-type scale and construct validity. *Journal of Sex Research, 16,* 245–257.

Larson, J. (2004, April 10). Behind the death of Timothy Thomas: Shooting of 19-year-old brings to light pattern of ticketing that raises questions of racial profiling. *Dateline NBC.* Retrieved September 24, 2005, from http://www.msnbc.msn.com/id/4703574/

Larson, J. A. (1932). *Lying and its detection.* Chicago: University of Chicago Press.

Lassiter, D., Diamond, S., Schmidt, H., & Elek, J. (2007). Evaluating videotaped confessions: Expertise provides no defense against the camera-perspective effect. *Psychological Science, 18,* 224–226.

Lassiter, G. D., & Geers, A. (2004). Bias and accuracy in the evaluation of confession evidence. In G. D. Lassiter (Ed.), *Interrogations, confessions, and entrapment* (pp. 197–214). New York: Kluwer/Plenum.

Lee, F. (1985, May 16). Women are put "on trial" in rape cases. *USA Today*, p. 1A.

Lees-Haley, P. (1991). A fake bad scale on the MMPI-2 for personal injury claimants. *Psychological Reports, 68*, 203–210.

Lees-Haley, P. (1992). Efficacy of MMPI-2 validity scales and MCMI-2 modifier scales for detecting spurious PTSD claims: F, F-K, Fake Bad Scale, Ego Strength, Subtle-Obvious subscales, DIS, and DEB. *Journal of Clinical Psychology, 48*, 681–689.

Lefkowitz, J. (1975). Psychological attributes of police-men: A review of research and opinion. *Journal of Social Issues, 31*, 3–26.

Leigey, M., & Bachman, R. (2007). The influence of crack cocaine on the likelihood of incarceration for a violent offense: An examination of a prison sample. *Criminal Justice Policy Review, 18*, 335–352.

Leipold, A., & Abbasi, H. (2006). The impact of joinder and severance on federal criminal cases: An empirical study. *Vanderbilt Law Review, 59*, 347–404.

Leippe, M. R., Eisenstadt, D., Rauch, S. M., & Stambush, M. A. (2006). Effects of social-comparative memory feedback on eyewitnesses' identification confidence, suggestibility, and retrospective memory reports. *Basic and Applied Social Psychology, 28*, 201–220.

Leistico, A., Salekin, R., DeCoster, J., & Rogers, R. (2008). A large-scale meta-analysis relating the Hare measures of psychopathy to antisocial conduct. *Law and Human Behavior, 32*, 28–45.

Lemert, E. M. (1951). *Social pathology*. New York: McGraw-Hill.

Lemert, E. M. (1972). *Human deviance, social problems, and social control* (2nd ed.). Englewood Cliffs, NJ: Prentice Hall.

Lempert, R. (1993). Civil juries and complex cases: Taking stock after twelve years. In R. E. Litan (Ed.), *Verdict: Assessing the civil jury system* (pp. 181–247). Washington, DC: The Brookings Institution.

Lentz, B., & Laband, D. (1995). *Sex discrimination in the legal profession*. Westport, CT: Quorum Books.

Leo, R. (1996). *Miranda's* revenge: Police interrogation as a confidence game. *Law and Society Review, 30*, 259–288.

Leo, R. (2007). The problem of false confession in America. *The Champion, 31*. Retrieved July 22, 2008, from http://www.nacdl.org/public.nsf/01c1e7698280d20385256d0b00789923/4a6e9aa597092057052573ed0056ffa3?OpenDocument

Leo, R. (2008). *Police interrogation and American justice.* Cambridge, MA: Harvard University Press.

Leo, R., & Ofshe, R. (1998). The consequences of false confessions: Deprivations of liberty and miscarriages of justice in the age of psychological interrogation. *Journal of Criminal Law and Criminology, 88*, 429–496.

Leo, R., & White, W. (1999). Adapting to *Miranda:* Modern interrogators' strategies for dealing with the obstacles posed by Miranda. *Minnesota Law Review, 84*, 397–472.

Leonard, K. E., Quigley, B. M., & Collins, R. L. (2002). Physical aggression in the lives of young adults. *Journal of Interpersonal Violence, 17*, 533–550.

Lerner, M. J. (1970). The desire for justice and reactions to victims. In J. Macaulay & L. Berkowitz (Eds.), *Altruism and helping behavior* (pp. 205–229). Orlando, FL: Academic Press.

Lerner, M. J. (1980). *The belief in a just world*. New York: Plenum.

Levenson, J. (2004). Reliability of sexually violent predator civil commitment criteria in Florida. *Law and Human Behavior, 28*, 357–368.

Levenson, J., & D'Amora, D. (2007). Social policies designed to prevent sexual violence: The emperor's new clothes? *Criminal Justice Policy Review, 18*, 168–199.

Levett, L., & Kovera, M. (2008). The effectiveness of opposing expert witnesses for educating jurors about unreliable expert evidence. *Law and Human Behavior, 32*, 363–374.

Levin, J., & Fox, J. A. (1985). *Mass murder*. New York: Plenum.

Levine, S. (2003, September 26). Death-row inmate hears hoped-for-words: We found killer. *The Washington Post*, p. A01.

Lewin, T. (1994, October 21). Outrage over 18 months for a killing. *The New York Times*, p. A18.

Lewis, A. (1964). *Gideon's trumpet*. New York: Knopf.

Lewis, A. (2005, June 21). Guantanamo's long shadow. *The New York Times*, p. A23.

Lieberman, J., & Arndt, J. (2000). Understanding the limits of limiting instructions: Social psychological explanations for the failures of instructions to disregard pretrial publicity and other inadmissible evidence. *Psychology, Public Policy, and Law, 6,* 677–711.

Lieberman, J., & Sales, B. (1997). What social sciences teaches us about the jury instruction process. *Psychology, Public Policy, and Law, 3,* 589–644.

Lieberman, J., & Sales, B. (2000). Jury instructions: Past, present, and future. *Psychology, Public Policy, and Law, 6,* 587–590.

Liebman, J. S. (2000). *A broken system: Error rates in capital cases, 1973–1995.* Retrieved October 1, 2005, from http://ccjr.policy.net/cjedfund/jpreport/

Lilly, J. R., Cullen, F. T., & Ball, R. A. (1989). *Criminological theory: Context and consequences.* Newbury Park, CA: Sage.

Lind, E. A. (1975). The exercise of information influence in legal advocacy. *Journal of Applied Social Psychology, 5,* 127–143.

Lind, E. A. (1982). The psychology of courtroom procedure. In N. L. Kerr & R. M. Bray (Eds.), *Psychology in the courtroom* (pp. 13–37). Orlando, FL: Academic Press.

Lind, E. A., Erickson, B. E., Friedland, N., & Dickenberger, M. (1978). Reactions to procedural models for adjudicative conflict resolution. *Journal of Conflict Resolution, 22,* 318–341.

Lind, E. A., Thibaut, J., & Walker, L. (1973). Discovery and presentation of evidence in adversary and non-adversary proceedings. *Michigan Law Review, 71,* 1129–1144.

Lind, E. A., & Tyler, T. R. (1988). *The social psychology of procedural justice.* New York: Plenum.

Lindsay, D., Hagen, L., Read, J., Wade, K., & Garry, M. (2004). True photographs and false memories. *Psychological Science, 15,* 149–154.

Lindsay, D. S., & Read, J. D. (1995). "Memory work" and recovered memories of childhood sexual abuse: Scientific evidence and public, professional, and personal issues. *Psychology, Public Policy, and Law, 1,* 846–908.

Lindsay, J. (2004, May 20). Man convicted in 1974 murder is released from prison. *The Associated Press State & Local Wire.* Retrieved July 18, 2005, from http://archive.southcoasttoday.com/daily/05-04/05-21-04/a16sr302.htm

Lindsay, R. C., Pozzulo, J. D., Craig, W., Lee, K., & Corber, S. (1997). Simultaneous lineups, sequential lineups, and showups: Eyewitness identification decisions of adults and children. *Law and Human Behavior, 21,* 391–404.

Lindsay, R., & Wells, G. (1985). Improving eyewitness identification from lineups: Simultaneous versus sequential lineup presentations. *Journal of Applied Psychology, 70,* 556–564.

Lipsey, M. (1992). Juvenile delinquency treatment: A meta-analytic inquiry into the variability of effects. In T. Cook, H. Cooper, S. Cordray, H. Hartmann, L. Hedges, R. Light, et al. (Eds.), *Meta-analysis for explanation: A casebook* (pp. 83–128). New York: Russell Sage Foundation.

Lipsey, M., & Wilson, D. (1998). Effective intervention for serious juvenile offenders: A synthesis of research. In R. Loeber & D. Farrington (Eds.), *Serious and violent juvenile offenders: Risk factors and successful interventions* (pp. 313–345). Thousand Oaks, CA: Sage.

Lipsitt, P. D., Lelos, D., & McGarry, A. L. (1971). Competency for trial: A screening instrument. *American Journal of Psychiatry, 128,* 105–109.

Liptak, A. (2005a). *Inmate's rising I.Q. score could mean his death.* Retrieved February 8, 2005, from http://www.nytimes.com/2005/02/06/national/06atkins.html/

Liptak, A. (2005b). *To more inmates, life term means dying behind bars.* Retrieved October 2, 2005, from www.nytimes/come/2005/10/12/national

Liptak, A. (2007, October 17). Lifers as teenagers, now seeking second chance. *The New York Times,* pp. A1, A24.

Liptak, A. (2008, May 25). *Rendering justice, with one eye on re-election.* Retrieved December 8, 2008, from www.nytimes.com/2008/05/25/us/25exception

Lisnek, P. (2003). *The hidden jury: And other secret tactics lawyers use to win.* Naperville, IL: Source Books.

Liss, M. B., & McKinley-Pace, M. J. (1999). Best interests of the child: New twists on an old theme. In R. Roesch, S. D. Hart, & J. R. P. Ogloff (Eds.), *Psychology and law: The state of the discipline* (pp. 341–372). New York: Kluwer Academic/Plenum.

Lockett v. Ohio, 438 U.S. 604 (1978).

Lockhart v. McCree, 106 S.Ct. 1758 (1986).

Loeber, R., & Stouthamer-Loeber, M. (1986). Family factors as correlates and predictors of juvenile conduct problems and delinquency. In M. Tonry & N. Morris (Eds.), *Crime and justice: An annual review of research* (Vol. 7, pp. 29–149). Chicago: University of Chicago Press.

Loewenstein, G., Issacharoff, S., Camerer, C., & Babcock, L. (1993). Self-serving assessments of fairness and pretrial bargaining. *Journal of Legal Studies, 22*, 135–159.

Loftus, E. F. (1974). Reconstructing memory: The incredible witness. *Psychology Today, 8*, 116–119.

Loftus, E. F. (1975). Leading questions and the eyewitness report. *Cognitive Psychology, 7*, 560–572.

Loftus, E. F. (1979). *Eyewitness testimony.* Cambridge, MA: Harvard University Press.

Loftus, E. F. (1984). Expert testimony on the eyewitness. In G. L. Wells & E. F. Loftus (Eds.), *Eyewitness testimony: Psychological perspectives* (pp. 273–282). New York: Cambridge University Press.

Loftus, E. F., & Greene, E. (1980). Warning: Even memory for faces may be contagious. *Law and Human Behavior, 4*, 323–334.

Loftus, E. F., & Pickrell, J. E. (1995). The formation of false memories. *Psychiatric Annals, 25*, 720–725.

Lombroso, C. (1876). *L' Uomo delinquente.* Milan: Hoepli.

London, K., Bruck, M., Ceci, S., & Shuman, D. (2005). Disclosure of child sexual abuse: What does the research tell us about the ways that children tell? *Psychology, Public Policy, and Law, 11*, 194–226.

London, K., & Nunez, N. (2000). The effect of jury deliberations on jurors' propensity to disregard inadmissible evidence. *Journal of Applied Psychology, 85*, 932–939.

Lott, B., Reilly, M. E., & Howard, D. R. (1982). Sexual assault and harassment: A campus community case study. *Signs: Journal of Women in Culture and Society, 8*, 296–319.

Loucks, A., & Zamble, E. (1994). Some comparisons of female and male serious offenders. *Forum on Corrections Research, 6*(1), 22–25.

Lowenkamp, C., & Latessa, E. (2005, April). Developing successful reentry programs: Lessons learned from the "what works" research. *Corrections Today, 67*, 72–77.

Ludwig, E. (2002). The changing role of the trial judge. *Judicature, 85*, 216–217.

Lurigio, A. J., & Skogan, W. G. (1994). Winning the hearts and minds of police officers: An assessment of staff perceptions of community policing in Chicago. *Crime and Delinquency, 40*, 315–330.

Lurigio, A., Watson, A., Luchins, D., & Hanrahan, P. (2001). Therapeutic jurisprudence in action. *Judicature, 84*, 184–189.

Luus, C. A. E., & Wells, G. L. (1994). The malleability of eyewitness confidence: Co-witness and perseverance effects. *Journal of Applied Psychology, 79*, 714–724.

Lykken, D. T. (1985). The probity of the polygraph. In S. M. Kassin & L. S. Wrightsman (Eds.), *The psychology of evidence and trial procedure* (pp. 95–123). Newbury Park, CA: Sage.

Lynam, D. (1996). Early identification of chronic offenders: Who is the fledgling psychopath? *Psychological Bulletin, 120*, 209–234.

Lynam, D. R. (1998). Early identification of the fledgling psychopath: Locating the psychopathic child in the current nomenclature. *Journal of Abnormal Psychology, 107*, 566–575.

Lynam, D., Moffitt, T., & Stouthamer-Loeber, M. (1993). Explaining the relation between IQ and delinquency: Class, race, test motivation, school failure, and self-control. *Journal of Abnormal Psychology, 102*, 187–196.

Lynch, M., & Haney, C. (2000). Discrimination and instructional comprehension: Guided discretion, racial bias, and the death penalty. *Law and Human Behavior, 24*, 337–358.

Lynch, T. (2003, Fall). The case against plea bargaining. *Regulation, 26*, 24–27.

MacCoun, R. J. (1996). Differential treatment of corporate defendants by juries: An examination of the "deep pockets" hypothesis. *Law and Society Review, 30*, 121–161.

MacCoun, R. J. (1999). Epistemological dilemmas in the assessment of legal decision making. *Law and Human Behavior, 23*, 723–730.

MacCoun, R. J., & Tyler, T. R. (1988). The basis of citizens' perceptions of the criminal jury: Procedural fairness, accuracy, and efficiency. *Law and Human Behavior, 12*, 333–352.

Madden-Derdich, D. A., Leonard, S. A., & Gunnell, G. A. (2002). Parents' and children's perceptions of family processes in inner-city families with delinquent youths: A qualitative investigation. *Journal of Marital and Family Therapy, 28*, 355–370.

Maddox, K., & Gray, S. (2002). Cognitive representations of Black Americans: Re-exploring the role of skin tone. *Personality and Social Psychology Bulletin, 28*, 250–259.

Magdol, L., Moffitt, T. E., Caspi, A., Newman, D. L., Fagan, J., & Silva, P. A. (1997). Gender differences in rates of partner violence in a birth cohort of 21-year-olds: Bridging the gap between clinical and epidemiological approaches. *Journal of Consulting and Clinical Psychology, 65*, 68–78.

Magdol, L., Moffitt, T. E., Caspi, A., & Silva, P. A. (1998). Developmental antecedents of partner abuse: A prospective-longitudinal study. *Journal of Abnormal Psychology, 107*, 373–389.

Mailer, N. (1979). *The executioner's song*. Boston, MA: Little, Brown.

Malpass, R. S., & Devine, P. G. (1981). Eyewitness identification: Lineup instructions and the absence of the offender. *Journal of Applied Psychology, 66*, 482–489.

Mankoff, M. (1971). Societal reaction and career deviance: A critical analysis. *Sociological Quarterly, 12*, 204–218.

Marcus, D. R., Lyons, P. M., & Guyton, M. R. (2000). Studying perceptions of juror influence *in vivo*: A social relations analysis. *Law and Human Behavior, 24*, 173–186.

Marder, N. S. (1999). The interplay of race and false claims of jury nullification. *University of Michigan Journal of Law Reform, 32*, 285–321.

Maricopa County Sheriff's Office. (2005). *Sheriff Joe Arpaio*. Retrieved October 5, 2009, from http://www.mcso.org/index.php?a=GetModule&mn=sheriff_bio

Mark, V. H., & Ervin, F. R. (1970). *Violence and the brain*. New York: Harper and Row.

Marlowe, D. B. (2002). Effective strategies for intervening with drug abusing offenders. *Villanova Law Review, 47*, 989–1026.

Marlowe, D., DeMatteo, D., & Festinger, D. (2003). A sober assessment of drug courts. *Federal Sentencing Reporter, 16*, 113–128.

Marshall, L. (2002). Do exonerations prove that the system works? *Judicature, 86*, 83–89.

Marshall, W. L., Fernandez, Y. M., & Cortoni, F. (1999). Rape. In V. Van Hasselt & M. Hersen (Eds.), *Handbook of psychological approaches with violent offenders* (pp. 245–266). New York: Kluwer/Plenum.

Marshall, W., Fernandez, Y., Marshall, L., & Serran, G. (2006). *Sexual offender treatment: Controversial issues*. West Sussex, UK: Wiley.

Marshall, W. L., Jones, R., Ward, T., Johnston, P., & Barbaree, H. E. (1991). Treatment outcome with sex offenders. *Clinical Psychology Review, 11*, 465–485.

Martin, C., Lurigio, A., & Olson, D. (2003). An examination of rearrests and reincarcerations among discharged day reporting center clients. *Federal Probation, 67*, 24–30.

Martin, S. S., Butzin, C. A., Saum, C. A., & Inciardi, J. A. (1999). Three-year outcomes of therapeutic community treatment for offenders in Delaware. *The Prison Journal, 79*, 294–320.

Martinson, R. (1974). What works? Questions and answers about prison reform. *Public Interest, 35*, 22.

Martinson, R. (1979). New findings, new views: A note of caution regarding sentencing reform. *Hofstra Law Review, 7*, 243.

Maryland v. Craig, 110 S.Ct. 3157 (1990).

Maslach, C., & Jackson, S. E. (1984). Burnout in organizational settings. In S. Oskamp (Ed.), *Applied social psychology annual* (pp. 133–154). Newbury Park, CA: Sage.

Mason, C., & Cheng, S. (2001). *Re-arrest rates among youth sentenced in adult court*. Miami, FL: Miami-Dade County Public Defender's Office.

Mauer, M., & King, R. S. (2007, July). *Uneven justice: State rates of incarceration by race and ethnicity*. Retrieved October 25, 2008, from http://www.sentencingproject.org

Maxfield, M. G., & Widom, C. S. (1996). The cycle of violence: Revisited 6 years later. *Archives of Pediatrics & Adolescent Medicine, 150*, 390–395.

Maxwell, C. D., Garner, J. H., & Fagan, J. A. (2002). The preventive effects of arrest on intimate partner violence: Research, policy and theory. *Criminology and Public Policy*. Retrieved June 23, 2005, from http://www.jcjs.org/Products/Domestic%20Violence/SARP/CCP.SARP%20article.pdf

Mazzoni, G. A., Loftus, E. F., Seitz, A., & Lynn, S. J. (1999). Changing beliefs and memories through dream interpretation. *Applied Cognitive Psychology, 13*, 125–144.

McAllister, H. (2008). Plea bargaining. In B. Cutler (Ed.), *Encyclopedia of psychology and law* (pp. 559–561). Thousand Oaks, CA: Sage Publications.

McAllister, H. A., & Bregman, N. J. (1986). Juror underutilization of eyewitness nonidentifications: Theoretical and practical implications. *Journal of Applied Psychology, 71,* 168–170.

McAree, D. (2004, May 31). Deadbeat dads face ban on procreation. *National Law Journal,* p. 4.

McCandless, S. R., & Sullivan, L. P. (1991, May 6). Two courts adopt new standard to determine sexual harassment. *National Law Journal,* pp. 18–20.

McCann, J. (1998). A conceptual framework for identifying various types of confessions. *Behavioral Sciences & the Law, 16,* 441–453.

McCann, T. (2004, August 21). *Jury consultants try to turn voir dire into a science.* Retrieved October 1, 2005, from http://www.zmf.com

McCleskey v. Kemp, 107 S. Ct. 1756 (1987).

McConahay, J. B., Mullin, C., & Frederick, J. (1977). The uses of social science in trials with political and racial overtones: The trial of Joan Little. *Law and Contemporary Problems, 41,* 205–229.

McCorkle, R. (1992). Personal precautions to violence in prison. *Criminal Justice and Behavior, 19,* 160–173.

McCoy, A. (2006). *A question of torture: CIA interrogation, from the cold war to the war on terror.* New York: Metropolitan Books/Henry Holt.

McDonough, M. (2004, October). Summary time blues. *American Bar Association Journal, 90,* 18.

McDonough, M. (2005, March). Demanding diversity. *American Bar Association Journal, 91,* 52.

McGee, H. (1971). Black lawyers and the struggle for racial justice in the American social order. *Buffalo Law Review, 20,* 423–433.

McGee, R., Feehan, M., Williams, S., & Anderson, J. (1992). DSM III disorders from age 11 to age 15 years. *Journal of the American Academy of Child and Adolescent Psychiatry, 31,* 50–59.

McGuire, J., Bilby, C., Hatcher, R., Hollin, C., Hounsome, J., & Palmer, E. (2008). Evaluation of structured cognitive-behavioural treatment programmes in reducing criminal recidivism. *Journal of Experimental Criminology, 4,* 21–40.

McKay v. Ashland Oil Inc., 120 F.R.D. 43, 49 (E.D.Ky. 1988).

McKinley, J. (2009). *Smoking ban hits home. Truly.* Retrieved April 22, 2009, from http://www.nytimes.com/2009/01/27/us/27belmont.html

McLaurin v. Oklahoma State Regents for Higher Education, 339 U.S. 637 (1950).

McNatt, D. (2000). Ancient Pygmalion joins contemporary management: A meta-analysis of the result. *Journal of Applied Psychology, 85,* 314–322.

McNiel, D., & Binder, R. (2007). Effectiveness of a mental health court in reducing criminal recidivism and violence. *American Journal of Psychiatry, 164,* 1395–1403.

McNiel, D. E., & Binder, R. L. (2005). Psychiatric emergency service use and homelessness, mental disorder, and violence. *Psychiatric Services, 56,* 699–704.

McQuiston-Surrett, D., Malpass, R., & Tredoux, C. (2006). Sequential vs. simultaneous lineups: A review of the methods, data, and theory. *Psychology, Public Policy, and Law, 12,* 137–169.

Meddis, S. S., & Kelley, J. (1985, April 8). Crime drops but fear on rise. *USA Today,* p. A1.

Medical News Today. (2007). *What level of mental illness should preclude execution and how to determine it?* Retrieved April 1, 2009, from www.medicalnewstoday.com

Medina v. California, 112 S.Ct. 2572 (1992).

Mednick, S. A., & Christiansen, K. O. (Eds.). (1977). *Biosocial bases of criminal behavior.* New York: Gardner Press.

Mednick, S. A., Gabrielli, W. F., Jr., & Hutchings, B. (1984). Genetic factors in the etiology of criminal behavior. In S. A. Mednick, T. E. Moffitt, & S. A. Stack (Eds.), *The causes of crime: New biological approaches* (pp. 74–91). Cambridge: Cambridge University Press.

Meissner, C., & Brigham, J. (2001). Thirty years of investigating the own-race bias in memory for faces: A meta-analytic review. *Psychology, Public Policy, and Law, 7,* 3–35.

Meissner, C., Brigham, J., & Pfeifer, J. (2003). Jury nullification: The influence of judicial instruction on the relationship between attitudes and juridic decision-making. *Basic and Applied Social Psychology, 25,* 243–254.

Meissner, C., & Kassin, S. (2002). He's guilty! Investigator bias in judgments of truth and deception. *Law and Human Behavior, 26*, 469–480.

Meissner, C., & Kassin, S. (2004). "You're guilty, so just confess!" Cognitive and behavioral confirmation biases in the interrogation room. In G. D. Lassiter (Ed.), *Interrogations, confessions, and entrapment* (pp. 85–106). New York: Kluwer Academic/Plenum.

Meissner, C., Tredoux, C., Parker, J., & MacLin, O. (2005). Eyewitness decisions in simultaneous and sequential lineups. *Memory and Cognition, 33*, 783–792.

Melilli, K. (1996). *Batson* in practice: What we have learned about *Batson* and peremptory challenges. *Notre Dame Law Review, 71*, 447–503.

Mellow, J., Mukamal, D. A., LoBuglio, S. F., Solomon, A. L., & Osborne, J. W. L. (2008, May). *The jail administrator's toolkit for reentry.* Washington, DC: Urban Institute.

Meloy, J. R., & Felthous, A. R. (2004). Introduction to this issue: Serial and mass homicide. *Behavioral Sciences & the Law, 22*(3), 289–290.

Meloy, J. R., Hempel, A. G., Gray, B. T., Mohandie, K., Shiva, A., & Richards, T. C. (2004). A comparative analysis of North American adolescent and adult mass murderers. *Behavioral Sciences & the Law, 22*(3), 291–309.

Melton, G., Petrila, J., Poythress, N., & Slobogin, C. (2007). *Psychological evaluations for the courts: A handbook for mental health professionals and lawyers* (3rd ed.). New York: Guilford.

Memon, A., Bartlett, J., Rose, R., & Gray, C. (2003). The aging eyewitness: Effects of age on face, delay, and source-memory ability. *The Journals of Gerontology Series B: Psychological Sciences and Social Sciences, 58B*, P338–P345.

Meritor Savings Bank v. Vinson, 106 S.Ct. 2399 (1986).

Merrick, R. A. (1985). The tort of outrage: Recovery for the intentional infliction of mental distress. *Behavioral Sciences & the Law, 3*, 165–175.

Mertens, R., & Allen, J. J. B. (2008). The role of psychophysiology in forensic assessments: Deception detection, ERPs, and virtual reality mock crime scenarios. *Psychophysiology, 45*, 286–298.

Merton, R. K. (1968). *Social theory and social structure.* New York: Free Press.

Meyer, P. (1982). *The Yale murder.* New York: Empire Books.

Mihalic, S., Irwin, K., Elliott, D., Fagan, A., & Hansen, D. (2001). *Blueprints for violence prevention.* Boulder, CO: Center for the Study and Prevention of Violence.

Milgram, S. (1963). Behavioral study of obedience. *Journal of Abnormal and Social Psychology, 67*, 371–378.

Miller, A. (1988, April 25). Stress on the job. *Newsweek*, pp. 40–45.

Miller, G. R., & Boster, F. J. (1977). Three images of a trial: Their implications for psychological research. In B. D. Sales (Ed.), *Psychology in the legal process* (pp. 19–38). New York: Spectrum.

Miller, H. A. (2001). *M-FAST: Miller Forensic Assessment of Symptoms Test professional manual.* Odessa, FL: Psychological Assessment Resources, Inc.

Miller, H. A. (2004). Examining the use of the M-FAST with criminal defendants incompetent to stand trial. *International Journal of Offender Therapy and Comparative Criminology, 48*(3), 268–280.

Miller, W. B. (1958). Lower-class culture as a generating milieu of gang delinquency. *Journal of Social Issues, 14*, 5–19.

Miller-El v. Cockrell, 537 U.S. 322 (2003).

Miller-El v. Dretke, 361 F.3d 849 (5th Cir. 2004); 545 U.S. 231 (2005).

Mills, L. G. (1998). Mandatory arrest and prosecution policies for domestic violence: A critical literature review and the case for more research to test victim empowerment approaches. *Criminal Justice and Behavior, 25*, 306–318.

Mills, R. B., McDevitt, R. J., & Tonkin, S. (1966). Situational tests in metropolitan police recruit selection. *Journal of Criminal Law, Criminology, and Police Science, 57*, 99–104.

Mills, S. (1998, April 29). "Killer" in jail when crime committed: Teen accuses cops of coercing him into admitting guilt. *Chicago Tribune*, p. 1.

Milne, R., & Bull, R. (2006). Interviewing victims of crime, including children and people with intellectual difficulties. In M. R. Kebbell & G. M. Davies (Eds.), *Practical psychology for forensic investigations* (pp. 7–24). Chichester, England: Wiley.

Milstein, V. (1988). EEG topography in patients with aggressive violent behavior. In T. E. Moffitt & S. A. Mednick (Eds.), *Biological contributions to crime causation.* Dordrecht, MA: Martinus Nihjoff.

Miranda v. Arizona, 384 U.S. 486 (1966).

Mitchell, P. (1976). *Act of love: The killing of George Zygmanik*. New York: Knopf.

Mitchell, T., Haw, R., Pfeifer, J., & Meissner, C. (2005). Racial bias in mock juror decision-making: A meta-analytic review of defendant treatment. *Law and Human Behavior, 29*, 621–637.

Miyake, Y., Mizutanti, M., & Yamahura, T. (1993). Event-related potentials as an indicator of detecting information in field polygraph examinations. *Polygraph, 22*, 131–149.

Mize, G. (1999, Spring). On better jury selection: Spotting UFO jurors before they enter the jury room. *Court Review, 36*, 10–15.

Moffitt, T., & Lynam, D. (1994). The neuropsychology of conduct disorder and delinquency: Implications for understanding antisocial behavior. In D. Fowles, P. Sutker, & S. Goodman (Eds.), *Psychopathy and antisocial behavior: A developmental perspective* (pp. 233–262). New York: Springer-Verlag.

Moffitt, T. E., & Mednick S. A. (1988). *Biological contributions to crime causation*. New York: Martinus Nijhoff.

Mohamed, F., Faro, S., Gordon, N., Platek, S., Ahmad, H., & Williams, J. (2006). Brain mapping of deception and truth telling about an ecologically valid situation: Functional MR imaging and polygraph investigation-initial experience. *Radiology, 238*, 679–688.

Monahan, J. (1984). The prediction of violent behavior: Toward a second generation of theory and practice. *American Journal of Psychiatry, 141*, 10–15.

Monahan, J., & Steadman, H. (Eds.). (1994). *Violence and mental disorder: Developments in risk assessment*. Chicago: University of Chicago Press.

Monahan, J., Steadman, H. J., Robbins, P. C., Appelbaum, P., Banks, S., Grisso, T., et al. (2005). An actuarial model of violence risk assessment for persons with mental disorders. *Psychiatric Services, 56*, 810–815.

Monahan, J., & Walker, L. (2005). *Social science in law: Cases and materials* (6th ed.). Westbury, NY: Foundation Press.

Moore, D., Kurtzberg, T., Thompson, L., & Morris, M. (1999). Long and short routes to success in electronically mediated negotiations: Group affiliations and good vibrations. *Organizational Behavior and Human Decision Processes, 77*, 22–43.

Moore, M., & Hiday, V. (2006). Mental health court outcomes: A comparison of re-arrest and re-arrest severity between mental health court and traditional court participants. *Law and Human Behavior, 30*, 659–674.

Moore, S. (2007, October 1). *DNA exoneration brings change in legal system*. Retrieved July 23, 2008, from http://www.nytimes.com/2007/10/01/us/01exonerate.html?scp=1&sq=%22dna%20exoneration%20brings%20change%22&st=cse

Moran, G., & Comfort, J. C. (1982). Scientific juror selection: Sex as a moderator of demographic and personality predictors of impaneled felony juror behavior. *Journal of Personality and Social Psychology, 43*, 1052–1063.

Moran, G., & Cutler, B. L. (1991). The prejudicial impact of pretrial publicity. *Journal of Applied Social Psychology, 21*, 345–367.

Morehouse, E., & Tobler, N. (2000). Preventing and reducing substance use among institutionalized adolescents. *Adolescence, 35*, 1–28.

Morgan, A. B., & Lilienfled, S. O. (2000). A meta-analytic review of the relation between antisocial behavior and neuropsychological measures of executive function. *Clinical Psychology Review, 20*, 113–136.

Morgan, C., Hazlett, G., Doran, A., Garrett, S., Hoty, G., Thomas, P., et al. (2004). Accuracy of eyewitness memory for persons encountered during exposure to highly intense stress. *International Journal of Law and Psychiatry, 27*, 265–279.

Morral, A., McCaffrey, D., & Ridgeway, G. (2004). Effectiveness of community-based treatment for substance abusing adolescents: 12-month outcomes from a case-control evaluation of a Phoenix academy. *Psychology of Addictive Behaviors, 18*, 257–268.

Morrison, P. (1995, August 21). The new chain gang. *National Law Journal*, pp. A1, A22.

Morse, S. J. (1978). Law and mental health professionals: The limits of expertise. *Professional Psychology, 9*, 389–399.

Morse, S. J. (1998). Fear of danger, flight from culpability. *Psychology, Public Policy, and Law, 4*, 250–267.

Mossman, D. (1987). Assessing and restoring competency to be executed: Should psychiatrists participate? *Behavioral Sciences & the Law, 5*, 397–410.

Mott, N. (2003). The current debate on juror questions: "To ask or not to ask, that is the question." *Chicago-Kent Law Review, 78*, 1099–1125.

Muehlenhard, C. L., & Linton, M. A. (1987). Date rape and sexual aggression in dating situations: Incidence and risk factors. *Journal of Counseling Psychology, 34,* 186–196.

Muir, W. K., Jr. (1977). *Police: Streetcorner politicians.* Chicago: University of Chicago Press.

Mulford, C. L., Lee, M. Y., & Sapp, S. C. (1996). Victim-blaming and society-blaming scales for social problems. *Journal of Applied Social Psychology, 26,* 1324–1336.

Mulvey, E., & Cauffman, E. (2001). The inherent limits of predicting school violence. *American Psychologist, 56,* 797–802.

Mu'Min v. Virginia, 111 S.Ct 1899 (1991).

Mumula, C. (2000). *Incarcerated parents and their children.* Washington, DC: U.S. Department of Justice.

Munetz, M., & Griffin, P. (2006). Use of the sequential intercept model as an approach to decriminalization of people with serious mental illness. *Psychiatric Services, 57,* 544–549.

Munsterman, G., & Hannaford-Agor, P. (2004). Building on bedrock: The continued evolution of jury reform. *The Judges' Journal, 43,* 10–16.

Murdoch, D., Pihl, R. O., & Ross, D. (1990). Alcohol and crimes of violence: Present issues. *International Journal of the Addictions, 25,* 1065–1081.

Murray, J. (2008). Media violence: The effects are both real and strong. *American Behavioral Scientist, 51,* 1212–1230.

Murrie, D., Cornell, D., & McCoy, W. (2005). Psychopathy, conduct disorder, and stigma: Does diagnostic labeling influence juvenile probation officer recommendations? *Law and Human Behavior, 25,* 323–342.

Mustard, D. (2001). Racial, ethnic, and gender disparities in sentencing: Evidence from the U.S. Federal Courts. *Journal of Law and Economics, 44,* 285–314.

Myers, B., Latter, R., & Abdollahi-Arena, M. K. (2006). The court of public opinion: Lay perceptions of polygraph testing. *Law and Human Behavior, 30,* 509–523.

Myers, D. L. (2001). *Excluding violent youths from juvenile court: The effectiveness of legislative waiver.* New York: LFB Scholarly.

Myers, J. (1996). A decade of international reform to accommodate child witnesses. *Criminal Justice and Behavior, 23,* 402–422.

Myers, M., Stewart, D., & Brown, S. (1998). Progression from conduct disorder to antisocial personality disorder following treatment for adolescent substance abuse. *American Journal of Psychiatry, 155,* 479–486.

Narby, D. J., Cutler, B. L., & Moran, G. (1993). A meta-analysis of the association between authoritarianism and jurors' perceptions of defendant culpability. *Journal of Applied Psychology, 78,* 34–42.

Nardulli, P., Eisenstein, J., & Fleming, R. (1988). *The tenor of justice: Criminal courts and the guilty plea process.* Champaign: University of Illinois Press.

National Advisory Commission on Criminal Justice Standards and Goals. (1973). *Corrections.* Washington, DC: U.S. Government Printing Office.

National Center for Education Statistics. (2003). *Indicators of school crime and safety: 2003.* Retrieved September 1, 2005, from http://nces.ed.gov/

National Center for Education Statistics. (2004). *Crime and safety in America's public schools: Selected findings from the School Survey on Crime and Safety.* Retrieved September 1, 2005, from http://nces.ed.gov/

National Institutes of Health. (2004). *Preventing violence and related health-risking social behaviors in adolescents: An NIH state-of-the-science conference.* Retrieved February 4, 2009, from http://consensus.nih.gov/2004/2004YouthViolencePreventionSOS023html.htm

National Jury Project. (1990). *Jurywork: Systematic techniques.* New York: Clark Boardman Company (Release No. 9).

National Offender Management Service. (2005). *Annual report for accredited programmes 2004–2005.* London: National Probation Directorate Interventions Unit, National Offender Management Service.

National Research Council. (1989). *Improving risk communication.* Washington, DC: National Academy Press.

National Research Council. (2003). *The polygraph and lie detection.* Washington, DC: National Academy of Sciences.

National Women's Study. (2000). *National Institute on Drug Abuse.* Retrieved October 1, 2005, from http://data.library.ubc.ca/java/jsp/database/production/detail.jsp?id=528

Neary, A. M. (1990). *DSM-II and psychopathology checklist assessment of antisocial personality disorder in black and white female felons.* Unpublished master's thesis, University of Missouri, St. Louis.

Nebraska Press Association v. Stuart, 427 U.S. 539 (1976).

Neil v. Biggers, 409 U.S. 188 (1972).

Neisser, U. (1976). *Cognition and reality: Principles and implications of cognitive psychology.* San Francisco: Freeman.

Nestor, P. G., Daggett, D., Haycock, J., & Price, M. (1999). Competence to stand trial: A neuropsychological inquiry. *Law and Human Behavior, 23,* 397–412.

Nettler, G. (1974). *Explaining crime.* New York: McGraw-Hill.

Neuschatz, J., Lawson, D., Fairless, A., Powers, R., Neuschatz, J., Goodsell, C., et al. (2007). The mitigating effects of suspicion on post-identification feedback and on retrospective eyewitness memory. *Law and Human Behavior, 31,* 231–247.

Newton, E. (2009). *Ban on drooping drawers faces legal challenge.* Retrieved April 20, 2009, from http://www.nytimes.com/2009/04/13/us/13pants.html

Nicholson, R. A. (1999). Forensic assessment. In R. Roesch, S. D. Hart, & J. R. Ogloff (Eds.), *Psychology and law: The state of the discipline* (pp. 122–173). New York: Kluwer/Plenum.

Nicholson, R. A., Briggs, S. R., & Robertson, H. C. (1988). Instruments for assessing competency to stand trial: How do they work? *Professional Psychology: Research and Practice, 19,* 383–394.

Nicholson, R. A., & Kugler, K. E. (1991). Competent and incompetent criminal defendants: A quantitative review of comparative research. *Psychological Bulletin, 109,* 355–370.

Nicholson, R. A., Norwood, S. (2000). The quality of forensic psychological assessments, reports, and testimony: Acknowledging the gap between promise and practice. *Law and Human Behavior, 24,* 9–44.

Nicholson, R. A., Norwood, S., & Enyart, C. (1991). Characteristics and outcomes of insanity acquittees in Oklahoma. *Behavioral Sciences & the Law, 9,* 487–500.

Niedermeier, K. E., Horowitz, I. A., & Kerr, N. L. (1999). Informing jurors of their nullification power: A route to a just verdict or judicial chaos? *Law and Human Behavior, 23,* 331–352.

Nietzel, M. T. (1979). *Crime and its modification: A social learning perspective.* New York: Pergamon Press.

Nietzel, M. T., & Dillehay, R. C. (1982). The effects of variations in voir dire procedures in capital murder trials. *Law and Human Behavior, 6,* 1–13.

Nietzel, M. T., & Dillehay, R. C. (1986). *Psychological consultation in the courtroom.* New York: Pergamon Press.

Nietzel, M. T., Hasemann, D., & Lynam, D. (1999). Behavioral perspectives on violent behavior. In J. B. Van Hasselt & M. Hersen (Eds.), *Handbook of psychological approaches with violent criminal offenders: Contemporary strategies and issues* (pp. 56–89). New York: Plenum.

Nietzel, M. T., Hasemann, D., & McCarthy, D. (1998). Psychology and capital litigation: Research contributions to courtroom consultation. *Applied and Preventive Psychology, 7,* 121–134.

Nietzel, M. T., McCarthy, D., & Kern, M. (1999). Juries: The current state of the empirical literature. In R. Roesch, S. D. Hart, & J. R. P. Ogloff (Eds.), *Psychology and law: The state of the discipline* (pp. 25–52). New York: Kluwer/Plenum.

Nishith, P., Mechanic, M. B., & Resick, P. A. (2000). Prior interpersonal trauma: The contribution to current PTSD symptoms in female rape victims. *Journal of Abnormal Psychology, 109,* 20–25.

Nix, C. (1987, July 9). 1000 new officers graduate to New York City streets. *The New York Times,* p. 15.

Nobile, P. (1989, July). The making of a monster. *Playboy,* 41–45.

Noble, K. B. (1987, March 23). High court to decide whether death penalty discriminates against blacks. *The New York Times,* p. 7.

Nordheimer, J. (1989, January 25). Bundy is put to death in Florida, closing murder cases across U.S. *The New York Times,* pp. 1, 11.

Northwestern University. (2007, June 29). New study shows how often juries get it wrong. *ScienceDaily.* Retrieved July 10, 2008, from http://www.sciencedaily.com/releases/2007/06/070628161330.htm

Norton, M., Sommers, S., Apfelbaum, E., Pura, N., & Ariely, D. (2006). Colorblindness and interracial interaction: Playing the "political correctness game." *Psychological Science, 17,* 949–953.

Norton, M., Vandello, J., & Darley, J. (2004). Cauistry and social category bias. *Journal of Personality and Social Psychology, 87,* 817–831.

Nunn, S. (2004). Thinking the inevitable: Suicide attacks in America and the design of effective public safety policies. *Journal of Homeland Security and Emergency Management, 1*(4), 401–423.

Obiakor, F., Merhing, T., & Schwenn, J. (1997). *Disruption, disaster, and death: Helping students deal with crises.* Reston, VA: Council for Exceptional Children.

O'Connell, C. (2004). *Murder trial renews division between Ivy Leaguers, blue-collar locals.* Retrieved October 11, 2005, from http://www.courttv.com/trials/pring-wilson/cambridge_091704_ctv.html

O'Connor v. Donaldson, 422 U.S. 563 (1975).

O'Connor, M., Sales, B. D., & Shulman, D. (1996). Mental health professional expertise in the courtroom. In B. D. Sales & D. W. Shulman (Eds.), *Law, mental health, and mental disorder* (pp. 40–60). Pacific Grove, CA: Brooks/Cole.

Odinot, G., & Wolters, G. (2006). Repeated recall, retention interval and the accuracy confidence relation in eyewitness memory. *Applied Cognitive Psychology, 20*, 973–985.

O'Donnell, P., & Lurigio, A. (2008). Psychosocial predictors of clinicians' recommendations and judges' placement orders in a juvenile court. *Criminal Justice and Behavior, 35*, 1429–1448.

Offe, H., & Offe, S. (2007). The comparison question test: Does it work and if so how? *Law and Human Behavior, 31*, 291–303.

Office of Juvenile Justice and Delinquency Prevention. (1995). *Guide for implementing the comprehensive strategy for serious, violent, and chronic juvenile offenders.* Washington, DC: Author.

Office of Juvenile Justice and Delinquency Prevention. (2008). *Model programs guide.* Retrieved June 11, 2008, from http://www.dsgonline.com/mpg2.5/mpg_index.htm

Ogloff, J. R. P. (1991). A comparison of insanity defense standards on juror decision making. *Law and Human Behavior, 15*, 509–532.

Ogloff, J. R. P., & Chopra, S. (2004). Stuck in the dark ages: Supreme Court decision making and legal developments. *Psychology, Public Policy, and Law, 10*, 379–416.

Ogloff, J. R. P., & Finkelman, D. (1999). Psychology and law: An overview. In R. Roesch, S. D. Hart, & J. R. Ogloff (Eds.), *Psychology and law: The state of the discipline* (pp. 1–20). New York: Kluwer.

Ogloff, J. R. P., & Otto, R. (1993). Psychological autopsy: Clinical and legal perspectives. *Saint Louis University Law Journal, 37*, 607–646.

Ogloff, J. R. P., & Vidmar, N. (1994). The impact of pretrial publicity on jurors: A study to compare the relative effects of television and print media in a child sex abuse case. *Law and Human Behavior, 18*, 507–525.

Olczak, P. V., Kaplan, M. F., & Penrod, S. (1991). Attorneys' lay psychology and its effectiveness in selecting jurors: Three empirical studies. *Journal of Social Behavior and Personality, 6*, 431–452.

Olsen-Fulero, L., & Fulero, S. (1997). Commonsense rape judgments: An empathy-complexity theory of rape juror story making. *Psychology, Public Policy, and Law, 3*, 402–427.

Olson, W. K. (1991). *The litigation explosion.* New York: Dutton.

Oncale v. Sundowner Offshore Services, Inc., 118 S. Ct. 998 (1998).

Orchowski, L. M., Gidycz, C. A., & Raffle, H. (2008). Evaluation of a sexual assault risk reduction and self-defense program: A prospective analysis of a revised protocol. *Psychology of Women Quarterly, 32*, 204–218.

Ornstein, P. A., Ceci, S. J., & Loftus, E. F. (1998). Adult recollections of childhood abuse: Cognitive and developmental perspectives. *Psychology, Public Policy, and Law, 4*, 1025–1051.

Ostrov, E. (1986). Police/law enforcement and psychology. *Behavioral Sciences & the Law, 4*, 353–370.

Otto, R., & Douglas, K. (Eds.). (2009). *Handbook of violence risk assessment tools.* New York: Routledge Press.

Otto, R., & Edens, J. (2003). Parenting capacity. In T. Grisso, *Evaluating competencies* (2nd ed., pp. 229–308). New York: Springer.

Otto, R., Poythress, N., Starr, K., & Darkes, J. (1993). An empirical study of the reports of APA's peer review panel in the congressional review of the *USS Iowa* incident. *Journal of Personality Assessment, 61*, 425–442.

Owen-Kostelnik, J., Reppucci, N. D., & Meyer, J. R. (2006). Testimony and interrogation of minors: Assumptions about maturity and morality. *American Psychologist, 61*, 286–304.

Packer, H. L. (1964). Two models of the criminal process. *University of Pennsylvania Law Review, 113*, 1–68.

Panetti v. Quarterman, 551 U.S. 930 (2007).

Parker, R. (2004). Alcohol and violence: Connections, evidence and possibilities for prevention. *Journal of Psychoactive Drugs* (Suppl. 2), 157–163.

Pasewark, R. A., Bieber, S., Bosten, K. J., Kiser, M., & Steadman, H. J. (1982). Criminal recidivism among insanity acquittees. *International Journal of Law and Psychiatry, 5,* 365–374.

Pasewark, R. A., & Pantle, M. L. (1981). Opinions about the insanity plea. *Journal of Forensic Psychology, 8,* 63.

Patterson, G. R. (1982). *Coercive family process.* Eugene, OR: Castalia.

Patterson, G. R. (1986). Performance models for antisocial boys. *American Psychologist, 41,* 432–444.

Paterson, H. M., & Kemp, R. I. (2006). Comparing methods of encountering post-event information: The power of co-witness suggestion. *Applied Cognitive Psychology, 20,* 1083–1099.

Patton v. Yount, 467 U.S. 1025 (1984).

Peak, K., Bradshaw, R., & Glensor, R. (1992). Improving citizen perceptions of the police: "Back to the basics" with a community policing strategy. *Journal of Criminal Justice, 20,* 24–40.

Pearce, J. B., & Snortum, J. R. (1983). Police effectiveness in handling disturbance calls: An evaluation of crisis intervention training. *Criminal Justice and Behavior, 10,* 71–92.

Pennington, N., & Hastie, R. (1986). Evidence evaluation in complex decision-making. *Journal of Personality and Social Psychology, 51,* 242–258.

Pennington, N., & Hastie, R. (1988). Explanation-based decision making: Effects of memory structure on judgment. *Journal of Experimental Psychology: Learning, Memory, and Cognition, 14,* 521–533.

Pennington, N., & Hastie, R. (1993). The story model for juror decision making. In R. Hastie (Ed.), *Inside the juror: The psychology of juror decision making* (pp. 192–221). New York: Cambridge University Press.

Penrod, S. D. (1990). Predictors of jury decision making in criminal and civil cases: A field experiment. *Forensic Reports, 3,* 261–278.

Penrod, S. D., Fulero, S. M., & Cutler, B. L. (1995). Expert psychological testimony on eyewitness reliability before and after *Daubert*: The state of the law and the science. *Behavioral Sciences & the Law, 13,* 229–260.

Penrod, S. D., Loftus, E. F., & Winkler, J. (1982). The reliability of eyewitness testimony: A psychological perspective. In N. L. Kerr & R. M. Bray (Eds.), *The psychology of the courtroom* (pp. 119–168). Orlando, FL: Academic Press.

People v. Falsetta, 986 P.2d 182 (1999).

Perkonigg, A., Kessler, R. C., Storz, S., & Wittchen, H. U. (2000). Traumatic events and post traumatic stress disorder in the community: Prevalence, risk factors and comorbidity. *Acta Psychiatrica Scandinavica, 101,* 46–59.

Perlin, M. (1996). The insanity defense: Deconstructing the myths and reconstructing the jurisprudence. In B. D. Sales & D. W. Shulman (Eds.), *Law, mental health, and mental disorder* (pp. 341–359). Pacific Grove, CA: Brooks/Cole.

Petersilia, J. (2001). When prisoners return to communities: Political, economic, and social consequences. *Federal Probation, 65,* 3–8.

Peterson, R., & Bailey, W. (2003). Is capital punishment an effective deterrent for murder? An examination of social science research. In J. Acker, R. Bohm, & C. Lanier (Eds.), *America's experiment with capital punishment: Reflections on the past, present, and future of the ultimate penal sanction* (pp. 251–282). Durham, NC: Carolina Academic Press.

Petrella, R. C., & Poythress, N. G. (1983). The quality of forensic evaluations: An interdisciplinary study. *Journal of Consulting and Clinical Psychology, 51,* 76–85.

Pfohl, S. J. (1984). Predicting dangerousness: A social deconstruction of psychiatric reality. In L. A. Teplin (Ed.), *Mental health and criminal justice* (pp. 201–225). Newbury Park, CA: Sage.

Pfohl, S. J. (1985). *Images of deviance and social control: A sociological history.* New York: McGraw-Hill.

Phan, K., Magalhaes, A., Ziemlewicz, T., Fitzgerald, D., Green, C., & Smith, W. (2005). Neural correlates of telling lies: A functional magnetic resonance imaging study at 4 Tesla. *Academic Radiology, 12,* 164–172.

Phares, E. J. (1976). *Locus of control in personality.* Morristown, NJ: General Learning Press.

Phares, E. J., & Wilson, K. G. (1972). Responsibility attribution: Role of outcome severity, situational ambiguity, and internal–external control. *Journal of Personality, 40,* 392–406.

Phillips, A. (2004, February 8). Training to be police officers: What does it take to join the force? These cadets are finding out. *The Austin American Statesman.* Retrieved July 15, 2005, from http://www.statesman.com/opinion/content/editorial/cadets/0208apdcadets.html

Phillips, C. (Producer). (2006, October 1). *Dexter* [Television Series]. Long Beach, CA: Showtime Network.

Phillips, D. A. (1979). *The great Texas murder trials: A compelling account of the sensational T. Cullen Davis case.* New York: Macmillan.

Phillips, M., McAuliff, B., Kovera, M., & Cutler, B. (1999). Double-blind photoarray administration as a safeguard against investigator bias. *Journal of Applied Psychology, 84,* 940–951.

Phillips, S., & Schneider, M. (1993). Sexual harassment of female doctors by patients. *New England Journal of Medicine, 329,* 1936–1939.

Pickel, K., French, T., & Betts, J. (2003). A cross-modal weapon focus effect: The influence of a weapon's presence on memory for auditory information. *Memory, 11,* 277–292.

Pierce, G., & Radelet, M. (2005). The impact of legally inappropriate factors on death sentencing for California homicides, 1990–1999. *Santa Clara Law Review, 46,* 1–47.

Pinizzotto, A. J., & Finkel, N. J. (1990). Criminal personality profiling: An outcome and process study. *Law and Human Behavior, 14,* 215–234.

Pizzi, W. T. (1987). Batson v. Kentucky: Curing the disease but killing the patient. In P. K. Kurland, G. Casper, & D. Hutchinson (Eds.), *The Supreme Court review, 1987* (pp. 97–156). Chicago: University of Chicago Press.

Platt, J. J., & Prout, M. F. (1987). Cognitive-behavioral theory and interventions for crime and delinquency. In E. K. Morris & C. J. Braukmann (Eds.), *Behavioral approaches to crime and delinquency: A handbook of application, research, and concepts* (pp. 477–497). New York: Plenum.

Plessy v. Ferguson, 163 U.S. 537 (1896).

Podkopacz, M., & Feld, B. (2001). The back-door to prison: Waiver reform, blended sentencing, and the law of unintended consequences. *Journal of Criminal Law & Criminology, 91,* 997–1071.

Poland, J. M. (1978). Police selection methods and the prediction of police performance. *Journal of Police Science and Administration, 6,* 374–393.

Police Psychological Services Section. (2004). *Psychological fitness-for-duty evaluation guidelines.* Retrieved July 1, 2005, from www.policepsych.com/ fitforduty.pdf

Porporino, F. (1990). Difference in response to long-term imprisonment: Implications for the management of long-term offenders. *The Prison Journal, 80,* 35–45.

Porter, B. (1983). Mind hunters. *Psychology Today, 17,* 44–52.

Posey, A., & Wrightsman, L. (2005). *Trial consulting.* New York: Oxford University Press.

Post, C. G. (1963). *An introduction to the law.* Englewood Cliffs, NJ: Prentice Hall.

Post, L. (2004a, June 7). Courts mix justice with social work. *National Law Journal,* p. 1.

Post, L. (2004b, November 8). *Spelling it out in plain English.* Retrieved November 11, 2004, from www.law.com/jsp/nlj

Post, L. (2004c, June 21). Report: Civil trials fall by half. *National Law Journal,* p. 6.

Powers v. Ohio, 111 S.Ct. 1364 (1991).

Poythress, N., Monahan, J., Bonnie, R., Otto, R. K., & Hoge, S. K. (2002). *Adjudicative competence: The MacArthur Studies.* New York: Kluwer/Plenum.

Poythress, N. G., Bonnie, R. J., Hoge, S. K., Monahan, J., & Oberlander, L. B. (1994). Client abilities to assist counsel and make decisions in criminal cases: Findings from three studies. *Law and Human Behavior, 18,* 437–452.

Poythress, N. G., Nicholson, R., Otto, R. K., Edens, J. F., Bonnie, R. J., Monahan, J., et al. (1999). *The MacArthur Competence Assessment Tool—Criminal Adjudication: Professional manual.* Odessa, FL: Psychological Assessment Resources.

Prentky, R. A., & Knight, R. A. (1991). Identifying critical dimensions for discriminating among rapists. *Journal of Consulting and Clinical Psychology, 59,* 643–661.

President's Commission on Law Enforcement and Administration of Justice. (1967). *Toward a just America.* Washington, DC: U.S. Government Printing Office.

Prettyman, E. B. (1960). Jury instructions—First or last? *American Bar Association Journal, 46,* 10–66.

Pryor, J. B. (1987). Sexual harassment proclivities in men. *Sex Roles, 17,* 269–290.

Pryor, J. B., Giedd, J. L., & Williams, K. B. (1995). A social psychological model for predicting sexual harassment. *Journal of Social Issues, 51,* 69–84.

Quas, J., Goodman, G., Ghetti, S., Alexander, K., Edelstein, R., Redlich, A., et al. (2005). Childhood sexual assault victims: Long-term outcomes after testifying in criminal court. *Monographs of the Society for Research in Child Development, 70*(2, Serial No. 280), pp. 1-145.

Quas, J., & Schaaf, J. (2002). Children's memories of experienced and nonexperienced events following repeated interviews. *Journal of Experimental Child Psychology, 83*, 304–338.

Quay, H. C. (1965). Personality and delinquency. In H. C. Quay (Ed.), *Juvenile delinquency* (pp. 139–169). Princeton, NJ: Van Nostrand.

Quinn, J. (1996). "Attitudinal" decision making in the federal courts: A study of constitutional self-representation claims. *San Diego Law Review, 33*, 701–754.

Quinsey, V. L. (1984). Sexual aggression: Studies of offenders against women. In D. Weisstub (Ed.), *Law and mental health: International perspectives* (Vol. 1, pp. 84–121). New York: Pergamon Press.

Quinsey, V. L., Harris, G. T., Rice, M. E., & Cormier, C. A. (1998). *Violent offenders: Appraising and managing risk.* Washington, DC: American Psychological Association.

Quinsey, V., Harris, G., Rice, M., & Cormier, C. (2006). *Violent offenders: Appraising and managing risk* (2nd ed.). Washington, DC: American Psychological Association.

Quinsey, V. L., Lalumiere, M. L., Rice, M. E., & Harris, G. T. (1995). Predicting violent offenses. In J. C. Campbell (Ed.), *Assessing dangerousness: Violence by sexual offenders, batterers, and child abusers* (pp.114–137). Thousand Oaks, CA: Sage.

Radelet, M., & Akers, R. (1996). Deterrence and the death penalty: The views of the experts. *Journal of Criminal Law and Criminology, 87*, 1–16.

Rafilson, F., & Sison, R. (1996). Seven criterion-related validity studies conducted with the National Police Officer Selection Test. *Psychological Reports, 78*, 163–176.

Raine, A. (2002). Annotation: The role of prefrontal deficits, low autonomic arousal, and early health factors in the development of antisocial and aggressive behavior in children. *Journal of Child Psychology & Psychiatry, 43*, 417–434.

Raine, A., Lencz, T., Bihrle, S., Lacasse, L., & Colletti, P. (2000). Reduced prefrontal gray matter volume and reduced autonomic activity in antisocial personality disorder. *Archives of General Psychiatry, 57*, 119–127.

Raine, A., Meloy, J., & Buchshaum, M. (1998). Reduced prefrontal and increased subcortical brain functioning using positron emission tomography in predatory and affective murderers. *Behavioral Sciences & the Law, 16*, 319–332.

Raine, A., Venables, P., & Williams, M. (1989). Relationships between N1, P300, and contingent negative variation recorded at age 15 and criminal behavior at age 24. *Psychophysiology, 27*, 567–574.

Rainville, J., Sobel, J. B., Hartigan, C., & Wright, A. (1997). The effect of compensation involvement on the reporting of pain and disability by patients referred for rehabilitation of chronic low back pain. *Spine, 22*, 2016–2024.

Ramirez, G., Zemba, D., & Geiselman, R. E. (1996). Judge's cautionary instructions on eyewitness testimony. *American Journal of Forensic Psychology, 14*, 31–66.

Raskin, D. C., & Honts, C. R. (2002). The comparison question test. In M. Kleiner (Ed.), *Handbook of polygraph testing* (pp. 1–47). San Diego, CA: Academic Press.

Rasul v. Bush, 542 U.S. 466 (2004).

Reardon, M., & O'Neil, K. (2008, March). *The "CSI Effect": Individual differences.* Paper presented at the annual conference of the American Psychology-Law Society, Jacksonville, FL.

Reaves, B. (2006). *Violent felons in large urban counties.* Washington, DC: U.S. Department of Justice, Bureau of Justice Statistics.

Reckless, W. C. (1967). *The crime problem* (4th ed.). New York: Meredith.

Redding, R. E., Floyd, M. Y., & Hawk, G. L. (2001). What judges and lawyers think about the testimony of mental health experts: A survey of the courts and bar. *Behavioral Sciences & the Law, 19*, 583–594.

Redding, R., & Mrozoski, B. (2005). Adjudicatory and dispositional decision making in juvenile justice. In K. Heilbrun, N. Goldstein, & R. Redding (Eds.), *Juvenile delinquency: Prevention, assessment, and intervention* (pp. 232–256). New York: Oxford University Press.

Reddy, M., Borum, R., Berglund, J., Vossekuil, B., Fein, R., & Modzeleski, W. (2001). Evaluating risk for targeted violence in schools: Comparing risk assessment, threat assessment, and other approaches. *Psychology in the Schools, 38*, 157–172.

Redlich, A. (2007a). Military and police interrogations: Similarities and differences. *Peace and Conflict, 13,* 423–428.

Redlich, A. (2007b). Double jeopardy in the interrogation room for youths with mental illness. *American Psychologist, 62,* 609–611.

Redlich, A., Silverman, M., Chen, J., & Steiner, H. (2004). The police interrogation of children and adolescents. In G. D. Lassiter (Ed.), *Interrogations, confessions, and entrapment* (pp. 107–126). New York: Kluwer Academic/Plenum.

Redlich, A., Steadman, A., Monahan, J., Robbins, P., & Petrila, J. (2006). Patterns of practice in mental health courts: A national survey. *Law and Human Behavior, 30,* 347–362.

Redlich, A., Steadman, H., Monahan, J., Petrila, J., & Griffin, P. (2005). The second generation of mental health courts. *Psychology, Public Policy, & Law, 11,* 527–538.

Redondo, S., Sanchez-Meca, J., & Garrido, V. (1999). The influence of treatment programs on the recidivism of juvenile and adult offenders: A European meta-analytic review. *Psychology, Crime and Law, 5,* 251–278.

Reibstein, L., & Foote, D. (1996, November 4). Playing the victim card. *Newsweek,* pp. 64, 66.

Reid, J. E., & Inbau, F. E. (1966). *Truth and deception: The polygraph ("lie-detector") technique.* Baltimore: Williams & Wilkins.

Reid, S. T. (1976). *Crime and criminology.* Hinsdale, IL: Dryden.

Reiser, M., & Geiger, S. (1984). Police officer as victim. *Professional Psychology: Research and Practice, 15,* 315–323.

Reiser, M., & Klyver, N. (1987). Consulting with police. In I. B. Weiner & A. K. Hess (Eds.), *Handbook of forensic psychology* (pp. 437–459). New York: Wiley.

Repko, G. R., & Cooper, R. (1983). A study of the average workers' compensation case. *Journal of Clinical Psychology, 39,* 287–295.

Reppucci, N. D., & Haugaard, J. J. (1989). Prevention of child sexual abuse: Myth or reality. *American Psychologist, 44,* 1266–1275.

Reske, H. (1996, January). Scarlet letter sentences. *American Bar Association Journal, 82,* 16–17.

Resnick, H. S., Kilpatrick, D. G., Dansky, B. S., Saunders, B., & Best, C. L. (1993). Prevalence of civilian trauma and posttraumatic stress disorder in a representative national sample of women. *Journal of Consulting and Clinical Psychology, 61,* 984–991.

Ressler, R. K., Burgess, A. W., & Douglas, J. E. (1988). *Sexual homicide: Patterns and motives.* Lexington, MA: Lexington Books.

Restrepo, L. F. (1995, April 17). Excluding bilingual jurors may be racist. *National Law Journal,* pp. A21, A22.

Reuben, R. (1996, August). The lawyer turns peacemaker. *American Bar Association Journal, 82,* 54–55.

Rhode Island v. Innis, 446 U.S. 291 (1980).

Rhode, D. (2001) *The unfinished agenda: Women and the legal profession.* Chicago, IL: ABA Commission of Women in the Profession.

Ribes-Inesta, E., & Bandura, A. (Eds.). (1976). *Analysis of delinquency and aggression.* Hillsdale, NJ: Erlbaum.

Rich, B. A. (1998). Personhood, patient-hood, and clinical practice: Reassessing advance directives. *Psychology, Public Policy, and Law, 4,* 610–628.

Richardson, A., & Budd, T. (2003). Young adults, alcohol, crime and disorder. *Criminal Behaviour & Mental Health, 13,* 5–16.

Richey, C. R. (1994). Proposals to eliminate the prejudicial effect of the use of the word "expert" under the federal rules of evidence in civil and criminal jury trials. *Federal Rules Decisions, 154,* 537–562.

Richmond Newspapers, Inc. v. Virginia, 448 U.S. 555 (1980).

Rideau v. Louisiana, 373 U.S. 723 (1963).

Rider, A. O. (1980). The firesetter: A psychological profile. *FBI Law Enforcement Bulletin, 49,* 123.

Ring v. Arizona, 536 U.S. 584 (2002).

Risinger, D. M. (2007). Innocents convicted: An empirically justified factual wrongful conviction rate. *Journal of Criminal Law and Criminology, 97,* 761–806.

Risinger, D., & Loop, J. (2002). Three card monte, Monty Hall, modus operandi, and "offender profiling": Some lessons of modern cognitive science for the law of evidence. *Cardozo Law Review, 24,* 193–253.

Risling, G. (2008). *Jury convicts mother of lesser charges in myspace suicide case.* Retrieved February 15, 2009, from http://www. law.com

Robbennolt, J. (2000). Outcome severity and judgments of "responsibility": A meta-analytic review. *Journal of Applied Social Psychology, 30,* 2575–2609.

Robbennolt, J. (2002). Punitive damage decision making: The decisions of citizens and trial court judges. *Law and Human Behavior, 26*, 315–342.

Robbennolt, J. (2003). Apologies and legal settlement: An empirical examination. *Michigan Law Review, 102*, 460–516.

Roberts, C. F., & Golding, S. L. (1991). The social construction of criminal responsibility and insanity. *Law and Human Behavior, 15*, 349–376.

Roberts, C. F., Golding, S. L., & Fincham, F. D. (1987). Implicit theories of criminal responsibility: Decision making and the insanity defense. *Law and Human Behavior, 11*, 207–232.

Roberts, C. F., Sargent, E. L., & Chan, A. S. (1993). Verdict selection processes in insanity cases: Juror construals and the effects of guilty but mentally ill instructions. *Law and Human Behavior, 17*, 261–275.

Roberts, J., & Stalans, L. (2004). Restorative sentencing: Exploring the views of the public. *Social Justice Research, 17*, 315–334.

Roberts, J., & Stanton, E. (2007, November 25). *A long road back after exoneration, and justice is slow to make amends.* Retrieved July 23, 2008, from http://www.nytimes.com/2007/11/25/us/25dna.html

Roberts, K. (2002). Children's ability to distinguish between memories from multiple sources: Implications for the quality and accuracy of eyewitness statements. *Developmental Review, 22*, 403–435.

Roesch, R., & Golding, S. L. (1980). *Competency to stand trial.* Urbana: University of Illinois Press.

Roesch, R., & Golding, S. L. (1987). Defining and assessing competence to stand trial. In I. Weiner & A. Hess (Eds.), *Handbook of forensic psychology* (pp. 378–394). New York: Wiley.

Roesch, R., Zapf, P., & Eaves, D. (2006). *Fitness Interview Test—Revised (FIT-R): A structured interview for assessing competency to stand trial.* Sarasota, FL: Professional Resource Press.

Rogers, J. (1998). Special report: Witness preparation memos raise questions about ethical limits. *ABA/BNA Manual on Lawyers' Professional Conduct, 14*, 48–54.

Rogers, R. (1986). *Conducting insanity evaluations.* New York: Van Nostrand.

Rogers, R. (1988). *Clinical assessment of malingering and deception.* New York: Guilford.

Rogers, R. (1992). *SIRS: Structured Interview of Reported Symptoms.* Odessa, FL: Psychological Assessment Resources, Inc.

Rogers, R. (Ed.). (1997). *Clinical assessment of malingering and deception* (2nd ed.). New York: Guilford.

Rogers, R. (2001). *Handbook of diagnostic and structured interviewing* (2nd ed.). New York: Guilford.

Rogers, R. (Ed.). (2008). *Clinical assessment of malingering and deception* (3rd ed.). New York: Guilford.

Rogers, R., & Ewing, C. P. (1989). Ultimate opinion proscriptions: A cosmetic fix and a plea for empiricism. *Law and Human Behavior, 13*, 357–374.

Rogers, R., Salekin, R. T., Sewell, K. W., Goldstein, A., & Leonard, K. (1998). A comparison of forensic and nonforensic malingerers: A prototypical analysis of exploratory models. *Law and Human Behavior, 22*, 253–267.

Rogers, R., & Shuman, D. (2000). *Conducting insanity evaluations* (2nd ed.). New York: Guilford.

Rogers, R., Tillbrook, C., & Sewell, K. (2004). *Evaluation of Competence to Stand Trial—Revised: Professional manual.* Lutz, FL: Psychological Assessment Resources, Inc.

Rohling, M. L., Binder, L. M., & Langhrinrichsen-Rohling, J. (1995). Money matters: A meta-analytic review of the association between financial compensation and the experience and treatment of chronic pain. *Health Psychology, 14*, 537–547.

Roper v. Simmons, 543 U.S. 551 (2005).

Rose, M. (2003). A voir dire of voir dire: Listening to jurors' views regarding the peremptory challenge. *Chicago-Kent Law Review, 78*, 1061–1098.

Rose, M. (2005). A dutiful voice: Justice in the distribution of jury service. *Law and Society Review, 39*, 601–634.

Rose, R., Bull, R., & Vrij, A. (2005). Non-biased lineup instructions do matter—A problem for older witnesses. *Psychology, Crime, and Law, 11*, 147–159.

Rosen, G. M. (1995). The *Aleutian Enterprise* sinking and posttraumatic stress disorder: Misdiagnosis in clinical and forensic settings. *Professional Psychology: Research and Practice, 26*, 82–87.

Rosenbaum, A., & Gearan, P. J. (1999). Relationship aggression between partners. In V. B. Van Hasselt & M. Hersen (Eds.), *Handbook of psychological approaches with violent offenders: Contemporary strategies and issues* (pp. 357–372). New York: Kluver Academic/Plenum.

Rosenfeld, J. P. (2005). Brain fingerprinting: A critical analysis. *Scientific Review of Mental Health Practice, 4,* 20–37.

Rosenfeld, J., Soskins, M., Bosh, G., & Ryan, A. (2004). Simple effective countermeasures to P300-based tests of detection of concealed information. *Psychophysiology, 41,* 205–219.

Rosenthal, R., & Jacobson, L. (1968). *Pygmalion in the classroom: Teacher expectation and pupils' intellectual development.* New York: Holt.

Ross, D., Ceci, S., Dunning, D., & Toglia, M. (1994). Unconscious transference and mistaken identify: When a witness misidentifies a familiar but innocent person. *Journal of Applied Psychology, 79,* 918–930.

Ross, L., & Ward, A. (1995). Psychological barriers to dispute resolution. *Advances in Experimental Social Psychology, 27,* 255–304.

Rotgers, F., & Barrett, D. (1996). *Daubert v. Merrell Dow* and expert testimony by clinical psychologists: Implications and recommendations for practice. *Professional Psychology: Research and Practice, 27,* 467–474.

Rotter, J. B. (1966). Generalized expectancies for internal versus external control of reinforcement. *Psychological Monographs, 80*(1, Whole No. 609).

Rottman, D., Flango, C., Cantrell, M., Hansen, R., & LaFountain, N. (1998). *State court organization.* Retrieved March 20, 2005, from http://www.ojp.usdoj.gov/bjs/pub/pdf/sco98.pdf

Rotundo, M., Nguyen, D., & Sackett, P. (2001). A meta-analytic review of gender differences in perceptions of sexual harassment. *Journal of Applied Psychology, 86,* 914–922.

Rowan, C. (1993). *Dream makers and dream breakers.* Boston, MA: Little, Brown.

Rowland, J. (1985). *The ultimate violation.* New York: Doubleday.

Rubinstein, M. L., Clarke, S. H., & White, T. J. (1980). *Alaska bans plea bargaining.* Washington, DC: National Institute of Justice, U.S. Department of Justice.

Ruby, C. L., & Brigham, J. C. (1996). A criminal schema: The role of chronicity, race, and socioeconomic status in law enforcement officials' perceptions of others. *Journal of Applied Social Psychology, 26,* 95–111.

Runda, J. (1991). *Personal affidavit filed with authors.* Lexington: University of Kentucky Press.

Rushton, J. (1996). Self-report delinquency and violence in adult twins. *Psychiatric Genetics, 6,* 87–89.

Russell, D. E. H. (1984). *Sexual exploitation: Rape, child sexual abuse, and workplace harassment.* Newbury Park, CA: Sage.

Ruva, C., McEvoy, C., & Bryant, J. (2007). Effects of pretrial publicity and collaboration on juror bias and source monitoring errors. *Applied Cognitive Psychology, 21,* 45–67.

Ryan, W. (1970). *Blaming the victim.* New York: Vintage.

Sachs, A. (1989, September 11). Doing the crime, not the time. *Time,* p. 81.

Sack, E. (2002). *Creating a domestic violence court: Guidelines and best practices.* San Francisco: Family Violence Prevention Fund.

Sack, K. (2001). *Research guided jury selection in church bombing trial.* Retrieved June 24, 2005, from http://www.nytimes.com/2001/05/03/national/03CHUR.html

Saks, M. (1997). What do jury experiments tell us about how juries (should) make decisions? *Southern California Interdisciplinary Law Journal, 6,* 1–53.

Salekin, R. (2004). *The Risk-Sophistication-Treatment Inventory.* Lutz, FL: PAR.

Salekin, R. T., Rogers, R., & Sewell, K. W. (1997). Construct validity of psychopathy in a female offender sample: A multitrait–multimethod evaluation. *Journal of Abnormal Psychology, 107,* 576–585.

Salekin, R., Trobst, K., & Krioukova, M. (2001). Construct validity of psychopathy in a community sample: A nomological net approach. *Journal of Personality Disorders, 15,* 425–441.

Sales, B. D., & Hafemeister, T. (1984). Empiricism and legal policy on the insanity defense. In L. A. Teplin (Ed.), *Mental health and criminal justice* (pp. 253–278). Newbury Park, CA: Sage.

Sales, B. D., & Shuman, D. W. (1993). Reclaiming the integrity of science in expert witnessing. *Ethics and Behavior, 3,* 223–229.

Salfati, C. G., & Canter, D. V. (1999). Differentiating stranger murders: Profiling offender characteristics from behavioral styles. *Behavioral Sciences & the Law, 17,* 391–406.

Samenow, S. E. (1984). *Inside the criminal mind.* New York: Times Books.

Sanborn, H. (2002, October). The vanishing trial. *American Bar Association Journal, 87,* 24–27.

Sanday, P. R. (1997). The socio-cultural context of rape: A cross-cultural study. In L. O'Toole & J. R. Schiffman (Eds.), *Gender violence: Interdisciplinary perspectives* (pp. 52–66). New York: New York University Press.

Sanders, J. (1993). The jury decision in a complex case: *Havener v. Merrell Dow Pharmaceuticals. The Justice System Journal, 16,* 45.

Sanschagrin, K., Stevens, T., Bove, A., & Heilbrun, K. (2006, March). *Quality of forensic mental health assessment of juvenile offenders: An empirical investigation.* Paper presented at the annual conference of the American Psychology-Law Society, Tampa, Florida.

Santiago, J. M., McCall-Perez, F., Gorcey, M., & Beigel, A. (1985). Long-term psychological effects of rape in 35 rape victims. *American Journal of Psychiatry, 142,* 1338–1340.

Santobello v. New York, 404 U.S. 257 (1971).

Satterfield, J. H., & Schella, A. M. (1984). Childhood brain function differences in delinquent and non-delinquent hyperactive boys. *Electroencephalography and Clinical Neurophysiology, 57,* 199–207.

Satterwhite v. Texas, 108 S. Ct. 1792 (1988).

Saum, C., & Hiller, M. (2008). Should violent offenders be excluded from drug court participation? An examination of the recidivism of violent and non-violent drug court participants. *Criminal Justice Review, 33,* 291–307.

Scheck, B., Neufeld, P., & Dwyer, J. (2000). *Actual innocence.* New York: Random House.

Schiavo ex rel. Schindler v. Schiavo, No. 05-116282005 WL 713153 (11th Circuit 2005).

Schmidt, F., Hunter, J., McKenzie, R., & Muldrow, T. (1979). Impact of valid selection procedures on workforce productivity. *Journal of Applied Psychology, 64,* 609–626.

Schoenwald, S., Henggeler, S., Brondino, M., & Rowland, M. (2000). Multisystemic therapy: Monitoring treatment fidelity. *Family Process, 39,* 83–103.

Schoenwald, S., Sheidow, A., & Letourneau, E. (2003). Toward effective quality assurance in multisystemic therapy: Links between expert consultation, therapist fidelity, and child outcomes. *Journal of Clinical Child and Adolescent Psychology, 33,* 94–104.

Schram, P. J., & Morash, M. (2002). Evaluation of a Life Skills Program for women inmates in Michigan. *Journal of Offender Rehabilitation, 34,* 47–70.

Schuller, R. (1995). Expert evidence and hearsay: The influence of "secondhand" information on jurors' decisions. *Law and Human Behavior, 19,* 345–362.

Schuller, R., & Hastings, P. (2002). Complainant sexual history evidence: Its impact on mock jurors' decisions. *Psychology of Women Quarterly, 25,* 252–261.

Schuller, R., & Klippenstine, M. (2004). The impact of complainant sexual history evidence on jurors' decisions: Considerations from a psychological perspective. *Psychology, Public Policy, and Law, 10,* 321–342.

Schuller, R., McKimmie, B., & Janz, T. (2004). The impact of expert testimony in trials of battered women who kill. *Psychiatry, Psychology and Law, 11,* 1–12.

Schulman, J., Shaver, P., Colman, R., Emrich, B., & Christie, R. (1973, May). Recipe for a jury. *Psychology Today,* pp. 37–44, 77–84.

Schwartz, J. (2009). *As jurors turn to Web, mistrials are popping up.* Retrieved March 23, 2009, from http://www.nytimes.com/2009/03/18/us/18juries.html

Schweitzer, N., & Saks, M. (2009). The gatekeeper effect: The impact of judges' admissibility decisions on the persuasiveness of expert testimony. *Psychology, Public Policy and Law, 15,* 1–18.

Scogin, F., Schumacher, J., Gardner, J., & Chaplin, W. (1995). Predictive validity of psychological testing in law enforcement settings. *Professional Psychology: Research and Practice, 26,* 68–71.

Scott, C., & Holmberg, T. (2003). Castration of sex offenders: Prisoners' rights versus public safety. *Journal of the American Academy of Psychiatry and the Law, 31,* 502–509.

Scrivner, E. M. (1994). *The role of police psychology in controlling excessive force.* Washington, DC: National Institute of Justice. Retrieved June 29, 2005, from http://www.ncjrs.org/txtfiles/ppsyc.txt

Seamon, J., Philbin, M., & Harrison, L. (2006). Do you remember proposing marriage to the Pepsi machine? False recollections from a college walk. *Psychonomic Bulletin & Review, 13,* 752–756.

Seedman, A. A., & Hellman, P. (1974). *Chief!* New York: Arthur Fields Books.

Segal, J., & Spaeth, H. (1993). *The Supreme Court and the attitudinal model.* New York: Cambridge University Press.

Segell, M. (1997, February). Homophobia doesn't lie. *Esquire,* 35.

Seiter, R. P., & Kadela, K. R. (2003). Prisoner reentry: What works, what does not, and what is promising. *Crime & Delinquency, 49,* 360–388.

Sell v. U.S., 539 U.S. 166 (2003).

Seltzer, R. (2006). Scientific jury selection: Does it work? *Journal of Applied Social Psychology, 36,* 2417–2435.

Semmler, C., Brewer, N., & Wells, G. (2004). Effects of postidentification feedback on eyewitness identification and nonidentification confidence. *Journal of Applied Psychology, 89,* 334–346.

Seventh Circuit American Jury Project. (2008). Retrieved January 30, 2009, from www.7thcircuitbar. org/associations/1507/files/7th%20Circuit% 20American%20Jury%20Project%20Final% 20Report.pdf

Shaffer, D. R. (1985). The defendant's testimony. In S. Kassin & L. Wrightsman (Eds.), *The psychology of evidence and trial procedure* (pp. 124–149). Beverly Hills, CA: Sage.

Shannon v. United States, 114 S.Ct. 2419 (1994).

Shapiro, P., & Penrod, S. (1986). Meta-analysis of racial identification studies. *Psychological Bulletin, 100,* 139–156.

Shaw, J., Appio, L., Zerr, T., & Pontoski, K. (2007). Public eyewitness confidence can be influenced by the presence of other witnesses. *Law and Human Behavior, 31,* 629–652.

Shaw, J., & Skolnick, P. (1995). Effects of prohibitive and informative judicial instructions on jury decision making. *Social Behavior and Personality, 23,* 319–326.

Shaw, J., & Skolnick, P. (1999). Weapon focus and gender differences in eyewitness accuracy: Arousal versus salience. *Journal of Applied Social Psychology, 29,* 2328–2341.

Sheidow, A., & Henggeler, S. (2005). Community-based treatments. In K. Heilbrun, N. Goldstein, & R. Redding (Eds.), *Juvenile delinquency: Prevention, assessment, and intervention* (pp. 257–281). New York: Oxford University Press.

Sheldon, K., & Krieger, L. (2004). Does legal education have undermining effects on law students? Evaluating changes in motivation, values, and well-being. *Behavioral Sciences & the Law, 22,* 261–286.

Sheldon, K., & Krieger, L. (2007). Understanding the negative effects of legal education on law students: A longitudinal test of self-determination theory. *Personality and Social Psychology Bulletin, 33,* 883–897.

Sheley, J. F. (1985). *America's "crime problem": An introduction to criminology.* Belmont, CA: Wadsworth.

Shepherd, J. (2007). Blakely's silver lining: Sentencing guidelines, judicial discretion, and crime. *Hastings Law Journal, 58,* 533–589.

Sheppard, B. H., & Vidmar, N. (1980). Adversary pretrial procedures and testimonial evidence: Effects of lawyer's role and Machiavellianism. *Journal of Personality and Social Psychology, 39,* 320–332.

Sheppard, B. H., & Vidmar, N. (1983, June). *Is it fair to worry about fairness?* Paper presented at the meeting of the Law and Society Association, Denver, CO.

Sherman, L. W., & Berk, R. A. (1984). *The Minneapolis domestic violence experiment.* Washington, DC: Police Foundation.

Shestowsky, D. (2004). Procedural preferences in alternative dispute resolution: A closer, modern look at an old idea. *Psychology, Public Policy, and Law, 10,* 211–249.

Shulman, K. I., Cohen, C. A., & Hull, I. (2004). Psychiatric issues in retrospective challenges of testamentary capacity. *International Journal of Geriatric Psychiatry, 20,* 63–69.

Shuman, D. (2000). The role of apology in tort law. *Judicature, 83,* 180–189.

Shuman, D. W., & Champagne, A. (1997). Removing the people from the legal process: The rhetoric and research on judicial selection and juries. *Psychology, Public Policy, and Law, 3,* 242–258.

Shusman, E., Inwald, R., & Landa, B. (1984). Correction officer job performance as predicted by the IPI and MMPI. *Criminal Justice and Behavior, 11,* 309–329.

Siegel, A. M., & Elwork, A. (1990). Treating incompetence to stand trial. *Law and Human Behavior, 14,* 57–65.

Silberman, C. E. (1978). *Criminal justice, criminal violence.* New York: Random House.

Silver, E. (1995). Punishment or treatment? Comparing the lengths of confinement of successful and unsuccessful insanity defendants. *Law and Human Behavior, 19,* 375–388.

Silver, E., Cirincione, C., & Steadman, H. J. (1994). Demythologizing inaccurate perceptions of the insanity defense. *Law and Human Behavior, 18,* 63–70.

Simon, R. J. (1967). *The jury and the defense of insanity.* Boston, MA: Little, Brown and Company.

Singleton, J. V., & Kass, M. (1986). Helping the jury understand complex cases. *Litigation, 12,* 11–13, 59.

Skeem, J., & Bibeau, L. (2008). How does violence potential relate to Crisis Intervention Team responses to emergencies? *Psychiatric Services, 59,* 201–204.

Skeem, J. L., & Golding, S. L. (2001). Describing jurors' personal conceptions of insanity and their relationship to case judgments. *Psychology, Public Policy, and Law, 7,* 561–621.

Skeem, J. L., Golding, S. L., Cohn, N. B., & Berge, G. (1998). Logic and reliability of evaluations of competence to stand trial. *Law and Human Behavior, 22,* 519–548.

Skeem, J., & Louden, J. (2006). Toward evidence-based practice for probationers and parolees mandated to mental health treatment. *Psychiatric Services, 57,* 1–10.

Skogan, W. G. (2006). *Police and community in Chicago: A tale of three cities.* New York: Oxford University Press.

Slade, M. (1994, February 25). Law firms begin reining in sex-harassing partners. *The New York Times,* p. B12.

Slater, D., & Hans, V. P. (1984). Public opinion of forensic psychiatry following the *Hinckley* verdict. *American Journal of Psychiatry, 141,* 675–679.

Sloat, L. M., & Frierson, R. L. (2005). Juror knowledge and attitudes regarding mental illness verdicts. *Journal of the American Academy of Psychiatry and Law, 33,* 208–213.

Slobogin, C., Melton, G., & Showalter, S. R. (1984). The feasibility of a brief evaluation of mental state at the time of the offense. *Law and Human Behavior, 8,* 305–321.

Slutske, W., Heath, A., Dinwiddie, S., Madden, P., Bucholz, K., Duhne, M., et al. (1998). Common genetic risk factors for conduct disorder and alcohol dependence. *Journal of Abnormal Psychology, 107,* 363–374.

Smith, A. (2008). *Case of a lifetime: A criminal defense lawyer's story.* New York: Palgrave Macmillan.

Smith, C. A., & Farrington, D. C. (2004). Continuities in antisocial behavior and parenting across three generations. *Journal of Child Psychology & Psychiatry, 45,* 230–247.

Smith, P., Goggin, C., & Gendreau, P. (2002). *The effects of prison sentences and intermediate sanctions on recidivism: General effects and individual differences.* Ottawa, Ontario: Public Safety Canada. (User Report 2002-01).

Smith, P. H., White, J. W., & Holland, L. J. (2003). A longitudinal perspective on dating violence among adolescent and college-age women. *American Journal of Public Health, 93,* 1104–1109.

Smith, S. (1989). Mental health expert witnesses: Of science and crystal balls. *Behavioral Sciences & the Law, 7,* 145–180.

Snyder v. Louisiana, Supreme Court No. 06-10119 (2008).

Snyder, H. N., & Sickmund, M. (1999). *Juvenile offenders and victims: 1999 national report.* Washington, DC: U.S. Department of Justice, Office of Juvenile Justice and Delinquency Prevention.

Snyder, H., & Sickmund, M. (2006). *Juvenile offenders and victims: 2006 national report.* Washington, DC: U.S. Department of Justice, Office of Justice Programs, Office of Juvenile Justice and Delinquency Prevention. (NCJ No. 212906).

Solomon, P., & Draine, J. (1995). Jail recidivism in a forensic case management program. *Health and Social Work, 20,* 167–173.

Solomon, P., Draine, J., & Marcus, S. (2002). Predicting incarceration of clients of a psychiatric probation and parole service. *Psychiatric Services, 53,* 50–56.

Solomon, R. C. (1990). *A passion for justice.* Reading, MA: Addison-Wesley.

Solomon, R. M., & Horn, J. M. (1986). Post-shooting traumatic reactions: A pilot study. In J. T. Reese & H. A. Goldstein (Eds.), *Psychological services for law enforcement* (pp. 383–394). Washington, DC: U.S. Government Printing Office.

Sommers, S. (2006). On racial diversity and group decision making: Identifying multiple effects of racial composition on jury deliberations. *Journal of Personality and Social Psychology, 90,* 597–612.

Sommers, S. (2007). Race and decision making of juries. *Legal and Criminological Psychology, 12,* 171–187.

Sommers, S. (2009). *Consequential conversations III.* Retrieved January 28, 2009, from http://blogs.psychologytoday.com/blog/science-of-small-talk/200901/consequential-conversations-part-iii

Sommers, S. R., & Ellsworth, P. C. (2000). Race in the courtroom: Perceptions of guilt and dispositional attributions. *Personality and Social Psychology Bulletin, 26,* 1367–1379.

Sommers, S., & Kassin, S. (2001). On the many impacts of inadmissible testimony: Selective compliance, need for cognition, and the overcorrection bias. *Personality and Social Psychology Bulletin, 27*, 1368–1377.

Sommers, S., & Norton, M. (2007). Race-based judgments, race-neutral justifications: Experimental examination of peremptory use and the *Batson* challenge procedure. *Law and Human Behavior, 31*, 261–273.

Sontag, S. (1978). *Illness as metaphor.* New York: Farrar, Straus, & Giroux.

Sorenson, S. B., & White, J. W. (1992). Adult sexual assault: Overview of research. *Journal of Social Issues, 48*(1), 1–8.

Soskis, D. A., & Van Zandt, C. R. (1986). Hostage negotiation: Law enforcement's most effective nonlethal weapon. *Behavioral Sciences & the Law, 4*, 423–436.

Sparf and Hansen v. United States, 156 U.S. 51 (1895).

Sparr, L. (1995). Post-traumatic stress disorder. *Neurologic Clinics, 13*, 413–429.

Spence, S. A., Hunter, M. D., Farrow, T. F. D., Green, R. D., Leung, D. H., Hughes, C. J., et al. (2004). A cognitive neurobiological account of deception: Evidence from functional neuroimaging. *Philosophical Transactions of the Royal Society, 359*, 1755–1762.

Spence, S. A., Kaylor-Hughes, C., Brook, M., Lankappa, S. T., & Wilkinson, I. D. (2008). "Munchausen's syndrome by proxy" or a "miscarriage of justice"? An initial application of functional neuroimaging to the question of guilt versus innocence. *European Psychiatry, 23*, 309–314.

Spencer, B. (2007). Estimating the accuracy of jury verdicts. *Journal of Empirical Legal Studies, 4*, 305–329.

Spielberger, C. D., Westberry, L. G., Grier, K. S., & Greenfield, G. (1980). *The police stress survey: Sources of stress in law enforcement.* Tampa, FL: Human Resources Institute.

Spilbor, J. M. (2004, October 28). *The sexual harassment case against Fox News's Bill O'Reilly: Why winning may be O'Reilly's costliest option.* Retrieved September 1, 2005, from http://writ.news.findlaw.com/commentary/20041028_spilbor.html

Spohn, C. (2000). Thirty years of sentencing reform: The quest for a racially neutral sentencing process. In J. Horney (Ed.), *Criminal justice 2000: Policies, processes, and decisions of the criminal justice system*

(Vol. 3, pp. 427–501). Washington DC: U.S. Department of Justice, National Institute of Justice.

Sporer, S. (2001). Recognizing faces of other ethnic groups: An integration of theories. *Psychology, Public Policy, and Law, 7*, 170–200.

Sporer, S., Penrod, S., Read, D., & Cutler, B. L. (1995). Choosing, confidence, and accuracy: A meta-analysis of the confidence–accuracy relation in eyewitness identification studies. *Psychological Bulletin, 118*, 315–327.

Sporer, S., & Schwandt, B. (2006). Paraverbal indicators of deception: A meta-analytic synthesis. *Applied Cognitive Psychology, 20*, 421–446.

Sprague, J., & Walker H. (2000). Early identification and intervention for youth with antisocial and violent behavior. *Exceptional Children, 66*, 367–380.

Stahl, A. L. (1999). *Offenders in juvenile court, 1996. OJJDP Bulletin.* Washington, DC: U.S. Department of Justice, Office of Juvenile Justice and Delinquency Prevention.

State v. Damms, 100 N.W.2d 592 (Wisc. 1960).

State v. Fuller, 862 A.2d 1130 (N.J. 2004).

State v. Lozano, 616 So.2d 73 (Fla. App. 1993).

State v. Michaels, 642 A.2d 1372 (N.J., 1994).

Steadman, H. J. (1979). *Beating a rap? Defendants found incompetent to stand trial.* Chicago: University of Chicago Press.

Steadman, H. J., & Braff, J. (1983). Defendants not guilty by reason of insanity. In J. Monahan & H. J. Steadman (Eds.), *Mentally disordered offenders: Perspectives from law and social science* (pp. 109–132). New York: Plenum.

Steadman, H. J., Cocozza, J., & Veysey, B. (1999). Comparing outcomes for diverted and nondiverted jail detainees with mental illnesses. *Law and Human Behavior, 23*, 615–627.

Steadman, H. J., Deane, D. W., Borum, R., & Morrissey, J. P. (2000). Comparing outcomes of major models of police responses to mental health emergencies. *Psychiatric Services, 51*, 5, 645–649.

Steadman, H. J., Keitner, L., Braff, J., & Arvanites, T. M. (1983). Factors associated with a successful insanity plea. *American Journal of Psychiatry, 140*, 401–405.

Steadman, H. J., McGreevy, M., Morrissey, J., Callahan, L., Robbin, P., & Cirincione, C. (1993). *Before and after Hinckley: Evaluating insanity defense reform.* New York: Guilford Press.

Steadman, H. J., Mulvey, E., Monahan, J., Robbins, P., Appelbaum, P., Grisso, T., et al. (1998). Violence by people discharged from acute psychiatric inpatient facilities and by others in the same neighborhoods. *Archives of General Psychiatry, 55,* 1–9.

Steadman, H. J., Rosenstein, M. J., MacAskill, R. L., & Manderscheid, R. W. (1988). A profile of mentally disordered offenders admitted to inpatient psychiatric services in the United States. *Law and Human Behavior, 12,* 91–99.

Steadman, H. J., & Veysey, B. (1997). *Providing services for jail inmates with mental disorders.* Retrieved February 8, 2009, from http://www.ncjrs.gov./txtfiles/162207.txt

Steblay, N. (1997). Social influence in eyewitness recall: A meta-analytic review of lineup instruction effects. *Law and Human Behavior, 21,* 283–298.

Steblay, N., Besirevic, J., Fulero, S., & Jiminez-Lorente, B. (1999). The effects of pretrial publicity on jury verdicts: A meta-analytic review. *Law and Human Behavior, 23,* 219–235.

Steblay, N., Dysart, J., Fulero, S., & Lindsay, R. (2001). Eyewitness accuracy rates in sequential and simultaneous lineup presentation: A meta-analytic comparison. *Law and Human Behavior, 25,* 459–473.

Steblay, N., Hosch, H., Culhane, S., & McWerthy, A. (2006). The impact on juror verdicts of judicial instruction to disregard inadmissible evidence: A meta-analysis. *Law and Human Behavior, 30,* 469–492.

Steele, W. W., & Thornburg, E. G. (1988). Jury instructions: A persistent failure to communicate. *North Carolina Law Review, 67,* 77–119.

Steffensmeier, D., & Demuth, S. (2006). Does gender modify the effects of race-ethnicity on criminal sanctioning? Sentences for male and female White, Black, and Hispanic defendants. *Journal of Quantitative Criminology, 22,* 241–261.

Steffensmeier, D., Ulmer, J., & Kramer, J. (1998). The interaction of race, gender, and age and criminal sentencing: The punishment cost of being young, black, and male. *Criminology, 36,* 763–797.

Steinberg, L., & Scott, E. (2003). Less guilty by reason of adolescence: Developmental immaturity, diminished responsibility, and the juvenile death penalty. *American Psychologist, 58,* 1009–1018.

Steiner, B., & Wright, E. (2006). Assessing the relative effects of state direct file waiver laws on violent juvenile crime: Deterrence or irrelevance? *The Journal of Criminal Law and Criminology, 96,* 1451–1477.

Stevens, R. (1983). *Law school: Legal education in America from the 1850s to the 1980s.* Chapel Hill: University of North Carolina Press.

Stevenson, M., Bottoms, B., Diamond, S., Stec, I., & Pimentel, P. (2008, March). *How jurors discuss a defendant's childhood maltreatment when they are deliberating on death.* Paper presented at the annual conference of the American Psychology-Law Society, Jacksonville, FL.

Stinchcomb, J. (2004). Searching for stress in all the wrong places: Combating chronic organizational stressors in policing. *Police Practice and Research, 5,* 259–277.

Stockdale, M. S., Visio, M., & Batra, L. (1999). The sexual harassment of men: Evidence for a broader theory of sexual harassment and sex discrimination. *Psychology, Public Policy, & Law, 5,* 630–664.

Storm, J., & Graham, J. (2000). Detection of coached general malingering on the MMPI-2. *Psychological Assessment, 12,* 158–165.

Stormo, K. J., Lang, A. R., & Stritzke, W. G. K. (1997). Attributions about acquaintance rape: The role of alcohol and individual differences. *Journal of Applied Social Psychology, 27,* 279–305.

Stratton, T. D., McLaughlin, M. A., Witte, F. M., Fosson, S. E., & Nora, L. M. (2005). Does students' exposure to gender discrimination and sexual harassment in medical school affect specialty choice and residency program selection? *Academic Medicine, 80,* 400–408.

Strauder v. West Virginia, 100 U.S. 303 (1880).

Straus, M. A., & Gelles, R. J. (1988). How violent are American families? Estimates from the National Family Violence Resurvey and other studies. In G. T. Hotaling, D. Finkelhor, J. T. Kirkpatrick, & M. A. Straus (Eds.), *Family abuse and its consequences* (pp. 14–36). Thousand Oaks, CA: Sage.

Streib V. (1983). Death penalty for children: The American experience with capital punishment for crimes committed while under age eighteen. *Oklahoma Law Review, 36,* 613–641.

Strier, F. (1996). *Reconstructing justice: An agenda for trial reform.* Westport, CN: Quorum Books.

Strier, F. (1999). Whither trial consulting? Issues and projections. *Law and Human Behavior, 23,* 93–115.

Strier, F. (2001). Why trial consultants should be licensed. *Journal of Forensic Psychology Practice, 1,* 69–76.

Stromwall, L., & Granhag, P. (2003). How to detect deception? Arresting the beliefs of police officers, prosecutors and judges. *Psychology, Crime, and Law, 9,* 19–36.

Studebaker, C. A., & Penrod, S. D. (1997). Pretrial publicity: The media, the law and common sense. *Psychology, Public Policy, and Law, 3,* 428–460.

Studebaker, C., & Penrod, S. (2005). Pretrial publicity and its influence on juror decision making. In N. Brewer & K. Williams (Eds.), *Psychology and law: An empirical perspective* (pp. 254–275). New York: Guilford.

Studebaker, C., Robbennolt, J., Penrod, S., Pathak-Sharma, M., Groscup, J., & Devenport, J. (2002). Studying pretrial publicity effects: New methods for improving ecological validity and testing external validity. *Law and Human Behavior, 26,* 19–42.

Sullivan, C. M., & Bybee, D. I. (1999). Reducing violence using community based advocacy for women with abusive partners. *Journal of Consulting and Clinical Psychology, 67,* 43–53.

Sullivan, D., & Tifft, L. (2006). Introduction: The healing dimension of restorative justice. A one-world body. In D. Sullivan & L. Tifft (Eds.), *Handbook of restorative justice: A global perspective* (pp. 1–16). London: Routledge.

Sunstein, C., Hastie, R., Payne, J., Schkade, D., & Viscusi, W. (2002). *Punitive damages: How juries decide.* Chicago: University of Chicago Press.

Susman, D. (1992). *Effects of three different legal standards on psychologists' determinations of competency for execution.* Unpublished doctoral dissertation, University of Kentucky, Lexington.

Sutherland, E. H. (1947). *Principles of criminology* (4th ed.). Philadelphia: Lippincott.

Sutherland, E. H., & Cressey, D. R. (1974). *Principles of criminology* (9th ed.). New York: Lippincott.

Sutker, P., Davis, J. M., Uddo, M., & Ditta, S. (1995). War zone stresses, personal resources, and PTSD in Persian Gulf returnees. *Journal of Abnormal Psychology, 104,* 444–452.

Swahn, M. H., Whitaker, D. J., Pippen, C. B., Leeb, R. T., Teplin, L. A., Abram, K. M., et al. (2006). Concordance between self-reported maltreatment and court records of abuse or neglect among high-risk youths. *American Journal of Public Health: Mental Health for Individuals and Communities, 96,* 1849–1853.

Swain v. Alabama, 380 U.S. 202 (1965).

Sydeman, S. J., Cascardi, M., Poythress, N. G., & Ritterband, L. M. (1997). Procedural justice in the context of civil commitment: A critique of Tyler's analysis. *Psychology, Public Policy, and Law, 3,* 207–221.

Tanford, J. A. (1991). Law reforms by courts, legislatures, and commissions following empirical research on jury instructions. *Law & Society Review, 25,* 155–175.

Tarasoff v. Regents of the University of California, 529 P.2d 553 (1974).

Tarasoff v. Regents of the University of California, 551 P.2d 334 (1976).

Taylor, G. (1992, March 2). Justice overlooked. *National Law Journal,* p. 43.

Taylor, S., Jr. (1986, May 6). Justices reject broad challenge in capital cases. *The New York Times,* pp. 1, 12.

Taylor, S. E., Klein, L. C., Lewis, B. P., Gruenewald, T. L., Gurung, R. A. R., & Updegraff, J. A. (2000). Biobehavioral responses to stress in females: Tend-and-befriend, not fight-or-flight. *Psychological Review, 107,* 411–429.

Taylor, T., & Hosch, H. (2004). An examination of jury verdicts for evidence of a similarity–leniency effect, an out-group punitiveness effect or a black sheep effect. *Law and Human Behavior, 28,* 587–598.

Tehrani, J., & Mednick, S. (2000). Genetic factors and criminality. *Federal Probation, 64,* 24–28.

Tennessee v. Garner, 471 U.S. 1 (1985).

Teplin, L. A. (1984). The criminalization of the mentally ill: Speculation in search of data. In L. A. Teplin (Ed.), *Mental health and criminal justice* (pp. 63–85). Newbury Park, CA: Sage.

Teplin, L. A. (1994). Psychiatric and substance abuse disorders among male urban jail detainees. *American Journal of Public Health, 84,* 290–293.

Teplin, L. (2000, July). Keeping the peace: Police discretion and mentally ill persons. *National Institute of Justice Journal,* 8–15.

Teplin, L. A., Abram, K. M., & McClelland, G. M. (1996). The prevalence of psychiatric disorder among incarcerated women. I: Pre-trial detainees. *Archives of General Psychiatry, 53,* 505–512.

Terman, L. M. (1917). A trial of mental and pedagogical tests in a civil service examination for policemen and firemen. *Journal of Applied Psychology, 1,* 17–29.

Terpstra, D. E., & Baker, D. D. (1987). A hierarchy of sexual harassment. *Journal of Psychology, 121,* 599–605.

Terpstra, D. E., & Baker, D. D. (1988). Outcomes of sexual harassment charges. *Academy of Management Journal, 31,* 185–194.

Terpstra, D. E., & Baker, D. D. (1992). Outcomes of federal court decisions on sexual harassment. *Academy of Management Journal, 35,* 181–190.

Tett, R., Jackson, D., & Rothstein, M. (1991). Personality measures as predictors of job performance: A meta-analytic review. *Personnel Psychology, 44,* 703–740.

Thibaut, J., & Walker, L. (1975). *Procedural justice: A psychological analysis.* Hillsdale, NJ: Erlbaum.

The Criminal Justice/Mental Health Consensus Project. (2005). Retrieved November 20, 2008, from http://justicecenter.csg.org/resources/mental_health

Thomas, C. (1996, April 8). *Judging.* Invited address, School of Law, University of Kansas, Lawrence, KS.

Thomas, E. (1991). *The man to see.* New York: Simon & Schuster.

Thompson v. Oklahoma, 487 U.S. 815 (1988).

Thompson, M., Osher, F., & Tomasini-Joshi, D. (2007). *Improving responses to people with mental illnesses: The essential elements of a mental health court.* New York: Council of State Governments Justice Center.

Thompson, W. C., Cowan, C. L., Ellsworth, P. C., & Harrington, J. C. (1984). Death penalty attitudes and conviction proneness: The translation of attitudes into verdicts. *Law and Human Behavior, 8,* 95–113.

Thornton, H. (1995). *Hung jury: The diary of a Menendez juror.* Philadelphia: Temple University Press.

Tietz, J. (2006). *The unending torture of Omar Khadr.* Retrieved July 16, 2008, from www.rollingstone.com/politics/story/11128331/follow_omar_khadr_from_an_al_qaeda_childhood_to_a_gitmo_cell

Tillbrook, C., Mumley, D., & Grisso, T. (2003). Avoiding expert opinions on the ultimate legal question: The case for integrity. *Journal of Forensic Psychology Practice, 3,* 77–87.

Tjaden, P., & Thoennes, N. (2000). *Full report of the prevalence, incidence, and consequences of violence against women.* Washington, DC: National Institute of Justice, Office of Justice Programs. (NCJ 13781).

Tjaden, P., & Thoennes, N. (2006). *Extent, nature, and consequences of rape victimization: Findings from the National Violence Against Women Survey.* Washington, DC: National Institute of Justice, Office of Justice Programs.

Toch, H. (1985). Warehouses for people? *The Annals of the American Academy of Political and Social Science, 478,* 58–72.

Tombaugh, T. (1997). *TOMM: Test of Memory Malingering manual.* Toronto: Multi-Health Systems.

Tonry, M. (1996). *Sentencing matters.* New York: Oxford University Press.

Tonry, M., & Melewski, M. (2008). The malign effects of drug and crime control policies on Black Americans. *Crime and Justice, 37,* 1–44.

Toobin, J. (1996, December 9). Asking for it. *New Yorker,* pp. 55–60.

Toot, J., Dunphy, G., Turner, M., & Ely, D. (2004). The SHR Y-chromosome increases testosterone and aggression, but decreases serotonin as compared to the WKY Y-chromosome in the rat model. *Behavioral Genetics, 34,* 515–524.

Torbet, P., Gable, R., Hurst, H., Montgomery, I., Szymanski, L., & Thomas, D. (1996). *State responses to serious and violent juvenile crime.* Washington, DC: U.S. Department of Justice, Office of Juvenile Justice and Delinquency Prevention.

Torkildson, J., & Kassin, S. (2008, March). *Inside interrogation: The outright lie, the bluff, and false confessions.* Paper presented at the annual conference of American Psychology-Law Society, Jacksonville, FL.

Trevethan, S. D., & Walker, L. J. (1989). Hypothetical versus real-life moral reasoning among psychopathic and delinquent youth. *Development and Psychopathology, 1,* 91–103.

Trupin, E., & Richards, H. (2003). Seattle's mental health courts: Early indicators of effectiveness. *International Journal of Law & Psychiatry, 26,* 33–53.

Trupin, E., Richards, H., Wertheimer, D., & Bruschi, D. (2001). *City of Seattle: Seattle Municipal Court, Mental Health Court: Evaluation report.* Retrieved May 3, 2005, from http://www.cityofseattle.net/courts/pdf/MHReport.pdf

Tsushima, W. T., Foote, R., Merrill, T. S., & Lehrke, S. A. (1996). How independent are independent psychological examinations? A workers' compensation dilemma. *Professional Psychology: Research and Practice, 27,* 626–628.

Tuohy, A. P., Wrennall, M. J., McQueen, R. A., & Stradling, S. G. (1993). Effect of socialization factors on decisions to prosecute: The organizational adaptation of Scottish police recruits. *Law and Human Behavior, 17,* 167–182.

Turkheimer, E., & Parry, C. D. H. (1992). Why the gap? Practice and policy in civil commitment hearings. *American Psychologist, 47,* 646–655.

Turner, R. J., & Lloyd, D. A. (1995). Lifetime trauma and mental health: The significance of cumulative adversity. *Journal of Health and Social Behavior, 36,* 360–376.

Turner, S., Greenwood, P., Fain, T., & Deschenes, E. (1999). Perceptions of drug court: How offenders view ease of program completion, strengths and weaknesses, and the impact on their lives. *National Drug Court Institute Review, 2,* 61–85.

Tversky, A., & Kahneman, D. (1974). Judgment under uncertainty: Heuristics and biases. *Science, 185,* 1124–1131.

Tyler, T., & Huo, Y. (2002). *Trust in the law: Encouraging public cooperation with the police and court.* New York: Russell Sage Foundation.

Uchida, C., & Brooks, L. (1988). *Violence against the police: Assaults on Baltimore County Police, 1984–86, final report.* Washington, DC: U.S. Department of Justice.

Umbreit, M., Vos, G., Coates, R., & Lightfoot, E. (2005). Restorative justice in the 21st century: A social movement full of opportunities and pitfalls. *Marquette Law Review, 89,* 251–304.

United States v. Angelos, 345 F.Supp. 2d 1227 (2004).

United States v. Booker, 125 S.Ct. 735 (2005).

United States v. Dougherty, 473 F.2d 1113 (1972).

United States v. Gementra, 379 F.3d 596 (2004).

United States v. Grubbs, 547 U.S. 90 (2006).

United States v. Lea, 249 F.3d 632 (2001).

United States v. McVeigh, 918 F. Supp. 1467 (1996).

United States v. Salerno, 481 U.S. 739 (1987).

United States v. Santiago-Martinez, 94–10350 (9th Cir. 1995).

United States v. Scheffer, 118 S.Ct. 1261 (1998).

United States v. Telfaire, 469 F.2d 552 (1972).

U.S. Department of Justice. (1999). *Eyewitness evidence: A guide for law enforcement.* Washington, DC: Author.

U.S. General Accounting Office. (1990). *Death penalty sentencing.* Washington, DC: U.S. Government Printing Office.

U.S. Public Health Service. (1999). *Mental health: A report of the Surgeon General.* Rockville, MD: U.S. Department of Health and Human Services, National Institutes of Health, National Institute of Mental Health.

Ustad, K. L., Rogers, R., Sewell, K. W., & Guarnaccia, C. A. (1996). Restoration of competency to stand trial: Assessment with the Georgia Court Competency Test and the Competency Screening Test. *Law and Human Behavior, 20,* 131–146.

Valentine, T., Pickering, A., & Darling, S. (2003). Characteristics of eyewitness identification that predict the outcome of real lineups. *Applied Cognitive Psychology, 17,* 969–993.

VanDuyn, A. L. (1999). The scarlet letter branding: A constitutional analysis of community notification provisions in sex offender statues. *Drake Law Review, 47,* 635–659.

Van Prooijen, J. (2006). Retributive reactions to suspected offenders: The importance of social categorizations and guilt probability. *Personality and Social Psychology Bulletin, 32,* 715–726.

Varela, J. G., Scogin, F. R., & Vipperman, R. K. (1999). Development and preliminary validation of a semi-structured interview for the screening of law enforcement candidates. *Behavioral Sciences & the Law, 17,* 467–481.

Vecchi, G., Van Hasselt, V., & Romano, S. (2005). Crisis (hostage) negotiation: Current strategies and issues in high-risk conflict resolution. *Aggression and Violent Behavior, 10,* 533–551.

Verlinden, S., Hersen, M., & Thomas, J. (2000). Risk factors in school shootings. *Clinical Psychology Review, 20,* 3–56.

Victor, T. L., & Abeles, N. (2004). Coaching clients to take psychological and neuropsychological tests: A clash of ethical obligations. *Practice Issues in Forensic Psychology, 35,* 373–379.

Vidmar, N. (1997). Generic prejudice and the presumption of guilt in sex abuse trials. *Law and Human Behavior, 21,* 5–25.

Vidmar, N. (1998). The performance of the American civil jury: An empirical perspective. *Arizona Law Review, 40,* 849–899.

Vidmar, N. (Ed.). (2000). *World jury systems.* Oxford: Oxford University Press.

Vidmar, N. (2002). Case studies of pre- and midtrial prejudice in criminal and civil litigation. *Law and Human Behavior, 26,* 73–106.

Vidmar, N., & Diamond, S. (2001). Juries and expert evidence. *Brooklyn Law Review, 66,* 1121–1180.

Vidmar, N., & Hans, V. P. (2007). *American juries: The verdict.* Amherst, NY: Prometheus.

Vidmar, N., & Rice, J. (1993). Assessments of non-economic damage awards in medical negligence: A comparison of jurors with legal professionals. *Iowa Law Review, 78,* 883–911.

Viljoen, J., Klaver, J., & Roesch, R. (2005). Legal decisions of preadolescent and adolescent defendants: Predictors of confessions, pleas, communication with attorneys, and appeals. *Law and Human Behavior, 29,* 253–277.

Viljoen, J. L., Roesch, R., Ogloff, J. R. P., & Zapf, P. A. (2003). The role of Canadian psychologists in conducting fitness and criminal responsibility evaluations. *Canadian Psychology, 44,* 369–381.

Viljoen, J., Zapf, P., & Roesch, R. (2007). Adjudicative competence and comprehension of *Miranda* rights in adolescent defendants: A comparison of legal safeguards. *Behavioral Sciences & the Law, 25,* 1–19.

Vinson, K. V., Costanzo, M. A., & Berger, D. E. (2008). Predictors of verdict and punitive damages in high-stakes civil litigation. *Behavioral Sciences & the Law, 26,* 167–186.

Violanti, J. M., & Aron, F. (1994). Ranking police stressors. *Psychological Reports, 75,* 824–826.

Vise, D. A. (1989, August 7). Using a Mafia law to bust high-flying stockbrokers. *The Washington Post National Weekly Edition,* p. 20.

Vitale, J. E., & Newman, J. P. (2001). Using the Psychopathy Checklist–Revised with female samples: Reliability, validity, and implications for clinical utility. *Clinical Psychology: Science & Practice, 8,* 117–132.

Vrig, A., Fisher, R., Mann, S., & Leal, S. (2006). Detecting deception by manipulating cognitive load. *Trends in Cognitive Sciences, 10,* 141–142.

Vrij, A. (2000). *Detecting lies and deceit: The psychology of lying and implications for professional practice.* Chichester, UK: Wiley.

Vrij, A., & Mann, S. (2001). Telling and detecting lies in a high-state situation: The case of a convicted murderer. *Applied Cognitive Psychology, 15,* 187–203.

Wade, K., Garry, M., Read, J., & Lindsay, D. (2002). A picture is worth a thousand lies: Using false photographs to create false childhood memories. *Psychonomic Bulletin & Review, 9,* 597–603.

Wainwright v. Witt, 469 U.S. 412 (1985).

Walker, L. (1979). *The battered woman.* New York: Harper & Row.

Walker, L. (1984). *The battered woman syndrome.* New York: Springer.

Walker, L., La Tour, S., Lind, E. A., & Thibaut, J. (1974). Reactions of participants and observers to modes of adjudication. *Journal of Applied Social Psychology, 4,* 295–310.

Wallendael, L., & Cutler, B. (2004). Limitations to empirical approaches to jury selection. *Journal of Forensic Psychology Practice, 4,* 79–86.

Walster, E. (1966). Assignment of responsibility for an accident. *Journal of Personality and Social Psychology, 3,* 73–79.

Waltz, J., Babcock, J. C., Jacobson, N. S., & Gottman, J. M. (2000). Testing a typology of batterers. *Journal of Consulting and Clinical Psychology, 68,* 658–669.

Ward, J. (1998, May 18). Boalt boosts minority enrollment by downplaying grades, scores. *National Law Journal,* p. A16.

Warner, W. J. (2005, April). Polygraph testing: A utilitarian tool. *FBI Law Enforcement Bulletin, 74,* 4.

Warren, E. (1977). *The memoirs of Earl Warren.* Garden City, NY: Doubleday.

Warshaw, R. (1988). *I never called it rape.* New York: Harper & Row.

Waterman, A., Blades, M., & Spencer, C. (2001). Interviewing children and adults: The effect of question format on the tendency to speculate. *Applied Cognitive Psychology, 15,* 521–531.

Watson, P. (1996). The search for justice—A case for reform in the civil justice system in Britain. *ILSA Journal of International and Comparative Law, 2*, 453.

Webster, C. D., Douglas, K. S., Eaves, D., & Hart, S. D. (1997). *HCR-20: Assessing risk for violence* (Version 2). Vancouver: Mental Health, Law, and Policy Institute (Simon Fraser University).

Weeks v. Angelone, 120 S.Ct. 1290 (2000).

Wegner, D. M. (1994). Ironic processes of mental control. *Psychological Review, 101*, 34–52.

Wegner, D. M., & Erber, R. (1992). The hyperaccessibility of suppressed thoughts. *Journal of Personality and Social Psychology, 63*, 903–912.

Wegner, D. M., Schneider, D. J., Carter, S., III, & White, T. (1987). Paradoxical effects of thought suppression. *Journal of Personality and Social Psychology, 53*, 5–13.

Weinberger, L., Sreenivasan, S., Garrick, T., & Osran, H. (2005). The impact of surgical castration on sexual recidivism risk among sexually violent predatory offenders. *Journal of the American Academy of Psychiatry and the Law, 33*, 16–36.

Weir, J. A., & Wrightsman, L. S. (1990). The determinants of mock jurors' verdicts in a rape case. *Journal of Applied Social Psychology, 20*, 901–919.

Weiss, W., Davis, R., Rostow, C., & Kinsman, S. (2003). The MMPI-2 L scale as a tool in police selection. *Journal of Police and Criminal Psychology, 18*, 57–60.

Weissman, H. N. (1985). Psycholegal standards and the role of psychological assessment in personal injury litigation. *Behavioral Sciences & the Law, 3*, 135–148.

Weissman, H. N. (1991). Child custody evaluations: Fair and unfair professional practices. *Behavioral Sciences & the Law, 9*, 469–476.

Weitzer, R., & Tuch, S. A. (1999). Race, class, and perceptions of discrimination by the police. *Crime & Delinquency, 45*, 494–507.

Wells, G. (1978). Applied eyewitness testimony research: System variables and estimator variables. *Journal of Personality and Social Psychology, 36*, 1546–1557.

Wells, G. L. (1993). What do we know about eyewitness identification? *American Psychologist, 48*, 553–571.

Wells, G. L., & Lindsay, R. C. L. (1980). On estimating the diagnosticity of eyewitness nonidentifications. *Psychological Bulletin, 88*, 776–784.

Wells, G. L., & Loftus, E. F. (1984). Eyewitness research: Then and now. In G. L. Wells & E. F. Loftus (Eds.). *Eyewitness testimony: Psychological perspectives* (pp. 1–11). New York: Cambridge University Press.

Wells, G., & Luus, C. (1990). Police lineups as experiments: Social methodology as a framework for properly conducted lineups. *Personality and Social Psychology Bulletin, 16*, 106–117.

Wells, G. L., Memon, A., & Penrod, S. D. (2006). Eyewitness evidence: Improving its probative value. *Psychological Science in the Public Interest, 7*, 45–75.

Wells, G., & Olson, E. (2003). Eyewitness testimony. *Annual Review of Psychology, 54*, 277–295.

Wells, G., Olson, E., & Charman, S. (2002). The confidence of eyewitnesses in their identifications from lineups. *Psychological Science, 11*, 151–154.

Wells, G. L., Small, M., Penrod, S., Malpass, R. S., Fulero, S. M., & Brimacombe, C. A. E. (1998). Eyewitness identification procedures: Recommendations for lineups and photospreads. *Law and Human Behavior, 22*, 603–647.

Wells, G. L., Wright, E. F., & Bradfield, A. L. (1999). Witnesses to crime: Social and cognitive factors governing the validity of people's reports. In R. Roesch, S. D. Hart, & J. Ogloff (Eds.), *Psychology and law: The state of the discipline* (pp. 54–89). New York: Kluwer Academic/Plenum.

Wells, G., Wrightsman, L., & Miene, P. (1985). The timing of the defense opening statement: Don't wait until the evidence is in. *Journal of Applied Social Psychology, 15*, 758–772.

Welsh, W. (2007). A multisite evaluation of prison-based therapeutic community drug treatment. *Criminal Justice and Behavior, 34*, 1481–1498.

Wenzel, M., Okimoto, T., Feather, N., & Platow, M. (2008). Retributive and restorative justice. *Law and Human Behavior, 32*, 375–389.

Wexler, D. B. (1992). Putting mental health into mental health law: Therapeutic jurisprudence. *Law and Human Behavior, 16*, 27–38.

Wexler, D., & Winick, B. (Eds.) (1996). *Law in a therapeutic key: Developments in therapeutic jurisprudence.* Durham, NC: Carolina Academic Press.

Whalen v. United States, 346 F.2d 812 (1965).

Whipple, S. B. (1937). *The trial of Bruno Richard Hauptmann.* New York: Doubleday.

White, J. W., & Sorenson, S. B. (1992). A sociocultural view of sexual assault: From discrepancy to diversity. *Journal of Social Issues, 48*, 187–195.

Whittemore, K. E., & Ogloff, J. R. P. (1995). Factors that influence jury decision making: Disposition instructions and mental state at the time of the trial. *Law and Human Behavior, 19*, 283–303.

Whren et al. v. United States, 517 U.S. 806 (1996).

Widom, C. S. (1989). Child abuse, neglect, and adult behavior: Research design and findings on criminality, violence, and child abuse. *American Journal of Orthopsychiatry, 59*, 355–367.

Widom, C. S. (1992). *The cycle of violence: National Institute of Justice Research in brief.* Washington, DC: U.S. Department of Justice.

Wiener, R., Arnot, L., Winter, R., & Redmond, B. (2006). Generic prejudice in the law: Sexual assault and homicide. *Basic and Applied Social Psychology, 28*, 145–155.

Wiener, R., Bornstein, B., & Voss, A. (2003). Emotion and the law: A framework for inquiry. *Law and Human Behavior, 30*, 231–248.

Wiener, R., & Gutek, B. (1999). Advance in sexual harassment research, theory, and policy. *Psychology, Public Policy, and Law, 5*, 507–518.

Wiener, R., Hurt, L., Russell, B., Mannen, K., & Gasper, C. (1997). Perceptions of sexual harassment: The effects of gender, legal standard, and ambivalent sexism. *Law and Human Behavior, 21*, 71–94.

Wiener, R., Rogers, M., Winter, R., Hurt, L., Hackney, A., Kadela, K., et al. (2004). Guided jury discretion in capital murder cases: The role of declarative and procedural knowledge. *Psychology, Public Policy, and Law, 10*, 516–576.

Wiener, R., Wiener, A., & Grisso, T. (1989). Empathy and biased assimilation of testimonies in cases of alleged rape. *Law and Human Behavior, 13*, 343–356.

Wiggins, E. (2006). The courtroom of the future is here: Introduction of emerging technologies in the legal system. *Law & Policy, 28*, 182–191.

Wilcock, R., Bull, R., & Vrij, A. (2007). Are old witnesses always poorer witnesses? Identification accuracy, context reinstatement, own age-bias. *Psychology, Crime, and Law, 13*, 305–316.

Wilkinson, R. (2001). Offender reentry: A storm overdue. *Corrections Management Quarterly, 5*, 46–51.

Will, G. (1984, January 22). Fitting laws to dynamic society likened to trousers on 10-year-old. *Lawrence Journal-World*, p. 6.

Williams, C. W., Lees-Haley, P. R., & Djanogly, S. E. (1999). Clinical scrutiny of litigants' self-reports. *Professional Psychology: Research and Practice, 30*, 361–367.

Williams, D. (1969). Neural factors related to habitual aggression: Consideration of those differences between those habitually aggressives and others who have committed crimes of violence. *Brain, 92*, 503–520.

Williams, L. M. (1994). Recall of childhood trauma: A prospective study of women's memories of child sexual abuse. *Journal of Consulting and Clinical Psychology, 62*, 1167–1176.

Williams, W., & Miller, K. S. (1981). The processing and disposition of incompetent mentally ill offenders. *Law and Human Behavior, 5*, 245–261.

Wilson, A. E., Calhoun, K. S., & Bernat, J. A. (1999). Risk recognition and trauma-related symptoms among sexually revictimized women. *Journal of Consulting and Clinical Psychology, 67*, 705–710.

Wilson, D., Mitchell, O., & Mackenzie, D. (2006). A systematic review of drug court effects on recidivism. *Journal of Experimental Criminology, 2*, 459–487.

Wilson, J. Q. (1975). *Thinking about crime.* New York: Basic Books.

Wilson, J. Q. (1978). *Varieties of police behavior* (2nd ed.). Cambridge, MA: Harvard University Press.

Wilson, J. Q., & Herrnstein, R. (1985). *Crime and human nature.* New York: Simon & Schuster.

Wilson, T. (2002). *Strangers to ourselves: Discovering the adaptive unconscious.* Cambridge, MA: Harvard University Press.

Wilt, S., & Olson, S. (1996). Prevalence of domestic violence in the United States. *Journal of the American Medical Women's Association, 51*, 77–82.

Winick, B. (1985). Restructuring competency to stand trial. *UCLA Law Review, 32*, 921–985.

Winick, B. (1996). Incompetency to proceed in the criminal process: Past, present, and future. In B. D. Sales & D. W. Shulman (Eds.), *Law, mental health, and mental disorder* (pp. 310–340). Pacific Grove, CA: Brooks/Cole.

Winkle, J., & Wedeking, J. (2003). Perceptions and experiences of gender fairness in Mississippi courts. *Judicature, 87,* 126–134.

Winslade, W. J., & Ross, J. W. (1983). *The insanity plea.* New York: Scribners.

Wise, R. A., & Safer, M. A. (2004). What U.S. judges know and believe about eyewitness testimony. *Applied Cognitive Psychology, 18,* 427–443.

Wissler, R., & Saks, M. (1985). On the inefficacy of limiting instructions. *Law and Human Behavior, 9,* 37–48.

Wistrich, A., Guthrie, C., & Rachlinski, J. (2005). Can judges ignore inadmissible information? The difficulty of deliberately disregarding. *University of Pennsylvania Law Review, 153,* 1251–1345.

Witherspoon v. Illinois, 391 U.S. 510 (1968).

Witt, P., & Barone, N. (2004). Assessing sex offender risk: New Jersey's methods. *Federal Sentencing Reporter, 16,* 170.

Wogalter, M., Malpass, R., & McQuiston, D. (2004). A national survey of U.S. police on preparation and conduct of identification lineups. *Psychology, Crime, and Law, 10,* 69–82.

Wood, J., Schreiber, N., Martinez, Y., McLaurin, K., Strok, R., Velarde, L., et al. (1998, March). *Child interviewing techniques in the McMartin Preschool and Kelly Michaels cases: A quantitative comparison.* Paper presented at the conference of the American Psychology Law Society, Redondo Beach, CA.

Woodrell, D. (1996). *Give us a kiss.* New York: Henry Holt.

Woodworth, M., & Porter, S. (2000). Historical foundations and current applications of criminal profiling in violent crime investigations. *Expert Evidence, 7,* 241–264.

Worden, A., & Carlson, B. (2005). Attitudes and beliefs about domestic violence: Results of a public opinion survey. *Journal of Interpersonal Violence, 20,* 1219–1243.

Wordsworth, A. (2005, January 7). Child-killer unfairly convicted, court rules: Expert witness misled jury in Andrea Yates trial. *National Post, Toronto Edition,* p. A13.

Worsnop, R. L. (1993, February 5). Community policing. *CQ Researcher,* p. 97.

Wright, D., & Skagerberg, E. (2007). Postidentification feedback affects real eyewitnesses. *Psychological Science, 18,* 172–178.

Wrightsman, L., & Kassin, S. (1993). *Confessions in the courtroom.* Thousand Oaks, CA: Sage.

Wyatt, G. E., Guthrie, D., & Notgrass, C. M. (1992). Differential effects of women's child sexual abuse and subsequent sexual revictimization. *Journal of Consulting and Clinical Psychology, 60,* 167–173.

www.abanet.org (2005).

www.adversity.net (2002).

www.nalp.org (2005).

Yegidis, B. L. (1986). Date rape and other forced sexual encounters among college students. *Journal of Sex Education and Therapy, 12,* 51–54.

Yochelson, S., & Samenow, S. E. (1976). *The criminal personality: A profile for change* (Vol. 1). New York: Aronson.

York, E., & Cornwell, B. (2006). Status on trial: Social characteristics and influence in the jury room. *Social Forces, 85,* 455–477.

Youngjohn, J. (1995). Confirmed attorney coaching prior to neuropsychological evaluation. *Assessment, 2,* 279–283.

Zamble, E. (1992). Behavior and adaptation in long-term prison inmates. *Criminal Justice and Behavior, 19,* 409–425.

Zapf, P., & Roesch, R. (1997). Assessing fitness to stand trial: Institution-based evaluations and brief screening interview. *Canadian Journal of Community Mental Health, 16,* 53–66.

Zhang, S., Roberts, R., & Callanan, V. (2006). Preventing parolees from returning to prison through community-based reintegration. *Crime & Delinquency, 52,* 551–571.

Zhao, J., Lovrich, N., & Thurman, Q. (1999). The status of community policing in American cities: Facilitators and impediments revisited. *Policing: An International Journal of Police Strategies and Management, 22,* 74–92.

Zinger, I., & Forth, A. E. (1998). Psychopathy and Canadian criminal proceedings: The potential for human rights abuses. *Canadian Journal of Criminology, 40,* 237–277.

Ziskin, J., & Faust, D. (1988). *Coping with psychiatric and psychological testimony* (4th ed.). Marina del Rey, CA: Law and Psychology Press.

Ziskin, J., & Faust, D. (1995). *Coping with psychiatric and psychological testimony* (5th ed.). Beverly Hills, CA: Law and Psychology Press.

Zlotnick, C., Clarke, J., Friedman, P., Roberts, M., Sacks, S., & Melnick, G. (2008). Gender differences in comorbid disorders among offenders in prison substance abuse treatment programs. *Behavioral Sciences & the Law, 26*, 403–412.

Zulawski, D. E., & Wicklander, D. E. (2001). *Practical aspects of interview and interrogation.* Boca Raton, FL: CRC Press.

Photo Credits

Name Index

Subject Index